standard catalog of ®
CAMARO
1967-2002

John Gunnell

Published by

krause publications

700 East State Street • Iola, WI 54990-0001
715/445-2214 • FAX: 715/445-4087   www.krause.com

Please call or write for our free catalog of publications. Our toll-free number to place an order or obtain a free catalog is (800) 258-0929.

Library of Congress Catalog Number: 2002105108
ISBN: 0-87349-495-4

Thanks

No project of this scope would be possible without the help and support of Camaro enthusiasts to check facts, proofread preliminary manuscripts, and help locate photos. Those involved in this project included Linda Clark of Iola, Wisconsin; Jerry Heasley of Pampa, Texas; Scott Moyer of Brooklyn Park, Minnesota; Tony Hossain of Rochester Hills, Michigan; Jim Mattison of Pontiac Historic Services, Sterling Heights, Michigan (who worked for Chevrolet during the early Camaro period), and Scott Settlemire, the Camaro Brand Manager for Chevrolet Motor Division.

Foreword

The concept behind Krause Publications' *Standard Catalogs of American Cars* series is to compile massive amounts of information about motor vehicles and present it in a standard format that the hobbyist, collector or professional dealer can use to answer some commonly asked questions.

Those questions include: What year, make and model is my vehicle? What did it sell for when it was new? How rare is it? What is special about it? In our general automotive catalogs, some answers are provided by photos and others are provided by the fact-filled text. In our special one-marque catalogs, such as *The Standard Catalog of Camaro 1967-2002*, additional information such as identification number charts and interesting facts about Chevrolet history are included throughout the book.

Chester L. Krause, the founder of Krause Publications, is responsible for the basic concept behind the *Standard Catalog of American Cars* series. Automotive historian David V. Brownell undertook preliminary work on the concept while editing *Old Cars Weekly* in the 1970s. John A. Gunnell edited the first of the *Standard Catalogs of American Cars* in 1978. Many well-known historians and car collectors have contributed to these books over the past 25 years.

No claims are made that these catalogs are infallible. They are not repair manuals or "bibles" for motor vehicle enthusiasts. They are meant as a contribution to the pursuit of greater knowledge about many wonderful vehicles. They are much larger in size, broader in scope and more deluxe in format than most other collector guides, buyer's guides or price guides.

The long-range goal of Krause Publications is to make all of our Standard Catalogs of American Cars as nearly perfect as possible. At the same time, we expect they will always raise new questions and bring forth new facts that were not previously unearthed. We maintain an ongoing file of new research, corrections and additional photos that are used, regularly, to update, refine and expand standard catalogs.

This first edition of *The Standard Catalog of Camaros 1967-2002* was compiled by the experienced editorial team at Krause Publication's books department. In this edition we have put particular emphasis on refining the Camaro vehicle identification number (VIN) information, on better organizing the Camaro engine options and on reducing the number of codes and abbreviations used so that the overall book is more "reader friendly."

Should you have knowledge or photos of cars that you wish to see in future editions of this book please don't hesitate to contact the editors at *The Standard Catalog of Camaro 1967-2002*, editorial department, 700 East State Street, Iola, WI 54990.

Contents

Introduction 6

1967 8

1968 16

1969 24

1970 34

1971 41

1972 47

1973 51

1974 55

1975 59

1976 63

1977 67

1978 73

1979 77

1980	81	1985	104
1981	87	1986	110
1982	91	1987	116
1983	96	1988	122
1984	100	1989	127

1990	133	1995	158
1991	138	1996	163
1992	143	1997	169
1993	149	1998	176
1994	154	1999	181

2000	187	35 Special Camaros	207
2001	192	Camaro Price Guide	220
2002	197		

Introduction

In 1963, when I was just 23 years old and working on special assignment for GM Vice President William Mitchell in a secret studio, I was asked to join a team in setting up a brand new Chevy II studio. Could that event be more exciting for a guy fresh out of college?

Irv Rybicki was head of all Chevrolet products and the product line was busting at the seams. More studio space was needed. The new Chevrolet studio was located on the east end of the south side of the design staff building. As a reference, all major production studios were located on the second floor, west end, facing north with a view over the lake and fountains. When we worked in the "warehouse" nobody else knew what we were doing. Bill Mitchell owned the keys to that castle and that's the way he wanted it. We worked on the future Corvettes, Camaros and shows cars. It was just stuff that wasn't meant to be shared.

Hank Haga, who became an excellent mentor, was chosen to head up this new Chevrolet studio. At the same time an interior studio was set up across the hall. A very good friend who I had worked with in that special, secret studio in the warehouse was also selected to join the interior studio. Bill Mitchell wanted an interior designer with gas in his blood to create exciting sports car interiors. George Angersbach was the right guy and he had a great sense of humor. Maybe George was a little concerned about going from exterior to interior design, however, he made a major impact on his first day on the job when he bolted a shifter to his design chair and entered the studio with car sounds. Those were the fun times.

Our new Chevrolet II studio was a great place to be at this time in history, working on an all-new Corvette theme and, unbeknownst to us, the first Camaro. We had four designers and probably three sculptors. It was a small team, but we worked hard and had a lot of fun. Without a doubt, Jerry Palmer ultimately became the king of Corvette design, but yours truly had his hand in a few of them.

The Chevrolet Studio had a small staff with two platforms in which to create two exciting products. We had what I would consider top talent. Great guys like Don Wood, Dave Stollery, Phil Garcia, Graham Bell, etc. They would rotate between Studios I and II, or come from other studios. Chevrolet II Studio was sort of out of the mainstream from exec visits, which allowed us more room for freedom to take risks and try many new design concepts. We still knew that management would have the last say. I believe Bill Mitchell and Chuck Jordan thought of us as their private sand box to play in and try things. This made for a very fun working relationship. We could sense their support and enthusiasm.

Just about the time Ford announced its Mustang show car in 1962, we were beginning to draw a bead on more sports car designs: low to the ground, tight seating package, and performance. We never knew that our zeal would eventually lead to the 1967

Camaro. Just before the Mustang came out in production, we were working on a small, hot, two-door performance coupe for the auto show. With the success of the Mustang and the acceptance of our show car, the stage was set to compete directly with Ford. Wow, Corvettes and Camaros! We thought we had died and gone to heaven. All the young designers wanted to get into the Chevrolet II Studio to show their stuff.

We had heard rumors about Ford, that they had a four-seater American Sports car coming that was definitely not a European sports car. Ford was very secretive, and at that time they had already announced the GT-40. That was a beautiful car.

When the Mustang came out I think there were a lot of us that were envious because we were sketching things like that. You didn't really see any stealing of designs or espionage, but if you have a lot of designers doing a lot of designs, you're going to have similarities.

Painfully, I remember my first full-size airbrush rendering. The side view was very big. I believe it gave me nightmares. It was a hard and demanding experience with plenty of mistakes, but I got it done.

The eyes were on us and the pressure was building. This Chevrolet had to be successful to go up against the Mustang. During this time, Hank gave me the title of "acting assistant designer" as his direct report.

To make sure that our Camaro was unique, we studied the Mustang's overall theme and details. The Mustang was very angular, and took the large-car design themes and made them into a sports look. Some of the detailing looked applied and cheap. Fit and finish left a lot to be desired. But we loved the overall proportions. They were on the mark. Long hood, short rear deck, wide stance, low roof and low to the ground. This car grabbed your attention, made you look, and made you buy.

When we were concepting our Camaro, we looked at what was going on in Europe for sports car design trends. We took the approach of simplicity as our main thrust. Being wheel-oriented was a must, with a taut, contoured skin covering the essentials — engine, wheels and people. The concept was to get a fairly squat car that was wide, short, and with a long front end. When we started we didn't have that. We had to come up with the proportions that we needed, and we worked hard to get it right.

The peak through the midsection of the body sides was a design feature you could find on many Chevrolets up to this time. That helped strengthen the Chevrolet brand recognition. To keep the design simple, a single opening mouth was used — a cue from many great sports machines.

Eventually, I was promoted to assistant chief designer. I was very proud and overwhelmed. Working with Chevrolet and design during this period of history was a great experience, especially with the emerging involvement of club and professional racing.

Aero design was starting to come of age, and we took our first scale model Camaro to a wind tunnel in Texas. We made some changes, like tapering the front, improving the front air intakes for cooling, and adjusting the rear profile. The data we gathered provided a good learning curve base and helped us as we continued to develop the overall exterior shape of the Camaro.

We thought the Camaro was great, but Ford really had a jump on us in the marketplace. They were really cooking hard.

One executive who really had an interest and focus on design was Chevrolet General Manager Bunkie Knudsen, who was eventually named executive vice president. He personally took the "old man look" out of Pontiac's vehicles. With the design staff's help, he made Pontiac's image more youthful and performance-oriented.

I really liked Bunkie and we got along well. He was very passionate about design, but he did not interfere. Bunkie would pick a design from several sketches we had produced. He was always polite and friendly and would ask your opinion. One morning at about 7:30 a.m. when I got to the studio I found Bunkie going through the designers' desks looking for a better solution for the Camaro front end. We always kept our sketches in our filing drawer and he knew it was OK to look.

That day he found two or three designs that looked good and we tried them. One was the hidden headlamp idea and it finally made it to production on our top-line series. Bunkie truly loved cars. It was good that Bill Mitchell and Chuck Jordan liked Bunkie. If they didn't, they would have kicked him out of the studio for messing with the design process.

There was a lot less stress than today. Design staff was made up of great, creative design teams and everybody had their oars in the water pulling together. Mitchell reported directly to the top, and they didn't have multi layers of management. Bill had a great vision about things, but he never, ever designed our cars. We had to do the sketches. The designers had to come up with the designs, then he would select the direction. And of course all the designers think they have the right ideas.

My gut feeling is that the car could have gone on forever. If you put out a great product, you can put out more than one version to select from and people will buy it. I'm really happy with the way the cars evolved. Today's versions are beautiful, but they're just a tad large for their market. Let's hope GM will revise these great names.

It saddens me that the Camaro and Firebird will be gone, but my personal experience with GM during these times will also be close to my heart. The passion and excitement of going to design staff every day and having the opportunity to create something great for all of us to drive was incredible. There will also be fond memories of the great, talented, and influential people that helped shape and support our beliefs and ideas, and those special folks are my unsung heroes.

—John Schinella
Former GM chief designer

The 1967 Z/28 was a favorite of racing enthusiasts.

The original 1967 Camaro was introduced to the public on Sept. 26, 1966, as Chevrolet's belated answer to Ford's enormously popular Mustang. "Camaro is bandbox new by Chevrolet and a freshly styled example of how fine an exciting road machine can look," said the first sales catalog for the new car, which described it as "a go as well as show machine."

It was the fourth totally new line of cars that Chevrolet had introduced since the Corvair first appeared late in 1959. Each of these cars — Corvair, Chevy II, Chevelle and Camaro — filled a different niche in Chevrolet's marketing scheme. While inspired by the "pony car" segment that the Mustang had carved out of the marketplace, the first Camaro was really promoted as more of a "Junior Corvette" that gave the family man with a hunkering for a real sports car the opportunity to buy one with four seats.

Chevrolet copywriters put major emphasis on the Camaro's "wide stance stability" and "big-car power" and explained how enthusiasts could personalize their Camaro Sport Coupe or convertible by adding extras and options packages. There was the base version with bucket seats and carpeting as standard equipment, the Rally Sport option with "hideaway" headlights and the SS 350 with its "bumblebee" stripes and powerful standard V-8. An optional 396-cid V-8 was released for the Super Sport after November 1966.

To these basic "building block" options the buyer could add a custom interior, a variety of engines and transmissions and accessories such as vinyl roofs and Rally wheels. Those who wanted to customize their Camaro even further could combine some extras to create such "model-options" as the now-highly-desirable RS/SS variant.

When all the possibilities were added up, Chevrolet reported the production of 154,698 Camaros in Lordstown, Ohio, 65,008 in Van Nuys, California. In its heyday — during the late 1970s — the Camaro would capture some 260,000 customers for smiling Chevrolet dealers.

The Camaro — along with its Pontiac counterpart the Firebird — would also go on to become an icon of America's blacktop highways and popular culture. It turned in memorable appearances on television series such as "Charlie's Angels" and "Betwitched" and starred in motion pictures such as the big-screen remake of "Charlie's Angels." The Chevy F-Car thrilled fans at racetracks and drag strips across the nation. And along the way it passed through four major styling "generations" that shaped its character for enthusiasts of different eras.

The first year of Camaro history gave us at least two other important elements of the Camaro legend. The first came in the spring when a Camaro convertible was selected to serve as the official pace car for the Indianapolis 500-Mile Race. This promotion was reinforced by the midyear introduction of the Camaro Z/28 model-option, which started life as a small-block-powered competitor in SCCA Trans-Am Challenge Series racing.

I.D. DATA

Camaros had a 13-symbol vehicle identification number (VIN) on the upper left surface of the instrument panel, visible through the windshield. The first symbol identifies the make: 1=Chevrolet Motor Division. The second symbol indicate the car line/series: 2=Camaro. The third symbol indicates the type of engine: odd number=inline six-cylinder, even number=V-8. The fourth and fifth symbols indicate body type: 37=two-door hardtop coupe and 67=convertible. The sixth symbol indicates model year: 7=1967. The seventh symbol indicates the assembly plant: N=Norwood, Ohio and L=Van Nuys (Los Angeles) Calif. The final six digits are the sequential serial number starting with 500001 at each plant regardless of series. The Fisher Body Style Number plate was located on the firewall below the rear of the hood. The code in the left upper position was ST 67 12337 NOR, ST 67 12367, ST 67 12437 NOR or ST 67 12467. The first two symbols ST stand for "Style." The third and fourth symbols indicate model year: 67=1967 model. The fifth symbol indicates the division: 1=Chevrolet. The sixth and seventh symbols indicate series: 23=Camaro six-cylinder or 24=Camaro V-8. The eighth and ninth symbols indicate body style: 37=two-door coupe, 67=two-door convertible. The last three symbols indicate the assembly plant: NOR=Norwood, Ohio, LOS=Van Nuys, California. This plate also carries codes indicating the body production sequence at the specific plant, interior trim (TR), exterior paint (PNT), the month and week of the month of production (1A=January, first week, etc.) and other special codes.

COLORS

A=Tuxedo Black, CC=Ermine White, DD=Nantucket Blue, EE=Deepwater Blue, FF=Marina Blue, GG=Granada Gold, HH=Mountain Green, KK=Emerald Turquoise, LL=Tahoe Turquoise, MM=Royal Plum, NN=Madeira Maroon, RR=Bolero Red, SS=Sierra Fawn, TT=Capri Cream and YY=Butternut Yellow.

CAMARO - SERIES 23/24 - SIX/V-8

The 1967 Camaro rode a 108-in. wheelbase and measured 185 in. stem to stern. Sport Coupe and convertible body styles were offered. It had a unitized body with a bolted-on front frame section to carry the engine, front suspension, steering and sheet metal components. Its overall appearance included a long hood and short rear deck with the popular "Coke bottle" shape dominating the design. Many options and options packages were available with some "model-options" that essentially turned the basic Camaro into several distinct models. Standard equipment included a satin silver horizontal bars grille with six vertical dividers, inset headlights and parking lights, twin-segment taillights with integral back-up lights on the inboard segment, all-vinyl front bucket seats, an all-vinyl rear bench seat, elegant new interior door styling with bright metal inserts, shielded door handles, a three-spoke steering wheel with circular "Camaro" horn button, a new gauge cluster with large round speedometer and fuel gauges and monitoring lights, Astro Ventilation with standard cowl side vents and two adjustable vent-ports mounted on the instrument panel, an energy-absorbing steering column, seat belts with push-button buckles for all passenger positions, shoulder belts for the driver and right front passenger with push-button buckles and a convenient storage provision on Sport Coupe models, passenger-guard door locks with deflecting lock buttons on all doors, a four-way hazard warning flasher, a dual master cylinder brake system with a warning light and corrosion-resistant brake lines, latches on the folding seat backs, dual-speed windshield wipers, windshield washers, an outside rearview mirror, back-up lights, a padded instrument panel, padded sun visors, padded windshield pillars, a reduced-glare instrument panel top, reduced-glare inside windshield moldings, a reduced-glare horn button, a reduced-glare steering wheel hub, an inside day/night rearview mirror with deflecting base, directional signals with a lane-change feature, safety armrests, a thick-laminate windshield, soft low-profile window control knobs and coat hooks, energy-absorbing seat backs, yielding door and window control handles, an energy-absorbing instrument panel with smooth-contoured knobs and levers, safety wheel rims, safety door latches and hinges, a uniform shift quadrant, an energy-absorbing steering wheel, snag-resistant steering wheel hardware, fuel tank and filler pipe security, an all-welded steel unit body with separate front rubber-mounted frame section, cross-braced Sport Coupe roof supports, heavy-gauge convertible rocker panels, an independent front coil spring suspension, Mono-Leaf rear leaf springs (multi-leaf rear springs with extra-cost V-8 engines), bias-mounted rear shock absorbers, Safety-Master self-adjusting brakes, a dual-chamber brake master cylinder, Rayon-reinforced front and rear brake hoses, a foot-

A total of 602 Z/28s were made for 1967, all of them were Sport Coupes.

A custom interior could be ordered in seven different colors.

operated parking brake, a long-life corrosion-resistant exhaust system with standard emission controls, a 12-volt electrical system with a 9-37-amp Delcotron diode-rectified generator, re-circulating ball-race steering with 28.3:1 manual gear ratio, a 230-cid 140-hp Turbo-Thrift inline six-cylinder engine or a 327-cid 210-hp Turbo-Fire V-8 and a fully synchronized three-speed manual transmission with column-mounted gearshift. The convertible also had a manual convertible top, bright windshield moldings, a bright windshield header with convertible top latches, special sun visors, special inside rear quarter panels with built-in armrests, dual courtesy lights and a convertible top boot.

Model Number	Body/Style Number	Body Type & Seating	Factory Price	Shipping Weight	Production Total
CAMARO - SERIES 23 - (L6)					
23	37	2d coupe	$2,466	2,770 lbs.	Notes 1/2
CAMARO - SERIES 23 - (L6)					
23	67	2d convertible	$2,704	3,025 lbs.	Notes 1/3
CAMARO - SERIES 24 - (V-8)					
24	37	2d coupe	$2,572	2,920 lbs.	Notes 1/2
CAMARO - SERIES 24 - (V-8)					
24	67	2d convertible	$2,809	3,180 lbs.	Notes 1/3

Note 1: Combined model-year production of all 1967 Camaros was 220,906.
Note 2: Combined model-year production of all 1967 Camaros included 160,648 base coupes.
Note 3: Combined model-year production of all 1967 Camaros included 25,141 base convertibles.

CAMARO RALLY SPORT - SERIES 23/24 + Z22 - V-6/V-8

"From hideaway headlights to unique taillights this Camaro says swinger from all angles," boasted the 1967 Camaro sales catalog in the section devoted to the Rally Sport model-option. The RPO Z22 Rally Sport package cost Chevrolet dealers $76 and retailed for $105.35. In addition to or in place of the standard equipment listed above for base Camaros, cars with the Rally Sport package also featured a vertical ornament with an "RS" emblem in the center of the grille, a similar emblem on the round gas filler cap at the center of the rear body panel, an "RS" emblem on the circular steering wheel horn button, a black-finished full-width lattice grille with electrically operated concealed headlights, lower body side moldings, a black accent below the body side moldings (with some body colors), color-keyed body accent stripes, sporty styling for the front parking and turning

lights, sports-style back-up lights, a distinctive edged-in-black taillight treatment with two lamps in each taillight unit for driving, braking and turn signal direction, bright metal front wheel opening moldings, bright metal rear wheel opening moldings and a bright drip rail molding on Sport Coupes. The Rally Sport option could be added to any Camaro with any engine. The prices given immediately below are for base Camaros with the Rally Sport package added. To determine the cost of other model-options with Rally Sport equipment installed add the package price of $105.35 to the factory prices for the specific SS or Z/28 model.

Model Number	Body/Style Number	Body Type & Seating	Factory Price	Shipping Weight	Production Total
CAMARO RALLY SPORT - SERIES 23 - (L6)					
23	37	2d coupe	$2,571	—	Notes 4/5
CAMARO RALLY SPORT - SERIES 23 - (L6)					
23	67	2d convertible	$2,809	—	Notes 4/5
CAMARO RALLY SPORT - SERIES 24 - (V-8)					
24	37	2d coupe	$2,677	—	Notes 4/5
CAMARO RALLY SPORT - SERIES 24 - (V-8)					
24	67	2d convertible	$2,914	—	Notes 4/5

Note 4: Combined model-year production of all 1967 Camaros was 220,906.
Note 5: Of the 220,906 cars built, 64,842 had the Rally Sport option.

CAMARO SS - SERIES 24 - V-8

"The go machine look outside tells everyone you've got the new 350 V-8 inside!" said Chevrolet about what was the hottest available option for its new Camaro – at least at the start of the year. The RPO Z27 SS 350 package cost Chevrolet dealers $152 and retailed for $210.65. In addition to or in place of all of the standard equipment listed above for base Camaros, the SS 350 package included a special hood with raised simulated air intakes, a big "SS 350" emblem for the center of the grille, a 350-cid 295-hp V-8, a color-keyed "bumblebee" type front accent band, "SS" identification inside the breaks on the bumblebee striping, "SS 350" identification on the round fuel filler cap at the center of the rear body panel, red stripe wide-oval tires on 14 x 6-in. wheels and the F41 suspension with stiffer shock absorbers and springs. After the beginning of the model year, two engine options based on the 396-cid "big-block" Turbo-Jet V-8 were offered. They included the L35 with 325 hp and the L78 with 375 hp. When either of these motors was added, the engine call-outs on the grille emblem and fuel cap emblem were deleted and the rear body panel carried flat black finish.

Model Number	Body/Style Number	Body Type & Seating	Factory Price	Shipping Weight	Production Total
CAMARO SS COUPE - SERIES 24 + Z27 - (RPO L48 "TURBO-FIRE 350" V-8/THREE-SPEED MANUAL TRANSMISSION)					
24	37	2d coupe	$2,783	—	Notes 6/7
24	67	2d convertible	$3,019	—	Notes 6/7
CAMARO SS COUPE - SERIES 24 + Z27 - (RPO L35 "TURBO-JET 396" V-8/ THREE-SPEED MANUAL TRANSMISSION)					
24	37	2d coupe	$2,835	—	Notes 6/7
24	67	2d convertible	3,072	—	Notes 6/7
CAMARO SS COUPE - SERIES 24 + Z27 - (RPO L78 "TURBO-JET 396" V-8/ THREE-SPEED MANUAL TRANSMISSION)					
24	37	2d coupe	$3,072	—	Notes 6/7
24	67	2d convertible	$3,309	—	Notes 6/7

Note 6: Combined model-year production of all 1967 Camaros was 220,906.
Note 7: Combined production of all 1967 Camaros included 34,411 total SS models (coupes and convertibles combined).

CAMARO Z/28 - SERIES 24 + Z/28 – V-8

The Z/28 package first appeared in December 1966. During the second half of 1967 a limited number of Camaros were built with the new option, which was available for Camaro Sport Coupes only. It was most sought after by enthusiasts with a serious interest in racing. In addition to or in place of the standard equipment listed above for the base Camaro, all Z/28s included a high-performance 302-cid small-block V-8 engine, a 2 1/4-in. diameter dual exhaust system, dual deep-tone mufflers, a heavy-duty suspension, special front coil springs, special Mono-Leaf rear springs, heavy-duty front and rear shock absorbers, 21.4:1 quick-ratio steering, 15 x 6-in. wheel rims, special 7.35 x 15 nylon white-stripe high-performance tires, a 3.73:1 rear axle ratio and paint stripes on the hood and rear deck lid. In the first year there were no Z/28 emblems on the exterior of the vehicle. Z/28s were also required to have the following extra-cost options: a close-ratio or heavy-duty close-ratio four-speed manual transmission and power front disc brakes or heavy-duty front disc brakes with metallic rear linings. Adding a positraction rear axle was recommended. The Z/28's 302-cid V-8 included a special camshaft,

mechanical valve lifters, an aluminum "tuned inlet" manifold, a high-capacity oil pump, special oil pan baffling, a dual-belt fan drive, an external bypass water pump, a thermostatically controlled five-blade cooling fan, a chrome-plated air cleaner cover, chrome-plated rocker arm covers, a chrome-plated oil filler tube and a chrome-plated oil cap.

Model Number	Body/Style Number	Body Type & Seating	Factory Price	Shipping Weight	Production Total
CAMARO Z/281 SPORT COUPE - SERIES 24 + Z/28 - (V-8 WITH 4-SPEED MANUAL TRANSMISSION AND POWER BRAKES)					
24	37	2d Coupe	3,273	3,520 lbs.	602

Note 8: Combined model-year production of all 1967 Camaros was 220,906.
Note 9: Combined production of all 1967 Camaros included 602 Z/28s.

ENGINES

STD Turbo-Thrift I6: Overhead-valve inline six-cylinder. Cast-iron block and head. Bore & stroke: 3.88 x 3.25 in. Displacement: 230 cid. Compression ratio: 8.5:1. Brake horsepower: 140 at 4400 rpm. Torque: 220 lbs.-ft. at 1600 rpm. Seven main bearings. Induction system: Rochester one-barrel carburetor. Standard in Camaro.

L22 Turbo-Thrift I6: Overhead-valve inline six-cylinder. Cast-iron block and head. Bore & stroke: 3.88 x 3.53 in. Displacement: 250 cid (4.1 liters). Compression ratio: 8.5:1. Brake horsepower: 155 at 4200 rpm. Torque: 235 lbs.-ft. at 1600 rpm. Seven main bearings. Induction system: Rochester No. 7040017 one-barrel carburetor. Optional in Camaro.

STD Turbo-Fire V-8: 90-degree, overhead-valve V-8. Cast-iron block and head. Bore & stroke: 4.00 x 3.25 in. Displacement: 327 cid. Compression ratio: 8.75:1. Brake horsepower: 210 at 4600 rpm. Torque: 320 lbs.-ft. at 2400 rpm. Five main bearings. Hydraulic valve lifters. Induction system: Rochester two-barrel carburetor. Standard V-8 in Camaro.

L30 Turbo-Fire V-8: 90-degree, overhead-valve V-8. Cast-iron block and head. Bore & stroke: 4.00 x 3.25 in. Displacement: 327 cid. Compression ratio: 10.0:1. Brake horsepower: 275 at 4800 rpm. Torque: 355 lbs.-ft. at 3200 rpm. Five main bearings. Hydraulic valve lifters. Induction system: Rochester four-barrel carburetor.

The 1967 convertible Camaro was chosen to pace the Indy 500.

Jerry Heasley photo

The SS 396 actually had a quicker 0 to 60-mph time than the Z/28.

Optional V-8 in Camaro.

L48 Turbo-Fire V-8: 90-degree, overhead-valve V-8. Cast-iron block and head. Bore & stroke: 4.00 x 3.48 in. Displacement: 350 cid (5.7 liters). Compression ratio: 10.25:1. Brake horsepower: 295 at 4800 rpm. Torque: 380 lbs.-ft. at 3200 rpm. Five main bearings. Hydraulic valve lifters. Induction system: Rochester four-barrel carburetor. Standard in Camaro SS; not available in other models.

L35 "396 Turbo-Jet" V-8: 90-degree, overhead-valve V-8. Cast-iron block and head. Bore & stroke: 4.09 x 3.76 in. Displacement: 396 cid. Compression ratio: 10.25:1. Brake horsepower: 325 at 4800 rpm. Torque: 410 lbs.-ft. at 3200 rpm. Five main bearings. Hydraulic valve lifters. Induction system: Rochester four-barrel carburetor. Optional in Camaro SS; not available in other models.

L78 "396 Turbo-Jet" V-8: 90-degree, overhead-valve V-8. Cast-iron block and head. Bore & stroke: 4.09 x 3.76 in. Displacement: 396 cid. Compression ratio: 11.0:1. Brake horsepower: 375 at 5600 rpm. Torque: 415 lbs.-ft. at 3600 rpm. Five main bearings. Solid valve lifters. Induction system: Holley four-barrel carburetor and high-rise aluminum intake manifold. Optional in Camaro SS; not available in other models.

Z28 Turbo-Fire V-8: 90-degree, overhead-valve V-8. Cast-iron block. Cast-iron head. Bore & stroke: 4.002 x 3.005 in. Displacement: 302 cid (5.0 liters). Compression ratio: 11.0:1. Brake horsepower: 290 at 5800 rpm. Torque: 290 lbs.-ft. at 4200 rpm. Five four-bolt main bearings with nodular iron main caps. Solid valve lifters. Induction system: 800-cfm Holley No. 3923289 (R4055A) four-barrel carburetor. Four-bolt main bearings. Special solid lifter camshaft. Cast-aluminum "high-rise" intake manifold. High-capacity oil pump. Special baffling in oil pan. Cooling system includes dual-belt fan drive, external bypass water pump and five-blade thermostatically controlled fan with operating range of 2300-2600 rpm. Also includes chrome-plated air cleaner, rocker covers, filler tube and cap. Dual exhaust system (2 1/4-in. diameter) with dual deep-tone mufflers. A 10.34-in.-diameter bent-finger diaphragm spring clutch with a 2300-2600-lb. rating. Standard in Camaro Z/28; not available in other Camaros.

CHASSIS

Base Sport Coupe: Wheelbase: (All) 108.0 in. Overall length: (All) 184.7 in. Height: (Sport Coupe) 51.0 in., (convertible) 50.9 in. Width: (All) 72.5 in. Front Tread: 59.0 in. Rear Tread: 58.9 in. Front headroom: (Sport Coupe) 37.7 in., (convertible) 37.6 in. Rear headroom: (Sport Coupe) 36.7 in., (convertible) 36.8 in. Front legroom: (Sport Coupe) 42.5 in., (convertible) 42.5 in. Rear legroom: (Sport Coupe) 29.9 in., (convertible) 29.6 in. Front hip room: (Sport Coupe) 56.3 in., (convertible)

56.3 in. Rear hip room: (Sport Coupe) 54.5 in., (convertible) 47.5 in. Front shoulder room: (Sport Coupe) 56.7 in., (convertible) 56.7 in. Rear shoulder room: (Sport Coupe) 53.8 in., (convertible) 47.3 in. Front entrance height: (Sport Coupe) 29.3 in., (convertible) 29.3 in. Usable luggage space: (Sport Coupe) 8.3 cu. ft., (convertible) 5.6 in. Rated fuel tank capacity: 18.5 gal. Standard Tires: 7.35 x 14.

Camaro SS: Wheelbase: (All) 108 in. Overall length: (All) 184.7 in. Height: (Sport Coupe) 51.0 in., (convertible) 50.9 in. Width: (All) 72.5 in. Front Tread: 59 in. Rear Tread: 58.9 in. Front headroom: (Sport Coupe) 37.7 in., (convertible) 37.6 in. Rear headroom: (Sport Coupe) 36.7 in., (convertible) 36.8 in. Front legroom: (Sport Coupe) 42.5 in., (convertible) 42.5 in. Rear legroom: (Sport Coupe) 29.9 in., (convertible) 29.6 in. Front hip room: (Sport Coupe) 56.3 in., (convertible) 56.3 in. Rear hip room: (Sport Coupe) 54.5 in., (convertible) 47.5 in. Front shoulder room: (Sport Coupe) 56.7 in., (convertible) 56.7 in. Rear shoulder room: (Sport Coupe) 53.8 in., (convertible) 47.3 in. Front entrance height: (Sport Coupe) 29.3 in., (convertible) 29.3 in. Usable luggage space: (Sport Coupe) 8.3 cu. ft., (convertible) 5.6 in. Rated fuel tank capacity: 18.5 gal. Standard Tires: 7.35 x 14.

Camaro Z/28: Wheelbase: (all) 108 in. Overall length: (all) 184.7 in. Height: (Sport Coupe) 51 in., (convertible) 50.9 in. Width: (all) 72.5 in. Front tread: 59 in. Rear tread: 58.9 in. Front headroom: (Sport Coupe) 37.7 in., (convertible) 37.6 in. Rear headroom: (Sport Coupe) 36.7 in., (convertible) 36.8 in. Front legroom: (Sport Coupe) 42.5 in., (convertible) 42.5 in. Rear legroom: (Sport Coupe) 29.9 in., (convertible) 29.6 in. Front hip room: (Sport Coupe) 56.3 in., (convertible) 56.3 in. Rear hip room: (Sport Coupe) 54.5 in., (convertible) 47.5 in. Front shoulder room: (Sport Coupe) 56.7 in., (convertible) 56.7 in. Rear shoulder room: (Sport Coupe) 53.8 in., (convertible) 47.3 in. Front entrance height: (Sport Coupe) 29.3 in., (convertible) 29.3 in. Usable luggage space: (Sport Coupe) 8.3 cu. ft., (convertible) 5.6 in. Rated fuel tank capacity: 18.5 gal. Standard tires: E70-15 special red stripe nylon tires.

TECHNICAL

Transmission: Three-speed manual transmission (column shift) standard with floor shift in Camaro six-cylinder. Three-speed manual transmission (column shift) standard with floor shift in Camaro V-8. Four-speed floor shift standard optional in Camaro V-8; mandatory in Camaro SS and Camaro Z/28 (choice of close-ratio or wide-ratio). Powerglide automatic transmission optional. Turbo-Hydra-Matic transmission optional with "big-block" V-8s. Steering: re-circulating ball. Front Suspension: coil springs and tube-type. Rear Suspension: Hotchkiss type with leaf springs and tube-type shock absorbers. Body construction: integral, with separate partial front box frame. Brakes: Drum (Front disc brakes included with Camaro SS package; front disc or four-wheel disc brakes required on Z/28 depending upon time of purchase). Fuel tank: 18.5 gal.

OPTIONS

AL4 Strato-Back front bench seat ($26.35). AS1 front shoulder belts ($23.20). AS2 Strato-Ease headrests ($52.70). A01 Soft-Ray all tinted glass ($30.55). A02 Soft-Ray tinted windshield only ($21.10). A31 power windows ($100.10). A39 custom deluxe front and rear belts ($6.35). A67 rear folding seat ($31.60). A85 custom deluxe front shoulder belts ($26.35). B37 color-keyed floor mats ($10.55). B93 door edge guards ($3.20). C06 power convertible top ($52.70). C08 vinyl roof cover ($73.75). C48 heater and defroster deletion ($31.65 credit). C50 rear window defroster with Sport Coupe ($21.10). C50 rear window defroster with convertible ($31.60). C60 air conditioning ($356). D33 left-hand remote-controlled outside rearview mirror ($9.50). D55 center front seat console ($47.40). D91 Front end "bumblebee" stripe ($14.75). F41 heavy-duty Sport suspension ($10.55). G80 Positraction rear axle ($42.15). Optional axle ratios 3.31:1, 3.55:1, 2.73:1, 3.07:1 and 7.73:1 ($2.15 each). J50 power brakes ($42.15). J52 front disc brakes ($79). J56 heavy-duty front disc brakes ($105.35) J65 special metallic brake facings ($36.90). K02 temperature-controlled de-clutching fan ($15.80). K19 Air Injector Reactor for California car ($44.75). K24

The standard Camaro Sport Coupe interior.

closed positive crankcase ventilation system ($5.25). K30 speed and cruise control ($50.05). K76 61-amp Delcotron alternator ($21.10). K79 42-amp Delcotron alternator ($10.55). L22 250-cid inline six-cylinder engine ($26.35). L30 327-cid 275-hp V-8 ($92.70). L35 396-cid 325-hp V-8 in Camaro SS only ($263.30). L48 350-cid 295-hp V-8 ($210.65). L78 396-cid 375-hp V-8 ($500.30). M11 floor-mounted gearshift lever ($10.55). M13 special three-speed manual transmission ($79). M20 wide-ratio four-speed manual transmission ($184.35). M21 close-ratio four-speed manual transmission ($184.35). M35 Powerglide automatic transmission with six-cylinder engines ($184.35). M35 Powerglide automatic transmission with small-block V-8s ($194.35). M40 Turbo-Hydra-Matic transmission ($226.45). N10 dual exhaust system ($22.10). N30 deluxe steering wheel ($7.40). N33 Comfortilt steering wheel ($42.15). N34 walnut grained steering wheel ($31.60). N40 power steering ($84.30). N44 "Quick-Response" variable-ratio steering ($15.80). N61 dual exhaust system ($21.10). N96 mag-style wheel covers ($73.75). PQ2 7.35 x 14 nylon white sidewall tires ($52). PW6 D70-14 red stripe tires ($62.50). P01 bright metal wheel covers ($21.10). P12 five 14 x 6 wheels ($5.30). P58 7.35 x 14 white sidewall tires ($31.35). T60 heavy-duty battery ($7.40). U03 tri-volume horn ($13.70). U15 speed warning indicator ($10.55). U17 special instrumentation ($79). U25 luggage compartment light ($2.65). U26 underhood light ($2.65). U27 glove compartment light ($2.65). U28 ashtray light ($2.65). U29 courtesy lights ($4.25). U35 electric clock ($15.80). U57 stereo tape player ($128.50). U63 AM radio ($57.40). U69 AM/FM radio ($133.80). U73 manual rear-mounted radio antenna ($9.50). U80 rear seat speaker ($13.90). V01 heavy-duty radiator ($10.55). V31 front bumper guard ($12.65). V32 rear bumper guard ($9.50). Z21 style trim ($40.05). Z22 Rally Sport package ($105.35). Z23 special interior group ($10.55). Z28 Special Performance package ($358.10). Z28 Special Performance package ($779.40). Z28 Special Performance package ($858.40). Z87 custom interior ($94.80).

HISTORICAL FOOTNOTES

In 1967, Elliot M. "Pete" Estes was general manager of Chevrolet Motor Division. It was a good year for the Camaro as production of 220,906 cars was realized in the model year. That represented 2.9 percent of total U.S. industry production. The total included 58,761 six-cylinder cars and 162,145 V-8-powered Camaros. Industry trade journals reported that 154,698 Camaros were built at the Norwood, Ohio, plant and 65,008 Camaros were made at a factory in Van Nuys (Los Angeles), California. In addition, the trade journals showed 1,200 Camaros "produced" at an assembly plant in Bloomfield, New Jersey. According to Camaro Brand Manager Scott Settlemire's sources, these 1,200 cars were actually units produced at the Norwood factory and shipped to a site near Bloomfield (possibly Little Ferry) where they were "knocked down" for shipment overseas. This means that the total number of cars built in Norwood was actually 155,898. Of the 220,906 Camaros built in the model year, 56.2 percent had automatic transmission, 21.5 percent had a four-speed manual transmission, 73.4 percent had a V-8, 26.6 percent had a six-cylinder engine, 78.8 percent had an AM radio, 2.8 percent had an AM/FM radio, 18.2 percent had a clock, 12.8 percent had air conditioning, 3.6 percent had a tilt steering wheel, 41.7 percent had power steering, 8.3 percent had power drum brakes, 6.7 percent had disc brakes, 2.2 percent had power side windows, 97.0 percent had front bucket seats, 23.7 percent had a vinyl roof, 63.0 percent had white sidewall tires, 37.1 percent had a tinted windshield only, 15.7 percent had all tinted glass, 16.3 percent had dual exhausts, 14.4 percent had a limited-slip differen-

The RS (Rally Sport) convertible with an optional 327 V-8 originally came with a sticker price of less than $3,000.

tial, 67.9 percent had wheel covers and 0.1 percent had cruise control. Camaro sales for calendar year 1967 came to 205,816 (2.7 percent of industry) in 1967 compared to 46,758 (0.6 percent) in the fall of 1966, right after it was first introduced. A total of 204,704 new Camaros were registered in the 1967 calendar year compared to 41,100 in the 1966 calendar year. The March 1967 edition of *Road & Track* featured a road test of a Camaro RS Sport Coupe with the 327-cid 275-hp V-8, four-speed manual transmission and 3.07:1 ratio rear axle. It did 0 to 30 mph in 3.7 sec., 0 to 60 mph in 9.1 sec. and the quarter mile in 16.9 sec. at 87 mph. The May 1967 edition of *Motor Trend* road tested a Camaro Z/28 coupe with the 302-cid 290-hp V-8 and four-speed manual transmission. It did 0 to 60 mph in 7.0 sec. and the quarter mile in 14.8 sec. at 96 mph. The magazine

noted that this engine was "rumored to bring more than 400 true hp to the starting line." It also pointed out that the Z/28 ran a slower 0 to 60 mph time than an SS 396 Camaro, but a faster quarter mile. A 1967 Camaro convertible was selected to pace the Indianapolis 500-Mile Race. A total of 104 similar convertibles were built for "official" use at the big race. The Camaro's front subframe was large enough to hold big-block Chevy V-8s like the 396-cid Turbo-Jet V-8. This meant that 427-cid V-8s could also be accommodated and a small number of 1967 Camaros were converted to 427 power by Yenko Chevrolet of Cannonsburg, Pennsylvania, Nickey Chevrolet of Chicago, Bill Thomas of Anaheim, California (who worked in connection with Nickey Chevrolet), and by Motion Performance of Baldwin, New York.

Jerry Heasley photo

The RS/SS 396 was a formidable machine for a first-year car.

Camaro

Jerry Healey photo

Chevrolet continued its commitment to building a fast, sporty car with the 1968 Z/28 Sport Coupe.

Camaro No. 2 came along in 1968 and was little more than a slightly modified version of the first edition that gained a "big-block" 396-cid V-8 during the year. To spot a 1967 model you can look for vent windows. To spot a 1968 model you should look for no vent windows, plus the addition of front and rear side marker lights (required to conform with new federal safety regulations). There were engineering refinements that Chevrolet said were "designed to keep the '68 Camaro the finest car in its field."

Glamour was the strong point of the 1968 Rally Sport package and husky performance was the calling card of the Camaro SS option. The base Camaro engine was again a 230-cid inline six-cylinder, while the 327-cid small-block remained the base V-8. A 350-cid V-8 was standard in the Camaro SS, but the Turbo-Jet 369-cid V-8 was the hot ticket for the lead-footed set. Cars with this engine were treated to a black-finished rear body panel to set them off as something special.

CAMARO - SERIES 23/24 - SIX/V-8

Standard equipment included a satin-silver horizontal bars grille with six vertical dividers, inset headlights and parking lights, twin-segment taillights with integral back-up lights on the inboard segment, new one-piece curved side windows, new rear side marker lights ahead of the rear bumper ends, new front side marker lights behind the front bumper ends, all-vinyl front bucket seats, an all-vinyl rear bench seat, new interior door styling with bright metal inserts, shielded door handles, a three-

spoke steering wheel with circular "Camaro" horn button, a new gauge cluster with large, round speedometer and fuel gauges and monitoring lights, Astro Ventilation with standard cowl side vents and two adjustable vent-ports mounted on the instrument panel, an energy-absorbing steering column, seat belts with push-button buckles for all passenger positions, shoulder belts for the driver and right front passenger with push-button buckles and a convenient storage provision on Sport Coupe models, passenger-guard door locks with deflecting lock buttons on all doors, a four-way hazard warning flasher, a dual master cylinder brake system with a warning light and corrosion-resistant brake lines, latches on the folding seat backs, dual-speed windshield wipers, windshield washers, an outside rearview mirror, back-up lights, new side marker lights and parking lights that illuminated with the headlights, a padded instrument panel, padded sun visors, padded windshield pillars, a reduced-glare instrument panel top, reduced-glare inside windshield moldings, a reduced-glare horn button, a reduced-glare steering wheel hub, an inside day/night rearview mirror with deflecting base, directional signals with a lane-change feature, safety armrests, a thick-laminate windshield, soft low-profile window control knobs and coat hooks, energy-absorbing seat backs, yielding door and window control handles, an energy-absorbing instrument panel with smooth-contoured knobs and levers, safety wheel rims, safety door latches and hinges, a uniform shift quadrant, an energy-absorbing steering wheel, snag-resistant steering wheel hardware, fuel tank and filler pipe security, an all-welded steel unit body with separate front rubber-mounted frame section, cross-braced Sport Coupe roof supports, heavy-gauge convertible rocker panels, an independent front coil spring suspension, Mono-Leaf rear leaf springs (multi-leaf rear springs with the V-8 engines), bias-mounted rear shock absorbers, Safety-Master self-adjusting brakes, a dual-chamber brake master cylinder, Rayon-reinforced front and rear brake hoses, a foot-operated parking brake, a long-life corrosion-resistant exhaust system with standard emission controls, a 12-volt electrical system with a 9-37 amp Delcotron diode-rectified generator, re-circulating ball-race steering with 28.3:1 manual gear ratio, a 230-cid 140-hp Turbo-Thrift inline six-cylinder engine or a 327-cid 210-hp Turbo-Fire V-8 and a fully synchronized three-speed manual transmission with column-mounted gearshift. The convertible also had a manual convertible top, bright windshield moldings, a bright windshield header with convertible top latches, special sun visors, special inside rear quarter panels with built-in armrests, dual courtesy lights and a convertible top boot.

I.D. DATA

Camaros had a 13-symbol vehicle identification number (VIN) on the upper left surface of the instrument panel, visible through the windshield. The first symbol identifies the make: 1=Chevrolet Motor Division. The second symbol indicate the car line/series: 2=Camaro. The third symbol indicates the type of engine: odd number=inline six-cylinder, even number=V-8. The fourth and fifth symbols indicate body type: 37=two-door hardtop coupe and 67=convertible. The sixth symbol indicates model year: 8=1968. The seventh symbol indicates the assembly plant: N=Norwood, Ohio and L=Van Nuys (Los Angeles) California. The final six digits are the sequential serial number starting with 500001 at each plant regardless of series. The Fisher Body Style Number plate was located on the firewall below the rear of the hood. The code in the left upper position was ST 68 12337 NOR, ST 68 12367, ST 68 12437 NOR or ST 68 12467. The first two symbols ST stand for "Style." The third and fourth symbols indicate model year: 68=1968 model. The fifth symbol indicates the division: 1=Chevrolet. The sixth and seventh symbols indicate series: 23=Camaro six-cylinder or 24=Camaro V-8. The eighth and ninth symbols indicate body style: 37=two-door coupe, 67=two-door convertible. The last three symbols indicate the assembly plant: NOR=Norwood, Ohio, LOS=Van Nuys, California. This plate also carries codes indicating the body production sequence at the specific plant, interior trim (TR), exterior paint (PNT), the month and week of the month of production (1A=January, first week, etc.) and other special codes.

COLORS

A=Tuxedo Black, CC=Ermine White, DD=Grotto Blue, EE=Fathom Blue, FF=Island Teal, GG=Ash Gold, HH=Grecian Gold, JJ=Rallye Green, KK=Tripoli Turquoise, LL=Teal Blue, NN=Cordovan Maroon, OO=Corvette Bronze, PP=Seafrost Green, RR=Matador Red, TT=Palomino Ivory, UU=LeMans Blue, VV=Sequoia Green, YY=Butternut Yellow and ZZ=British Green.

Model Number	Body/Style Number	Body Type & Seating	Factory Price	Shipping Weight	Production Total
CAMARO - SERIES 23 - (L6)					
23	37	2d coupe	$2,565	3,040 lbs.	Note 1/2
CAMARO - SERIES 23 - (L6)					
23	67	2d convertible	$2,802	3,160 lbs.	Note 1/3
CAMARO - SERIES 24 - (V-8)					
24	37	2d coupe	$2,670	3,050 lbs.	Note 1/2
CAMARO - SERIES 24 - (V-8)					
24	67	2d convertible	$2,908	3,295 lbs.	Note 1/3

Note 1: Combined model-year production of all 1968 Camaros was 235,147. (See historical footnotes)

Note 2: Combined model-year production of all 1968 Camaros included 176,813 base coupes.

Note 3: Combined model-year production of all 1968 Camaros included 20,440 base convertibles.

CAMARO RALLY SPORT - SERIES 23/24 + Z22 - V-6/V-8

Chevrolet described cars equipped with the optional Rally Sport package as "a more glamorous version" of the Camaro. The RPO Z22 Rally Sport package cost Chevrolet dealers $81.35 and retailed for $105.35. In addition to or place of the standard equipment listed above for base Camaros, cars with the Rally Sport package also featured concealed headlights, a special full-width grille, small rectangular parking and directional signal lights mounted below the bumper instead of in the grille, an RS emblem on the center of the grille, small rectangular back-up lamps mounted below the rear bumper (both taillight segments had red lenses), an "RS" emblem on the round gas filler cap in the center of the rear body panel, bright lower body side moldings with black lower body finish under the molding, bright "Rally Sport" scripts on the upper front fenders behind the wheel openings, a bright roof drip molding on Sport Coupes and a bright belt line molding. The Rally Sport option could be added to any Camaro with any engine. The prices given immediately below are for base Camaros with the Rally Sport package added. To determine the cost of other model-options with Rally Sport equipment installed add the package price of $105.35 to the factory prices for the specific SS or Z/28 model.

Model Number	Body/Style Number	Body Type & Seating	Factory Price	Shipping Weight	Production Total
CAMARO RALLY SPORT - SERIES 23 - (L6)					
23	37	2d coupe	$2,670	—	Note 4/5
CAMARO RALLY SPORT - SERIES 23 - (L6)					
23	67	2d convertible	$2,907	—	Note 4/5
CAMARO RALLY SPORT - SERIES 24 - (V-8)					
24	37	2d coupe	$2,775	—	Note 4/5
CAMARO RALLY SPORT - SERIES 24 - (V-8)					
24	67	2d convertible	$3,013	—	Note 4/5

Note 4: Combined model-year production of all 1968 Camaros was 235,147. (See historical footnotes)

Note 5: Of the 235,147 cars built, 40,977 had the Rally Sport option.

CAMARO SS - SERIES 24 - V-8

Chevrolet boasted that the 1968 Camaro SS (Super Sport) was dedicated to the "fun crowd." The sales catalog said it was "a husky performer and looks it." Big engines, a beefed-up suspension and special equipment features made this model-option stand out. The prices of the RPO Z27 SS package varied according to engine. With the L48 V-8 the dealer paid $152 and got $210.65 at retail. With the L35 engine the dealer cost was $190 and the retail price was $263.30. With the L34 V-8 the

The Rally Sport convertible, this one with a 327 V-8, had hidden headlights and a few other "classy" features.

dealer cost was $266 and the retail price was $368.65. The L78 version of the SS wholesaled for $361 and retailed for $500.30. The L78/L89 version with aluminum cylinder heads retailed for $868.95 (dealer cost unknown). In addition to, or in place of, all of the standard equipment listed above for base Camaros, the SS 350 package included the same special hood with raised simulated air intakes used on 1967 SS models, a big SS emblem for the center of the grille, special hood insulation, special chassis components, a 350-cid 295-hp V-8 engine, a color-keyed bumblebee-type front accent band (black with light colors and white with darker colors), SS identification below the Camaro front fender script, SS identification on the round fuel filler cap at the center of the rear body panel, red stripe or white stripe wide-oval tires and multi-leaf rear springs. In addition to, or in place of, all of the standard equipment listed above for base Camaros, the SS 396 package included unique hood with twin banks of four square simulated air intakes, a big SS emblem for the center of the grille, special hood insulation, special chassis components, a 396-cid V-8 engine, a color-keyed bumblebee type front accent band (black with light colors and white with darker colors), SS identification below the Camaro front fender script, SS identification on the round fuel filler cap at the center of the rear body panel, red stripe or white stripe wide-oval tires, multi-leaf rear springs and a black-painted rear body panel. A dual exhaust system was included with all Camaro SS models at no additional cost.

Model Number	Body/Style Number	Body Type & Seating	Factory Price	Shipping Weight	Production Total
CAMARO SS COUPE - SERIES 24 + Z27 - (RPO L48 "TURBO-FIRE 350" V-8/THREE-SPEED MANUAL TRANSMISSION)					
24	37	2d coupe	$2,881	—	Note 6/7
24	67	2d convertible	$3,119	—	Note 6/7
CAMARO SS COUPE - SERIES 24 + Z27 - (RPO L35 "TURBO-JET 396" V-8/ THREE-SPEED MANUAL TRANSMISSION)					
24	37	2d coupe	$2,933	—	Note 6/7
24	67	2d convertible	$3,171	—	Note 6/7
CAMARO SS COUPE - SERIES 24 + Z27 - (RPO L34 "TURBO-JET 396" V-8/ THREE-SPEED MANUAL TRANSMISSION)					
24	37	2d coupe	$3,039	—	Note 6/7
24	67	2d convertible	$3,277	—	Note 6/7
CAMARO SS COUPE - SERIES 24 + Z27 - (RPO L78 "TURBO-JET 396" V-8/ THREE-SPEED MANUAL TRANSMISSION)					
24	37	2d coupe	$3,170	—	Note 6/7
24	67	2d convertible	$3,408	—	Note 6/7
CAMARO SS COUPE - SERIES 24 + Z27 - (RPO L78/L89 "TURBO-JET 396" V-8/ THREE-SPEED MANUAL TRANSMISSION)					
24	37	2d coupe	$3,539	—	Note 6/7
24	67	2d convertible	$3,777	—	Note 6/7

Note 6: Combined model-year production of all 1968 Camaros was 235,147. (See historical footnotes)

Note 7: Combined production of all 1968 Camaros included 30,695 total SS models (coupes and convertibles combined).

CAMARO Z/28 - SERIES 24 + Z/28 – V-8

In 1968, the popularity of the Camaro Z/28 Special Performance package started to climb based on the car's first-year racing reputation. During the later part of the 1967 model year, only 602 Z/28s had been released and Chevrolet wasn't sure if it wanted to market the option strictly for racing or to the public. Output climbed to 7,199 cars in 1968, making it clear that a decision had been made. The Z/28 package was available for Camaro Sport Coupes only. It came in four different variations. In addition to, or in place of, the standard equipment listed above for the base Camaro, all Z/28s included a high-performance 302-cid small-block V-8 engine, a dual exhaust system, deep-tone mufflers, special front and rear suspensions, a heavy-duty radiator, a temperature-controlled de-clutching radiator fan, quick-ratio steering, 15 x 6-in. wheel rims, E70 x 15 special white-letter nylon tires, a 3.73:1 rear axle ratio, paint stripes on the hood and paint stripes on the rear deck lid. Z/28s were also required to have the following extra-cost options: a close-ratio four-speed manual transmission and power front disc brakes or heavy-duty front disc brakes with metallic rear linings. Adding a Positraction rear axle was recommended. The least expensive version of the Z/28 was the standard Z/281 option as described above. It cost dealers $288.80 and retailed for $400.25. Next came the Z/282 option with a plenum air intake. It cost Chevy dealers $345.80 and retailed for $479.25. The Z/283 version came with exhaust headers. It wholesaled for $562.40 and retailed for $779.40. Finally, there was the Z/284 version with both the plenum air intake and exhaust headers. This "ultimate" Z/28 had a dealer cost of $619.40 and retailed for $858.40.

Model Number	Body/Style Number	Body Type & Seating	Factory Price	Shipping Weight	Production Total
CAMARO Z/281 SPORT COUPE - SERIES 24 + Z/28 - (V-8 WITH 4-SPEED MANUAL TRANSMISSION AND POWER BRAKES)					
24	37	2d coupe	$3,297	—	Note 8/9
CAMARO Z/282 SPORT COUPE - SERIES 24 + Z/28 - (V-8 WITH 4-SPEED MANUAL TRANSMISSION AND POWER BRAKES)					
24	37	2d coupe	$3,376	—	Note 8/9
CAMARO Z/283 SPORT COUPE - SERIES 24 + Z/28 - (V-8 WITH 4-SPEED MANUAL TRANSMISSION AND POWER BRAKES)					
24	37	2d coupe	$3,755	—	Note 8/9
CAMARO Z/283 SPORT COUPE - SERIES 24 + Z/28 - (V-8 WITH 4-SPEED MANUAL TRANSMISSION AND POWER BRAKES)					
24	37	2d coupe	$3,834	—	Note 8/9

Note 8: Combined model-year production of all 1968 Camaros was 235,147. (See historical footnotes)
Note 9: Combined production of all 1968 Camaros included 7,199 Camaro Z/28s.

ENGINES

STD Turbo-Thrift I6: Overhead-valve inline six-cylinder. Cast-iron block and head. Bore & stroke: 3.88 x 3.25 in. Displacement: 230 cid. Compression ratio: 8.5:1. Brake horsepower: 140 at 4400 rpm. Torque: 220 lbs.-ft. at 1600 rpm. Seven main bearings. Induction system: Rochester one-barrel carburetor. Standard in Camaro.

L22 Turbo-Thrift I6: Overhead-valve inline six-cylinder. Cast-iron block and head. Bore & stroke: 3.88 x 3.53 in. Displacement: 250 cid (4.1 liters). Compression ratio: 8.5:1. Brake horsepower: 155 at 4200 rpm. Torque: 235 lbs.-ft. at 1600 rpm. Seven main bearings. Induction system: Rochester No. 7040017 one-barrel carburetor. Optional in Camaro.

STD Turbo-Fire V-8: 90-degree, overhead-valve V-8. Cast-iron block and head. Bore & stroke: 4.00 x 3.25 in. Displacement: 327 cid. Compression ratio: 8.75:1. Brake horsepower: 210 at 4600 rpm. Torque: 320 lbs.-ft. at 3400 rpm. Five main bearings. Hydraulic valve lifters. Induction system: Rochester two-barrel carburetor. Standard V-8 in Camaro.

L30 Turbo-Fire V-8: 90-degree, overhead-valve V-8. Cast-iron block and head. Bore & stroke: 4.00 x 3.25 in. Displacement: 327 cid. Compression ratio: 8.75:1. Brake horsepower: 250 at 4600 rpm. Torque: 335 lbs.-ft. at 3200 rpm. Five main bearings. Hydraulic valve lifters. Induction system: Rochester two-barrel carburetor. Optional V-8 in Camaro.

L48 Turbo-Fire V-8: 90-degree, overhead-valve V-8. Cast-iron block and head. Bore & stroke: 4.00 x 3.48 in. Displacement: 350 cid (5.7 liters). Compression ratio: 10.25:1. Brake horsepower: 295 at 4800 rpm. Torque: 380 lbs.-ft. at 3200 rpm. Five main bearings. Hydraulic valve lifters. Induction system: Rochester four-barrel carburetor. Standard in Camaro SS; not available in other models.

L35 "396 Turbo-Jet" V-8: 90-degree, overhead-valve V-8. Cast-iron block and head. Bore & stroke: 4.09 x 3.76 in. Displacement: 396 cid. Compression ratio: 10.25:1. Brake horsepower: 325 at 4800 rpm. Torque: 410 lbs.-ft. at 3200 rpm. Five main bearings. Hydraulic valve lifters. Induction system: Rochester four-barrel carburetor. Optional in Camaro SS; not available in other models.

L34 "396 Turbo-Jet" V-8: 90-degree, overhead-valve V-8. Cast-iron block and head. Bore & stroke: 4.09 x 3.76 in. Displacement: 396 cid. Compression ratio: 10.25:1. Brake horsepower: 350 at 5200 rpm. Torque: 415 lbs.-ft. at 3400 rpm. Five main bearings. Hydraulic valve lifters. Induction system: Rochester four-barrel carburetor. Optional in Camaro SS; not available in other models.

L78 "396 Turbo-Jet" V-8: 90-degree, overhead-valve V-8. Cast-iron block and head. Bore & stroke: 4.09 x 3.76

The Camaro SS had several distinct exterior features, including a bumblebee stripe on the front end, fender script, and SS emblem on the black grille. The version had the 350-cid V-8 and four-speed transmission.

The SS-350 Sport Coupe with a three-speed could be purchased new for about $2,800.

in. Displacement: 396 cid. Compression ratio: 11.0:1. Brake horsepower: 375 at 5600 rpm. Torque: 415 lbs.-ft. at 3600 rpm. Five main bearings. Solid valve lifters. Induction system: Holley four-barrel carburetor and a high-rise aluminum manifold. Optional in Camaro SS; not available in other models.

L78/L89 "396 Turbo-Jet" V-8: 90-degree, overhead-valve V-8. Cast-iron block. Aluminum head with large valves. Bore & stroke: 4.09 x 3.76 in. Displacement: 396 cid. Compression ratio: 11.0:1. Brake horsepower: 375 at 5600 rpm. Torque: 415 lbs.-ft. at 3600 rpm. Five main bearings. Solid valve lifters. Induction system: Holley four-barrel carburetor and a high-rise aluminum manifold. Optional in Camaro SS; not available in other models. This option was installed in only 272 Camaros in 1968.

Z28 Turbo-Fire V-8: 90-degree, overhead valve V-8. Cast-iron block. Cast-iron head. Bore & stroke: 4.002 x 3.005 in. Displacement: 302 cid (5.0 liters). Compression ratio: 11.0:1. Brake horsepower: 290 at 5800 rpm. Torque: 290 lbs.-ft. at 4200 rpm. Five four-bolt main bearings with nodular iron main caps. Solid valve lifters. Induction system: 800-cfm Holley No. 3923289 (R4055A) four-barrel carburetor. Four-bolt main bearings. Special solid lifter camshaft. Cast-aluminum "high-rise" intake manifold. High-capacity oil pump. Special baffling in oil pan. Cooling system includes dual-belt fan drive, external bypass water pump and five-blade thermostatically controlled fan with operating range of 2300-2600 rpm. Also includes chrome-plated air cleaner, rocker covers, filler tube and cap. Dual exhaust system (2 1/4-in. diameter) with dual deep-tone mufflers. A 10.34-in. diameter bent-finger diaphragm spring clutch with a 2,300-2,600-lb. rating. Standard in Camaro Z/28; not available in other Camaros.

L72 "427 Turbo-Jet" V-8: 90-degree, overhead-valve V-8. Cast-iron block and head. Bore & stroke: 4.251 x 3.76 in. Displacement: 427 cid. Compression ratio: 11.00:1. Brake horsepower: 425 at 5400 rpm. Torque: 460 lbs.-ft. at 3600 rpm. Five main bearings. Solid valve lifters. Induction system: Rochester four-barrel carburetor. No 1968 Camaros left a Chevrolet assembly line with this engine, but it was used in a handful of Camaros built by Chevrolet dealers who specialized in performance such as Fred Gibb Chevrolet, Don Yenko Sportscars and Nickey Chevrolet.

L72 "427 Turbo-Jet" V-8: 90-degree, overhead-valve V-8. Cast-iron block and head. Bore & stroke: 4.251 x 3.76 in. Displacement: 427 cid. Compression ratio: 11.25:1. Brake horsepower: 435 at 5800 rpm. Torque: 460 lbs.-ft. at 4000 rpm. Five main bearings. Solid valve lifters. Induction system: Rochester four-barrel carburetor. A very few 1968 Camaros left a Chevrolet assembly line with this engine, custom-built for Yenko Sportscars under COPO 9737. The (L72) 427-cid engine was also installed in a handful of Camaros built by Chevrolet dealers who specialized in performance installations, such as Fred Gibb Chevrolet, Don Yenko Sportscars and Nickey Chevrolet.

CHASSIS

Base Sport Coupe: Wheelbase: (all) 108 in. Overall length: (all) 184.6 in. Height: (Sport Coupe) 51.5 in., (convertible) 50.9 in. Width: (all) 72.3 in. Front Tread: 59.6 in. Rear Tread: 59.5 in. Front headroom: (Sport Coupe) 37.7 in., (convertible) 37.6 in. Rear headroom: (Sport Coupe) 36.5 in., (convertible) 36.8 in. Front legroom: (Sport Coupe) 42.5 in., (convertible) 42.5 in. Rear legroom: (Sport Coupe) 29.9 in., (convertible) 29.6 in. Front hip room: (Sport Coupe: 56.3 in., (convertible) 56.3 in. Rear hip room: (Sport Coupe) 54.5 in., (convertible) 47.5 in. Front shoulder room: (Sport Coupe) 56.7 in., (convertible) 56.7 in. Rear shoulder room: (Sport Coupe) 53.8 in., (convertible) 47.3 in. Front entrance height: (Sport Coupe) 29.3 in., (convertible) 29.3 in. Usable luggage space: (Sport Coupe) 8.3 cu. ft., (convertible) 5.6 in. Rated fuel tank capacity: 18.5 gal. Standard tires: 7.35 x 14.

Camaro SS: Wheelbase: (all) 108 in. Overall length: (all) 184.6 in. Height: (Sport Coupe) 51.5 in., (convertible) 50.9 in. Width: (all) 72.3 in. Front Tread: 59.6 in. Rear Tread: 59.5 in. Front headroom: (Sport Coupe) 37.7 in., (convertible) 37.6 in. Rear headroom: (Sport Coupe) 36.5 in., (convertible) 36.8 in. Front legroom: (Sport Coupe) 42.5 in., (convertible) 42.5 in. Rear legroom: (Sport Coupe) 29.9 in., (convertible) 29.6 in. Front hip room: (Sport Coupe) 56.3 in., (convertible) 56.3 in. Rear hip room: (Sport Coupe) 54.5 in., (convertible) 47.5 in. Front shoulder room: (Sport Coupe) 56.7 in., (convertible) 56.7 in. Rear shoulder room: (Sport Coupe) 53.8 in., (convertible) 47.3 in. Front entrance height: (Sport Coupe) 29.3 in., (convertible) 29.3 in. Usable luggage space: (Sport Coupe) 8.3 cu. ft., (convertible) 5.6 in. Rated fuel tank capacity: 18.5 gal. Standard tires: 7.35 x 14.

Camaro Z/28: Wheelbase: (all) 108 in. Overall length: (all) 184.6 in. Height: (Sport Coupe) 51.5 in., (convertible) 50.9 in. Width: (all) 72.3 in. Front tread: 59.6 in. Rear tread: 59.5 in. Front headroom: (Sport Coupe) 37.7 in., (convertible) 37.6 in. Rear headroom: (Sport Coupe) 36.5 in., (convertible) 36.8 in. Front legroom: (Sport Coupe) 42.5 in., (convertible) 42.5 in. Rear legroom: (Sport Coupe) 29.9 in., (convertible) 29.6 in. Front hip room: (Sport Coupe): 56.3 in., (convertible) 56.3 in. Rear hip room: (Sport Coupe) 54.5 in., (convertible) 47.5 in. Front shoulder room: (Sport Coupe) 56.7 in., (convertible) 56.7 in. Rear shoulder room: (Sport Coupe) 53.8 in., (convertible) 47.3 in. Front entrance height: (Sport Coupe) 29.3 in., (convertible) 29.3 in. Usable luggage space: (Sport Coupe) 8.3 cu. ft., (convertible) 5.6 in. Rated fuel tank capacity: 18.5 gal. Standard tires: E70 x 15 special red stripe nylon tires.

TECHNICAL

Transmission: Three-speed manual transmission (column shift) standard with floor shift in Camaro six-cylinder. Three-speed manual transmission (column shift) standard with floor shift in Camaro V-8. Four-speed floor shift standard optional in Camaro V-8; mandatory in Camaro SS and Camaro Z/28 (choice of close-ratio or wide-ratio). Powerglide automatic transmission optional with all engines except Turbo-Jet 396 V-8. Turbo-Hydra-Matic transmission optional with Turbo-Jet 396 V-8. Steering: re-circulating ball. Front suspension: coil springs and tube-type. Rear suspension: Hotchkiss-type with leaf springs and tube-type shock absorbers. Body construction: integral, with separate partial front box frame. Brakes: Drum (front disc brakes required on Z/28). Fuel tank: 18.5 gal.

OPTIONS

AK1 custom deluxe seat and shoulder belts ($11.10). AL4 Strato-Back front bench seat ($32.65). AS1 front shoulder belts ($23.20). AS2 Strato-Ease headrests ($52.70). AS4 custom deluxe rear shoulder belts ($26.35). AS5 standard rear shoulder belts ($23.20). A01 Soft-Ray all tinted glass ($30.55). A02 Soft-Ray tinted windshield only ($21.10). A31 power windows ($100.10). A39 custom deluxe front and rear belts ($7.90). A67 rear folding seat ($42.15). A85 custom deluxe front shoulder belts ($26.35). B37 color-keyed floor mats ($10.55). B93 door edge guards ($4.25). C06 power convertible top ($52.70). C08 vinyl roof cover ($73.75). C50 rear window defroster with Sport Coupe ($21.10). C50 rear window defroster with convertible ($31.60). C60 air conditioning ($360.20). D33 left-hand remote-controlled outside rearview mirror ($9.50). D55 center front seat console ($50.60). D80 rear deck lid spoiler ($32.65). D90 Sport striping ($25.30). D91 Front end "bumblebee" stripe ($14.75). D96 accent striping ($13.70). F41 heavy-duty Sport suspension ($10.55). G31 special heavy-duty rear springs ($20.05). G80 positraction rear axle ($42.15). Optional axle ratios ($2.15). J50 power brakes ($42.15). J52 front disc brakes ($100.10). KD5 positive crankcase ventilation ($6.35). K02 temperature-controlled de-clutching fan ($15.80). K30 speed and cruise control ($52.70). K76 61-amp Delcotron alternator ($26.35). K79 42-amp Delcotron alternator ($10.55). L30 327-cid 275-hp V-8 ($92.70). L34 396-cid 350-hp in Camaro SS only ($368.65). L35 396-cid 325-hp V-8 in Camaro SS only ($263.30). L48 350-cid 295-hp V-8 ($210.65). L78 396-cid 375-hp V-8 ($500.30). L78/L89 396-cid 375-hp V-8 with aluminum cylinder heads in Camaro SS only ($868.95). MB1 Torque drive transmission ($68.65). M11 floor-mounted gearshift lever ($10.55). M13 special three-speed manual transmission ($79). M20 wide-ratio four-speed manual transmission ($184.35). M21 close-ratio four-speed manual transmission ($184.35). M22 close-ratio heavy-duty four-speed manual transmission ($310.70). M35 Powerglide automatic transmission with six-cylinder engines ($184.35). M35 Powerglide automatic transmission with small-block V-8s ($194.35). M40 Turbo-Hydra-Matic transmission ($237.00). NF2 Deep-Tone dual exhaust system ($27.40). N10 dual exhaust system ($27.40). N33 Comfortilt steering wheel ($42.15). N34 walnut grained steering wheel ($31.60). N40 power steering ($84.30). N44 "Quick-Response" variable-ratio steering ($15.80). N65 Spacesaver spare tire ($19.35). N95 simulated wire wheel covers ($73.75). N96 mag-style wheel covers ($73.75). PA2 mag-spoke wheel covers ($73.75). PW7 F70-14 white sidewall tires ($64.75).

Cordovan Maroon was one of 19 color choices.

Hal Andrews photo

PW8 F70-14 red stripe tires ($64.75). PY4 F70-14 fiberglass-belted tires ($26.55). PY5 fiberglass-belted red stripe tires ($26.55). P01 bright metal wheel covers ($21.10). P58 7.35 x 14 white sidewall tires ($31.35). T60 heavy-duty battery ($7.40). U03 tri-volume horn ($13.70). U15 speed warning indicator ($10.55). U17 special instrumentation ($94.80). U46 light monitoring system ($26.35). U57 stereo tape player ($133.80). U63 AM radio ($61.10). U69 AM/FM radio ($133.80). U73 manual rear-mounted radio antenna ($9.50). U79 push-button AM/FM stereo radio ($239.15). U80 rear seat speaker ($13.20). V01 heavy-duty radiator ($13.70). V31 front bumper guard ($12.65). V32 rear bumper guard ($12.65). ZJ7 Rally wheels ($31.60). ZJ9 auxiliary lighting in Sport Coupe without custom interior option ($13.70). ZJ9 auxiliary lighting in Sport Coupe with custom interior option ($11.10). ZJ9 auxiliary lighting in convertible without custom interior option ($9.50). ZJ9 auxiliary lighting in convertible with custom interior option ($6.85). Z21 style trim ($47.40). Z22 Rally Sport package ($105.35). Z23 special interior group ($17.95). Z27 Camaro Super Sport package ($210.65-$868.95). Z28 Special Performance package ($400.25-$858.40). Z87 custom interior ($110.60).

HISTORICAL FOOTNOTES

In late 1968, John Z. DeLorean became general manager of Chevrolet Motor Division, taking over from Elliott M. "Pete" Estes. It was a good year for the redesigned Camaro as production of 235,147 Camaros was realized in the model year. (Note: Industry trade journals also printed the figure 235,151, but 235,147 seems to be

more accurate; also note that other figures, such as production by factory and production by type of engine, do not add up to either of these figures). The total represented 2.8 percent of total U.S. industry production and compared to 220,906 cars and 2.9 percent of industry in 1967. According to automotive trade journals of the day, the total included 50,937 six-cylinder cars and 184,178 V-8-powered Camaros, although this adds up to only 235,115 cars. Industry trade journals reported that 184,735 Camaros were built at the Norwood, Ohio, plant and 49,064 Camaros were made at a factory in Van Nuys (Los Angeles), California. In addition, the trade journals showed 1,248 Camaros "produced" at an assembly plant in Bloomfield, New Jersey. According to Camaro Brand Manager Scott Settlemire's sources, these 1,248 cars were actually units produced at the Norwood factory and shipped to a site near Bloomfield (possibly Little Ferry), where they were "knocked down" for shipment overseas. This means that the total number of cars built in Norwood, Ohio, was actually 185,983. Of the Camaros built in the model year, 56.4 percent had automatic transmission, 20.2 percent had a four-speed manual transmission, 78.3 percent had a V-8, 21.7 percent had a six-cylinder engine, 82.0 percent had an AM radio, 3.1 percent had an AM/FM radio, 1.8 percent had a factory tape deck, 15.3 percent had air conditioning, 2.3 percent had a tilt steering wheel, 49.0 percent had power steering, 10.2 percent had power drum brakes, 8.6 percent had disc brakes, 1.4 percent had power side windows, 97.9 percent had front bucket seats, 32.8 percent had a vinyl roof, 85.3 percent had white sidewall tires, 25.8 percent had a tinted windshield only, 27.8 percent had all tinted

Jerry Heasley photo

The white seats and door panels made for a sharp interior combination.

This car was the only 1968 Z/28 convertible made. It was dark blue with white stripes and a white convertible top.

Jerry Heasley photo

glass, 21.7 percent had dual exhausts, 15.6 percent had a limited-slip differential, 62.9 percent had wheel covers and 0.1 percent had cruise control. Camaro sales for calendar year 1968 came to a new high of 213,980 units (2.50 percent of industry) compared to 205,816 (2.7 percent of industry) in 1967. A total of 209,822 new Camaros were registered in the 1968 calendar year compared to 204,862 in the 1967 calendar year and 41,100 in the 1966 calendar year. The 1968 Camaro Z/28 was road tested by three major magazines with varying results. *Road & Track* (June 1968) recorded a 3.4-second 0 to 30-mph time, a 6.9-second 0 to 60-mph time, a 15-second 0 to 100-mph time and a 14.90-second quarter mile at 100 mph. *Car Life* (July 1968) recorded a 3.5-second 0 to 30-mph time, a 7.4-second 0 to 60-mph time, a 14.2-second 0 to 100-mph time and a 14.85-second quarter mile at 101.40 mph. *Car and Driver* (June 1968) recorded a 2.2-second 0 to 30-mph time, a 5.3-second 0 to 60-mph time, a 12.3-second 0 to 100-mph time and a 13.77-second quarter mile at 107.39 mph. The *Car and Driver* car was specially prepped by the factory, but beat out a Mustang with similar modifications. A single 1968 Camaro Z/28 convertible was specially built for Chevrolet general manager Elliott "Pete" Estes.

Gene Stransky photo

A '68 RS/SS 396 with yellow and black exterior. This one has an automatic transmission and deluxe interior package.

Chip Myers photo

The 1969 Camaro was the last of the first-generation Camaros and is a favorite among enthusiasts. This RS/SS is a show winner that boasts a 350-cid L48 engine and four-speed transmission.

The SS 396 Camaro was big news for the go-fast set, but the 1969 model went one step further with big news for every class of buyer. It sported a heavy exterior facelift featuring muscular-looking new sheet metal.

The last of the first-generation Camaros is considered by many enthusiasts to be the most popular one. The concept behind the new design was to make the Camaro look more "aggressive." The new body provided a longer, lower and wider appearance and had sculpted body sides. The wheel wells were flattened with sculptured feature lines flowing off them toward the rear of the car and rear-slanting air slots ahead of the rear wheel. An RS/SS convertible with a 396-cid Turbo-Jet V-8 under its hood paced the 1969 Indy 500 and this time Chevrolet sold replicas of the pace car to the public starting on Feb. 4, 1969. Experts say 3,675 of these Z11 convertibles were made, along with a few hundred hardtops with a rare Z10 Indy Sport Coupe package.

Chevrolet started promoting the Camaro as the "Hugger" this year and even had a Hugger Orange paint color for those who really wanted to catch attention on the street. The name, however, did not really stick and was rarely heard after 1970.

A new 307-cid base V-8 was added to the Camaro's engines list, as was an optional 250-cid straight six with 15 hp more than the standard inline six. Performance buffs could chose between the 350-cid and 396-cid V-8 offerings. Those who wanted to go even faster down a drag strip had the option of visiting a handful of dealerships across the country that would gladly stuff a 427-cid "Rat" motor into a Camaro for mucho bucks.

Chevy built 211,922 Camaros at Norwood in 1969, plus 31,163 more in Van Nuys.

I.D. DATA

Camaros had a 13-symbol vehicle identification number (VIN) on the upper left surface of the instrument panel, visible through the windshield. The first symbol identifies the make: 1=Chevrolet Motor Div. The second symbol indicates the car line/series: 2=Camaro. The third symbol indicates the type of engine: odd number=inline six-cylinder, even number=V-8. The fourth and fifth symbols indicate body type: 37=two-door hardtop coupe and 67=convertible. The sixth symbol indicates model year: 9=1969. The seventh symbol indicates the assembly plant: N=Norwood, Ohio and L=Van Nuys (Los Angeles) California. The final six digits are the sequential serial number starting with 500001 at each plant regardless of series. The Fisher Body Style Number plate was located on the firewall below the rear of the hood. The code in the left upper position was ST 69 12337 NOR, ST 69 12367, ST 69 12437 NOR or ST 69 12467. The first two symbols ST stand for "Style." The third and fourth symbols indicate model year: 69=1969 model. The fifth symbol indicates the division: 1=Chevrolet. The sixth and seventh symbols indicate series: 23=Camaro six-cylinder or 24=Camaro V-8. The eighth and ninth symbols indicate body style: 37=two-door coupe, 67=two-door convertible. The last three symbols indicate the assembly plant: NOR=Norwood, Ohio, LOS=Van Nuys, California. This plate also carries codes indicating the body production sequence at the specific plant, interior trim (TR), exterior paint (PNT), the month and week of the month of production (1A=January, first week, etc.) and other special codes.

COLORS

10=Tuxedo Black, 40=Butternut Yellow, 50=Dover White, 51=Dusk Blue, 52=Garnet Red, 53=Glacier Blue, 55=Azure Turquoise, 57=Fathom Green, 59=Frost Green, 61=Burnished Brown, 63=Champagne, 65= Olympic Gold, 67=Burgundy, 69=Cortez Silver, 71= LeMans Blue, 72=Hugger Orange, 76=Daytona Yellow, 79=Rallye Green. Two-tone color combinations available were 53/50 (Glacier Blue/ Dover White), 55/50 (Azure Turquoise/Dover White), 53/51 Glacier Blue/Dusk Blue, 51/53 Dusk Blue/Glacier Blue, 65/50 Olympic Gold/Dover White and 61/63 Burnished Brown/Champagne.

CAMARO - SERIES 23/24 - SIX/V-8

At the front of standard Camaros was a grille with 13 slender vertical moldings and five horizontal moldings forming a grid surrounded by a bright molding. A badge with the Chevrolet bow-tie emblem was in the center. There were single round headlamps near both outer ends of the grille. The full-width bumper integrated with the body-color outer grille surround and there was a license plate holder in the center of the valance panel. Round parking lights were positioned on either side of the license plate. At the rear were wider taillight bezels with triple-segment lenses. Standard equipment included an Argent Silver radiator grille, a bow-tie radiator emblem, valance-mounted parking lights with a clear lens and amber bulb, a "Camaro by Chevrolet" radiator grille header panel nameplate, bright windshield reveal moldings, Argent Silver headlight bezels, integrated front headlights and parking lights, a bright radiator grille outline molding, amber front and red rear sidemarker lights, white-painted front fender engine call-outs, "Camaro" front fender nameplates, hub caps, rocker panel moldings, a left-hand outside rearview mirror, a "Camaro by Chevrolet" rear deck lid nameplate, rear bumper guards, a bright backlight molding, taillights with bright moldings mounted in rear-end body panel, back-up lights mounted in the taillights, a rear panel bow-tie emblem, a prismatic 10-in. inside rearview mirror with padded edges, a satin-finished rearview mirror support, a color-coordinated rearview mirror center support, padded sun visors, color-coordinated padded windshield pillars, a dome light with a bright bezel, bright front seat shoulder belt clips, color-coordinated plastic seat belt anchor covers, left- and right-hand door jamb light switches, all-vinyl front Strato-bucket seats, an all-vinyl rear bench seat, a bright seat adjuster handle, bright front seat back latches, seat belts in all passenger positions, shoulder belts for driver and front passenger, luggage compartment with spatter paint finish, passenger compartment floor carpeting, all-vinyl head rests on front seat (as a mandatory option), color-coordinated all-vinyl door and quarter panel trim, padded front door arm rests, silver-accented clear plastic window regulator knobs, bright door lock buttons, "Camaro" nameplates on doors, a blended-air heater and defroster with illuminated controls, a "Camaro" nameplate on the right-hand side of the instrument panel, bright vent controls, a color-coordinated padded dashboard with reduced-glare elements, warning lights (for temperature, generator, oil pressure and parking brake), a lockable glove compartment, a high-beam indicator lamp, directional signals with indicator lamp on instrument board, two-speed windshield wipers with sliding control lever, windshield washers, a cigar lighter (in ashtray), an Astro Ventilation system, a bright light with black accents, front courtesy lights, a clock cover with "Camaro" nameplate, a steering column ignition with anti-theft lock, a color-coordinated turn signal lever knob, a color-coordinated floor shift knob, a two-spoke plastic steering wheel with built-in horn tabs, an energy-absorbing steering column, a bow-tie steering wheel emblem, a bright hazard lights control, Magic-Mirror acrylic lacquer finish, flush-and-dry rocker panels, curved side windows with full door-glass styling, keyless locking of all doors, inner fenders front and rear, a separate front frame unit, cushioned body mountings, an all-welded Fisher body, self-adjusting brakes with bonded linings, precise ball-race steering, 6,000-mile or four-month chassis lubrication, a foot-operated parking brake, a Delco Energizer battery, a long-life exhaust system, exhaust emission controls on all engines, a dual master cylinder brake system, corrosion resistant brake lines, a dual-action safety hood latch, a 230-cid 145-hp Turbo-Thrift inline six-cylinder engine or a 327-cid 210-hp Turbo-Fire V-8 engine, a three-speed manual transmission and E78 x 14 two-ply (four-ply-rated) black side-

The SS-396 was available with three different engines, generating between 325 and 375 hp.

Jerry Heasley photo

wall tires. Convertibles also had a folding convertible top, a clip-on top boot, bright windshield pillar moldings, a bright windshield header with convertible top latches, rear belt molding, courtesy lights under the instrument panel, radio speakers in the front kick panels, narrower sun visors, rear inside body panels with built-in armrests and ashtrays, E78-14 tires and a strengthening floor brace. They did not have color-coordinated roof rails with shoulder belt clips and coat hooks, plastic seat belt anchor covers or a dome light. A power-operated convertible top was optional. (Note: In January 1969 a 307-cid 200-hp Turbo-Fire V-8 replaced the 327-cid V-8 as the base V-8 engine).

Model Number	Body/Style Number	Body Type & Seating	Factory Price	Shipping Weight	Production Total
CAMARO - SERIES 23 - (L6)					
23	37	2d coupe	$2,621	3,005 lbs.	Note 1/2
CAMARO - SERIES 23 - (L6)					
23	67	2d convertible	$2,835	3,255 lbs.	Note 1/3
CAMARO - SERIES 24 - (V-8)					
24	37	2d coupe	$2,727	3,135 lbs.	Note 1/2
CAMARO - SERIES 24 - (V-8)					
24	67	2d convertible	$2,940	3,385 lbs.	Note 1/3

Note 1: Combined model-year production of all 1969 Camaros was 243,085.
Note 2: Combined model-year production of all 1969 Camaros included 165,226 base coupes.
Note 3: Combined model-year production of all 1969 Camaros included 17,573 base convertibles.

CAMARO RALLY SPORT - SERIES 23/24 + Z22 – V-6/V-8

The RPO Z22 Rally Sport package initially cost Chevrolet dealers $101.65 and retailed for $131.65. In May, after automakers issued revised prices, the dealer cost of this option rose to $104.15, but the retail price remained unchanged. The Rally Sport package included a special grille that filled only the space between where the headlights normally appeared in full view, instead of going fully across the front of the car like the standard grille. The grille had an "RS" emblem in its center. The license plate was still mounted below the center of the full-width bumper and the round parking lamps flanked it. The headlights were actually there, but they were hidden behind triple segmented "doors" that flanked the grille. Chevrolet even included a "fail safe" system to open the headlight doors if the vacuum motor failed and headlight washers. The headlamp covers actually consisted of a body-color outer door with three horizontal openings in it and a chrome door that was slotted to allow light to shine through if it if the system wasn't operating. Other Rally Sport content included fender striping (except when the sport striping or Z/28 options were added), bright accents on the air vents ahead of the rear wheel opening, front and rear wheel opening moldings, black body sills (except on cars painted Dusk Blue, Fathom Green, Burnished Brown or Burgundy), "Rally Sport" fender nameplates, bright taillight accents, bright parking light accents, back-up lights below the rear bumper, an RS steering wheel emblem, black steering wheel accents and bright roof drip moldings on coupes. Other Rally Sport features included an all-vinyl Stratobucket seat interior, bright accents on the instrument panels and doors, foam-cushioned front and rear seats, Astro Ventilation, color-keyed deep-twist carpeting, a lockable glove compartment, an ashtray with cigar lighter, a center dome light, front fender engine call-outs (except with the 140-hp six-cylinder engine), amber parking and directional signal lamps with white lenses, "Rally Sport" front fender nameplates, a windshield molding, full door-glass styling, a rectangular left-hand outside rearview mirror, hub caps, front and rear side marker lights, triple-unit taillights, rear bumper guards and a concealed fuel filler. The RS convertible had a courtesy light under the instrument panel in place of a dome light. Most other features listed above for the base Camaro were also included on the Rally Sport unless another feature was substituted by the package itself. The Rally Sport option could be added to any Camaro with any engine. The prices given immediately below are for base Camaros with the Rally Sport package added. To determine the cost of other model-options with Rally Sport equipment installed add the package price of $131.65 to the factory prices for the specific SS or Z/28 model.

The special COPO Camaros are valuable collector cars today.

Jerry Heasley photo

Jerry Heasley photo

The powerful, and scarce, ZL1 Camaros are among the great American muscle cars.

Model Number	Body/Style Number	Body Type & Seating	Factory Price	Shipping Weight	Production Total
CAMARO RALLY SPORT - SERIES 23 + Z22 - (L6)					
23	37	2d coupe	$2,753	—	Note 4/5
CAMARO RALLY SPORT - SERIES 23 + Z22 - (L6)					
23	67	2d convertible	$2,967	—	Note 4/5
CAMARO RALLY SPORT - SERIES 24 + Z22 - (V-8)					
24	37	2d coupe	$2,859	—	Note 4/5
CAMARO RALLY SPORT - SERIES 24 + Z22 - (V-8)					
24	67	2d convertible	$3,072	—	Note 4/5

Note 4: Combined model-year production of all 1969 Camaros was 243,085.
Note 5: Of the 243,085 cars built, 37,773 had the Rally Sport option.

CAMARO SS - SERIES 24 - V-8

The Camaro SS (Super Sport) was a performance-oriented option package that initially cost Chevrolet dealers $228.51 and retailed for $295.95 early in the 1969 model year. On May 1, 1969, there was an increase in Chevrolet pricing and the dealer cost of the Z27 package rose to $246.63, which increased the retail price to $311.75. Standard equipment for Rally Sport models included all of the base equipment, such as seat belts with push-button buckles for all passenger positions, shoulder belts with push-button buckles for the driver and front passenger, two front seat head restraints, an energy-absorbing steering column, passenger-guard door locks with forward-mounted lock buttons, safety door latches and hinges, folding seat back latches, an energy-absorbing instrument panel and front seat back tops, contoured roof rails, a thick-laminate windshield, padded sun visors, safety armrests, a safety steering wheel, side-guard beam door structures, a cargo-guard luggage compartment, side markers with reflectors (front side marker lights flash with directional signals), parking lights that illuminate with the headlights, a four-way hazard warning flasher, back-up lights, a lane-change feature in the directional signal control, a windshield defroster, windshield washers, dual-speed windshield wipers, a vinyl-edged wide-view inside day/night mirror with shatter resistant glass, a left-hand outside rearview mirror, a dual master cylinder brake system with a warning light, dual-action safety hood latches, a double-panel acoustically engineered roof with built-in headers, side-guard beam door structures, flush door handles, an advanced-design front suspension with forward-mounted steering linkage, E78-14 bias-belted ply tires, a precision-molded instrument panel, wide doors, all-vinyl bucket seats, bucket-styled rear seats, multi-leaf rear springs, a transverse muffler mounted behind the rear axle, full door-glass styling, Magic-Mirror acrylic lacquer finish, flush-and-dry rocker panels, double-panel door and deck lid construction, a flush-mounted windshield and rear window bonded to the body, a blended-air heater and defroster system, front and rear springs tailored to match individual models and equipment, a sealed side-terminal Delco Energizer battery, safety wheel rims, inner front and rear fenders, vinyl-trimmed inside door panels and carpeting. In addition, the SS option added a 300-hp Turbo-Fire 350 V-8, a neat-looking hood with exclusive bright-finished simulated intake ports, "hockey-stick" sport striping, simulated rear fender louvers, power front disc brakes, F70-14 raised white-letter tires on 7-in. wide wheels, a black-finished grille with a bright outline and SS identification, black-painted body sills (except on cars painted Dusk Blue, Fathom Green, Burnished Brown or Burgundy), a special three-speed manual transmission with 2.42:1 low gear, "SS" front fender emblems, an "SS" rear panel emblem and an "SS" steering wheel emblem (except with the optional wood-grained steering wheel). Three different "Turbo-Jet 396" (396-cid) V-8s were available as options for the Camaro SS. The RPO L34 version was rated at 350 hp, the RPO L78 version was rated at 375 hp and the RPO L89 version also carried a 375-hp rating. When these engines were added, the rear panel of the standard Camaro SS was painted black (except on Indy 500 Pace Cars).

Model Number	Body/Style Number	Body Type & Seating	Factory Price	Shipping Weight	Production Total
CAMARO SS COUPE - SERIES 24 + Z27 - (RPO L48 "TURBO-FIRE 350" V-8/THREE-SPEED MANUAL TRANSMISSION)					
24	37	2d coupe	$3,023	—	Note 6/7
24	67	2d convertible	$3,236	—	Note 6/7
CAMARO SS COUPE - SERIES 24 + Z27 - (RPO L34 "TURBO-JET 396" V-8/ THREE-SPEED MANUAL TRANSMISSION)					
24	37	2d coupe	$3,207	—	Note 6/7
24	67	2d convertible	$3,420	—	Note 6/7
CAMARO SS COUPE - SERIES 24 + Z27 - (RPO L35 "TURBO-JET 396" V-8/ THREE-SPEED MANUAL TRANSMISSION)					

24	37	2d coupe	$3,086	—	Note 6/7
24	67	2d convertible	$3,299	—	Note 6/7

CAMARO SS COUPE - SERIES 24 + Z27 - (RPO L34 "TURBO-JET 396" V-8/ THREE-SPEED MANUAL TRANSMISSION)

24	37	2d coupe	$3,207	—	Note 6/7
24	67	2d convertible	$3,420	—	Note 6/7

CAMARO SS COUPE - SERIES 24 + Z27 - (RPO L89 "TURBO-JET 396" V-8/ THREE-SPEED MANUAL TRANSMISSION)

24	37	2d coupe	$3,734	—	Note 6/7
24	67	2d convertible	$3,947	—	Note 6/7

Note 6: Combined model-year production of all 1969 Camaros was 243,085.
Note 7: Combined production of all 1969 Camaros included 36,309 total SS models (coupes and convertibles combined).
Note 8: The initial price for the SS package was used in computing prices above; the price climbed $15.80 after May 1, 1969.

CAMARO INDY SPORT CONVERTIBLE (INDY 500 OFFICIAL PACE CAR REPLICA) – MODEL 12467 + Z11 – V-8

The first Camaro had served as Official Pace Car for the 1967 Indianapolis 500-Mile Race and Indianapolis Motor Speedway. That year, only a limited number of actual Indy 500 Pace Cars and "Official Cars" were made and these were not intended for sale to the public as new cars. In 1969, Chevrolet was invited to supply a Camaro Pace Car once again. By this time auto sales were in a slump and the company decided to get extra mileage out of the promotional effort by creating the RPO Z11 "Indy Sport Convertible" package. A confidential Chevrolet Passenger Car Product Bulletin issued on Feb. 4, 1969, described this option as "Midseason Change No. 13" and stated the following: "A new Regular Production Option (Z11) will be released to provide a modified Camaro SS/RS Convertible similar to the Indianapolis 500 Pace Car. The RPO Z11 is comprised of: Camaro SS/Rally Sport (Camaro SS RPO Z27 with Rally Sport equipment RPO Z22). With exceptions: Add hood and deck lid Hugger Orange paint stripes, same as used with RPO Z28. Body sill to be white instead of black. Rear panel to be white instead of black, as specified with 396 V-8 engine options. Remove Sport Striping (reference RPO D90). Add Hugger Orange fender striping (reference RPO D96, part of RPO Z22). Exterior body color, Dover White, Code 911. Custom interior, RPO Z87 with exceptions: Orange houndstooth trim, Code 720. Air Induction Hood, RPO ZL2. Rally wheel, hub cap and trim ring, RPO ZJ7. To be identical with the actual pace car, additional

options are required: Turbo-Hydra-Matic RPO M40, Positraction rear Axle RPO G80, power steering RPO N40, power convertible top RPO C06, Console RPO D55, special instrumentation RPO U17, AM radio RPO U63, air spoiler, front and rear RPO D80, Sport styled steering wheel RPO N34, custom deluxe seat and front shoulder belts (A39 & A85) RPO YA1, Soft-Ray tinted glass RPO A01. — R.C. Mumbrum, Sales Liaison Engineer." The Z11 option was available for SS/RS convertibles with the 350-cid 300-hp V-8 or with 396-cid V-8s. Pace car door decals that read "Chevrolet Camaro OFFICIAL PACE CAR, 53rd ANNUAL INDIANAPOLIS 500 MILE RACE MAY 30, 1969" were available with the Z11 option, but not mandatory. The decals were shipped inside the trunk of the cars for installation at the dealership level, if the customer desired the lettering. Pace cars were produced at both the Norwood and Van Nuys assembly plants. The cars built in Ohio had "Z11" stamped on the Fisher Body cowl tag and the California built cars did not.

Model Number	Body/Style Number	Body Type & Seating	Factory Price	Shipping Weight	Production Total
24	67	2d convertible	$3,405	—	3,675

Note 9: Two actual Indy 500 Official Pace Cars were also built for use at the Indianapolis Motor Speedway on May 30, 1969.

CAMARO INDY SPORT COUPE – MODEL 12437 + Z10 – V-8

Camaro club enthusiasts have documented that a Pace Car Sport Coupe was offered as a promotional model by the Chevrolet Southwest Sales Zone and sold in a number of states, including Arizona, Oklahoma, Texas and Wisconsin. The package was coded as RPO Z10 and was for the Camaro coupe with RS/SS equipment. These were similar to the Z11 convertible on the outside, but had some interior differences such as black (standard, custom or houndstooth) and ivory (standard and houndstooth) interior choices, in addition to orange houndstooth. They also came with the optional wood-grained steering wheel, ComforTilt steering wheel, a vinyl top and other options. It is believed that the Norwood factory built 200 to 300 of these cars.

Model Number	Body/Style Number	Body Type & Seating	Factory Price	Shipping Weight	Production Total
24	37	2d coupe	$3,192	—	200-300

Note 10: Production of cars with the Z10 option is an estimate.

A Rallye Green 350 Sport Coupe with white interior and automatic transmission.

Stephen King photo

More than 20,000 1969 Z/28s were sold, marking a three-year high for the hot Camaro.

CAMARO Z/28 - SERIES 24 + Z/28 – V-8

In 1969, the popularity of the Camaro Z/28 achieved a three-year high with production climbing from 602 in 1967 to 7,199 in 1968 to 20,302 in 1969. To a large degree, the boom in interest was generated by the 1969 Z/28s that Roger Penske's racing team campaigned in the Sports Car Club of America's Trans-Am series. Penzke's dark blue and yellow Camaros appeared in Sunoco gasoline advertisements, as well as in promotions for Sears Die-Hard batteries. The Z/28 package was available for Camaro Sport Coupes with power disc brakes and a four-speed manual transmission. A Positraction rear axle (as an extra-cost option) was recommended to go with the package. In addition to or in place of that model's standard equipment, the Z/28 featured a special 302-cid V-8, a dual exhaust system with deep-tone mufflers, a special front suspension, a special rear suspension, rear bumper guards, a heavy-duty radiator, a temperature-controlled de-clutching fan, quick-ratio steering, 15 x 7-in. Rally wheel rims, special E70-15 white-letter tires, a 3.73:1 ratio rear axle and special Rally stripes on the hood and rear deck lid. Some changes were made to the content and prices of the Z/28 package during the model year. The original cost in September, 1968, was $458.15. In October, the engine got bright accents, a chambered exhaust system became available, as did four-wheel disc brakes. In January 1969, due to problems with noise regulations, the chambered exhaust system was dropped, a tachometer was required at extra cost and the price went up $15.80. On April 1 the price climbed by $32.65 and a front valance panel and rear deck lid spoiler became mandatory options. In May, chrome exhaust pipe tips were made standard Z/28 equipment. September 1969 of the stretched model year brought another $15.80 price increase.

Model Number	Body/Style Number	Body Type & Seating	Factory Price	Shipping Weight	Production Total
24	37	2d coupe	$3,588	—	20,302

Note 11: Price column reflects computed price with least expensive mandatory options array early in model year.

ENGINE

STD Turbo-Thrift I6: Overhead-valve inline six-cylinder. Cast-iron block and head. Bore & stroke: 3.88 x 3.25 in. Displacement: 230 cid. Compression ratio: 8.5:1. Brake horsepower: 140 at 4400 rpm. Torque: 220 lbs.-ft. at 1600 rpm. Seven main bearings. Induction system: Rochester one-barrel carburetor. Standard in Camaro.

L22 Turbo-Thrift I6: Overhead-valve inline six-cylinder. Cast-iron block and head. Bore & stroke: 3.88 x 3.53 in. Displacement: 250 cid (4.1 liters). Compression ratio: 8.5:1. Brake horsepower: 155 at 4200 rpm. Torque: 235 lbs.-ft. at 1600 rpm. Seven main bearings. Induction system: Rochester No. 7040017 one-barrel carburetor. Optional in Camaro.

STD Turbo-Fire V-8: 90-degree, overhead-valve V-8. Cast-iron block and head. Bore & stroke: 3.87 x 3.25 in. Displacement: 307 cid (5.7 liters). Compression ratio: 9.0:1. Brake horsepower: 200 at 4600 rpm. Torque: 300 lbs.-ft. at 2400 rpm. Five main bearings. Hydraulic valve lifters. Induction system: Rochester two-barrel carburetor. Standard V-8 in Camaro starting in January 1969.

STD Turbo-Fire V-8: 90-degree, overhead-valve V-8. Cast-iron block and head. Bore & stroke: 4.00 x 3.25 in. Displacement: 327 cid. Compression ratio: 8.75:1. Brake horsepower: 210 at 4600 rpm. Torque: 320 lbs.-ft. at 3400 rpm. Five main bearings. Hydraulic valve lifters. Induction system: Rochester two-barrel carburetor. Standard V-8 in Camaro prior to January 1969, then replaced by 307-cid V-8.

LM1 Turbo-Fire V-8: 90-degree, overhead-valve V-8. Cast-iron block and head. Bore & stroke: 4.00 x 3.48 in. Displacement: 350 cid (5.7 liters). Compression ratio: 9.0:1. Brake horsepower: 255 at 4800 rpm. Torque: 365 lbs.-ft. at 3200 rpm. Five main bearings. Hydraulic valve lifters. Induction system: Rochester two-barrel carburetor. Optional in Camaro; dropped during the model year.

L65 Turbo-Fire V-8: 90-degree, overhead-valve V-8. Cast-iron block and head. Bore & stroke: 4.00 x 3.48 in. Displacement: 350 cid (5.7 liters). Compression ratio: 9.0:1. Brake horsepower: 250 at 4800 rpm. Torque: 345 lbs.-ft. at 2800 rpm. Five main bearings. Hydraulic valve lifters. Induction system: Rochester no. 7040113 two-barrel carburetor. Optional in Camaro late in the model year.

L48 Turbo-Fire V-8: 90-degree, overhead-valve V-8. Cast-iron block and head. Bore & stroke: 4.00 x 3.48 in. Displacement: 350 cid (5.7 liters). Compression ratio: 10.25:1. Brake horsepower: 300 at 4800 rpm. Torque: 380 lbs.-ft. at 4000 rpm. Five main bearings. Hydraulic valve lifters. Induction system: Rochester four-barrel carburetor. Standard in Camaro SS; not available in other models.

L35 "396 Turbo-Jet" V-8: 90-degree, overhead-valve V-8. Cast-iron block and head. Bore & stroke: 4.09 x 3.76 in. Displacement: 396 cid. Compression ratio: 10.25:1. Brake horsepower: 325 at 4800 rpm. Torque: 410 lbs.-ft. at 3200 rpm. Five main bearings. Hydraulic valve lifters. Induction system: Rochester four-barrel carburetor. Optional in Camaro SS; not available in other models. Installed in 6,752 Camaros.

L34 "396 Turbo-Jet" V-8: 90-degree, overhead-valve V-8. Cast-iron block and head. Bore & stroke: 4.09 x 3.76 in. Displacement: 396 cid. Compression ratio: 10.25:1. Brake horsepower: 350 at 5200 rpm. Torque: 415 lbs.-ft. at 3400 rpm. Five main bearings. Hydraulic valve lifters. Induction system: Rochester four-barrel carburetor. Optional in Camaro SS; not available in other models. Installed in 2,018 Camaros.

L78 "396 Turbo-Jet" V-8: 90-degree, overhead-valve V-8. Cast-iron block and head. Bore & stroke: 4.09 x 3.76 in. Displacement: 396 cid. Compression ratio: 11.0:1. Brake horsepower: 375 at 5600 rpm. Torque: 415 lbs.-ft. at 3600 rpm. Five main bearings. Solid valve lifters. Induction system: Holley four-barrel carburetor and high-rise aluminum intake manifold. Optional in Camaro SS; not available in other models. Installed in 4,889 Camaros.

L78/L89 "396 Turbo-Jet" V-8: 90-degree, overhead-valve V-8. Cast-iron block. Aluminum head with large valves. Bore & stroke: 4.09 x 3.76 in. Displacement: 396 cid. Compression ratio: 11.0:1. Brake horsepower: 375 at 5600 rpm. Torque: 415 lbs.-ft. at 3600 rpm. Five main bearings. Solid valve lifters. Induction system: Holley four-barrel carburetor and high-rise aluminum intake manifold. Installed in 311 Camaros. Optional in Camaro SS; not available in other models.

Z28 Turbo-Fire V-8: 90-degree, overhead-valve V-8. Cast-iron block. Large-port cylinder head with 2.02-in. intake valves and 1.60-in. exhaust valves. Bore & stroke: 4.002 x 3.005 in. Displacement: 302 cid (5.0 liters). Compression ratio: 11.1:1. Brake horsepower: 290 at 5800 rpm. Torque: 290 lbs.-ft. at 4200 rpm. Five four-bolt main bearings with nodular iron main caps. Solid valve lifters. Induction system: Holley No. 4053 four-barrel carburetor. Four-bolt main bearings. Special 30/30 lash solid lifter camshaft. Aluminum high-rise manifold. Aluminum impact extruded pistons. Large-port heads.

Standard in Camaro Z/28; not available in other Camaros.

L72 "427 Turbo-Jet" V-8: 90-degree, overhead-valve V-8. Cast-iron block and head. Bore & stroke: 4.251 x 3.76 in. Displacement: 427 cid. Compression ratio: 11.00:1. Brake horsepower: 400 at 5400 rpm. Torque: 460 lbs.-ft. at 3600 rpm. Five main bearings. Solid valve lifters. Induction system: Rochester four-barrel carburetor. There are no records to verify that any Camaros left the assembly line with this engine, but it was used in Berger, Motion/Baldwin, Fred Gibb, Dana/Nickey and Yenko Camaros that were built as Central Office Production Option (COPD) cars.

L72 "427 Turbo-Jet" V-8: 90-degree, overhead-valve V-8. Cast-iron block and head. Bore & stroke: 4.251 x 3.76 in. Displacement: 427 cid. Compression ratio: 11.25:1. Brake horsepower: 435 at 5800 rpm. Torque: 460 lbs.-ft. at 4000 rpm. Five main bearings. Solid valve lifters. Induction system: Holley four-barrel carburetor. This engine was originally released for use by Don Yenko's Yenko Sportscars under Central Office Production Order (COPO) 9561. Eventually other Chevrolet dealers such as Berger, Nickey, Emmert and others were given permission to order this special engine package as well.

ZL1 "427 Turbo-Jet" V-8: 90-degree, overhead-valve V-8. Aluminum block and "open-chamber" aluminum heads. Bore & stroke: 4.251 x 3.76 in. Displacement: 427 cid. Compression ratio: 12.5:1. Brake horsepower: 430 at 5800 rpm. Torque: 460 lbs.-ft. at 4000 rpm. Five main bearings. Solid valve lifters. Induction system: special 850 cfm Holley four-barrel carburetor on top of a special high-rise aluminum manifold. This very special engine package was originally released for Fred Gibb Chevrolet under Central Office Production Order (COPO) 9560. A total of only 69 Camaros received this special engine package.

CHASSIS

Base Sport Coupe: Wheelbase: (all) 108 in. Overall length: (all) 186 in. Height: (Sport Coupe) 51.1 in., (convertible) 50.9 in. Width: (all) 74 in. Front tread: 59.6 in. Rear tread: 59.5 in. Front headroom: (Sport Coupe) 37.1 in., (convertible) 37.5 in. Front legroom: (all) 42.5 in. Front shoulder room: (all) 56.5 in. Front hip room: (all) 56.3 in. Rear headroom: (Sport Coupe) 36.7 in., (con-

This SS-396 was loaded with almost all the available options and original SS wheels.

Doug Christenson photo

Chip Myers photo

The Camaro line got some aggressive styling updates for 1969, but the big remake would come a year later.

vertible) 36.8 in. Rear legroom: (Sport Coupe) 29.2 in., (convertible) 29.5 in. Rear shoulder room: (Sport Coupe) 53.6 in., (convertible) 47.3 in. Rear hip room: (Sport Coupe) 54.6 in., (convertible) 47.5 in. Usable trunk capacity: (Sport Coupe) 8.5 cu. ft., (convertible) 6.1 cu. ft. Rated fuel tank capacity: 18 gal. Standard tires: (Sport Coupe) E78 x 14, (convertible) D78 x 14.

Camaro SS: Wheelbase: (all) 108 in. Overall length: (all) 186 in. Height: (Sport Coupe) 51.1 in., (convertible) 50.9 in. Width: (all) 74.0 in. Front tread: 59.6 in. Rear tread: 59.5 in. Front headroom: (Sport Coupe) 37.1 in., (convertible) 37.5 in. Front legroom: (all) 42.5 in. Front shoulder room: (all) 56.5 in. Front hip room: (all) 56.3 in. Rear headroom: (Sport Coupe) 36.7 in., (convertible) 36.8 in. Rear legroom: (Sport Coupe) 29.2 in., (convertible) 29.5 in. Rear shoulder room: (Sport Coupe) 53.6 in., (convertible) 47.3 in. Rear hip room: (Sport Coupe) 54.6 in., (convertible) 47.5 in. Usable trunk capacity: (Sport Coupe) 8.5 cu. ft., (convertible) 6.1 cu. ft. Rated fuel tank capacity: 18 gal. Standard tires: F70-14 raised white-letter tires on 14 x 7-in. wheels.

Camaro Z/28: Wheelbase: (all) 108 in. Overall length: (all) 186 in. Height: (Sport Coupe) 51.1 in., (convertible) 50.9 in. Width: (all) 74.0 in. Front tread: 59.6 in. Rear tread: 59.5 in. Front headroom: (Sport Coupe) 37.1 in., (convertible) 37.5 in. Front legroom: (all) 42.5 in. Front shoulder room: (all) 56.5 in. Front hip room: (all) 56.3 in. Rear headroom: (Sport Coupe) 36.7 in., (convertible)

36.8 in. Rear legroom: (Sport Coupe) 29.2 in., (convertible) 29.5 in. Rear shoulder room: (Sport Coupe) 53.6 in., (convertible) 47.3 in. Rear hip room: (Sport Coupe) 54.6 in., (convertible) 47.5 in. Usable trunk capacity: (Sport Coupe) 8.5 cu. ft., (convertible) 6.1 cu. ft. Rated fuel tank capacity: 18 gal. Standard tires: Special E70-15 white-letter tires on 15 x 7-in. Rally wheels.

TECHNICAL

Transmission: Three-speed manual transmission (column shift) standard with floor shift in Camaro six-cylinder. Three-speed manual transmission (column shift) standard with floor shift in Camaro V-8. Four-speed floor shift standard optional in Camaro V-8; mandatory in Camaro SS and Camaro Z/28 (choice of close-ratio or wide-ratio). Turbo-Hydra-Matic transmission optional. Steering: re-circulating ball. Turning diameter wall-to-wall, outside front: 38 ft. 8 in. Turning diameter curb to curb, outside front: 37 ft. 4 in. Front suspension: coil springs and tube-type. Rear suspension: leaf springs and tube-type shock absorbers. Body construction: integral, with separate partial front box frame. Brakes: Drum (Front disc brakes included with Camaro SS package; front disc or four-wheel disc brakes required on Z/28 depending upon time of purchase). Fuel tank: 18 gal.

OPTIONS

AS1 front shoulder belts ($23.20). AS4 custom deluxe

rear shoulder belts ($26.35). AS5 standard rear shoulder belts ($23.20). A01 Soft-Ray tinted glass ($32.65). A31 power windows ($105.35). A39 custom deluxe front and rear belts ($9). A67 rear folding seat ($42.15). A85 custom deluxe front shoulder belts ($26.35). B37 color-keyed floor mats ($11.60). B93 door edge guards ($4.25). CE1 headlight flasher ($15.80). C06 power convertible top ($52.70). C08 vinyl roof cover ($84.30). C50 rear window defroster with Sport Coupe ($22.15). C50 rear window defroster with convertible ($32.65). C60 air conditioning ($376). DX1 front accent striping ($25.30). D33 left-hand remote-controlled outside rearview mirror ($10.55). D34 visor-vanity mirror ($3.20). D55 center front seat console ($53.75). D90 Sport striping ($25.30). D96 fender striping ($15.80). F41 heavy-duty Sport suspension ($10.55). G31 special heavy-duty rear springs ($20.05). G80 positraction rear axle ($42.15). Optional axle ratios ($2.15). JL8 power four-wheel disc brakes ($500.30). J52 power front disc brakes ($64.25). J50 power brakes ($42.15). KD5 positive crankcase ventilation ($6.35). K02 temperature-controlled de-clutching fan ($15.80). K05 engine block heater ($10.55). K79 42-amp Delcotron alternator ($10.55). K85 63-amp Delcotron alternator ($26.35). LM1 350-cid 255-hp V-8 ($52.70). L22 250-cid 155-hp six-cylinder engine ($26.35). L34 396-cid 350-hp in Camaro SS only ($184.35). L35 396-cid 325-hp V-8 in Camaro SS only ($63.20). L65 350-cid 250-hp V-8 ($21.10). L78 396-cid 375-hp V-8 ($316). L78/L89 396-cid 375-hp V-8 with aluminum cylinder heads in Camaro SS only ($710.95). MB1 Torque drive transmission ($68.65). MC1 special three-speed manual transmission ($79). MC11 floor-mounted gearshift lever ($10.55). M20 wide-ratio four-speed manual transmission ($195.40). M21 close-ratio four-speed manual transmission ($195.40). M22 close-ratio heavy-duty four-speed manual transmission ($322.10). M35 Powerglide automatic transmission with six-cylinder engines ($163.70). M35 Powerglide automatic transmission with small-block V-8s ($14.25). M40 Turbo-Hydra-Matic transmission ($190.10). NC8 chambered dual exhaust system ($15.80). N10 dual exhaust system ($30.55). N33 Comfortilt steering wheel ($45.30). N34 woodgrained steering wheel ($34.80). N40 power steering ($94.80). N44 "Quick-Response" variable-ratio steering ($15.80). N65 Spacesaver spare tire ($19). N95 simulated wire wheel covers ($73.75). N96 mag-style wheel covers ($73.75). PA2 mag-spoke wheel covers ($73.75). PK8 E78-14 white sidewall tires ($32.10). PL5 F70-14 white-letter tires ($63.05). PW7 F70-14 white sidewall tires ($62.60). PW8 F70-14 red stripe tires ($62.60). PY4 F70-14 fiberglass-belted tires ($88.60). PY4 F0-14 fiberglass-belted white sidewall tires on Camaro SS ($26.25). PY5 fiberglass-belted red stripe tires ($88.60). PY5 fiberglass-belted red stripe tires on Camaro SS ($26.25). P01 bright metal wheel covers ($21.10). P06 wheel trim rings ($21.10). T60 heavy-duty battery ($8.45). U15 speed warning indicator ($11.60). U17 special instrumentation ($94.80). U35 electric clock ($15.80). U16 tachometer ($52.70). U46 light monitoring system ($26.35). U57 stereo tape player ($133.80). U63 AM radio ($61.10). U69 AM/FM radio ($133.80). U73 manual rear-mounted radio antenna ($9.50). U79 push-button AM/FM stereo radio ($239.10). U80 rear

The "Hugger" tag only stuck with the Camaro for 1969. The nickname was gone by 1970.

seat speaker ($13.20). VE3 special body-color front bumper ($42.15). V01 heavy-duty radiator ($14.75). V31 front bumper guard ($12.65). V32 rear bumper guard ($12.65). ZJ9 auxiliary lighting in Sport Coupe without custom interior option ($13.70). ZJ9 auxiliary lighting in Sport Coupe with custom interior option ($11.10). ZJ9 auxiliary lighting in convertible without custom interior option ($9.50). ZJ9 auxiliary lighting in convertible with custom interior option ($6.85). ZK3 custom deluxe seat and shoulder belts ($12.15). ZL2 special cold-air-induction hood for Camaro SS or Camaro Z/28 ($79). Z11 special Indy 500 convertible package ($36.90). Z21 style trim ($47.40). Z22 Rally Sport package ($131.65). Z23 special interior group ($17.95). Z27 Camaro Super Sport package ($295.95). Z28 Special Performance package ($458.15). Z87 custom interior ($110.60). Two-tone paint ($31.60).

HISTORICAL FOOTNOTES

In 1969, John Z. DeLorean was general manager of Chevrolet Motor Division. It was another good year for the redesigned Camaro as production of 243,085 cars was realized in the model year. That represented 2.9 percent of total U.S. industry production and compared to 235,151 cars and 2.8 percent of industry in 1968 and 220,906 cars and 2.9 percent of industry in 1967. In round numbers the total included 36,500 six-cylinder cars and 206,500 V-8-powered Camaros. Of the total production, 211,922 Camaros were built at the Norwood, Ohio, plant (which also built 23,516 Firebirds). Another 31,163 Camaros (and 21,366 Firebirds) were made at a factory in Van Nuys (Los Angeles), California. The total included 12,316 cars built for export. Of the 200,213 Camaros built in the model year, 57.6 percent had automatic transmission, 23.9 percent had a four-speed manual transmission, 45.8 percent had a standard V-8, 39.2 percent had an optional V-8, 15 percent had a six-cylinder engine, 84.6 percent had an AM radio, 3.6 percent had an AM/FM radio, 2.8 percent had a stereo tape player, 57.3 percent had power steering, 6.7 percent had power drum brakes, 29 percent had front disc brakes, 1.4 percent had power side windows, 100 percent had bucket seats, 41.1 percent had a vinyl top, 47.5 percent had white sidewall tires, 1.2 percent had a tinted windshield only, 47.2 percent had all-tinted glass, 18.1 percent had air conditioning, 21 percent had a limited-slip differential, 46.2 percent had optional wheel covers, 19.2 percent had optional styled wheels, 21.7 percent had an optional clock, 3 percent had tilt steering and 26.4 percent had dual exhausts. Camaro sales for calendar year

1969 came to 171,598 units for a 2.03 percent share of the industry total. That compared to 213,980 (2.50 percent of industry) in 1968 and 205,816 (2.7 percent of industry) in 1967. A total of 172,459 new Camaros were registered in the U.S. during calendar year 1969, down from, 209,822 in the 1968 calendar year, 204,862 in the 1967 calendar year and 41,100 in the 1966 calendar year. In May 1969 *Car Life* magazine road tested a 375-hp SS 396 Camaro with the close-ratio four-speed manual transmission and cold-air-induction hood. The car did 0 to 30 mph in 2.6 sec., 0 to 60 mph in 6.8 sec., 0 to 100 mph in 15.6 sec. and the quarter mile in 14.77 sec. at 98.72 mph. It had a top speed of 126 mph. Many special high-performance 1969 Camaros were created by performance-oriented Chevrolet dealers as so-called COPO (Central Office Production Option) cars. For more information on these cars, see the "Special Camaros" chapter.

Jerry Heasley photo

An SS-396 convertible (right) was chosen as the Indy Pace Car and marketed to the public. An SS-350 was also produced (left).

C a m a r o

Jerry Heasley photo

In one magazine test, the 1970 Z/28 outperformed the Mustang.

An all-new second-generation Camaro arrived later than usual in the 1970 model year. The announcement day for the new Camaro was Feb. 26, 1970. Luckily, it was a hit! The revamped Camaro had a smooth European sports car image and came only as a coupe. The sleek long hood-short deck fastback body was longer, lower and wider than the first-generation Camaro.

Driver safety was enhanced by the use of side-guard door beams, while the performance-options list gained a 350-cid 360-hp LT1 engine for the Z/28 model, which had formerly relied on a hot "302." More importantly, the gorgeous new body would survive for 11 long model years, ultimately bringing the Camaro to one of its high points in both popularity and profitability.

I.D. DATA

Camaros had a 13-symbol vehicle identification number (VIN) on the upper left surface of the instrument panel, visible through the windshield. The first symbol identifies the make: 1=Chevrolet Motor Div. The second symbol indicate the car line/series: 2=Camaro. The third symbol indicates the type of engine: odd number=inline six-cylinder, even number=V-8. The fourth and fifth symbols indicate body type: 87=two-door hardtop coupe. The sixth symbol indicates model year: 0=1970. The seventh symbol indicates the assembly plant: N=Norwood, Ohio. The final six digits are the sequential serial number. The Fisher Body Style Number plate was located on the firewall below the rear of the hood. The code in the left upper position was ST 70 12387 NOR or ST 70 12487 NOR. The first two symbols ST stand for "Style." The third and fourth symbols indicate model year: 70=1970 model. The fifth symbol indicates the division: 1=Chevrolet. The sixth and seventh symbols indicate series: 23=Camaro six-cylinder or 24=Camaro V-8. The eighth and ninth symbols indicate body style:

87=two-door coupe. The last three symbols indicate the assembly plant: NOR=Norwood, Ohio, LOS=Van Nuys, California. This plate also carries codes indicating the body production sequence at the specific plant, interior trim (TR), exterior paint (PNT), the month and week of the month of production (1A=January, first week, etc.) and other special codes.

COLORS

10=Classic White, 14=Cortez Silver, 17=Shadow Gray, 25=Astro Blue, 26=Mulsanne Blue, 43=Citrus Green, 45=Green Mist, 48=Forest Green, 51=Daytona Yellow, 53=Camaro Gold, 58=Autumn Gold, 63=Desert Sand, 65=Hugger Orange, 67=Classic Copper and 75=Cranberry Red.

CAMARO - SERIES 23/24 - SIX/V-8

Standard equipment included seat belts with push-button buckles for all passenger positions, shoulder belts with push-button buckles for the driver and front passenger, two front seat head restraints, an energy-absorbing steering column, passenger-guard door locks with forward-mounted lock buttons, safety door latches and hinges, folding seat back latches, an energy-absorbing instrument panel and front seat back tops, contoured roof rails, a thick-laminate windshield, padded sun visors, safety armrests, a safety steering wheel, side-guard beam door structures, a cargo-guard luggage compartment, side markers with reflectors (front side marker lights flash with directional signals), parking lights that illuminate with the headlights, a four-way hazard warning flasher, back-up lights, a lane-change feature in the directional signal control, a windshield defroster, windshield washers, dual-speed windshield wipers, a vinyl-edged wide-view inside day/night mirror with shatter resilient glass, a left-hand outside rearview mirror, a dual master cylinder brake system with a warning light, dual-action safety hood latches, a double-panel acoustically-engineered roof with built-in headers, side-guard beam door structures, flush door handles, an advanced-design front suspension with forward-mounted steering linkage, E78-14 bias-belted ply tires, a precision-molded instrument panel, wide doors, all-vinyl bucket seats, bucket-styled rear seats, multi-leaf rear springs, a transverse muffler mounted behind the rear axle, high-output Power-Beam single-unit headlights, full door-glass styling, Magic Mirror acrylic lacquer finish, flush-and-dry rocker panels, double-panel door and deck lid construction, a flush-mounted windshield and rear window bonded to the body, a blended-air heater and defroster system, front and rear springs tailored to match individual models and equipment, a sealed side-terminal Delco Energizer battery, safety wheel rims, inner front and rear fenders, vinyl-trimmed inside door panels in black, blue, jade, saddle or sandlewood (matching seats), deep-twist floor carpeting, a 250-cid 155-hp inline six-cylinder engine or a 307-cid 200-hp V-8 and a three-speed manual transmission with floor shift.

Model Number	Body/Style Number	Body Type & Seating	Factory Price	Shipping Weight	Production Total
CAMARO SPORT COUPE - SERIES 23 - (L6)					
23	87	2d coupe	$2,749	3,058 lbs.	Note 1
CAMARO SPORT COUPE - SERIES 24 - (V-8)					
24	87	2d coupe	$2,839	3,172 lbs.	Note 1

Note 1: Model year production of 1970 base Camaro coupes was 100,967.

CAMARO RALLY SPORT - SERIES 23/24 + Z22 – SIX/V-8

The RPO Z22 Rally Sport package was a factory option designed to make the Camaro a bit flashier and more luxurious. The 1970 version retailed for $168.55. It was available separately for the base Sport Coupe or it could also be combined with the SS or Z/28 packages. Standard equipment for Rally Sport models included all of the base equipment, such as seat belts with push-button buckles for all passenger positions, shoulder belts with push-button buckles for the driver and front passenger, two front seat head restraints, an energy-absorbing steering column, passenger-guard door locks with forward-mounted lock buttons, safety door latches and hinges, folding seat back latches, an energy-absorbing instrument panel and front seat back tops, contoured roof rails, a thick-laminate windshield, padded sun visors, safety armrests, a safety steering wheel, side-guard beam door structures, a cargo-guard luggage com-

partment, side markers with reflectors (front side marker lights flash with directional signals), parking lights that illuminate with the headlights, a four-way hazard warning flasher, back-up lights, a lane-change feature in the directional signal control, a windshield defroster, windshield washers, dual-speed windshield wipers, a vinyl-edged wide-view inside day/night mirror with shatter resistant glass, a left-hand outside rearview mirror, a dual master cylinder brake system with a warning light, dual-action safety hood latches, a double-panel acoustically engineered roof with built-in headers, side-guard beam door structures, flush door handles, an advanced-design front suspension with forward-mounted steering linkage, E78-14 bias-ply belted tires, a precision-molded instrument panel, wide doors, all-vinyl bucket seats, bucket-styled rear seats, multi-leaf rear springs, a transverse muffler mounted behind the rear axle, high-output Power-Beam single-unit headlights, full door-glass styling, Magic Mirror acrylic lacquer finish, flush-and-dry rocker panels, double-panel door and deck lid construction, a flush-mounted windshield and rear window bonded to the body, a blended-air heater and defroster system, front and rear springs tailored to match individual models and equipment, a sealed side-terminal Delco Energizer battery, safety wheel rims, inner front and rear fenders, vinyl-trimmed inside door panels in black, blue, jade, saddle or sandlewood (to match the seats), deep-twist floor carpeting, a 250-cid 155-hp inline six-cylinder engine or a 307-cid 200-hp V-8 and a three-speed manual transmission with floor shift. In addition to all of this, the Rally Sport package added the Style Trim group, roadlight-styled parking lights mounted adjacent to the headlights, left and right front bumpers (replacing the standard full-width bumper), a color-matched resilient grille frame, Hide-A-Way windshield wipers, RS identification and more. Shown below are the prices for base Camaro Sport Coupes with the Rally Sport option. For RS/SS or RS/Z28 combinations add the package price to the factory prices for the SS and Z/28 model-options listed further below.

Model Number	Body/Style Number	Body Type & Seating	Factory Price	Shipping Weight	Production Total
CAMARO RALLY SPORT COUPE - SERIES 23 + Z22 - (L6)					
23	87	2d coupe	$2,918	—	Note 2/3
CAMARO RALLY SPORT COUPE - SERIES 24 + Z22 - (V-8)					
24	87	2d coupe	$3,008	—	Note 2/3

Note 2: Combined model-year production of all 1970 Camaros was 124,901.
Note 3: The production total given above included 27,136 Camaros with the Rally Sport package.

The 1970 (or 1970 1/2) Z28 with the 360-hp LT1 engine lived up to Chevrolet's vision for a true sports car.

Tim Mellem photo

CAMARO SS - SERIES 24 - V-8

The Camaro SS, or Super Sport, was a real muscle car for the streets. The RPO Z27 SS package was a factory option that retailed for $289.65 in 1970. It was available for V-8-powered Camaros with four-speed or Turbo-Hydra-Matic transmission. Standard equipment for Rally Sport models included all of the base equipment such as seat belts with push-button buckles for all passenger positions, shoulder belts with push-button buckles for the driver and front passenger, two front seat head restraints, an energy-absorbing steering column, passenger-guard door locks with forward-mounted lock buttons, safety door latches and hinges, folding seat back latches, an energy-absorbing instrument panel and front seat back tops, contoured roof rails, a thick-laminate windshield, padded sun visors, safety armrests, a safety steering wheel, side-guard beam door structures, a cargo-guard luggage compartment, side markers with reflectors (front side marker lights flash with directional signals), parking lights that illuminate with the headlights, a four-way hazard warning flasher, back-up lights, a lane-change feature in the directional signal control, a windshield defroster, windshield washers, dual-speed windshield wipers, a vinyl-edged wide-view inside day/night mirror with shatter resistant glass, a left-hand outside rearview mirror, a dual master cylinder brake system with a warning light, dual-action safety hood latches, a double-panel acoustically engineered roof with built-in headers, side-guard beam door structures, flush door handles, an advanced-design front suspension with forward-mounted steering linkage, a precision-molded instrument panel, wide doors, all-vinyl bucket seats, bucket-styled rear seats, multi-leaf rear springs, a transverse muffler mounted behind the rear axle, high-output Power-Beam single-unit headlights, full door-glass styling, Magic Mirror acrylic lacquer finish, flush-and-dry rocker panels, double-panel door and deck lid construction, a flush-mounted windshield and rear window bonded to the body, a blended-air heater and defroster system, front and rear springs tailored to match individual models and equipment, a sealed side-terminal Delco Energizer battery, safety wheel rims, inner front and rear fenders, vinyl-trimmed inside door panels in black, blue, jade, saddle or sandlewood (to match the seats), deep-twist floor carpeting, a 250-cid 155-hp inline six-cylinder engine or a 307-cid 200-hp V-8 and a three-speed manual transmission with floor shift. In addition, the SS option added the 300-hp Turbo-Fire 350 V-8, a black-finished grille with a bright outline and SS identification, a remote-control left-hand outside sport type rearview mirror, power disc brakes, special hood insulation, dual exhaust outlets, Hide-A-Way windshield wipers, 14 x 7-in. wheels, F70 x 14 wide-oval white-letter bias-belted tires and special SS ornamentation on fenders, steering wheel and rear deck lid. A 350-hp (L34) and a 375-hp (L89) "396 Turbo-Jet" V-8 were optional for cars with the SS package. Both engines available with the package came with a bright air cleaner cover. On Camaro SS models with the bigger engine the buyer got a heavy-duty Sport suspension with front and rear stabilizer bars and special shock absorbers.

Model Number	Body/Style Number	Body Type & Seating	Factory Price	Shipping Weight	Production Total
CAMARO SS COUPE - SERIES 24 + Z27 - (RPO L48 "TURBO-FIRE 350" V-8/FOUR-SPEED MANUAL TRANSMISSION)					
23	87	2d coupe	$3,336	—	Note 4
CAMARO SS COUPE - SERIES 24 + Z22 - (RPO L34 "TURBO-JET 396" V-8/FOUR-SPEED MANUAL TRANSMISSION)					
24	87	2d coupe	$3,491	—	Note 4
CAMARO SS COUPE - SERIES 24 + Z22 - (RPO L78 "TURBO-JET 396" V-8/FOUR-SPEED MANUAL TRANSMISSION)					
24	87	2d coupe	$3,724	—	Note 4

Note 4: Model-year production of 1970 Camaro SS coupes was 15,201.

CAMARO Z/28 - SERIES 24 + Z/28 – V-8

The Camaro Z/28 grew out of Chevrolet's desire to field a car in the popular Sports Car Club of America Trans-Am racing series. SCCA rules put maximum displacement restrictions on the so-called sedan racers. The rules were changed in 1970 and, as a result, the Z/28's high-performance small-block V-8 was increased from 302-cid to 350-cid. However, it was a very special 350-cid engine that was virtually identical to the LT1 Corvette engine. The major difference was that the Camaro had a more restrictive exhaust system that robbed away about 10 hp and gave the engine a 360-hp rating. The combination of the new body with this outstanding motor made the 1970 Z/28 an instant classic. The engine featured bright accents, finned aluminum valve covers, four-bolt main bearings, impact extruded aluminum pistons, forged steel bearings, solid valve lifters, a 780-cfm Holley four-barrel carburetor, a high-

The Rally Sport package was a $168.55 option for the 1970 Camaro.

rise aluminum intake manifold, a dual exhaust system and extra-large 2.02-in. intake valves and 1.60-in. exhaust valves. The RPO Z/28 Special Performance package retailed for $572.95 in 1970. It was available for V-8-powered Camaros with special instrumentation, a four-speed manual or Turbo-Hydra-Matic transmission, power disc brakes and a 3.73:1 Positraction rear axle (4.10:1 optional). Standard equipment started with most of the items that were standard on the base Sport Coupe (as listed above). In addition, the Z/28 option added a heavy-duty radiator, a black-painted grille, a Z/28 grille emblem, Z/28 front fender emblems, a Z/28 rear deck lid emblem, rear bumper guards, the F41 performance suspension, heavy-duty front and rear springs, 15 x 7-in. wheels, bright lug nuts, special center wheel caps, wheel trim rings, hood insulation, F60 x 15 white-letter bias-belted tires, a rear deck lid spoiler and special paint stripes on the hood and rear deck lid.

Model Number	Body/Style Number	Body Type & Seating	Factory Price	Shipping Weight	Production Total
CAMARO Z/28 SPORT COUPE - SERIES 24 + Z/28 - (V-8 WITH FOUR-SPEED MANUAL TRANSMISSION)					
24	87	2d coupe	$3,794	—	Note 5
CAMARO Z/28 SPORT COUPE - SERIES 24 + Z/28 - (V-8 WITH TURBO-HYDRA-MATIC TRANSMISSION)					
24	87	2d coupe	$3,878	—	Note 5

Note 5: Model-year production of 1970 Camaro Z/28 coupes was 8,733.

ENGINES

L22 Turbo-Thrift I6: Overhead-valve inline six-cylinder. Cast-iron block and head. Bore & stroke: 3.88 x 3.53 in. Displacement: 250 cid (4.1 liters). Compression ratio: 8.5:1. Brake horsepower: 155 at 4200 rpm. Torque: 235 lbs.-ft. at 1600 rpm. Seven main bearings. Induction system: Rochester No. 7040017 one-barrel carburetor. Standard in Camaro Sport Coupe.

Base Turbo-Fire V-8: 90-degree, overhead-valve V-8. Cast-iron block and head. Bore & stroke: 3.87 x 3.25 in. Displacement: 307 cid (5.7 liters). Compression ratio: 9.0:1. Brake horsepower: 200 at 4600 rpm. Torque: 300 lbs.-ft. at 2400 rpm. Five main bearings. Hydraulic valve lifters. Induction system: Rochester two-barrel carburetor. Standard V-8 in base Camaro Sport Coupe.

L65 Turbo-Fire V-8: 90-degree, overhead-valve V-8. Cast-iron block and head. Bore & stroke: 4.00 x 3.48 in. Displacement: 350 cid (5.7 liters). Compression ratio: 9.0:1. Brake horsepower: 250 at 4800 rpm. Torque: 345 lbs.-ft. at 2800 rpm. Five main bearings. Hydraulic valve lifters. Induction system: Rochester No. 7040113 two-barrel carburetor. Optional in Camaro Sport Coupe and Rally Sport.

L48 Turbo-Fire V-8: 90-degree, overhead-valve V-8. Cast-iron block and head. Bore & stroke: 4.00 x 3.48 in. Displacement: 350 cid (5.7 liters). Compression ratio: 10.25:1. Brake horsepower: 300 at 4800 rpm. Torque: 380 lbs.-ft. at 4000 rpm. Five main bearings. Hydraulic valve lifters. Induction system: Rochester four-barrel carburetor. Standard in Camaro SS; not available in other models.

Z28 Turbo-Fire V-8: 90-degree, overhead-valve V-8. Cast-iron block and head. Bore & stroke: 4.00 x 3.48 in. Displacement: 350 cid (5.7 liters). Compression ratio: 11.0:1. Brake horsepower: 360 at 6000 rpm. Torque: 380 lbs.-ft. at 4000 rpm. Five main bearings. Solid valve lifters. Induction system: Holley four-barrel carburetor. Four-bolt main bearings. Big valve heads. Special cam. Aluminum high-rise manifold. Standard in Camaro Z/28; not available in other Camaros.

L34 "396 Turbo-Jet" V-8: 90-degree, overhead-valve V-8. Cast-iron block and head. Bore & stroke: 4.13 x 3.76 in. Displacement: 402 cid. Compression ratio: 10.25:1. Brake horsepower: 350 at 5200 rpm. Torque: 415 lbs.-ft. at 3400 rpm. Five main bearings. Hydraulic valve lifters. Induction system: Rochester four-barrel carburetor. Optional in Camaro SS; not available in other models. (Promoted at "Turbo-Jet 396" V-8 but actually 402 cid).

L78 "396 Turbo-Jet" V-8: 90-degree, overhead-valve V-8. Cast-iron block and head. Bore & stroke: 4.13 x 3.76 in. Displacement: 402 cid. Compression ratio: 11.0:1. Brake horsepower: 375 at 5600 rpm. Torque: 415 lbs.-ft. at 3600 rpm. Five main bearings. Solid valve lifters. Induction system: Holley four-barrel carburetor. Optional in Camaro SS; not available in other models. (Promoted at "Turbo-Jet 396" V-8 but actually 402 cid).

LS6 "454 Turbo-Jet" V-8: 90-degree, overhead-valve V-8. Cast-iron block and head. Bore & stroke: 4.251 x 4.00 in. Displacement: 454 cid. Compression ratio: 11.25:1. Brake horsepower: 450 at 5600 rpm. Torque: 500 lbs.-ft. at 3600 rpm. Five main bearings. Solid valve lifters. Induction system: Rochester four-barrel carbure-

The Camaro got a redesign that brought a sleeker, more refined look for 1970.

Jerry Heasley photo

The SS option added the 300-hp Turbo-Fire 350 V-8, a black-finished grille with a bright outline and SS identification. There were two other available SS engines for 1970 - a 350-hp V-8 and 375-hp V-8 - making the Camaro SS one of the most muscular cars around.

tor. There are no records to verify that any Camaros left the assembly line with this engine, but it was used in the Motion/Baldwin Camaro and other car with the 454-cid V-8 that were built as Central Office Production Option (COPD) cars.

CHASSIS

Base Sport Coupe: Wheelbase: 108 in. Overall length: 186 in. Height: 50.9 in. Width: 74 in. Front tread: 59.6 in. Rear tread: 59.5 in. Front headroom: 37.3 in. Front legroom: 43.9 in. Front shoulder room: 56.7 in. Front hip room: 56.7 in. Rear headroom: 36 in. Rear legroom: 29.6 in. Rear shoulder room: 54.4 in. Rear hip room: 47.3 in. Usable trunk capacity: 6.4 cu. ft. Rated fuel tank capacity: 18 gal. Standard tires: E78 x 14/B tires.

Camaro SS: Wheelbase: 108 in. Overall length: 186 in. Height: 50.9 in. Width: 74 in. Front tread: 59.6 in. Rear tread: 59.5 in. Front headroom: 37.3 in. Front legroom: 43.9 in. Front shoulder room: 56.7 in. Front hip room: 56.7 in. Rear headroom: 36 in. Rear legroom: 29.6 in. Rear shoulder room: 54.4 in. Rear hip room: 47.3 in. Usable trunk capacity: 6.4 cu. ft. Rated fuel tank capacity: 18 gal. Standard tires: F70 x 14 wide-oval white-letter bias-belted tires.

Camaro Z/28: Same as above (depending upon which model the package was ordered for) with the following changes or additions: sport suspension with heavy-duty springs and front and rear stabilizer bars, special 15 x 7-in. wheels (with center caps, wheel trim rings and bright-finished lug nuts) and F60 x 15 bias-ply white letter tires.

TECHNICAL

Transmission: Three-speed manual transmission (column shift) standard with floor shift in Camaro six-cylinder. Three-speed manual transmission (column shift) standard with floor shift in Camaro V-8. Four-speed floor shift standard optional in Camaro V-8; mandatory in Camaro SS and Camaro Z/28 (choice of close-ratio or wide-ratio). Turbo-Hydra-Matic transmission optional. Steering: re-circulating ball. Turning diameter wall-to-wall, outside front: 39 ft. 11 in. Turning diameter curb to

curb, outside front: 37 ft. 8 in. Front suspension: coil springs and tube-type. Rear suspension: leaf springs and tube-type shock absorbers. Body construction: integral, with separate partial front box frame. Brakes: Front disc/rear drum (1970 1/2). Fuel tank: 19 gal.

OPTIONS

AK1 color-keyed seat and shoulder belts ($12.15). AS4 rear shoulder belts ($26.35). A01 Soft-Ray tinted glass ($37.95). B37 color-keyed floor mats ($11.60). B93 door edge guard moldings ($5.30). C08 vinyl roof cover ($89.55). C24 Hide-A-Way windshield wipers ($19). C50 rear window defogger ($26.35). C60 Four-Season air conditioning ($380.25). D34 visor-vanity mirror ($3.20). D35 sport mirrors ($26.35). D55 center console ($59). D80 rear deck lid spoiler ($32.65). F41 Sport suspension ($30.55). G80 Positraction rear axle ($44.25). J50 power brakes ($47.30). L34 "396 Turbo-Jet" 402-cid 350-hp V-8 ($152.75). L65 350-cid 350 250-hp Turbo-Fire four-barrel V-8 ($31.60). L78 "396 Turbo-Fire" 402-cid 375-hp V-8 ($385.50). M20 four-speed wide-ratio manual transmission ($205.95). M35 Powerglide automatic transmission with six-cylinder engine ($174.25). M40 Turbo-Hydra-Matic automatic transmission with Z/28 ($290.40). M40 Turbo-Hydra-Matic automatic transmission with Camaros SS with optional L34 V-8 ($221.80). M40 Turbo-Hydra-Matic automatic transmission with other Camaros ($200.65). NA9 California emission controls ($36.90). N33 Comfortilt steering wheel ($45.30). N40 power steering ($105.35). PL3 E78 x 14 white sidewall tires ($26.05). PL4 F70 x 14 white letter tires ($65.35). PX6 F78 x 14 white sidewall tires ($43.30). PY4 F70 x 14 white sidewall tires ($65.70). PO1 bright metal wheel trim covers ($26.35). P02 custom wheel trim covers ($79). T60 heavy-duty battery ($15.80). U14 special instrumentation ($84.30). U35 electric clock ($15.80). U63 AM radio ($61.10). U69 AM/FM radio ($133.80). U80 rear seat speaker ($14.75). VF3 deluxe front and rear bumpers ($36.90). V01 heavy-duty radiator ($14.75). YD1 trailering axle ratio ($12.65). ZJ7 Rally wheels with trim rings ($42.15). ZJ9 auxiliary lighting without custom interior option ($13.70). ZJ9 auxiliary lighting with custom interior option ($11.10). ZQ9 performance axle ratio ($12.65). Z21 style trim ($52.70). Z22 Rally Sport package ($168.55). Z23 interior accent group ($21.10). Z27 Camaro Super Sport package ($289.65). Z28 Special Performance package ($572.95). Z87 custom interior ($115.90).

HISTORICAL FOOTNOTES

Due to the late startup of 1970 Camaro production, the 1970 models were marketed for only half a year. They entered production on Jan. 5, 1970, and were introduced to the public on Feb. 26, 1970. Model-year production included 12,615 six-cylinder Camaros, 56,330 cars with the standard V-8 and 55,956 cars with an optional V-8 for a total of 124,901 units. Of these, 92,249 were built at the Norwood, Ohio, plant (which also built 37,215 Firebirds). Another 32,652 Camaros (and 11,524 Firebirds) were made at a factory in Van Nuys (Los Angeles), California. Production included 7,147 cars built for export. Of these Camaros, 73.1 percent had automatic transmission, 15 percent had a four-speed manual transmission, 45.1 percent had a standard V-8, 44.8 percent had an optional V-8, 10.1 percent had a six-cylinder engine, 88.7 percent had an AM radio, 6.9 percent had an AM/FM radio, 74.2 percent had power steering, 47.7 percent had standard front disc brakes as 1970 1/2 models, 100 percent had bucket seats, 34.6 percent had a vinyl top, 91.6 percent had white sidewall tires, 57.1 percent had all-tinted glass, 30.9 percent had air conditioning, 15.8 percent had a limited-slip differential, 61.5 percent had optional wheel covers, 12.2 percent had optional styled wheels, 12.4 percent had an optional clock, 5.4 percent had tilt steering and 17.0 percent had dual exhausts. Camaro sales for calendar year 1970 came to 145,826 units for a 2.05 percent share of the industry total. That compared to 171,598 (2.03 percent of industry) in 1969. A total of 142,281 new Camaros were registered in the U.S. during calendar year 1970, down from 172,459 in the 1969 calendar year, 209,822 in the 1968 calendar year, 204,862 in the

The hot Z28 was recognizable by its rear spoiler and special paint stripes on the hood and rear deck lid.

1967 calendar year and 41,100 in the 1966 calendar year. In May 1970, *Car Life* tested a Z/28 with Turbo-Hydra-Matic transmission and a 4.10:1 rear axle. This car did 0 to 30 mph in 2.9 sec., 0 to 60 mph in 6.5 sec and the quarter mile in 14.51 sec. at 98.79 mph. Top speed was given as 119 mph. *Car and Driver* tested a similar car the same month and registered a 2.1 sec. 0 to 30-mph time, a 5.8 sec. 0 to 60-mph time and a 14.2-sec. quarter mile at 100.3 mph. In this article top speed was given as 118 mph. *Motor Tend* (March 1970) tested a Z/28 with Turbo-Hydra-Matic and a 3.73:1 axle. It did 0 to 30 mph in 3.0 sec., 0 to 60 mph in 7.0 sec. And the quarter mile in 15.4 sec. at 94 mph. *Motor Trend* did not estimate top speed. A comparison test against a Mustang in *Car Life* magazine the Camaro Z/28 came out on top. The Z/28 did the quarter mile in 14.50 sec. at 100.22 mph. According to *Ward's 1970 Automotive Yearbook* the bucket seats introduced on the 1970 1/2 Camaro and Firebird were the first full-foam bucket seats to appear on a domestic car. They were developed by the Fisher Body Division. of GM and contained 85 percent fewer parts than conventional bucket seats.

The Camaro RS came with either a 250-cid inline six-cylinder or 307-cid V-8.

Jerry Heasley photo

Chevrolet rolled out 4,862 new Z/28s for 1971.

Chevrolet added high-back bucket seats (pirated from its sub-compact Vega) in 1971 and a new steering wheel with a cushioned hub. There were few other basic changes. In mid-1971, the Camaro front end was changed to accept "big Chevrolet" steering parts. The steering knuckles were switched to nodular iron castings, rather than forgings, and the tread was widened accordingly.

There were also new nameplates and new paint colors. The front side marker lights blinked in unison with the directional signals. A new type of thinner windshield glass was used. Technical changes were more important, as the engines were modified to operate on low-lead or lead-free gasoline blends. This meant lower compression ratios and horsepower ratings.

This was a great year for Chevrolet sales in general, but the Camaro didn't bask in the glory of Chevrolet Motor Division's first 3 million-unit year and its production dropped by more than 50 percent due to a lengthy strike in the fall of 1970. Also, the government and insurance companies were making life very hard for muscle car fans.

I.D. DATA

Camaros had a 13-symbol vehicle identification number (VIN) on the upper left surface of the instrument panel, visible through the windshield. The first symbol identifies the make: 1=Chevrolet Motor Division. The second symbol indicates the car line/series: 2=Camaro. The third symbol indicates the type of engine: odd number=inline six-cylinder, even number=V-8. The fourth and fifth symbols indicate body type: 87=two-door plainback hardtop coupe. The sixth symbol indicates model year: 1=1971. The seventh symbol indicates the assembly plant: N=Norwood, Ohio. The final six digits are the sequential serial number. The Fisher Body Style Number plate was located on the firewall below the rear

of the hood. The code in the left upper position was ST 71 12387 NOR or ST 71 12487 NOR. The first two symbols ST stand for "Style." The third and fourth symbols indicate model year: 71=1971 model. The fifth symbol indicates the division: 1=Chevrolet. The sixth and seventh symbols indicate series: 23=Camaro six-cylinder or 24=Camaro V-8. The eighth and ninth symbols indicate body style: 87=two-door coupe. The last three symbols indicate the assembly plant: NOR=Norwood, Ohio. This plate also carries codes indicating the body production sequence at the specific plant, interior trim (TR), exterior paint (PNT), the month and week of the month of production (1A=January, first week, etc.) and other special codes.

COLORS

11=White, 13=Steel Silver, 19=Tuxedo Black, 24=Medium Blue, 26=Bright Blue, 42=Palm Green, 43=Lime Green, 49=Dark Green, 52=Bright Yellow, 53=Bright Yellow Metallic, 61=Light Sandalwood, 62=Burnt Orange, 67=Sienna, 75=Red and 78=Dark Rosewood.

CAMARO - SERIES 23/24 - SIX/V-8

Standard equipment included seat belts with push-button buckles for all passenger positions, shoulder belts with push-button buckles for the driver and front passenger, two front seat head restraints, an energy-absorbing steering column, passenger-guard door locks with forward-mounted lock buttons, safety door latches and hinges, folding seat back latches, an energy-absorbing instrument panel and front seat back tops, contoured roof rails, a thick-laminate windshield, padded sun visors, safety armrests, a safety-cushioned steering wheel, side-guard beam door structures, a cargo-guard luggage compartment, side markers with reflectors (front side marker lights flash with directional signals), parking

The 1971 Camaro Sport Coupe could be purchased with either a standard inline six or 307-cid V-8, or an optional 350-cid V-8 like this car has.

Daniel B. Lyons photo

lights that illuminate with the headlights, a four-way hazard warning flasher, back-up lights, a lane-change feature in the directional signal control, a windshield defroster, windshield washers, dual-speed windshield wipers, a vinyl-edged wide-view inside day/night mirror with shatter resilient glass, a left-hand outside rearview mirror, a dual master cylinder brake system with a warning light, dual-action safety hood latches, a double-panel acoustically engineered roof with built-in headers, side-guard beam door structures, flush door handles, an advanced-design front suspension with forward-mounted steering linkage, E78-14 bias-belted ply tires, a precision-molded instrument panel, wide doors, all-vinyl bucket seats, bucket-styled rear seats, multi-leaf rear springs, a transverse muffler mounted behind the rear axle, high-output Power-Beam single-unit headlights, full door-glass styling, Magic-Mirror acrylic lacquer finish, flush-and-dry rocker panels, double-panel door and deck lid construction, a flush-mounted windshield and rear window bonded to the body, a blended-air heater and defroster system, front and rear springs tailored to match individual models and equipment, a sealed side-terminal Delco Energizer battery, safety wheel rims, inner front and rear fenders, new door trim panels with a built-in coin holder and map pocket in the armrest in black, blue, jade, saddle or sandlewood (matching seats), deep-twist floor carpeting, a 250-cid 155-hp (110 SAE net horsepower) inline six-cylinder engine or a 307-cid 200-hp (140 SAE net horsepower) V-8 and a three-speed manual transmission with floor shift.

Model Number	Body/Style Number	Body Type & Seating	Factory Price	Shipping Weight	Production Total
CAMARO SPORT COUPE - SERIES 23 - (L6)					
23	87	2d coupe	$2,758	3,016 lbs.	Note 1
CAMARO SPORT COUPE - SERIES 24 - (V-8)					
24	87	2d coupe	$2,848	3,218 lbs.	Note 1

Note 1: Model-year production of 1971 base Camaro coupes was 91,481.

CAMARO RALLY SPORT - SERIES 23/24 + Z22 - SIX/V-8

The RPO Z22 Rally Sport package was a factory option that cost Chevrolet dealers $141.65 and retailed for $179.05. Standard equipment included most items provided with the base Sport Coupe such as seat belts with push-button buckles for all passenger positions, shoulder belts with push-button buckles for the driver and front passenger, two front seat head restraints, an energy-absorbing steering column, passenger-guard door locks with forward-mounted lock buttons, safety door latches and hinges, folding seat back latches, an energy-absorbing instrument panel and front seat back tops, contoured roof rails, a thick-laminate windshield, padded sun visors, safety armrests, a safety-cushioned steering wheel, side-guard beam door structures, a cargo-guard luggage compartment, side markers with reflectors (front side marker lights flash with directional signals), parking lights that illuminate with the headlights, a four-way hazard warning flasher, back-up lights, a lane-change feature in the directional signal control, a windshield defroster, windshield washers, dual-speed windshield wipers, a vinyl-edged wide-view inside day/night mirror with shatter resilient glass, a left-hand outside rearview mirror, a dual master cylinder brake system with a warning light, dual-action safety hood latches, a double-panel acoustically engineered roof with built-in headers, side-guard beam door structures, flush door handles, an advanced-design front suspension with forward-mounted steering linkage, E78-14 bias-belted ply tires, a precision-molded instrument panel, wide doors, all-vinyl bucket seats, bucket-styled rear seats, multi-leaf rear springs, a transverse muffler mounted behind the rear axle, high-output Power-Beam single-unit headlights, full door-glass styling, Magic Mirror acrylic lacquer finish, flush-and-dry rocker panels, double-panel door and deck lid construction, a flush-mounted windshield and rear window bonded to the body, a blended-air heater and defroster system, front and rear springs tailored to match individual models and equipment, a sealed side-terminal Delco Energizer battery, safety wheel rims, inner front and rear fenders, new door trim panels with a built-in coin holder and map pocket in the armrest in black, blue, jade, saddle or sandlewood (matching seats), deep-twist floor carpeting, a 250-cid 155-hp (110 SAE net horsepower) inline six-cylinder engine or a 307-cid 200-hp (140 SAE net horsepower) V-8 and a three-speed manual transmission with floor shift. In addition, the Rally Sport option added a special black-finished grille with Argent Silver accents, a special rubber-tipped vertical grille center bar, parking lights with bright accents mounted on the grille panel between the headlights, independent right- and left-hand front bumpers replacing the standard full-width bumper, a license plate bracket mounted below the right-hand bumper, a resilient body-color hard rubber grille frame, an RS front fender nameplate, bright roof drip moldings, bright window moldings, bright hood panel moldings, body-color inserts on the door handles, an RS emblem on the steering wheel, bright-accented taillights, bright-accented back-up lights and Hide-A-Way concealed windshield wipers. The RS package could be added to six-cylinder or V-8 Camaros as shown immediately below. It could also be combined with the SS package or the Z/28 Special Performance package by adding $179.05 to the prices shown further below for these model-options. RS emblems were deleted from the package when it was ordered in combination with the Camaro SS package or when the Z/28 Special Performance package was also ordered.

Model Number	Body/Style Number	Body Type & Seating	Factory Price	Shipping Weight	Production Total
CAMARO RALLY SPORT COUPE - SERIES 23 + Z22 - (L6)					
23	87	2d coupe	$2,937	—	Note 2/3
CAMARO RALLY SPORT COUPE - SERIES 24 + Z22 - (V-8)					
24	87	2d coupe	$3,027	—	Note 2/3

Note 2: Combined model year production of all 1971 Camaros was 114,630.
Note 3: The production total given above included 18,404 Camaros with the Rally Sport package.

CAMARO SS - SERIES 24 - V-8

The RPO Z27 Super Sport or SS package was a factory option that cost Chevrolet dealers $248.34 and retailed for $313.90. It was available for V-8-powered Camaros with four-speed or Turbo-Hydra-Matic transmission. Standard equipment included most items standard on the base Sport Coupe such as seat belts with push-button buckles for all passenger positions, shoulder belts with push-button buckles for the driver and front passenger, two front seat head restraints, an energy-absorbing steering column, passenger-guard door locks with forward-mounted lock buttons, safety door latches and hinges, folding seat back latches, an energy-absorbing instrument panel and front seat back tops, contoured roof rails, a thick-laminate windshield, padded sun visors, safety armrests, a safety-cushioned steering wheel, side-guard beam door structures, a cargo-guard luggage compartment, side markers with reflectors (front side marker lights flash with directional signals), parking lights that illuminate with the headlights, a four-way hazard warning flasher, back-up lights, a lane-change feature in the directional signal control, a windshield defroster, windshield washers, dual-speed windshield wipers, a vinyl-edged wide-view inside day/night mirror with shatter resilient glass, a dual master cylinder brake system with a warning light, dual-action safety hood latches, a double-panel acoustically engineered roof with built-in

The SS option for 1971 added the 270-hp 350 V-8 and a host of other dress-up items.

The Z/28 was actually a product of the RPO Z/28 Special Performance package. It was a factory option that cost Chevrolet dealers $622.41 and retailed for $786.75.

Daniel B. Lyons photo

headers, side-guard beam door structures, flush door handles, an advanced-design front suspension with forward-mounted steering linkage, a precision-molded instrument panel, wide doors, all-vinyl bucket seats, bucket-styled rear seats, multi-leaf rear springs, a dual-outlet transverse muffler mounted behind the rear axle, high-output Power-Beam single-unit headlights, full door-glass styling, Magic-Mirror acrylic lacquer finish, flush-and-dry rocker panels, double-panel door and deck lid construction, a flush-mounted windshield and rear window bonded to the body, a blended-air heater and defroster system, front and rear springs tailored to match individual models and equipment, a sealed side-terminal Delco Energizer battery, safety wheel rims, inner front and rear fenders, new door trim panels with a built-in coin holder and map pocket in the armrest in black, blue, jade, saddle or sandlewood (matching seats) and deep-twist floor carpeting. In addition, the SS option added the 270-hp (210 SAE net horsepower) Turbo-Fire 350 V-8, a black-finished grille, a remote-control left-hand outside rearview mirror, power brakes, special hood insulation, dual exhausts, Hide-A-Way windshield wipers, 14 x 7-in. wheels, F70 x 14 wide-oval white-letter bias-belted tires and special SS ornamentation. A 300-hp (260 SAE net horsepower) "396 Turbo-Jet" V-8 was optional for cars with the SS package. Both engines available with the package came with chrome dress-up parts. On Camaro SS models with the bigger engine the buyer got a heavy-duty Sport suspension with front and rear stabilizer bars and special shock absorbers.

Note 4: Model year production of 1971 Camaro SS coupes was 18,287.

CAMARO Z/28 - SERIES 24 + Z/28 – V-8

The RPO Z/28 Special Performance package was a factory option that cost Chevrolet dealers $622.41 and retailed for $786.75. It was available for V-8-powered Camaros with a four-speed manual or Turbo-Hydra-Matic transmission. Standard equipment included most items standard on the base Sport Coupe, such as seat belts for all passengers, shoulder belts for front passengers, an energy-absorbing steering column, seat back latches, a padded instrument panel, padded sun visors, side-guard door beams, a cargo-guard luggage compartment, a full roof inner panel, side marker lights and reflectors, rear marker lights, parking lights that illuminated with the headlights, four-way hazard warning flashers, flush-and-dry rocker panels, rocker panel moldings, front bumper guards, back-up lights, a windshield defroster, dual-speed windshield wipers, windshield washers, an inside rearview mirror, a dual master brake cylinder, a brake warning lamp, an ignition key anti-theft warning, all-vinyl front bucket seats, all-vinyl rear bucket type seats, new door trim panels with a built-in coin holder and map pocket in the armrest, front disc/rear drum brakes, a coil spring front suspension and a leaf spring rear suspension. In addition, the Z/28 came with an exclusive 330-hp Turbo-Fire 350 V-8, bright engine accents, finned aluminum valve covers, a left-hand remote-controlled sport style outside rearview mirror, special instrumentation, power brakes, a 3.73:1 positraction rear axle (4.10:1 optional), a heavy-duty radiator, dual exhausts, a black-finished grille, Z/28 emblems on the front fender, rear bumper guards, a Sport suspension, heavy-duty springs and front and rear springs, 15 x 7-in. wheels with bright lug nuts, special wheel center caps, wheel trim rings, F60-15/B bias-belted white-letter tires, a rear deck lid spoiler with Z/28 decal and special

Model Number	Body/Style Number	Body Type & Seating	Factory Price	Shipping Weight	Production Total
CAMARO SUPER SPORT COUPE - SERIES 24 + Z27 - (RPO L48 "TURBO-FIRE 350" V-8)					
23	87	2d coupe	$3,126	—	Note 4
CAMARO SUPER SPORT COUPE - SERIES 24 + Z22 - (RPO LS3 "TURBO-JET 396" V-8)					
24	87	2d coupe	$3,222	—	Note 4

black or white paint stripes (except with a vinyl top or a black or white painted roof). The four-speed manual or Turbo-Hydra-Matic transmission was required at extra cost. Air conditioning, wheel covers and Rally wheels were not available.

Model Number	Body/Style Number	Body Type & Seating	Factory Price	Shipping Weight	Production Total
CAMARO Z/28 SPORT COUPE - SERIES 24 + Z/28 - (V-8 WITH FOUR-SPEED MANUAL TRANSMISSION)					
24	87	2d coupe	$3,841	—	Note 5
CAMARO Z/28 SPORT COUPE - SERIES 24 + Z/28 - (V-8 WITH TURBO-HYDRA-MATIC TRANSMISSION)					
24	87	2d coupe	$3,941	—	Note 5

Note 5: Model year production of 1971 Camaro Z/28 coupes was 4,862.

ENGINES

L22 I6: Overhead-valve inline six-cylinder. Cast-iron block and head. Bore & stroke: 3.88 x 3.53 in. Displacement: 250 cid (4.1 liters). Compression ratio: 8.5:1. Gross horsepower: 145 at 4200 rpm. Net horsepower: 110 at 3800 rpm. Gross torque: 230 lbs.-ft. at 1600 rpm. Net torque: 185 lbs.-ft. at 1600 rpm. Seven main bearings. Induction system: Rochester No. 7041017 one-barrel carburetor. Standard in Camaro Sport Coupe.

Base Turbo-Fire V-8: 90-degree, overhead-valve V-8. Cast-iron block and head. Bore & stroke: 3.87 x 3.25 in. Displacement: 307 cid (5.7 liters). Compression ratio: 8.5:1. Gross horsepower: 200 at 4600 rpm. Net horsepower: 140 at 4400 rpm. Gross torque: 300 lbs.-ft. at 2400 rpm. Net torque: 235 lbs.-ft. at 2400 rpm. Five main bearings. Hydraulic valve lifters. Induction system: Rochester two-barrel carburetor. Standard V-8 in base Camaro Sport Coupe.

L65 V-8: 90-degree, overhead-valve V-8. Cast-iron block and head. Bore & stroke: 4.00 x 3.48 in. Displacement: 350 cid (5.7 liters). Compression ratio: 8.5:1. Gross horsepower: 245 at 4800 rpm. Net horsepower: 165 at 4000 rpm. Gross torque: 350 lbs.-ft. at 2400 rpm. Net torque: 275 lbs.-ft. at 2200 rpm. Five main bearings. Hydraulic valve lifters. Induction system: Rochester No. 7041113 two-barrel carburetor. Optional in Camaro Sport Coupe and Rally Sport.

L48 V-8: 90-degree, overhead-valve V-8. Cast-iron block and head. Bore & stroke: 4.00 x 3.48 in. Displacement: 350 cid (5.7 liters). Compression ratio: 8.5:1. Gross horsepower: 270 at 4800 rpm. Net horsepower: 210 at 4400 rpm. Gross torque: 360 lbs.-ft. at 3200 rpm. Net torque: 300 lbs.-ft. at 2800 rpm. Five main bearings. Hydraulic valve lifters. Induction system: Rochester four-barrel carburetor. Standard in Camaro SS; not available in other models.

Z28 V-8: 90-degree, overhead-valve V-8. Cast-iron block and head. Bore & stroke: 4.00 x 3.48 in. Displacement: 350 cid (5.7 liters). Compression ratio: 9.0:1. Gross horsepower: 330 at 5600 rpm. Net horsepower: 275 at 5600 rpm. Gross torque: 360 lbs.-ft. at 4000 rpm. Net torque: 300 lbs.-ft. at 4000 rpm. Five main bearings. Hydraulic valve lifters. Induction system: Rochester No. 7042202 four-barrel carburetor. Four-bolt main bearings. Big valve heads. Special cam. Aluminum high-rise manifold. Standard in Camaro Z/28; not available in other Camaros.

LS3 V-8: 90-degree, overhead-valve V-8. Cast-iron block and head. Bore & stroke: 4.13 x 3.76 in. Displacement: 402 cid. Compression ratio: 8.5:1. Gross horsepower: 300 at 4800 rpm. Net horsepower: 260 at 4400 rpm. Gross torque: 400 lbs.-ft. at 3200 rpm. Net torque: 345 lbs.-ft. at 3200 rpm. Five main bearings. Hydraulic valve lifters. Induction system: Rochester No. 7042118 four-barrel carburetor. Optional in Camaro SS; not available in other models.

CHASSIS

Base Sport Coupe: Wheelbase: 108 in. Overall length: 188 in. Height: 50.5 in. Width: 74.4 in. Front tread: 59.6 in. Rear tread: 59.5 in. Front headroom: 37.3 in. Front legroom: 43.9 in. Front shoulder room: 56.7 in. Front hip room: 56.7 in. Rear headroom: 36 in. Rear legroom: 29.6 in. Rear shoulder room: 54.4 in. Rear hip room: 47.3 in. Usable trunk capacity: 6.4 cu. ft. Rated fuel tank capacity: 18 gal. Standard tires: E78-14/B steel-belted radial

Daniel B. Lyons photo

The 1971 Z/28 had hot looks and a hot 350-cid, 330-hp V-8.

tires.

Camaro SS: Wheelbase: 108 in. Overall length: 188.5 in. Height: 49.1 in. Width: 74.4 in. Front tread: 61.3 in. Rear tread: 60 in. Front headroom: 37.3 in. Front legroom: 43.9 in. Front shoulder room: 56.7 in. Front hip room: 56.7 in. Rear headroom: 36 in. Rear legroom: 29.6 in. Rear shoulder room: 54.4 in. Rear hip room: 47.3 in. Usable trunk capacity: 6.4 cu. ft. Rated fuel tank capacity: 18 gal. Standard tires: F70-14 wide-oval white-letter bias-belted tires.

Camaro Z/28: Same as above (depending upon which model the package was ordered for) with the following changes or additions: sport suspension with heavy-duty springs and front and rear stabilizer bars, special 15 x 7-in. wheels (with center caps, wheel trim rings and bright-finished lug nuts) and F60 x 15 bias-ply white letter tires.

TECHNICAL

Transmission: Three-speed manual transmission (column shift) standard with floor shift in Camaro six-cylinder. Three-speed manual transmission (column shift) standard with floor shift in Camaro V-8. Four-speed floor shift standard optional in Camaro V-8; mandatory in Camaro SS and Camaro Z/28 (choice of close-ratio or wide-ratio). Turbo-Hydra-Matic transmission optional. Steering: re-circulating ball. Turning diameter wall to wall, outside front: 41 ft. Turning diameter curb to curb, outside front: 39 ft. Front suspension: coil springs and tube-type. Rear suspension: leaf springs and tube-type shock absorbers. Body construction: integral, with separate partial front box frame. Brakes: Front disc, rear drum. Fuel tank: 18 gal.

OPTIONS

AK1 color-keyed seat and shoulder belts ($15.30). AN6 adjustable seatback ($19). AS4 rear shoulder belts ($26.35). A01 Soft-Ray tinted glass ($40.05). B37 color-keyed floor mats ($12.65). B93 door edge guard moldings ($6.35). C08 vinyl roof cover ($89.55). C24 Hide-A-Way windshield wipers ($21.10). C50 rear window defogger ($31.60). C60 Four-Season air conditioning ($402.35). D34 visor-vanity mirror ($3.20). D35 sport mirror ($15.80). D55 center console ($59). D80 front and rear spoilers ($79). F41 Sport suspension ($30.55). G80 Positraction rear axle ($44.25). J50 power brakes ($47.30). LS3 "396 Turbo-Jet V-8 ($99.05). L65 350-cid 350 Turbo-Fire four-barrel V-8 ($26.35). M20 four-speed wide-ratio manual transmission ($205.95). M21 four-speed close-ratio manual transmission ($205.95). M22 heavy-duty four-speed close-ratio manual transmission ($237.60). M35 Powerglide automatic transmission with six-cylinder engine ($179.55). M35 Powerglide automatic transmission with V-8 engine ($190.10). M40 Turbo-Hydra-Matic automatic transmission with Z/28 ($306.25). M40 Turbo-Hydra-Matic automatic transmission with Camaros SS with optional LS3 V-8 ($237.60). M40 Turbo-Hydra-Matic automatic transmission with other Camaros ($216.50). NK2 custom steering wheel ($15.80). NK4 sport steering wheel ($15.80). N33 Comfortilt steering wheel ($45.30). N40 power steering ($110.60). PL3 E-78-14 white sidewall tires ($26.05).

PL4 F70-14 white letter tires ($81.50). PY4 F70-14 white sidewall tires ($68.05). PO1 bright metal wheel trim covers ($26.35). P02 custom wheel trim covers ($84.30). T60 heavy-duty battery ($15.80). U14 special instrumentation ($84.30). U35 electric clock ($16.90). U63 AM radio ($66.40). U69 AM/FM radio ($139.05). U80 rear seat speaker ($15.80). VF3 deluxe front and rear bumpers ($36.90). V01 heavy-duty radiator ($14.75). YD1 trailering axle ratio ($12.65). ZJ7 Rally wheels with trim rings ($45.30). ZJ9 auxiliary lighting without custom interior option ($18.45). ZJ9 auxiliary lighting with custom interior option ($15.80). ZQ9 performance axle ratio ($12.65). Z21 style trim ($57.95). Z22 Rally Sport package ($179.05). Z23 interior accent group ($21.10). Z27 Camaro Super Sport package ($313.90). Z28 Special Performance package ($786.75). Z87 custom interior ($115.90).

HISTORICAL FOOTNOTES

Due to the late startup of 1970 Camaro production, the 1970 models were marketed for only half a year and, as a result, few changes were made in the 1971 models. Chevrolet bounced back in 1971, when it became the first automaker to build more than 3,000,000 cars and trucks combined. Truck deliveries were the highest ever, but car deliveries (including those of the Camaro) were far from the all-time record level. Industry trade journals of the era reported model-year production of 11,177 six-cylinder Camaros and 103,466 Camaro V-8s for a total of 114,643 units. The same sources reported that 93,741 of these cars were built at the Ohio, plant (which also built 38,258 Firebirds) and that 20,889 Camaros (and 14,886 Firebirds) were made at the factory in California. This also totals 114,643 cars, which is 13 more than the Chevrolet production total of 114,630. Camaro production included 7,147 cars built for export. Of these Camaros, 79.4 percent had automatic transmission, 9.3 percent had a four-speed manual transmission, 49 percent had a standard V-8, 41.2 percent had an optional V-8, 9.8 percent had a six-cylinder engine, 83.6 percent had an AM radio, 11.6 percent had an AM/FM radio, 81.3 percent had power steering, 36.3 percent had optional front disc brakes, 100 percent had bucket seats, 33.4 percent had a vinyl top, 92.2 percent had white sidewall tires, 0.7 percent had a tinted windshield only, 58.7 percent had all-tinted glass, 37.1 percent had air conditioning, 10.3 percent had a limited-slip differential, 49.9 percent had optional wheel covers, 34.4 percent had optional styled wheels, 9 percent had an optional clock, 7.3 percent had tilt steering and 12.9 percent had dual exhausts. Camaro sales for calendar year 1971 came to 128,106 units for a 1.5 percent share of the industry total. That compared to 145,826 units (2.1 percent of industry) in 1970 and 171,598 (2.03 percent of industry) in 1969. A total of 120,803 new Camaros were registered in the U.S. during calendar year 1971, down from 142,281 in 1970. A road test in the August 1972 issue of *Motor Trend* involved a Z/28 with the 350-cid 255-hp V-8, four-speed manual transmission and 3.73:1 rear axle. The car did 0 to 30 mph in 3.1 sec. 0 to 60 mph in 7.7 sec. and the quarter mile in 15.2 sec. at 86.6 mph.

Camaro

Daniel B. Lyons photo

A strike-marred production schedule was one reason why few changes came to the Z/28 (or the rest of the Camaro line) for 1972.

The 1972 run was horrible for Camaro production, which slid to 68,651 units. For many years, this was the low point in the nameplate's popularity, although there would be worse years later on. Three-point safety belts were one new feature, but there were few changes overall.

GM didn't have the time or money to think about product changes because of outside factors. First, there was a massive strike by the United Auto Workers Union that shut down the Camaro factory in Ohio for 117 days. By the time the labor dispute was settled, cars left sitting on the assembly line could not be finished and sold. New government safety and emissions standards had come into law during the strike period and it was impossible to modify the half-built cars to meet the new regulations. More than 1,000 F-Cars were simply scrapped.

This situation left a bad taste in the mouths of GM brass, who contemplated killing off both cars and being done with the problem. Luckily, a group of passionate enthusiasts who worked within the corporation lobbied for keeping the Camaro and Firebird. In the end, this faction won the battle and engineers devised a cheaper way to satisfy the government standards. The Camaro and its Pontiac cousin were saved.

The 1972 Camaro was promoted as "the closest thing to a Vette yet." It was almost identical in general appearance to the 1971 model, but had a slightly coarser grille mesh and high-back bucket seats.

CAMARO - SERIES 23/24 - SIX/V-8

Standard equipment for the base Camaro Sport Coupe included seat belts for all passengers, shoulder belts for front passengers, an energy-absorbing steering column, seat back latches, a padded instrument panel, padded sun visors, side-guard door beams, a cargo-guard luggage compartment, a full roof inner panel, side marker lights and reflectors, rear marker lights, parking lights that illuminated with the headlights, four-way hazard warning flashers, flush-and-dry rocker panels, rocker panel moldings, front bumper guards, back-up lights, a windshield defroster, dual-speed windshield wipers, windshield washers, an inside rearview mirror, an left-hand outside rearview mirror, a dual master brake cylinder, a brake warning lamp, an ignition key anti-theft warning, all-vinyl front bucket seats, all-vinyl rear bucket type seats, new door trim panels with a built-in coin holder and map pocket in the armrest, a coil spring front suspension, a leaf spring rear suspension, front disc/rear drum brakes, E78-14 black sidewall tires, a 250-cid 110-hp inline six-cylinder engine and a three-speed manual transmission with a floor shifter.

I.D. DATA

Camaros had a 13-symbol vehicle identification number (VIN) on the upper left surface of the instrument panel, visible through the windshield. The first symbol identifies the make: 1=Chevrolet Motor Division. The second symbol indicate the car line/series: Q=Camaro. The third and fourth symbols indicate body type: 87=two-door plainback hardtop coupe. The fifth symbol indicates the engine type: D=RPO L22 Turbo-Thrift 250-cid 100-hp inline six-cylinder with one-barrel carburetor, F=RPO Turbo-Fire 307-cid 130-hp two-barrel V-8, H=L65 Turbo-Fire 350-cid 165-hp two-barrel V-8, K=RPO L48 Turbo-Fire 350-cid 200-hp V-8 with four-barrel carburetor, L=RPO Z28 Turbo-Fire 350-cid 255-hp V-8 with four-barrel carburetor (Z/28 only), U=RPO LS3 "Turbo-Jet 396" 402-cid 240-hp V-8 with special four-barrel carburetor (not available in California). The sixth symbol indicates model year: 2=1972. The final six digits are the sequential serial number. The Fisher Body Style Number plate was located on the firewall below the

Chuck Dunlap photo

There were only 68,651 Camaros built for 1972, which makes an all-original Z/28 like this one a nice prize.

rear of the hood. The code in the left upper position was ST 72 12387 NOR or ST 72 12487 NOR. The first two symbols ST stand for "Style." The third and fourth symbols indicate model year: 72=1972 model. The fifth symbol indicates the division: 1=Chevrolet. The sixth and seventh symbols indicate series: 23=Camaro six-cylinder or 24=Camaro V-8. The eighth and ninth symbols indicate body style: 87=two-door coupe. The last three symbols indicate the assembly plant: NOR=Norwood, Ohio. This plate also carries codes indicating the body production sequence at the specific plant, interior trim (TR), exterior paint (PNT), the month and week of the month of production (1A=January, first week, etc.) and other special codes.

COLORS

11=Antique White, 14=Pewter Silver, 24=Ascot Blue, 26=Mulsanne Blue, 36=Spring Green, 43=Gulf Green, 48=Sequoia Green, 50=Covert Tan, 53=Placer Gold, 56=Cream Yellow, 57=Golden Brown, 63=Mohave Gold, 65=Flame Orange, 68=Midnight Bronze and 75=Cranberry Red.

Model Number	Body/Style Number	Body Type & Seating	Factory Price	Shipping Weight	Production Total
CAMARO SPORT COUPE - SERIES 23 - (L6)					
23	87	2d coupe	$2,730	3,121 lbs.	Note 1
CAMARO SPORT COUPE - SERIES 24 - (V-8)					
24	87	2d coupe	$2,820	3,248 lbs.	Note 1

Note 1: Combined model-year production of all 1972 base Camaros was 58,544.

CAMARO RALLY SPORT - SERIES 23/24 + Z22 – SIX/V-8

The RPO Z22 Rally Sport package was a factory option that cost Chevrolet dealers $92.04 and retailed for $118. Standard equipment included most items standard on the base Sport Coupe such as seat belts for all passengers, shoulder belts for front passengers, an energy-absorbing steering column, seat back latches, a padded instrument panel, padded sun visors, side-guard door beams, a cargo-guard luggage compartment, a full roof inner panel, side marker lights and reflectors, rear marker lights, parking lights that illuminated with the headlights, four-way hazard warning flashers, flush-and-dry rocker panels, rocker panel moldings, front bumper guards, back-up lights, a windshield defroster, dual-speed windshield wipers, windshield washers, an inside rearview mirror, an left-hand outside rearview mirror, a dual master brake cylinder, a brake warning lamp, an ignition key anti-theft warning, all-vinyl front bucket seats, all-vinyl rear bucket type seats, new door trim panels with a built-in coin holder and map pocket in the armrest, a coil spring front suspension, a leaf spring rear suspension, front disc/rear drum brakes, E78-14 black sidewall tires, a 250-cid 110-hp inline six-cylinder engine and a three-speed manual transmission with a floor shifter. In addition, the Rally Sport option added a special black-finished grille with Argent Silver accents, a special rubber-tipped vertical grille center bar, a smaller grille grid pattern (identical to the 1971 Rally Sport grille), parking lights with bright accents mounted on the grille panel between the headlights, independent right-and left-hand front bumpers replacing the standard full-width bumper, a license plate bracket, a dent-resistant body-color hard rubber grille frame, Rally Sport emblems on the sides of the fenders and Hide-A-Way concealed windshield wipers. The RS package could be added to six-cylinder or V-8 Camaros as shown immediately below. It could also be combined with the SS package by adding $118 to the SS prices shown further below.

Model Number	Body/Style Number	Body Type & Seating	Factory Price	Shipping Weight	Production Total
CAMARO RALLY SPORT COUPE - SERIES 23 + Z22 - (L6)					
23	87	2d coupe	$2,848	3,121 lbs.	Note 2/3
CAMARO RALLY SPORT COUPE - SERIES 24 + Z22 - (V-8)					
24	87	2d coupe	$2,938	3,248 lbs.	Note 2/3

Note 2: Combined model-year production of all 1972 Camaros was 68,651.
Note 3: The production total given above included 11,364 Camaros with the Rally Sport package.

CAMARO SS - SERIES 24 - V-8

The RPO Z27 Super Sport or SS package was a factory option that cost Chevrolet dealers $237.90 and retailed for $306.35. It was available for V-8-powered Camaros with four-speed or Turbo-Hydra-Matic transmission. Standard equipment included most items standard on the base Sport Coupe, such as seat belts for all passengers, shoulder belts for front passengers, an energy-absorbing steering column, seat back latches, a padded instrument panel, padded sun visors, side-guard door beams, a cargo-guard luggage compartment, a full roof inner panel, side marker lights and reflectors, rear marker lights, parking lights that illuminated with the headlights, four-way hazard warning flashers, flush-and-dry rocker panels, rocker panel moldings, front bumper guards, back-up lights, a windshield defroster, dual-speed windshield wipers, windshield washers, an inside rearview mirror, a dual master brake cylinder, a brake warning lamp, an ignition key anti-theft warning, all-vinyl front bucket seats, all-vinyl rear bucket type seats, new door trim panels with a built-in coin holder and map pocket in the armrest, a coil spring front suspension, a leaf spring rear suspension and front disc/rear drum brakes. In addition, the SS option added the 200-hp Turbo-Fire 350 V-8, Hide-A-Way windshield wipers, a black-finished grille, a remote-control left-hand outside rearview mirror, front and rear spoilers, power brakes, special hood insulation, dual exhausts, 14 x 7-in. wheels, F70-14 wide-oval white-letter bias-belted tires and SS fender emblems. A 240-hp "396 Turbo-Jet" (actually 402-cid) V-8 was optional for cars with the SS package. Both engines available with the package came with chrome dress-up parts, heavy-duty engine mounts and a heavy-duty starter. On Camaro SS models with the bigger engine the rear body panel was finished in black and the buyer got a heavy-duty Sport suspension with front and rear stabilizer bars and special shock absorbers. The 240-hp engine was not available for cars being registered in the State of California. Both SS engines required a four-speed manual or Turbo-Turbo-Hydra-Matic transmission attachment.

1972 Z/28s with white interior are scarce today.

Model Number	Body/Style Number	Body Type & Seating	Factory Price	Shipping Weight	Production Total
CAMARO SUPER SPORT COUPE - SERIES 24 + Z27 - (RPO L48 "TURBO-FIRE 350" 350-CID 200-HP V-8)					
23	87	2d coupe	$3,126	—	Note 4
CAMARO SUPER SPORT COUPE - SERIES 24 + Z22 - (RPO LS3 "TURBO-JET 396" 402-CID 240-HP V-8)					
24	87	2d Coupe	$3,222	—	Note 4

Note 4: Model year production of 1972 Camaro SS coupes was 7,532.

CAMARO Z/28 - SERIES 24 + Z/28 – V-8

The RPO Z/28 Special Performance package was a factory option that cost Chevrolet dealers $597.48 and retailed for $769.15. It was available for V-8-powered Camaros in two versions. The Z28/YF8 version included black striping and the Z28/ZR8 version included white striping. Standard equipment included most items standard on the base Sport Coupe, such as seat belts for all passengers, shoulder belts for front passengers, an energy-absorbing steering column, seat back latches, a padded instrument panel, padded sun visors, side-guard door beams, a cargo-guard luggage compartment, a full roof inner panel, side marker lights and reflectors, rear marker lights, parking lights that illuminated with the headlights, four-way hazard warning flashers, flush-and-dry rocker panels, rocker panel moldings, front bumper guards, back-up lights, a windshield defroster, dual-speed windshield wipers, windshield washers, an inside rearview mirror, a dual master brake cylinder, a brake warning lamp, an ignition key anti-theft warning, all-vinyl front bucket seats, all-vinyl rear bucket type seats, new door trim panels with a built-in coin holder and map pocket in the armrest, a coil spring front suspension, a leaf spring rear suspension and front disc/rear drum brakes. In addition, the Z/28 came with an exclusive 255-hp Turbo-Fire 350 V-8, finned aluminum rocker covers, bright engine accents, dual sport style outside rearview mirrors (left-hand remote-control), special instrumentation, power brakes, a 3.73:1 positraction rear axle, dual exhausts, a black-finished grille, Z/28 emblems, rear bumper guards, a Sport suspension with heavy-duty springs and front and rear stabilizer bars, heavy-duty engine mounts, a heavy-duty starter, a heavy-duty radiator, 15 x 7-in. wheels with bright lug nuts, special wheel center caps, wheel trim rings, F60-15/B bias-belted white-letter tires, Z/28 decals and special paint stripes on the hood and rear deck lid. A four-speed manual or Turbo-Hydra-Matic transmission was required at extra cost and air conditioning, wheel covers or Rally wheels were not available. It was possible to order a Z/28 in 1972 and delete the hood and deck lid stripes.

Model Number	Body/Style Number	Body Type & Seating	Factory Price	Shipping Weight	Production Total
CAMARO Z/28 SPORT COUPE - SERIES 24 + Z/28 - (V-8 WITH FOUR-SPEED MANUAL TRANSMISSION)					
24	87	2d coupe	$3,789	—	Note 6
CAMARO Z/28 SPORT COUPE - SERIES 24 + Z/28 - (V-8 WITH TURBO-HYDRA-MATIC TRANSMISSION)					
24	87	2d coupe	$3,886	—	Note 6

Note 6: Model-year production of 1972 Camaro Z/28 coupes was 2,575.

ENGINES

L22 I6: Overhead-valve inline six-cylinder. Cast-iron block and head. Bore & stroke: 3.88 x 3.53 in. Displacement: 250 cid (4.1 liters). Compression ratio: 8.5:1.

Chuck Dunlap photo

Daniel B. Lyons photo

The 1972 Z/28 could be ordered with either black or white stripes, but the 5.7-liter V-8 was the only engine available.

Brake horsepower: 110 at 3600 rpm. Torque: 185 lbs.-ft. at 1600 rpm. Seven main bearings. Induction system: Rochester No. 7042014 one-barrel carburetor. Standard in Camaro Sport Coupe; not available in Type LT or base Sport Coupe with Z/28 option. VIN Code D.

Base Turbo-Fire V-8: 90-degree, overhead-valve V-8. Cast-iron block and head. Bore & stroke: 3.87 x 3.25 in. Displacement: 307 cid (5.7 liters). Compression ratio: 8.5:1. Brake horsepower: 130 at 4000 rpm. Torque: 230 lbs.-ft. at 2400 rpm. Five main bearings. Hydraulic valve lifters. Induction system: Rochester no. 7042100 two-barrel carburetor. Standard V-8 in base Camaro Sport Coupe. VIN Code: F.

L65 V-8: 90-degree, overhead-valve V-8. Cast-iron block and head. Bore & stroke: 4.00 x 3.48 in. Displacement: 350 cid (5.7 liters). Compression ratio: 8.5:1. Brake horsepower: 165 at 4000 rpm. Torque: 280 lbs.-ft. at 2400 rpm. Five main bearings. Hydraulic valve lifters. Induction system: Rochester No. 7042112 two-barrel carburetor. Optional in Camaro Sport Coupe and Rally Sport. VIN Code: H.

L48 V-8: 90-degree, overhead-valve V-8. Cast-iron block and head. Bore & stroke: 4.00 x 3.48 in. Displacement: 350 cid (5.7 liters). Compression ratio: 8.5:1. Brake horsepower: 200 at 4000 rpm. Torque: 280 lbs.-ft. at 2400 rpm. Five main bearings. Hydraulic valve lifters. Induction system: Rochester four-barrel carburetor. Standard in Camaro SS; not available in other models. VIN Code: K.

Z28 V-8: 90-degree, overhead-valve V-8. Cast-iron block and head. Bore & stroke: 4.00 x 3.48 in. Displacement: 350 cid (5.7 liters). Compression ratio: 9.0:1. Brake horsepower: 255 at 5600 rpm. Torque: 280 lbs.-ft. at 4000 rpm. Five main bearings. Hydraulic valve lifters. Induction system: Rochester No. 7042202 four-barrel carburetor. Standard in Camaro Z/28; not available in other Camaros. VIN Code: L.

LS3 V-8: 90-degree, overhead-valve V-8. Cast-iron block and head. Bore & stroke: 4.13 x 3.76 in. Displacement: 402 cid. Compression ratio: 8.5:1. Brake horse-power: 240 at 4400 rpm. Torque: 345 lbs.-ft. at 3200 rpm. Five main bearings. Hydraulic valve lifters. Induction system: Rochester No. 7042118 four-barrel carburetor. Optional in Camaro SS; not available in other models. VIN Code: U.

CHASSIS

Base Sport Coupe: Wheelbase: 108 in. Overall length: 188 in. Height: 50.5 in. Width: 74.4 in. Front tread: 61.3 in. Rear tread: 60 in. Front headroom: 37.3 in. Front legroom: 43.9 in. Front shoulder room: 56.7 in. Front hip room: 56.7 in. Rear headroom: 36 in. Rear legroom: 29.6 in. Rear shoulder room: 54.4 in. Rear hip room: 47.3 in. Usable trunk capacity: 6.4 cu. ft. Rated fuel tank capaci-ty: 18 gal. Standard tires: E78 x 14/B steel-belted radial tires.

Camaro SS: Wheelbase: 108 in. Overall length: 188.5 in. Height: 49.1 in. Width: 74.4 in. Front Tread: 61.3 in. Rear tread: 60 in. Front headroom: 37.3 in. Front legroom: 43.9 in. Front shoulder room: 56.7 in. Front hip room: 56.7 in. Rear headroom: 36 in. Rear legroom: 29.6 in. Rear shoulder room: 54.4 in. Rear hip room: 47.3 in. Usable trunk capacity: 6.4 cu. ft. Rated fuel tank capaci-ty: 18 gal. Standard tires: F70-14 wide-oval white-letter bias-belted tires.

Camaro Z/28: Same as above (depending upon which model the package was ordered for) with the following changes or additions: Sport suspension with heavy-duty springs and front and rear stabilizer bars, special 15 x 7-in. wheels (with center caps, wheel trim rings and bright-finished lug nuts) and F60-15 bias-ply white-letter tires.

TECHNICAL

Transmission: Three-speed manual transmission (col-umn shift) standard with floor shift in Camaro six-cylin-der. Three-speed manual transmission (column shift) standard with floor shift in Camaro V-8. Four-speed floor shift standard optional in Camaro V-8; mandatory in Camaro SS and Camaro Z/28 (choice of close-ratio or wide-ratio). Turbo-Hydra-Matic transmission optional.

Steering: re-circulating ball. Turning diameter wall to wall, outside front: 40 ft. 2 in. Turning diameter curb to curb, outside front: 38 ft. Front Suspension: coil springs and tube-type. Rear suspension: leaf springs and tube-type shock absorbers. Body construction: integral, with separate partial front box frame. Brakes: Front disc, rear drum. Fuel tank: 18 gal.

OPTIONS

AK1 color-keyed seat and shoulder belts ($14.50). AN6 adjustable seatback ($18). A01 Soft-Ray tinted glass ($39). 37 color-keyed floor mats ($12). B84 body side moldings ($33). B93 door edge guard moldings ($6). C08 vinyl roof cover ($87). C24 Hide-A-Way windshield wipers ($21). C50 rear window defogger ($31). C60 Four-Season air conditioning ($397). D34 visor-vanity mirror ($3). D35 sport mirror ($15). D55 center console ($57). D80 front and rear spoilers ($77). F41 sport suspension ($30). G80 positraction rear axle ($45). J50 power brakes ($46). LS3 402-cid "396 Turbo-Jet 240-hp V-8 ($96). L65 350-cid 165-hp four-barrel V-8 ($26). M20 four-speed wide-ratio manual transmission ($200). M21 four-speed close-ratio manual transmission ($200). M22 heavy-duty four-speed close-ratio manual transmission. M35 Powerglide automatic transmission with six-cylinder engine ($174). M35 Powerglide automatic transmission with V-8 engine ($185). M40 Turbo-Hydra-Matic automatic transmission with Z/28 ($297). M40 Turbo-Hydra-Matic automatic transmission with Camaros SS with optional LS3 V-8 ($231). M40 Turbo-Hydra-Matic automatic transmission with other Camaros ($210). NK4 sport steering wheel ($15). N33 Comfortilt steering wheel ($44). N40 power steering ($130). PL3 E-78-14 white sidewall tires ($28). PL4 F70-14 white-letter tires ($82.85). PY4 F70-14 white sidewall tires ($69.85). PO1 bright metal wheel trim covers ($26). P02 custom wheel trim covers ($82). U35 electric clock ($16). U63 AM radio ($65). U69 AM/FM radio ($135). U80 rear seat speaker ($15). VF3 deluxe front and rear bumpers ($36). V01 heavy-duty radiator ($14). YD1 trailering axle ratio ($12). YF5 California emissions test ($15). ZJ7 Rally wheels with trim rings ($44). ZJ9 auxiliary lighting ($17.50). ZJ9 auxiliary lighting with Z54 Quiet Sound group or Type LT ($15). Z21 style trim ($56). Z22 Rally Sport package ($118). Z27 Camaro Super Sport package ($306.35). Z/28 special performance package ($769.15). Z87 custom interior ($113).

HISTORICAL FOOTNOTES

In 1972, F.J. McDonald was general manager of Chevrolet Motor Division. For that year, the division based in the General Motors Building in Detroit actually had only one Chevrolet assembly plant and it built only trucks. Other Chevrolet products were made at various General Motors Assembly Division (GMAD) plants across the country. All Camaros were made at the Norwood, Ohio, factory, which had previously built only GM F-Cars (Camaros and Firebirds). However, another name-plate was also produced there in 1972. In the 1972 *Ward's Automotive Yearbook* it was stated, "In January-February of 1972, Nova was put into the Norwood plant with Camaro, which reportedly will be phased out by 1974." Along with the belief that the end of the muscle car era in 1972 would devastate Camaro sales, there were other factors inspiring Chevrolet management to consider dropping the sports-personal model. For example, no Camaros were built from mid-April through mid-October of that year. Management was hit with a 174-day United Auto Workers (UAW) union strike at the Norwood factory that closed it starting on April 7. The strike was not settled until Sept. 24, 1972. The work stoppage left 1,100 partially assembled Camaros sitting on the production line. When the strike was over in October, those cars (along with numerous sub-assemblies and parts) had to be scrapped since they did not meet U.S. emissions and safety standards going into effect for model-year 1973. GM determined that it would not be cost effective to upgrade the cars. Model-year production included 4,821 six-cylinder Camaros and 63,830 Camaro V-8s for a total of 68,651 units all made at the Norwood factory (which also built 29,951 Firebirds and 2,852 Novas). The totals included 3,698 units built for export. Of the 68,651 Camaros, 82.7 percent had automatic transmission, 8.5 percent had a four-speed manual transmission, 40.3 percent had a standard V-8, 52.7 percent had an optional V-8, 7 percent had a six-cylinder engine, 79.1 percent had an AM radio, 15.2 percent had an AM/FM radio, 87.2 percent had power steering, 42.6 percent had power disc brakes, 57.4 percent had manual disc brakes, 100 percent had bucket seats, 34.8 percent had a vinyl top, 93.1 percent had white sidewall tires, 0.8 percent had a tinted windshield only, 64.3 percent had all-tinted glass, 46.2 percent had air conditioning, 11.1 percent had a limited-slip differential, 41.6 percent had optional wheel covers, 44.3 percent had optional styled wheels, 10.8 percent had an optional clock, 5.4 percent had tilt steering and 13.3 percent had dual exhausts. Camaro sales for calendar year 1972 came to 45,330 units for a 0.5 percent share of the industry total. That compared to 128,106 car (1.5 percent of industry) in 1971 and 145,826 units (2.1 percent of industry) in 1970. A total of 45,184 new Camaros were registered in the U.S. during calendar year 1972, down from 120,803 in 1971. A road test in the August 1972 issue of *Motor Trend* involved a Z/28 with the 350-cid 255-hp V-8, four-speed manual transmission and 3.73:1 rear axle. The car did 0 to 30 mph in 3.1 sec. 0 to 60 mph in 7.7 sec. and the quarter mile in 15.2 sec. At 86.6 mph.

Camaro

Jerry Heasley photo

Despite an oil embargo in the Middle East, Chevrolet still produced 96,752 Camaros for 1973, including 11,574 Z/28s.

The resurrected Camaro entered 1973 as a coupe only — the last of the so-called "steel bumper" cars. A new Type LT "luxury touring" version was added to the product mix and it was truly a separate 1S87 model, whereas the RS and Z/28 were considered to be options for the base 1Q87 model. The SS package was dropped entirely.

The Type LT Camaro was aimed at female buyers and later took the Berlinetta name to move even further in that direction. It featured such add-ons as rocker panel accent moldings, Rally wheels and windshield wipers that parked out of view under the cowl panel. With the right engine options, the Type LT could still be made into quite a "macho" performance machine rivaling the old SS. In fact, RS, SS or Z/28 equipment could be added to the Type LT.

Chevy's other hot-running Camaro — the Z/28 — got a new Holley four-barrel carburetor as a performance upgrade, but the aluminum intake model used on previous Zs was replaced with a cast-iron type. Chevy also replaced the neat Z/28 emblems on the rear body panel with foil-type stickers, although the metal emblems were still used on the sides of the front fenders.

Calendar-year sales of Camaros didn't exactly zoom in 1973, although they started heading in the right direction once again and peaked at 108,381 units. That was more than double the 45,330 sales in calendar 1972. Model-year production climbed to 96,751 cars.

I.D. DATA

Camaros had a 13-symbol vehicle identification number (VIN) on the upper left surface of the instrument panel, visible through the windshield. The first symbol identifies the make: 1=Chevrolet Motor Div. The second symbol indicate the car line/series: Q=Camaro and S=Camaro Type LT. The third and fourth symbols indicate body type: 87=two-door four-passenger two-door hardtop. The fifth symbol indicates the engine type: D=RPO L22 250-cid 100-hp inline six-cylinder with one-barrel carburetor, F=RPO 307-cid 115-hp two-barrel V-8, H=L65 350-cid 145-hp two-barrel V-8, K=RPO L48 350-cid 175 hp V-8 with four-barrel carburetor and T=RPO Z28 350-cid 245-hp V-8 with four-barrel carburetor. The sixth symbol indicates model year: 3=1973. The seventh symbol indicates the assembly plant: L=Van Nuys, California, N=Norwood, Ohio. The final six digits are the sequential serial number.

COLORS

11=Antique White, 24=Light Blue Metallic, 26=Bright Blue Metallic, 29=Midnight Blue Metallic, 42=Dark Green Metallic, 46=Green-Gold Metallic, 48=Midnight Green, 51=Light Yellow, 56=Chamois, 60=Light Copper, 64=Silver Metallic, 68=Dark Brown Metallic, 74=Dark Red Metallic, 75=Medium Red and 97=Medium Orange.

CAMARO - SERIES 1FQ - SIX/V-8

The last of the steel-bumper Camaros was the 1973. It continued using the body introduced in 1970 and added rubber-faced vertical guards to the standard, full-across bumper to satisfy new government frontal impact standards. Other changes included a conventional automatic transmission shifter replacing the "can-crusher" style and new options like power windows. Base Camaro engines were the 250-cid inline six or the 307-cid V-8. Standard equipment for the base Camaro Sport Coupe included seat belts, two built-in front-seat head restraints, an energy-absorbing steering column, passenger-guard door locks, safety door latches and hinges, folding seat back latches, an energy-absorbing padded instrument panel, energy-absorbing padded front-seat back tops, a contoured windshield header, a thick-laminate windshield, safety armrests, a safety steering wheel, a cargo-guard luggage compartment, side-guard door beams, a contoured inner roof panel, side marker lights and reflectors, parking lights that illuminated with the headlights, four-way hazard warning flashers, back-up lights, directional signals, a windshield defroster, windshield washers, dual-speed windshield wipers, a vinyl-edged wide-view inside day/night mirror with shatterproof glass, a left-hand outside rearview mirror, a dual master cylinder brake system with a warning light, a starter safety switch, dual-action safety hood latches, an anti-theft ignition key reminder buzzer, an anti-theft steering column lock, a catalytic converter, a fuel tank nozzle restrictor, a carburetor air intake extension (to bring in cooler outside air), steel-belted radial tires, posh wall-to-wall cut-pile carpeting, recessed headlights and parking lights, Camaro emblems, a Delcotron generator with built-in solid state regulator, corrosion-fighting inner fender liners, a four-spoke sport steering wheel, an independent front suspension with coil springs, minor-impact-cushioning front and rear bumper systems, contoured full-foam Strato-bucket front seats, rear leaf springs, self-adjusting front disc brakes with audible wear indicators, drum-type rear brake, a coolant recovery system, tight all-welded unit-body construction, front ball joints with wear indicators, self-cleaning rocker panels, a 21-gal. gas tank, a power ventilation system, a perforated acoustical headliner, double-panel construction doors and hood and deck lid, a Delco Energizer sealed side-terminal battery and a floor-mounted three-speed manual transmission.

Model Number	Body/Style Number	Body Type & Seating	Factory Price	Shipping Weight	Production Total
CAMARO SPORT COUPE - SERIES 1FQ - (L6)					
FQ	87	2d coupe	$2,781	3,119 lbs.	Note 1
CAMARO SPORT COUPE - SERIES 1FQ - (V-8)					
FQ	87	2d coupe	$2,872	3,238 lbs.	Note 1

Note 1: Model-year production of 1973 base Camaro coupes was 52,850 or 52,851 (See historical footnotes).

CAMARO TYPE LT - SERIES 1FS - V-8

The Camaro Type LT or luxury touring model was seen for the first time in 1973 and filled a gap in the model lineup left by the elimination of the SS package. It was a separate model, rather than an option package, and had a distinct model number 1FS87 instead of the 1Q87 used for other Camaros. In addition to the features that were standard on the base Camaro Sport Coupe, the Type LT included special trim, special LT identification (on the front, the roof rear quarter and the rear end panel), Hide-A-Way windshield wipers, dual sport style outside rearview mirrors (left-hand remote-controlled),

rocker panel accents, 14 x 7-in. Rally wheels with caps and trim rings, variable-ratio power steering, a sport steering wheel, deluxe seat trim, woodgrained trim on the doors and instrument panel, extra sound insulation, a glove compartment lamp and special instrumentation (including a tachometer, an ammeter, a temperature gauge and an electric clock). The front bucket seats in the Type LT were of a full-foam, molded design with a choice of two upholstery options. A mixed-tone cloth-and-vinyl selection was available in black and white, black and blue or green and black. Also available was all-vinyl trim in neutral or black. Color-keyed deep-twist carpeting protected the floor. Red or blue accent carpeting was optional. The standard engine in the Type LT Camaro was the Turbo-Fire 350-cid V-8 with a two-barrel carburetor.

Model Number	Body/Style Number	Body Type & Seating	Factory Price	Shipping Weight	Production Total
1FS	87	2d coupe	$3,268	3,349 lbs.	Note 2

Note 2: The production total given above included 32,327 or 32,328 Type LT Camaros (See historical footnotes).

CAMARO RALLY SPORT - SERIES 1FQ OR 1FS WITH Z22 – SIX/V-8

All 1973 Camaro Sport Coupes and Type LT coupes could be equipped with the Rally Sport package. It included a special black-finished grille with silver accents, a resilient grille surround, split bumpers (one on each side with no bumper across the grille) and Hide-A-Way windshield wipers. The front parking lights were repositioned from the normal location under the bumper to a space between the headlights and grille.

Model Number	Body/Style Number	Body Type & Seating	Factory Price	Shipping Weight	Production Total
CAMARO RALLY SPORT COUPE - SERIES 1FQ WITH Z22 - (L6)					
FQ	87	2d coupe	—	2,899 lbs.	Note 3/4
CAMARO RALLY SPORT COUPE - SERIES 1FQ WITH Z22- (V-8)					
FQ	87	2d coupe	—	2,990 lbs.	Note 3/4
CAMARO TYPE LTRALLY SPORT - SERIES 1FS WITH Z22 - (V-8)					
1FS	87	2d coupe	—	3,365 lbs.	Note 3/4

Note 3: Combined model-year production of all 1973 Camaros was 96,751 or 96,752 (See historical footnotes).
Note 4: The production total given above included 16,133 Camaros with the Rally Sport option.

CAMARO Z/28 - SERIES 1FQ - V-8

In 1973, the Camaro Z/28 special performance package was a $598 option for the base Camaro Sport Coupe or a $502 option for the Camaro Type LT coupe. In addition to or in place of the base model's standard equip-

The Z/28 again had several upgrades that set it apart, including a rear deck lid spoiler, special striping and a beefed-up suspension.

Jerry Heasley photo

Thomas Glatch Productions photo

This 1973 Z/28 featured the Midnight Blue Metallic exterior with black interior. It features the 350-cid automatic and still has the original tires. Z/28s could have a split bumper and finer-mesh grille, along with the circular turn signals, if the Z/28 package was ordered on a car with the RS package.

ment listed above, the Z/28 package included bright engine accents, finned aluminum valve covers, a heavy-duty radiator, dual exhausts, a black-finished grille, Z/28 emblems, a sport suspension, heavy-duty front and rear springs, 15 x 7-in. wheels, special center caps and trim rings, hood insulation, F60 x 15/B white-letter, a rear deck lid spoiler and special paint stripes on the hood and rear deck lid. The 1973 Z/28 engine had hydraulic valve lifters, which lowered horsepower to 245, but permitted the addition of air conditioning at extra cost. A Rochester four-barrel carburetor and a cast-iron intake manifold were used instead of a Holley carb and aluminum intake manifold.

Model Number	Body/Style Number	Body Type & Seating	Factory Price	Shipping Weight	Production Total
Z/28 CAMARO SPORT COUPE - SERIES 1FQ - (V-8)					
FQ	87	2d coupe	$3,379	—	Note 5
Z/28 CAMARO TYPE LT COUPE - SERIES 1FS - (V-8)					
FQ	87	2d coupe	$3,770	—	Note 5

Note 5: Model-year production of 1973 Camaro Z/28 coupes was 11,574.

ENGINES

L22 I6: Overhead-valve inline six-cylinder. Cast-iron block and head. Bore & stroke: 3.88 x 3.53 in. Displacement: 250 cid (4.1 liters). Compression ratio: 8.25:1. Brake horsepower: 100 at 3600 rpm. Torque: 175 lbs.-ft. at 1600 rpm. Seven main bearings. Induction system: Rochester 1ME one-barrel carburetor. Standard in Camaro Sport Coupe; not available in Type LT or base Sport Coupe with Z/28 option. VIN Code D.

Base Turbo-Fire V-8: 90-degree, overhead-valve V-8. Cast-iron block and head. Bore & stroke: 3.87 x 3.25 in. Displacement: 307 cid (5.7 liters). Compression ratio: 8.5:1. Brake horsepower: 115 at 3600 rpm. Five main bearings. Hydraulic valve lifters. Induction system: Rochester two-barrel carburetor. Standard V-8 in base Camaro Sport Coupe. VIN Code: F.

L65 V-8: 90-degree, overhead-valve V-8. Cast-iron block and head. Bore & stroke: 4.00 x 3.48 in. Displacement: 350 cid (5.7 liters). Compression ratio: 8.5:1. Brake horsepower: 145 at 3800 rpm. Torque: 250 lbs.-ft. at 2200 rpm Five main bearings. Hydraulic valve lifters. Induction system: Rochester two-barrel carburetor.

Standard in Camaro Type LT coupe. VIN Code: H.

L48 V-8: 90-degree, overhead-valve V-8. Cast-iron block and head. Bore & stroke: 4.00 x 3.48 in. Displacement: 350 cid (5.7 liters). Compression ratio: 8.5:1. Brake horsepower: 175. Five main bearings. Hydraulic valve lifters. Induction system: Rochester four-barrel carburetor. Optional in Camaro Type LT and Camaro Sport Coupe. VIN Code: K.

Z/28 V-8: 90-degree, overhead-valve V-8. Cast-iron block and head. Bore & stroke: 4.00 x 3.48 in. Displacement: 350 cid (5.7 liters). Compression ratio: 9.0:1. Brake horsepower: 245 at 5200 rpm. Torque: 285 lbs.-ft. at 4000 rpm. Five main bearings. Hydraulic valve lifters. Induction system: Rochester four-barrel carburetor. Standard in Camaro Z/28; not available in other Camaros. VIN Code: T.

CHASSIS

Base Sport Coupe: Wheelbase: 108 in. Overall length: 188.5 in. Height: 49.1 in. Width: 74.4 in. Front tread: 61.3 in. Rear tread: 60 in. Front headroom: 37.3 in. Front legroom: 43.9 in. Front shoulder room: 56.7 in. Front hip room: 56.7 in. Rear headroom: 36 in. Rear legroom: 29.6 in. Rear shoulder room: 54.4 in. Rear hip room: 47.3 in. Usable trunk capacity: 6.4 cu. ft. Rated fuel tank capacity: 18 gal. Standard tires: E78 x 14/B steel-belted radial tires.

Camaro Type LT: Wheelbase: 108 in. Overall length: 188.5 in. Height: 49.1 in. Width: 74.4 in. Front tread: 61.6 in. Rear tread: 60.3 in. Front headroom: 37.3 in. Front legroom: 43.9 in. Front shoulder room: 56.7 in. Front hip room: 56.7 in. Rear headroom: 36 in. Rear legroom: 29.6 in. Rear shoulder room: 54.4 in. Rear hip room: 47.3 in. Usable trunk capacity: 6.4 cu. ft. Rated fuel tank capacity: 18 gal. Standard tires: E78 x 14/B steel-belted radial whitewall tires.

Camaro Z/28: Same as above (depending upon which model the package was ordered for) with the following changes or additions: Sport suspension, special 15 x 7-in. wheels (with center caps, wheel trim rings and bright-finished lug nuts) and F60 x 15 bias-ply white-letter tires.

TECHNICAL

Transmission: Three-speed manual transmission (column shift) standard with floor shift in Camaro six-cylinder. Three-speed manual transmission (column shift) standard with floor shift in Camaro V-8. Four-speed floor shift standard optional in Camaro V-8; standard in Camaro Z/28 (choice of close-ratio or wide-ratio). Turbo-Hydra-Matic transmission optional. Steering: re-circulating ball. Front suspension: coil springs and tube-type. Rear Suspension: leaf springs and tube-type shock absorbers. Body construction: integral, with separate partial front box frame. Brakes: Front disc, rear drum. Fuel tank: 18 gal.

OPTIONS

AK1 color-keyed seat and shoulder belts ($14.50). AN6 adjustable seat back ($18). A01 Soft-Ray tinted glass ($39). A31 power windows ($75). B37 color-keyed floor mats ($12). B84 body-side moldings ($33). B93 door edge guard moldings ($6). C08 vinyl roof cover ($87). C24 Hide-A-Way windshield wipers ($21). C50 rear window defogger ($31). C60 Four-Season air conditioning ($397). D34 visor-vanity mirror ($3). D35 sport mirrors ($26). D55 center console ($57). D80 front and rear spoilers ($77). D88 black striping ($77). F41 sport suspension ($30). G80 positraction rear axle ($45). J50 power brakes ($46). L48 350-cid 175-hp four-barrel V-8 in base Sport Coupe ($102). L48 350-cid 175-hp four-barrel V-8 in Type LT coupe ($76). L65 350-cid 145-hp V-8 ($26). M20 four-speed wide-ratio manual transmission ($200). M21 four-speed close-ratio manual transmission ($200). M40 Turbo-Hydra-Matic automatic transmission with Z/28 ($297). M40 Turbo-Hydra-Matic automatic transmission with Camaros except Z/28 ($210). N33 Comfortilt steering wheel ($44). N40 power steering ($113). N65 Space-Saver spare tire ($14.16). N95 wire wheel covers ($82). PE1 Turbine I wheels and trim with Sport Coupe ($110.50). PE1 Turbine I wheels with wheel trim on Type LT ($75). PO1 full wheel covers ($26). QEH E78-14 white sidewall tires on Sport Coupe with Stowaway spare ($22.40). QEH E78-14 white sidewall tires on Sport Coupe without Stowaway spare ($28). QFC F70-14 white sidewall tires on Type LT with Space-Saver spare ($51). QFC F70-14 white sidewall tires on Type LT coupe with Space-Saver spare ($65). QFC F70-14 white sidewall tires on Sport Coupe with Space-Saver spare ($56). QFC F70-14 white sidewall tires on Sport Coupe with Space-Saver spare ($70). QFD F70-14 white-letter tires on Type LT coupe with Space-Saver spare ($61.40). QFD F70-14 white-letter tires on Type LT coupe without Space-Saver spare ($78). QFD F70-14 white-letter tires on Sport Coupe with Space-Saver spare ($66.40). QFD F70-14 white-letter tires on Sport Coupe without Space-Saver spare ($83). UA1 heavy-duty battery ($15). U14 Special Instrumentation ($82). U35 electric clock ($16). U63 AM radio ($65). U69 AM/FM radio ($135). U80 rear seat speaker ($15). V01 heavy-duty radiator without Z/28 ($14). V01 heavy-duty radiator with Z/28 ($7.50). YA7 California emissions equipment ($15). YD1 trailering axle ratio ($12). ZJ4 trailer towing package ($41). ZJ7 Rally wheels with trim rings ($44). ZJ9 auxiliary lighting ($17.50). ZJ9 auxiliary lighting with Z54 Quiet Sound group or Type LT ($15). Z21 style trim ($56). Z22 Rally Sport package on base Sport Coupe ($118). Z22 Rally Sport package on Type LT ($97). Z/28 special performance package with base Sport Coupe ($598.05). Z/28 special performance package with Type LT ($502.05). Z54 Quiet Sound interior décor group ($35).

HISTORICAL FOOTNOTES

In 1973, F.J. McDonald was general manager of Chevrolet Motor Division. The 1973 Camaro went into production the week ending Sept. 1, 1972, and was introduced to the public 20 days later. Total Chevrolet sales climbed to 2,281,517 cars and 14.9 percent of those vehicles were sports models like the Camaro. In fact, the most dramatic gain in production over 1973 totals was realized by the Camaro due to the fact that its 1972 output had been curtailed by the strike at the Norwood, Ohio, assembly plant. The strike inspired GM to stop building Novas at Norwood, so the factory built only Camaros and Firebirds during 1973. Another factor that actually helped Camaro sales in 1973 was the Arab oil embargo coupled with cuts in domestic gasoline production. Industry trade journals of the era reported that model year production in the United States included 3,614 six-cylinder Camaros and 93,138 V-8s for a total of 96,752 units. Other sources say one less (96,751). *Car and Driver* (September 1973) tested a Camaro Z/28 with the wide-ratio four-speed transmission and a 3.42:1 axle. The car did 0 to 60 mph in 6.7 sec. and the quarter mile in 15.2 sec. at 94.6 mph.

The 1973 Camaro (this is a Z/28) was known as the last of the "steel bumper" cars.

Thomas Glatch Productions photo

Camaro

The 1974 Camaro Z/28 Sport Coupe ran a 15.2-second quarter mile in one magazine test.

Bigger changes came along for 1974, when the Camaro received new styling fore and aft. The revised nose and tail incorporated stronger, impact-absorbing aluminum-faced bumpers that were designed to keep Uncle Sam happy. Although the bumpers themselves were lighter in weight, the overall bumper system added performance-robbing pounds to the F-Cars and also made them 7 in. longer.

There was a body-color fascia above the front bumper. At the rear, new taillights that replaced the trademark round units of 1970-1973 were more rectangular and notched into the body sides

Power selections were reduced in number to keep the industry watchdogs happy, and while Camaro engines actually gained cubic inches and horsepower, they did not make the cars appreciably faster. A 350-cid 145-hp engine replaced the "307" as the base V-8, while the L48 engine had 10 more horsepower than it did in 1973. The Z/28 used the same V-8 as the year before and gained a breakerless HEI ignition system during the model run. Radial tires were introduced, along with front brake pad sensors. A seat belt interlock system that forced front-seat passengers to buckle up before the car could be operated was a very unpopular new safety feature.

I.D. DATA

Camaros had a 13-symbol vehicle identification number (VIN) on the upper left surface of the instrument panel, visible through the windshield. The first symbol identifies the make: 1=Chevrolet Motor Div. The second symbol indicate the car line/series: Q=Camaro and S=Camaro Type LT. The third and fourth symbols indicate body type: 87=two-door four-passenger two-door hardtop. The fifth symbol indicates the engine type: D=RPO L22 250-cid 100-hp inline six-cylinder with one-barrel carburetor, V=RPO L65 350-cid 145-hp V-8 with two-barrel carburetor (in 49 states; not in California), L=RPO LM1 350-cid 160-hp V-8 with four-barrel carburetor (California cars only), K=RPO L48 350-cid 185 hp V-8 with four-barrel carburetor and T=RPO Z28 350-cid 245-hp V-8 with four-barrel carburetor. The sixth symbol indicates model year: 4=1974. The seventh symbol indicates the assembly plant: L=Van Nuys, California, N=Norwood, Ohio. The final six digits are the sequential serial number. A body number plate on the upper horizontal surface of the shroud identifies model year, car division, series, style, body assembly plant, body number, trim combination, modular seat code, paint code, and date build code. A two- or three-symbol code (combined with a serial number) identifies each engine. On sixes, the pad is at the right side of the block, to rear of distributor. On V-8s, that pad is just forward of the right cylinder head.

COLORS

11=Antique White, 26=Bright Blue Metallic, 29=Midnight Blue Metallic, 36=Aqua Blue Metallic, 40=Lime Yellow, 46=Bright Green Metallic, 49=Medium Dark Green Metallic, 50=Cream Beige, 55=Sandstone, 59=Golden Brown Metallic, 64=Silver Metallic, 66=Bronze Metallic, 74=Medium Red Metallic and 75=Medium Red.

CAMARO - SERIES 1FQ - SIX/V-8

Standard equipment for the base Camaro Sport Coupe included seat belts with push-button buckles for all passengers, two combination seat and shoulder belts for the driver and front passenger with a belt reminder and inertia reel, two built-in front seat head restraints, an energy-absorbing steering column, passenger-guard door locks, safety door latches and hinges, folding seat back latches, an energy-absorbing padded instrument panel, energy-absorbing padded front seat back tops, a contoured windshield header, a thick-laminate windshield, safety armrests, a safety steering wheel, a cargo-guard luggage compartment, side-guard door beams, a contoured inner roof panel, side marker lights and reflectors, parking lights that illuminated with the headlights, four-way hazard warning flashers, back-up lights, directional signals with a lane-change feature, a windshield defroster, windshield washers, dual-speed windshield wipers, a vinyl-edged wide-view inside day/night mirror with shatterproof glass, a left-hand outside rearview mirror, a dual master cylinder brake system with a warning light, a starter safety switch, dual-action safety hood latches, an anti-theft ignition key reminder buzzer, an anti-theft steering column lock, a catalytic converter, a fuel tank nozzle restrictor, a High Energy Ignition (HEI) system, a carburetor air intake extension (to bring in cooler outside air), steel-belted radial tires, posh wall-to-wall cut-pile carpeting, recessed headlights and parking lights, Camaro emblems, a Delcotron generator with built-in solid state regulator, corrosion-fighting inner fender liners, a four-spoke sport steering wheel, an independent front suspension with coil springs, minor-impact-cushioning front and rear bumper systems, contoured full-foam Strato-bucket front seats, rear leaf springs, self-adjusting front disc brakes with audible wear indicators, drum-type rear brake, a coolant recovery system, tight all-welded unit body construction, Saginaw variable-ratio power steering (on cars with a V-8 engine), front ball joints with wear indicators, self-cleaning rocker panels, a 21-gal. gas tank, a power ventilation system a perforated acoustical headliner, double-panel construction doors and hood and deck lid, a Delco Energizer sealed side-terminal battery, a standard 250-cid inline six-cylinder engine and a floor-mounted three-speed manual transmission.

Model Number	Body/Style Number	Body Type & Seating	Factory Price	Shipping Weight	Production Total
CAMARO SPORT COUPE - SERIES 1FQ - (L6)					
FQ	87	2d coupe	$2,828	3,119 lbs.	Note 1
CAMARO SPORT COUPE - SERIES 1FQ - (V-8)					
FQ	87	2d coupe	$3,040	3,238 lbs.	Note 1

Note 1: Model-year production of 1974 base Camaro coupes was 88,243.

CAMARO TYPE LT - SERIES 1FS - V-8

The Camaro Type LT was the luxury touring model for 1974. Its upscale image was enhanced through the use of additional sound-deadening materials, wood-grained interior trim, knit vinyl or cord-ridge fabric upholstery, a color-coordinated instrument panel and a color-coordinated steering wheel and column. The 307-cid base V-8 of 1973 was dropped and a 350-cid V-8 with a two-barrel carburetor was standard. This was the L65 engine in all states except California. In California, the LM1 350-cid V-8 was standard, but cost $49 extra. Standard equipment started along the same lines as the base Sport Coupe with seat belts with push-button buckles for all passengers, two combination seat and shoulder belts for the driver and front passenger with a belt reminder and inertia reel, two built-in front seat head restraints, an energy-absorbing steering column, passenger-guard door locks, safety door latches and hinges, folding seat back latches, an energy-absorbing padded instrument

panel, energy-absorbing padded front seat back tops, a contoured windshield header, a thick-laminate windshield, safety armrests, a safety steering wheel, a cargo-guard luggage compartment, side-guard door beams, a contoured inner roof panel, side marker lights and reflectors, parking lights that illuminated with the headlights, four-way hazard warning flashers, back-up lights, directional signals with a lane-change feature, a windshield defroster, windshield washers, dual-speed windshield wipers, a vinyl-edged wide-view inside day/night mirror with shatterproof glass, a left-hand outside rearview mirror, a dual master cylinder brake system with a warning light, a starter safety switch, dual-action safety hood latches, an anti-theft ignition key reminder buzzer, an anti-theft steering column lock, a catalytic converter, a fuel tank nozzle restrictor, a High Energy Ignition (HEI) system, a carburetor air intake extension (to bring in cooler outside air), steel-belted radial tires, posh wall-to-wall cut-pile carpeting, recessed headlights and parking lights, Camaro emblems, a Delcotron generator with built-in solid state regulator, corrosion-fighting inner fender liners, a four-spoke sport steering wheel, an independent front suspension with coil springs, minor-impact-cushioning front and rear bumper systems, contoured full-foam Strato-bucket front seats, rear leaf springs, self-adjusting front disc brakes with audible wear indicators, rear drum brakes, a coolant recovery system, tight all-welded unit body construction, Saginaw variable-ratio power steering, front ball joints with wear indicators, self-cleaning rocker panels, a 21-gal. gas tank, a power ventilation system a perforated acoustical headliner, double-panel construction doors and hood and deck lid and a Delco Energizer sealed side-terminal battery. In addition to the above, the Type LT Camaro came standard with an especially well-trimmed interior with LT bucket seats having distinctive deep-contour seat backs, dressed-up door panels with map pockets and door pulls, a special instrument panel with a clock and a tachometer, sport mirrors on both sides (left-hand remote controlled), variable-ratio power steering, a steering wheel with an LT emblem on the hub, Rally wheels with center caps, bright wheel trim rings, bright parking light trim, bright vertical bars on the parking lights, a lighted glove box, Hide-A-Way windshield wipers, Type LT nameplates on the sides and back, a base 350-cid two-barrel V-8 and a floor-mounted three-speed manual transmission.

Model Number	Body/Style Number	Body Type & Seating	Factory Price	Shipping Weight	Production Total
1FS	87	2d coupe	$3,380	3,349 lbs.	Note 2

Note 2: Model-year production of 1974 Camaro Type LT coupes was 48,963.

CAMARO Z/28 - SERIES 1FQ - V-8

Technically the Camaro Z/28 was an option for the base Camaro Sport Coupe or the Camaro Type LT coupe in 1974. It was available throughout the United States. Major elements of the Z/28 package included special trim and badges, engine and drive train upgrades and suspension and tire upgrades. The package added $572 to the price of the Sport Coupe and $502 to the price of the Type LT coupe. The difference was attributable to the fact that the Type LT model already included some of the same content. Standard equipment for a Z/28 started with either the base Sport Coupe or Type LT coupe standard equipment listed above. In addition, all cars with the Z/28 option had the following major elements of the package: a 350-cid 245-hp V-8 with finned aluminum rocker covers and dual exhausts, bright engine accents, a four-speed manual transmission (close-ratio or wide-ratio), a heavy-duty cooling system, a heavy-duty starter, a heavy-duty clutch with manual transmission, Z/28 fender emblems, RPO J50 power brakes, a sport suspension, special 15 x 7-in. wheels (with center caps, wheel trim rings and bright-finished lug nuts), F60 x 15 bias-ply white-letter tires, a Positraction rear axle, a black-finished radiator grille with an Argent Silver outline, dual sport style outside rearview mirrors and additional Z/28 identification. A breakerless High Energy Ignition system was added to the Z/28 package contents during the 1974 model run. Z/28s with air conditioning had a 3.42:1 rear axle ratio in place of the standard 3.73:1 axle ratio. Popular options for Z/28s included the D80 rear deck lid spoiler and the D88 striping package. The latter included extremely bold four-color "Z/28" graphics on the hood and rear deck lid.

Model Number	Body/Style Number	Body Type & Seating	Factory Price	Shipping Weight	Production Total
Z/28 CAMARO SPORT COUPE - SERIES 1FQ - (V-8)					
FQ	87	2d coupe	$3,612	—	Note 3
Z/28 CAMARO TYPE LT COUPE - SERIES 1FS - (V-8)					
FQ	87	2d coupe	$3,883	—	Note 3

Note 3: Model-year production of 1974 Camaro Z/28 coupes was 13,802.

ENGINES

L22 I6: Overhead-valve inline six-cylinder. Cast-iron block and head. Bore & stroke: 3.88 x 3.53 in. Displacement: 250 cid (4.1 liters). Compression ratio: 8.25:1. Brake horsepower: 100 at 3600 rpm. Torque: 175 lbs.-ft. at 1800 rpm. Seven main bearings. Induction system: Rochester 1ME one-barrel carburetor. Standard in Camaro Sport Coupe; not available in Type LT or base Sport Coupe with Z/28 option. VIN Code D.

L65 V-8: 90-degree, overhead-valve V-8. Cast-iron block and head. Bore & stroke: 4.00 x 3.48 in. Displacement: 350 cid (5.7 liters). Compression ratio: 8.5:1. Brake horsepower: 145 at 3800 rpm. Torque: 250 lbs.-ft. at 2200 rpm Five main bearings. Hydraulic valve lifters. Induction system: Rochester two-barrel carburetor. Standard in Camaro Type LT in 49 states; Optional in Camaro Sport Coupe in 49 states. VIN Code: V.

LM1 V-8: 90-degree, overhead-valve V-8. Cast-iron block and head. Bore & stroke: 4.00 x 3.48 in. Displacement: 350 cid (5.7 liters). Compression ratio: 8.5:1. Brake horsepower: 160 at 3800 rpm. Torque: 250 lbs.-ft. at 2400 rpm. Five main bearings. Hydraulic valve lifters. Induction system: Rochester four-barrel carburetor. Standard at extra cost in Camaro Type LT in California and optional in Camaro Sport Coupe in California. VIN Code: L.

L48 V-8: 90-degree, overhead-valve V-8. Cast-iron block and head. Bore & stroke: 4.00 x 3.48 in. Displacement: 350 cid (5.7 liters). Compression ratio: 8.5:1. Brake horsepower: 185 at 4000 rpm. Torque: 270 lbs.-ft. at 2600 rpm. Five main bearings. Hydraulic valve lifters. Induction system: Rochester four-barrel carburetor. Optional in Camaro Type LT and Camaro Sport Coupe. VIN Code: K.

Z28 V-8: 90-degree, overhead-valve V-8. Cast-iron block and head. Bore & stroke: 4.00 x 3.48 in. Displacement: 350 cid (5.7 liters). Compression ratio: 9.0:1. Brake horsepower: 245 at 5200 rpm. Torque: 280 lbs.-ft. at 4000 rpm. Five main bearings. Hydraulic valve lifters. Induction system: Rochester four-barrel carburetor. Standard in Camaro Z/28; not available in other Camaros. VIN Code: T.

CHASSIS

Base Sport Coupe: Wheelbase: 108 in. Overall length: 195.4 in. Height: 49.1 in. Width: 74.4 in. Front tread: 61.3 in. Rear tead: 60 in. Front headroom: 37.3 in. Front legroom: 43.9 in. Front shoulder room: 56.7 in. Front hip room: 56.7 in. Rear headroom: 36 in. Rear legroom: 29.6 in. Rear shoulder room: 54.4 in. Rear hip room: 47.3 in. Usable trunk capacity: 6.4 cu. ft. Rated fuel tank capacity: 21 gal. Standard tires: FR78 x 14/B steel-belted radial tires.

Camaro Type LT: Wheelbase: 108 in. Overall length: 195.4 in. Height: 49.1 in. Width: 74.4 in. Front tread: 61.6 in. Rear tread: 60.3 in. Front headroom: 37.3 in. Front legroom: 43.9 in. Front shoulder room: 56.7 in. Front hip room: 56.7 in. Rear headroom: 36 in. Rear legroom: 29.6 in. Rear shoulder room: 54.4 in. Rear hip room: 47.3 in. Usable trunk capacity: 6.4 cu. ft. Rated fuel tank capacity: 21 gal. Standard Tires: FR78 x 14/B steel-belted radial whitewalls tires.

John R. Poletto photo

This 1974 Camaro LT Sport Coupe features a 350-V-8 with Quadra-Jet four-barrel carburetor, dual exhaust, automatic transmission and Rally wheels.

Camaro Z/28: Same as above (depending upon which model the package was ordered for) with the following changes or additions: Sport suspension, special 15 x 7-in. wheels (with center caps, wheel trim rings and bright-finished lug nuts) and F60 x 15 bias-ply white-letter tires.

TECHNICAL

Transmission: Three-speed manual transmission (column shift) standard with floor shift in Camaro six-cylinder. Three-speed manual transmission (column shift) standard with floor shift in Camaro V-8. Four-speed floor shift standard optional in Camaro V-8; standard in Camaro Z/28 (choice of close-ratio or wide-ratio). Turbo Hydra-Matic transmission optional. Steering: re-circulating ball. Front suspension: unequal-length control arms, coil springs and stabilizer bar. Rear suspension: semi-elliptic leaf springs, stabilizer bar, rigid axle. Body construction: integral, with separate partial front box frame. Brakes: Front disc, rear drum. Fuel tank: 21 gal.

OPTIONS

AK1 color-keyed seat and shoulder belts ($14.50). AN6 adjustable seatback ($18). A01 Soft-Ray tinted glass ($39). A31 power windows ($75). B37 color-keyed floor mats ($12). B84 body side moldings ($33). B93 door edge guard moldings ($6). C08 vinyl roof cover ($87). C24 Hide-A-Way windshield wipers ($21). C50 rear window defogger ($31). C60 Four-Season air conditioning ($397). D34 visor-vanity mirror ($3). D35 sport mirrors ($26). D55 center console ($57). D80 front and rear spoilers ($77). D88 black striping ($77). F41 sport suspension ($30). G80 Positraction rear axle ($45). G92 high-altitude rear axle ($12). J50 power brakes ($46). LM1 350-cid 160-hp four-barrel V-8 ($46). L48 350-cid 185-hp four-barrel V-8 ($76). M20 four-speed wide-ratio manual transmission ($200). M21 four-speed close-ratio manual transmission ($200). M40 Turbo-Hydra-Matic automatic transmission with Z/28 ($297). M40 Turbo-Hydra-Matic automatic transmission with Camaros except Z/28 ($210). N33 Comfortilt steering wheel ($44). N41 power steering ($113). N65 Space-Saver spare tire ($14.16). PE1 Turbine I wheels and trim with Sport Coupe ($110.50). PE1 Turbine I wheels with wheel trim on Type LT ($75). PO1 full wheel covers ($26). QBT FR78-14 white-letter tires without Space-Saver spare ($147.15). QBT FR78-14 white-letter tires on Sport Coupe with Space-Saver spare ($117.72). QBT FR78-14 white-letter tires on Type LT with Space-Saver spare ($116.72). QDV FR78-14 black sidewall tires without Space-Saver spare ($104.15). QDV FR78-14 black sidewall tires on Sport Coupe with Space-Saver spare ($83.32). QDV FR78-14 black sidewall tires on Type LT with Space-Saver spare ($82.32). QDW FR78-14 white sidewall tires without Space-Saver spare ($134.15). QDW FR78-14 white sidewall tires on Sport Coupe with Space-Saver spare ($107.32). QDW FR78-14 white sidewall tires on Type LT with Space-Saver spare ($106.32). QEH E78-14 white sidewall tires on Sport Coupe with Stowaway spare ($22.40). QEH E78-14 white sidewall tires on Sport Coupe without Stowaway spare ($28). QFC F70-14 white sidewall tires on Sport Coupe with Space-Saver spare ($56). QFC F70-14 white sidewall tires on Sport Coupe with Space-Saver spare ($70). QFD F70-14 white-letter tires on Sport Coupe with Space-Saver spare ($66.40). QFD F70-14 white-letter tires on Sport Coupe without Space-Saver spare ($83). UA1 heavy-duty battery ($15). U05 dual horns ($4). U14 Special Instrumentation ($82). U35 electric clock ($16). U58 AM/FM stereo radio ($233). U63 AM stereo radio ($65). U69 AM/FM radio ($135). U80 rear seat speaker ($15). V01 heavy-duty radiator without Z/28 ($14). V01 heavy-duty radiator with Z/28 ($7.50). V30 front and rear bumper guards ($31). YF5 California emissions equipment ($15). ZJ4 trailer towing package ($41). ZJ7 Rally wheels with trim rings ($44). ZJ9 auxiliary lighting ($17.50). ZJ9 auxiliary lighting with Z54 Quiet Sound group or Type LT ($15). Z21 style trim ($52). Z/28 special performance package with base Sport Coupe ($572.05). Z/28 special performance package with Type LT ($502.05). Z54 Quiet Sound interior décor group ($35).

HISTORICAL FOOTNOTES

At the start of 1974, F.J. McDonald was general manager of Chevrolet Motor Division, but by 1975 Robert L. Lund took over the post when McDonald became executive vice president of GM's Car, Truck, Body & Assembly Division. The 1974 Camaro was introduced to the public on Sept. 21, 1973. The Camaro Rally Sport model was dropped, but would return as an option package in 1975. As the gas crisis drove buyers away from the large full-size cars of the day, sports models like the Camaro came to represent a larger (29.4 percent vs. 14.9 percent) portion of the Chevrolet model mix. Model-year production of 151,008 Camaros reflected a large swing towards six-cylinder models, with 22,210 such cars being built. Model-year production of Camaro V-8s also rose to a total of 128,798 units. All of these cars were made at the Norwood factory (which also built 73,729 Firebirds). The totals included 4,412 units built for export. Of the 151,008 Camaros, 85.2 percent had automatic transmission, 7.4 percent had a four-speed manual transmission, 56.5 percent had a standard V-8, 28.8 percent had an optional V-8, 14.7 percent had a six-cylinder engine, 100 percent had power steering, 91.3 percent had power disc brakes, 13.4 percent had a limited-slip differential, 22.7 percent had dual exhausts, 32.9 percent had steel-belted radial tires, 15.7 percent had tilt steering, 100 percent had bucket seats, 1.6 percent had a tinted windshield only, 78.3 percent had all-tinted glass, 52.5 percent had air conditioning, 25.2 percent had a vinyl top, 60.6 percent had an AM radio, 19.2 percent had an AM/FM radio, 7.1 percent had an AM/FM stereo radio, 33.1 percent had a standard clock, 42 percent had an optional clock, 22.5 percent had a rear window defogger, 93 percent had a remote-control outside rearview mirror, 22.8 percent had optional wheel covers, 33.1 percent had optional styled wheels. Camaro sales for calendar year 1974 came to 136,404 for a 1.8 percent market share. A total of 130,446 new Camaros were registered in the U.S. during calendar year 1974. *Car and Driver* (September 1973) tested a 1974 Camaro Z/28 with the wide-ratio four-speed transmission and a 3.42:1 axle. The car did 0 to 60 mph in 6.7 sec. and covered the quarter mile in 15.2 sec. at 94.6 mph.

Camaro

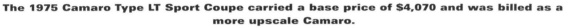

The 1975 Camaro Type LT Sport Coupe carried a base price of $4,070 and was billed as a more upscale Camaro.

Chevy temporarily killed the Z/28 starting in 1975. Some say that this was due to the fact that a catalytic converter was required this year and Camaro lovers at the division felt they could not build a true performance car with a converter-clogged exhaust system. Others say it was simply a bad marketing decision — bad because Pontiac stuck with the Trans Am and it sold great. The Z-car would return in mid-1977.

The ninth annual edition of the Camaro continued with a good-looking design dominated by a low profile, a wide stance and a sloping rear deck. The '75 models also got a new wraparound rear window to reduce a blind spot that had troubled many drivers. A new Rally Sport option with multi-color paint schemes and bold stripes bowed in the middle of the season. There was also a rare factory interior selection that was the only leather upholstery option offered for first- or second-generation Camaros.

A breakerless HEI ignition system was standard on all 1975 Camaros as were radial tires. You could get air conditioning in a six-cylinder Camaro this year and power door locks were a new option.

I.D. DATA

Camaros had a 13-symbol vehicle identification number (VIN) on the upper left surface of the instrument panel, visible through the windshield. The first symbol identifies the make: 1=Chevrolet Motor Div. The second symbol indicate the car line/series: Q=Camaro and S=Camaro Type LT. The third and fourth symbols indicate body type: 87=two-door four-passenger two-door hardtop. The fifth symbol indicates the engine type: D=RPO L22 250-cid 105-hp inline six-cylinder with one-barrel carburetor, V=RPO L65 350-cid 145-hp V-8 with two-barrel carburetor, L=RPO LM1 350-cid 155-hp V-8 with four-barrel carburetor. The sixth symbol indicates model year: 5=1975. The seventh symbol indicates the

assembly plant: L=Van Nuys, Calif., N=Norwood, Ohio. The final six digits are the sequential serial number. A Body Number Plate on the upper horizontal surface of the shroud identifies model year, car division, series, style, body assembly plant, body number, trim combination, modular seat code, paint code, and date build code. A two- or three-symbol code (combined with a serial number) identifies each engine. On sixes, the pad is at the right side of the block, to rear of distributor. On V-8s, that pad is just forward of the right cylinder head.

COLORS

11=Antique White, 13=Silver, 15=Light Gray, 24=Medium Blue, 26=Bright Blue Metallic, 29=Midnight Blue Metallic, 44=Medium Green, 49=Dark Green Metallic, 50=Cream Beige, 51=Bright Yellow, 55=Sandstone, 58=Dark Sandstone Metallic, 63=Light Saddle Metallic, 64=Medium Orange Metallic, 74=Dark Red Metallic and 75=Light Red.

CAMARO - SERIES 1FQ - SIX/V-8

Standard equipment for the base Camaro Sport Coupe included seatbelts with push-button buckles for all passengers, two combination seat and shoulder belts for the driver and front passenger with a belt reminder and inertia reel, two built-in front seat head restraints, an energy-absorbing steering column, passenger-guard door locks, safety door latches and hinges, folding seat back latches, an energy-absorbing padded instrument panel, energy-absorbing padded front seat back tops, a contoured windshield header, a thick-laminate windshield, safety armrests, a safety steering wheel, a cargo-guard luggage compartment, side-guard door beams, a contoured inner roof panel, side marker lights and reflectors, parking lights that illuminated with the headlights, four-way hazard warning flashers, back-up lights, directional signals with a lane-change feature, a windshield defroster, windshield washers, dual-speed windshield wipers, a vinyl-edged wide-view inside day/night mirror with shatterproof glass, a left-hand outside rearview mirror, a dual master cylinder brake system with a warning light, a starter safety switch, dual-action safety hood latches, an anti-theft ignition key reminder buzzer, an anti-theft steering column lock, a catalytic converter, a fuel tank nozzle restrictor, a High Energy Ignition (HEI) system, a carburetor air intake extension (to bring in cooler outside air), steel-belted radial tires, posh wall-to-wall cut-pile carpeting, recessed headlights and parking lights, distinctive new red, white and blue Chevrolet Camaro emblems, a Delcotron generator with built-in solid state regulator, corrosion-fighting inner fender liners, a four-spoke sport steering wheel, an independent front suspension with coil springs, minor-impact-cushioning front and rear bumper systems, contoured full-foam Strato-bucket front seats, rear leaf springs, self-adjusting front disc brakes with audible wear indicators, new finned rear brake drums, a coolant recovery system, tight all-welded unit-body construction, Saginaw variable-ratio power steering, front ball joints with wear indicators, self-cleaning rocker panels, a 21-gal. gas tank, a power ventilation system, a perforated acoustical headliner, double-panel construction doors and hood and deck lid, a Delco Energizer sealed side-terminal battery, a standard 250-cid inline six-cylinder engine, a floor-mounted three-speed manual transmission and a 2.73:1 or 3.08:1 rear axle (depending on engine).

Model Number	Body/Style Number	Body Type & Seating	Factory Price	Shipping Weight	Production Total
CAMARO SPORT COUPE - SERIES 1FQ - (L6)					
FQ	87	2d coupe	$3,553	3,421 lbs.	Note 1
CAMARO SPORT COUPE - SERIES 1FQ - (V-8)					
FQ	87	2d coupe	$3,698	3,532 lbs.	Note 1

Note 1: Model-year production of 1975 Camaro base coupes was 105,927.

CAMARO RALLY SPORT - SERIES 1FQ/Z85 - SIX/V-8

Big news for Camaro lovers in 1975 was the return of the Rally Sport as an option package. Designated the Z85 package, it was available for the base Sport Coupe at $238. The Rally Sport features included a flat black hood, a flat black forward roof section, a flat black grille, a flat black rear end panel, tri-color trim stripes, Rally wheels, dual sport mirrors and assorted decals. Front and rear spoilers that looked great with this package were available at extra cost.

Model Number	Body/Style Number	Body Type & Seating	Factory Price	Shipping Weight	Production Total
CAMARO RALLY SPORT COUPE - SERIES 1FQ/Z85 - (L6)					
1FQ/Z85	87	2d coupe	$3,791	—	Note 2/3
CAMARO RALLY SPORT COUPE - SERIES 1FQ/Z85 - (V-8)					
1FQ/Z85	87	2d coupe	$3,936	—	Note 2/3

Note 2: Combined model-year production of all 1975 Camaros was 145,770.
Note 3: The production total given in Note 2 above included 7,000 Camaros with the Rally Sport package.

CAMARO TYPE LT - SERIES 1FS - V-8

Chevrolet literature described the Type LT (Luxury Touring) Camaro as "a step up" car that represented "everything the Sport Coupe is, plus an interesting mix of tasteful touches outside and in." Standard equipment started along the same lines as the base Sport Coupe

with seat belts with push-button buckles for all passengers, two combination seat and shoulder belts for the driver and front passenger with a belt reminder and inertia reel, two built-in front seat head restraints, an energy-absorbing steering column, passenger-guard door locks, safety door latches and hinges, folding seat back latches, an energy-absorbing padded instrument panel, energy-absorbing padded front seat back tops, a contoured windshield header, a thick-laminate windshield, safety armrests, a safety steering wheel, a cargo-guard luggage compartment, side-guard door beams, a contoured inner roof panel, side marker lights and reflectors, parking lights that illuminated with the headlights, four-way hazard warning flashers, back-up lights, directional signals with a lane-change feature, a windshield defroster, windshield washers, dual-speed windshield wipers, a vinyl-edged wide-view inside day/night mirror with shatterproof glass, a left-hand outside rearview mirror, a dual master cylinder brake system with a warning light, a starter safety switch, dual-action safety hood latches, an anti-theft ignition key reminder buzzer, an anti-theft steering column lock, a catalytic converter, a fuel tank nozzle restrictor, a High Energy Ignition (HEI) system, a carburetor air intake extension (to bring in cooler outside air), steel-belted radial tires, posh wall-to-wall cut-pile carpeting, recessed headlights and parking lights, distinctive new red, white and blue Chevrolet Camaro emblems, a Delcotron generator with built-in solid state regulator, corrosion-fighting inner fender liners, a four-spoke sport steering wheel, an independent front suspension with coil springs, minor-impact-cush-

The 1975 Camaro line continued with the second-generation theme of a more sloping front end and sturdier bumper.

ioning front and rear bumper systems, contoured full-foam Strato-bucket front seats, rear leaf springs, self-adjusting front disc brakes with audible wear indicators, new finned rear brake drums, a coolant recovery system, tight all-welded unit body construction, Saginaw variable-ratio power steering, front ball joints with wear indicators, self-cleaning rocker panels, a 21-gal. gas tank, a power ventilation system, a perforated acoustical headliner, double-panel construction doors and hood and deck lid and a Delco Energizer sealed side-terminal battery. In addition to the above list, the Type LT Camaro came standard with an especially well-trimmed interior with standard plaid knit-cloth seat and door trim (knit vinyl was also available as well as, for a short time, genuine leather), LT bucket seats with distinctive deep-contour seat backs, dressed-up door panels with map pockets and door pulls, a special instrument panel insert with simulated bird's-eye maple accents, a clock, a tachometer, added sound deadeners and insulation, sport mirrors on both sides (left-hand remote controlled), variable-ratio power steering, a color-keyed steering wheel with an LT emblem on the hub, Rally wheels with center caps, bright wheel trim rings, bright parking light trim, bright vertical bars on the parking lights, a lighted glove box, Hide-A-Way windshield wipers, Type LT nameplates on the sides and back, a base 350-cid two-barrel V-8 and a floor-mounted three-speed manual transmission.

Model Number	Body/Style Number	Body Type & Seating	Factory Price	Shipping Weight	Production Total
1FS	87	2d coupe	$4,070	3,753 lbs.	Note 4

Note 4: Combined model-year production of all 1975 Camaros was 141,629.

CAMARO TYPE LT RALLY SPORT - SERIES 1FS/Z85 - SIX/V-8

The return of the Rally Sport was also good news for Camaro Type LT buyers. They could get it on the V-8-only Type LT for $165. The lower price was explained by the fact that the Type LT model already had some of the ingredients, such as Rally wheels. Except for the base engine, this version of the Z85 package was identical to the version offered for the Sport Coupe and included the same content such as a flat black hood, a flat black forward roof section, a flat black grille, a flat black rear end panel, tri-color trim stripes, Rally wheels, dual sport mirrors and assorted decals.

Model Number	Body/Style Number	Body Type & Seating	Factory Price	Shipping Weight	Production Total
CAMARO TYPE LT RALLY SPORT COUPE - SERIES 1FS/Z85 - (V-8)					
1FS/Z85	87	2d coupe	$4,235	—	Note 4

Note 4: Model-year production of 1975 Camaro Type LT coupes was 39,843.

ENGINES

L22 I6: Overhead-valve inline six-cylinder. Cast-iron block and head. Bore & stroke: 3.88 x 3.53 in. Displacement: 250 cid (4.1 liters). Compression ratio: 8.25:1. Brake horsepower: 105 at 3800 rpm. Torque: 185 lbs.-ft. at 1200 rpm. Seven main bearings. Induction system: Rochester 1ME one-barrel carburetor. Standard in Camaro Sport Coupe and Camaro Sport Coupe with Rally Sport package; not available in Type LT or Type LT with Rally Sport package. VIN Code D.

L65 V-8: 90-degree, overhead-valve V-8. Cast-iron block and head. Bore & stroke: 4.00 x 3.48 in. Displace-

ment: 350 cid (5.7 liters). Compression ratio: 8.5:1. Brake horsepower: 145 at 3800 rpm. Torque: 250 lbs.-ft. at 2200 rpm Five main bearings. Hydraulic valve lifters. Induction system: Rochester two-barrel carburetor. Standard in Camaro Type LT; Optional in Camaro Sport Coupe. VIN Code: V.

LM1 V-8: 90-degree, overhead-valve V-8. Cast-iron block and head. Bore & stroke: 4.00 x 3.48 in. Displacement: 350 cid (5.7 liters). Compression ratio: 8.5:1. Brake horsepower: 155 at 3800 rpm. Torque: 250 lbs.-ft. at 2400 rpm Five main bearings. Hydraulic valve lifters. Induction system: Rochester M4MC four-barrel carburetor. Optional in Camaro Type LT and Camaro Sport Coupe. VIN Code: L.

CHASSIS:

Base Sport Coupe: Wheelbase: 108 in. Overall length: 195.4 in. Height: 49.1 in. Width: 74.4 in. Front tread: 61.3 in. Rear tread: 60 in. Front headroom: 37.3 in. Front legroom: 43.9 in. Front shoulder room: 56.7 in. Front hip room: 56.7 in. Rear headroom: 36 in. Rear legroom: 29.6 in. Rear shoulder room: 54.4 in. Rear hip room: 47.3 in. Usable trunk capacity: 6.4 cu. ft. Rated fuel tank capacity: 21 gal. Standard tires: FR78 x 14/B steel-belted radial tires.

Camaro Rally Sport: Wheelbase: 108 in. Overall length: 195.4 in. Height: 49.1 in. Width: 74.4 in. Front tread: 61.3 in. Rear tread: 60 in. Front headroom: 37.3 in. Front legroom: 43.9 in. Front shoulder room: 56.7 in. Front hip room: 56.7 in. Rear headroom: 36 in. Rear legroom: 29.6 in. Rear shoulder room: 54.4 in. Rear hip room: 47.3 in. Usable trunk capacity: 6.4 cu. ft. Rated fuel tank capacity: 21 gal. Standard tires: FR78 x 14/B steel-belted radial tires.

Camaro Type LT: Wheelbase: 108 in. Overall length: 195.4 in. Height: 49.1 in. Width: 74.4 in. Front tread: 61.6 in. Rear tread: 60.3 in. Front headroom: 37.3 in. Front legroom: 43.9 in. Front shoulder room: 56.7 in. Front hip room: 56.7 in. Rear headroom: 36 in. Rear legroom: 29.6 in. Rear shoulder room: 54.4 in. Rear hip room: 47.3 in. Usable trunk capacity: 6.4 cu. ft. Rated fuel tank capacity: 21 gal. Standard tires: FR78 x 14/B steel-belted radial whitewalls tires.

Camaro Type LT Rally Sport: Wheelbase: 108 in. Overall length: 195.4 in. Height: 49.1 in. Width: 74.4 in. Front tread: 61.6 in. Rear tread: 60.3 in. Front headroom: 37.3 in. Front legroom: 43.9 in. Front shoulder room: 56.7 in. Front hip room: 56.7 in. Rear headroom: 36 in. Rear legroom: 29.6 in. Rear shoulder room: 54.4 in. Rear hip room: 47.3 in. Usable trunk capacity: 6.4 cu. ft. Rated fuel tank capacity: 21 gal. Standard tires: FR78 x 14/B steel-belted radial whitewalls tires.

TECHNICAL

Transmission: Three-speed manual transmission (column shift) standard with floor shift in Camaro six-cylinder: (First) 3.11:1; (Second) 1.84:1; (Third) 1.00:1. Three-speed manual transmission (column shift) standard with floor shift in Camaro V-8: (First) 2.85:1; (Second) 1.68:1; (Third) 1.00:1. Four-speed floor shift standard optional in Camaro V-8: (First) 2.54:1; (Second) 1.80:1; (Third) 1.44:1; (Fourth) 1.00:1. Turbo Hydra-Matic gear ratios: (First) 2.52:1; (Second) 1.52:1; (Third)

The 1975 Camaro was not lacking in ammenities. Buyers could pick from an option list that included power windows and door locks, hidden windshield wipers, and leather upholstery.

1.00:1; (Reverse) 1.94:1. Standard final drive ratio: (Camaro Six) 3.08:1, (Camaro 350-cid two-barrel V-8) 2.73:1, (Camaro 350-cid four-barrel V-8) 3.08:1. Steering: re-circulating ball. Front suspension: unequal-length control arms, coil springs and stabilizer bar. Rear suspension: semi-elliptic leaf springs, stabilizer bar, rigid axle. Body construction: integral, with separate partial front box frame. Brakes: Front disc, rear drum. Fuel tank: 21 gal.

OPTIONS

AK1 color-keyed seat and shoulder belts ($16). AN6 adjustable seatback ($18). AU3 power door lock system ($56). A01 Soft-Ray tinted glass ($45). A31 power windows ($91). B37 color-keyed floor mats ($14). B84 body side moldings ($38). B93 door edge guard moldings ($7). C09 vinyl roof cover ($87). C24 Hide-A-Way windshield wipers ($21). C50 rear window defogger ($41). C60 Four-Season air conditioning ($435). D34 visor-vanity mirror ($3). D35 sport mirrors ($27). D55 center console ($68). D80 front and rear spoilers ($77). D88 black striping ($77). FE8 Radial Tuned Suspension ($35). G80 Positraction rear axle ($49). G92 high-altitude rear axle ($12). G96 highway axle ($12). J50 power brakes ($55). LM1 350-cid four-barrel V-8 ($54). M20 four-speed wide-ratio manual transmission ($219). M40 Turbo-Hydra-Matic automatic transmission ($235). N33 Comfortilt steering wheel ($49). N65 Stowaway spare tire ($14.10). PE1 turbine wheels and trim with Sport Coupe ($110.50). PE1 turbine styled wheels with wheel trim on Type LT ($75). PO1 full wheel covers ($30). QBT FR78-14 white-letter tires ($46). QDW FR78-14 white sidewall tires with ($33). QEG E78-14 black sidewall tires on Sport Coupe with Stowaway spare ($105.42 credit). QEG E78-14 black sidewall tires on Sport Coupe without Stowaway spare ($105.90 credit). QEH E78-14 white sidewall tires on Sport Coupe with Stowaway spare ($74.42 credit). QEH E78-14 white sidewall tires on Sport Coupe without Stowaway spare ($74.90 credit). UA1 heavy-duty battery ($15). UM1 AM stereo radio with 8-track tape ($199). UM2 AM/FM stereo sound system with tape player ($363). U05 dual horns ($4). U14 Special Instrumentation ($88). U35 electric clock ($17). U58 AM/FM stereo radio ($233). U63 AM stereo radio ($69). U69 AM/FM radio ($135). U80 rear seat speaker ($19). V01 heavy-duty radiator ($15). V30 front and rear bumper guards ($34). YF5 California emissions equipment ($45). ZJ7 Rally wheels with trim rings ($46). ZJ9 auxiliary lighting ($22.50). ZJ9 auxiliary lighting with Z54 Quiet Sound group or Type LT ($20). Z21 Z08 Sport décor package for Sport Coupe with Z21 ($40). Z08 Sport décor package for Sport Coupe without Z21 ($42). Z08 Sport décor package for Type LT with Z21 ($13). Z08 Sport décor package for Type LT without Z21 ($15). Z21 style trim ($55). Z54 Quiet Sound interior décor group ($35). Z85 Rally Sport package on Sport Coupe ($238). Z85 Rally Sport package on Type LT ($165). Z86 Gymkhana suspension without Rally Sport package ($112). Z86 Gymkhana suspension with Rally Sport package ($66). Z86 Gymkhana suspension with Type LT ($66).

HISTORICAL FOOTNOTES

Robert L. Lund was general manager of Chevrolet Motor Division in 1975. Model-year production of 145,770 Camaros again reflected a large swing towards six-cylinder models, with 29,749 such cars being built. Model-year production of Camaro V-8s dropped to a total of 116,021 units. All 1975 Camaros were made at the Norwood factory (which also built 84,063 Firebirds). The totals included 4,160 units built for export. Of the Camaros built, 86.8 percent had automatic transmission, 6 percent had a four-speed manual transmission, 58.2 percent had a standard V-8, 21.7 percent had an optional V-8, 21.7 percent had a six-cylinder engine, 100 percent had power steering, 14.6 had manual disc brakes, 85.4 percent had power disc brakes, 6.1 percent had a limited-slip differential, 86.2 percent had steel-belted radial tires, 21.6 percent had tilt steering, 3.8 percent had power door locks, 7.3 percent had power windows, 100 percent had bucket seats, 1.8 percent had a tinted windshield only, 77.6 percent had all-tinted glass, 53 percent had air conditioning, 18.4 percent had a vinyl top, 53.5 percent had an AM radio, 17.9 percent had an AM/FM radio, 5.6 percent had an AM/FM stereo radio, 4.1 percent had a stereo tape player, 27.3 percent had a standard clock, 19.3 percent had an optional clock, 24.1 percent had a rear window defogger, 88.5 percent had a remote-control outside rearview mirror, 20.3 percent had optional wheel covers, 25.3 had standard styled wheels and 45.7 percent had optional styled wheels. Camaro sales for model year 1975 came to 135,102 units. Camaro sales for calendar year 1975 came to 145,029. A total of 138,679 new Camaros were registered in the U.S. during calendar year 1975.

Camaro

The 1976 Camaro Type LT Sport Coupe got a new 305-cid V-8 and had a few interior amenities designed to make it a "Luxury Touring" vehicle.

Chevrolet really had little motivation to change anything on the Camaro for 1976, since production of 182,959 cars — the highest total since 1969 — was realized. In fact, production of Camaros at the Van Nuys, California, factory had to be resumed in August of 1975 just to keep up with demand.

The base Sport Coupe looked similar to the 1975 version. The crosshatch grille was made up of thin bars that peaked forward at the center. The grille was surrounded by a bright molding with rounded upper corners. Round, deeply recessed parking lamps sat between the grille and the recessed round headlamps. Front fenders held small side marker lenses. Taillights with bright moldings wrapped around the body sides, tapering to a point. Small vertical back-up lights were in the taillight housings. Rectangular emblems sat on the hood and deck. The body styling incorporated a long hood and short deck appearance with a swept-back roofline.

There were only three engine options for 1976 models, including a new 305-cid 140-hp V-8. The LM1 350-cid V-8 gained 10 hp, while the base inline six was unchanged. Power brakes were now standard and cruise control was now optional. The vinyl top option was revised to incorporate a canopy look with a painted rear band. The Type LT had a new bright aluminum rear body panel and simulated leather dashboard.

I.D. DATA

Camaros had a 13-symbol vehicle identification number (VIN) on the upper left surface of the instrument panel, visible through the windshield. The first symbol identifies the make: 1=Chevrolet Motor Division. The second symbol indicate the car line/series: Q=Camaro and S=Camaro Type LT. The third and fourth symbols indicate body type: 87=two-door four-passenger Sport Coupe. The fifth symbol indicates the engine type: D=RPO L22 250-cid 105-hp inline six-cylinder with one-barrel carburetor, Q=RPO LG3 305-cid 140-hp V-8 with

two-barrel carburetor and L=RPO LM1 350-cid 165-hp V-8 with four-barrel carburetor. The sixth symbol indicates model year: 6=1976. The seventh symbol indicates the assembly plant: L=Van Nuys, California, N=Norwood, Ohio. The final six digits are the sequential serial number. A body number plate on the upper horizontal surface of the shroud identifies model year, car division, series, style, body assembly plant, body number, trim combination, modular seat code, paint code, and date build code. A two- or three-symbol code (combined with a serial number) identifies each engine. On sixes, the pad is at the right side of the block, to rear of distributor. On V-8s, that pad is just forward of the right cylinder head.

COLORS

11=Antique White, 13=Silver, 19=Black, 28=Light Blue Metallic, 35=Dark Blue Metallic, 36=Firethorn Metallic, 37=Mahogany Metallic, 40=Lime Green Metallic, 49=Dark Green Metallic, 50=Cream, 51=Bright Yellow, 65=Buckskin, 67=Medium Saddle Metallic and 78=Medium Orange Metallic.

CAMARO - SERIES 1FQ - SIX/V-8

Standard equipment for the Camaro Sport Coupe included new narrow bright rocker panel moldings, a padded vinyl-covered four-spoke steering wheel with a crest, a left-hand outside rearview mirror, a wide-tread suspension, front disc brakes, finned rear drum brakes, variable-ratio power steering, contoured full-foam Stra-to-bucket front bucket seats, bucket-styled full-foam rear seats, standard all-vinyl seat trim, bright bumpers with protective black rubber strips, right top and side windshield moldings, bright side window moldings, bright full rear window moldings, Magic-Mirror acrylic finish, a built-in heater-defroster system, flow-through power ventilation, wall-to-wall cut-pile carpeting, double-panel steel construction (in the roof, doors, hood and deck lid), protective inner fenders, self-cleaning rocker panels, a front stabilizer bar, a coil spring front suspension, a leaf spring rear suspension, 14 x 6 in. wheels, FR78-14 steel-belted radial ply black sidewall tires, High Energy ignition, hydraulic valve lifters, a coolant recovery system, a Delco Energizer battery with sealed side terminals, front seat and shoulder belts, an energy-absorbing steering column, passenger-guard door locks, safety door latches and hinges, folding seat back latches, a padded instrument panel, energy-absorbing front seat back tops, a contoured windshield header, a thick laminate windshield, safety armrests, side marker lights and reflectors, parking lamps that illuminated with the headlights, four-way hazard warning flashers, signal lights with a lane-change feature, windshield washers, dual-speed windshield wipers, a wide-view inside day/night rearview mirror, an outside rearview mirror, a dual-chamber brake master cylinder, a starter safety switch, a dual-action safety hood latch, an ignition key reminder buzzer and a steering column lock. As before, the 250-cid inline six was the base engine. A new 305-cid small-block V-8 engine replaced the 350-cid V-8 as the standard V-8.

Model Number	Body/Style Number	Body Type & Seating	Factory Price	Shipping Weight	Production Total
CAMARO SPORT COUPE - SERIES 1FQ - (L6)					
FQ	87	2d coupe	$3,762	3,421 lbs.	Note 1
CAMARO SPORT COUPE - SERIES 1FQ - (V-8)					
FQ	87	2d coupe	$3,927	3,511 lbs.	Note 1

Note 1: Model-year production of 1976 base Camaro Sport Coupes was 130,538.

CAMARO RALLY SPORT - SERIES 1FQ/Z85 - SIX/V-8

A Rally Sport package was available. In addition to the standard Sport Coupe equipment listed above, the Rally Sport package included Low Gloss Black finish on the forward section of the roof, the hood, the radiator grille, the header panel, the headlight bezels, the upper fenders, the rocker panels and the rear panel. Rally wheels were standard. Tri-color striping separated the black-accented areas from the basic body color. The package also included bright headlamp trim, "Rally Sport" decals on the rear deck lid, "Rally Sport" front fender decals and Argent Silver paint accents. Rally Sport Camaros came in a limited range of base colors, including Antique White, Silver, Light Blue Metallic, Firethorn Metallic and Bright Yellow. The package was $260 for the base Camaro Sport Coupe.

Model Number	Body/Style Number	Body Type & Seating	Factory Price	Shipping Weight	Production Total
CAMARO RALLY SPORT COUPE - SERIES 1FQ/Z85 - (L6)					
1FQ/Z85	87	2d coupe	$4,022	—	Note 2/3
CAMARO RALLY SPORT COUPE - SERIES 1FQ/Z85 - (V-8)					
1FQ/Z85	87	2d coupe	$4,187	—	Note 2/3

Note 2: Combined model-year production of all 1976 Camaros was reported by most sources as 182,959. (See historical footnotes).
Note 3: The production total given above in Note 2 included 15,855 cars with the Rally Sport package.

CAMARO TYPE LT - SERIES 1FS - V-8

The Type LT (Luxury Touring) Camaro also looked similar to the 1975 version. Standard equipment included a wide-tread suspension, front disc brakes, finned rear drum brakes, variable-ratio power steering, a soft-rim vinyl-covered four-spoke sport steering wheel, contoured full-foam front bucket seats, bucket-styled full-foam rear seats, standard all-vinyl seat trim, wraparound taillights with bright moldings, bright bumpers with protective black rubber strips, bright lower body moldings, bright top and side windshield moldings, bright side window moldings, bright full rear window moldings, Magic-Mirror acrylic finish, a built-in heater-defroster system, flow-through power ventilation, wall-to-wall cut-pile carpeting, double-panel steel construction (in the roof, doors, hood and deck lid), protective inner fenders, self-cleaning rocker panels, a front stabilizer bar, a coil spring front suspension, a leaf spring rear suspension, FR78-14 steel-belted radial ply black sidewall tires, High Energy ignition, hydraulic valve lifters, a coolant recovery system, a Delco Energizer battery with sealed side terminals, front seat and shoulder belts, an energy-absorbing steering column, passenger-guard door locks, safety door latches and hinges, folding seat back latches, a padded instrument panel, energy-absorbing front seat back tops, a contoured windshield header, a thick lami-

Not much new was added to the 1976 Camaro Sport Coupe, which could still be had new with a V-8 for less than $4,000.

nate windshield, safety armrests, side marker lights and reflectors, parking lamps that illuminated with the headlights, four-way hazard warning flashers, signal lights with a lane-change feature, back-up lights, windshield washers, dual-speed windshield wipers, a wide-view inside day/night rearview mirror, an outside rearview mirror, a dual-chamber brake master cylinder, a starter safety switch, a dual-action safety hood latch, an ignition key reminder buzzer and a steering column lock. In addition, every Type LT Camaro had a "Type LT" nameplate on the right side of the bright rear end panel and a brushed aluminum appliqué across the full width of the rear end panel. Type LT seat trim now used vertical stitching for both cloth and vinyl upholstery. The Type LT Camaro offered three Dover knit cloth-and-vinyl interiors in black, dark blue and dark firethorn as well as all-vinyl interiors in black, white or light buckskin. The Type LT interiors also had special bucket seats with deep-contour seat backs and built-in padded armrests. Hide-A-Way windshield wipers, sport-style outside rearview mirrors (left-hand remote-controlled) and 14 x 7 in. Rally wheels were also standard. Inside the LT was a tachometer, a clock, a voltmeter and a temperature gauge, plus a color-keyed steering wheel, a glove compartment light and simulated leather instrument panel trim. The new 305-cid V-8 was standard in the Type LT.

Model Number	Body/Style Number	Body Type & Seating	Factory Price	Shipping Weight	Production Total
1FS	87	2d coupe	$4,320	3,576 lbs.	Note 4

Note 4: Model year production of 1976 Camaro Type LT coupes was 52,421.

CAMARO TYPE LT RALLY SPORT - SERIES 1FS/Z85 - V-8

The Rally Sport model-option package included Low Gloss Black finish on the forward section of the roof, the hood, the radiator grille, the header panel, the headlight bezels, the upper fenders, the rocker panels and the rear panel. Rally wheels were standard. Tri-color striping separated the black-accented areas from the basic body color. The package also included bright headlamp trim, "Rally Sport" decals on the rear deck lid, "Rally Sport" front fender decals and Argent Silver paint accents. Rally Sport Camaros came in a limited range of base colors, including Antique White, Silver, Light Blue Metallic, Firethorn Metallic and Bright Yellow. The package could be ordered for the Camaro Type LT. This combination added the special contents of the Rally Sport package to the special contents of the Type LT equipment list (described above). Since the Type LT model already included shared features such as Rally Wheels, the Rally Sport package cost a little less when added to a Type LT. The suggested retail price was $173.

Model Number	Body/Style Number	Body Type & Seating	Factory Price	Shipping Weight	Production Total
1FS	87	2d coupe	$4,493	3,477 lbs.	Note 5/6

Note 5: Combined model-year production of all 1976 Camaros was reported by most sources as 182,959. (See historical footnotes).

Note 6: The production total given above in Note 5 included 15,855 cars with the Rally Sport package.

ENGINES

L22 I6: Overhead-valve inline six-cylinder. Cast-iron block and head. Bore & stroke: 3.88 x 3.53 in. Displacement: 250 cid (4.1 liters). Compression ratio: 8.25:1. Brake horsepower: 105 at 3800 rpm. Torque: 185 lbs.-ft. at 1200 rpm. Seven main bearings. Induction system: Rochester 1ME one-barrel carburetor. Standard in Camaro Sport Coupe and Camaro Sport Coupe with Rally Sport package; not available in Type LT or Type LT with Rally Sport package. VIN Code D.

LG3 BASE V-8: 90-degree, overhead-valve V-8. Cast-iron block and head. Bore & stroke: 3.74 x 3.48 in. Displacement: 305 cid (5.0 liters). Compression ratio: 8.5:1. Brake horsepower: 140 at 3800 rpm. Torque: 245 lbs.-ft. at 2000 rpm Five main bearings. Hydraulic valve lifters. Induction system: Rochester 2GC two-barrel carburetor. Standard in Camaro V-8 Sport Coupe and Camaro V-8 Sport Coupe with Rally Sport package; Standard in Type LT and Type LT with Rally Sport package. VIN Code: Q.

LM1 V-8: 90-degree, overhead-valve V-8. Cast-iron block and head. Bore & stroke: 4.00 x 3.48 in. Displacement: 350 cid (5.7 liters). Compression ratio: 8.5:1. Brake horsepower: 165 at 3800 rpm. Torque: 260 lbs.-ft. at 2400 rpm Five main bearings. Hydraulic valve lifters. Induction system: Rochester M4MC four-barrel carburetor. Optional for all Camaro V-8s. VIN Code: L.

The stylish 1976 Camaro Rally Sport had T-tops, a flashy paint scheme that included tri-color striping, and a black finish on the hood, roof, front end and rocker panels.

CHASSIS

Base Sport Coupe: Wheelbase: 108 in. Overall length: 195.4 in. Height: 49.2 in. Width: 74.4 in. Front tread: 61.3 in. Rear tread: 60 in. Front headroom: 37.2 in. Front legroom: 43.9 in. Front shoulder room: 56.7 in. Front hip room: 52.4 in. Rear headroom: 36 in. Rear legroom: 28.4 in. Rear shoulder room: 54.4 in. Rear hip room: 45.8 in. Usable trunk capacity: 6.4 cu. ft. Rated fuel tank capacity: 21 gal. Standard tires: FR78 x 14/B steel-belted radial tires.

Camaro Rally Sport: Wheelbase: 108 in. Overall length: 195.4 in. Height: 49.2 in. Width: 74.4 in. Front Tread: 61.3 in. Rear tread: 60 in. Front headroom: 37.2 in. Front legroom: 43.9 in. Front shoulder room: 56.7 in. Front hip room: 52.4 in. Rear headroom: 36 in. Rear legroom: 28.4 in. Rear shoulder room: 54.4 in. Rear hip room: 45.8 in. Usable trunk capacity: 6.4 cu. ft. Rated fuel tank capacity: 21 gal. Standard tires: FR78 x 14/B steel-belted radial tires.

Camaro Type LT: Wheelbase: 108 in. Overall length: 195.4 in. Height: 49.2 in. Width: 74.4 in. Front tread: 61.6 in. Rear tread: 60.3 in. Front headroom: 37.2 in. Front legroom: 43.9 in. Front shoulder room: 56.7 in. Front hip room: 52.4 in. Rear headroom: 36 in. Rear legroom: 28.4 in. Rear shoulder room: 54.4 in. Rear hip room: 45.8 in. Usable trunk capacity: 6.4 cu. ft. Rated fuel tank capacity: 21 gal. Standard tires: FR78 x 14/B steel-belted radial whitewalls tires.

Camaro Type LT Rally Sport: Wheelbase: 108 in. Overall length: 195.4 in. Height: 49.2 in. Width: 74.4 in. Front tread: 61.6 in. Rear tread: 60.3 in. Front headroom: 37.2 in. Front legroom: 43.9 in. Front shoulder room: 56.7 in. Front hip room: 52.4 in. Rear headroom: 36 in. Rear legroom: 28.4 in. Rear shoulder room: 54.4 in. Rear hip room: 45.8 in. Usable trunk capacity: 6.4 cu. ft. Rated fuel tank capacity: 21 gal. Standard tires: FR78 x 14/B steel-belted radial whitewalls tires.

TECHNICAL

Transmission: Three-speed manual transmission (column shift) standard with floor shift on Camaro: (First) 3.11:1; (Second) 1.84:1; (Third) 1.00:1; (Reverse) 3.22:1. Four-speed floor shift standard optional on Camaro V-8: (First) 2.85:1; (Second) 2.02:1; (Third) 1.35:1; (4th) 1.00:1; (Reverse) 2.85:1. Three-speed Turbo Hydra-Matic gear ratios: (First) 2.52:1; (Second) 1.52:1; (Third) 1.00:1; (Reverse) 1.94:1. Standard final drive ratio: (Camaro Six) 3.08:1, (Camaro V-8) 2.73:1. Steering: re-circulating ball. Front suspension: unequal-length control arms, coil springs and stabilizer bar. Rear suspension: semi-elliptic leaf springs, stabilizer bar, rigid axle. Body construction: integral, with separate partial front box frame. Brakes: Front disc, rear drum. Fuel tank: 21 gal.

OPTIONS

AK1 color-keyed seat and shoulder belts ($17). AN6 adjustable seatback ($19). AU3 power door lock system ($62). A01 Soft-Ray tinted glass ($46). A31 power windows ($99). B37 color-keyed floor mats ($15). B80 roof drip moldings ($16). B84 body side moldings ($38). B93 door edge guard moldings ($7). C24 Hide-A-Way windshield wipers ($22). C50 rear window defogger ($43). C60 Four-Season air conditioning ($470 without V-8; $452 with V-8). D35 sport mirrors ($27). D55 center console ($71). D80 front and rear spoilers ($81). F41 sport suspension ($32). G80 Positraction rear axle ($51). G92 high-altitude rear axle ($13). J50 power brakes ($58). K30 cruise control ($73). LG3 305-cid V-8 (standard V-8). LM1 350-cid V-8 ($85). M20 four-speed wide-ratio manual transmission ($242). M40 Turbo-Hydra-Matic automatic transmission ($260). N33 Comfortilt steering wheel ($57). N65 Stowaway spare tire ($15.11 without radial tires or $1.13 credit on cars with radial tires). PE1 custom styled wheels without Rally Sport package ($116). PE1 custom styled wheels with Rally Sport package ($79). PE1 custom styled wheels with Type LT Camaro ($79). PO1 full wheel covers ($30). QBT FR78-14 white-letter tires with Stowaway spare ($39). QBT FR78-14 white-letter tires without Stowaway spare ($49). QDW FR78-14 white sidewall tires with Stowaway spare ($28). QDW FR78-14 white sidewall tires without Stowaway spare ($35). QEG E78-14 black sidewall tires with Stowaway spare ($84.40 credit). QEG E78-14 black sidewall tires without Stowaway spare ($105.75 credit). QEH E78-14 white sidewall tires with Stowaway spare ($72.75 credit). QEH E78-14 white sidewall tires without Stowaway spare ($58.40 credit). UA1 heavy-duty battery ($16). UM1 AM stereo radio with 8-track tape ($209). UM2 AM/FM stereo sound system with tape player ($324). U05 dual horns ($6). U14 Special Instrumentation ($92). U35 electric clock ($18). U58 AM/FM stereo radio ($226). U63 AM stereo radio ($75). U69 AM/FM radio ($137). U76 windshield antenna ($16). U80 rear seat speaker ($21). V01 heavy-duty radiator ($27). V30 front and rear bumper guards ($36). YF5 California emissions equipment ($50). ZJ7 Rally Sport wheels ($60). ZJ9 auxiliary lighting ($30). ZJ9 auxiliary lighting with Z54 Quiet Sound group or Type LT ($26). Z21 style trim ($58). Z54 Quiet Sound interior décor group ($53). Z85 Rally Sport package on Sport Coupe ($260). Z85 Rally Sport package on Type LT ($173).

HISTORICAL FOOTNOTES

Robert L. Lund was general manager of Chevrolet Motor Division in 1976. Camaro production started Aug. 16, 1975 at the Norwood factory and the same date was also the start of Camaro production at a second plant in Van Nuys, California. This was called the Los Angeles plant and had not built Camaros in several years. Chevrolet realized a hefty comeback in sales this year and so did the Camaro. Model-year production of 1976 Camaros is reported by most sources as 182,959. The engine breakouts reported in one industry trade journal reflected a further swing towards six-cylinder models, with production of 38,047 such cars being recorded. This source showed that model-year production of Camaro V-8s also rose to a total of 144,912 units. The trade journals reported production at Norwood (which also built all 110,775 Firebirds made in 1976) as 141,701 Camaros and showed that an additional 41,280 Camaros were assembled in California. This totals 182,981 units, which is 22 cars more than the production total reported by most sources. Of the Camaros built, 87.5 percent had automatic transmission, 6.2 percent had a four-speed manual transmission, 48.2 percent had a standard V-8, 31 percent had an optional V-8, 20.8 percent had a six-cylinder engine, 100 percent had power steering, 8.3 percent had manual disc brakes, 91.7 percent had power disc brakes, 7 percent had a limited-slip differential, 91 percent had radial tires, 25.5 percent had tilt steering, 7.6 percent had power door locks, 10.4 percent had power windows, 100 percent had bucket seats, 1.8 percent had a tinted windshield only, 78.5 percent had all-tinted glass, 80.6 percent had air conditioning, 13.6 percent had a vinyl top, 38 percent had an AM radio, 17.5 percent had an AM/FM radio, 7.6 percent had an AM/FM stereo radio, 13.8 percent had a stereo tape player, 28.6 percent had a standard clock, 19.3 percent had an optional clock, 30.7 percent had a rear window defogger, 89.9 percent had a remote-control outside rearview mirror, 14.6 percent had optional wheel covers and 78.9 had styled wheels. Camaro sales for model year 1976 came to 163,653 units. Camaro sales for calendar year 1976 came to 172,846 for a 2 percent market share. A total of 166,689 new Camaros were registered in the U.S. during calendar year 1976.

Camaro

Gerry West photo

This gold 1977 base Camaro with an automatic transmission and 305 V-8 came with an original sticker price of $6,004. It has had the original Rally wheels replaced with Superior wheels and Firestone Wide-Oval tires.

Does excitement sell automobiles? It must, if the 1977 Camaro model year is any example. In the middle of the year, Chevrolet brought back the Z28 (the / was dropped starting this year) to stir up enthusiasts and production zoomed to 218,853 units.

The new version of the "Z" was merchandised as a separate model, although it was factory coded as an option for the base Camaro. It did not have an exclusive engine like earlier Z28s, but the badges, stripes and decals made it look exciting and a heavy-duty suspension setup made for some heart-racing road manners.

The Camaro changed little for 1977. When the new models were introduced in the fall the lineup included the standard Camaro Sport Coupe and the upscale Camaro Type LT (or Luxury Touring edition). The familiar 250-cid inline six-cylinder engine was the standard power plant for 1977 Camaros. Options included a 305-cid V-8 and a 350-cid V-8. Transmission choices ranged from a standard three-speed manual gearbox, to four-speed manual gearbox to a Turbo-Hydra-Matic transmission. The standard axle ratio for both V-8s with automatic changed from 2.73:1 to 2.56:1 to help boost fuel economy. The four-speed transmission shift pattern was revised and reverse gear was now engaged by a rearward (toward the driver) lifting motion, rather than forward as before. A new refillable carbon-dioxide canister replaced the disposable freon-filled unit used to inflate the Stowaway spare tire. Intermittent windshield wipers joined the Camaro's option list and all models had Hide-A-Way windshield wipers.

I.D. DATA

Camaros had a 13-symbol vehicle identification number (VIN) on the upper left surface of the instrument panel, visible through the windshield. The first symbol identifies the make: 1=Chevrolet Motor Division. The second symbol indicate the car line/series: Q=Camaro, Camaro Rally Sport and Camaro Z28 and S=Camaro Type LT. The third and fourth symbols indicate body type: 87=two-door four-passenger Sport Coupe. The fifth symbol indicates the engine type: D=RPO L22 250-cid inline six-cylinder with one-barrel carburetor (110 hp except 90 hp in California), U=RPO LG3 305-cid V-8 with two-barrel carburetor (145 hp except 135 hp in California) and L=RPO LM1 350-cid V-8 with four-barrel carburetor (170 hp except 160 hp in California). The sixth symbol indicates model year: 7=1977. The seventh symbol indicates the assembly plant: L=Van Nuys, California, N=Norwood, Ohio. The final six digits are the sequential serial number. A body number plate on the upper horizontal surface of the shroud identifies model year, car division, series, style, body assembly plant, body number, trim combination, modular seat code, paint code, and date build code. A two- or three-symbol code (combined with a serial number) identifies each engine. On sixes, the pad is at the right side of the block, to rear of distributor. On V-8s, that pad is just forward of the right cylinder head.

COLORS

11=Antique White, 13=Silver, 19=Black, 22=Light Blue Metallic, 29=Dark Blue Metallic, 36=Firethorn Metallic, 38=Aqua Metallic, 44=Medium Green Metallic, 51=Bright Yellow, 61=Light Buckskin, 63=Buckskin Metallic, 69=Brown Metallic, 75=Light Red and 78=Orange Metallic.

CAMARO SPORT COUPE - SERIES 1FQ - SIX/V-8

Standard equipment for the Camaro Sport Coupe included a wide-tread suspension, front disc brakes, finned rear drum brakes, variable-ratio power steering, a soft-rim vinyl-covered four-spoke sport steering wheel, contoured full-foam front bucket seats, bucket-styled

Like the Sport Coupe and Rally Sport, the 1977 Type LT Camaro could be had with a straight six, 305-cid V-8, or 350-cid V-8.

full-foam rear seats, standard all-vinyl seat trim, wraparound taillights with bright moldings, bright bumpers with protective black rubber strips, bright lower body moldings, bright top and side windshield moldings, bright side window moldings, bright full rear window moldings, Magic-Mirror acrylic finish, a built-in heater-defroster system, flow-through power ventilation, wall-to-wall cut-pile carpeting, double-panel steel construction (in the roof, doors, hood and deck lid), protective inner fenders, self-cleaning rocker panels, a front stabilizer bar, a coil spring front suspension, a leaf spring rear suspension, FR78-14 steel-belted radial ply black sidewall tires, High Energy ignition, hydraulic valve lifters, a coolant recovery system, a Delco Energizer battery with sealed side terminals, front seat and shoulder belts, an energy-absorbing steering column, passenger-guard door locks, safety door latches and hinges, folding seat back latches, a padded instrument panel, energy-absorbing front seat back tops, a contoured windshield header, a thick laminate windshield, safety armrests, side marker lights and reflectors, parking lamps that illuminated with the headlights, four-way hazard warning flashers, signal lights with a lane-change feature, back-up lights, windshield washers, dual-speed windshield wipers, a wide-view inside day/night rearview mirror, an outside rearview mirror, a dual-chamber brake master cylinder, a starter safety switch, a dual-action safety hood latch, an ignition key reminder buzzer and a steering column lock.

Model Number	Body/Style Number	Body Type & Seating	Factory Price	Shipping Weight	Production Total
CAMARO SPORT COUPE - SERIES 1FQ - (I6)					
FQ	87	2d coupe	$4,113	3,369 lbs.	Note 1
CAMARO SPORT COUPE - SERIES 1FQ - (V-8)					
FQ	87	2d coupe	$4,223	3,476 lbs.	Note 1

Note 1: Model-year production of 1977 base Camaro coupes was 131,717.

CAMARO RALLY SPORT - SERIES 1FQ/Z85 - SIX/V-8

The Rally Sport package was actually an option that added $281 to the price of the base Sport Coupe, but many Camaro fans viewed it as a separate model. Some call this a "model-option." Standard equipment included a wide-tread suspension, front disc brakes, finned rear drum brakes, variable-ratio power steering, a soft-rim vinyl-covered four-spoke sport steering wheel, contoured full-foam front bucket seats, bucket-styled full-foam rear seats, standard all-vinyl seat trim, wraparound taillights with bright moldings, bright bumpers with protective black rubber strips, bright lower body moldings, bright top and side windshield moldings, bright side window moldings, bright full rear window moldings, Magic-Mirror acrylic finish, a built-in heater-defroster system, flow-through power ventilation, wall-to-wall cut-pile carpeting, double-panel steel construction (in the roof, doors, hood and deck lid), protective inner fenders, self-cleaning rocker panels, a front stabilizer bar, a coil spring front suspension, a leaf spring rear suspension, FR78-14 steel-belted radial black sidewall tires, High Energy ignition, hydraulic valve lifters, a coolant recovery system, a Delco Energizer battery with sealed side terminals, front seat and shoulder belts, an energy-absorbing steering column, passenger-guard door locks, safety door latches and hinges, folding seat back latches, a padded instrument panel, energy-absorbing front seat back tops, a contoured windshield header, a thick laminate windshield, safety armrests, side marker lights and reflectors, parking lamps that illuminated with the headlights, four-way hazard warning flashers, signal lights with a lane-change feature, back-up lights, windshield washers, dual-speed windshield wipers, a wide-view inside day/night rearview mirror, an outside rearview mirror, a dual-chamber brake master cylinder, a starter safety switch, a dual-action safety hood latch, an ignition key reminder buzzer and a steering column lock. The Rally Sport package added a dramatic appearance to the Camaro Sport Coupe or Camaro Type LT coupe. It featured special contrasting paint areas with the buyer's choice of Low Gloss Black or new-for-1977 Gray Metallic, Dark Blue Metallic or Buckskin Metallic finish on the forward top surfaces of the body as well as the rear end panel and standard dual sport mirrors. The grille and lower body area were also finished in Low Gloss Black and a distinctive tri-color striping package separated the contrasting color from the body color in appropriate areas. The Rally Sport package also included bright-edged headlight bezels, Rally wheels and Rally Sport decals on the deck lid and front fenders. Exterior colors available with the Rally Sport package were limited.

Model Number	Body/Style Number	Body Type & Seating	Factory Price	Shipping Weight	Production Total
CAMARO RALLY SPORT COUPE - SERIES 1FQ/Z85 - (I6)					
1FQ/Z85	87	2d coupe	$4,394	—	Note 2/3
CAMARO RALLY SPORT COUPE - SERIES 1FQ/Z85 - (V-8)					
1FQ/Z85	87	2d coupe	$4,504	—	Note 2/3

Note 2: Combined model-year production of all 1977 Camaros was 218,853.
Note 3: The production total given in Note 2 above includes 17,026 Camaros with the Rally Sport package.

CAMARO TYPE LT - SERIES 1FS SIX/V-8

The Camaro Type LT was the Luxury Touring model. Standard equipment included a wide-tread suspension, front disc brakes, finned rear drum brakes, variable-ratio power steering, a soft-rim vinyl-covered four-spoke sport steering wheel, contoured full-foam front bucket seats, bucket-styled full-foam rear seats, standard all-vinyl seat trim, wraparound taillights with bright moldings, bright bumpers with protective black rubber strips, bright lower body moldings, bright top and side windshield moldings, bright side window moldings, bright full rear window moldings, Magic-Mirror acrylic finish, a built-in heater-defroster system, flow-through power ventilation, wall-to-wall cut-pile carpeting, double-panel steel construction (in the roof, doors, hood and deck lid), protective inner fenders, self-cleaning rocker panels, a front stabilizer bar, a coil spring front suspension, a leaf spring rear suspension, FR78-14 steel-belted radial ply black sidewall tires, High Energy ignition, hydraulic valve lifters, a coolant recovery system, a Delco Energizer battery with sealed side terminals, front seat and shoulder belts, an energy-absorbing steering column, passenger-guard door locks, safety door latches and hinges, folding seat back latches, a padded instrument panel, energy-absorbing front seat back tops, a contoured windshield header, a thick laminate windshield, safety armrests, side marker lights and reflectors, parking lamps that illuminated with the headlights, four-way hazard warning flashers, signal lights with a lane-change feature, back-up lights, windshield washers, dual-speed windshield wipers, a wide-view inside day/night rearview mirror, an outside rearview mirror, a dual-chamber brake master cylinder, a starter safety switch, a dual-action safety hood latch, an ignition key reminder buzzer and a steering column lock. In addition, every Type LT coupe had dual sport mirrors (left-hand remote-controlled), dual horns, Rally wheels with bright center caps and trim rings, special instrumentation (including a tachometer, voltmeter, temperature gauge and electric clock), the interior décor Quiet Sound group (including simulated leather trim on the instrument cluster, additional instrument lighting, additional body sound insulation and a one-piece hood insulator), bright radiator grille outline moldings, a black-finished accent panel under a bright lower body molding, a brushed-aluminum trim panel between the taillights (with bright upper ands lower moldings), a bright trim ring with a vertical center bar on the parking lights, a "Type LT" nameplate behind the side window, a "Type LT" nameplate on the rear trim panel, special Type LT front bucket seats with deep-contoured backs and a special color-coordinated interior trim treatment.

Model Number	Body/Style Number	Body Type & Seating	Factory Price	Shipping Weight	Production Total
CAMARO TYPE LT - SERIES 1FS - (I6)					
1FS	87	2d coupe	$4,478	3,422 lbs.	Note 4

The 1977 Camaro International Race of Champions competition coupe with the IROC series drivers.

The Z28 returned after a two-year absence in 1977, boasting a 350-cid V-8 and Borg-Warner four-speed transmission.

CAMARO TYPE LT - SERIES 1FS - (V-8)

1FS	87	2d coupe	$4,598	3,529 lbs.	Note 4

Note 4: Model-year production of 1977 Camaro Type LT coupes was 72,787.

CAMARO TYPE LT RALLY SPORT SERIES 1FS/Z85 - SIX/V-8

The Rally Sport model-option package could also be ordered for the Camaro Type LT. This combination added the special contents of the Rally Sport package to the special contents of the Type LT equipment list, as described above. Since the Type LT model already included shared features such as Rally Wheels, the Rally Sport package cost a little less when added to a Type LT. The suggested retail price was $186.

Model Number	Body/Style Number	Body Type & Seating	Factory Price	Shipping Weight	Production Total
CAMARO TYPE LT RALLY SPORT - SERIES 1FS/Z85 - (I6)					
1FS	87	2d coupe	$4,664	3,352 lbs.	Note 5/6
CAMARO TYPE LT RALLY SPORT - SERIES 1FS/Z85 - (V-8)					
1FS	87	2d coupe	$4,784	3,477 lbs.	Note 5/6

Note 5: Combined model-year production of all 1977 Camaros was 218,853.
Note 6: The production total given in Note 2 above includes 17,026 Camaros with the Rally Sport package.

CAMARO Z28 - SERIES 1FQ - V-8

After being away from the lineup for two years, the high-performance Camaro Z28 returned as a 1977 1/2 model. It made its debut at the Chicago Auto Show. Standard equipment included a wide-tread suspension, front disc brakes, finned rear drum brakes, variable-ratio power steering, a soft-rim vinyl-covered four-spoke sport steering wheel, contoured full-foam front bucket seats, bucket-styled full-foam rear seats, standard all-vinyl seat trim, wraparound taillights with bright moldings, bright bumpers with protective black rubber strips, bright lower body moldings, bright top and side windshield moldings, bright side window moldings, bright full rear window moldings, Magic-Mirror acrylic finish, a built-in heater-defroster system, flow-through power ventilation, wall-to-wall cut-pile carpeting, double-panel steel construction (in the roof, doors, hood and deck lid), protective inner fenders, self-cleaning rocker panels, a coil spring front suspension, a leaf spring rear suspension, High Energy ignition, hydraulic valve lifters, a coolant recovery system, a Delco Energizer battery with sealed side terminals, front seat and shoulder belts, an energy-absorbing steering column, passenger-guard door locks, safety door latches and hinges, folding seat back latches, a padded instrument panel, energy-absorbing front seat back tops, a contoured windshield header, a thick laminate windshield, safety armrests, side marker lights and reflectors, parking lamps that illuminated with the headlights, four-way hazard warning flashers, signal lights with a lane-change feature, back-up lights, windshield washers, dual-speed windshield wipers, a wide-view inside day/night rearview mirror, an outside rearview mirror, a dual-chamber brake master cylinder, a starter safety switch, a dual-action safety hood latch, an ignition key reminder buzzer and a steering column lock. The Camaro Z28 rode on special GR70-15 white-lettered wide-profile steel-belted radial tires that were mounted on color-keyed 15 x 7-in. mag-style wheels. Under the hood was a special 350-cid V-8 that had an identifying decal. It was linked to a Borg-Warner four-speed manual transmission and 3.73:1 rear axle. Turbo-Hydra-Matic transmission was required in California. The chassis held front and rear stabilizer bars, special spring rates and quicker steering. This new Camaro Z28 also had body-color bumpers, body-color spoilers, body-color mirrors, body-color wheels, a black-out grille, a blacked-out rear-end panel, black-finished rocker panels, black moldings, black headlamp bezels, black taillight bezels, a

Stowaway spare tire and "open" exhausts with dual resonators. Rounding out the Z28's appearance were stripes on the rocker panels and wheel housings, special emblems and a Z28 badge on the driver's side of the grille. The Z28 came only in seven body colors with bumpers to match. The special "Z28" identification was available in four tri-color variations.

Model Number	Body/Style Number	Body Type & Seating	Factory Price	Shipping Weight	Production Total
1FP	87	2d coupe	$5,170	—	Note 5

Note 5: Total production of Camaro Z28s was 14,349.

ENGINES

L22 I6: Overhead-valve inline six-cylinder. Cast-iron block and head. Bore & stroke: 3.88 x 3.53 in. Displacement: 250 cid (4.1 liters). Compression ratio: 8.3:1. Brake horsepower: 110 at 3800 rpm (90 hp in California). Torque: 195 lbs.-ft. at 1600 rpm. Seven main bearings. Induction system: Rochester 1ME one-barrel carburetor. Standard in Camaro Sport Coupe, Rally Sport and Type LT. VIN Code D

LG3 base V-8: 90-degree, overhead-valve V-8. Cast-iron block and head. Bore & stroke: 3.74 x 3.48 in. Displacement: 305 cid (5.0 liters). Compression ratio: 8.4:1. Brake horsepower: 145 at 3800 rpm (135 hp in California). Torque: 245 lbs.-ft. at 2400 rpm Five main bearings. Hydraulic valve lifters. Induction system: Rochester 2GC two-barrel carburetor. Optional in Camaro Sport Coupe, Rally Sport and Type LT. VIN Code: U.

LM1 V-8: 90-degree, overhead-valve V-8. Cast-iron block and head. Bore & stroke: 4.00 x 3.48 in. Displacement: 350 cid (5.7 liters). Compression ratio: 8.2:1. Brake horsepower: 170 at 3800 rpm (160 hp in California). Torque: 270 lbs.-ft. at 2400 rpm Five main bearings. Hydraulic valve lifters. Induction system: Rochester M4MC four-barrel carburetor. Optional in Camaro Sport Coupe, Rally Sport and Type LT. VIN Code: L.

LM1 V-8: 90-degree, overhead-valve V-8. Cast-iron block and head. Bore & stroke: 4.00 x 3.48 in. Displacement: 350 cid (5.7 liters). Compression ratio: 8.2:1. Brake horsepower: 185 at 4000 rpm. Torque: 280 lbs.-ft. at 2400 rpm Five main bearings. Hydraulic valve lifters. Induction system: Rochester four-barrel carburetor. Standard and exclusive in Camaro Z28. VIN Code: L.

CHASSIS

Base Sport Coupe: Wheelbase: 108 in. Overall length: 195.4 in. Height: 49.2 in. Width: 74.4 in. Front tread: 61.3 in. Rear tread: 60 in. Front headroom: 37.2 in. Front legroom: 43.9 in. Front shoulder room: 56.7 in. Front hip room: 52.4 in. Rear headroom: 36 in. Rear legroom: 28.4 in. Rear shoulder room: 54.4 in. Rear hip room: 45.8 in. Usable trunk capacity: 6.4 cu. ft. Rated fuel tank capacity: 21 gal. Standard tires: FR78 x 14/B steel-belted radial tires.

Camaro Rally Sport: Wheelbase: 108 in. Overall length: 195.4 in. Height: 49.2 in. Width: 74.4 in. Front tread: 61.3 in. Rear tread: 60 in. Front headroom: 37.2 in. Front legroom: 43.9 in. Front shoulder room: 56.7 in. Front hip room: 52.4 in. Rear headroom: 36 in. Rear legroom: 28.4 in. Rear shoulder room: 54.4 in. Rear hip room: 45.8 in. Usable trunk capacity: 6.4 cu. ft. Rated fuel tank capacity: 21 gal. Standard tires: FR78 x 14/B steel-belted radial tires.

Camaro Type LT: Wheelbase: 108 in. Overall length: 195.4 in. Height: 49.2 in. Width: 74.4 in. Front tead: 61.6 in. Rear tread: 60.3 in. Front headroom: 37.2 in. Front legroom: 43.9 in. Front shoulder room: 56.7 in. Front hip room: 52.4 in. Rear headroom: 36 in. Rear legroom: 28.4 in. Rear shoulder room: 54.4 in. Rear hip room: 45.8 in. Usable trunk capacity: 6.4 cu. ft. Rated fuel tank capacity: 21 gal. Standard tires: FR78-14/B steel-belted radial whitewalls tires.

Camaro Type LT Rally Sport: Wheelbase: 108 in. Overall length: 195.4 in. Height: 49.2 in. Width: 74.4 in. Front tread: 61.6 in. Rear tread: 60.3 in. Front headroom: 37.2 in. Front legroom: 43.9 in. Front shoulder room: 56.7 in. Front hip room: 52.4 in. Rear headroom: 36 in. Rear legroom: 28.4 in. Rear shoulder room: 54.4 in. Rear hip room: 45.8 in. Usable trunk capacity: 6.4 cu. ft. Rated fuel tank capacity: 21 gal. Standard tires: FR78 x 14/B steel-belted radial whitewalls tires.

Camaro Z28: Wheelbase: 108 in. Overall length: 195.4 in. Height: 49.2 in. Width: 74.4 in. Front tread: 61.3 in. Rear tread: 60 in. Front headroom: 37.2 in. Front legroom: 43.9 in. Front shoulder room: 56.7 in. Front hip room: 52.4 in. Rear headroom: 36 in. Rear legroom: 28.4 in. Rear shoulder room: 54.4 in. Rear hip room: 45.8 in. Usable trunk capacity: 6.4 cu. ft. Rated fuel tank capacity: 21 gal. Standard tires: P225/70R15 steel-belted radial white-letter.

TECHNICAL

Transmission: Three-speed manual transmission (column shift) standard with floor shift on Camaro: (First) 3.11:1; (Second) 1.84:1; (Third) 1.00:1; (Reverse) 3.22:1. Four-speed floor shift standard optional on Camaro V-8: (First) 2.85:1; (Second) 2.02:1; (Third) 1.35:1; (4th) 1.00:1; (Reverse) 2.85:1. Three-speed Turbo Hydra-Matic gear ratios: (First) 2.52:1; (Second) 1.52:1; (Third) 1.00:1; (Reverse) 1.94:1. Standard final drive ratio: (Camaro Six) 2.73:1, (Camaro V-8/automatic transmission) 2.56:1, (Camaro Z28) 3.73:1; Steering: re-circulating ball. Front suspension: unequal-length control arms, coil springs and stabilizer bar. Rear suspension: semi-elliptic leaf springs, stabilizer bar, rigid axle. Body construction: integral, with separate partial

The standard Camaro vinyl interior.

front box frame. Brakes: Front disc, rear drum. Fuel tank: 21 gal.

OPTIONS

AK1 color-keyed seat and shoulder belts ($19). AN6 adjustable seat back ($20). AU3 power door lock system ($68). A01 Soft-Ray tinted glass ($50). A31 power windows ($108). B37 color-keyed floor mats ($16). B80 roof drip moldings ($17). B84 body side moldings ($40). B93 door edge guard moldings ($8). CD4 intermittent windshield wipers ($30). C50 rear window defogger ($48). C60 Four-Season air conditioning ($507 without V-8; $478 with V-8). D35 sport mirrors ($30). D55 center console ($75). D80 rear deck lid spoiler ($87). F41 sport suspension ($36). G80 Positraction rear axle ($54). G92 performance ratio rear axle ($14). J50 power brakes ($61). K30 cruise control ($80). LG3 305-cid 145-hp/135-hp California. V-8 ($120). LM1 350-cid 170-hp/160-hp in California. V-8 ($210). M20 four-speed wide-ratio manual transmission ($252). M21 four-speed close-ratio manual transmission with Z28 ((no cost). M40 Turbo-Hydra-Matic automatic transmission in Z28 ($30). M40 Turbo-Hydra-Matic automatic transmission in Camaros except Z28 ($282). NA6 high-altitude emissions ($22). N33 Comfortilt steering wheel ($57). N65 Stowaway spare tire (no cost). PE1 custom styled wheels without Rally Sport package ($125). PE1 custom styled wheels with Rally Sport package ($85). PE1 custom styled wheels with Type LT Camaro ($85). PO1 full wheel covers ($33). QBT FR78-14 white-letter tires with Stowaway spare ($44). QBT FR78-14 white-letter tires without Stowaway spare ($55). QDW FR78-14 white sidewall tires with Stowaway spare ($33). QDW FR78-14 white sidewall tires without Stowaway spare ($41). QEG E78-14 black sidewall tires with Stowaway spare ($86.94 credit). QEG E78-14 black sidewall tires without Stowaway spare ($107.10 credit credit). QEH E78-14 white sidewall tires with Stowaway spare ($55.94 credit). QEH E78-14 white sidewall tires without Stowaway spare ($68.10 credit). UA1 heavy-duty battery ($17). UM1 AM stereo radio with 8-track tape ($209). UM2 AM/FM stereo sound system with tape player ($324). U05 dual horns ($6). U14 special instrumentation ($99). U35 electric clock ($19). U58 AM/FM stereo radio ($226). U63 AM stereo radio ($72). U69 AM/FM radio ($137). U76 windshield antenna ($17). U80 rear seat speaker ($23). V01 heavy-duty radiator ($29). V30 front and rear bumper guards ($39). YF5 California emissions equipment ($70). ZJ7 Rally Sport wheels ($65). ZJ9 auxiliary lighting ($32). ZJ9 auxiliary lighting with Z54 Quiet Sound group or Type LT ($27). Z21 style trim ($61). Z54 Quiet Sound interior décor group ($57). Z85 Rally Sport package on Sport Coupe ($281). Z85 Rally Sport package on Type LT ($186).

HISTORICAL FOOTNOTES

Camaro sales climbed. Model-year production of 218,853 Camaros included 31,389 six-cylinder models and 187,464 Camaro V-8s. This model-year production at Van Nuys was higher than production at Norwood. Industry trade journals reported that the California plant built 153,671 Camaros and the Ohio factory built 65,183 Camaros. (In addition, all 155,736 Firebirds made in 1977 were built at Norwood.) Of the Camaros built, 89.8 percent had automatic transmission, 6.2 percent had a four-speed manual transmission, 6.6 percent had a standard V-8, 79.1 percent had an optional V-8, 14.3 percent had a six-cylinder engine, 100 percent had power steering, 4.9 percent had manual disc brakes, 95.1 percent had power disc brakes, 8 percent had a limited-slip differential, 93.5 percent had radial tires, 9.2 percent had power door locks, 14.2 percent had power windows, 100 percent had bucket seats, 2 percent had a tinted windshield only, 83 percent had all-tinted glass, 66.1 percent had manual air conditioning, 9 percent had a vinyl top, 31.0 percent had an AM radio, 15 percent had an AM/FM radio, 10 percent had an AM/FM stereo radio, 14 percent had a stereo tape player, 58 percent had a analog clock, 33.0 percent had a rear window defogger, 94 percent had a remote-control outside rearview mirror, 11.5 percent had cruise control, 12.4 percent had a tachometer, 7.4 percent had delay-type windshield wipers, 100 percent had electronic ignition, 10 percent had optional wheel covers and 79 had styled wheels. Camaro sales for model year 1977 came to 198,755 units. Camaro sales for calendar year 1977 came to 208,511 for a 2.3 percent market share. A total of 199,186 new Camaros were registered in the U.S. during calendar year 1977. Top racing drivers who piloted Camaros in the International Race of Champions (IROC) Series in 1977 included Benny Parsons, Brian Redman, James Hunt, Richard Petty, Jody Scheckter, A.J. Foyt, Mario Andretti, Bobby Allison, Al Unser and David Pearson.

Camaro

Phil Kunz photo

The Z28 added a new pointed hood panel air scoop with a black throat and functional slanted front fender air louvers.

The 1978 Camaros continued the second generation, but got a heavy facelift to make them look more up to date. Though unchanged in basic design, the 1978 Camaro managed a fresh look with a new body-colored soft nose section and rear bumper. The new design used the same cellular urethane as the Corvette to replace the former aluminum face bar and spring bumper system. The Camaro grille was similar to the 1977 grille, but had fewer horizontal bars, larger openings (10 rows across) and a deeper repeated lower section below the narrow bumper. At the rear of the car were wedge-shaped wrap-around taillights with amber-colored inboard directional signal lamps and clear back-up lamp lenses. This became a new Camaro trademark, replacing the characteristic round taillights of the early '70s.

Model-options were expanded to Sport Coupe, Rally Sport, Type LT, Type LT Rally Sport and Z28 using about the same power teams as in 1977.

A new option was a hatch roof with removable glass panels that soon became popularly known as the "T-top." The 305-cid V-8 got a new aluminum intake manifold and a 350-cid V-8 with a four-barrel carburetor and dual exhausts was used in the Z28. There were also suspension improvements designed to increase front-end rigidity and reduce rear axle hop.

I.D. DATA

Camaros again had a 13-symbol vehicle identification number (VIN) on the upper left surface of the instrument panel, visible through the windshield. The first symbol identifies the make: 1=Chevrolet Motor Division. The second symbol indicates the car line/series: Q=Camaro, Camaro Rally Sport and Camaro Z28 and S=Camaro Type LT. The third and fourth symbols indicate body type: 87=two-door four-passenger Sport Coupe. The fifth symbol indicates the engine type: D=RPO L22 250-cid inline six-cylinder with one-barrel carburetor (110 hp except 90 hp in California), U=RPO LG3 305-cid V-8 with two-barrel carburetor (145 hp except 135 hp in California) and L=RPO LM1 350-cid V-8 with four-barrel carburetor (170 hp except 160 hp in California). The sixth symbol indicates model year: 8=1978. The seventh symbol indicates the assembly plant: L=Van Nuys, California, N=Norwood, Ohio. The final six digits are the sequential serial number. A body number plate on the upper horizontal surface of the shroud identifies model year, car division, series, style, body assembly plant, body number, trim combination, modular seat code, paint code, and date build code. A two- or three-symbol code (combined with a serial number) identifies each engine. On sixes, the pad is at the right side of the block, to rear of distributor. On V-8s, that pad is just forward of the right cylinder head.

COLORS

11=White, 15=Silver, 19=Black, 22=Light Blue, 24=Bright Blue, 34=Orange-Yellow, 48=Dark Blue-Green, 51=Bright Yellow, 63=Camel, 67=Saffron, 69=Dark Camel, 75=Light Red and 77=Carmine.

CAMARO SPORT COUPE - SERIES 1FQ - SIX/V-8

The standard Camaro engine was a 250-cid inline six rated at 110 hp and linked to a three-speed manual transmission. Options included 305- and 350-cid V-8s. A four-speed manual gearbox was standard with both V-8s. Camaros sold in California came only with automatic transmission. Car buyerss in so-called high-altitude counties were limited to the 350-cid V-8 and automatic transmission. The six-cylinder engine had improved exhaust system isolation this year. An aluminum intake manifold helped cut the 305-cid V-8's weight by 35 lbs. Chassis improvements included front frame reinforcements. The brake-pressure differential switch was now made of nylon. Axle ratios for all Camaros were lowered in an attempt to boost gas mileage. Base Camaros had new standard cloth seat trim, a new door trim design and optional new aluminum wheels. Also joining the option list was a T-bar twin hatch roof with tinted glass lift-out roof panels. A single latch on each panel operated this "T-top." A total of 9,875 T-bar roofs were installed.

Model Number	Body/Style Number	Body Type & Seating	Factory Price	Shipping Weight	Production Total
CAMARO SPORT COUPE - SERIES 1FQ - (I6)					
FQ	87	2d coupe	$4,414	3,300 lbs.	Note 1
CAMARO SPORT COUPE - SERIES 1FQ - (V-8)					
FQ	87	2d coupe	$4,599	3,425 lbs.	Note 1

Note 1: Model-year production of 1978 base Camaro coupes without the RS option was 134,491.

CAMARO RALLY SPORT - SERIES 1FQ/Z85 - SIX/V-8

The Camaro Rally Sport became a model this year rather than an option. It featured new paint striping. Rally Sport Coupe models had a bold contrasting paint scheme. The forward roof section, hood surface and front header (to below the grille opening) were black metallic. Tri-color striping separated those black surfaces from the basic body color. Rally Sport decals were on front fenders and rear deck lid. Engines were the same as on the base Camaro.

Model Number	Body/Style Number	Body Type & Seating	Factory Price	Shipping Weight	Production Total
CAMARO RALLY SPORT COUPE - SERIES 1FQ/Z85 - (I6)					
1FQ/Z85	87	2d coupe	$4,784	—	Note 2
CAMARO RALLY SPORT COUPE - SERIES 1FQ/Z85 - (V-8)					
1FQ/Z85	87	2d coupe	$4,969	—	Note 2

Note 2: Model year production of 1978 base coupes with the RS option was 11,902.

CAMARO TYPE LT - SERIES 1FS - SIX/V-8

The Camaro Type LT (Luxury Touring) model included special identification and trim, concealed windshield wipers, dual sport mirrors, Rally wheels with caps and trim rings, a sport steering wheel, deluxe interior trim, woodgrain accents, a glove compartment lamp, added sound insulation and special instrumentation.

Model Number	Body/Style Number	Body Type & Seating	Factory Price	Shipping Weight	Production Total
CAMARO TYPE LT - SERIES 1FS - (I6)					
1FS	87	2d coupe	$4,814	3,352 lbs.	Note 3
CAMARO TYPE LT - SERIES 1FS - (V-8)					
1FS	87	2d coupe	$4,999	3,477 lbs.	Note 3

Note 3: Model year production of 1978 Camaro Type LT coupes without the RS option was 65,635.

CAMARO TYPE LT RALLY SPORT - SERIES 1FS - SIX/V-8

Like the standard Type LT, the Type LT Rally Sport Coupe also had the bold Rally Sport paint scheme with contrasting colors. The forward roof section, hood surface and front header (to below the grille opening) were done in metallic black paint. Tri-color striping separated those black surfaces from the basic body color. Rally Sport decals were seen on the front fenders and rear deck lid. This model-option also included special identification and trim, concealed windshield wipers, dual sport mirrors, Rally wheels with caps and trim rings, a sport steering wheel, deluxe interior trim, woodgrain

accents, a glove compartment lamp, added sound insulation and special instrumentation.

Model Number	Body/Style Number	Body Type & Seating	Factory Price	Shipping Weight	Production Total
CAMARO TYPE LT RALLY SPORT - SERIES 1FS/Z85 - (I6)					
1FS	87	2d coupe	$5,065	3,352 lbs.	Note 4
CAMARO TYPE LT RALLY SPORT - SERIES 1FS/Z85 - (V-8)					
1FS	87	2d coupe	$5,250	3,477 lbs.	Note 4

Note 4: Model-year production of 1978 Type LT coupes with the RS option was 5,696.

CAMARO Z28 - SERIES 1F - SIX/V-8

The high-performance Camaro Z28 added a new pointed hood panel air scoop with a black throat, functional slanted front fender air louvers, a body-color rear deck lid spoiler, modified body striping and a simulated string-wrapped steering wheel. The base Z28 power plant was the 350-cid V-8 with four-barrel carburetor and dual exhaust outlets, which put out 185 hp. Z28s also had a 3.42:1 or 3.73:1 rear axle ratio, a special handling suspension and GR70-15/B white-letter tires. Suspension revisions this year increased the Z28's front-end rigidity and limited transverse movement of the rear axle. A Z28 decal was placed below the air louvers.

Model Number	Body/Style Number	Body Type & Seating	Factory Price	Shipping Weight	Production Total
CAMARO Z28 - SERIES 1FP - (5.7-LITER V-8)					
1FP	87	2d coupe	$5,604	—	Note 5

Note 5: Model-year production of 1978 Camaro Z28 coupes was 54,907.

ENGINES

L22 I6: Overhead-valve inline six-cylinder. Cast-iron block and head. Bore & stroke: 3.88 x 3.53 in. Displacement: 250 cid (4.1 liters). Compression ratio: 8.1:1. Brake horsepower: 110 at 3800 rpm (90 hp in California). Torque: 190 lbs.-ft. at 1600 rpm. Seven main bearings. Induction system: Rochester 1ME one-barrel carburetor. Standard in Camaro Sport Coupe, Rally Sport and Type LT. VIN Code D

LG3 base V-8: 90-degree, overhead-valve V-8. Cast-iron block and head. Bore & stroke: 3.74 x 3.48 in. Displacement: 305 cid (5.0 liters). Compression ratio: 8.4:1. Brake horsepower: 145 at 3800 rpm (135 hp in California). Torque: 245 lbs.-ft. at 2400 rpm. Five main bearings. Hydraulic valve lifters. Induction system: Rochester 2GC two-barrel carburetor. Optional in Camaro Sport Coupe, Rally Sport and Type LT. VIN Code: U.

LM1 V-8: 90-degree, overhead-valve V-8. Cast-iron block and head. Bore & stroke: 4.00 x 3.48 in. Displacement: 350 cid (5.7 liters). Compression ratio: 8.2:1. Brake horsepower: 170 at 3800 rpm (160 hp in California). Torque: 270 lbs.-ft. at 2400 rpm. Five main bearings. Hydraulic valve lifters. Induction system: Rochester M4MC four-barrel carburetor. Optional in Camaro Sport Coupe, Rally Sport and Type LT. VIN Code: L.

LM1 V-8: 90-degree, overhead-valve V-8. Cast-iron block and head. Bore & stroke: 4.00 x 3.48 in. Displacement: 350 cid (5.7 liters). Compression ratio: 8.2:1. Brake horsepower: 185 at 4000 rpm. Torque: 280 lbs.-ft. at 2400 rpm. Five main bearings. Hydraulic valve lifters. Induction system: Rochester four-barrel carburetor. Standard in Z28. VIN Code: L.

The 1978 Camaro Rally Sport (left) and Type LT featured paint schemes that used black around the hood, roof and nose.

CHASSIS

Base Sport Coupe: Wheelbase: 108 in. Overall length: 197.6 in. Height: 49.2 in. Width: 74.5 in. Front tread: 61.3 in. Rear tread: 60 in. Standard tires: FR78 x 14/B steel-belted radial tires.

Camaro Rally Sport: Wheelbase: 108 in. Overall length: 197.6 in. Height: 49.2 in. Width: 74.5 in. Front tread: 61.3 in. Rear tread: 60 in. Standard tires: FR78 x 14/B steel-belted radial tires.

Camaro Type LT: Wheelbase: 108 in. Overall length: 197.6 in. Height: 49.2 in. Width: 74.5 in. Front tread: 61.6 in. Rear tread: 60.3 in. Standard tires: FR78-14/B steel-belted radial whitewalls tires.

Camaro Type LT Rally Sport: Wheelbase: 108 in. Overall length: 197.6 in. Height: 49.2 in. Width: 74.5 in. Front tread: 61.6 in. Rear tread: 60.3 in. Standard tires: FR78-14/B steel-belted radial whitewalls tires.

Camaro Z28: Wheelbase: 108 in. Overall length: 197.6 in. Height: 49.2 in. Width: 74.5 in. Front tread: 61.3 in. Rear tread: 60 in. Standard tires: P225/70R15 steel-belted radial white-letter.

TECHNICAL

Transmission: Three-speed manual transmission with floor shift standard with six-cylinder: (First) 3.50:1; (Second) 1.81:1; (Third) 1.00:1; (Reverse) 3.62:1. Four-speed manual transmission with floor shift standard with V-8: (First) 2.85:1; (Second) 2.02:1; (Third) 1.35:1; (4th) 1.00:1; (Reverse) 2.85:1. Four-speed manual transmission with floor shift standard with Z28: (First) 2.64:1; (Second) 1.75:1; (Third) 1.34:1; (4th) 1.00:1; (Reverse) 2.55:1. Three-speed automatic transmission optional: (First) 2.52:1; (Second) 1.52:1; (Third) 1.00:1; (Reverse) 1.94:1. Standard final drive ratio: (Camaro six) 2.73:1; (Camaro V-8, except Z28) 3.08:1; (Camaro Z28) 3.42:1 or 3.73:1. Steering: re-circulating ball. Front suspension: unequal-length control arms, coil springs, stabilizer bar. Rear suspension: semi-elliptic leaf springs, stabilizer bar and rigid axle. Body construction: integral, with separate partial front box frame. Brakes: Front disc, rear drum. Fuel tank: 21 gal.

OPTIONS

AK1 color-keyed seat and shoulder belts ($21). AN6 adjustable seat back ($21). AU3 power door lock system ($80). A01 Soft-Ray tinted glass ($56). A31 power windows ($124). B37 color-keyed floor mats ($20). B80 roof drip moldings ($23). B84 body side moldings ($42). B93 door edge guard moldings ($11). CC1 removable glass roof panels ($625). CD4 intermittent windshield wipers ($32). C50 rear window defogger ($51). C60 Four-Season air conditioning ($539 without V-8; $508 with V-8). D35 sport mirrors ($33). D55 center console ($80). D80 rear deck lid spoiler ($55). F41 Sport suspension ($38). G80 positraction rear axle ($59). G92 performance ratio rear axle ($15). J50 power brakes ($69). K30 cruise control ($90). LG3 305-cid 145-hp/135-hp California V-8 ($185). LM1 350-cid 170-hp/160-hp in California V-8 ($300). MM4 four-speed wide-ratio manual transmission ($125). MX1 automatic transmission in Z28 ($45). MX1 automatic transmission in Camaros except Z28 ($307). M21 close-ratio four-speed manual transmission in Z28 (no cost). NA6 high-altitude emissions ($33). N33 Comfortilt steering wheel ($69). N65 Stowaway spare tire (no cost). PE1 custom styled wheels with Camaro Sport Coupe ($133). PE1 custom styled wheels with Type LT or Rally Sport ($91). PO1 full wheel covers ($37). QBT FR78-14 white letter tires with Stowaway spare ($49). QBT FR78-14 white letter tires without Stowaway spare ($61). QDW FR78-14 white sidewall tires with Stowaway spare ($37). QDW FR78-14 white sidewall tires without Stowaway spare ($46). QEG E78-14 black sidewall tires with Stowaway spare ($89.56 credit). QEG E78-14 black sidewall tires without Stowaway spare ($112.95 credit). QEH E78-14 white sidewall tires with Stowaway spare ($54.56 credit). QEH E78-14 white sidewall tires without Stowaway spare ($68.95 credit). UA1 heavy-duty battery ($18). UM1 AM stereo radio with 8-track tape ($229). UM2 AM/FM stereo sound system with tape player ($328). U05 dual horns ($7). U14 Special Instrumentation ($106). U35 electric clock ($20). U58 AM/FM stereo radio ($229). U63 AM stereo radio ($79). U69 AM/FM radio ($149). U76 windshield antenna ($25). U80 rear seat speaker ($24). V01 heavy-duty radiator ($31). YF5 California emissions equipment ($75). YJ8 Color-keyed aluminum wheels with Sport Coupe ($265). YJ8 Color-keyed aluminum wheels with Z28 ($195). YJ8 Color-keyed aluminum wheels with Rally Sport or Type LT ($180). ZJ7 Rally wheels trim ($85). ZJ9 auxiliary lighting ($34). ZJ9 auxiliary lighting with Z54 Quiet Sound group or Type LT ($28). Z21 style trim ($70). Z54 Quiet Sound interior décor group ($61). J-2 cloth seats with Sport Coupe or Z28 ($21). F-2 Custom cloth seats with Type LT ($21). F-2 Custom cloth seats with Z28 ($315). S-2 custom cloth seats with Type LT ($21). S-2 custom sport seats with Z28 ($315). X-2 custom vinyl seats with Z28 ($294).

HISTORICAL FOOTNOTES

Introduced: Oct. 6, 1977. Chevrolet's overall model-year sales rose by 4.6 percent (from 2,239,538 to 2,342,035), making 1978 the third highest year in Chevrolet history. In recent years, other GM divisions had been using more shared components and body style offerings. Chevrolet continued to retain more individuality, at least for the time being. Robert D. Lund stayed at the helm of the division in 1978 and Camaro sales climbed. Model-year sales came to 247,437 units. Calendar year sales wound up at 260,201 for a 2.8 percent market share. Model-year production of 272,631 Camaros included 36,982 six-cylinder models and 235,649 Camaro V-8s. The Van Nuys plant reported building 130,258 Camaros (and 90,272 Firebirds). The Norwood factory reported building 142,375 Camaros (and 97,013 Firebirds). Of the Camaros built, 87.9 percent had automatic transmission, 9.7 percent had a four-speed manual transmission, 20.1 percent had a standard V-8, 66.3 percent had an optional V-8, 13.6 percent had a six-cylinder engine, 100 percent had power steering, 3.8 percent had manual disc brakes, 96.2 percent had power disc brakes, 12 percent had a limited-slip differential, 94.1 percent had radial tires, 11.7 percent had power door locks, 18.7 percent had power windows, 100 percent had bucket seats, 2.4 percent had a tinted windshield only, 85.5 percent had all-tinted glass, 71.4 percent had manual air conditioning, 42.9 percent had tilt steering, 17.2 percent had cruise control, 4.3 percent had a vinyl top, 27.3 percent had an AM radio, 13.1 percent had an AM/FM radio, 11.9 percent had an AM/FM stereo radio, 3.7 percent had an AM 8-track tape player, 11.8 percent had an AM/FM 8-track tape player, 61.8 percent had a analog clock, 34.9 percent had a rear window defogger, 95.3 percent had a remote-control outside rearview mirror, 5.4 percent had optional wheel covers and 88.4 percent had styled steel wheels, 8.7 percent had styled aluminum wheels and 3.6 percent had a hatch roof. A total of 251,983 new Camaros were registered in the U.S. during calendar year 1978.

Eugene Stansky photo

The 1978 Camaro Z28 Sport Coupe had its own signature exterior and a 350-cid four-barrel V-8 with a stiffer suspension.

Camaro

The Berlinetta took the place of the Type LT in 1979.

The new Camaro Berlinetta Sport Coupe with pin striping, a bright grille and black rocker panels replaced the Type LT in 1979. All Camaros got a new instrument panel and anti-theft steering column. The performance Z28 had a new blackout grille, flared front wheel openings and a three-piece front air dam that wrapped around the sides. New options included a CB radio, a cassette player and an AM/FM stereo with a built-in clock.

The base inline six had a lower axle ratio to raise gas mileage. Both 305 and 350-cid V-8s were available. The Z28 came with a standard 350-cid four-barrel V-8, a four-speed transmission and body-color front and rear spoilers. This would be the last year of the second-generation Camaro's production boom. Chevy built 152,657 cars in California and 129,925 in Ohio.

It was a great year for business, as the 1979 models proved to be the best-selling Camaros in history. In addition, an important change in sales patterns was realized this season when the Z28 became the second best-selling Camaro models. With the Z-car's higher price, that added up to more profits for Chevrolet.

I.D. DATA

Camaros again had a 13-symbol vehicle identification number (VIN) on the upper left surface of the instrument panel, visible through the windshield. The first symbol identifies the make: 1=Chevrolet Motor Division. The second symbol indicates the car line/series: Q=Camaro, Camaro Rally Sport and Camaro Z28 and S=Camaro Berlinetta. The third and fourth symbols indicate body type: 87=two-door four-passenger Sport Coupe. The fifth symbol indicates the engine type: D=RPO L22 250-cid inline six-cylinder with one-barrel carburetor (100 hp except 90 hp in California), G=RPO LG3 305-cid V-8 with two-barrel carburetor (135 hp except 130 hp in California) and L=RPO LM1 350-cid V-8 with four-barrel

carburetor (170 hp except 165 hp in California). The sixth symbol indicates model year: 9=1979. The seventh symbol indicates the assembly plant: L=Van Nuys, California, N=Norwood, Ohio. The final six digits are the sequential serial number.

COLORS

11=White, 15=Silver, 19=Black, 22=Light Blue, 24=Bright Blue, 29=Dark Blue, 40=Light Green, 44=Medium Green, 51=Bright Yellow, 57=Gold, 61=Beige, 63=Camel, 69=Dark Brown, 75=Red and 77=Carmine.

CAMARO SPORT COUPE - SERIES 1FQ - SIX/V-8

Standard equipment for the base Sport Coupe included power steering, a Delco Freedom battery, a front stabilizer bar, concealed two-speed windshield wipers, carpeting, a heater and defroster, front bucket seats, a center dome light, a four-spoke sport steering wheel, a day/night mirror and FR78 x 14 steel-belted radial tires. The base 250-cid (4.1-liter) inline six had a lower axle ratio this year to increase its gas mileage. Optional V-8s included 305- and 350-cid engines. Only 2,438 Camaros were produced with a performance axle ratio, while 33,584 had optional removable glass roof panels, which most people called "T-tops." New audio options included Citizen's Band (CB) radio, cassette player or clock built into an AM/FM stereo. Mast and windshield type radio antennas were available.

Model Number	Body/Style Number	Body Type & Seating	Factory Price	Shipping Weight	Production Total
CAMARO SPORT COUPE - SERIES 1FQ - (I6)					
FQ	87	2d coupe	$4,677	3,305 lbs.	Note 1
CAMARO SPORT COUPE - SERIES 1FQ - (V-8)					
FQ	87	2d coupe	$4,912	3,435 lbs.	Note 1

Note 1: Most sources show model-year production of 1979 base Camaro Sport Coupes was 111,357. (See historical footnotes.)

CAMARO RALLY SPORT - SERIES 1FQ/Z85 - SIX/V-8

Standard equipment for the 1979 Camaro Rally Sport Coupe included power steering, a Delco Freedom battery, a front stabilizer bar, concealed two-speed windshield wipers, carpeting, a heater and defroster, front bucket seats, a center dome light, a four-spoke sport steering wheel, a day/night mirror, FR78-14 steel-belted radial tires, a rear deck lid spoiler, a sport suspension, black-finished rocker panels, a black grille, black headlamp bezels, bright reveal moldings, sport mirrors, color-keyed Rally wheels and a bold two-tone paint scheme. Engine options were the same as those for the base model.

Model Number	Body/Style Number	Body Type & Seating	Factory Price	Shipping Weight	Production Total
CAMARO RALLY SPORT COUPE - SERIES 1FQ/Z85 - (I6)					
1FQ/Z85	87	2d coupe	$5,073	—	Note 2
CAMARO RALLY SPORT COUPE - SERIES 1FQ/Z85 - (V-8)					
1FQ/Z85	87	2d coupe	$5,308	—	Note 2

Note 2: Most sources show model-year production of 1979 Camaro Rally Sport Coupes was 19,101. (See historical footnotes.)

CAMARO BERLINETTA - SERIES 1FS - SIX/V-8

A new Camaro Berlinetta model took the place of the Type LT. The Berlinetta was promoted as the "new way to take your pulse." It had body pin striping, a bright grille and black-finished rocker panels. Standard equipment included power steering, a Delco Freedom battery, a front stabilizer bar, concealed two-speed windshield wipers, carpeting, a heater and defroster, front bucket seats, a center dome light, a four-spoke sport steering wheel, a day/night mirror, FR78-14 steel-belted radial whitewall tires, color-keyed custom styled wheels, body-color sport mirrors (left-hand remote-controlled), dual pin stripes, chrome headlamp bezels, a soft fascia front bumper system, a soft fascia rear bumper system, bright windshield moldings, bright back window moldings and an Argent Silver rear-panel appliqué.

Model Number	Body/Style Number	Body Type & Seating	Factory Price	Shipping Weight	Production Total
CAMARO BERLINETTA - SERIES 1FS - (I6)					
1FS	87	2d coupe	$5,396	3,358 lbs.	Note 3
CAMARO BERLINETTA - SERIES 1FS - (V-8)					
1FS	87	2d coupe	$5,631	3,488 lbs.	Note 3

Note 3: Most sources show model-year production of 1979 Camaro Berlinetta coupes was 67,236. (See historical footnotes.)

CAMARO Z28 - SERIES 1FQ - V-8

The high-performance Camaro Z28 had new flared front wheel openings as well as a three-piece front air dam that wrapped around the sides and up into wheel openings. The Z28 also had a blacked-out front end with a center grille emblem. Its identifying decal was moved from the front fender to the door. A rear spoiler was standard equipment, but 81 cars were produced without this item. In addition to the equipment that was standard on the base model the Camaro Z28 came with a special 350-cid 175-hp (170-hp in California) four-barrel V-8, a four-speed close-ratio manual gearbox, a bolt-on simulated hood air scoop with a black "throat," black windshield moldings, black back window moldings, two-tone front fender striping, front fender flares, an air dam, door panels, a rear deck lid panel, front fender air louvers, body-color spoilers (front and rear), a black-out style grille, black headlamp bezels, black taillight bezels, a black rear end panel, a black-finished license plate mount, body-color sport mirrors, body-color door handle inserts, a body-color back bumper, P225/70R15 steel-belted white-letter tires and 7-in. body-color wheels.

Model Number	Body/Style Number	Body Type & Seating	Factory Price	Shipping Weight	Production Total
1FP	87	2d coupe	$6,115	—	Note 4

Note 4: Most sources show model-year production of 1979 Camaro Z28 coupes was 84,877. (See historical footnotes.)

ENGINE

L22 I6: Overhead-valve inline six-cylinder. Cast-iron block and head. Bore & stroke: 3.88 x 3.53 in. Displacement: 250 cid (4.1 liters). Compression ratio: 8.0:1. Brake horsepower: 110 at 3800 rpm (90 hp in California). Torque: 200 lbs.-ft. at 1600 rpm. Seven main bearings. Induction system: Rochester 1ME one-barrel carburetor. Standard in Camaro Sport Coupe, Rally Sport and Berlinetta. VIN Code D

LG3 base V-8: 90-degree, overhead-valve V-8. Cast-iron block and head. Bore & stroke: 3.74 x 3.48 in. Displacement: 305 cid (5.0 liters). Compression ratio: 8.4:1. Brake horsepower: 135 at 3200 rpm (130 hp in California). Torque: 245 lbs.-ft. at 2000 rpm Five main bearings. Hydraulic valve lifters. Induction system: Rochester M2MC two-barrel carburetor. Optional in Camaro Sport Coupe, Rally Sport and Berlinetta. VIN Code: G.

LM1 V-8: 90-degree, overhead-valve V-8. Cast-iron block and head. Bore & stroke: 4.00 x 3.48 in. Displace-

The 1979 Camaro lineup included the Z28, Rally Sport, Berlinetta and base Sport Coupe.

Thomas Glatch Productions photo

The 1979 Z28 had its identifying decal moved from the front fender to the door. A rear spoiler was standard equipment.

ment: 350 cid (5.7 liters). Compression ratio: 8.2:1. Brake horsepower: 170 at 4000 rpm (165 hp in California). Torque: 270 lbs.-ft. at 2400 rpm Five main bearings. Hydraulic valve lifters. Induction system: Rochester M4MC four-barrel carburetor. Standard in Z28. VIN Code: L.

CHASSIS

Base Camaro Sport Coupe: Wheelbase: 108 in. Overall length: 197.6 in. Height: 49.2 in. Width: 74.5 in. Front tread: 61.3 in. Rear tread: 60 in. Standard tires: FR78 x 14 steel-belted radial tires.

Camaro Rally Sport: Wheelbase: 108 in. Overall length: 197.6 in. Height: 49.2 in. Width: 74.5 in. Front tread: 61.3 in. Rear tread: 60 in. Standard tires: FR78 x 14 steel-belted radial tires.

Camaro Berlinetta: Wheelbase: 108 in. Overall length: 197.6 in. Height: 49.2 in. Width: 74.5 in. Front tread: 61.6 in. Rear tread: 60.3 in. Standard tires: FR78 x 14 steel-belted radial whitewalls tires.

Camaro Z28: Wheelbase: 108 in. Overall length: 197.6 in. Height: 49.2 in. Width: 74.5 in. Front tread: 61.3 in. Rear tread: 60 in. Standard tires: P225/70R15 steel-belted radial white-letter tires.

TECHNICAL

Base Sport Coupe: Transmission: Three-speed manual transmission with inline six-cylinder: (First) 3.50:1, (Second) 1.89:1, (Third) 1.00:1, (Reverse) 3.62:1. Standard final drive ratio: (six-cylinder) 2.56:1, (V-8 with four-speed manual transmission) 3.08:1, (with Turbo-Hydra-Matic transmission) 3.08:1. Steering: re-circulating ball. Brakes: Front disc/rear drum. Fuel tank: 21 gal.

Camaro Rally Sport: Transmission: Three-speed manual transmission with inline six-cylinder: (First) 3.50:1, (Second) 1.89:1, (Third) 1.00:1, (Reverse) 3.62:1. Standard final drive ratio: (six-cylinder) 2.56:1, (V-8 with four-speed manual transmission) 3.08:1, (with Turbo-Hydra-Matic transmission) 3.08:1. Steering: re-circulating ball. Brakes: Front disc/rear drum. Fuel tank: 21 gal.

Camaro Berlinetta: Transmission: Three-speed man-

ual transmission with inline six-cylinder: (First) 3.50:1, (Second) 1.89:1, (Third) 1.00:1, (Reverse) 3.62:1. Standard final drive ratio: (six-cylinder) 2.56:1, (V-8 with four-speed manual transmission) 3.08:1, (with Turbo-Hydra-Matic transmission) 3.08:1. Steering: re-circulating ball. Brakes: Front disc/rear drum. Fuel tank: 21 gal.

Camaro Z28: Transmission: Four-speed manual transmission with 350-cid V-8: (First) 3.42:1, (Second) 2.28:1, (Third) 1.45:1, (Fourth) 1.00:1, (Reverse) 3.51:1. Standard final drive ratio: (with three-speed manual transmission) 2.73:1, (with four-speed transmission) 3.73:1, (with Turbo-Hydra-Matic transmission) 3.42:1. Front suspension: Coil springs and tube-type shock absorbers. Rear suspension: Leaf springs and tube-type shock absorbers. Steering: re-circulating ball. Brakes: Front disc/rear drum. Fuel tank: 21 gal.

OPTIONS

AK1 color-keyed seat and shoulder belts ($23). AN6 adjustable seat back ($23). AU3 power door lock system ($86). A01 Soft-Ray tinted glass ($64). A31 power windows ($132). B37 color-keyed floor mats ($23). B80 roof drip moldings ($24). B84 body side moldings ($43). B93 door edge guard moldings ($13). CC1 removable glass roof panels ($655). CD4 intermittent windshield wipers ($38). C49 rear window defogger ($99). C60 Four-Season air conditioning ($562 without V-8; $529 with V-8). D35 sport mirrors ($43). D55 center console ($80). D80 rear deck lid spoiler ($58). F41 Sport suspension ($41). G80 Positraction rear axle ($64). G92 performance ratio rear axle ($18). J50 power brakes ($76). K30 cruise control ($103). LG3 305-cid 135-hp/130-hp Calif. V-8 ($235). LM1 350-cid 170-hp/165-hp in Calif. V-8 ($360). MM4 four-speed wide-ratio manual transmission ($135). MX1 automatic transmission in Z28 ($59). MX1 automatic transmission in Camaros except Z28 ($335). M21 close-ratio four-speed manual transmission in Z28 (no cost). N33 Comfortilt steering wheel ($75). N65 Stowaway spare tire (no cost). N90 aluminum wheels with Berlinetta ($172). N90 aluminum wheels with Sport Coupe ($315). N90 aluminum wheels with Z28 ($242). N90 aluminum wheels with Z28 ($222). PE1 custom styled wheels with Camaro Sport Coupe ($143). PE1 custom styled wheels with Rally Sport ($100). PO1 full wheel covers ($43). QBT FR78-14 white letter tires on Camaro Sport Coupe or Rally Sport with Stowaway spare ($52). QBT FR78-14 white letter tires on Camaro Sport Coupe or Rally Sport without Stowaway spare ($65). QBT FR78-14 white letter tires on Berlinetta with Stowaway spare ($13). QBT FR78-14 white-letter tires on Berlinetta without Stowaway spare ($16). QDW FR78-14 white sidewall tires with Stowaway spare ($40). QDW FR78-14 white sidewall tires without Stowaway spare ($49). QEG E78-14 black sidewall tires with Stowaway spare ($94.56 credit). QEG E78-14 black sidewall tires without Stowaway spare ($118.95 credit). QEH E78-14 white sidewall tires with Stowaway spare ($57.56). QEH E78-14 white sidewall tires without Stowaway spare ($71.95). TR9 auxiliary lighting ($39). TR9 auxiliary lighting with Berlinetta or Quiet Sound Group ($31). UA1 heavy-duty battery ($20). UM1 AM stereo radio with 8-track tape ($248). UM2 AM/FM stereo sound system with tape player ($335). UN3 AM/FM stereo radio with cassette player ($341). UP5 AM/FM radio with CB ($489). UP6 AM/FM stereo radio with CB ($570). UY8 AM/FM stereo radio with clock with Z28, Special Instrumentation or Berlinetta ($372). U05 dual horns ($9). U14 Special Instrumentation ($112). U35 electric clock ($23). U58 AM/FM stereo radio ($232). U63 AM stereo radio ($85). U69 AM/FM radio ($158). U75 power antenna ($47). U76 windshield antenna ($27). U80 rear seat speaker ($25). V01 heavy-duty radiator ($33). YF5 California emissions equipment ($83). ZJ7 Rally wheels with wheel trim rings ($93). Z21 style trim ($73). Z54 Quiet Sound interior décor group ($64). J-2 cloth seats with Sport Coupe, Rally Sport or Z28 ($23). S-2 custom cloth seats with Berlinetta ($23). S-2 custom cloth seats with Sport Coupe, Rally Sport or Z28 ($330). X-2 custom vinyl seats with Sport Coupe, Rally Sport or Z28 ($307).

HISTORICAL FOOTNOTES

Robert D. Lund was general manager of Chevrolet Motor Division in 1979. This was a year in which consumers experienced a mid-summer gasoline crisis and the Camaro, although in tune with the times, was not immune to such pressure. Its model-year sales declined from 247,437 in 1978 to 233,802 in 1979. Calendar-year sales wound up at 204,742 (a 2.5 percent share of industry). Industry trade journals of the era reported model-year production of 282,582 Camaros including 22,041 six-cylinder models and 260,541 Camaro V-8s. The trade journals say that the Van Nuys, California, plant built 152,657 Camaros (and 114,673 Firebirds) and that the Norwood, Ohio, factory built 129,925 Camaros (and 96,781 Firebirds). Most sources show model-year production at a slightly lower 282,571 units. Of the Camaros built, 88.1 percent had automatic transmission, 10.5 percent had a four-speed manual transmission, 92.2 percent had a V-8, 7.8 percent had a six-cylinder engine, 100 percent had power steering, 1.8 percent had manual disc brakes, 98.2 percent had power disc brakes, 13.7 percent had a limited-slip differential, 97.5 percent had steel-belted radial tires, 18.9 percent had power door locks, 28.8 percent had power windows, 100 percent had bucket seats, 3.4 percent had a tinted windshield only, 87.6 percent had all-tinted glass, 78.2 percent had manual air conditioning, 51.6 percent had tilt steering, 26.5 percent had cruise control, 1.9 percent had a vinyl top, 21.9 percent had an AM radio, 11 percent had an AM/FM radio, 13.6 percent had an AM/FM stereo radio, 2.4 percent had an AM 8-track tape player, 20.1 percent had an AM/FM 8-track tape player, 68.0 percent had a analog clock, 0.4 percent had a digital clock, 45 percent had a rear window defogger, 96.5 percent had a remote-control outside rearview mirror, 3.7 percent had optional wheel covers, 20.5 percent had aluminum styled wheels, 73 percent had styled steel wheels and 11.9 percent had a hatch roof. A total of 203,647 new Camaros were registered in the U.S. during calendar year 1979.

Nancy Glueck photo

Chevrolet sold more than 111,000 Camaro Sport Coupes for 1979. They could be had with a straight six, 305-cid V-8, or a 350-cid V-8, like this car has.

Camaro

Gene Stransky photo

The Z28 was billed as "the maximum Camaro" and had a functional rear-facing hood scoop.

Camaro entered 1980 wearing a new grille with tighter crosshatch pattern and offering a revised engine selection. A lighter, more economical 3.8-liter (229-cid) V-6 rated at 115 hp replaced the old familiar 250-cid inline six as the standard power plant. Camaros sold in California also had a base 3.8-liter V-6, but it was Buick's 231-cid engine. There was also a new 4.4-liter (267-cid) V-8 option with a 120-hp rating, plus a 305-cid 155-hp V-8. Camaros with automatic transmission had a new torque converter clutch to eliminate slippage. The grille used on the standard Camaro Sport Coupe had an emblem in the upper corner. Berlinettas had wire wheel covers as standard equipment.

Chevrolet billed the 1980 Z28 as "the maximum Camaro!" It had a new rear-facing functional hood scoop facing with an electrically activated flap that opened when the gas pedal was pounded on. Also available was the Rally Sport package with a rear spoiler, a sport suspension, black rocker panels, a black grille, black headlamp bezels, bright reveal moldings, sport mirrors and color-keyed Rally wheels.

Production tapered off to 152,005 units due to a second gas crisis in the Middle East combined with the start of a deep economic recession.

I.D. DATA

Camaros again had a 13-symbol vehicle identification number (VIN) on the upper left surface of the instrument panel, visible through the windshield. The first symbol identifies the make: 1=Chevrolet Motor Div. The second symbol indicates the car line/series: Q=Camaro, S=Camaro Berlinetta. The third and fourth symbols indicate body type: 87=two-door four-passenger Sport Coupe. The fifth symbol indicates the engine type: A=RPO LD5 3.8-liter (231-cid) Buick-built V-6 with two-barrel carburetor [base engine in California], J=RPO L39 4.4-liter (267-cid) Chevrolet/GM Canada-built V-8 with two-barrel carburetor, H=RPO LG4 5.0-liter (305-cid

155-hp) V-8 with four-barrel carburetor, H=RPO LG4 5.0-liter (305-cid 165-hp) V-8 with four-barrel carburetor, K=RPO LC3 3.8-liter (229-cid) Chevrolet/GM Canada-built V-6 with two-barrel carburetor (base engine in 49 states), L=RPO LM1 5.7-liter V-8 with four-barrel carburetor. The sixth symbol indicates model year: A=1980. The seventh symbol indicates the assembly plant: L=Van Nuys, California, N=Norwood, Ohio. The final six digits are the sequential serial number.

COLORS

11=White, 15=Silver, 19=Black, 24=Bright Blue, 29=Dark Blue, 40=Lime Green, 51=Bright Yellow, 57=Gold, 67=Dark Brown, 72=Red, 76=Dark Claret, 79=Red Orange, 80=Bronze and 84=Charcoal.

CAMARO SPORT COUPE - SERIES 1FP - V-6/V-8

Standard Camaro equipment included a V-6 engine, a three-speed manual transmission, P205/705R14 SBR tires, body-color front and rear bumper covers, bucket seats, a console, a day/night mirror and a cigarette lighter.

Model Number	Body/Style Number	Body Type & Seating	Factory Price	Shipping Weight	Production Total
CAMARO SPORT COUPE - SERIES 1FP - (V-6)					
FP	87	2d coupe	$5,499	3,218 lbs.	Note 1
CAMARO SPORT COUPE - SERIES 1FP - (V-8)					
FP	87	2d coupe	$5,679	3,346 lbs.	Note 1

Note 1: Model-year production of 1980 base Camaro Sport Coupes was 80,189. (44,027 six-cylinder and 36,162 V-8)

CAMARO RALLY SPORT - SERIES 1FP/Z85 - V-6/V-8

Rally Sport Camaros came with an all-black "thin-line" grille. Standard equipment included a V-6 engine, a three-speed manual transmission, P205/705R14 steel-belted radial tires, body-color front and rear bumper covers, bucket seats, a console, a day/night mirror, a cigarette lighter, a rear spoiler, a sport suspension, black-finished rocker panels, a black grille, black headlamp bezels, bright reveal moldings, sport mirrors and color-keyed Rally wheels. Rally Sport engine options included the new 4.4-liter (267-cid) V-8 and the 305-cid 155-hp V-8.

Model Number	Body/Style Number	Body Type & Seating	Factory Price	Shipping Weight	Production Total
CAMARO RALLY SPORT COUPE - SERIES 1FP/Z85 - (V-6)					
1FP	87	2d coupe	$5,916	—	Note 2
CAMARO RALLY SPORT COUPE - SERIES 1FP/Z85 - (V-8)					
1FP	87	2d coupe	$6,069	—	Note 2

Note 2: Model-year production of 1980 base Camaro Sport Coupes was 80,189. (44,027 six-cylinder and 36,162 V-8)
Note 3: Of the cars listed in Note 2 above 12,015 had the Rally Sport package.

CAMARO BERLINETTA - SERIES 1FS V-6/V-8

The 1980 Camaro Berlinetta carried a version of the new Rally Sport grille with bright finish and the emblem in the center. Berlinettas also had new standard wire wheel covers. Standard equipment included a V-6, a three-speed manual transmission, P205/705R14 white sidewall steel-belted radial tires, body-color front and rear bumper covers, front bucket seats, a console, a day/night mirror, a cigarette lighter, bright headlamp bezels, bright upper and lower grille moldings, bright windshield moldings, bright window reveal moldings, black-finished rocker panels, dual horns, an electric clock, special instrumentation, the quiet sound group, sport mirrors and wire wheel covers. Engine choices included the new 4.4-liter (267-cid) V-8 and the 305-cid 155-hp V-8.

Model Number	Body/Style Number	Body Type & Seating	Factory Price	Shipping Weight	Production Total
CAMARO BERLINETTA - SERIES 1FS - (V-6)					
1FS	87	2d coupe	$6,662	3,253 lbs.	Note 3
CAMARO BERLINETTA - SERIES 1FS - (V-8)					
1FS	87	2d coupe	$6,442	3,381 lbs.	Note 3

Note 3: Model-year production of 1980 Camaro Berlinetta coupes was 26,679. (7,077 six-cylinder and 19,602 V-8)

CAMARO Z28 - SERIES 1FP - V-8

The 1980 Z28 grille had a pattern of horizontal bars with a large Z28 emblem in the upper corner. The high-performance Z28 model was billed as "the maximum Camaro." A new functional hood air-intake scoop faced to the rear and had an electrically activated flap that opened up when the driver stepped harder on the gas. A side fender port allowed hot engine air to exit and boosted acceleration at the same time. Also new to the Z28 were rear fender flares. Economy-conscious buyers could order their Z28 with a 165-hp version of the RPO LG4 305-cid V-8 that had a Rochester M4ME four-barrel carburetor and get a $50 credit off base price. The RPO LM1 350-cid that produced 190 hp was standard and available in Z28s only. The hot Camaro model also came with P225/70R15 white-letter tires, body-color 15 x 7-in. wheels, black headlamp bezels, black upper and lower grille moldings, black reveal moldings, sport mirrors, a body-color front spoiler, body-color front flares, a hood scoop decal, front fender louvers, a rear spoiler, a Sport suspension, power brakes and a four-speed manual transmission with floor-mounted gear shifter.

Model Number	Body/Style Number	Body Type & Seating	Factory Price	Shipping Weight	Production Total
CAMARO Z28 - SERIES 1FP - (5.0-LITER V-8)					

The Z28 came with white-letter tires and body-color wheels for 1980.

Daniel B. Lyons photo

1FP	87	2d coupe	$7,071	—	Note 4

CAMARO Z28 - SERIES 1FP - (5.7-LITER V-8)

1FP	87	2d coupe	$7,121	—	Note 4

Note 4: Model-year production of 1980 Camaro Z28 coupes was 45,137. (All V-8)

ENGINES

LD5 V-6: Overhead-valve V-6. Cast-iron block and head. Bore & stroke: 3.80 x 3.40 in. Displacement: 231 cid (3.8 liters). Compression ratio: 8.0:1. Brake horsepower: 110 at 4200 rpm. Torque: 170 lbs.-ft. at rpm. Four main bearings. Induction system: Rochester E2ME two-barrel carburetor. Standard in Camaro Sport Coupe, Rally Sport and Berlinetta sold in California. VIN Code A

LC3 V-6: 90-degree overhead-valve V-6. Cast-iron block and head. Bore & stroke: 3.74 x 3.48 in. Displacement: 229 cid (3.8 liters). Compression ratio: 8.6:1. Brake horsepower: 115 at 4000 rpm. Torque: 175 lbs.-ft. at 2000 rpm. Four main bearings. Induction system: Rochester M2ME two-barrel carburetor. Standard in Camaro Sport Coupe, Rally Sport and Berlinetta sold outside California. VIN Code K.

L39 V-8: 90-degree overhead-valve V-8. Cast-iron block and head. Bore & stroke: 3.50 x 3.48 in. Displacement: 267 cid (4.4 liters). Compression ratio: 8.3:1. Brake horsepower: 120 at 3600 rpm. Torque: 215 lbs.-ft.

Gerald West photo

This Rally Sport had an unusual interior/exterior color combination. It also had every factory option available for 1980, including the 305-cid V-8.

Black headlamp bezels, and black upper and lower grille moldings were prominent on the front of the 1980 Z28.

Daniel B. Lyons photo

at 2000 rpm. Five main bearings. Induction system: Rochester M2ME two-barrel carburetor. Optional in Camaro Sport Coupe, Rally Sport and Berlinetta. VIN Code J.

LG4 BASE V-8: 90-degree, overhead-valve V-8. Cast-iron block and head. Bore & stroke: 3.74 x 3.48 in. Displacement: 305 cid (5.0 liters). Compression ratio: 8.6:1. Brake horsepower: 155 at 4000 rpm Torque: 240 lbs.-ft. at 1600 rpm. Five main bearings. Hydraulic valve lifters. Induction system: Rochester 4ME four-barrel carburetor. Optional in Sport Coupe and Camaro Berlinetta. VIN Code: H.

LG4 BASE V-8: 90-degree, overhead-valve V-8. Cast-iron block and head. Bore & stroke: 3.74 x 3.48 in. Displacement: 305 cid (5.0 liters). Compression ratio: 8.6:1. Brake horsepower: 165 at 4000 rpm Torque: 245 lbs.-ft. at 2400 rpm Five main bearings. Hydraulic valve lifters. Induction system: Rochester M4ME four-barrel carburetor. Delete option in Z28. VIN Code: H.

LM1 V-8: 90-degree, overhead-valve V-8. Cast-iron block and head. Bore & stroke: 4.00 x 3.48 in. Displacement: 350 cid (5.7 liters). Compression ratio: 8.2:1. Brake horsepower: 190 at 4200 rpm Torque: 280 lbs.-ft. at 2400 rpm Five main bearings. Hydraulic valve lifters. Induction system: Rochester M4ME four-barrel carburetor. Standard in Z28. VIN Code: L.

CHASSIS

Base Camaro Sport Coupe: Wheelbase: 108 in. Overall length: 197.6 in. Height: 49.2 in. Width: 74.5 in. Front tread: 61.3 in. Rear tread: 60 in. Standard tires: P205/75R14 steel-belted radial.

Camaro Berlinetta: Wheelbase: 108 in. Overall length: 197.6 in. Height: 49.2 in. Width: 74.5 in. Front tread: 61.6 in. Rear tread: 60.3 in. Standard tires: (Camaro) P205/75R14 steel-belted radial whitewalls.

Camaro Z28: Wheelbase: 108 in. Overall length: 197.6 in. Height: 49.2 in. Width: 74.5 in. Front tread: 61.3 in. Rear tread: 60 in. Standard tires: P225/70R15 steel-belted radial white-letter.

TECHNICAL

Transmission: Three-speed manual transmission. Gear ratios: (First) 3.50:1, (Second) 1.89:1, (Third) 1.00:1, (Reverse) 3.62:1. Four-speed floor shift with 305-cid V-8: (First) 2.85:1, (Second) 2.02:1, (Third) 1.35:1, (Fourth) 1.00:1, (Reverse) 2.85:1. Four-speed floor shift with 350-cid V-8: (First) 3.42:1, (Second) 2.28:1, (Third) 1.45:1, (Fourth) 1.00:1, (Reverse) 3.51:1. Standard final drive ratio: (Camaro V-6) 2.73:1, (Camaro V-8) 2.56:1, Steering: re-circulating ball. Front suspension: control arms, coil springs and stabilizer bar. Rear suspension: rigid axle, semi-elliptic leaf springs and stabilizer bar. Brakes: Front disc, rear drum. Body construction: unit-body with separate partial box frame. Fuel tank: 21 gal.

OPTIONS

AN6 adjustable seat back ($25). AU3 power door lock system ($93). A01 Soft-Ray tinted glass ($68). A31 power windows ($143). B37 color-keyed floor mats ($25). B80 roof drip moldings ($26). B84 body side moldings ($46). B93 door edge guard moldings ($14). CC1 removable glass roof panels ($695). CD4 intermittent windshield wipers ($41). C49 rear window defogger ($107). C60 Four-Season air conditioning ($566). D35 sport mirrors ($46). D80 rear deck lid spoiler ($62). F41 sport suspension ($44). G80 Positraction rear axle ($68). G92 performance ratio rear axle ($19). J50 power brakes ($81). K35 cruise control ($112). LG4 305-cid 155-hp V-8 ($295). LG4 305-cid 165-hp V-8 with Z28

($50 credit in Z28 in place of standard LM1 350-cid V-8). LM1 350-cid 175-hp V-8 with Z28 (no cost). L39 267-cid 115-hp V-8 ($180). MM4 four-speed wide-ratio manual transmission in Z28 (no cost); in other Camaros ($144). MX1 automatic transmission in Z28 ($63). MX1 automatic transmission, in Camaros except Z28 ($358). N33 Comfortilt steering wheel ($81). N65 Stowaway spare tire (no cost). N90 aluminum wheels on Camaro Berlinetta ($184). N90 aluminum wheels on base Camaro Sport Coupe ($337). N90 aluminum wheels on Camaro Rally Sport ($237). N90 aluminum wheels on Camaro Z28 ($257). PE1 custom styled wheels on base Camaro Sport Coupe ($153). PE1 custom styled wheels on Camaro Rally Sport ($107). PQ1 full wheel covers ($46). QGR P255/70R-15 white-letter tires on Z28 (no cost). QJY P20575R14 white sidewall tires on Berlinetta (no cost). QJY P20575R14 white sidewall tires on Camaros other than Berlinetta without Stowaway spare ($63). QJY P20575R14 white sidewall tires on Camaros other than Berlinetta with Stowaway spare ($65). QKL P205/75R14 tires with Berlinetta ($15). QKL P205/75R14 tires on Camaros other than Berlinetta with Stowaway spare ($65). QKL P205/75R14 tires on Camaros other than Berlinetta without Stowaway spare ($81). TR9 auxiliary lighting with Berlinetta or Quiet Sound Group ($40). TR9 auxiliary lighting without Berlinetta or Quiet Sound Group ($33). UA1 heavy-duty battery ($21). UM1 AM stereo radio with 8-track tape ($249). UM2 AM/FM stereo sound system with 8-track player ($272). UN3 AM/FM stereo radio with cassette player ($285). UP5 AM/FM radio with CB ($473). UP6 AM/FM stereo radio with CB ($525). UY8 AM/FM stereo radio with clock ($328-353). U05 dual horns ($10). U14 gauge package with tachometer ($120). U35 electric clock ($25). U58 AM/FM stereo radio ($192). U63 AM stereo radio (97). U69 AM/FM radio ($153). U75 power antenna ($51). U76 windshield antenna ($27). U80 rear seat speaker ($20). V08 heavy-duty cooling without air conditioning ($63). V08 heavy-duty cooling with air conditioning ($36). YF5 California emissions equipment ($250). ZJ7 Rally wheels with wheel trim rings ($100). Z21 style trim ($78). Z54 Quiet Sound interior décor group ($69). C-2 cloth seats with Sport Coupe, Rally Sport or Z28 ($25). F-2 custom cloth seats with Berlinetta ($25). F-2 custom cloth seats with Sport Coupe, Rally Sport or Z28 ($353). X-2 custom vinyl seats with Sport Coupe, Rally Sport or Z28 ($328).

HISTORICAL FOOTNOTES

This year the rising popularity of small cars combined with an auto industry downturn put a pinch on Chevrolet's business. The Camaro suffered mightily as its model-year sales declined from 233,802 in 1979 to 131,066 in 1980. Calendar-year sales wound up at 116,824 (a 1.8 percent share of industry). Trade journals of the era listed model-year production of 152,005 Camaros in tables showing production by series and engine, by engine or by body style. However, the same sources listed production of a slightly higher 152,021 units when broken out by model year or by factory of origin. The engine breakouts given in such sources were 51,104 six-cylinder Camaros and 100,901 Camaro V-8s, or 152,005 total cars. However, the trade journals recorded the Van Nuys, California, plant as building 84,178 Camaros (and 57,912 Firebirds) and the Norwood, Ohio, factory as building 67,303 Camaros (and 49,428 Firebirds). That means Camaro numbers by factory total 152,021. The figures used by most enthusiasts show production by each of the four Camaro model-options and total 152,005. Of the Camaros built, 87.3 percent had automatic transmission, 8.1 percent had a four-speed manual transmission, 66.4 percent had a V-8,

The 1980 Camaro Berlinetta Sport Coupe came standard with a V-6 that could be upgraded to a 305-cid V-8. All the new Camaros got a revamped grille on the front end.

33.6 percent had a six-cylinder engine, 100 percent had power steering, 3.8 percent had manual disc brakes, 96.2 percent had power disc brakes, 11.6 percent had a limited-slip differential, 100 percent had steel-belted radial tires, 18.1 percent had power door locks, 29.4 percent had power windows, 100 percent had bucket seats, 2.3 percent had a tinted windshield only, 85.9 percent had all-tinted glass, 70.5 percent had manual air conditioning, 52.3 percent had tilt steering, 25.1 percent had cruise control, none had a vinyl top, 24.6 percent had an AM radio, 10.1 percent had an AM/FM radio, 14.5 percent had an AM/FM stereo radio, 1.1 percent had an AM 8-track tape player, 12 percent had an AM/FM 8-track tape player, 10.1 percent had an AM/FM cassette player, 0.3 percent had an AM/FM stereo with a CB radio, 59.4 percent had a analog clock, 0.2 percent had a digital clock, 51.3 percent had an electric rear window defogger, 97 percent had a remote-control outside rearview mirror, 18.6 percent had optional wheel covers, 17.2 percent had aluminum styled wheels, 61.6 percent had styled steel wheels and 16.3 percent had T-tops. A total of 117,164 new Camaros were registered in the U.S. during calendar year 1980. That was down from 203,904 in 1979 and 251,983 in 1978.

Daniel B. Lyons photo

Some of the exterior items on the Z28 included body-color Sport mirrors, fender flares and a rear spoiler.

Camaro

For 1981, Chevrolet built only 20,253 of the styish Camaro Z28 Sport Coupes.

The Rally Sport left the Camaro lineup this year, leaving only the base Sport Coupe, Berlinetta and Z28 to represent the final year of the second-generation Camaro. Not much else changed, beyond the use of GM's new Computer Command Control engine management system on all models. Power brakes, a lightweight Freedom II battery, new low-drag front disc brakes and a stowaway spare tire became standard on all Camaros. Halogen headlamps were a new option.

Optional automatic transmissions added a lock-up torque converter clutch in third gear. The basic Camaro Sport Coupe had an Argent Silver grille that was split into upper and lower sections, plus wraparound taillights.

The base engine for the Sport Coupe and fancier Berlinetta remained a 229-cid V-6, while Z28s had a standard four-barrel 305-cid V-8 teamed with a new wide-ratio four-speed manual transmission. Z28 buyers could add a 350-cid V-8 at no charge, but only if they wanted an automatic transmission. In a reversal of recent buying habits, Chevrolet built only 20,253 Z28s compared to 62,614 Sport Coupes and 43,272 Berlinettas. America was on an economy binge again!

I.D. DATA

Camaros again had a 17-symbol vehicle identification number (VIN) on the upper left surface of the instrument panel, visible through the windshield. The first symbol identifies country of origin: 1=U.S.A., 2=Canada. The second symbol identifies the manufacturer: G=General Motors. The third symbol indicates make: 1=Chevrolet, 7=GM of Canada. The fourth symbol indicates restraint system: A=non-passive manual belts, B=Passive automatic belts, C=passive inflatable airbags. The fifth symbol indicates the car line/series: P=Camaro, S=Camaro Berlinetta. The sixth and seventh symbols indicate body type: 87=two-door plain back special coupe. The eighth

symbol indicates the engine type: A=RPO LD5 3.8-liter (231-cid) Buick-built V-6 with two-barrel carburetor [base engine in California], J=RPO L39 4.4-liter (267-cid) Chevrolet/GM Canada-built V-8 with two-barrel carburetor, H=RPO LG4 5.0-liter (305-cid/150-hp) V-8 with four-barrel carburetor, H=RPO LG4 5.0-liter (305-cid/165 hp) V-8 with four-barrel carburetor, K=RPO LC3 3.8-liter (229-cid) Chevrolet/GM Canada-built V-6 with two-barrel carburetor [base engine in 49 states], L=RPO LM1 5.7-liter V-8 with four-barrel carburetor. The ninth symbol is a check digit. The 10th symbol indicates model year: B=1981. The 11th symbol indicates the assembly plant: L=Van Nuys, California, N=Norwood, Ohio. The final six digits are the sequential serial number.

COLORS

11=White, 16=Silver, 19=Black, 20=Bright Blue, 21=Light Blue, 29=Dark Blue, 51=Bright Yellow, 54=Gold, 57=Orange, 67=Dark Brown, 75=Red, 77=Maroon and 84=Charcoal.

CAMARO - SERIES 1FP - V-6-/V-8

Base Camaro Sport Coupes used the 229-cid V-6 as standard equipment. It came linked to a three-speed manual transmission. Also featured were power steering, power brakes, P205/75R14 steel-belted radial tires, a front stabilizer bar, multi-leaf rear springs, concealed two-speed wipers, front bucket seats with a console, a dome light, a four-spoke sport steering wheel, a day/night mirror and body-colored bumpers. Halogen headlamps were a new option. Cloth or vinyl interiors came in beige, black, dark blue, camel, red or silver.

Model Number	Body/Style Number	Body Type & Seating	Factory Price	Shipping Weight	Production Total
CAMARO SPORT COUPE - SERIES 1FP - (V-6)					
1FP	87	2d coupe	$6,780	3,222 lbs.	Note 1

CAMARO SPORT COUPE - SERIES 1FP - (V-8)

1FP	87	2d coupe	$6,830	3,392 lbs.	Note 1

Note 1: Model-year production of 1981 base Camaro Sport Coupes was 62,614 (43,126 six-cylinder and 19,488 V-8).

CAMARO BERLINETTA - SERIES 1FS - V-6-/V-8

The Berlinetta's Argent Silver grille had bright accent moldings. The upscale Camaro came with a standard Quiet Sound Group that included a layer of sound-absorbing materials inside the roof and a soft foam-backed headliner. Special paint and striping emphasized its "sculptured lines." Body stripes came in silver, black, blue, beige, gold or red. Berlinetta identification was seen on the grille header panel, on the side pillars and on the rear deck lid. The body sills were black as opposed to the bright-finished sills on the base Camaro Sport Coupe. The standard engine for the posh Berlinetta was the standard 3.8-liter V-6 (229 cid/115 hp in 49 states or 231 cid/110 hp in California) hooked to a three-speed manual transmission. Options included the 4.4-liter (267-cid) V-8 and the 5.0-liter (305-cid) V-8 with an automatic or four-speed manual transmission required in either case. Standard equipment on the Camaro Berlinetta coupe included power steering, power brakes, P205/75R14 steel-belted radial whitewall tires, a front stabilizer bar, multi-leaf rear springs, concealed two-speed wipers, front bucket seats with a console, a dome light, a four-spoke sport steering wheel, a day/night mirror, body-color bumpers, wire wheel covers, a gauge package including a tachometer, dual horns, sport mirrors (left-hand remote control), an electric clock, bright door pillar moldings, bright upper fender moldings, a bright hood panel molding, bright belt moldings and bright roof drip moldings.

Model Number	Body/Style Number	Body Type & Seating	Factory Price	Shipping Weight	Production Total
CAMARO BERLINETTA - SERIES 1FS - (V-6)					
1FS	87	2d coupe	$7,576	3,275 lbs.	Note 2
CAMARO BERLINETTA - SERIES 1FS - (V-8)					
1FS	87	2d coupe	$7,626	3,445 lbs.	Note 2

Note 2: Model-year production of 1981 Camaro Berlinetta coupes was 20,253 (8,878 six-cylinder and 11,375 V-8).

CAMARO Z28 - SERIES 1FP - V-6-/V-8

The Camaro Z28's distinctive grille was body-colored with horizontal bars. There was Z28 identification on the driver's side of the grille and a Z28 decal on the doors. Other Z28 features included black headlamp bezels, black taillight bezels, a black rear end panel, a black-finished license plate opening, black parking light bezels, black body sill moldings, black window moldings, black windshield moldings, tri-tone striping on the rear spoiler, tri-tone striping on the lower body side, tri-tone striping ond the front air dam and tri-tone striping on the fender flares. The front and rear bumper covers were formed of body-color urethane plastic. The Z28's solenoid-activated hood air intake actually drew in cold air.

Daniel B. Lyons photo

The 1981 Camaro Z28's distinctive grille was body-colored with horizontal bars.

So did its fender air scoops. Seven Z28 striping colors were available: silver, charcoal, blue, dark gold, gold, red and orange. The Z28's torque converter clutch was computer-controlled in both second and third gears. Standard equipment nationwide included a 5.0-liter (305-cid four-barrel V-8) and a new wide-ratio four-speed manual transmission (optional on other Camaros) with a 3.42:1 low-gear ratio that delivered both economy and low-end performance. Z28 buyers could also get a 5.7-liter (350-cid) V-8 at no extra charge, but only with automatic transmission, which added $61 to the price. The Camaro Z28 also included a front air dam, front fender flares, air louvers, a hood scoop with decal, a rear deck lid spoiler, P225/70R15 raised-white-letter tires on body-color 15 x 7-in. sport wheels and contour bucket seats. A heavy-duty cooling system, a clock, a gauge package and sport mirrors were also part of the Z28 image.

Model Number	Body/Style Number	Body Type & Seating	Factory Price	Shipping Weight	Production Total
CAMARO Z28 - SERIES 1FP - (5.0-LITER V-8)					
1FP	87	2d coupe	$8,263	—	Note 3
CAMARO Z28 - SERIES 1FP - (5.7-LITER V-8)					
1FP	87	2d coupe	$8,324	—	Note 3

Note 3: Model-year production of 1981 Camaro Z28 coupes was 43,271 (All V-8).

ENGINE

LD5 V-6: Overhead-valve V-6. Cast-iron block and head. Bore & stroke: 3.80 x 3.40 in. Displacement: 231 cid (3.8 liters). Compression ratio: 8.0:1. Brake horsepower: 110 at 4200 rpm. Torque: 170 lbs.-ft. at rpm. Four main bearings. Induction system: Rochester E2ME two-barrel carburetor. Standard in Camaro Sport Coupe and Berlinetta sold in California. VIN Code A

LC3 V-6: Overhead-valve V-6. Cast-iron block and head. Bore & stroke: 3.74 x 3.48 in. Displacement: 229 cid (3.8 liters). Compression ratio: 8.6:1. Brake horsepower: 110 at 3800 rpm. Torque: 190 lbs.-ft. at 1600 rpm. Four main bearings. Induction system: Rochester 2ME two-barrel carburetor. Standard in Camaro Berlinetta and Camaro Sport Coupe outside California.

VIN Code K.

L39 V-8: 90-degree overhead-valve V-8. Cast-iron block and head. Bore & stroke: 3.50 x 3.48 in. Displacement: 267 cid (4.4 liters). Compression ratio: 8.3:1. Brake horsepower: 115 at 4000 rpm. Torque: 200 lbs.-ft. at 2400 rpm. Five main bearings. Induction system: Rochester 2ME two-barrel carburetor. Optional in Camaro Berlinetta and Camaro Sport Coupe. VIN Code J.

LG4 base V-8: 90-degree, overhead-valve V-8. Cast-iron block and head. Bore & stroke: 3.74 x 3.48 in. Displacement: 305 cid (5.0 liters). Compression ratio: 8.6:1. Brake horsepower: 150 at 3800 rpm Torque: 240 lbs.-ft. at 2400 rpm Five main bearings. Hydraulic valve lifters. Induction system: Rochester 4ME four-barrel carburetor. Optional in Camaro Sport Coupe and Camaro Berlinetta. VIN Code: H.

LG4 base V-8: 90-degree, overhead-valve V-8. Cast-iron block and head. Bore & stroke: 3.74 x 3.48 in. Displacement: 305 cid (5.0 liters). Compression ratio: 8.6:1. Brake horsepower: 165 at 4000 rpm Torque: 245 lbs.-ft. at 2400 rpm Five main bearings. Hydraulic valve lifters. Induction system: Rochester M4ME four-barrel carburetor. Standard in Z28. VIN Code: H.

LM1 V-8: 90-degree, overhead-valve V-8. Cast-iron block and head. Bore & stroke: 4.00 x 3.48 in. Displacement: 350 cid (5.7 liters). Compression ratio: 8.2:1. Brake horsepower: 175 at 4000 rpm Torque: 275 lbs.-ft. at 2400 rpm Five main bearings. Hydraulic valve lifters. Induction system: Rochester 4ME four-barrel carburetor. Standard in Z28. VIN Code: L.

CHASSIS

Base Sport Coupe: Wheelbase: 108 in. Overall length: 197.6 in. Height: 49.2 in. Width: 74.5 in. Front tread: 61.3 in. Rear tread: 60 in. Standard tires: P205/75R14 steel-belted radial.

Berlinetta: Wheelbase: 108 in. Overall length: 197.6 in. Height: 49.2 in. Width: 74.5 in. Front tread: 61.6 in.

The back end of the Z28 was marked by black bezels and trim, and tri-color striping.

Daniel B. Lyons photo

Rear tread: 60.3 in. Standard tires: (Camaro) P205/75R14 steel-belted radial whitewalls.

Z28: Wheelbase: 108 in. Overall length: 197.6 in. Height: 49.2 in. Width: 74.5 in. Front tread: 61.3 in. Rear tread: 60 in. Standard tires: P225/70R15 steel-belted radial white-letter.

TECHNICAL

Sport Coupe: Standard transmission: Three-speed manual. Standard final drive ratio: 2.56:1 (2.73:1 in California). Front suspension: Coil springs and tube-type shock absorbers. Rear suspension: Leaf springs and tube-type shock absorbers. Brakes: Power front disc/rear drum. Steering: re-circulating ball. Fuel tank capacity: 20.8 gal.

Berlinetta: Standard transmission: Three-speed manual. Standard final drive ratio: 2.56:1 (2.73:1 in California). Front suspension: Coil springs and tube-type shock absorbers. Rear suspension: Leaf springs and tube-type shock absorbers. Brakes: Power front disc/rear drum. Steering: re-circulating ball. Fuel tank capacity: 20.8 gal.

Z28: Standard transmission: Four-speed wide-ratio manual. Standard final drive ratio: 3.42:1 (2.73:1 in California). Front suspension: Coil springs and tube-type shock absorbers. Rear suspension: Leaf springs and tube-type shock absorbers. Brakes: Power front disc/rear drum. Steering: re-circulating ball. Fuel tank capacity: 20.8 gal.

OPTIONS

AN6 adjustable seatback ($24). AU3 power door lock system ($93). A01 Soft-Ray tinted glass ($75). A31 power windows ($140). B37 color-keyed floor mats ($25). B80 roof drip moldings ($25). B84 body side moldings ($44). B93 door edge guard moldings ($13) CC1 removable glass roof panels ($695). CD4 intermittent windshield wipers ($41). C49 rear window defogger ($107). C60 Four-Season air conditioning ($560). D35 sport mirrors ($47). D80 rear deck lid spoiler ($60). F41 Sport suspension ($43). G80 Positraction rear axle ($67). G92 performance ratio rear axle ($19). K35 cruise control with resume feature ($132). LG4 305-cid 150-hp V-8 ($50). LG4 305-cid 165-hp V-8 with Z28 (no cost replacement for standard LM1 V-8). LM1 350-cid 175-hp V-8 with Z28 (standard equipment). L39 267-cid 115-hp V-8 ($50). MM4 four-speed wide-ratio manual transmission in Z28 (no cost); in other Camaros ($141). MX1 automatic transmission in Z28 ($61). MX1 automatic transmission, in Camaros except Z28 ($349). N18 wheel cover locks ($34). N33 Comfortilt steering wheel ($81). N90 aluminum wheels on Berlinetta ($180). N90 aluminum wheels on base Sport Coupe ($331). N90 aluminum wheels on Z28 ($253). PE1 custom styled wheels ($151). PQ1 full wheel covers ($46). QGR P225/70R-15 white-letter tires on Z28 (no cost). QJY P20575R14 white sidewall tires on Berlinetta (no cost). QJY P20575R14 white sidewall tires on Camaros other than Berlinetta ($54). QKL P205/75R14 tires with Berlinetta ($15). QKL P205/75R14 tires on Camaros other than Berlinetta ($69). TR9 auxiliary lighting with Berlinetta or Quiet Sound Group ($33). TR9 auxiliary lighting without Berlinetta or Quiet Sound Group ($39). TT4 halogen headlights ($36). UA1 heavy-duty battery ($20). UM2 AM/FM stereo sound system with 8-track player ($252). UN3 AM/FM stereo radio with cassette player ($264). UP6 AM/FM stereo radio with CB ($487). U05 dual horns ($10). U14 gauge package with tachometer ($118). U35 electric clock ($23). U58 AM/FM stereo radio ($178). U63 AM stereo radio (90). U69 AM/FM radio ($142). U75 power antenna ($47). U76 windshield antenna ($25). U80 rear seat speaker ($19). V08 heavy-duty cooling without air conditioning ($61). V08 heavy-duty cooling with air conditioning ($34). YF5 California emissions equipment ($46). ZJ7 Rally wheels with wheel trim rings ($99). Z21 style trim ($76). Z54 Quiet Sound interior décor group ($67). C-2 cloth seats with Sport Coupe or Z28 ($26). F-2 custom cloth seats with Berlinetta ($26). F-2 custom cloth seats with Sport Coupe or Z28 ($330). X-2 custom vinyl seats with Sport Coupe or Z28 ($304).

HISTORICAL FOOTNOTES

The 1981 Camaro line was introduced on Sept. 25, 1980. Robert D. Lund was general manager of Chevrolet Motor Division in 1980, but would pass the title on to Robert C. Stempel by 1982. Lund then joined the General Motors Sales and Marketing Staff. Chevrolet projected a sales increase for 1981, but failed to realize its goal. The Camaro's popularity deteriorated further, with model year sales sliding from 131,066 in 1980 to 109,707 in 1981. That was a 17.9 percent decline, which was attributed to the fact that the basic Camaro body was 11 years old and that its technology was out of step with modern times. A racy-looking Camaro with all-new styling and engineering was in the works for 1982. Calendar-year sales wound up at 94,606 (a 1.5 percent share of industry). Model-year production was 126,138 Camaros, although some sources show 126,139. The Camaro earned a 1.89 percent share of the industry total. The Van Nuys, California, plant reported building 86,126 Camaros (and 45,098 Firebirds). The Norwood, Ohio, factory reported building 40,012 Camaros (and 25,801 Firebirds). Of the Camaros built, 87 percent had automatic transmission, 8.5 percent had a four-speed manual transmission, 58.8 percent had a V-8, 41.2 percent had a six-cylinder engine, 100 percent had power steering, 100 percent had power front disc brakes, 9.6 percent had a limited-slip differential, 100 percent had steel-belted radial tires, 19.6 percent had power door locks, 30.5 percent had power windows, 86.8 percent had non-reclining bucket seats, 13.2 percent had reclining bucket seats, 1 percent had a tinted windshield only, 89.5 percent had all-tinted glass, 76.2 percent had manual air conditioning, 59.8 percent had tilt steering, 32.4 percent had cruise control, 19.8 percent had an AM radio, 6.6 percent had an AM/FM radio, 20.6 percent had an AM/FM stereo radio, 6.5 percent had an AM/FM 8-track tape player, 18.8 percent had an AM/FM cassette player, 0.2 percent had an AM/FM stereo with a CB radio, 59 percent had a analog clock, 47.6 percent had an electric rear window defogger, 97.8 percent had a remote-control outside rearview mirror, 16 percent had optional wheel covers, 24.7 percent had aluminum styled wheels, 57 percent had styled steel wheels and 24.1 percent had T-tops. A total of 93,706 new Camaros were registered in the U.S. during calendar year 1981. That was down from 117,164 in 1980.

Camaro

Scott Moyer photo

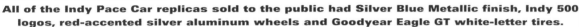

All of the Indy Pace Car replicas sold to the public had Silver Blue Metallic finish, Indy 500 logos, red-accented silver aluminum wheels and Goodyear Eagle GT white-letter tires.

An all-new rear-wheel-drive Camaro with a lighter-weight fastback format arrived late in the 1982 model year. Chevy said it captured "the essence of the contemporary American performance expression."

The flush-mounted 62-degree windshield produced one of the lowest drag coefficient readings ever measured by GM. The new Camaro was 10 in. shorter and 470 lbs. lighter. Instead of a rear window, it had a new lift-up hatch back with a huge piece of curved glass. A hatch release lock was located behind the license plate. The fuel filler door was on the driver's side quarter panel.

A 151-cid inline four with electronic fuel injection was the base engine. Options included a 173-cid 102-hp EFI V-6 and a 305-cid 145-hp V-8 with a four-barrel carburetor. Z28 buyers could pay $450 for an optional 305-cid 165-hp Crossfire fuel-injected V-8.

The Camaro's interior space was similar to before, even though the outside was smaller. The all-new fastback body was nearly 10 in. shorter than that of the previous Camaro. It rode on a 7-in. shorter 101-in. wheelbase. Each model had its own styling features, including a specific front air dam and rear fascia. The Z28 front end had no upper grille opening, its "ground effects" hugged the ground and it rode on special five-spoke aluminum wheels.

The new body featured unit construction with bolt-on front sheet metal. The front suspension was of a modified MacPherson strut design with coil springs and a stabilizer bar. At the rear, coil springs replaced leaf springs and the suspension used longitudinal torque tubes, short control arms ahead of the solid axle and lateral track rods. Z28s added a link-type rear stabilizer bar.

There were Sport Coupe, Berlinetta and Z28 models. A Z28 paced the Indy 500 and 6,360 commemorative editions of the Z28 were sold on a one-per-dealer basis. They were silver and blue with Indy 500 logos, red-

accented silver aluminum wheels and Goodyear Eagle GT white-letter tires.

I.D. DATA

Camaros again had a 17-symbol Vehicle Identification Number (VIN) on the upper left surface of the instrument panel, visible through the windshield. The first symbol identifies country of origin: 1=U.S.A., 2=Canada. The second symbol identifies the manufacturer: G=General Motors. The third symbol indicates make: 1=Chevrolet, 7=GM of Canada. The fourth symbol indicates restraint system: A=non-passive manual belts, B=Passive automatic belts. The fifth symbol indicates the car line/series: P=Camaro, S=Camaro Berlinetta. The sixth and seventh symbols indicate body type: 87=two-door plain back special coupe. The eighth symbol indicates the engine type: 2=RPO LQ9 2.5-liter (151-cid) inline four-cylinder with electronic fuel injection; 1=RPO LC1 2.8-liter (173-cid) HO V-6 with two-barrel carburetor, 7=RPO LU5 5.0-liter V-8 with Crossfire fuel injection, H=RPO LG4 5.0-liter (305-cid) V-8 with four-barrel carburetor. The ninth symbol is a check digit. The 10th symbol indicates model year: C=1982. The 11th symbol indicates the assembly plant: L=Van Nuys, California, N=Norwood, Ohio. The final six digits are the sequential serial number.

COLORS

White, Silver Metallic, Black, Light Blue Metallic, Dark Blue Metallic, Light Jade Metallic, Dark Jade Metallic, Gold Metallic, Dark Gold Metallic, Red, Maroon Metallic and Charcoal Metallic.

CAMARO - SERIES 1F - FOUR/V-6/V-8

The standard engine for the base Sport Coupe model was a Pontiac-built 151-cid (2.5-liter) 90-hp "Iron Duke" four with electronic fuel injection. Optional engines included a variant of the Citation's 173-cid (2.8-liter) V-6 rated at 102 hp or a 305-cid V-8 with a four-barrel carburetor that produced 145 hp. A four-speed manual gearbox was standard in the base Camaro and the old three-speed manual transmission was gone for good. Four-wheel disc brakes were available with V-8-powered cars. Inside, a new center console held a glove box, a parking brake lever and controls for the heater, optional stereo radio and air conditioning. The instrument panel had a black finish to minimize reflections. Twin speedometer needles showed both miles and kilometers per hour. Interior space was similar to before, even though the car's outside dimensions had shrunk. The rear seat backrest folded down, turning the rear section into a cargo area that was accessible through the hatch. Each model had its own styling features, including specific front air dam and rear fascia. All Camaros had deeply recessed quad rectangular headlamps and tri-color wraparound taillights (not far removed from prior designs). The optional F41 Sport suspension added a link-type rear stabilizer bar. Standard equipment for the base Sport Coupe included the four-speed manual transmission, power brakes, power steering, a front stabilizer bar, dual black sport mirrors, a black windshield molding, concealed windshield wipers, body-color wheels, hubcaps, P195/75R14 fiberglass-belted radial tires, reclining front bucket seats, and a day/night mirror.

Model Number	Body/Style Number	Body Type & Seating	Factory Price	Shipping Weight	Production Total
CAMARO SPORT COUPE - SERIES 1F - (L-4)					
P	87	2d coupe	$7,631	2,798 lbs.	Note 1
CAMARO SPORT COUPE - SERIES 1F - (V-6)					
P	87	2d coupe	$7,755	2,846 lbs.	Note 1
CAMARO SPORT COUPE - SERIES 1F - (V-8)					
P	87	2d coupe	$7,925	3,025 lbs.	Note 1

Note 1: Model-year production of 1982 base Camaros was 78,749 (802 four-cylinder, 45,820 six-cylinder and 11,127 V-8).

CAMARO BERLINETTA - SERIES 1F - V-6/V-8

The concept behind the Berlinetta was to enhance the Camaro's appeal to female buyers. When it replaced the LT in 1979, it became the "luxury touring" version of the sporty Chevy. The new-for-1982 Berlinetta played the same role in the Camaro model lineup. In addition to the features that were standard on the base Sport Coupe, the Berlinetta added the V-6, P205/70R14 steel-belted radial tires, body pin striping, body-color sport mirrors, black lower-body accenting (with stripes), gold-accented cast-aluminum spoked wheels and a higher-level acoustical package.

Model Number	Body/Style Number	Body Type & Seating	Factory Price	Shipping Weight	Production Total
CAMARO BERLINETTA - SERIES 1F - (V-6)					
S	87	2d coupe	$9,266	2,880 lbs.	Note 2
CAMARO BERLINETTA - SERIES 1F - (V-8)					
S	87	2d coupe	$9,436	3,094 lbs.	Note 2

Note 2: Model-year production of 1982 Camaro Berlinettas was 39,744 (23,945 six-cylinder and 15,799 V-8).

CAMARO Z28 - SERIES 1F - V-8

The Camaro Z28 front end had no upper grille opening and its ground effects air dams reached nearly to the ground. It also had operating air inlets. Four-wheel disc brakes were available. For an extra $611, Z28 buyers could even order an optional Lear-Siegler "Conteur" seat with six adjustments (backrest bolster, thigh support, cushion bolster, lumbar and recliner). A six-way power seat was optional. Z28s rode on special 15-in. five-spoke aluminum wheels with gold or charcoal accents. The suspension added a link-type rear stabilizer bar. Other standard equipment included P215/65R15 white-letter tires, a rear stabilizer bar, a specially tuned suspension, dual mufflers and tailpipes, body-color sport mirrors, a front air dam, a ground effects rocker molding area and a rear deck spoiler. Twin air scoops adorned the special Z28 hood. A 305-cid (5.0-liter) V-8 was standard in the Camaro Z28. It could also have an optional Cross-Fire injected 305-cid V-8 rated at 165 hp. That version carried a Cross-Fire Injection decal below the Z28 badge just behind the front wheel housing.

The Z28 front end had no upper grille opening.

Jerry Heasley photo

The Camaro received a complete redesign for 1982. The cars were shorter, lighter, had a sleeker front end, and hatch back. This Berlinetta was still marketed as a more stylish touring car.

Model Number	Body/Style Number	Body Type & Seating	Factory Price	Shipping Weight	Production Total
CAMARO Z28 - SERIES 1F - (V-8)					
1P	87	2d coupe	$9,700	3,005 lbs.	Note 3
CAMARO Z28 - SERIES 1F - (CFI V-8)					
1P	87	2d coupe	$10,150	3,107 lbs.	Note 3

Note 3: Model-year production of non-Indy Pace Car 1982 Camaro Z28s was 64,882. (All V-8)

Note 4: Chevrolet figures also show 1,300 Z28E hatchback models built for export (not included in other U.S. production totals).

CAMARO Z28 INDY PACE CAR - SERIES 1F - V-8

A total of 6,360 Indy 500 Commemorative Editions of the Z28 were built this year, marking the use of the new Camaro Z28 as the year's "Official Pace Car" for the Indy 500. All of the Indy Pace Car replicas sold to the public had Silver Blue Metallic finish, Indy 500 logos, red-accented silver aluminum wheels and Goodyear Eagle GT white-letter tires. The Indy Pace Car's blue cloth and silver vinyl interior included the Lear-Siegler Conteur driver's seat, along with special instruments, a leather-wrapped steering wheel and an AM/FM radio.

Model Number	Body/Style Number	Body Type & Seating	Factory Price	Shipping Weight	Production Total
CAMARO Z28 INDY PACE CAR - SERIES 1F - (V-8)					
1P	87	2d coupe	-	3,107 lbs.	6,360

Note 5: The total of 6,360 Indy 500 Commemorative Editions built is included in Note 3 figures above.

ENGINE

LQ9 base four: Inline. Overhead-valve. Four-cylinder. Cast-iron block and head. Bore & stroke: 4.00 x 3.00 in. Displacement: 151 cid (2.5 liters). Compression ratio: 9.0:1. Brake horsepower: 90 at 4000 rpm. Torque: 132 lbs.-ft. at 2800 rpm. Five main bearings. Hydraulic valve lifters. Induction system: Throttle-body fuel injection. Pontiac-built. Standard in Sport Coupe. VIN Code 2.

LC1 V-6: 60-degree, overhead-valve V-6. Cast-iron block and head. Bore & stroke: 3.50 x 2.99 in. Displacement: 173 cid (2.8 liters). Compression ratio: 8.5:1. Brake horsepower: 102 at 5100 rpm. Torque: 142 lbs.-ft.

at 2400 rpm. Four main bearings. Induction system: Two-barrel carburetor. Standard in Berlinetta. Optional in Sport Coupe. VIN Code 1.

LG4 base V-8: 90-degree, overhead-valve V-8. Cast-iron block and head. Bore & stroke: 3.74 x 3.48 in. Displacement: 305 cid (5.0 liters). Compression ratio: 8.6:1. Brake horsepower: 145 at 4000 rpm Torque: 240 lbs.-ft. at 2000 rpm Five main bearings. Hydraulic valve lifters. Induction system: four-barrel carburetor. Standard in Z28. Optional in Sport Coupe and Berlinetta. VIN Code: H.

LU5 V-8: 90-degree, overhead-valve V-8. Cast-iron block and head. Bore & stroke: 3.74 x 3.48 in. Displacement: 305 cid (5.0 liters). Compression ratio: 8.6:1. Brake horsepower: 165 at 4200 rpm Torque: 240 lbs.-ft. at 2400 rpm Five main bearings. Hydraulic valve lifters. Induction system: Cross-Fire fuel injection. Optional in Z28. VIN Code: 7.

CHASSIS

Sport Coupe: Wheelbase: 101 in. Overall length: 187.8 in. Overall height: 50 in. Overall width: 72.8 in. Front tread: 60.7 in. Rear tread: 61.6 in. Front head-room: 37 in. Rear headroom: 35.6 in. Front legroom: 43 in. Rear legroom: 28.9 in. Front shoulder room: 57.5 in. Rear shoulder room: 56.3 in. Front hip room: 56.3 in. Rear hip room: 42.8 in. Cargo volume: 12.4 cu. ft. (31 cu. ft. with rear seatback down). Standard tires: P195/75R-14 steel-belted radial. Wheel size: 14 x 6-in.

Berlinetta: Wheelbase: 101 in. Overall length: 187.8 in. Overall height: 50 in. Overall width: 72.8 in. Front tread: 60.7 in. Rear tread: 61.6 in. Front headroom: 37 in. Rear headroom: 35.6 in. Front legroom: 43 in. Rear legroom: 28.9 in. Front shoulder room: 57.5 in. Rear shoulder room: 56.3 in. Front hip room: 56.3 in. Rear hip room: 42.8 in. Cargo volume: 12.4 cu. ft. (31 cu. ft. with rear seatback down). Standard tires: P205/70R14 steel-belted radial. Wheel size: Berlinetta 14 x 7-in.

Z28: Wheelbase: 101 in. Overall length: 187.8 in.

Jerry Heasley photo

This 1982 Z/28 received the new flush-mounted 62-degree windshield that produced one of the lowest drag coefficient readings ever measured by GM. The '82 Camaros were 10 in. shorter and 470 lbs. lighter.

Overall height: 50 in. Overall width: 72.8 in. Front tread: 60.7 in. Rear tread: 61.6 in. Front headroom: 37 in. Rear headroom: 35.6 in. Front legroom: 43 in. Rear legroom: 28.9 in. Front shoulder room: 57.5 in. Rear shoulder room: 56.3 in. Front hip room: 56.3 in. Rear hip room: 42.8 in. Cargo volume: 12.4 cu. ft. (31 cu. ft. with rear seatback down). Standard tires: P215/65R15 white-letter steel-belted radial. Wheel size: Z28 15 x 7-in.

TECHNICAL

Sport Coupe: Standard transmission: Four-speed manual. Standard final drive ratio: 3.73:1. Front suspension: Modified MacPherson strut with 1.106-in. diameter stabilizer bar. Rear suspension: Torque arm with 0.71-in. rear anti-roll bar, plus link-type rear stabilizer bar with optional F41 Sport suspension. Brakes: Power front disc/rear drum. Fuel tank capacity: 15.8 gal. with four-cylinder engine; 16.2 gal. with V-6 or V-8.

Berlinetta: Standard transmission: Five-speed manual. Standard final drive ratio: (five-speed) 3.23:1, (automatic) 3.08:1. Front suspension: Modified MacPherson strut with 1.106-in. diameter stabilizer bar. Rear suspension: Torque arm, solid axle, lower control arms, track bar and coil springs with 0.71-in. rear anti-roll bar, plus link-type rear stabilizer bar with optional F41 Sport suspension. Brakes: Power front disc/rear drum. Fuel tank capacity: 16.2 gal.

Z28: Standard transmission: Five-speed manual. Standard final drive ratio: (Five-speed) 3.23:1, (Automatic) 3.08:1, (TPI V-8) 3.23:1. Front suspension: Modified MacPherson strut with 1.22-in. diameter stabilizer bar. Rear suspension: Torque arm with 0.83-in. rear anti-roll bar, plus link-type rear stabilizer bar. Brakes Power front disc/rear drum. Fuel tank capacity: 16.2 gal.

OPTIONS

LC1 173-cid V-6 ($125). LG4 305-cid four-barrel base V-8 ($170 in Berlinetta; $295 in Sport Coupe). LU5 305-cid Cross-Fire fuel-injected V-8, Camaro Z28 only ($450). MXO four-speed overdrive automatic transmission in Berlinetta or Z28 ($295). MXO four-speed overdrive automatic transmission in base Camaro Sport

There were 6,300 1982 Camaro Z28 T-top Indy 500 Pace Cars produced.

Coupe ($525). MX3 three-speed automatic transmission in base Sport Coupe ($425). MX3 three-speed automatic transmission in Berlinetta ($195). MM5 five-speed manual transmission, in base Camaro Sport Coupe ($125). AG9 six-way power seat ($197). AU3 power door locks ($106). AO1 tinted glass ($88). A90 power hatch release ($32). BS1 Quiet Sound group ($72-$80). B34 color-keyed front floor mats ($16). B35 color-keyed rear floor mats ($11). B84 body side moldings ($47). CC1 removable glass roof panels ($790). CD4 intermittent windshield wipers ($47). C25 rear window wiper and washer ($117). C49 electric rear window defogger ($125). C60 air conditioning ($675). D67 twin electric remote-control sport style outside rearview mirrors ($88-$137). D80 rear deck lid spoiler ($69). F41 Sport suspension system ($49). G80 limited-slip differential ($76). J65 four-wheel power disc brakes ($179). N33 Comfortilt steering wheel ($95). UO5 dual horns ($12). UO5 gauge package ($149). ZJ7 Rally wheels ($112). PO1 full-wheel covers ($52).

HISTORY

The all-new Camaro was introduced on Jan. 14, 1982. In one illuminating survey that held portents of the future, Chevrolet discovered that nearly 37 percent of Camaros purchased in 1980 were bought by women. That was higher than any other Chevrolet passenger car and well above the industry average of 24.5 percent. Twin slogans for the restyled Camaro also suggested what was to come as the decade unrolled. "Excess is out. Efficiency is in!" predicted the rising emphasis on fuel-efficiency and modest size. "Brute power is out. Precision is in!" seemed to toll the death knell for the big V-8, although it would stay around for some time yet. Robert C. Stempel was general manager of Chevrolet Motor Division in 1982. While Chevy's overall model-year sales declined by more than 300,000 vehicles, the redesigned Camaro's popularity rose. Model-year sales went from 109,707 in 1981 to 148,649 in 1982. Unfortunately, that was below the target number of 155,000 units. Part of the reason for missing the goal was that the Camaro was not introduced until Jan. 14, 1982, while other Chevy products bowed on Sept. 24, 1981. Calendar-year sales wound up at 182,848. Industry trade journals of the era show model-year production of 189,735 Camaros, which represented a 3.68 percent share of the industry total. Other sources show a slightly higher production total of 189,747. The Van Nuys, California, plant reported building 121,512 Camaros (and 76,445 Firebirds). The Norwood, Ohio, factory reported building 68,223 Camaros (and 39,919 Firebirds). Of the Camaros built, 82 percent had automatic transmission, 18 percent had a four-speed manual transmission, 11.5 percent had a four-cylinder engine, 51.7 percent had a V-8, 36.8 percent had a V-6, 100 percent had power steering, 96.7 percent had power front disc brakes, 3.3 percent had power four-wheel disc brakes, 11.6 percent had a limited-slip differential, 91 percent had steel-belted radial tires, 9 percent had fiberglass belted tires, 33.9 percent had power door locks, 44.8 percent had power windows, 100 percent had reclining bucket seats, 8.3 percent had a power front driver's seat, 70.6 percent had tilt steering, 1 percent had a tinted windshield only, 89.5 percent had all-tinted glass, 84.1 percent had manual air conditioning, 32.4 percent had cruise control, 11.4 percent had an AM radio, 5.8 percent had an AM/FM radio, 27.8 percent had an AM/FM stereo radio, 1.9 percent had an AM/FM 8-track tape player, 5.1 percent had a stereo cassette player, 29.4 percent had a analog clock, 44.5 percent had a digital clock, 61.8 percent had an electric rear window defogger, 7.4 percent had a rear window washer, 97 percent had a remote-control left-hand outside rearview mirror, 10.1 percent also had a remote-control right-hand outside rearview mirror, 35.5 percent had aluminum styled wheels, 58.5 percent had styled steel wheels and 28.1 percent had T-tops. A total of 173,686 new Camaros were registered in the U.S. during calendar year 1982. That was up from 93,706 in 1981.

Camaro

Phil Kunz photo

The 1983 Z28s could have the standard 305-cid V-8, the fuel-injected V-8, or a 305-cid H.O. V-8.

The Camaro's looks changed little following its 1982 restyling, but more power train combinations were available. Engine choices were essentially the same until a new 305-cid 190-hp H.O. V-8 with cam revisions and a four-barrel carburetor arrived late in the model year. A five-speed overdrive manual transmission was now optional for the base Sport Coupe and standard on other models. Also new was an available four-speed overdrive automatic with lockup torque converter.

Maroon was dropped from the body color list and brown replaced maroon as an interior choice, but color choices otherwise remained the same as before. Production, which had raced up to 189,747 in the third generation's first year, tapered back down (but only temporarily) to 154,381 units.

I.D. DATA

Chevrolets again had a 17-symbol Vehicle Identification Number (VIN) on the upper left surface of the instrument panel, visible through the windshield. The first symbol identifies country of origin: 1=U.S.A., 2=Canada. The second symbol identifies the manufacturer: G=General Motors. The third symbol indicates make: 1=Chevrolet, 7=GM of Canada. The fourth symbol indicates restraint system: A=non-passive manual belts. The fifth symbol indicates the car line/series: P=Camaro, S=Camaro Berlinetta. The sixth and seventh symbols indicate body type: 87=two-door plain back special coupe. The eighth symbol indicates the engine type: 2=RPO LQ9 2.5-liter (151-cid) inline four-cylinder with electronic fuel injection; 1=RPO LC1 2.8-liter (173-cid) HO V-6 with two-barrel carburetor, 7=RPO LB9 5.0-liter V-8 with Crossfire fuel injection, H=RPO LG4 5.0-liter

(305-cid) V-8 with four-barrel carburetor; S=RPO L69 5.0-liter (305-cid) High Output V-8 with four-barrel carburetor. The ninth symbol is a check digit. The 10th symbol indicates model year: D=1983. The 11th symbol indicates the assembly plant: L=Van Nuys, California, N=Norwood, Ohio. The final six digits are the sequential serial number.

COLORS

White, Silver Metallic, Black, Light Blue (not available on Z28), Dark Blue Metallic (not available on Berlinetta), Beige, Light Brown Metallic, Dark Brown Metallic (not available on Berlinetta), Red and Charcoal Metallic.

CAMARO - SERIES 1F - V-6/V-8

Camaros again had a rear glass hatch, reclining front bucket seats, and standard power steering. Joining the option list: a rear compartment cover to hide cargo. Optional mats now were carpeted instead of plain rubber. The standard equipment list included all GM safety, occupant protection, accident avoidance and anti-theft features plus dual black outside rearview mirrors, quad headlamps, a carpeted cargo floor with a storage well, a hinged stowage compartment in the front center console, a power ventilation system, reclining front bucket seats, side window defoggers, a front stabilizer bar, P195/75R-14 black sidewall tires, a power front disc/rear drum braking system with audible front wear sensors, fast-ratio power steering, a rear suspension with a torque arm to handle driving and braking forces and 14 x 6-in. body-color wheels with hubcaps.

Model Number	Body/Style Number	Body Type & Seating	Factory Price	Shipping Weight	Production Total
CAMARO SPORT COUPE - SERIES 1F - (L-4)					
P	87	2d coupe	$7,845	2,798 lbs.	Note 1
CAMARO SPORT COUPE - SERIES 1F - (V-6)					
P	87	2d coupe	$8,186	2,878 lbs.	Note 1
CAMARO SPORT COUPE - SERIES 1F - (V-8)					
P	87	2d coupe	$8,386	3,035 lbs.	Note 1

Note 1: Model-year production of 1983 base Camaros was 64,356 (9,926 four-cylinder, 39,859 six-cylinder and 14,571 V-8).

CAMARO BERLINETTA - SERIES 1F - V-6/V-8

Berlinettas came standard with the 173-cid (2.8-liter) V-6. A five-speed overdrive manual transmission was also standard. Berlinetta equipment included an AM/FM stereo electronic-tuning radio, a digital clock, hood and sail panel decals, a lockable fuel filler door, a sport aluminum hood, dual horns, a five-speed manual gearbox, a smooth-ride suspension, intermittent windshield wipers, custom vinyl reclining front bucket seats with adjustable head restraints, a front stabilizer bar and P205/70R-14 black sidewall tires, color-keyed sport mirrors, lower accent body paint with striping and 14 x 7-in. finned aluminum wheels with gold accents.

Model Number	Body/Style Number	Body Type & Seating	Factory Price	Shipping Weight	Production Total
CAMARO BERLINETTA - SERIES 1F - (V-6)					
S	87	2d coupe	$9,881	2,864 lbs.	Note 2
CAMARO BERLINETTA - SERIES 1F - (V-8)					
S	87	2d coupe	$10,106	3,056 lbs.	Note 2

Note 2: Model-year production of 1983 Camaro Berlinettas was 27,925. (14,473 six-cylinder and 13,452 V-8)

CAMARO Z28 - SERIES 1F - V-6/V-8

The standard Camaro V-8 was carbureted, but Z28s could have the Cross-Fire fuel-injected V-8. Camaros with this CFI engine had functional dual air intake hood scoops. Five-speed overdrive manual transmission was standard. New four-speed overdrive automatic (with lockup torque converter) was also available. A new high-output 305 V-8 engine with revised cam and four-barrel carburetor arrived late in the model year. It developed 190 hp. A total of 3,223 H.O. V-8s were installed in 1983 Camaros. Optional "Conteur" multi-adjustment driver's

seats got matching passenger seats. Stereo radios offered electronic tuning. Z28 had new three-tone upholstery featuring multiple Camaro logos. The Z28 standard equipment list included all GM safety, occupant protection, accident avoidance and anti-theft features, plus dual body-color Sport outside rearview mirrors (left-hand remote controlled), a front air dam and ground effects rocker molding in silver or gold, quad headlamps, a rear deck lid spoiler, a carpeted cargo floor with a storage well, a hinged stowage compartment in the front center console, a power ventilation system, reclining front bucket seats, side window defoggers, a 1.22-in. diameter front stabilizer bar, P215/65R-15 steel-belted radial-ply white letter tires, a power front disc/rear drum braking system with audible front wear sensors, fast-ratio power steering, a rear suspension with a torque arm to handle driving and braking forces and 15 x 7-in. five-spoke cast-aluminum wheels with gold, charcoal or silver accent color.

Model Number	Body/Style Number	Body Type & Seating	Factory Price	Shipping Weight	Production Total
CAMARO Z28 - SERIES 1F - (V-8)					
1P	87	2d coupe	$10,336	3,061 lbs.	Note 3
CAMARO Z28 - SERIES 1F - (CFI V-8)					
1P	87	2d coupe	$10,786	3,107 lbs.	Note 3
CAMARO Z28 - SERIES 1F - (H.O. V-8)					
1P	87	2d coupe	$10,841	3,107 lbs.	Note 3

Note 3: Model-year production of 1983 Camaro Z28s was 62,100 (all V-8).
Note 4: Chevrolet production figures also show 550 Z28E hatchback Sport Coupes built for export (not included in U.S. totals).

ENGINE

LQ9 base four: Inline. Overhead valve. Four-cylinder. Cast-iron block and head. Bore & stroke: 4.00 x 3.00 in. Displacement: 151 cid (2.5 liters). Compression ratio: 9.0:1. Brake horsepower: 92 at 4000 rpm. Torque: 134 lbs.-ft. at 2800 rpm. Five main bearings. Hydraulic valve lifters. Induction system: Throttle-body fuel injection. Pontiac-built. Standard in Camaro Sport Coupe. VIN Code 2.

LC1 V-6: 60-degree, overhead-valve V-6. Cast-iron block and head. Bore & stroke: 3.50 x 2.99 in. Displacement: 173 cid (2.8 liters). Compression ratio: 8.5:1. Brake horsepower: 107 at 4800 rpm. Torque: 145 lbs.-ft.

After a major facelift in 1982, the 1983 Camaro received only minor changes.

at 2100 rpm. Four main bearings. Induction system: Two-barrel carburetor. Standard in Camaro Berlinetta. Optional in Camaro Sport Coupe. VIN Code 1.

LG4 base V-8: 90-degree, overhead-valve V-8. Cast-iron block and head. Bore & stroke: 3.74 x 3.48 in. Displacement: 305 cid (5.0 liters). Compression ratio: 8.6:1. Brake horsepower: 150 at 4000 rpm Torque: 240 lbs.-ft. at 2400 rpm Five main bearings. Hydraulic valve lifters. Induction system: four-barrel carburetor. Standard in Z28. Optional in Sport Coupe and Berlinetta. VIN Code: H.

LB9 V-8: 90-degree, overhead-valve V-8. Cast-iron block and head. Bore & stroke: 3.74 x 3.48 in. Displacement: 305 cid (5.0 liters). Compression ratio: 8.6:1. Brake horsepower: 175 at 4800 rpm Torque: 235 lbs.-ft. at 3200 rpm Five main bearings. Hydraulic valve lifters. Induction system: Cross-Fire fuel injection. Optional in Z28. VIN Code: 7.

L69 H.O. V-8: 90-degree, overhead-valve V-8. Cast-iron block and head. Bore & stroke: 3.74 x 3.48 in. Displacement: 305 cid (5.0 liters). Compression ratio: 9.5:1. Brake horsepower: 190 at 4800 rpm Torque: 249 lbs.-ft. at 3200 rpm Five main bearings. Hydraulic valve lifters. Induction system: 650-cfm quadrajet four-barrel carburetor. Optional in Z28. VIN Code: S.

CHASSIS

Sport Coupe: Wheelbase: 101 in. Overall length: 187.8 in. Overall height: 50 in. Overall width: 72.8 in. Front tread: 60.7 in. Rear tread: 61.6 in. Front headroom: 37 in. Rear headroom: 35.6 in. Front legroom: 43 in. Rear legroom: 28.9 in. Front shoulder room: 57.5 in. Rear shoulder room: 56.3 in. Front hip room: 56.3 in. Rear hip room: 42.8 in. Cargo volume: 12.4 cu. ft. (31 cu. ft. with rear seat back down). Standard tires: P195/75R-14 steel-belted radial.

Berlinetta: Wheelbase: 101 in. Overall length: 187.8 in. Overall height: 50 in. Overall width: 72.8 in. Front tread: 60.7 in. Rear tread: 61.6 in. Front headroom: 37 in. Rear headroom: 35.6 in. Front legroom: 43 in. Rear legroom: 28.9 in. Front shoulder room: 57.5 in. Rear

Reclining bucket seats were standard in 1983.

The 1983 Camaro cockpit.

shoulder room: 56.3 in. Front hip room: 56.3 in. Rear hip room: 42.8 in. Cargo volume: 12.4 cu. ft. (31 cu. ft. with rear seat back down). Standard tires: P205/70R14 steel-belted radial.

Z28: Wheelbase: 101 in. Overall length: 187.8 in. Overall height: 50 in. Overall width: 72.8 in. Front tread: 60.7 in. Rear tread: 61.6 in. Front headroom: 37 in. Rear headroom: 35.6 in. Front legroom: 43 in. Rear legroom: 28.9 in. Front shoulder room: 57.5 in. Rear shoulder room: 56.3 in. Front hip room: 56.3 in. Rear hip room: 42.8 in. Cargo volume: 12.4 cu. ft. (31 cu. ft. with rear seat back down). Standard tires: P215/65R15 white-letter steel-belted radial.

TECHNICAL

Sport Coupe: Standard transmission: Five-speed manual. Standard final drive ratio: 3.73:1. Front suspension: Modified MacPherson strut with 1.106-in. diameter stabilizer bar. Rear suspension: Torque arm. Brakes: Power front disc/rear drum. Fuel tank capacity: 15.8 gal. with four-cylinder engine; 16.2 gal. with V-6 or V-8.

Berlinetta: Standard transmission: Five-speed manual. Standard final drive ratio: (Five-speed) 3.23:1, (Automatic) 3.08:1. Front suspension: Modified MacPherson strut with 1.106-in. diameter stabilizer bar. Rear suspension: Torque arm. Brakes: Power front disc/rear drum. Fuel tank capacity: 16.2 gal.

Z28: Standard transmission: Five-speed manual. Standard final drive ratio: (Five-speed) 3.23:1, (Automatic) 3.08:1, (TPI V-8) 3.23:1. Front suspension: Modified MacPherson strut with 1.22-in. diameter stabilizer bar. Rear suspension: Torque arm. Brakes Power front disc/rear drum. Fuel tank capacity: 16.2 gal.

OPTIONS

LC1 173-cid V-6 ($150). LG4 305-cid four-barrel base V-8 ($225 in Berlinetta; $350 in Sport Coupe). LB9 305-cid Cross-Fire Injected V-8, Camaro Z28 only ($450). L69 305-cid H.O. four-barrel V-8 ($505). MXO four-speed overdrive automatic transmission in Berlinetta or Z28 ($295). MXO four-speed overdrive automatic transmission in base Camaro Sport Coupe ($525). MX3 three-speed automatic transmission in Base Sport Coupe ($425). MX3 three-speed automatic transmission in Berlinetta ($195). MM5 five-speed manual transmission, in base Camaro Sport Coupe ($125). AG9 six-way power seat ($210). AU3 power door locks ($120). AO1 tinted glass ($105). A90 power hatch release ($40). BS1 Quiet

Linda Phillips photo

A 1983 Camaro Z28 convertible conversion by Custom Form.

Sound Group ($72-$82). B34 color-keyed front floor mats ($20). B35 color-keyed rear floor mats ($15). CC1 removable glass roof panels ($825). CD4 intermittent windshield wipers ($49). C25 rear window wiper and washer ($120). C49 electric rear window defogger ($135). C60 air conditioning ($725). D67 twin electric remote-control sport style outside rearview mirrors ($89-$137). D80 rear deck lid spoiler ($69). F41 Sport suspension system ($49). G80 limited-slip differential ($95). J65 four-wheel power disc brakes ($179). N33 Comfortilt steering wheel ($105). UO5 dual horns ($12). UO5 gauge package ($149). ZJ7 Rally wheels ($112). PO1 full wheel covers ($52).

HISTORICAL FOOTNOTES

The 1983 Camaro line was introduced on Nov. 8, 1982. The nation's economic condition may have improved during 1983, but Chevrolet's status remained shaky. Model-year sales rose by only 6 percent. Robert C. Stempel, Chevrolet's general manager, promoted a new "pricing strategy which finds more than half of Chevrolet's 1983 passenger car models carrying lower sticker prices than they did in '82." Some of the reduction, though, was due to elimination of formerly standard equipment, a practice that would become common in the years ahead. The Camaro was named *Motor Trend* "Car of the Year." In a GM reshuffling, Chevrolet became part of the new Chevrolet-Pontiac-GM of Canada Group, which was to emphasize small cars. That group was headed by Lloyd E. Reuss, formerly Buick's general manager. Bob Stempel moved over to the new Buick-Oldsmobile-Cadillac group, which focused on large cars. Robert D. Burger became Chevrolet's general manager. Model-year sales rose from 148,649 in 1982 to 175,004 in 1983. Calendar-year sales wound up at 178,266 or 8.8 percent of the industry total. Model-year production of 154,381 Camaros represented a 2.72 percent share of the industry's total. The Van Nuys plant reported building 68,810 Camaros (and 37,548 Firebirds). The Norwood factory reported building 85,571 Camaros (and 37,349 Firebirds). Of the Camaros built, 76.7 percent had automatic transmission, 2.5 percent had a four-speed manual transmission, 20.8 percent had a five-speed manual transmission, 6.4 percent had a four-cylinder engine, 58.4 percent had a V-8, 35.2 percent had a V-6, 100 percent had power steering, 93.6 percent had power front disc brakes, 6.4 percent had power four-wheel disc brakes, 12.3 percent had a limited-slip differential, 94.8 percent had steel-belted radial tires, 5.2 percent had fiberglass belted tires, 34.2 percent had power door locks, 45.1percent had power windows, 100 percent had reclining bucket seats, 12 percent had a power front driver's seat, 73.2 percent had tilt steering, 93.8 percent had all-tinted glass, 83.4 percent had manual air conditioning, 47 percent had cruise control, 7 percent had an AM radio, 2.6 percent had an AM/FM radio, 28.1 percent had an AM/FM stereo radio, 48.1 percent had a stereo cassette player. A total of 175,690 new Camaros were registered in the U.S. during calendar year 1983. That was up from 173,686 in 1982.

Jerry Heasley photo

Chevrolet sold more than 100,000 1984 Z28s — an all-time high never hit again.

The Camaro took off in popularity again in 1984, when 261,591 were made. This included more than 100,000 Z28s — an all-time high never hit again. The Berlinetta gained the most attention in 1984 with its new "space-age instrumentation," including digital readouts, a pivoting pedestal-mounted radio and dual adjustable fingertip control pods that could be moved close to the steering wheel. This Corvette-inspired cockpit also sported a roof console and adjustable low-back seats.

The Camaro's modest "grille" hardly qualified as a grille. It consisted of no more than three side-by-side slots in the front panel. The grille was flanked by rectangular headlamps. Body colors were the same as 1983, but Dark Gold was added to the palette. Buyers could enhance the interior of their Camaro Sport Coupe with an elegant new low-back seating option that came with adjustable head restraints. The stylish striped seat bolsters characterized the standard front reclining bucket seats.

On the mechanical side, Cross-Fire injection was dropped, but the Z28 offered an optional 5.0-liter 190-hp H.O. V-8. It came hooked to either a five-speed manual or four-speed automatic transmission. This engine, introduced in the spring, was the most powerful carbureted engine offered in an '84 Chevy. The standard 2.5-liter four-cylinder engine featured an electronic fuel injection system that was so advanced it compared in principle to the new Corvette engine. A 173-cid (2.8-liter) V-6 was also a popular option. A hydraulic clutch was now used with all manual gearboxes.

I.D. DATA

Chevrolets again had a 17-symbol vehicle identification number (VIN) on the upper left surface of the instrument panel, visible through the windshield. The first symbol identifies country of origin: 1=U.S.A., 2=Canada. The second symbol identifies the manufacturer: G=General Motors. The third symbol indicates make: 1=Chevrolet, 7=GM of Canada. The fourth symbol indicates restraint system: A=non-passive manual belts. The fifth symbol indicates the car line/series: P=Camaro, S=Camaro Berlinetta. The sixth and seventh symbols indicate body type: 87=two-door plain back special coupe. The eighth symbol indicates the engine type: 2=RPO LQ9 2.5-liter (151-cid) inline four-cylinder with Electronic Fuel Injection; 1=RPO LB8 2.8-liter (173-cid) HO V-6 with Multiport Fuel Injection; H=RPO LG4 5.0-liter (305-cid) V-8 with four-barrel carburetor; G=RPO L69 5.0-liter (305-cid) High Output V-8 with four-barrel carburetor. The ninth symbol is a check digit. The 10th symbol indicates model year: E=1984. The 11th symbol indicates the assembly plant: L=Van Nuys, California, N=Norwood, Ohio. The final six digits are the sequential serial number.

COLORS

White, Silver Metallic, Black, Light Blue (not available on Z28), Dark Blue Metallic (not available on Berlinetta), Beige, Light Brown Metallic, Dark Gold Metallic, Dark Brown Metallic (not available on Berlinetta), Red and Charcoal Metallic. Available standard interior colors for the base Sport Coupe and Z28 were Charcoal, Dark Blue, Camel, Sand Gray and Dark Brown in a choice of standard vinyl or optional cloth. The Custom interior (which was standard in Berlinettas and optional in other models) offered the same color and material choices except for Camel vinyl. The optional L/S interior for the Z28 came in Charcoal/Red Orange, Dark Blue and Dark Brown in a choice of cloth or deluxe cloth.

CAMARO SPORT COUPE - SERIES 1F - FOUR/V-6/V-8

Chevrolet promoted the 1984 Camaro as "the best-selling 2+2 on the road." The base Camaro Sport Coupe featured a chassis and suspension configuration derived from the Z28 and combined it with clean aesthetics that made it the "purest" Camaro. Steel-belted fourth-generation all-season radial tires were became standard on the Sport Coupe. Base Sport Coupe equipment was otherwise similar to 1983. The standard equipment list included all GM safety, occupant protection, accident avoidance and anti-theft features plus dual black outside rearview mirrors, quad headlamps, a carpeted cargo floor with a storage well, a hinged stowage compartment in the front center console, a power ventilation system, reclining front bucket seats, side window defoggers, a 1.06-in. diameter front stabilizer bar, P195/75R-14 steel-belted radial-ply black sidewall tires, a power front disc/rear drum braking system with audible front wear sensors, fast-ratio power steering, a rear suspension with a torque arm to handle driving and braking forces and 14 x 6-in. body-color wheels with hubcaps.

Model Number	Body/Style Number	Body Type & Seating	Factory Price	Shipping Weight	Production Total
CAMARO SPORT COUPE - SERIES 1F - (L-4)					
P	87	2d coupe	$7,995	2,813 lbs.	Note 1
CAMARO SPORT COUPE - SERIES 1F - (V-6)					
P	87	2d coupe	$8,245	2,907 lbs.	Note 1
CAMARO SPORT COUPE - SERIES 1F - (V-8)					
P	87	2d coupe	$8,545	3,091 lbs.	Note 1

Note 1: Model-year production of 1984 base Camaros was 127,775. (10,687 four-cylinder, 86,447 six-cylinder and 30,611 V-8)

CAMARO BERLINETTA - SERIES 1F - V-6

Berlinettas could be spotted by their gold-colored body trim. This model got the most attention this year. It had new "space-age instrumentation" that included digital readouts, a pivoting pedestal-mounted radio and dual adjustable fingertip control pods that could be moved close to the steering wheel. The Corvette-inspired cockpit also sported a roof console and adjustable low-back bucket seats. A digital display ahead of the driver showed road speed in miles or kilometers per hour, plus odometer or engine speed. An adjoining vertical-bar tachometer flashed more urgently as engine speed increased, while a monitor farther to the right signaled low fluid levels or other trouble spots. At the left were conventional needle-type gauges. The twin pods contained switches for lights and instrument displays, plus wiper and climate control. Other push-button controls were in the floor console, while the overhead console contained a swivel map light and small storage pouch. A remote-controlled, electronically tuned AM/FM stereo radio with digital clock was standard. Options included a tape player and a graphic equalizer. The radio could swivel for easy operation by either the driver or passenger. Buttons for the optional cruise control were on the Berlinetta's steering wheel, not the steering column. In addition to the electronic instrumentation and roof console, Berlinetta equipment included an AM/FM stereo electronic-tuning radio, a digital clock, hood and sail panel decals, a lockable fuel filler door, a sport aluminum hood, dual horns, a five-speed manual gearbox, a smooth-ride suspension, intermittent windshield wipers, custom vinyl reclining front bucket seats with adjustable head restraints, a 1.06-in. diameter front stabilizer bar and P205/70R-14 steel-belted radial black sidewall tires. Berlinettas carried color-keyed sport mirrors and lower accent body paint with striping. Their 14 x 7 in. finned aluminum wheels were gold accented. Other models could have the Berlinetta style roof console for $50 extra, while a lockable rear storage cover cost $80 additional.

Model Number	Body/Style Number	Body Type & Seating	Factory Price	Shipping Weight	Production Total
CAMARO BERLINETTA - SERIES 1F - (V-6)					
S	87	2d coupe	$10,895	2,919 lbs.	Note 2
CAMARO BERLINETTA - SERIES 1F - (V-8)					
S	87	2d coupe	$11,270	3,157 lbs.	Note 2

Note 2: Model-year production of 1984 Camaro Berlinettas was 33,400. (11,994 six-cylinder and 21,406 V-8)

Camaro Z28 - Series 1F - V-8

The basic 1984 Camaro grille was simple enough, but the Z28 didn't even have slots in its upper panel. The performance model displayed subtle 5.0-Liter H.O. badges on its back bumper, rocker panels and air cleaner. It also had dual tailpipes. Standard features were similar to 1983. On the mechanical side, Crossfire Fuel Injection was dropped, but the Z28 could have an optional high-output 5.0-liter engine (RPO code L69) that was rated at 190 hp. It came hooked to either a five-

The 1984 Z28 had no upper grille openings.

speed manual gearbox or a four-speed automatic transmission. That H.O. V-8 (introduced in the spring of 1983) was the most powerful carbureted engine offered in a Chevrolet. It had a higher-lift, longer-duration camshaft, retuned valve system and 9.5:1 compression. The H.O. engine also had a specially calibrated Rochester Quadrajet carburetor, dual-snorkel cold-air intake, large-diameter exhaust and tailpipes and wide-mouth (Corvette-type) catalytic converter. Z28s could have Berlinetta's roof console for an extra $50, while a locking rear storage cover cost $80. The Z28 standard equipment list included all GM safety, occupant protection, accident avoidance and anti-theft features plus dual body-color sport outside rearview mirrors (left-hand remote controlled), a front air dam and ground effects rocker molding in silver or gold, quad headlamps, a rear deck lid spoiler, a carpeted cargo floor with a storage well, a hinged stowage compartment in the front center console, a power ventilation system, reclining front bucket seats, side window defoggers, a 1.22-in. diameter front stabilizer bar, P215/65R-15 steel-belted radial-ply white letter tires, a power front disc/rear drum braking system with audible front wear sensors, fast-ratio power steering, a rear suspension with a torque arm to handle driving and braking forces and 15 x 7-in. five-spoke cast-aluminum wheels with gold, charcoal or silver accent color.

Model Number	Body/Style Number	Body Type & Seating	Factory Price	Shipping Weight	Production Total
CAMARO Z28 - SERIES 1F - (V-8)					
1P	87	2d coupe	$10,620	3,107 lbs.	Note 3
CAMARO Z28 - SERIES 1F - (H.O. V-8)					
1P	87	2d coupe	$11,150	3,107 lbs.	Note 3

Note 3: Model year production of 1984 Camaro Z28s was 100,416 (all V-8).
Note 4: Chevrolet production figures also show 478 Z28E hatchback Sport Coupes (not included in U.S. production).

ENGINE

LQ9 base four: Inline. Overhead valve. Four-cylinder. Cast iron block and head. Bore & stroke: 4.00 x 3.00 in. Displacement: 151 cid (2.5 liters). Compression ratio: 9.0:1. Brake horsepower: 92 at 4000 rpm. Torque: 134 lbs.-ft. at 2800 rpm. Five main bearings. Hydraulic valve lifters. Induction system: Throttle-body fuel injection. Pontiac-built. Standard in Sport Coupe. VIN Code 2.

LB8 V-6: 60-degree, overhead-valve V-6. Cast-iron block and head. Bore & stroke: 3.50 x 2.99 in. Displace-

The base Camaro front end featured three narrow slots on the upper grille between rectangular headlights.

ment: 173 cid (2.8 liters). Compression ratio: 8.5:1. Compression ratio: 8.9:1. Brake horsepower: 107 at 4800 rpm. Torque: 145 lbs.-ft. at 2100 rpm. Four main bearings. Induction system: Two-barrel carburetor. Standard in Berlinetta. Optional in Sport Coupe. VIN Code 1.

LG4 base V-8: 90-degree, overhead-valve V-8. Cast-iron block and head. Bore & stroke: 3.74 x 3.48 in. Displacement: 305 cid (5.0 liters). Compression ratio: 8.8:1. Brake horsepower: 150 at 4000 rpm Torque: 240 lbs.-ft. at 2400 rpm Five main bearings. Hydraulic valve lifters. Induction system: four-barrel carburetor. Standard in Z28. Optional in Sport Coupe and Camaro Berlinetta. VIN Code: H.

L69 H.O. V-8: 90-degree, overhead-valve V-8. Cast-iron block and head. Bore & stroke: 3.74 x 3.48 in. Displacement: 305 cid (5.0 liters). Compression ratio: 9.5:1. Brake horsepower: 190 at 4800 rpm Torque: 240 lbs.-ft. at 3200 rpm Five main bearings. Hydraulic valve lifters. Induction system: four-barrel carburetor. Optional in Z28. VIN Code: G.

CHASSIS

Sport Coupe: Wheelbase: 101 in. Overall length: 187.8 in. Overall height: 50 in. Overall width: 72.8 in. Front tread: 60.7 in. Rear tread: 61.6 in. Front headroom: 37 in. Rear headroom: 35.6 in. Front legroom: 43 in. Rear legroom: 28.9 in. Front shoulder room: 57.5 in. Rear shoulder room: 56.3 in. Front hip room: 56.3 in. Rear hip room: 42.8 in. Cargo volume: 12.4 cu. ft. (31 cu. ft. with rear seat back down). Standard tires: P195/75R-14 steel-belted radial.

Berlinetta: Wheelbase: 101 in. Overall length: 187.8 in. Overall height: 50 in. Overall width: 72.8 in. Front tread: 60.7 in. Rear tread: 61.6 in. Front headroom: 37 in. Rear headroom: 35.6 in. Front legroom: 43 in. Rear legroom: 28.9 in. Front shoulder room: 57.5 in. Rear shoulder room: 56.3 in. Front hip room: 56.3 in. Rear hip room: 42.8 in. Cargo volume: 12.4 cu. ft. (31 cu. ft. with rear seat back down). Standard tires: P205/70R14 steel-belted radial.

Z28: Wheelbase: 101 in. Overall length: 187.8 in. Overall height: 50 in. Overall width: 72.8 in. Front tread: 60.7 in. Rear tread: 61.6 in. Front headroom: 37 in. Rear headroom: 35.6 in. Front legroom: 43 in. Rear legroom: 28.9 in. Front shoulder room: 57.5 in. Rear shoulder room: 56.3 in. Front hip room: 56.3 in. Rear hip room: 42.8 in. Cargo volume: 12.4 cu. ft. (31 cu. ft. with rear seat back down). Standard tires: P215/65R15 white-letter steel-belted radial.

TECHNICAL

Sport Coupe: Standard Transmission: Five-speed manual. Standard final drive ratio: 3.73:1. Front suspension: Modified MacPherson strut with 1.106-in. diameter stabilizer bar. Rear suspension: Torque arm. Brakes: Power front disc/rear drum. Fuel tank capacity: 15.8 gal. with four-cylinder engine; 16.2 gal. with V-6 or V-8.

Berlinetta: Standard transmission: Five-speed manual. Standard final drive ratio: (Five-speed) 3.23:1, (Automatic) 3.08:1. Front suspension: Modified MacPherson strut with 1.106-in. diameter stabilizer bar. Rear suspension: Torque arm. Brakes: Power front disc/rear drum. Fuel tank capacity: 16.2 gal.

Phil Kunz photo

The Camaro base coupe was available with four-, six- and eight-cylinder engines for the third straight year in 1984.

Z28: Standard transmission: Five-speed manual. Standard final drive ratio: (Five-speed) 3.23:1, (Automatic) 3.08:1, (TPI V-8) 3.23:1. Front suspension: Modified MacPherson strut with 1.22-in. diameter stabilizer bar. Rear suspension: Torque arm. Brakes Power front disc/rear drum. Fuel tank capacity: 16.2 gal.

OPTIONS

173-cid two-barrel V-6 ($250). 305-cid four-barrel V-8 ($550). 305-cid four-barrel H.O. V-8 in Z28 ($530). Five-speed manual transmission in base Camaro ($125). Four-speed overdrive automatic transmission in base Camaro ($525). Limited-slip differential ($95). Performance axle ratio ($21). Power four-wheel disc brakes in Camaro V-8 ($179). F41 Sport suspension ($49). Heavy-duty cooling ($40-$70). Engine block heater ($20). Air conditioning ($730). Rear defogger, electric ($140). Cruise control ($175-$185). Tinted glass ($110). Comfortilt steering wheel ($110). Six-way power driver's seat ($215). Power windows ($185). Power door locks ($125). Power hatch release ($40). Electric clock ($35). Gauge package with tachometer ($149). Intermittent windshield wipers ($50). Rear wiper/washer ($120). Quiet Sound group ($72-$82). Halogen high-beam headlamps ($10). Auxiliary lighting ($37-$72). Dual horns ($12). Twin sport mirrors left-hand remote controlled, on base Camaro ($53). Twin electric remote sport mirrors ($91-$139). AM radio ($112). AM/FM radio ($171). Electronic-tuning AM/FM stereo radio ($263); with clock ($267-$302); with cassette and clock ($367-$402); with cassette, clock and seek/scan ($570-$605). Dual rear speakers ($30). Fixed mast antenna, included with radios ($41). Power antenna ($60). Removable glass roof panels ($825). Rear spoiler ($69). Black body side moldings ($55). Door edge guards ($15). Roof drip molding ($29). Console ($50). Cloth bucket seats ($28). Custom cloth or vinyl bucket seats in base Camaro ($359); in Z28 ($287). Cloth LS contour bucket seats ($375). Custom cloth LS contour bucket seats Camaro ($650). Front mats with carpeted inserts ($20). Rear mat with carpeted inserts ($15). Cargo area cover ($69). Deluxe trunk trim in Camaro ($164); in Z28 ($84). Locking rear storage cover ($80). Rally wheels ($112). Full wheel covers ($52). Wire wheel covers ($159). P195/75R14 GBR WSW: Camaro ($62). P195/75R14 SBR WSW: Monte ($62). P205/70R14 steel-belted radial black sidewall tires on base Camaro ($58). P205/70R14 steel-belted radial white sidewall tires ($124). P205/70R14 white-letter steel-belted radial tires ($146). P215/65R15 steel-belted black sidewall tires on Z28 ($92 credit).

HISTORICAL FOOTNOTES

Introduced: Sept. 22, 1983. Chevrolet Motor Division's model-year sales finished nearly 23 percent higher than the 1983 result, with all lines (except Citation) performing well. To help plan for the enthusiast's market, surveys revealed that nearly two-thirds of Camaro buyers were under age 35. *Road & Track* magazine called the '84 Camaro one of the dozen top enthusiast cars, and it tied with Trans Am for best Sports GT in its price league. The International Race of Champions returned to the racing circuit during 1984 after a three-year absence. Co-sponsored by Chevrolet, Anheuser-Busch, Goodyear and True Value Hardware, the races would put a dozen of the world's top drivers behind the wheel of identically prepared Camaro Z28s. The IROC racing series had begun in 1974 using Porsches, then switched to Camaros. With heavy TV coverage, this year's races would draw considerable attention to Camaro and perhaps help pave the way for the soon-to-come IROC-Z production models. On another level, Chevrolet hosted a traveling Chevy Sports Hall of Fame show in urban shopping malls this year as part of greatly increased advertising and promotional expenditures. Robert D. Burger remained Chevrolet's general manager. Model-year sales rose from 175,004 in 1983 to 207,285 in 1984. Calendar year sales wound up at 202,172 or 8.5 percent of the industry total. Model-year production of 261,591 Camaros represented a 3.21 percent share of the industry's total. The Van Nuys plant reported building 160,862 Camaros (and 77,542 Firebirds). The Norwood factory built 100,729 Camaros (and 50,762 Firebirds). Of the Camaros built, 79.7 percent had automatic transmission, 2 percent had a four-speed manual transmission, 18.3 percent had a five-speed manual transmission, 3.9 percent had a four-cylinder engine, 57.4 percent had a V-8, and 38.7 percent had a V-6.

The 1985 IROC-Z had rocker panel striping and some other exterior features that set it apart.

A hotter IROC-Z version of the Z28 arrived in 1985. It was styled along the lines of the Camaros that competed in the International Race of Champions. Front fog lights, a ground-hugging front air dam, ornamental hood louvers, door decals and rocker panel striping set it off. Special 16 x 8-in. aluminum wheels carried P245-/50VR16 Goodyear Eagle GT unidirectional tires. The chassis featured Delco/Bilstein rear shocks, special struts and springs, a special rear stabilizer and reinforced front frame rails.

Any of three 5.0-liter (305-cid) V-8s were available and the top TPI version came only with a four-speed automatic transmission. Individually tuned runners channeled incoming air to each cylinder and computer-controlled port injectors delivered precisely metered fuel. The Berlinetta got a 2.8-liter MFI V-6 as standard equipment. Also new were body graphics and subtly patterned interior fabrics. The Sport Coupe offered V-6 and V-8 engines. Like the Z28, it had new styling, a wider selection of sound systems and revised optional instrument cluster graphics. The double-needle speedometer was abandoned.

All Camaros had new "wet arm" windshield wipers with washer outlets on the blades. Split rear seat backs were a new option and Z28-style cast-aluminum wheels were available on the base Camaro.

I.D. DATA

Chevrolets again had a 17-symbol vehicle identification number (VIN) on the upper left surface of the instrument panel, visible through the windshield. The first symbol identifies country of origin: 1=U.S.A., 2=Canada. The second symbol identifies the manufacturer: G=General Motors. The third symbol indicates make: 1=Chevrolet, 7=GM of Canada. The fourth symbol indicates restraint system: A=non-passive manual belts, B=passive automatic belts, C=passive inflatable (airbag). The fifth symbol indicates the car line/series: P=Camaro,

S=Camaro Berlinetta. The sixth and seventh symbols indicate body type: 87=two-door plain back special coupe. The eighth symbol indicates the engine type: 2=RPO LQ9 2.5-liter (151-cid) inline four-cylinder with Electronic Fuel Injection; S=RPO LB8 2.8-liter (173-cid) HO V-6 with Multiport Fuel Injection; H=RPO LG4 5.0-liter (305-cid) V-8 with four-barrel carburetor; G=RPO L69 5.0-liter (305-cid) High Output V-8 with four-barrel carburetor; F=RPO LB9 5.0-liter (305-cid) V-8 with Tuned Port Injection. The ninth symbol is a check digit. The 10th symbol indicates model year: F=1985. The 11th symbol indicates the assembly plant: L=Van Nuys, California, N=Norwood, Ohio. The final six digits are the sequential serial number.

COLORS

White, Silver Metallic, Medium Gray Metallic, Black, Dark Blue, Bright Blue Metallic, Yellow, Light Yellow, Light Brown Metallic, Copper Metallic, Red and Maroon.

CAMARO SPORT COUPE - SERIES 1F - FOUR/V-6/V-8

The base Camaro Sport Coupe had new body styling, a wider selection of optional sound systems with electronic-tuning radios and revised optional instrument cluster graphics. Standard equipment included manual lap/shoulder belts for driver and front passenger, driver side audible and visible safety belt warning system, manual lap belts at each rear seating position, an energy-absorbing steering column, an energy-absorbing instrument panel, energy-absorbing front seat tops, laminated safety glass (windshield, side glass and rear glass), safety interlocking door latches, passenger-guard inside door handles, inertia-locking folding front seatbacks, safety armrests, safety strength seat attachments, front seat head restraints, side marker lights and reflectors, parking lamps that illuminated with the headlights, a four-way hazard warning flasher, back-up lights, directional signals with lane-change feature, windshield defroster, windshield washer, dual-speed windshield wipers, an inside rearview mirror with vinyl bonded glass, black outside left and right rearview mirrors, a brake system with a dual master cylinder and warning light, a starter safety switch, a dual-action hood latch system, low-glare instrument panel finish, low-glare inside windshield moldings, low-glare wiper arms and blades, low-glare metallic steering wheel surfaces, illuminated heater and defroster controls, tires with built-in tread-wear indicators, an audible reminder for ignition key removal, an anti-theft steering column lock, a visible VIN, Argent Silver wheels and hubcaps, an AM radio (could be deleted for credit), a carpeted cargo floor with storage well, a hinged-cover front stowage console, reclining front bucket seats, front disc brake audible wear sensors, a 1.1-in. diameter front stabilizer bar, P195/75R-14 all-season steel-belted radial ply black sidewall tires, a power front disc/rear drum braking system, power steering, a torque arm rear suspension, an RPO LQ9 2.5-liter inline four-cylinder engine with electronic fuel injection (EFI) and a five-speed manual transmission.

Model Number	Body/Style Number	Body Type & Seating	Factory Price	Shipping Weight	Production Total
CAMARO SPORT COUPE - SERIES 1F - (L-4)					
P	87	2d coupe	$8,363	2,813 lbs.	Note 1
CAMARO SPORT COUPE - SERIES 1F - (V-6)					
P	87	2d coupe	$8,698	2,907 lbs.	Note 1
CAMARO SPORT COUPE - SERIES 1F - (V-8)					
P	87	2d coupe	$8,998	3,091 lbs.	Note 1

Note 1: Model-year production of 1985 base Camaros was 97,966 (3,318 four-cylinder, 72,652 six-cylinder and 21,996 V-8).

CAMARO BERLINETTA - SERIES 1F - V-6

Chevrolet described the 1985 Camaro Berlinetta as the "fullest expression of poetry in motion." The Berlinetta got a new standard 173-cid (2.8-liter) V-6 with Multiport Fuel Injection and only one engine option: the carbureted 5.0-liter V-8. Also new were body graphics and subtly patterned interior fabrics. Basic standard equipment for the Berlinetta included manual lap/shoulder belts for driver and front passenger, driver side audible and visible safety belt warning system, manual lap belts at each rear seating position, an energy-absorbing steering column, an energy-absorbing instrument panel, energy-absorbing front seat tops, laminated safety glass (windshield, side glass and rear glass), safety interlocking door latches, passenger-guard inside door handles, inertia-locking folding front seatbacks, safety armrests, safety strength seat attachments, front seat head restraints, side marker lights and reflectors, parking lamps that illuminated with the headlights, a four-way hazard warning flasher, backup lights, directional signals with lane-change features, windshield defroster, windshield washer, dual-speed windshield wipers, an inside rearview mirror with vinyl bonded glass, outside left and right rearview mirrors, a brake system with a dual master cylinder and warning light, a starter safety switch, a dual-action hood latch system, low-glare instrument panel finish, low-glare inside windshield moldings, low-glare wiper arms and blades, low-glare metallic steering wheel surfaces, illuminated heater and defroster controls, tires with built-in tread-wear indicators, an audible reminder for ignition key removal, an anti-theft steering column lock and a visible VIN. The Berlinetta also came standard with body pin striping, a color-accented lower body, a carpeted cargo floor with stowage well, hinged-cover console stowage, an electronically tuned four-speaker AM/FM stereo radio (with swivel remote control, seek-and-scan, digital display and clock, tuning graphs, front coaxial speakers and extended-range rear speakers), reclining front bucket seats, a 2.8-liter Multiport Fuel-Injected V-6, a five-speed manual transmission, a front disc/rear drum brake system with audible front wear sensors, P205/70R-14 all-season steel-belted radial-ply black sidewall tires, power steering, a torque arm rear suspension and a tachometer.

Model Number	Body/Style Number	Body Type & Seating	Factory Price	Shipping Weight	Production Total
CAMARO BERLINETTA - SERIES 1F - (V-6)					
S	87	2d coupe	$11,060	2,919 lbs.	Note 2
CAMARO BERLINETTA - SERIES 1F - (V-8)					
S	87	2d coupe	$11,360	3,157 lbs.	Note 2

Note 2: Model-year production of 1985 Camaro Berlinettas was 13,649 (5,663 six-cylinder and 7,986 V-8).

CAMARO Z28 - SERIES 1F - V-8

The Z28 came with the standard or TPI versions of the 5.0-liter V-8, but not the carbureted H.O. version.

The Z28 sported a front air dam and "ground-effects" rocker moldings, a rear deck lid spoiler, and silver- or gold-accented lower body with striping.

Jerry Heasley photo

The IROC-Z was the muscle car of the Camaro line, and could be had with three different 305-cid engines.

Z28s in general had a selection of changes in appearance details, including grille and parking lamps, deeper ground-effects rocker panels, hood louvers, a deeper chin spoiler, three-element taillights, a larger rear bumper fascia and new body nameplates. Inside were new speedometer graphics and a tachometer. Standard equipment included manual lap/shoulder belts for driver and front passenger, driver side audible and visible safety belt warning system, manual lap belts at each rear seating position, an energy-absorbing steering column, an energy-absorbing instrument panel, energy-absorbing front seat tops, laminated safety glass (windshield, side glass and rear glass), safety interlocking door latches, passenger-guard inside door handles, inertia-locking folding front seat backs, safety armrests, safety strength seat attachments, front seat head restraints, side marker lights and reflectors, parking lamps that illuminated with the headlights, a four-way hazard warning flasher, back-up lights, directional signals with lane-change features, windshield defroster, windshield washer, dual-speed windshield wipers, an inside rearview mirror with vinyl bonded glass, outside left and right rearview mirrors, a brake system with a dual master cylinder and warning light, a starter safety switch, a dual-action hood latch system, low-glare instrument panel finish, low-glare inside windshield moldings, low-glare wiper arms and blades, low-glare metallic steering wheel surfaces, illuminated heater and defroster controls, tires with built-in tread-wear indicators, an audible reminder for ignition key removal, an anti-theft steering column lock and a visible VIN. Also included as standard Z28 features were dual sport mirrors (left-hand remote control and right-hand manual). A front air dam and "ground-effects" rocker moldings, a rear deck lid spoiler, a Silver- or Gold-accented lower body with striping, an AM radio (could be deleted for credit), a carpeted cargo floor with stowage

well, hinged-cover console stowage, reclining front bucket seats, a 5.0-liter four-barrel V-8, a five-speed manual transmission, a front disc/rear drum braking system with audible front break pad wear sensors, a 1.3-in. front stabilizer bar, P215/65R-15 all-season steel-belted radial-ply black sidewall tires, a torque arm rear suspension, power steering and a tachometer.

Model Number	Body/Style Number	Body Type & Seating	Factory Price	Shipping Weight	Production Total
CAMARO Z28 - SERIES 1F - (V-8)					
1P	87	2d coupe	$11,060	3,107 lbs.	Note 3

Note 3: Model-year production of 1985 Camaro Z28s was 47,226 (all V-8).

CAMARO IROC-Z - SERIES 1F - V-8

The most appealing model-option for real Camaro connoisseurs was the new IROC-Z. This car was styled along the lines of the racing models that performed in the International Race of Champions. The IROC-Z was packaged as a Z28 option. In appearance, it could be spotted by twin fog lamps inset in the grille opening (alongside the license plate mount), a low front air dam, ornamental hood louvers and striping at rocker panel level. IROC-Zs had a solid angled front panel between deeply recessed quad headlamps, with parking lamps just below the crease line. Deep body-color "ground effects" skirting encircled the entire car. Special 16 x 8-in. aluminum wheels held Corvette-inspired P245-/50VR16 Goodyear Eagle GT unidirectional tires. Near the base of each door were large "IROC-Z" decals. The IROC-Z chassis featured Delco-Bilstein rear shock absorbers, special struts and springs, special rear stabilizer, and reinforced front frame rails. The IROC-Z could have any of three 305-cid (5.0-liter) V-8s. The standard engine had a four-barrel carburetor and five-speed manual gearbox (a four-speed overdrive automatic was available). The other choices were a High Output L69 carbureted V-8 with a five-speed transmission or the new LB9 Tuned Port Injection (TPI) version. The TPI came only with a four-speed automatic transmission. Individually tuned runners channeled incoming air to each cylinder in the TPI V-8, while computer-controlled port injectors delivered precisely metered fuel. In limited-production IROC-Z dress, the factory claimed a 0 to 60-mph time in the 7-sec. bracket and 15-sec. quarter-mile acceleration times. Basic standard equipment included manual lap/shoulder belts for driver and front passenger, a driver side audible and visible safety belt warning system, manual lap belts at each rear seating position, an energy-absorbing steering column, an energy-absorbing instrument panel, energy-absorbing front seat tops, laminated safety glass (windshield, side glass and rear glass), safety interlocking door latches, passenger-guard inside door handles, inertia-locking folding front seat backs, safety armrests, safety strength seat attachments, front seat head restraints, side marker lights and reflectors, parking lamps that illuminated with the headlights, a four-way hazard warning flasher, back-up lights, directional signals with lane-change features, windshield defroster, windshield washer, dual-speed windshield wipers, an inside rearview mirror with vinyl bonded glass, outside left and right rearview mirrors, a brake system with a dual master cylinder and warning light, a starter safety switch, a dual-action hood latch system, low-glare instrument panel finish, low-glare inside windshield moldings, low-glare wiper arms and blades, low-glare metallic steering wheel surfaces, illuminated heater and defroster controls, tires with built-in tread-wear indicators, an audible reminder for ignition key removal, an anti-theft steering column lock and a visible VIN. Also included as standard equipment on the IROC-Z were dual sport mirrors (left-hand remote-control mirror and right-hand manual-adjustable mirror), new extended Z28-type "ground-effects" rocker panels, a larger front air dam, fog lamps, special IROC-Z badges inside and out, hood louvers, a leather-wrapped steering wheel, a rear deck lid spoiler, an AM radio (could be deleted for credit), a carpeted cargo floor with stowage well, hinged-cover console stowage, reclining front bucket seats, a five-speed manual transmission, a front disc/rear drum braking system with audible front break pad wear sensors, P245/50VR-16 unidirectional high-performance

The Camaro Custom interior included a Comfortilt steering wheel and new striped fabric, and was available with a six-way power driver's seat.

tires (that had been pioneered on the Corvette), 16-in. aluminum wheels, quick-response power steering with 2.5 turns lock to lock and high-effort valving, a modified MacPherson-strut front suspension with increased camber for optimal response, specific strut valving to provide excellent wheel control, a mass-efficient rear suspension with two short control arms and Bilstein gas shocks, a larger-diameter stabilizer bar, power front disc/rear drum brakes and a tachometer.

Model Number	Body/Style Number	Body Type & Seating	Factory Price	Shipping Weight	Production Total
1P	87	2d coupe	$11,719	3,157 lbs.	Note 4

Note 4: Model-year production of 1985 Camaro IROC-Zs was 21,177 (all V-8).
Note 5: Chevrolet production figures also show 204 Z28E hatchback Sport Coupes (not included in U.S. production).

ENGINE

LQ9 Base four cylinder: Inline. Overhead-valve four-cylinder. Cast-iron block and head. Bore & stroke: 4.00 x 3.00 in. Displacement: 151 cid (2.5 liters). Compression ratio: 9.0:1. Brake horsepower: 88 at 4400 rpm. Torque: 132 lbs.-ft. at 2800 rpm. Five main bearings. Hydraulic valve lifters. Induction system: Throttle body injection. Pontiac-built. Standard in Sport Coupe. VIN Code 2.

LB8 V-6: 60-degree, overhead-valve V-6. Cast-iron block and head. Bore & stroke: 3.50 x 2.99 in. Displacement: 173 cid (2.8 liters). Compression ratio: 8.5:1. Compression ratio: 8.9:1. Brake horsepower: 135 at 5100 rpm. Torque: 165 lbs.-ft. at 3600 rpm. Induction system: Multiport Fuel Injection. Standard in Berlinetta. Optional in Sport Coupe. VIN Code S.

LG4 Base V-8: 90-degree, overhead-valve V-8. Cast-iron block and head. Bore & stroke: 3.74 x 3.48 in. Displacement: 305 cid (5.0 liters). Compression ratio: 9.5:1. Brake horsepower: 155 at 4200 rpm Torque: 245 lbs.-ft. at 2000 rpm Five main bearings. Hydraulic valve lifters. Induction system: four-barrel carburetor. Standard in Z28 and IROC Z. Optional in Sport Coupe and Berlinetta. VIN Code: H.

L69 H.O. V-8: 90-degree, overhead-valve V-8. Cast-iron block and head. Bore & stroke: 3.74 x 3.48 in. Displacement: 305 cid (5.0 liters). Compression ratio: 9.5:1. Brake horsepower: 190 at 4800 rpm Torque: 240 lbs.-ft. at 3200 rpm Five main bearings. Hydraulic valve lifters. Induction system: four-barrel carburetor. Optional in Z28. Optional in IROC-Z. VIN Code: G.

LB9 Optional TPI V-8: 90-degree, overhead-valve V-8. Cast-iron block and head. Bore & stroke: 3.74 x 3.48 in. Displacement: 305 cid (5.0 liters). Compression ratio: 9.5:1. Brake horsepower: 215 at 4400 rpm Torque: 275 lbs.-ft. at 3200 rpm Five main bearings. Hydraulic valve lifters. Electronic spark control. 3.0-in. front exhaust pipes and dual outlet muffler. Induction system: Tuned Port Injection. Optional in Z28. Optional in IROC-Z. VIN Code: F.

CHASSIS

Sport Coupe: Wheelbase: 101 in. Overall length: 188 in. Overall height: 50 in. Overall width: 72.8 in. Front tread: 60.7 in. Rear tread: 61.6 in. Front headroom: 37 in. Rear headroom: 35.6 in. Front legroom: 43 in. Rear legroom: 28.9 in. Front shoulder room: 57.5 in. Rear shoulder room: 56.3 in. Front hip room: 56.3 in. Rear hip room: 42.8 in. Cargo volume: 12.4 cu. ft. (31 cu. ft. with rear seatback down). Standard tires: P195/75R14 steel-belted radial.

Berlinetta: Wheelbase: 101 in. Overall length: 188 in. Overall height: 50 in. Front tread: 60 in. Rear Tread: 60.9 in. Front headroom: 37 in. Rear headroom: 35.6 in. Front legroom: 43 in. Rear legroom: 28.9 in. Front shoulder room: 57.5 in. Rear shoulder room: 56.3 in. Front hip room: 56.3 in. Rear hip room: 42.8 in. Cargo volume: 12.4 cu. ft. (31 cu. ft. with rear seatback down). Standard tires: P205/70R14 steel-belted radial.

Z28: Wheelbase: 101 in. Overall length: 192 in. Overall height: 50.3 in. Front tread: 60 in. Rear tread: 60.9 in. Front headroom: 37 in. Rear headroom: 35.6 in. Front legroom: 43 in. Rear legroom: 28.9 in. Front shoulder room: 57.5 in. Rear shoulder room: 56.3 in. Front hip room: 56.3 in. Rear hip room: 42.8 in. Cargo volume: 12.4 cu. ft. (31 cu. ft. with rear seatback down). Standard tires: P215/65R15 white-letter steel-belted radial.

IROC-Z: Wheelbase: 101 in. Overall length: 192 in. Overall height: 50.3 in. Front tread: 60 in. Rear tread: 60.9 in. Front headroom: 37 in. Rear headroom: 35.6 in. Front legroom: 43 in. Rear legroom: 28.9 in. Front shoulder room: 57.5 in. Rear shoulder room: 56.3 in. Front hip room: 56.3 in. Rear hip room: 42.8 in. Cargo volume: 12.4 cu. ft. (31 cu. ft. with rear seatback down). Standard tires: P245/50VR16 white-letter steel-belted radial.

TECHNICAL

Sport Coupe: standard transmission: Five-speed manual (1st) 3.50:1; (2nd) 2.48:1; (3rd) 1.66:1; (4th) 1.00:1; (Rev) 3.50:1. Standard final drive ratio: 3.73:1. Front suspension: Modified MacPherson strut with 1.1-in. diameter stabilizer bar. Rear suspension: Torque arm. Brakes: Power front disc/rear drum. Fuel tank capacity: 15.5 gal.

Berlinetta: Standard transmission: Five-speed manual (1st) 3.50:1; (2nd) 2.14:1; (3rd) 1.36:1; (4th) 1.00:1; (5th) 0.78:1; (Rev) 3.39:1. Automatic transmission: Four-speed (1st) 3.06:1; (2nd) 1.63:1; (3rd) 1.00:1; (4th) 0.70:1; (Rev) 2.29:1. Standard final drive ratio: (Five-speed) 3.23:1, (Automatic) 3.08:1. Front suspension: Modified MacPherson strut with 1.1-in. diameter stabilizer bar. Rear suspension: Torque arm. Brakes: Power front disc/rear drum. Fuel tank capacity: 15.5 gal.

Z28: Standard transmission: Five-speed manual (1st) 2.95:1; (2nd) 1.94:1; (3rd) 1.34:1; (4th) 1.00:1; (5th) 0.73:1; (Rev) 2.76:1. Automatic transmission: Four-speed (1st) 3.06:1; (2nd) 1.63:1; (3rd) 1.00:1; (4th) 0.70:1; (Rev) 2.29:1. Standard final drive ratio: (Five-speed) 3.23:1, (Automatic) 3.08:1, (TPI V-8) 3.23:1. Front suspension: Modified MacPherson strut with 1.3-in. diameter stabilizer bar. Rear suspension: Torque arm. Brakes: Power front disc/rear drum. Fuel tank capacity: 16.2 gal.

IROC-Z: Standard transmission: Five-speed manual (1st) 2.95:1; (2nd) 1.94:1; (3rd) 1.34:1; (4th) 1.00:1; (5th) 0.73:1; (Rev) 2.76:1. Automatic transmission: Four-speed (1st) 3.06:1; (2nd) 1.63:1; (3rd) 1.00:1; (4th) 0.70:1; (Rev) 2.29:1. Standard final drive ratio: (Five-speed) 3.23:1, (Automatic) 3.08:1, (TPI V-8) 3.23:1, (H.O. V-8) 3.73:1. Front suspension: Modified MacPherson strut with increased caster for optimal steering response and 1.3-in. diameter stabilizer bar. Rear suspension: Mass-efficient torque arm type with Delco/Bilstein gas-filled shocks, two short control arms and larger diameter stabilizer bar. Brakes: Power front disc/rear drum. Fuel tank capacity: 16.2 gal.

OPTIONS

IROC-Z sport equipment package for Camaro Z28 ($659). Air conditioning ($730). Rear defogger ($140). Cruise control with resume ($175-$185). Tinted glass ($110). Comfortilt steering wheel ($110). Six-way power

Chuck Dunlap photo

An all-original 1985 Z/28 with T-tops and a five-speed like this one is a good bet to become a hit with collectors.

The Z28 had Conteur bucket seats that were available in three different colors.

driver's seat ($215). Power windows ($185). Power door locks ($125). Power hatch release ($40). Electric clock ($35). Gauge package including tachometer in Camaro Sport Coupe ($149). Intermittent wipers ($50). Rear wiper/washer on Camaro Sport Coupe ($120). Quiet sound group in Camaro ($72-$82). Halogen headlamps ($22). Auxiliary lighting: Camaro ($37-$72). Dual horns with Camaro Sport Coupe ($12). Twin sport mirrors (left remote control) with Camaro Sport Coupe ($53). Twin electric remote sport mirrors with Camaro Sport Coupe ($91-$139). AM/FM radio ($82). Electronic-tuning AM/FM stereo radio with Camaro Sport Coupe or Z28 ($173); with clock ($177-$212); with cassette, clock and seek-and-scan ($319-$354). AM stereo/FM with cassette, graphic equalizer and clock ($469-$504). Seek-and-scan AM/FM stereo with remote control in Berlinetta ($242). Dual rear speakers ($30). Power antenna ($60). Radio delete in Camaro Sport Coupe ($56 credit); in Berlinetta ($256 credit). Removable glass roof panels ($825). Rear spoiler on Camaro Sport Coupe ($69). Black body side moldings on Camaro Sport Coupe ($55). Door edge guards ($15). Roof console in Camaro Sport Coupe/Z28 ($50). Cloth bucket seats in Camaro Sport Coupe ($28). Custom cloth bucket seats in Camaro Sport Coupe or Z28 ($359). Custom cloth LS conteur bucket seats in Camaro Sport Coupe or Z28 ($650). Split folding back seat with Camaro Sport Coupe ($50). Mats with carpeted inserts for Camaro Sport Coupe front ($20); rear ($15). Cargo area cover with Camaro Sport Coupe ($69). Deluxe trunk trim with Camaro Sport Coupe ($164); with Z28 ($84). Locking rear storage cover for Camaro Sport Coupe ($80). Aluminum wheels, standard Z28, other models ($225). Rally wheels on Camaro Sport Coupe ($112). Full wheel covers on Camaro Sport Coupe ($52). P195/75R14 steel-belted-radial white sidewall on Camaro Sport Coupe ($62). P205/70R14 steel-belted-radial black sidewall on Camaro Sport Coupe ($58). P205/70R14 steel-belted-radial white sidewall on Camaro Sport Coupe ($124); on Berlinetta ($66). P205/70R14 steel-belted-radial white-letter on Camaro Sport Coupe ($146). P235/60VR15 steel-belted-radial black sidewall: Z28 ($85). LB8 173-cid V-6 in Camaro Sport Coupe ($435). LG4 305-cid V-8 in Camaro Sport Coupe ($635); in Berlinetta ($300). L69 305-cid H.O. V-8 in IROC-Z ($680). LB9 350-cid TPI V-8 in Z28 or

IROC-Z ($680). Five-speed manual transmission in Camaro Sport Coupe (no cost). Four-speed overdrive automatic transmission ($395). Limited-slip differential ($95). Performance axle ratio ($21). Power four-wheel disc brakes ($179). F41 heavy-duty suspension: ($49). Heavy-duty cooling ($40-$70). Engine block heater ($20). Heavy-duty battery ($26). California emission system ($99).

HISTORICAL FOOTNOTES

General introduction was Oct. 2, 1984, but the Camaro debuted on Nov. 8. During 1985, Chevrolet capitalized on its involvement with the International Race of Champions by creating the IROC-Z model-option for the Camaro Z28. This year's ad theme, "Today's Chevrolet," was focused on the new IROC-Z. The association between the racing series and the new Camaro model was enhanced by the syndication of a 30-minute-long IROC racing television program. A prototype "Customer Communications System" began test operation at selected Chevrolet dealerships. Prospects could view the benefits of Chevrolet ownership via touch-screen computer videodiscs with bold graphics. A "Commitment to Excellence" program provided enhanced pre-delivery inspection of each new car sold by a dealer, an orientation drive by the salesperson, and customer benefit package mailed to the owner after purchase. Robert D. Burger remained Chevrolet's general manager. Model-year sales fell slightly from 207,285 in 1984 to 206,082 in 1985. Calendar-year sales also wound up slightly down at 199,985, or 7.8 percent of the industry total. Model-year production of 180,018 Camaros represented a 2.30 percent share of the industry's total. The Van Nuys plant reported building 103,767 Camaros (and 54,874 Firebirds). The Norwood factory reported building 76,251 Camaros (and 41,006 Firebirds). Of the Camaros built, 84.8 percent had automatic transmission, 15.2 percent had a five-speed manual transmission, 1.8 percent had a four-cylinder engine, 36.5 percent had a V-8 with a carburetor, 18.2 percent had a fuel-injected V-8, 43.5 percent had a V-6, 100 percent had power steering, 88 percent had power front disc brakes, 11.2 percent had power four-wheel disc brakes, 8.6 percent had a limited-slip differential, 100 percent had steel-belted radial tires, 39.3 percent had power door locks, 49.2 percent had power windows, 100 percent had reclining bucket seats, 17.9 percent had a power front driver's seat, 75.4 percent had tilt steering, 92.9 percent had all-tinted glass, 81.3 percent had manual air conditioning, 47.2 percent had cruise control, 8.2 percent had an AM radio, 6.3 percent had an AM/FM radio, 25.2 percent had an AM/FM stereo radio, 34.8 percent had a stereo cassette player, 19.3 had a Bose premium sound system, 4.7 percent had a analog clock, 69.6 percent had a digital clock, 66.3 percent had an electric rear window defogger, 4.1 percent had a rear window wiper, 97.8 percent had a remote-control left-hand outside rearview mirror, 12.1 percent also had a remote-control right-hand outside rearview mirror, 42.4 percent had aluminum styled wheels, 50.5 percent had styled steel wheels and 35.3 percent had T-tops. A total of 200,091 new Camaros were registered in the U.S. during calendar year 1985. That was up from 198,624 in 1984.

Camaro

Jerry Heasley photo

The IROC-Z had distinctive twin fog lamps inset into the grille opening, a low front air dam, ornamental hood louvers and striping at the rocker panel level.

Base Camaros could be optioned to look like Z28s this year. When ordered with either the 2.8-liter V-6 or 5.0-liter V-8 they came with a sport suspension, P215/65R15 tires, 15 x 7-in. styled steel wheels and a sport-tone exhaust system. Even four-cylinder Camaros got the sport suspension and 14-in. styled wheels. All Camaros got an air conditioning cutout switch, for use when full power was needed, and an upshift indicator was added to stick shift models. The rear hatch got a new automatic pull-down latch. Also new was a soft-feel leather steering wheel, shift lever and parking brake lever. Body side moldings now came in eight colors (or black on Sport Coupes).

The IROC-Z and Z28 were virtually unchanged except for new colors. The base coupe included black lower body accents, black windshield and drip moldings and color-keyed bumpers. Berlinettas added an electronic-tuning AM/FM stereo with a digital clock, dual horns, electronic instrumentation, a roof console, full wheel covers and a tachometer.

This was the last time that Camaro production totals approached the 200,000 level, although they fell short of that goal by nearly 8,000. The figures included 99,608 Sport Coupes, 4,479 Berlinettas, 88,132 Z28s and 49,585 IROC-Zs.

I.D. DATA

Chevrolets again had a 17-symbol vehicle identification number (VIN) on the upper left surface of the instrument panel, visible through the windshield. The first symbol identifies country of origin: 1=USA, 2=Canada. The second symbol identifies the manufacturer: G=General Motors. The third symbol indicates make: 1=Chevrolet, 7=GM of Canada. The fourth and fifth symbols now indicated the car line and series: F/P=Camaro Sport Coupe and F/S=Camaro Berlinetta. The sixth and seventh symbols indicated body type and restraint system: 87=two-door plain back special coupe. The eighth symbol indicates the engine type: 2=RPO LQ9 2.5-liter (151-cid) inline four-cylinder with Electronic Fuel Injection; S=RPO LB8 2.8-liter (173-cid) HO V-6 with Multi-Port Fuel Injection; H=RPO LG4 5.0-liter (305-cid) V-8 with four-barrel carburetor; G=RPO L69 5.0-liter (305-cid) High Output V-8 with four-barrel carburetor; F=RPO LB9 5.0-liter (305-cid) V-8 with Tuned Port Injection. The ninth symbol is a check digit. The 10th symbol indicates model year: G=1986. The 11th symbol indicates the assembly plant: L=Van Nuys, California, N=Norwood, Ohio. The final six digits are the sequential serial number.

COLORS

White, Silver Metallic, Medium Gray Metallic, Black, Dark Blue Metallic, Bright Blue Metallic, Yellow, Light Brown Metallic, Copper Metallic, Dark Brown Metallic, Dark Red Metallic and Bright Red.

CAMARO SPORT COUPE - SERIES F/P - FOUR/V-6/V-8

The 1986 Camaro Sport Coupe was identified by a new black accent band on the taillights and the use of Chevrolet lettering in place of the Camaro name on the rear fascia. It also gained the F41 sports suspension, P215/656-15 black sidewall steel-belted radial tires with raised white letters, 15 x 7-in. Rally wheels, wheel trim rings, black sport style outside rearview mirrors, black-out rocker panels, black-out-style fascias, special striping and a "sport tone" exhaust system. The standard interior used in the Sport Coupe featured new solid-tone trim materials and design. Wet-arm windshield wipers were made standard equipment on all Camaros. A new automatic closure feature was adopted for the rear hatch. At the rear, a new center high-mounted stoplight was seen. Black body side moldings were used on the

Sport Coupe and all Camaros now had basecoat/clearcoat finish. Standard equipment included manual lap/shoulder belts for driver and front passenger, driver side audible and visible safety belt warning system, manual lap belts at each rear seating position, an energy-absorbing steering column, an energy-absorbing instrument panel, energy-absorbing front seat tops, laminated safety glass (windshield, side glass and rear glass), safety interlocking door latches, passenger-guard inside door handles, inertia-locking folding front seat backs, safety armrests, safety strength seat attachments, front seat head restraints, side marker lights and reflectors, parking lamps that illuminated with the headlights, a four-way hazard warning flasher, back-up lights, directional signals with lane-change feature, windshield defroster, windshield washer, dual-speed windshield wipers, an inside rearview mirror with vinyl bonded glass, a brake system with a dual master cylinder and warning light, a starter safety switch, a dual-action hood latch system, low-glare instrument panel finish, low-glare inside windshield moldings, low-glare wiper arms and blades, low-glare metallic steering wheel surfaces, illuminated heater and defroster controls, tires with built-in tread-wear indicators, an audible reminder for ignition key removal, an anti-theft steering column lock, a visible VIN, Argent Silver wheels and hubcaps, an AM radio (could be deleted for credit), a carpeted cargo floor with storage well, a hinged-cover front stowage console, reclining front bucket seats, front disc brake audible wear sensors, a 1.1-in. diameter front stabilizer bar, a power front disc/rear drum braking system, power steering and a torque arm rear suspension. Historical sources indicate that the RPO LQ9 2.5-liter inline four-cylinder engine with electronic fuel injection (EFI) and a five-speed manual transmission was listed as the standard drive train for 1986 Camaros, although production totals seem to indicate that no four-cylinder cars were built.

Model Number	Body/Style Number	Body Type & Seating	Factory Price	Shipping Weight	Production Total
CAMARO SPORT COUPE - SERIES F/P - (L-4)					
F/P	87	2d coupe	$9,035	2,871 lbs.	Note 1
CAMARO SPORT COUPE - SERIES F/P - (V-6)					
F/P	87	2d coupe	$9,285	2,912 lbs.	Note 1
CAMARO SPORT COUPE - SERIES F/P - (V-8)					
F/P	87	2d coupe	$9,685	3,071 lbs.	Note 1

Note 1: Model-year production of 1986 base Camaros was 99,608.

CAMARO BERLINETTA SERIES 1F/S - V-6

The Berlinetta added a few items to the standard equipment list such as an electronic-tuning AM/FM stereo radio with a digital clock, dual horns, electronic instruments, a locking rear storage cover, dome and map lights, color-keyed sport mirrors (left-hand remote controlled), intermittent windshield wipers, a roof console, full wheel covers and a tachometer. It also featured body-color belt moldings in any of eight colors or black, color-keyed lower accent paint with striping and custom cloth reclining front bucket seats. It lacked rocker panel moldings or a rear stabilizer bar. Other standard equipment for the Berlinetta included manual lap/shoulder belts for driver and front passenger, driver side audible and visible safety belt warning system, manual lap belts at each rear seating position, an energy-absorbing steering column, an energy-absorbing instrument panel, energy-absorbing front seat tops, laminated safety glass (windshield, side glass and rear glass), safety interlocking door latches, passenger-guard inside door handles, inertia-locking folding front seat backs, safety armrests, safety strength seat attachments, front seat head restraints, side marker lights and reflectors, parking lamps that illuminated with the headlights, a four-way hazard warning flasher, back-up lights, directional signals with lane-change features, a windshield defroster, windshield washers, dual-speed windshield wipers, an inside

The 1986 Camaro Sport Coupe received a new suspension and Rally wheels.

Jerry Heasley photo

rearview mirror with vinyl bonded glass, a brake system with a dual master cylinder and warning light, a starter safety switch, a dual-action hood latch system, low-glare instrument panel finish, low-glare inside windshield moldings, low-glare wiper arms and blades, low-glare metallic steering wheel surfaces, illuminated heater and defroster controls, tires with built-in tread-wear indicators, an audible reminder for ignition key removal, an anti-theft steering column lock, a visible VIN, a carpeted cargo floor with stowage well, a 2.8-liter Multiport Fuel-Injected V-6, a five-speed manual transmission, a front disc/rear drum brake system with audible front wear sensors, P205/70R-14 all-season steel-belted radial-ply black sidewall tires, power steering and a torque-arm rear suspension.

Model Number	Body/Style Number	Body Type & Seating	Factory Price	Shipping Weight	Production Total
CAMARO BERLINETTA - SERIES F/S - (V-6)					
F/S	87	2d coupe	$11,902	2,983 lbs.	Note 2
CAMARO BERLINETTA - SERIES F/S - (V-8)					
F/S	87	2d coupe	$12,302	3,162 lbs.	Note 2

Note 2: Model-year production of 1986 Camaro Berlinettas was 99,608.

CAMARO Z28 - SERIES 1F - V-8

The solid-tone interior introduced on the 1986 Camaro Sport Coupe was also new on the Z28, which was technically an option package for the base Camaro. It also offered body side moldings in eight colors and black. Standard equipment included manual lap/shoulder belts for driver and front passenger, driver side audible and visible safety belt warning system, manual lap belts at each rear seating position, an energy-absorbing steering column, an energy-absorbing instrument panel, energy-absorbing front seat tops, laminated safety glass (windshield, side glass and rear glass), safety interlocking door latches, passenger-guard inside door handles, inertia-locking folding front seat backs, safety armrests, safety strength seat attachments, front seat head restraints, side marker lights and reflectors, parking lamps that illuminated with the headlights, a four-way

hazard warning flasher, back-up lights, directional signals with lane-change feature, windshield defroster, windshield washer, dual-speed windshield wipers, an inside rearview mirror with vinyl bonded glass, outside left and right rearview mirrors, a brake system with a dual master cylinder and warning light, a starter safety switch, a dual-action hood latch system, low-glare instrument panel finish, low-glare inside windshield moldings, low-glare wiper arms and blades, low-glare metallic steering wheel surfaces, illuminated heater and defroster controls, tires with built-in tread-wear indicators, an audible reminder for ignition key removal, an anti-theft steering column lock and a visible VIN. Also included as standard Z28 features were dual Sport mirrors (left-hand remote control and right-hand manual). A front air dam and "ground effects" rocker moldings, a rear deck lid spoiler, a silver- or gold-accented lower body with striping, an AM radio (could be deleted for credit), a carpeted cargo floor with stowage well, hinged-cover console stowage, reclining front bucket seats, a 5.0-liter four-barrel V-8, a five-speed manual transmission, a front disc/rear drum braking system with audible front break pad wear sensors, a 1.3-in. front stabilizer bar, P215/65R-15 all-season steel-belted radial ply black sidewall tires, a torque arm rear suspension, power steering and a tachometer.

Model Number	Body/Style Number	Body Type & Seating	Factory Price	Shipping Weight	Production Total
F/P	87	2d coupe	$11,902	3,121 lbs.	Note 3

Note 3: Combined model-year production of 1986 Camaros Z28s and IROC-Zs was 88,132.

CAMARO IROC-Z - SERIES F/P - V-8

The IROC-Z was once again a Z28 option package. It featured twin fog lamps inset into the grille opening (alongside the license plate mount), a low front air dam, ornamental hood louvers and striping at rocker panel level. IROC-Z had a solid angled front panel between deeply recessed quad headlamps, with parking lamps just below the crease line. Deep body-color "ground

The Z28 (above) and IROC-Z models continued to be popular for 1987, with a combined 88,132 Z-cars being produced.

Sport Coupes could be had with four-, six-, and eight-cylinder engines for 1987.

effects" skirting encircled the entire car. Special 16 x 8-in. aluminum wheels held Corvette-inspired P245-/50VR16 Goodyear Eagle GT unidirectional tires. Near the base of each door were large "IROC-Z" decals. The IROC-Z chassis featured Delco-Bilstein rear shock absorbers, special struts and springs, special rear stabilizer and reinforced front frame rails. The IROC-Z could have any of three 305-cid (5.0-liter) V-8s: a standard four-barrel with five-speed manual gearbox (four-speed overdrive automatic available), an optional High Output L69 carbureted V-8 with five-speed or the new LB9 Tuned Port Injected (TPI) version. The TPI V-8 came only with four-speed automatic transmission. Individually tuned runners channeled incoming air to each cylinder in the TPI V-8, while computer-controlled port injectors delivered precisely metered fuel. In limited-production IROC-Z dress, the factory claimed a 0 to 60-mph time in the 7-sec. neighborhood and 15-sec. quarter-mile acceleration times. Basic standard equipment included manual lap/shoulder belts for driver and front passenger, driver side audible and visible safety belt warning system, manual lap belts at each rear seating position, an energy-absorbing steering column, an energy-absorbing instrument panel, energy-absorbing front seat tops, laminated safety glass (windshield, side glass and rear glass), safety interlocking door latches, passenger-guard inside door handles, inertia-locking folding front seat backs, safety armrests, safety strength seat attachments, front seat head restraints, side marker lights and reflectors, parking lamps that illuminated with the headlights, a four-way hazard warning flasher, back-up lights, directional signals with lane-change feature, windshield defroster, windshield washer, dual-speed windshield wipers, an inside rearview mirror with vinyl bonded glass, outside left and right rearview mirrors, a brake system with a dual master cylinder and warning light, a starter safety switch, a dual-action hood latch system, low-glare instrument panel finish, low-glare inside windshield moldings, low-glare wiper arms and blades, low-glare metallic steering wheel surfaces, illuminated heater and defroster controls, tires with built-in tread-wear indicators, an audible reminder for ignition key removal, an anti-theft steering column lock and a visible VIN. Also

included as standard on the IROC-Z were dual sport mirrors (left-hand remote control and right-hand manual), new extended Z28-type ground-effects rocker panels, a larger front air dam, fog lamps, special IROC-Z badges inside and out, hood louvers, a leather-wrapped steering wheel, a rear deck lid spoiler, an AM radio (could be deleted for credit), a carpeted cargo floor with stowage well, hinged-cover console stowage, reclining front bucket seats, a five-speed manual transmission, a front disc/rear drum braking system with audible front break pad wear sensors, P245/50VR-16 unidirectional high-performance tires (that had been pioneered on the Corvette), 16-in. aluminum wheels, quick-response power steering with 2.5 turns lock to lock and high-effort valving, a modified MacPherson strut front suspension with increased camber for optimal response, specific strut valving to provide excellent wheel control, a mass-efficient rear suspension with two short control arms and Bilstein gas shocks, a larger-diameter stabilizer bar, power front disc/rear drum brakes and a tachometer.

Model Number	Body/Style Number	Body Type & Seating	Factory Price	Shipping Weight	Production Total
CAMARO IROC-Z - SERIES F/P - (V-8)					
F/P	87	2d coupe	$12,561	3,157 lbs.	Note 4

Note 4: Combined model-year production of 1986 Camaros Z28s and IROC-Zs was 88,132.

ENGINES

LQ9 base four: Inline. Overhead-valve four-cylinder. Cast-iron block and head. Bore & stroke: 4.00 x 3.00 in. Displacement: 151 cid (2.5 liters). Compression ratio: 9.0:1. Brake horsepower: 88 at 4400 rpm. Torque: 130 lbs.-ft. at 2800 rpm. Five main bearings. Hydraulic valve lifters. Induction system: Throttle body injection. Pontiac-built. Standard in Camaro Sport Coupe. VIN Code 2. Note: Production total by engines indicate no cars were built with four-cylinder engines.

LB8 V-6: 60-degree, overhead-valve V-6. Cast-iron block and head. Bore & stroke: 3.50 x 2.99 in. Displacement: 173 cid (2.8 liters). Compression ratio: 8.5:1. Compression ratio: 8.9:1. Brake horsepower: 135 at 5100 rpm. Torque: 160 lbs.-ft. at 3900 rpm. Induction system: Multiport Fuel Injection. Standard in Camaro Berlinetta. Optional in Camaro Sport Coupe. VIN Code

S.

LG4 base V-8: 90-degree, overhead-valve V-8. Cast-iron block and head. Bore & stroke: 3.74 x 3.48 in. Displacement: 305 cid (5.0 liters). Compression ratio: 9.5:1. Brake horsepower: 165 at 4400 rpm Torque: 250 lbs.-ft. at 2000 rpm Five main bearings. Hydraulic valve lifters. Induction system: four-barrel carburetor. Standard in Z28 and IROC-Z. Optional in Camaro Sport Coupe and Camaro Berlinetta. VIN Code: H.

L69 H.O. V-8: 90-degree, overhead-valve V-8. Cast-iron block and head. Bore & stroke: 3.74 x 3.48 in. Displacement: 305 cid (5.0 liters). Compression ratio: 9.5:1. Brake horsepower: 190 at 4800 rpm Torque: 240 lbs.-ft. at 3200 rpm Five main bearings. Hydraulic valve lifters. Induction system: four-barrel carburetor. Optional in Z28. Optional in IROC-Z. VIN Code: G.

LB9 optional TPI V-8: 90-degree, overhead-valve V-8. Cast-iron block and head. Bore & stroke: 3.74 x 3.48 in. Displacement: 305 cid (5.0 liters). Compression ratio: 9.5:1. Brake horsepower: 190 at 4000 rpm Torque: 285 lbs.-ft. at 2800 rpm Five main bearings. Hydraulic valve lifters. Electronic spark control. 3.0-in. front exhaust pipes and dual outlet muffler. Induction system: Tuned Port Injection. Optional in Z28. Optional in IROC-Z. VIN Code: F.

CHASSIS

Sport Coupe: Wheelbase: 101 in. Overall length: 188 in. Overall height: 50 in. Overall width: 72.8 in. Front tread: 60.7 in. Rear tread: 61.6 in. Front headroom: 37 in. Rear headroom: 35.6 in. Front legroom: 43 in. Rear legroom: 28.9 in. Front shoulder room: 57.5 in. Rear shoulder room: 56.3 in. Front hip room: 56.3 in. Rear hip room: 42.8 in. Cargo volume: 12.4 cu. ft. (31 cu. ft. with rear seat back down). Standard tires: P195/75R14 steel-belted radial.

Berlinetta: Wheelbase: 101 in. Overall length: 188 in. Overall height: 50 in. Front tread: 60 in. Rear Tread: 60.9 in. Front headroom: 37 in. Rear headroom: 35.6 in. Front legroom: 43 in. Rear legroom: 28.9 in. Front shoulder room: 57.5 in. Rear shoulder room: 56.3 in. Front hip room: 56.3 in. Rear hip room: 42.8 in. Cargo volume: 12.4 cu. ft. (31 cu. ft. with rear seat back down). Standard tires: P205/70R14 steel-belted radial.

Z28: Wheelbase: 101 in. Overall length: 192 in. Overall height: 50.3 in. Front tread: 60 in. Rear tread: 60.9 in. Front headroom: 37 in. Rear headroom: 35.6 in. Front legroom: 43 in. Rear legroom: 28.9 in. Front shoulder room: 57.5 in. Rear shoulder room: 56.3 in. Front hip room: 56.3 in. Rear hip room: 42.8 in. Cargo volume: 12.4 cu. ft. (31 cu. ft. with rear seat back down). Standard tires: P215/65R15 white-letter steel-belted radial.

IROC-Z: Wheelbase: 101 in. Overall length: 192 in. Overall height: 50.3 in. Front tread: 60 in. Rear tread: 60.9 in. Front headroom: 37 in. Rear headroom: 35.6 in. Front legroom: 43 in. Rear legroom: 28.9 in. Front shoulder room: 57.5 in. Rear shoulder room: 56.3 in. Front hip room: 56.3 in. Rear hip room: 42.8 in. Cargo volume: 12.4 cu. ft. (31 cu. ft. with rear seat back down). Standard tires: P245/50VR16 white-letter steel-belted radial.

TECHNICAL

Sport Coupe: Standard Transmission: Five-speed manual (1st) 3.50:1; (2nd) 2.48:1; (3rd) 1.66:1; (4th) 1.00:1; (Rev) 3.50:1. Standard final drive ratio: 3.73:1. Front suspension: Modified MacPherson strut with 1.1-in. diameter stabilizer bar. Rear suspension: Torque arm. Brakes: Power front disc/rear drum. Fuel tank capacity: 15.5 gal.

Berlinetta: Standard transmission: Five-speed manual (1st) 3.50:1; (2nd) 2.14:1; (3rd) 1.36:1; (4th) 1.00:1; (5th) 0.78:1; (Rev) 3.39:1. Automatic transmission: Four-speed (1st) 3.06:1; (2nd) 1.63:1; (3rd) 1.00:1; (4th) 0.70:1; (Rev) 2.29:1. Standard final drive ratio: (Five-speed) 3.23:1, (Automatic) 3.08:1. Front suspension: Modified MacPherson strut with 1.1-in. diameter stabilizer bar. Rear suspension: Torque arm. Brakes: Power front disc/rear drum. Fuel tank capacity: 15.5 gal.

Z28: Standard transmission: Five-speed manual (1st) 2.95:1; (2nd) 1.94:1; (3rd) 1.34:1; (4th) 1.00:1; (5th) 0.73:1; (Rev) 2.76:1. Automatic transmission: Four-speed (1st) 3.06:1; (2nd) 1.63:1; (3rd) 1.00:1; (4th) 0.70:1; (Rev) 2.29:1. Standard final drive ratio: (Five-speed) 3.23:1, (Automatic) 3.08:1, (TPI V-8) 3.23:1. Front suspension: Modified MacPherson strut with 1.3-in. diameter stabilizer bar. Rear suspension: Torque arm. Brakes Power front disc/rear drum. Fuel tank capacity: 16.2 gal.

IROC-Z: Standard transmission: Five-speed manual (1st) 2.95:1; (2nd) 1.94:1; (3rd) 1.34:1; (4th) 1.00:1; (5th) 0.73:1; (Rev) 2.76:1. Automatic transmission: Four-speed (1st) 3.06:1; (2nd) 1.63:1; (3rd) 1.00:1; (4th) 0.70:1; (Rev) 2.29:1. Standard final drive ratio: (Five-speed) 3.23:1, (Automatic) 3.08:1, (TPI V-8) 3.23:1, (H.O. V-8) 3.73:1. Front suspension: Modified MacPherson strut with increased caster for optimal steering response and 1.3-in. diameter stabilizer bar. Rear suspension: Mass-efficient torque arm type with Delco/Bilstein gas-filled shocks, two short control arms and larger diameter stabilizer bar. Brakes: Power front disc/rear drum. Fuel tank capacity: 16.2 gal.

OPTIONS

IROC-Z sport equipment package for Camaro Z28 ($659). Air conditioning ($750). Electric rear window defogger ($145). Cruise control with resume ($175-$185). Tinted glass ($115). Comfortilt steering wheel ($115). Six-way power driver's seat ($225). Power windows ($195). Power door locks ($130). Power hatch release ($40). Gauge package including tachometer in Camaro Sport Coupe ($149). Intermittent windshield wipers ($50). Rear wiper/washer ($125). Quiet sound group ($82). Halogen fog lamps ($60). Auxiliary lighting ($37-$72). Dual horns ($12). Twin electric remote sport mirrors ($91). Automatic day/night mirror ($80). AM radio with digital clock: base ($39). Electronic-tuning seek-and-scan AM/FM stereo radio in Camaro Sport Coupe ($193). Electronic-tuning seek-and-scan AM/FM stereo radio with clock ($197-$232); with cassette and clock ($319-$354); with AM/FM stereo and cassette ($469-$504). Seek-and-scan AM/FM stereo with remote control and cassette in Berlinetta ($242). Power antenna ($60). Radio delete ($56 credit) except Berlinetta ($256 credit); Z28 ($95 credit). Removable glass roof panels ($846). Rear spoiler ($69). Rear window louvers ($210). Black body side moldings ($55). Door edge guards ($15).

Roof console in Camaro Sport Coupe or Z28 ($50). Cloth bucket seats ($28). Custom cloth bucket seats in Camaro Sport Coupe or Z28 ($359). Split folding back seat ($50). Mats with carpeted inserts: front ($20); rear ($15). Cargo area cover ($69). Deluxe trunk trim ($164); Z28 ($84). Locking rear storage cover in Z28 ($80). Aluminum wheels on Berlinetta ($225). Wheel locks on Berlinetta or Z28 ($16). P195/70R14 steel-belted-radial black sidewall Eagle GT tires on Berlinetta ($80). P205/70R14 steel-belted-radial white sidewall tires on Berlinetta ($66). P215/65R15 steel-belted-radial black sidewall tires on Z28 ($92 credit). P215/65R15 steel-belted-radial raised-white-letter tires on Camaro four ($92). P235/60VR15 steel-belted-radial black sidewall tires on Z28 ($85). LB8 173-cid V-6 in Camaro Sport Coupe ($350). LG4 305-cid V-8 in Camaro Sport Coupe ($750); in Berlinetta ($400). L69 305-cid H.O. V-8 in IROC-Z ($695). LB9 350-cid TPI V-8 in Z28 or IROC-Z ($680). Five-speed manual transmission in Camaro Sport Coupe (no cost). Four-speed overdrive automatic transmission ($695). Limited-slip differential. Performance axle ratio. Power four-wheel disc brakes ($179). F41 heavy-duty suspension: ($49). Heavy-duty cooling ($40-$70). Engine block heater ($20). Heavy-duty battery ($26). California emission system ($99).

HISTORICAL FOOTNOTES

In 1986, Chevrolet claimed to have America's fastest car (Corvette), most popular car (Cavalier), most popular mid- and full-sized cars (Celebrity and Caprice) and favorite sporty 2 + 2 (Camaro). Low-interest loans (7.7 percent) were offered by GM late in the 1985 model year and 8.8 percent rates arrived for 1986. One Illinois dealer opened experimental operations in a shopping mall in an attempt to lure buyers who might otherwise be missed. A Women's Marketing Committee was formed to develop approaches to attract female buyers, whose role in auto purchasing was gaining steadily by the mid-1980s. Among other innovations was a pre-approved credit plan for women customers through the General Motors Acceptance Corporation. Dealers also held "Car Care Clinics" for women. Robert D. Burger continued as Chevrolet's general manager. Model-year sales fell 206,082 in 1985 to 173,674. Calendar-year sales also wound up lower at 163,204, or 6.7 percent of the industry total. Model-year production of 192,219 Camaros represented a 2.43 percent share of the industry's total. The Van Nuys, California, plant reported building 103,446 Camaros (and 59,110 Firebirds). The Norwood, Ohio, factory reported building 88,773 Camaros (and 51,373 Firebirds). Industry trade journals recorded 1986 model-year production of 114,741 Camaros with V-8 engines and 77,478 Camaros with V-6 engines. Note that these numbers *do not* match up with percentage figures given for different engine installations. Of the Camaros built, 85.1 percent had automatic transmission, 14.9 percent had a five-speed manual transmission, 39.6 percent had a V-8 with a carburetor, 33.8 percent had a fuel-injected V-8, 26.6 percent had a V-6, 100 percent had power steering, 81.4 percent had power front disc brakes, 18.6 percent had power four-wheel disc brakes, 19.9 percent had a limited-slip differential, 100 percent had steel-belted radial tires, 44.8 percent had power door locks, 57.6 percent had power windows, 100 percent had reclining bucket seats, 16.6 percent had a power front driver's seat, 78.2 percent had tilt steering, 95.2 percent had all-tinted glass, 94.7 percent had manual air conditioning, 54.9 percent had cruise control, 2.4 percent had a conventional AM radio, 1.4 percent had an ETR AM radio, 21.1 percent had an ETR AM/FM radio, 27.1 percent had an ETR AM/FM stereo radio, 40.4 percent had a ETR stereo cassette player, 84.2 percent had a digital clock, 68.9 percent had an electric rear window defogger, 0.7 percent had a rear window wiper, 100 percent had a remote-control left-hand outside rearview mirror, 20.4 percent also had a remote-control right-hand outside rearview mirror, 64.5 percent had aluminum styled wheels, 35.5 percent had styled steel wheels and 46.8 percent had T-tops. A total of 165,883 new Camaros were registered in the U.S. during calendar year 1986. That was down from 200,091 in 1985.

Jerry Heasley photo

The Z28 featured a rear deck lid spoiler, ground effects rocker panels, and lower body striping.

Scott Moyer photo

This 1987 IROC-Z came fully loaded with leather, automatic transmission, four-wheel disc brakes, Positraction and a 5.7-liter V-8.

Camaro coupes changed little in appearance in 1987, but got new wet-arm windshield wipers and a federally required center high-mount stoplight mounted on the rear deck lid spoiler. The biggest news for ragtop fans was the return of a convertible to the lineup. It was built by the Automobile Specialty Co. and didn't appear in the sales catalog because it was introduced very late. However, it was available through dealers on a limited-orders basis.

The arrival of a 5.7-liter (350-cid) V-8 with roller lifters as an option for the IROC-Z was another of this year's exciting changes. Both the four-cylinder engine and the 5.0-liter H.O. V-8 were dropped. Consequently, the 2.8-liter Generation II V-6 became the base power plant.

A new LT model-option replaced the Berlinetta which, ironically, had come into the world as a replacement for the Type LT. A 5.0-liter 165-hp four-barrel V-8 was optional in the Sport Coupe and the LT and standard under the Z28's hood. The Z28 could also be ordered with a 5.0-liter 215-hp TPI V-8.

All 1987 Camaros (except the IROC-Z with the 5.7 liter V-8) could be had with either a five-speed manual gearbox or four-speed overdrive automatic transmission. The big-engined IROC-Z came only with the automatic transmission.

I.D. DATA

Chevrolets again had a 17-symbol vehicle identification number (VIN) on the upper left surface of the instrument panel, visible through the windshield. The first symbol identifies country of origin: 1=USA, 2=Canada. The second symbol identifies the manufacturer: G=General Motors. The third symbol indicates make: 1=Chevrolet, 7=GM of Canada. The fourth and fifth symbols indicated the car line and series: F/P=Camaro Sport Coupe. The sixth symbol indicated body type: 2=two-door hatchback style 87. The seventh symbol indicated the type of restraint system: 1=manual belts and 4=automatic belts. The eighth symbol indicates the engine type: S=RPO LB8 2.8-liter (173-cid) H.O. V-6 with Multi-Port Fuel Injection; H=RPO LG4 5.0-liter (305-cid) V-8 with four-barrel carburetor; F=RPO LB9 5.0-liter (305-cid) V-8 with Tuned Port Injection; 8=RPO L98 5.7-liter (350-cid) V-8 with TPI (Interim availability). The ninth symbol is a check digit. The 10th symbol indicates model year: H=1987. The 11th symbol indicates the assembly plant: L=Van Nuys, California, N=Norwood, Ohio. The final six digits are the sequential serial number.

COLORS

Silver Metallic, Bright Blue Metallic, Dark Blue Metallic, White, Black, Yellow, Dark Brown Metallic, Dark Red Metallic, Bright Red and Medium Gray Metallic.

CAMARO SPORT COUPE - SERIES F/P - V-6/V-8

Camaro Sport Coupes could have either a five-speed manual gearbox or four-speed overdrive automatic transmission. Otherwise, Camaros changed little in appearance, aside from the arrival of a convertible. A leather seat option was also available for the first time in years. A Delco-Bose music system was available as a premium sound option. All V-8 engines were equipped with friction-reducing roller hydraulic lifters. Standard equipment included manual lap/shoulder front safety belts with a visual and audible warning system, manual rear lap belts, an energy-absorbing steering column, energy-absorbing front seat tops, safety glass windshield, safety glass side windows, safety glass rear window, safety interlocking door latches, passenger-guard inside door lock handles, inertia locking folding front seat backs, safety armrests, front head restraints, side marker lights

The Camaro lineup for 1987 (from left): the IROC-Z, the LT, the Sport Coupe and the Z28.

Model Number	Body/Style Number	Body Type & Seating	Factory Price	Shipping Weight	Production Total
CAMARO SPORT COUPE - SERIES F/P - (V-6)					
F/P	87	2d coupe	$9,995	3.062 lbs.	Note 1
CAMARO SPORT COUPE - SERIES F/P - (V-8)					
F/P	87	2d coupe	$10,395	3,181 lbs.	Note 1
CAMARO CONVERTIBLE - SERIES F/P - (V-8)					
F/P	87	2d convertible	$14,794	N/A lbs.	Note 2

Note 1: Combined model-year production of 1987 Camaro coupes was 136,753 (60,439 V-6s and 76,314 V-8s).
Note 2: Combined model-year production of 1987 Camaro convertibles was 1,007 (all V-8s).

CAMARO LT - SERIES F/P - V-6

A new LT model (actually a set of option packages) replaced the former Berlinetta. A 165-hp carbureted 5.0-liter V-8 was optional in the LT. The V-6 was standard. LT's had specific upper and lower body striping, specific lower accent paint and LT badges on the roof sail panels. A handling suspension was included. Standard equipment included manual lap/shoulder front safety belts with visual and audible warning system, manual rear lap belts, an energy-absorbing steering column, energy-absorbing front seat tops, safety glass windshield, safety glass side windows, safety glass rear window, safety interlocking door latches, passenger-guard inside door lock handles, inertia locking folding front seat backs, safety armrests, front head restraints, side marker lights and reflectors, parking lamps that illuminated with the headlights, hazard warning flashers, a center high-mounted stop lamp, direction signals with lane-change feature, a defroster, dual-speed windshield wipers, an inside rearview mirror with vinyl bonded glass, dual outside rearview mirrors, a dual-chamber brake master cylinder, a starter safety switch, a dual-action hood latch system, low-glare instrument panel finish, low-glare windshield moldings, low-glare wiper arms and blades, low-glare metallic steering wheel surfaces, illuminated heater and defroster controls, tires with built-in wear indicators, an audible reminder for ignition key removal, a theft-deterrent steering column lock, a visible VIN number, the V-6 engine, quad rectangular headlights with black or gray metallic headlamp openings, an auxiliary lighting package, black windshield reveal moldings, black concealed windshield wipers, 14 x 7-in. steel wheels with full wheel covers, P205/70R-14 black sidewall radial tires, dual body-color sport mirrors (left-hand remote control), tri-color taillights with black accents,

and reflectors, parking lamps that illuminated with the headlights, hazard warning flashers, a center high-mounted stop lamp, direction signals with lane-change feature, a defroster, dual-speed windshield wipers, an inside rearview mirror with vinyl bonded glass, dual outside rearview mirrors, a dual-chamber brake master cylinder, a starter safety switch, a dual-action hood latch system, low-glare instrument panel finish, low-glare windshield moldings, low-glare wiper arms and blades, low-glare metallic steering wheel surfaces, illuminated heater and defroster controls, tires with built-in wear indicators, an audible reminder for ignition key removal, a theft-deterrent steering column lock, a visible VIN number, the V-6 engine, quad rectangular headlights, black windshield reveal moldings, black concealed windshield wipers, 15 x 7-in. styled steel Rally wheels with trim rings, P215/65R-15 black sidewall steel-belted Eagle GT radial tires, dual black sport mirrors (left-hand remote control), special accent tape stripes, chip-resistant gray or black lower body accent finish, an automatic hatch power pull-down latch, vinyl reclining bucket seats, amber parking light lenses, power steering, power front disc/rear drum brakes, a headlamp-on warning, an AM radio (could be deleted for credit), basecoat-/clearcoat finish, an inside hood release, black or gray finish on headlight openings, a carpeted cargo floor, a deep-well luggage area, a console with hinged-cover storage area, side window defoggers, Computer Command Control, the five-speed manual transmission, front disc brake audible wear sensors, a power ventilation system, the F41 sport suspension and a torque arm rear suspension.

The IROC-Z coupe came with a base $13,488 window price for 1987.

Jerry Heasley photo

special accent tape stripes, chip-resistant gray or black lower body accent finish, an automatic power hatch pull-down latch, reclining bucket seats with custom cloth trim, amber parking light lenses, power steering, power front disc/rear drum brakes, a headlamp-on warning, an AM/FM stereo radio with a clock, air conditioning, basecoat/clearcoat finish, an inside hood release, a carpeted cargo floor, a deep-well luggage area, a console with hinged-cover storage area, side window defoggers, Computer Command Control, the five-speed manual transmission, front disc brake audible wear sensors, a power ventilation system, front and rear stabilizer bars and a torque arm rear suspension.

Model Number	Body/Style Number	Body Type & Seating	Factory Price	Shipping Weight	Production Total
CAMARO LT - SERIES F/P - (V-6)					
F/P	87	2d coupe	$11,517	—	Note 3
CAMARO LT - SERIES F/P - (V-8)					
F/P	87	2d coupe	$11,917	—	Note 3

Note 3: Combined model-year production of 1987 Camaro coupes was 136,753 (60,439 V-6s and 76,314 V-8s).

CAMARO Z28 - SERIES 1F - V-8

The 5.0-liter 165-hp four-barrel V-8 that was optional in the Camaro Sport Coupe and Camaro LT was standard under the hood of the Z28. The Z28 could also be ordered with a TPI version of that V-8 that delivered 215 hp. Standard equipment also included manual lap/shoulder front safety belts with a visual and audible warning system, manual rear lap belts, an energy-absorbing steering column, energy-absorbing front seat tops, safety glass windshield, safety glass side windows, safety glass rear window, safety interlocking door latches, passenger-guard inside door lock handles, inertia locking folding front seat backs, safety armrests, front head restraints, side marker lights and reflectors, parking lamps that illuminated with the headlights, hazard warning flashers, a center high-mounted stop lamp, direction signals with lane-change feature, a defroster, dual-speed windshield wipers, an inside rearview mirror with vinyl bonded glass, dual outside rearview mirrors, a dual-chamber brake master cylinder, a starter safety switch, a dual-action hood latch system, low-glare instrument panel finish, low-glare windshield moldings, low-glare wiper arms and blades, low-glare metallic steering wheel surfaces, illuminated heater and defroster controls, tires with built-in wear indicators, an audible reminder for ignition key removal, a theft-deterrent steering column lock, a visible VIN number, quad rectangular headlights, black windshield reveal moldings, black concealed windshield wipers, 15 x 7-in. aluminum wheels in Silver, Gold or Charcoal, P215/65R-15 white-outline-lettered steel-belted Eagle GT radial tires, specific wide-accent body striping, an accent color (Silver, Charcoal or Gold) on the lower body, a rear hatch lid spoiler with integral high-mounted stoplight, a front wraparound air dam, ground effects body extensions (on the rocker panels, fenders, doors and quarter panels), simulated hood louvers, a unique front fascia and black grille, dual black sport mirrors (left-hand remote control), a visor-vanity mirror, an automatic hatch power pull-down latch, vinyl reclining bucket seats, special instrumentation with a tachometer, a leather-wrapped steering wheel, amber parking light lenses, power steering, power front disc/rear drum brakes, a headlamp-on warning, an AM radio with clock, basecoat/clearcoat finish, an inside hood release, black or gray finish on headlight openings, a carpeted cargo floor, a deep-well luggage area, a console with hinged-cover storage area, side window defoggers, Computer Command Control, a five-speed manual transmission, front disc brake audible wear sensors, a power ventilation system, the F41 sport suspension and a torque arm rear suspension.

Model Number	Body/Style Number	Body Type & Seating	Factory Price	Shipping Weight	Production Total
CAMARO Z28 - SERIES F/P - (V-8)					
F/P	87	2d coupe	$12,819	3,121 lbs.	52,863
CAMARO Z28 CONVERTIBLE - SERIES F/P - (V-8)					
F/P	87	2d convertible	$17,218	—	744

Note 4: Combined model-year production of 1987 Camaro coupes was 136,753 (60,439 V-6s and 76,314 V-8s).
Note 5: Combined model-year production of 1987 Camaro convertibles was 1,007 (all V-8s).

CAMARO IROC-Z - SERIES F/P - V-8

Biggest news for Camaro performance fans in 1987 was the arrival of the 350-cid (5.7-liter) V-8 with roller lifters as an option for the IROC-Z. It came only with automatic transmission. Otherwise, Camaros changed little in appearance apart from new wet-arm wipers and the mounting of the required center high-mount stop lamp on the rear spoiler (if a rear spoiler was installed). Standard equipment also included manual lap/shoulder

The IROC-Z convertible was the crown jewel of the 1987 Camaro lineup.

Daniel B. Lyons photo

This Z28 came decked out in Black with Silver. Charcoal and Gold were the other two accent colors for 1987.

front safety belts with a visual and audible warning system, manual rear lap belts, an energy-absorbing steering column, energy-absorbing front seat tops, safety glass windshield, safety glass side windows, safety glass rear window, safety interlocking door latches, passenger-guard inside door lock handles, inertia locking folding front seat backs, safety armrests, front head restraints, side marker lights and reflectors, parking lamps that illuminated with the headlights, hazard warning flashers, a center high-mounted stop lamp, direction signals with lane-change feature, a defroster, dual-speed windshield wipers, an inside rearview mirror with vinyl bonded glass, dual outside rearview mirrors, a dual-chamber brake master cylinder, a starter safety switch, a dual-action hood latch system, low-glare instrument panel finish, low-glare windshield moldings, low-glare wiper arms and blades, low-glare metallic steering wheel surfaces, illuminated heater and defroster controls, tires with built-in wear indicators, an audible reminder for ignition key removal, a theft-deterrent steering column lock, a visible VIN number, quad rectangular headlights, halogen fog lamps, black windshield reveal moldings, black concealed windshield wipers, 16 x 8-in. aluminum wheels in Argent Silver or Gold, P245/50VR-16 black-letter steel-belted radial tires, specific body striping and color-coordinated IROC-Z door decals, an accent color (Silver, Charcoal or Gold) on the lower body, a rear hatch lid spoiler with integral high-mounted stoplight, a front wraparound air dam, ground effects body extensions (on the rocker panels, fenders, doors and quarter panels), simulated hood louvers, a unique front fascia, a black grille with Gold or Silver Camaro lettering on it, dual black sport mirrors (left-hand remote control), a visor vanity mirror, an automatic hatch power pull-down latch, vinyl reclining bucket seats, special instrumentation with a tachometer, a leather-wrapped steering wheel, amber parking light lenses, power steering, power front disc/rear drum brakes, a headlamp-on warning, an AM radio with clock, basecoat/clearcoat finish, an inside hood release, black or gray finish on headlight openings, a carpeted cargo floor, a deep-well luggage area, a console with hinged-cover storage area, side window defoggers, Computer Command Control, the five-speed manual transmission, front disc brake audible wear sensors, a power ventilation system, a special performance and ride suspension and a torque arm rear suspension.

Model Number	Body/Style Number	Body Type & Seating	Factory Price	Shipping Weight	Production Total
CAMARO IROC-Z - SERIES F/P - (V-8)					
F/P	87	2d coupe	$13,488	—	Note 6
CAMARO IROC-Z CONVERTIBLE - SERIES F/P - (V-8)					
F/P	87	2d convertible	$17,917	—	Note 6

Note 6: Combined model-year production of 1987 IROC-Zs was 38,889.

ENGINE

LB8 V-6: 60-degree, overhead-valve V-6. Cast-iron block and head. Bore & stroke: 3.50 x 2.99 in. Displacement: 173 cid (2.8 liters). Compression ratio: 8.5:1. Compression ratio: 8.9:1. Brake horsepower: 135 at 5100 rpm. Torque: 160 lbs.-ft. at 3900 rpm. Induction system: Multiport Fuel Injection. Standard in Camaro Sport Coupe and Camaro LT. VIN Code S.

LG4 base V-8: 90-degree, overhead-valve V-8. Cast-iron block and head. Bore & stroke: 3.74 x 3.48 in. Displacement: 305 cid (5.0 liters). Compression ratio: 9.5:1. Brake horsepower: 165 at 4400 rpm Torque: 250 lbs.-ft. at 2000 rpm Five main bearings. Hydraulic valve lifters. Induction system: four-barrel carburetor. Standard in Z28 and IROC-Z. VIN Code: H.

LB9 TPI V-8: 90-degree, overhead-valve V-8. Cast-iron block and head. Bore & stroke: 3.74 x 3.48 in. Displacement: 305 cid (5.0 liters). Compression ratio: 9.5:1. Brake horsepower: 190 at 4000 rpm Torque: 285 lbs.-ft. at 2800 rpm Five main bearings. Hydraulic valve lifters. Electronic spark control. 3-in. front exhaust pipes and dual outlet muffler. Induction system: Tuned Port Injection. Optional in Z28. Optional in IROC-Z. VIN Code: F.

L98 TPI V-8: 90-degree, overhead-valve V-8. Cast-iron block and head. Bore & stroke: 4.00 x 3.48 in. Displacement: 350 cid (5.7 liters). Compression ratio: 9.0:1. Brake horsepower: 225 at 4400 rpm Torque: 330 lbs.-ft. at 2800 rpm Five main bearings. Hydraulic valve lifters.

Electronic spark control. 3.0-in. front exhaust pipes and dual outlet muffler. Induction system: Tuned Port Injection. Optional in IROC-Z VIN Code: 8. Limited interim availability.

Base Camaro: Wheelbase: 101 in. Overall length: 188 in. Overall height: 50 in. Overall width: 72.8 in. Front tread: 60.7 in. Rear tread: 61.6 in. Front headroom: 37 in. Rear headroom: 35.6 in. Front legroom: 43 in. Rear legroom: 28.9 in. Front shoulder room: 57.5 in. Rear shoulder room: 56.3 in. Front hip room: 56.3 in. Rear hip room: 42.8 in. Cargo volume: 12.4 cu. ft. (31 cu. ft. with rear seat back down). Standard tires: P215/65R-15 black sidewall steel-belted Eagle GT radial.

CHASSIS

Camaro LT: Wheelbase: 101 in. Overall length: 188 in. Overall height: 50 in. Front tread: 60 in. Rear tread: 60.9 in. Front headroom: 37 in. Rear headroom: 35.6 in. Front legroom: 43 in. Rear legroom: 28.9 in. Front shoulder room: 57.5 in. Rear shoulder room: 56.3 in. Front hip room: 56.3 in. Rear hip room: 42.8 in. Cargo volume: 12.4 cu. ft. (31 cu. ft. with rear seat back down). Standard tires: P205/70R-14 black sidewall radial.

Z28: Wheelbase: 101 in. Overall length: 192 in. Overall height: 50.3 in. Front tread: 60 in. Rear tread: 60.9 in. Front headroom: 37 in. Rear headroom: 35.6 in. Front legroom: 43 in. Rear legroom: 28.9 in. Front shoulder room: 57.5 in. Rear shoulder room: 56.3 in. Front hip room: 56.3 in. Rear hip room: 42.8 in. Cargo volume: 12.4 cu. ft. (31 cu. ft. with rear seat back down). Standard tires: P215/65R-15 white-outline-lettered steel-belted Eagle GT radial.

IROC-Z: Wheelbase: 101 in. Overall length: 192 in. Overall height: 50.3 in. Front tread: 60 in. Rear tread: 60.9 in. Front headroom: 37 in. Rear headroom: 35.6 in. Front legroom: 43 in. Rear legroom: 28.9 in. Front shoulder room: 57.5 in. Rear shoulder room: 56.3 in. Front hip room: 56.3 in. Rear hip room: 42.8 in. Cargo volume: 12.4 cu. ft. (31 cu. ft. with rear seat back down). Standard tires: P245/50VR-16 black-letter steel-belted radial.

TECHNICAL

Base: Transmission: (Standard): Five-speed manual. (Optional) Four-speed overdrive automatic. Steering: re-circulating ball. Front suspension: MacPherson struts with coil springs, lower control arms and stabilizer bar.

The IROC-Z received a new 350-cid engine for 1987, but was otherwise largely unchanged.

Rear suspension: rigid axle and torque tube with longitudinal control arms, Panhard rod, coil springs and stabilizer bar; Brakes: front disc, rear drum; four-wheel discs available. Body construction: unibody. Fuel tank capacity: 15.5 gal.

LT: Transmission: (Standard, except with LG4 V-8): Five-speed manual. (Optional) Four-speed overdrive automatic. Steering: re-circulating ball. Front suspension: MacPherson struts with coil springs, lower control arms and stabilizer bar. Rear suspension: rigid axle and torque tube with longitudinal control arms, Panhard rod, coil springs and stabilizer bar; Brakes: front disc, rear drum; four-wheel discs available. Body construction: unibody. Fuel tank capacity: 15.5 gal.

Z28: Transmission: (Standard): Five-speed manual. (Optional) Four-speed overdrive automatic. Steering: re-circulating ball. Front suspension: MacPherson struts with coil springs, lower control arms and stabilizer bar. Rear suspension: rigid axle and torque tube with longitudinal control arms, Panhard rod, coil springs and stabilizer bar; Brakes: front disc, rear drum; four-wheel discs available. Body construction: unibody. Fuel tank capacity: 16.2 gal.

IROC-Z: Transmission: (Standard): Five-speed manual. (Optional) Four-speed overdrive automatic. (Required option with L98 V-8) Four-speed overdrive automatic. Steering: re-circulating ball. Front suspension: MacPherson struts with coil springs, lower control arms and stabilizer bar. Rear suspension: rigid axle and torque tube with longitudinal control arms, Panhard rod, coil springs and stabilizer bar; Brakes: front disc, rear drum; four-wheel discs available. Body construction: unibody. Fuel tank capacity: 16.2 gal.

OPTIONS

Air conditioning ($775). Heavy-duty battery ($26). Engine oil cooler ($110). Locking rear storage cover ($80). Rear defogger ($145). Power door locks ($145). California emissions pkg. ($99). Gauge package in Sport Coupe ($149). Tinted glass ($120). Rear window louvers ($210). Deluxe luggage compartment trim, Sport Coupe ($164). Z28 ($84). Body side moldings ($60). Power antenna ($70). T-top roof ($866). Split folding rear seat back ($50). Rear spoiler on Sport Coupe ($69). Cast aluminum wheels with locks ($215). AM/FM stereo cassette ($364). AM/FM stereo with electronic tuning and graphic equalizer ($242). AM/FM stereo electronic tuning with cassette and graphic equalizer ($514). Delco-GM/Bose music system ($1127). AM mono radio ($39). Sport Coupe option package 2 includes tinted glass, air conditioning, tilt steering column and AM/FM stereo ($1,212). AM/FM stereo cassette ($122). AM/FM stereo with cassette and graphic equalizer ($272). Delco-GM/Bose music system ($885). AM/FM stereo delete ($298 credit). Sport Coupe option package 3 includes package 2 plus four floor mats, body side moldings, intermittent wipers, rear spoiler, cruise control, AM/FM stereo w/cassette and extended range speakers ($1,628). Sport Coupe option package 4 includes package 3 plus power windows and door locks, power hatch release and cargo cover ($2,126). Halogen headlamps. Auxiliary lighting. Sound systems with Sport Coupe option packages 3 or 4. AM/FM stereo with cassette and graphic equalizer

($150). Delco-GM/Bose music system ($763). AM/FM stereo delete ($420 credit). LT option package 1, includes tinted glass, air conditioning, tilt steering column, AM-FM stereo, full wheel covers, body side stripes, custom interior and quiet sound group ($1,522). Sound systems with LT option package 1. AM/FM cassette ($122). AM/FM with cassette with graphic equalizer ($272). Delco-GM/Bose music system ($885). AM/FM delete ($298 credit). LT option package 2 includes package 1 plus floor mats, body side moldings, intermittent wipers, rear spoiler, cruise control, and electronic tuning AM/FM stereo cassette with extended-range speakers ($1,938). LP option package 3 includes package 2 plus power windows and door locks, power hatch release, cargo cover and halogen headlamps ($2,387). LT option package 4 includes package 3 plus power seat, interior roof console, automatic day/night mirror, power remote mirrors, and halogen fog lamps ($2,858). Sound systems with LT option package 2, 3 or 4: Electronic tuning AM/FM stereo with cassette and graphic equalizer ($150). Delco-GM/Bose music system ($763). AM/FM stereo ET cassette delete ($420 credit). Sound Systems in Z28: AM/FM ET cassette ($325); AM/FM stereo ET ($203); AM/FM with cassette and graphic equalizer ($475); Delco-GM/Bose music system ($1,088). Z28 option package 2 includes sport equipment, tinted glass, air conditioning, tilt steering wheel, floor mats, body side moldings, intermittent wipers, cruise control and AM/FM stereo electronic tuning cassette with extended range speakers ($1,999). Z28 option package 3 includes package 2 plus power windows and door locks, power hatch release, auxiliary lighting, halogen headlamps, cargo cover, power mirrors, power seat, automatic day/night mirror, interior roof console and halogen fog lamps ($2,470 without cargo area cover or $2,539 with cargo area cover). Sound system with Z28 option package 2 or 3 includes electronic tuning AM/FM stereo with cassette and graphic equalizer ($150). Delco-GM/Bose music system ($763). AM/FM electronic tuning with cassette deleted ($381 credit). IROC-Z option package 1 includes halogen fog lamps, uprated suspension and P245/50VR16 tires on aluminum wheels ($669). Sound systems with IROC-Z package 1 includes electronic tuning AM/FM stereo with cassette ($325). Electronic tuning AM/FM stereo ($203). Electronic tuning AM-FM stereo with cassette and graphic equalizer ($475). Delco-GM/Bose music system ($1088). IROC-Z option package 2 includes package 1 plus sport equipment, tinted glass, air conditioning, tilt steering column, floor mats, intermittent wipers, AM/FM stereo electronic tuning cassette with extended range speakers, power windows and door locks and power hatch release ($2,409). Sound Systems with IROC-Z package 2 includes electronic tuning AM/FM stereo with cassette and graphic equalizer ($150). Delco-GM/Bose music system ($763). Electronic tuning AM/FM stereo with cassette and graphic equalizer ($150). Delco-GM/Bose music system ($763). Electronic tuning AM/FM stereo with cassette, deleted for credit ($381 credit). IROC-Z option package 3 includes package 2 plus power mirrors, cruise control, body side moldings, cargo cover, auxiliary lighting, automatic day/night mirror, power seat, interior roof console, electronic tun-

ing AM/FM stereo with cassette and graphic equalizer and extended range speakers ($3,273 with cargo cover or $3,204 without cargo cover). Sound systems with IROC-Z package 3 includes Delco-GM/Bose music system ($613). Electronic tuning AM/FM stereo with cassette and graphic equalizer deleted for credit ($531 credit). 5.0-liter four-barrel V-8 ($400). 5.0-liter TPI V-8 in Camaro or Z28 ($745). 5.7-liter TPI V-8 in IROC-Z only ($1,045). Four-speed overdrive automatic transmission ($490). Performance axle ratio ($21). Power four-wheel disc brakes ($179).

HISTORICAL FOOTNOTES

Robert D. Burger continued as Chevrolet's general manager during 1987. Model-year sales fell from 173,674 in 1986 to 122,761 in 1987. Calendar year sales also wound up lower at 117,324 or 4.9 percent of the industry total. Model-year production of 137,760 Camaros represented a 1.87 percent share of the industry's total. The Van Nuys plant reported building 51,936 Camaros (and 35,610 Firebirds). The Norwood factory reported building 85,824 Camaros (and 53,013 Firebirds). This would be the last year of operation for the Norwood plant. Of the Camaros built, 83.6 percent had automatic transmission, 16.4 percent had a five-speed manual transmission, 26.7 percent had a V-8 with a carburetor, 29.4 percent had a fuel-injected V-8, 43.9 percent had a fuel-injected V-6, 100 percent had power steering, 82.7 percent had power front disc brakes, 17.3 percent had power four-wheel disc brakes, 29.6 percent had a limited-slip differential, 100 percent had steel-belted radial tires, 47.2 percent had power door locks, 48.1 percent had power windows, 100 percent had reclining bucket seats, 22.7 percent had a power front driver's seat, 78.2 percent had tilt steering, 94.6 percent had all-tinted glass, 90.4 percent had manual air conditioning, 56.7 percent had cruise control, 66 percent had delay windshield wipers, 3 percent had a conventional AM radio, 0.7 percent had an ETR AM radio, 15.8 percent had an ETR AM/FM radio, 51.1 percent had a ETR stereo cassette player, 6.2 percent had a Bose/JBL sound system, 19.8 percent had a premium sound system, 93.6 percent had a digital clock, 62.5 percent had an electric rear window defogger, 0.7 percent had a rear window wiper, 100 percent had a remote-control left-hand outside rearview mirror, 22.8 percent also had a remote-control right-hand outside rearview mirror, 47.1 percent had aluminum styled wheels and 44 percent had T-tops. A total of 116,656 new Camaros were registered in the U.S. during calendar year 1987. That was down from 165,883 in 1986. With the closing of the General Motors Assembly Division plant in Norwood, Ohio, the only remaining source of Camaros and Firebirds after 1987 was the Van Nuys, California, factory. GM also cancelled its GM80 development program for plastic-bodied, front-wheel-drive Camaros and Firebirds, and industry observers began to speculate that the end of both nameplates was in sight. As we now know, it would take 15 years for the end to arrive, but in 1987 the speculation alone was enough to lead to a reduction of models for 1988. As a result, only the base Sport Coupe and IROC-Z were marketed in model year 1988.

Paul Plasek photo

The IROC-Z convertible went for about $18,000 in 1988.

Chevy offered only the base Sport Coupe and the IROC-Z in its 1988 Camaro line. With the demise of the Z28, the base model came with a rear spoiler, aluminum wheels, lower body side panels, and body-color mirrors. It had a standard 2.8-liter 125-hp V-6. The optional 5.0-liter V-8 was standard in the IROC-Z. It now had throttle-body fuel injection and five more horsepower. Two MFI V-8 options were offered for the IROC-Z. They were a 5.0-liter H.O. (which put out 220 hp with a five-speed manual gearbox and 195 hp with automatic transmission) and a 5.7-liter 230-hp edition that came only with four-speed automatic.

Barely 1,000 Camaro convertibles had been produced during the 1987 model year, but the numbers rose to 5,620 in 1988 when the revived body style had its first full-year run.

I.D. DATA

Chevrolets again had a 17-symbol vehicle identification number (VIN) on the upper left surface of the instrument panel, visible through the windshield. The first symbol identifies country of origin: 1=USA, 2=Canada. The second symbol identifies the manufacturer: G=General Motors. The third symbol indicates make: 1=Chevrolet, 7=GM of Canada. The fourth and fifth symbols indicated the car line and series: F/P=Camaro Sport Coupe and Camaro convertible, the sixth symbol indicated body type: 2=two-door hatchback style 87, 3=two-door convertible style 67. The seventh symbol indicated the type of restraint system: 1=manual belts, 3=driver airbag and 4=automatic belts. The eighth symbol indicates the engine type: S=RPO LB8 2.8-liter (173-cid) H.O. V-6 with Multiport Fuel Injection; E=RPO LO3 5.0-liter (305-cid) V-8 with electronic fuel injection; F=RPO LB9 5.0-liter (305-cid) V-8 with Tuned Port Injection; 8=RPO B2L 5.7-liter (350-cid) V-8 with TPI. The ninth symbol is a check digit. The 10th symbol indicates model year: J=1988. The 11th symbol indicates the assembly plant: L=Van Nuys, California, N=Norwood, Ohio. The final six digits are the sequential serial number.

COLORS

Silver Metallic, Bright Blue Metallic, Dark Blue Metallic, White, Black, Yellow, Medium Orange Metallic, Dark Red Metallic, Bright Red and Medium Gray Metallic. (Silver Metallic, Bright Blue Metallic and Yellow were not available on the IROC-Z model).

CAMARO SPORT COUPE - SERIES F/P V-6/V-8

Standard equipment included manual lap/shoulder front safety belts with a visual and audible warning system, manual rear lap belts, an energy-absorbing steering column, an energy-absorbing instrument panel, energy-absorbing front seat tops, laminated safety windshield glass, safety glass side windows, safety glass rear window, safety interlocking door latches, passenger-guard inside door lock handles, inertia locking folding front seat backs, safety armrests, front head restraints, side marker lights and reflectors, parking lamps that illuminated with the headlights, four-way hazard warning flashers, backup lights, a center high-mounted stop lamp, direction signals with a lane-change feature, a windshield defroster, a windshield washer system, multi-speed windshield wipers, an inside rearview mirror with vinyl bonded glass, dual outside rearview mirrors, a dual-chamber brake master cylinder and brake system warning light, a starter safety switch, a dual-action hood latch system, low-glare instrument panel finish, low-glare windshield moldings, low-glare wiper arms and blades, low-glare metallic steering wheel surfaces, illuminated heater and defroster controls, tires with built-in wear indicators, an audible reminder for ignition key removal,

The base Camaro came as both a Sport Coupe and convertible, and had a choice of V-6 and 305-cid V-8 engines.

a theft-deterrent steering column lock, a visible VIN number, marked body parts, a 2.8-liter V-6 engine with multiport fuel injection, an AM/FM stereo (with seek-and-scan, a digital clock and an extended-range sound system), basecoat/clearcoat paint, a black windshield molding, black concealed windshield wipers, body tape striping, a carpeted cargo floor, cloth reclining bucket seats, Computer Command Control, a deep-well luggage area, dual color-keyed sport style outside rearview mirrors (left-hand remote and right-hand manual), 15 x 7-in. aluminum wheels in silver or gold, a five-speed manual transmission, a front air dam, ground-effects type rocker panel moldings, front disc brakes with audible wear sensors, hinged cover console stowage, improved corrosion protection including the use of pre-coated steel, power front disc/rear drum brakes, power steering, a power ventilation system, P215/65R-15 steel-belted radial ply tires, a rear deck lid spoiler, a rear hatch with automatic pull-down, side window defoggers, special instrumentation with a tachometer, a Sport suspension, a vinyl-coated shift knob and a vinyl-wrapped steering wheel.

Model Number	Body/Style Number	Body Type & Seating	Factory Price	Shipping Weight	Production Total
CAMARO SPORT COUPE - SERIES F/P - (V-6)					
F/P	87	2d coupe	$10,995	3,054 lbs.	Note 1
CAMARO SPORT COUPE - SERIES F/P - (V-8)					
F/P	87	2d coupe	$11,395	3,228 lbs.	Note 1
CAMARO CONVERTIBLE - SERIES F/P-Z08 - (V-8)					
F/P	87/Z08	2d convertible	$16,255	3,350 lbs.	1,859

Note 1: Model-year production of 1986 base Camaro coupes was 66,605.

CAMARO IROC-Z - SERIES F/P - V-8

Most noticeable of the Camaro changes this year may have been the absence of a Z28. The IROC-Z was still offered, but was still technically an option for the base Camaro as both were coded with the F/P designation for car line and series. However, the IROC-Z was promoted as a separate model line in the 1988 Camaro sales catalog. A new 5.0-liter V-8 was standard on the IROC-Z. It had throttle body injection and gained five horsepower over the base 1987 V-8. Two Multiport Fuel Injected V-8 options were also offered for the IROC-Z. The first was a 5.0-liter H.O. V-8 rated at 220 hp with a five-speed manual shift and 195 hp with automatic transmission. The second was the new RPO B2L engine. This was a 350-cid (5.7-liter) TPI V-8 that came only with the four-speed automatic transmission. The 5,620 Camaro convertibles made in 1988 included 3,761 IROC-Z ragtops. Standard equipment included manual lap/shoulder front safety belts with visual/audible warning system, manual rear lap belts, an energy-absorbing steering column, an energy-absorbing instrument panel, energy-absorbing front seat tops, laminated safety windshield glass, safety glass side windows, safety glass rear window, safety interlocking door latches, passenger-guard inside door lock handles, inertia locking folding front seat backs, safety armrests, front head restraints, side marker lights and reflectors, parking lamps that illuminated with the headlights, halogen fog lamps, four-way hazard warning flashers, back-up lights, a center high-mounted stop lamp, direction signals with lane-change feature, a windshield defroster, a windshield washer system, multi-speed windshield wipers, an inside rearview mirror with vinyl bonded glass, dual outside rearview mirrors, a dual-chamber brake master cylinder and brake system warning light, a starter safety switch, a dual-action hood latch system, low-glare instrument panel finish, low-glare windshield moldings, low-glare wiper arms and blades, low-glare metallic steering wheel surfaces, illuminated heater and defroster controls, tires with built-in wear indicators, an audible reminder for ignition key removal, a theft-deterrent steering column lock, a visible VIN number, marked body parts, the 5.0-liter V-8 with electronic fuel injection, an AM/FM stereo (with seek-and-scan, a digital clock and an extended-range sound system), basecoat/clearcoat paint, a black windshield molding, black concealed windshield wipers, black-painted headlight openings, body tape striping, black simulated

Jerry Heasley photo

The Camaro line included only the IROC-Z (left) and Sport Coupe for 1988.

hood louvers, a carpeted cargo floor, cloth reclining bucket seats, Computer Command Control, a deep-well luggage area, dual color-keyed Sport-style outside rearview mirrors (left-hand remote and right-hand manual), a visor-vanity mirror, 15 x 7-in aluminum wheels in silver or gold, a five-speed manual transmission, a front air dam, body-color ground effects panels, specific body striping and color-coordinated IROC-Z door decals, Camaro gold or silver lettering on the grille, ground effects type rocker panel moldings, front disc brakes with audible wear sensors, hinged-cover console stowage, improved corrosion protection, including the use of pre-coated steel, power front disc/rear drum brakes, power steering, a power ventilation system, P215/65R-15 steel-belted radial ply tires, a specific rear deck lid spoiler, a rear hatch with automatic pull-down, side window defoggers, special instrumentation with a tachometer, a special performance ride and handling suspension, a leather-wrapped shift knob, a leather-wrapped steering wheel and specific taillights. The convertible also had a manually operated cloth top and a flush-fitting fiberglass top boot.

Model Number	Body/Style Number	Body Type & Seating	Factory Price	Shipping Weight	Production Total
CAMARO IROC-Z - SERIES F/P - (V-8)					
F/P	87	2d coupe	$13,490	3,229 lbs.	24,050
CAMARO IROC-Z CONVERTIBLE - SERIES F/P - (V-8)					
F/P	87	2d convertible	$18,015	3,352 lbs.	3,761

ENGINES

LB8 V-6: 60-degree, overhead-valve V-6. Cast-iron block and head. Bore & stroke: 3.50 x 2.99 in. Displacement: 173 cid (2.8 liters). Compression ratio: 8.9:1. Brake horsepower: 135 at 4900 rpm. Torque: 160 lbs.-ft. at 3900 rpm. Induction system: Multiport Fuel Injection. Standard in Camaro Sport Coupe. VIN Code S.

LO3 base V-8: 90-degree, overhead-valve V-8. Cast-iron block and head. Bore & stroke: 3.74 x 3.48 in. Displacement: 305 cid (5.0 liters). Compression ratio: 9.3:1. Brake horsepower: 170 at 4400 rpm Torque: 255 lbs.-ft. at 2400 rpm Five main bearings. Hydraulic valve lifters. Induction system: electronic fuel injection. Standard in

Camaro convertible and IROC-Z. Optional in base Camaro. VIN Code: H.

LB9 TPI V-8: 90-degree, overhead-valve V-8. Cast-iron block and head. Bore & stroke: 3.74 x 3.48 in. Displacement: 305 cid (5.0 liters). Compression ratio: 9.3:1. Brake horsepower: 220 at 4400 rpm (195 hp with automatic transmission). Torque: 290 lbs.-ft. at 3200 rpm. Five main bearings. Hydraulic valve lifters. Electronic spark control. Induction system: Tuned Port Injection. Optional in IROC-Z. VIN Code: F.

B2L TPI V-8: 90-degree, overhead-valve V-8. Cast-iron block and head. Bore & stroke: 4.00 x 3.48 in. Displacement: 350 cid (5.7 liters). Compression ratio: 9.3:1. Brake horsepower: 230 at 4400 rpm Torque: 330 lbs.-ft. at 3200 rpm Five main bearings. Hydraulic valve lifters. Electronic spark control. 3-in. front exhaust pipes and dual outlet muffler. Induction system: Tuned Port Injection option package for IROC-Z. VIN Code: 8.

CHASSIS

Base Sport Coupe: Wheelbase: 101 in. Overall length: 192 in. Overall height: 50.3 in. Overall width: 72.8 in. Front tread: 60 in. Rear tread: 60.9 in. Front headroom: 37 in. Rear headroom: 35.6 in. Front legroom: 43 in. Rear legroom: 29.8 in. Front shoulder room: 57.5 in. Rear shoulder room: 56.3 in. Front hip room: 56.3 in. Rear hip room: 42.8 in. Cargo volume: 12.4 cu. ft. (31 cu. ft. with rear seat back down). Standard tires: P215/65R-15 black sidewall steel-belted radial.

Base Camaro convertible: Wheelbase: 101 in. Overall length: 192 in. Overall height: 50.3 in. Overall width: 72.8 in. Front tread: 60 in. Rear tread: 60.9 in. Front headroom: 37 in. Rear headroom: 35.6 in. Front legroom: 43 in. Rear legroom: 29.8 in. Front shoulder room: 57.5 in. Rear shoulder room: 56.3 in. Front hip room: 56.3 in. Rear hip room: 42.8 in. Cargo volume: 5.2 cu. ft. Standard tires: P215/65R-15 black sidewall steel-belted radial.

IROC-Z Coupe: Wheelbase: 101 in. Overall length: 192 in. Overall height: 50.3 in. Overall width: 72.8 in. Front tread: 60 in. Rear tread: 60.9 in. Front headroom: 37 in. Rear headroom: 35.6 in. Front legroom: 43 in.

The IROC-Z package again included exterior features like body-color ground effects panels, specific body striping and color-coordinated IROC-Z door decals.

Daniel B. Lyons photo

Rear legroom: 29.8 in. Front shoulder room: 57.5 in. Rear shoulder room: 56.3 in. Front hip room: 56.3 in. Rear hip room: 42.8 in. Cargo volume: 12.4 cu. ft. (31 cu. ft. with rear seat back down). Standard tires: P215/65R-15 black-letter steel-belted radial.

IROC-Z convertible: Wheelbase: 101 in. Overall length: 192.0 in. Overall height: 50.3 in. Overall width: 72.8 in. Front tread: 60 in. Rear tread: 60.9 in. Front headroom: 37 in. Rear headroom: 35.6 in. Front legroom: 43 in. Rear legroom: 29.8 in. Front shoulder room: 57.5 in. Rear shoulder room: 56.3 in. Front hip room: 56.3 in. Rear hip room: 42.8 in. Cargo volume: 5.2 cu. ft. Standard tires: P215/65R-15 black-letter steel-belted radial.

TECHNICAL

Base Sport Coupe: Transmission: (Standard): Five-speed manual. (Optional) Four-speed overdrive automatic. Steering: re-circulating ball. Front suspension: MacPherson struts with coil springs, lower control arms and stabilizer bar. Rear suspension: rigid axle and torque tube with longitudinal control arms, Panhard rod, coil springs and stabilizer bar; Brakes: front disc, rear drum; four-wheel discs available. Body construction: unibody. Fuel tank capacity: 15.5 gal.

Base convertible: Transmission: (Standard): Five-speed manual. (Optional) Four-speed overdrive automatic. Steering: re-circulating ball. Front suspension: MacPherson struts with coil springs, lower control arms and stabilizer bar. Rear suspension: rigid axle and torque tube with longitudinal control arms, Panhard rod, coil springs and stabilizer bar. Brakes: front disc, rear drum; four-wheel discs available. Body construction: unibody. Fuel tank capacity: 15.5 gal.

IROC-Z coupe: Transmission: (Standard): Five-speed manual. (Optional) Four-speed overdrive automatic. (Required option with L98 V-8) Four-speed overdrive automatic. Steering: re-circulating ball. Front suspension: Modified MacPherson strut with coil springs, lower control arms and large-diameter stabilizer bar. Rear suspension: rigid axle and torque arm with longitudinal control arms, Panhard rod, coil springs, large-diameter stabilizer bar and Delco-Bilstein gas-pressure shock absorbers. Brakes: front disc, rear drum; four-wheel discs available. Body construction: unibody. Fuel tank capacity: 15.5 gal.

IROC-Z convertible: Transmission: (Standard): Five-speed manual. (Optional) Four-speed overdrive automatic. (Required option with L98 V-8) Four-speed overdrive automatic. Steering: re-circulating ball. Front suspension: Modified MacPherson strut with coil springs, lower control arms and large-diameter stabilizer bar. Rear suspension: rigid axle and torque arm with longitudinal control arms, Panhard rod, coil springs, large-diameter stabilizer bar and Delco-Bilstein gas-pressure shock absorbers. Brakes: front disc, rear drum; four-wheel discs available. Body construction: unibody. Fuel tank capacity: 15.5 gal.

OPTIONS

Air conditioning ($775). Heavy-duty battery ($26). Engine oil cooler ($110). Locking rear storage cover ($80). Rear defogger ($145). Power door locks ($145).

California emissions package ($99). Gauge package in Sport Coupe ($149). Tinted glass ($120). Rear window louvers ($210). Deluxe luggage compartment trim for Sport Coupe ($164). Body side moldings ($60). Power antenna ($70). T-top roof ($866). Split folding rear seat back ($50). Rear spoiler in Sport Coupe ($69). Cast aluminum wheels with locks ($215). AM/FM stereo cassette ($364). Electronic-tuning AM/FM stereo ET with graphic equalizer ($242). Electronic-tuning AM/FM stereo with cassette and graphic equalizer ($514). Delco-GM/Bose music system ($1,127). AM mono radio ($39). Sport Coupe option package 2 includes tinted glass, air conditioning, tilt steering column and AM/FM stereo ($1,212). Sound systems with Sport Coupe package 2, AM/FM stereo cassette ($122). AM/FM stereo with cassette graphic equalizer ($272). Delco-GM/Bose music system ($885). AM/FM stereo delete ($298 credit). Sport Coupe option package 3 ($1,628) includes package 2 plus four floor mats, body side moldings, intermittent wipers, rear spoiler, cruise control, AM/FM stereo w/cassette and extended range speakers. Sport Coupe option package 4 ($2,126) includes package 3 plus power windows and door locks, power hatch release and cargo cover. Halogen headlamps. Auxiliary lighting. Sound systems with Sport Coupe option packages 3 or 4, AM/FM stereo with cassette and graphic equalizer ($150). Delco-GM/Bose music system ($763). AM/FM stereo delete ($420 credit). IROC-Z option package 1 ($669) includes halogen fog lamps, up-rated suspension and P245/50VR16 tires on aluminum wheels. Sound systems with IROC package 1, AM/FM stereo ET with cassette ($325). Electronic-tuning AM/FM stereo ($203). AM-FM stereo ET with cassette and graphic equalizer ($475). Delco-GM/Bose music system ($1,088). IROC option package 2 ($2,409), includes package 1 plus sport equipment, tinted glass, air conditioning, tilt steering column, floor mats, intermittent wipers, AM/FM stereo ET cassette with extended range speakers, power windows and door locks, and power hatch release. Sound Systems with IROC package 2, electronic-tuning AM/FM stereo with cassette and graphic equalizer ($150). Delco-GM/Bose music system ($763). Electronic-tuning AM/FM stereo with cassette and graphic equalizer ($150). Delco-GM/Bose music system ($763). AM/FM stereo ET with cassette deleted ($381 credit). IROC option package 3 ($3,273 or without cargo area cover $3,204) includes package 2 plus power mirrors, cruise control, body side moldings, cargo cover, auxiliary lighting, automatic day/night mirror, power seat, interior roof console, electronic-tuning AM/FM stereo with cassette and equalizer and extended range speakers. Sound systems with IROC package 3, Delco-GM/Bose music system ($613). Electronic-tuning AM/FM stereo with cassette and graphic equalizer delete ($531 credit).

HISTORICAL FOOTNOTES

Robert D. Burger continued as Chevrolet's general manager during 1988. Model-year sales fell from 122,761 in 1987 to 93,617 in 1988. Calendar-year sales were 101,665 units or 3.7 percent of the industry total. Model year production of 96,275 Camaros represented a 1.38 percent share of the industry's total. The Van Nuys, California, plant built all of these cars (and all 62,467 Fire-

Daniel B. Lyons photo

This IROC-Z hardtop came in Medium Gray Metallic.

birds made in model year 1988). Of the Camaros built, 80.2 percent had automatic transmission, 19.8 percent had a five-speed manual transmission, 55.5 percent had a fuel-injected V-8, 44.5 percent had a fuel-injected V-6, 100 percent had power steering, 86.1 percent had power front disc brakes, 13.9 percent had power four-wheel disc brakes, 29.5 percent had a limited-slip differential, 100 percent had steel-belted radial tires, 45.7 percent had power door locks, 63 percent had power windows, 100 percent had reclining bucket seats, 16.8 percent had a power front driver's seat, 61.7 percent had tilt steering, 94.6 percent had all-tinted glass, 91.9 percent had manual air conditioning, 58.9 percent had cruise control,

61.7 percent had delay windshield wipers, 16.6 percent had an ETR AM/FM radio, 54.9 percent had a ETR stereo cassette player, 4.6 percent had a Bose/JBL sound system, 19.8 percent had a premium sound system, 91.3 percent had premium speakers, 95.9 percent had a digital clock, 55 percent had an electric rear window defogger, 0.7 percent had a rear window wiper, 100 percent had a remote-control left-hand outside rearview mirror, 18.7 percent also had a remote-control right-hand outside rearview mirror, 22.6 percent had aluminum styled wheels and 42.6 percent had T-tops. A total of 99,052 new Camaros were registered in the U.S. during calendar year 1988. That was down from 117,060 in 1987.

The Z28 was not offered in 1988, but the IROC-Z (above) helped make up for that void by offering three different engine options, including a 5.0-liter H.O. and new B2L 5.7-liter power plant.

Camaro

Camaro buyers could pick between the RS (above) and IROC-Z in 1989.

Jerry Heasley photo

Two versions of the rear-drive Camaro were available again this year and the less-expensive version was now called the RS. Like the IROC-Z, it came in hatchback coupe or convertible forms. Both models added a PASS-Key theft-deterrent system as standard equipment since the Camaro ranked as the most popular vehicle among car thieves. The RS coupe with a standard 2.8-liter V-6 engine debuted first in California and was designed to lower skyrocketing insurance costs there.

Both IROC-Z models and the RS ragtop had a standard 170-hp V-8. IROC-Z buyers could add the 220-hp 5.0-liter V-8 or the big 5.7-liter V-8 with 230 hp. Chevy built 110,580 Camaros and more than 7,000 had folding tops.

I.D. DATA

Chevrolets again had a 17-symbol vehicle identification number (VIN) on the upper left surface of the instrument panel, visible through the windshield. The first symbol identifies country of origin: 1=USA, 2=Canada. The second symbol identifies the manufacturer: G=General Motors. The third symbol indicates make: 1=Chevrolet, 7=GM of Canada. The fourth and fifth symbols indicated the car line and series: F/P=Camaro Sport Coupe and Camaro convertible. The sixth symbol indicated body type: 2=two-door hatchback style 87, 3=two-door convertible style 67. The seventh symbol indicated the type of restraint system: 1=manual belts, 3=driver airbag and 4=automatic belts. The eighth symbol indicates the engine type: S=RPO LB8 2.8-liter (173-cid) HO V-6 with Multiport Fuel Injection, E=RPO LO3 5.0-liter (305-cid) V-8 with electronic fuel injection, F=RPO LB9 5.0-liter (305-cid) V-8 with Tuned Port Injection, 8=RPO B2L 5.7-liter (350-cid) V-8 with TPI. The ninth symbol is a check digit. The 10th symbol indicates model year:

K=1989. The 11th symbol indicates the assembly plant: L=Van Nuys, California, N=Norwood, Ohio. The final six digits are the sequential serial number.

COLORS

Silver Metallic, Bright Blue Metallic, Dark Blue Metallic, White, Black, Yellow, Medium Orange Metallic, Dark Red Metallic, Bright Red and Medium Gray Metallic. (Silver Metallic, Bright Blue Metallic and Yellow were not available on the IROC-Z model).

CAMARO RS - SERIES F/P - V-6/V-8

The RS hatchback coupe actually debuted first, in California, as a model intended to keep insurance costs down. Its standard engine was the 2.8-liter V-6 engine. However, a 170-hp V-8 was standard in the RS convertible. Standard equipment included manual lap/shoulder front safety belts with a visual and audible warning system, manual rear lap belts, an energy-absorbing steering column, an energy-absorbing instrument panel, energy-absorbing front seat tops, laminated safety windshield glass, safety glass side windows, safety glass rear window, safety interlocking door latches, passenger-guard inside door lock handles, inertia locking folding front seat backs, safety armrests, front head restraints, side marker lights and reflectors, parking lamps that illuminated with the headlights, four-way hazard warning flashers, back-up lights, a center high-mounted stop lamp, direction signals with lane-change feature, a windshield defroster, a windshield washer system, multi-speed windshield wipers, an inside rearview mirror with vinyl bonded glass, dual outside rearview mirrors, a dual-chamber brake master cylinder and brake system warning light, a starter safety switch, a dual-action hood latch system, low-glare instrument panel finish, low-glare windshield moldings, low-glare wiper arms and blades, low-glare metallic steering wheel surfaces, illuminated heater and defroster controls, tires with built-in wear indicators, an audible reminder for ignition key removal, a theft-deterrent steering column lock, a visible VIN number, marked body parts, a PASS-Key vehicle anti-theft (VATS) system, a 2.8-liter V-6 engine with Multi-port Fuel Injection, an AM/FM stereo (with seek-and-scan, a digital clock and an extended-range sound system), basecoat/clearcoat paint, a black windshield molding, black concealed windshield wipers, body tape striping, a carpeted cargo floor, cloth reclining bucket seats, dual color-keyed sport style outside rearview mirrors (left-hand remote and right-hand manual), 15 x 7-in. cast-aluminum wheels, a five-speed manual transmission, a front air dam, ground-effects type rocker panel moldings, power front disc brakes with audible wear sensors, power rear drum brakes, power steering, a power ventilation system, P215/65R-15 steel-belted radial-ply touring tires, a rear deck lid spoiler, a rear hatch with automatic pull-down, side window defoggers, special instrumentation with a tachometer and a Sport suspension.

Model Number	Body/Style Number	Body Type & Seating	Factory Price	Shipping Weight	Production Total
CAMARO RS SPORT COUPE - SERIES F/P - (V-6)					
F/P	87	2d coupe	$11,495	3,082 lbs.	Note 1
CAMARO RS SPORT COUPE - SERIES F/P - (V-8)					
F/P	87	2d coupe	$11,895	3,285 lbs.	Note 1
CAMARO RS CONVERTIBLE - SERIES F/P-Z08 - (V-8)					
F/P	67	2d convertible	$16,995	3,116 lbs.	3,245

Note 1: Model-year production of 1989 Camaro RS coupes was 83,487.

CAMARO IROC-Z - SERIES F/P - V-8

The IROC-Z was back for 1989 and came in hatch-back coupe or convertible models, both with the PASS-Key theft-deterrent system as standard equipment. The base engine was the 170-hp V-8. The IROC-Z also had a choice of 220-hp 5.0-liter TPI V-8 or the big 5.7-liter TPI V-8 with 240 hp. Standard equipment included manual lap/shoulder front safety belts with a visual and audible warning system, manual rear lap belts, an energy-absorbing steering column, an energy-absorbing instrument panel, energy-absorbing front seat tops, laminated safety windshield glass, safety glass side windows, safety glass rear window, safety interlocking door latches, passenger-guard inside door lock handles, inertia locking folding front seat backs, safety armrests, front head restraints, side marker lights and reflectors, parking lamps that illuminated with the headlights, black painted headlight openings, halogen fog lamps, black simulated louvers on the hood, Camaro gold or silver letters on the lower front fascia, four-way hazard warning flashers, back-up lights, a center high-mounted stop lamp, direction signals with lane-change feature, a windshield defroster, a windshield washer system, multi-speed windshield wipers, an inside rearview mirror with vinyl bonded glass, dual outside rearview mirrors, a dual-chamber brake master cylinder and brake system warning light, a starter safety switch, a dual-action hood latch system, low-glare instrument panel finish, low-glare windshield moldings, low-glare wiper arms and blades, low-glare metallic steering wheel surfaces, illuminated heater and defroster controls, tires with built-in wear indicators, an audible reminder for ignition key removal, a theft-deterrent steering column lock, a visible VIN number, marked body parts, a PASS-Key vehicle anti-theft system (VATS), a 5.0-liter V-6 engine with electronic fuel injection, an AM/FM stereo (with seek-and-scan, a digital clock and an extended-range sound system), basecoat/clearcoat paint, a black windshield molding, black concealed windshield wipers, body tape striping, a carpeted cargo floor, cloth reclining bucket seats,

Chevy produced more than 83,000 RS Camaros in 1989, but only 3,245 of them were convertibles.

dual color-keyed sport style outside rearview mirrors (left-hand remote and right-hand manual), 15 x 7-in. cast-aluminum wheels, a five-speed manual transmission, a leather-wrapped gearshift knob, specific body striping, color-coordinated IROC-Z door decals, special instrumentation with a tachometer, a front air dam, ground-effects type rocker panel moldings, power front disc brakes with audible wear sensors, power rear drum brakes, power steering, a power ventilation system, P215/65R-15 steel-belted radial-ply touring tires, a rear deck lid spoiler, a rear hatch with automatic pull-down, side window defoggers, a special performance ride and handling suspension, a visor-vanity mirror and specific taillights.

Model Number	Body/Style Number	Body Type & Seating	Factory Price	Shipping Weight	Production Total
CAMARO IROC-Z - SERIES F/P - (V-8)					
F/P	87	2d coupe	$14,145	3,264 lbs.	20,067
CAMARO IROC-Z CONVERTIBLE - SERIES F/P - (V-8)					
F/P	67	2d convertible	$18,945	—	3,940

Note 2: The optional 1LE competition package was installed on 111 of the IROC-Zs built in model year 1989.

ENGINES

LB8 V-6: 60-degree, overhead-valve V-6. Cast-iron block and head. Bore & stroke: 3.50 x 2.99 in. Displacement: 173 cid (2.8 liters). Compression ratio: 8.9:1. Brake horsepower: 135 at 4900 rpm. Torque: 160 lbs.-ft. at 3900 rpm. Induction system: Multiport Fuel Injection. Standard in Camaro RS Sport Coupe. VIN Code S.

LO3 base V-8: 90-degree, overhead-valve V-8. Cast-iron block and head. Bore & stroke: 3.74 x 3.48 in. Displacement: 305 cid (5.0 liters). Compression ratio: 9.3:1. Brake horsepower: 170 at 4000 rpm Torque: 255 lbs.-ft. at 2400 rpm Five main bearings. Hydraulic valve lifters. Induction system: electronic fuel injection. Standard in Camaro RS convertible and IROC-Z. Optional in RS Sport Coupe. VIN Code: H.

LB9 TPI V-8: 90-degree, overhead-valve V-8. Cast-iron block and head. Bore & stroke: 3.74 x 3.48 in. Displacement: 305 cid (5.0 liters). Compression ratio: 9.3:1. Brake horsepower: 220 at 4400 rpm (195 hp with automatic transmission). Torque: 290 lbs.-ft. at 3200 rpm. Five main bearings. Hydraulic valve lifters. Electronic spark control. Induction system: Tuned Port Injection. Optional in IROC-Z. VIN Code: F.

B2L TPI V-8: 90-degree, overhead-valve V-8. Cast-iron block and head. Bore & stroke: 4.00 x 3.48 in. Displacement: 350 cid (5.7 liters). Compression ratio: 9.3:1. Brake horsepower: 240 at 4400 rpm Torque: 330 lbs.-ft. at 3200 rpm. Hydraulic valve lifters. Electronic spark control. Induction system: Tuned Port Injection. Optional in IROC-Z. VIN Code: 8.

CHASSIS

Base RS Coupe: Wheelbase: 101 in. Overall length: 192 in. Overall height: 50.3 in. Overall width: 72.8 in. Front tread: 60 in. Rear tread: 60.9 in. Front headroom: 37 in. Rear headroom: 35.6 in. Front legroom: 43 in. Rear legroom: 29.8 in. Front shoulder room: 57.5 in. Rear shoulder room: 56.3 in. Front hip room: 56.3 in. Rear hip room: 42.8 in. Cargo volume: 12.4 cu. ft. (31 cu. ft. with rear seat back down). Standard tires: P215/65R-15 black sidewall steel-belted radial.

Base RS Convertible: Wheelbase: 101 in. Overall length: 192 in. Overall height: 50.3 in. Overall width: 72.8 in. Front tread: 60 in. Rear tread: 60.9 in. Front headroom: 37 in. Rear headroom: 35.6 in. Front legroom: 43 in. Rear legroom: 29.8 in. Front shoulder room: 57.5 in. Rear shoulder room: 56.3 in. Front hip room: 56.3 in. Rear hip room: 42.8 in. Cargo volume: 5.2 cu. ft. Standard tires: P215/65R-15 black sidewall steel-belted radial.

This 1989 IROC-Z convertible came with a flashy black and pink paint scheme.

The IROC-Z came with a long list of goodies, including T-tops.

IROC-Z Coupe: Wheelbase: 101 in. Overall length: 192 in. Overall height: 50.3 in. Overall width: 72.8 in. Front tread: 60 in. Rear Tread: 60.9 in. Front headroom: 37 in. Rear headroom: 35.6 in. Front legroom: 43 in. Rear legroom: 29.8 in. Front shoulder room: 57.5 in. Rear shoulder room: 56.3 in. Front hip room: 56.3 in. Rear hip room: 42.8 in. Cargo volume: 12.4 cu. ft. (31 cu. ft. with rear seat back down). Standard tires: P215/65R-15 black-letter steel-belted radial.

IROC-Z Convertible: Wheelbase: 101 in. Overall length: 192 in. Overall height: 50.3 in. Overall width: 72.8 in. Front tread: 60 in. Rear tread: 60.9 in. Front headroom: 37 in. Rear headroom: 35.6 in. Front legroom: 43 in. Rear legroom: 29.8 in. Front shoulder room: 57.5 in. Rear shoulder room: 56.3 in. Front hip room: 56.3 in. Rear hip room: 42.8 in. Cargo volume: 5.2 cu. ft. Standard tires: P215/65R-15 black-letter steel-belted radial.

TECHNICAL

Base RS Coupe: Transmission: (Standard): Five-speed manual. (Optional) Four-speed overdrive automatic. Steering: re-circulating ball. Front suspension: MacPherson struts with coil springs, lower control arms and stabilizer bar. Rear suspension: rigid axle and torque tube with longitudinal control arms, Panhard rod, coil springs and stabilizer bar, Brakes: front disc, rear drum, four-wheel discs available. Body construction: unibody. Fuel tank capacity: 15.5 gal.

Camaro RS Convertible: Transmission: (Standard): Five-speed manual. (Optional) Four-speed overdrive automatic. Steering: re-circulating ball. Front suspension: MacPherson struts with coil springs, lower control arms and stabilizer bar. Rear suspension: rigid axle and torque tube with longitudinal control arms, Panhard rod, coil springs and stabilizer bar, Brakes: front disc, rear drum, four-wheel discs available. Body construction: unibody. Fuel tank capacity: 15.5 gal.

IROC-Z Coupe: Transmission® (Standard): Five-speed manual. (Optional) Four-speed overdrive automatic. (Required option with L98 V-8) Four-speed overdrive automatic. Steering: re-circulating ball. Front suspension: Modified MacPherson strut with coil springs, lower control arms and large-diameter stabilizer bar. Rear suspension: rigid axle and torque arm with longitudinal control arms, Panhard rod, coil springs, large-diameter stabilizer bar and Delco-Bilstein gas-pressure shock absorbers. Brakes: front disc, rear drum, four-wheel discs available. Body construction: unibody. Fuel tank capacity: 15.5 gal.

IROC-Z Convertible: Transmission: (Standard): Five-speed manual. (Optional) Four-speed overdrive automatic. (Required option with L98 V-8) Four-speed overdrive automatic. Steering: re-circulating ball. Front suspension: Modified MacPherson strut with coil springs, lower control arms and large-diameter stabilizer bar. Rear suspension: rigid axle and torque arm with longitudinal control arms, Panhard rod, coil springs, large-diameter stabilizer bar and Delco-Bilstein gas-pressure shock absorbers. Brakes: front disc, rear drum, four-wheel discs available. Body construction: unibody. Fuel tank capacity: 15.5 gal.

OPTIONS

RS coupe preferred equipment group 1, including heavy-duty battery, tinted glass, auxiliary lighting and body side moldings ($255). RS coupe preferred equipment group 2, including air conditioning, power door locks, a heavy-duty battery, front and rear color-keyed carpet mats, tinted glass, auxiliary lighting, body side moldings, electronically tuned AM/FM stereo radio (with seek-and-scan, stereo cassette tape, digital clock and extended-range sound system), speed control with resume feature, a Comfortilt steering wheel and an intermittent windshield wiper system ($1,727). RS coupe preferred equipment group 3, including air conditioning, a heavy-duty battery, a cargo cover, a power door lock system, front and rear carpet mats, tinted glass, halogen headlamps, high and low-beam auxiliary lighting, a mirror with dual reading lamps, body side moldings, an electronically tuned AM/FM stereo radio (with seek-and-scan, stereo cassette tape, digital clock and extended-

About 20 percent of 1989 Camaros had a manual transmission.

range sound system), electronic speed control with resume speed feature, a Comfortilt steering wheel and an intermittent windshield wiper system. IROC-Z preferred equipment group 1 including tinted glass, a heavy-duty battery, auxiliary lighting and body side moldings (without 5.7-liter engine $255; with 5.7-liter engine $229). IROC-Z preferred equipment group 2, including air conditioning, a power door lock system, front and rear carpet mats, tinted glass, a power hatch release, auxiliary lighting, body side moldings, electronically tuned AM/FM stereo radio (with seek-and-scan, stereo cassette tape, digital clock and extended-range sound system), speed control with resume feature, a heavy-duty battery, a Comfortilt steering wheel and an intermittent windshield wiper system, without 5.7-liter engine ($1,777). IROC-Z preferred equipment group 3, including air conditioning, power door lock system, a cargo cover, color-keyed front and rear carpet mats, tinted glass, halogen high- and low-beam headlamps, a power hatch release, auxiliary lighting, a mirror with dual reading lamps, twin remote-control sport-style outside rearview mirrors, body side moldings, an electronically tuned AM/FM

stereo radio (with seek-and-scan, stereo cassette tape, search-and-repeat, graphic equalizer, digital clock and extended-range sound system), a power driver's seats, electronic speed control with resume speed, a heavy-duty battery, a Comfortilt steering wheel, power windows and an intermittent windshield wiper system (without 5.7-liter engine $2,605, with 5.7-liter engine $2,579). Camaro RS convertible preferred equipment group 1, including heavy-duty battery, tinted glass and body side moldings ($206). RS convertible preferred equipment group 2, includes air conditioning, heavy-duty battery, power door lock system, front and rear color-keyed carpet mats, tinted glass, body side moldings, electronically tuned AM/FM stereo radio, (with seek-and-scan, stereo cassette tape, digital clock, and extended-range sound system), electronic speed control, with resume feature, a Comfortilt steering wheel and an intermittent windshield wiper system ($1,678). RS convertible preferred equipment group 3, including air conditioning, a heavy-duty battery, a power door lock system, color-keyed front and rear carpet mats. Tinted glass, halogen high- and low-beam headlights, body side moldings, an electronically tuned AM/FM stereo radio (with seek-and-scan, cassette tape player, digital clock and an extended-range sound system). Electronic speed control with resume speed, a Comfortilt steering wheel, power windows and an intermittent windshield wiper system ($1,923). IROC-Z convertible preferred equipment group 1, including heavy-duty battery, tinted glass and body side moldings ($206). IROC-Z convertible preferred equipment group 2, including air conditioning, heavy-duty battery, power door lock system, front and rear carpet mats, tinted glass, body side moldings, electronically tuned AM/FM stereo radio (with seek-and-scan, cassette, digital clock and extended-range sound system), speed control with resume, Comfortilt steering wheel and intermittent windshield wiper system ($1,678). IROC-Z convertible preferred equipment

This IROC-Z came in Dark Red Metallic.

Daniel B. Lyons photo

The IROC-Z convertible was the highest-priced 1989 Camaro. It started at $18,945.

group 3, including air conditioning, heavy-duty battery, power door lock system, front and rear carpet mats, tinted glass, halogen high- and low-beam headlamps, twin remote sport mirrors, body side moldings, electronically tuned AM/FM stereo radio (with seek-and-scan, stereo cassette tape, search-and-repeat, graphic equalizer, digital clock and extended-range sound system), power driver's seat, speed control with resume feature, Comfortilt steering wheel, power windows, and intermittent windshield wiper system ($2,414). Custom cloth bucket seats ($277). Custom leather bucket seats ($750). Air conditioning ($795). Limited-slip differential ($100). Performance axle ratio including dual exhausts ($177). Front license plate bracket (no cost). Power four-wheel disc brakes ($179). Engine oil cooler ($110). Locking rear storage cover ($80). Decal and stripe delete ($60 credit). Electric rear window defogger ($150). Power door lock system ($155). California emission system ($100). Power hatch release ($50). Engine block heater ($20). Rear window louvers ($210). Deluxe luggage compartment trim, RS coupe only, includes locking rear compartment storage cover ($164). IROC-Z coupe ($84). Sport twin remote mirrors ($91). Black door edge guards ($15). Electronically tuned AM/FM stereo radio with seek-and-scan, stereo cassette tape, search-and-repeat, graphic equalizer and digital clock ($150/$272). Electronically tuned AM/FM stereo with seek-and-scan, stereo cassette tape and digital clock ($122). Electronically tuned GM Delco/Bose music system, including AM/FM stereo with seek-and-scan, stereo cassette tape, digital clock, special tone and balance control and four speakers ($613/$885). Electronically tuned AM/FM stereo radio (with seek-and-scan, compact disc player and digital clock ($124/$396). Power antenna ($70). Removable roof panels, including locks ($866). Split folding rear seatback ($50). Cast-aluminum 16-in. wheels with wheel locks and P245/50 VF16 SBR black sidewall tires ($520).

HISTORICAL FOOTNOTES

Robert D. Burger was Chevrolet's general manager at the start of 1989, but by 1990, Jim C. Perkins would assume this position. The company lost nearly a full point of overall market share this year, however model-year sales of Camaros rose from 93,617 in 1988 to 110,034 in 1989. Calendar-year sales were 95,469 units or 3.7 percent of the industry total for the specialty model segment. Model-year production of 110,739 Camaros represented a slightly higher 1.55 percent share of the industry's total than the previous year. The Van Nuys plant built all of these cars (and all 64,406 Firebirds). Of the Camaros built, 79.9 percent had automatic transmission, 20.1 percent had a five-speed manual transmission, 61.5 percent had a fuel-injected V-8, 38.5 percent had a fuel-injected V-6, 100 percent had power steering, 88.4 percent had power front disc brakes, 11.6 percent had power four-wheel disc brakes, 27.9 percent had a limited-slip differential, 100 percent had steel-belted radial tires, 89.7 percent had power door locks, 55.7 percent had power windows, 100 percent had reclining bucket seats, 17.8 percent had a power front driver's seat, 89.9 percent had tilt steering, 99.8 percent had tinted glass, 94.5 percent had manual air conditioning, 58.9 percent had cruise control, 61.7 percent had delay windshield wipers, 5.5 percent had an ETR AM/FM radio, 66.3 percent had a ETR stereo cassette player, 4.1 percent had a Bose/JBL sound system, 21.8 percent had a premium sound system, 2.3 percent had a CD player, 100 percent had a digital clock, 53.8 percent had an electric rear window defogger, 0.7 percent had a rear window wiper, 100 percent had a remote-control left-hand outside rearview mirror, 26 percent also had a remote-control right-hand outside rearview mirror, 14.9 percent had aluminum styled wheels and 40.3 percent had T-tops. A total of 98,735 new Camaros were registered in the U.S. during calendar year 1989. That was down from 99,052 in 1988.

Camaro

Jerry Heasley photo

The 1990 IROC-Z got new alloy wheels and a limited-slip differential. It also had an optional leather interior for the first time.

With face-lifted '91 Camaros due to arrive in the spring, the 1990 model year was abbreviated and only 35,048 were built. The Camaro RS got a larger 3.1-liter (190-cid) base V-6. All Camaros now incorporated a driver's side airbag. A five-speed manual gearbox remained standard, but Camaros with the optional four-speed overdrive automatic got a modified torque converter with higher lockup points for improved gas mileage.

New standard equipment included halogen headlamps, tinted glass, intermittent wipers and a tilt steering wheel. New 16-in. alloy wheels became standard on the IROC-Z convertible and optional on the coupe. IROC-Z models also had a standard limited-slip differential. Leather upholstery joined the interior options list, while the instrument panel switched to new yellow graphics.

I.D. DATA

Chevrolets again had a 17-symbol vehicle identification number (VIN) on the upper left surface of the instrument panel, visible through the windshield. The first symbol identifies country of origin: 1=USA, 2=Canada. The second symbol identifies the manufacturer: G=General Motors. The third symbol indicates make: 1=Chevrolet, 7=GM of Canada. The fourth and fifth symbols indicated the car line and series: F/P=Camaro Sport Coupe and Camaro convertible. The sixth symbol indicated body type: 2=two-door hatchback style 87, 3=two-door convertible style 67. The seventh symbol indicated the type of restraint system: 1=manual belts, 3=driver airbag and 4=automatic belts. The eighth symbol indicates the engine type: T=RPO LH0 3.1-liter (190-cid) V-6 with Multiport Fuel Injection, E=RPO LO3 5.0-liter (305-cid) V-8 with electronic fuel injection, F=RPO LB9 5.0-liter (305-cid) V-8 with Tuned Port Injection, 8=RPO B2L 5.7-liter (350-cid) V-8 with TPI. The ninth symbol is a check digit. The 10th symbol indicates model year:

L=1989. The 11th symbol indicates the assembly plant: L=Van Nuys, California.

COLORS

White, Black, Dark Red Metallic, Bright Red, Medium Gray Metallic, Light Blue Bright Blue Metallic (Light Blue Metallic and Medium Gray Metallic not available on IROC-Z).

CAMARO RS - SERIES F/P - V-6/V-8

Standard equipment included manual lap/shoulder front safety belts with visual and audible warning system, manual rear lap belts, an energy-absorbing steering column, an energy-absorbing instrument panel, energy-absorbing front seat tops, laminated safety windshield glass, safety glass side windows, safety glass rear window, safety interlocking door latches, passenger-guard inside door lock handles, inertia locking folding front seat backs, safety armrests, front head restraints, side marker lights and reflectors, parking lamps that illuminated with the headlights, four-way hazard warning flashers, back-up lights, a center high-mounted stop lamp, direction signals with a lane-change feature, a windshield defroster, a windshield washer system, multi-speed windshield wipers, an inside rearview mirror with vinyl bonded glass, dual outside rearview mirrors, a dual-chamber brake master cylinder and brake system warning light, a starter safety switch, a dual-action hood latch system, low-glare instrument panel finish, low-glare windshield moldings, low-glare wiper arms and blades, low-glare metallic steering wheel surfaces, illuminated heater and defroster controls, tires with built-in wear indicators, an audible reminder for ignition key removal, a theft-deterrent steering column lock, a visible VIN number, marked body parts, a PASS-Key vehicle anti-theft system (VATS), a 2.8-liter V-6 engine with Multiport Fuel Injection, an AM/FM stereo (with seek-and-scan, a digital clock and an extended-range sound system), basecoat/clearcoat paint, a black windshield molding, black concealed windshield wipers, body tape striping, a carpeted cargo floor, cloth reclining bucket seats, dual color-keyed sport style outside rearview mirrors (left-hand remote and right-hand manual), 15 x 7-in. cast-aluminum wheels, a front air dam, ground-effects type rocker panel moldings, power front disc brakes with audible wear sensors, power rear drum brakes, power steering, a power ventilation system, P215/65R-15 steel-belted radial-ply touring tires, a rear deck lid spoiler, a rear hatch with automatic pull-down, side window defoggers, special instrumentation with a tachometer and a sport suspension. The 5.0-liter TBI V-8 engine was standard in the RS convertible and optional in the RS coupe.

Model Number	Body/Style Number	Body Type & Seating	Factory Price	Shipping Weight	Production Total
CAMARO RS SPORT COUPE - SERIES F/P - (V-6)					
F/P	87	2d coupe	$10,995	2,975 lbs.	Note 1
CAMARO RS SPORT COUPE - SERIES F/P - (V-8)					
F/P	87	2d coupe	$11,345	3,143 lbs.	Note 1
CAMARO RS CONVERTIBLE - SERIES F/P-Z08 - (V-8)					
F/P	67	2d convertible	$16,880	3,270 lbs.	Note 2

Note 1: Model-year production of 1990 Camaro RS coupes was most likely 28,750.
Note 2: Model-year production of 1990 Camaro RS convertibles was most likely 729.

CAMARO IROC-Z - SERIES F/P - V-8

The IROC-Z got the same new equipment as the Camaro RS including the available four-speed overdrive automatic transmission with a modified torque converter having higher lock-up points for improved gas mileage. New 16-in. alloy wheels became standard on the IROC-Z convertible and optional on the hatchback coupe. Also new for the IROC-Z was a standard limited-slip differential. Leather upholstery joined the interior options list, while the instrument panel (RS and IROC-Z) switched to new yellow graphics. Other standard IROC-Z equipment included manual lap/shoulder front safety belts with a visual and audible warning system, manual rear lap belts, an energy-absorbing steering column, an energy-absorbing instrument panel, energy-absorbing front seat tops, laminated safety windshield glass, safety glass side windows, safety glass rear window, safety interlocking door latches, passenger-guard inside door lock handles, inertia locking folding front seat backs, safety armrests, front head restraints, side marker lights and reflectors, parking lamps that illuminated with the headlights, black painted headlight openings, halogen fog lamps, black simulated louvers on the hood, Camaro gold or silver letters on the lower front fascia, four-way hazard warning flashers, back-up lights, a center high-mounted stop lamp, direction signals with lane-

change feature, a windshield defroster, a windshield washer system, multi-speed windshield wipers, an inside rearview mirror with vinyl bonded glass, dual outside rearview mirrors, a dual-chamber brake master cylinder and brake system warning light, a starter safety switch, a dual-action hood latch system, low-glare instrument panel finish, low-glare windshield moldings, low-glare wiper arms and blades, low-glare metallic steering wheel surfaces, illuminated heater and defroster controls, tires with built-in wear indicators, an audible reminder for ignition key removal, a theft-deterrent steering column lock, a visible VIN number, marked body parts, a PASS-Key vehicle anti-theft system (VATS), a 5.0-liter V-6 engine with electronic fuel injection, an AM/FM stereo (with seek-and-scan, a digital clock and an extended-range sound system), basecoat/clearcoat paint, a black windshield molding, black concealed windshield wipers, body tape striping, a carpeted cargo floor, cloth reclining bucket seats, dual color-keyed sport style outside rearview mirrors (left-hand remote and right-hand manual), 15 x 7-in. cast-aluminum wheels, a five-speed manual transmission, a leather-wrapped gearshift knob, specific body striping, color-coordinated IROC-Z door decals, special instrumentation with a tachometer, a front air dam, ground-effects type rocker panel moldings, power front disc brakes with audible wear sensors, power rear drum brakes, power steering, a power ventilation system, P215/65R-15 steel-belted radial ply touring tires, a rear deck lid spoiler, a rear hatch with automatic pull-down, side window defoggers, a special performance ride and handling suspension, a visor-vanity mirror and specific taillights.

Model Number	Body/Style Number	Body Type & Seating	Factory Price	Shipping Weight	Production Total
CAMARO IROC-Z - SERIES F/P - (V-8)					
F/P	87/Z28	2d coupe	$14,145	3,264 lbs.	Note 3
CAMARO IROC-Z CONVERTIBLE - SERIES F/P - (V-8)					
F/P	67/Z28	2d convertible	$18,945	3,272 lbs.	Note 4

Note 3: Model-year production of 1990 Camaro IROC-Z coupes was most likely 4,213 (see production chart in rear of catalog).
Note 4: Model-year production of 1990 Camaro IROC-Z convertibles was most likely 1,294 (see production chart in rear of catalog).
Note 5: The optional 1LE competition package was installed on 62 Camaro IROC-Zs in the 1990 model year.

ENGINES

LH0 V-6: 60-degree, overhead-valve V-6. Cast-iron block and head. Bore & stroke: 3.50 x 3.31 in. Displacement: 191 cid (3.1 liters). Compression ratio: 8.8:1. Brake horsepower: 144 at 4400 rpm. Torque: 180 lbs.-ft. at 3600 rpm. Induction system: Multiport Fuel Injection. Standard in Camaro RS hatchback coupe. VIN Code T.

LO3 base V-8: 90-degree, overhead-valve V-8. Cast-

The Camaro RS received a larger standard V-6 engine. Chevrolet sold more than 28,000 of the coupes in an abbreviated production run.

iron block and head. Bore & stroke: 3.74 x 3.48 in. Displacement: 305 cid (5.0 liters). Compression ratio: 9.3:1. Brake horsepower: 170 at 4000 rpm Torque: 255 lbs.-ft. at 2400 rpm Five main bearings. Hydraulic valve lifters. Induction system: electronic fuel injection. Optional in Camaro RS hatchback coupe, standard in Camaro RS convertible and IROC-Z. VIN Code: E.

LB9 TPI V-8: 90-degree, overhead-valve V-8. Cast-iron block and head. Bore & stroke: 3.74 x 3.48 in. Displacement: 305 cid (5.0 liters). Compression ratio: 9.3:1. Brake horsepower: 220 at 4400 rpm (195 hp with automatic transmission). Torque: 290 lbs.-ft. at 3200 rpm. Five main bearings. Hydraulic valve lifters. Electronic spark control. Induction system: Tuned Port Injection. Optional in IROC-Z. VIN Code: F.

B2L TPI V-8: 90-degree, overhead-valve V-8. Cast-iron block and head. Bore & stroke: 4.00 x 3.48 in. Displacement: 350 cid (5.7 liters). Compression ratio: 9.3:1. Brake horsepower: 230 at 4400 rpm Torque: 330 lbs.-ft. at 3200 rpm. Optional in IROC-Z. VIN Code: 8.

CHASSIS:

Base RS Coupe: Wheelbase: 101 in. Overall length: 192.0 in. Overall height: 50.3 in. Overall width: 72.8 in. Front tread: 60 in. Rear tread: 60.9 in. Front headroom: 37 in. Rear headroom: 35.6 in. Front legroom: 43 in. Rear legroom: 29.8 in. Front shoulder room: 57.5 in. Rear shoulder room: 56.3 in. Front hip room: 56.3 in. Rear hip room: 42.8 in. Cargo volume: 12.4 cu. ft. (31 cu. ft. with rear seat back down). Standard tires: P215/65R-15 black sidewall steel-belted radial.

Base RS Convertible: Wheelbase: 101 in. Overall length: 192 in. Overall height: 50.3 in. Overall width: 72.8 in. Front tread: 60 in. Rear tread: 60.9 in. Front headroom: 37 in. Rear headroom: 35.6 in. Front legroom: 43 in. Rear legroom: 29.8 in. Front shoulder room: 57.5 in. Rear shoulder room: 56.3 in. Front hip room: 56.3 in. Rear hip room: 42.8 in. Cargo volume: 5.2 cu. ft. Standard tires: P215/65R-15 black sidewall steel-belted radial.

IROC-Z Coupe: Wheelbase: 101 in. Overall length: 192 in. Overall height: 50.3 in. Overall width: 72.8 in. Front tread: 60 in. Rear tread: 60.9 in. Front headroom: 37 in. Rear headroom: 35.6 in. Front legroom: 43 in. Rear legroom: 29.8 in. Front shoulder room: 57.5 in. Rear shoulder room: 56.3 in. Front hip room: 56.3 in. Rear hip room: 42.8 in. Cargo volume: 12.4 cu. ft. (31 cu. ft. with rear seat back down). Standard tires: P215/65R-15 black-letter steel-belted radial.

IROC-Z Convertible: Wheelbase: 101 in. Overall length: 192 in. Overall height: 50.3 in. Overall width: 72.8 in. Front tread: 60 in. Rear tread: 60.9 in. Front headroom: 37 in. Rear headroom: 35.6 in. Front legroom: 43 in. Rear legroom: 29.8 in. Front shoulder room: 57.5 in. Rear shoulder room: 56.3 in. Front hip room: 56.3 in. Rear hip room: 42.8 in. Cargo volume: 5.2 cu. ft. Standard tires: P215/65R-15 black-letter steel-belted radial.

TECHNICAL

Base RS Coupe: Transmission: (Standard): Five-speed manual. (Optional) Four-speed overdrive automatic. Steering: re-circulating ball. Front suspension: MacPherson struts with coil springs, lower control arms and stabilizer bar. Rear suspension: rigid axle and torque tube with longitudinal control arms, Panhard rod, coil springs and stabilizer bar. Brakes: front disc, rear drum, four-wheel discs available. Body construction: unibody. Fuel tank capacity: 15.5 gal.

Camaro RS Convertible: Transmission: (Standard): Five-speed manual. (Optional) Four-speed overdrive automatic. Steering: re-circulating ball. Front suspension: MacPherson struts with coil springs, lower control arms and stabilizer bar. Rear suspension: rigid axle and torque tube with longitudinal control arms, Panhard rod, coil springs and stabilizer bar. Brakes: front disc, rear drum, four-wheel discs available. Body construction: unibody. Fuel tank capacity: 15.5 gal.

IROC-Z Coupe: Transmission: (Standard): Five-speed manual. (Optional) Four-speed overdrive automatic. (Required option with L98 V-8) Four-speed overdrive automatic. Steering: re-circulating ball. Front suspension: Modified MacPherson strut with coil springs, lower control arms and large-diameter stabilizer bar. Rear suspension: rigid axle and torque arm with longitudinal control arms, Panhard rod, coil springs, large-diameter stabilizer bar and Delco-Bilstein gas-pressure shock absorbers. Brakes: front disc, rear drum, four-wheel discs available. Body construction: unibody. Fuel tank capacity: 15.5 gal.

IROC-Z Convertible: Transmission: (Standard): Five-speed manual. (Optional) Four-speed overdrive automatic. (Required option with L98 V-8) Four-speed overdrive automatic. Steering: re-circulating ball. Front suspension: Modified MacPherson strut with coil springs, lower control arms and large-diameter stabilizer bar. Rear suspension: rigid axle and torque arm with longitudinal control arms, Panhard rod, coil springs, large-diameter stabilizer bar and Delco-Bilstein gas-pressure shock absorbers. Brakes: front disc, rear drum, four-wheel discs available. Body construction: unibody. Fuel tank capacity: 15.5 gal.

OPTIONS

RS coupe base equipment group included with model (no cost). RS coupe base equipment group with UM6 radio (add $140). RS coupe base equipment group with UU8 radio (add $1,015). RS coupe base equipment group with UL5 radio delete ($165 credit). RS coupe preferred equipment group number 1, including air conditioning, ETR AM/FM stereo (with seek-and-scan, cassette tape, digital clock and extended-range sound system), power door locks, speed control with resume, body side moldings and front and rear color-keyed carpeted floor mats for package price of $1,410 or $875 additional with UU8 radio. RS coupe preferred equipment group number 2, including air conditioning, ETR AM/FM stereo (with seek-and-scan, cassette tape, digital clock and extended-range sound system), power door locks, speed control with resume, power hatch release, cargo area cover, body side moldings, front and rear color-keyed carpeted floor mats and mirror with dual reading lamps for package price of $1,782 or $875 additional with UU8 radio. IROC-Z base equipment group included with model (no cost). IROC-Z base equipment group with UM6 radio (add $140). IROC-Z base equipment group with UU8

The IROC-Z coupe had a base price of $14,145.

radio (add $1,015). IROC-Z base equipment group with UL5 radio delete ($165 credit). IROC-Z preferred equipment group number 1 includes air conditioning and body side moldings for package price of $865 (with UM6 radio add $140 or with UU8 radio add $1,015). IROC-Z coupe preferred equipment group number 2, including air conditioning, ETR AM/FM stereo (with seek-and-scan, cassette tape, digital clock and extended-range sound system), power door locks, speed control with resume, power hatch release, cargo area cover, body side moldings and front and rear color-keyed carpeted floor mats for package price of $1,759 or $875 additional with UU8 radio. IROC-Z coupe preferred equipment group number 3, including air conditioning, ETR AM/FM stereo (with seek-and-scan, cassette tape, digital clock and extended-range sound system), power windows, power driver's seat, power door locks, speed control with resume, power hatch release, dual power sport-type outside rearview mirrors, cargo area cover, body side moldings, front and rear color-keyed carpeted floor mats and mirror with dual reading lamps for package price of $2,143 or $875 additional with UU8 radio. RS convertible base equipment group (no cost). RS convertible base equipment group with UM6 radio (add $140). RS convertible base equipment group with UL5 radio delete ($165 credit). RS convertible preferred equipment group number 1, including air conditioning, ETR AM/FM stereo (with seek-and-scan, cassette tape, digital clock and extended-range sound system), body side moldings and front and rear color-keyed carpeted floor mats for package price of $1,040. RS convertible preferred equipment group number 2, including air conditioning, ETR AM/FM stereo (with seek-and-scan, cassette tape, digital clock and extended-range sound system), power windows, power door locks, speed control with resume, body side moldings and front and rear color-keyed carpeted floor mats for package price of $1,640. IROC-Z convertible base equipment group (no cost). IROC-Z convertible base equipment group with UM6 radio (add $140). IROC-Z convertible base equipment group with UL5

radio delete ($165 credit). IROC-Z convertible preferred equipment group number 1, including air conditioning and body side moldings for package price of $865 or add $140 for UM6 radio. IROC-Z convertible preferred equipment group number 2, including air conditioning, ETR AM/FM stereo (with seek-and-scan, cassette tape, digital clock and extended-range sound system), power windows, power door locks, speed control with resume, body side moldings and front and rear color-keyed carpeted floor mats for package price of $1,640. IROC-Z convertible preferred equipment group number 3, including air conditioning, ETR AM/FM stereo (with seek-and-scan, cassette tape, digital clock and extended-range sound system), power windows, power driver's seat, power door locks, speed control with resume, dual power sport-type outside rearview mirrors, body side moldings and front and rear color-keyed carpeted floor mats for package price of $2,001. C2 cloth bucket seats (no cost). F2 custom cloth bucket seats ($327). A2 custom leather bucket seats ($800). Solid color exterior paint (no cost). LHO 3.1-liter MFI V-6 in RS coupe only, as standard equipment (no cost). LB9 5.0-liter TPI V-8 in IROC-Z coupe and convertible only, as standard equipment (no cost). L03 5.0-liter EFI V-8, standard in RS convertible, in RS coupe ($350). B2L 5.7-liter V-8 in IROC-Z ($300). C60 air conditioning, including increased-capacity cooling system ($805). G92 performance ratio and dual exhausts ($466). VK3 front license plate bracket (no cost). DX3 decals and stripes delete ($60 credit). C49 electric rear window defogger ($160). AU3 electric power door lock system ($175). YF5 California emissions requirements, including all testing and certification necessary for registration in California ($100). NA5 standard emissions equipment (no cost). A90 power hatch release ($50). K05 engine block heater ($20). DE1 rear window louvers ($210). DG7 electric twin remote sport mirrors ($91). [Note: All stereo radios include extended-range sound system.] UM6 ETR AM/FM stereo with seek-and-scan, cassette tape and digital clock (available in packages only). UU8 ETR Delco-

Bose music system, including AM/FM ETR stereo with seek-and-scan, stereo cassette tape, digital clock, special tone balance and four speakers (available in packages only). UL5 radio delete (available in packages only). CC1 removable glass roof panels including, locks ($866). QYZ P215/65R15 steel-belted radial-ply black sidewall tires (no cost). QLC P245/50ZR16 steel-belted radial-ply black sidewall tires (no cost). MM5 five-speed manual transmission (no cost). MXO automatic overdrive transmission ($515). N96 16-in. cast-aluminum wheels with locks and P245/50ZR16 steel-belted radial-ply black sidewall tires ($520).

HISTORICAL FOOTNOTES

Jim C. Perkins was Chevrolet's general manager during 1990. This was an unusual year, with production of 1990 models starting on Aug. 14, 1989, at the Van Nuys, California, factory and ending Dec. 22, 1989. Officially, no 1990 Camaros were actually built in 1990. However, 39 cars were produced in January 1990 before production of 1991 models officially started on Feb. 22, 1990. It is not clear if these cars were 1990 Camaros, 1991 Camaro pilot models or a combination of both. Calendar-year sales of Camaros totaled 77,599 units or 2.4 percent of the domestic total for the specialty model segment. Model-year sales were 78,654 units or 1.2 percent of the industry total. Model-year production totals available for 1990 from various sources reflect a wide variation. The actual number of 1990 Camaros built was around 35,000. However, trade journals counted early '91 with the '90 models. Of the Camaros built, 90.3 percent had automatic transmission, 9.7 percent had a five-speed manual transmission, 46.8 percent had a 5.0-liter TBI V-8, 11.1 percent had a 5.0-liter TPI V-8, 8.1 percent had a 5.7-liter TPI V-8, 34 percent had a 3.1-liter fuel-injected V-6, 100 percent had power steering, 90.6 percent had power front disc brakes, 9.4 percent had power four-wheel disc brakes, 19.4 percent had a limited-slip differential, 100 percent had steel-belted radial tires, 80.2 percent had power door locks, 67 percent had power windows, 100 percent had reclining bucket seats, 14.2 percent had a power seats, 100 percent had a driver's side airbag, 97.9 percent had tilt steering, 100 percent had tinted glass, 97.4 percent had manual air conditioning, 78.7 percent had cruise control, 100 percent had delay windshield wipers, 4.5 percent had an ETR AM/FM radio, 88.3 percent had a ETR stereo cassette player, 1.2 percent had a Bose/JBL sound system, 0.8 percent had a premium sound system, 4.6 percent had a CD player, 38.2 percent had premium speakers, 100 percent had a digital clock, 23.4 percent had an electric rear window defogger, 0.7 percent had a rear window wiper, 74.4 percent had a manual remote-control left-hand outside rearview mirror, 25.6 percent had a power left-hand rearview mirror, 25.6 percent had a power right-hand rearview mirror, 42.1 percent had aluminum styled wheels and 15 percent had T-tops. A total of 76,415 new Camaros were registered in the U.S. during calendar year 1990.

Camaro

The 1991 Camaro RS came with a base 5.0-liter V-8.
The RS coupe had a standard V-6.

The 1991 Camaro lineup debuted in early 1990 and the IROC-Z was replaced by a new Z28. The Z28 and RS series each offered coupe and convertible models. New equipment included 16-in. wheels for the Z28 (optional on the RS), aero-styled rocker panels, a high-profile rear deck lid spoiler for the Z28 and a heavy-duty battery. There were two new exterior colors and the high-mounted stop lamp was relocated.

The RS coupe came standard with a 3.1-liter V-6. A 5.0-liter V-8 was base power plant in the RS convertible and both Z28 models. The 5.7-liter TPI V-8 was optional in Z28s. A five-speed manual transmission was standard, while a four-speed automatic was optional.

I.D. DATA

Chevrolets again had a 17-symbol vehicle identification number (VIN) on the upper left surface of the instrument panel, visible through the windshield. The first symbol identifies country of origin: 1=USA, 2=Canada. The second symbol identifies the manufacturer: G=General Motors. The third symbol indicates make: 1=Chevrolet, 7=GM of Canada. The fourth and fifth symbols indicated the car line and series: F/P=Camaro Sport Coupe and Camaro convertible. The sixth symbol indicated body type: 2=two-door hatchback style 87, 3=two-door convertible style 67. The seventh symbol indicated the type of restraint system: 1=manual belts, 3=driver airbag and 4=automatic belts. The eighth symbol indicates the engine type: T=RPO LH0 3.1-liter (190-cid) V-6 with Multiport Fuel Injection, E=RPO LO3 5.0-liter (305-cid) V-8 with electronic fuel injection, F=RPO LB9 5.0-liter (305-cid) V-8 with Tuned Port Injection, 8=RPO B2L 5.7-liter (350-cid) V-8 with TPI. The ninth symbol is a check digit. The 10th symbol indicates model year: M=1991. The 11th symbol indicates the assembly plant: L=Van Nuys, California.

COLORS

Arctic White, Black, Bright Red, Dark Red Metallic, Dark Teal Metallic, Light Blue Metallic, Medium Gray Metallic, Ultra Blue Metallic.

CAMARO RS - SERIES F/P - V-6/V-8

Standard equipment included manual lap/shoulder front safety belts with visual/audible warning system, manual rear lap belts, an energy-absorbing steering column, an energy-absorbing instrument panel, energy-absorbing front seat tops, laminated safety windshield glass, safety glass side windows, safety glass rear window, safety interlocking door latches, passenger-guard inside door lock handles, inertia locking folding front seat backs, safety armrests, front head restraints, side marker lights and reflectors, parking lamps that illuminated with the headlights, four-way hazard warning flashers, back-up lights, a center high-mounted stop lamp, direction signals with lane-change feature, a windshield defroster, a windshield washer system, multi-speed windshield wipers, an inside rearview mirror with vinyl bonded glass, dual outside rearview mirrors, a dual-chamber brake master cylinder and brake system warning light, a starter safety switch, a dual-action hood latch system, low-glare instrument panel finish, low-glare windshield moldings, low-glare wiper arms and blades, low-glare metallic steering wheel surfaces, illuminated heater and defroster controls, tires with built-in wear indicators, an audible reminder for ignition key removal, a theft-deterrent steering column lock, a visible VIN number, marked body parts, a PASS-Key vehicle anti-theft system (VATS), a 3.1-liter V-6 engine with Multiport Fuel Injection, an AM/FM stereo (with seek-and-scan, a digital clock and an extended-range sound system), basecoat/clearcoat paint, a black windshield molding, black concealed windshield wipers, body tape striping, a carpeted cargo floor, cloth reclining bucket seats, dual color-keyed Sport-style outside rearview mirrors (left-hand remote and right-hand manual), 15 x 7-in. cast-aluminum wheels, a front air dam, ground-effects type rocker panel moldings, power front disc brakes with audible wear sensors, power rear drum brakes, power steering, a power ventilation system, P215/65R-15 steel-belted radial-ply touring tires, a rear deck lid spoiler, a rear hatch with automatic pull-down, side window defoggers, special instrumentation with a tachometer and a sport suspension.

Model Number	Body/Style Number	Body Type & Seating	Factory Price	Shipping Weight	Production Total
CAMARO RS SPORT COUPE - SERIES F/P - (V-6)					
F/P	87	2d coupe	$12,180	3,103 lbs.	Note 1
CAMARO RS SPORT COUPE - SERIES F/P - (V-8)					
F/P	87	2d coupe	$12,530	3,263 lbs.	Note 1
CAMARO RS CONVERTIBLE - SERIES F/P-Z08 - (V-6)					
F/P	67	2d convertible	$17,960	3,203 lbs.	Note 2
CAMARO RS CONVERTIBLE - SERIES F/P-Z08 - (V-8)					
F/P	67	2d convertible	$18,310	3,363 lbs.	Note 2

Note 1: Total Camaro coupe production was 92,306. (Excluding 1991 models introduced in the 1990 model year.)
Note 2: Total Camaro convertible production was 8,532. (Excluding 1991 models introduced in the 1990 model year.)

CAMARO Z28 SERIES F/P - V-8

Release of the 1991 Camaro marked the return of the Z28. Coupe and convertible models were offered. New equipment included 16-in. wheels for the Z28, aero-styled rocker panels, a high-profile rear spoiler, two new exterior colors, a heavy-duty battery and a relocated high-mounted stop lamp. The 5.0-liter V-8 was the base engine for the Z28 line. The Z28 could also be ordered with the 5.7-liter TPI V-8. Base transmission was the five-speed manual and a four-speed automatic was optional. Removable T-tops were also offered as optional equipment. Other standard equipment included manual lap/shoulder front safety belts with visual/audible warning system, manual rear lap belts, an energy-absorbing steering column, an energy-absorbing instrument panel, energy-absorbing front seat tops, laminated safety windshield glass, safety glass side windows, safety glass rear window, safety interlocking door latches, passenger-guard inside door lock handles, inertia locking folding front seat backs, safety armrests, front head restraints, side marker lights and reflectors, parking lamps that illu-minated with the headlights, black painted headlight openings, halogen fog lamps, four-way hazard warning flashers, backup lights, a center high-mounted stop lamp, direction signals with lane-change feature, a windshield defroster, a windshield washer system, multi-speed windshield wipers, an inside rearview mirror with vinyl bonded glass, dual outside rearview mirrors, a dual-chamber brake master cylinder and brake system warning light, a starter safety switch, a dual-action hood latch system, low-glare instrument panel finish, low-glare windshield moldings, low-glare wiper arms and blades, low-glare metallic steering wheel surfaces, illuminated heater and defroster controls, tires with built-in wear indicators, an audible reminder for ignition key removal, a theft-deterrent steering column lock, a visible VIN number, marked body parts, a PASS-Key vehicle anti-theft (VATS) system, a 5.0-liter V-8 engine with electronic fuel injection, an AM/FM stereo (with seek-and-scan, a digital clock and an extended-range sound system), basecoat/clearcoat paint, a black windshield molding, black concealed windshield wipers, body tape striping, a carpeted cargo floor, cloth reclining bucket seats, dual color-keyed sport style outside rearview mirrors (left-hand remote and right-hand manual), 16-in. cast-aluminum wheels, P235/55R-16 black-letter steel-belted radial tires, a five-speed manual transmission, a leather-wrapped gearshift knob, specific body striping, special instrumentation with a tachometer, a front air dam, ground-effects type rocker panel moldings, power front disc brakes with audible wear sensors, power rear drum brakes, power steering, a power ventilation system, a rear deck lid spoiler, a rear hatch with automatic pull-down, side window defoggers, a special performance ride and handling suspension, a visor vanity mirror and specific taillights.

Model Number	Body/Style Number	Body Type & Seating	Factory Price	Shipping Weight	Production Total
CAMARO Z28 - SERIES F/P - (V-8)					
F/P	87/Z28	2d coupe	$15,455	3,319	Note 3
CAMARO Z28 CONVERTIBLE - SERIES F/P - (V-8)					
F/P	67/Z28	2d convertible	$20,815	3,400	Note 4

Note 3: Total Camaro coupe production was 92,306. (Excluding 1991 models introduced in the 1990 model year)
Note 4: Total Camaro convertible production was 3,400. (Excluding 1991 models introduced in the 1990 model year)

Jerry Heasley photo

The RS convertible retained a sporty exterior design and came with a standard five-speed manual transmission.

ENGINES

LH0 V-6: 60-degree, overhead-valve V-6. Cast-iron block and head. Bore & stroke: 3.50 x 3.31 in. Displacement: 191 cid (3.1 liters). Compression ratio: 8.8:1. Brake horsepower: 140 at 4400 rpm. Torque: 180 lbs.-ft. at 3800 rpm. Induction system: Multiport Fuel Injection. Standard in Camaro RS hatchback coupe. VIN Code T.

LO3 base V-8: 90-degree, overhead-valve V-8. Cast-iron block and head. Bore & stroke: 3.74 x 3.48 in. Displacement: 305 cid (5.0 liters). Compression ratio: 9.3:1. Brake horsepower: 170 at 4000 rpm Torque: 255 lbs.-ft. at 2400 rpm Five main bearings. Hydraulic valve lifters. Induction system: electronic fuel injection. Optional in Camaro RS hatchback coupe, standard in Camaro RS convertible and Z28. VIN Code: E.

LB9 TPI V-8: 90-degree, overhead-valve V-8. Cast-iron block and head. Bore & stroke: 3.74 x 3.48 in. Displacement: 305 cid (5.0 liters). Compression ratio: 9.3:1. Brake horsepower: 230 at 4400 rpm (195 hp with automatic transmission). Torque: 255 lbs.-ft. at 2400 rpm. Five main bearings. Hydraulic valve lifters. Electronic spark control. Induction system: Tuned Port Injection. Optional in Z28. VIN Code: F.

B2L TPI V-8: 90-degree, overhead-valve V-8. Cast-iron block and head. Bore & stroke: 4.00 x 3.48 in. Displacement: 350 cid (5.7 liters). Compression ratio: 9.3:1. Brake horsepower: 245 at 4400 rpm Torque: 345 lbs.-ft. at 3200 rpm. Five main bearings. Hydraulic valve lifters. Electronic spark control. Induction system: Tuned Port Injection. Optional in Z28. VIN Code: 8.

CHASSIS

Base Camaro RS Coupe: Wheelbase: 101 in. Overall length: 192.6 in. Overall height: 50.3 in. Overall width: 72.8 in. Front tread: 60 in. Rear tread: 60.9 in. Front headroom: 37 in. Rear headroom: 35.6 in. Front legroom: 43 in. Rear legroom: 29.8 in. Front shoulder room: 57.5 in. Rear shoulder room: 56.3 in. Front hip room: 56.3 in. Rear hip room: 42.8 in. Cargo volume: 12.4 cu. ft. (31 cu. ft. with rear seat back down). Standard tires: P215/65R-15 black sidewall steel-belted radial.

Base Camaro RS Convertible: Wheelbase: 101 in. Overall length: 192.6 in. Overall height: 50.3 in. Overall width: 72.8 in. Front tread: 60 in. Rear tread: 60.9 in. Front headroom: 37 in. Rear headroom: 35.6 in. Front legroom: 43 in. Rear legroom: 29.8 in. Front shoulder room: 57.5 in. Rear shoulder room: 56.3 in. Front hip room: 56.3 in. Rear hip room: 42.8 in. Cargo volume: 5.2 cu. ft. Standard tires: P215/65R-15 black sidewall steel-belted radial.

Z28 Coupe: Wheelbase: 101 in. Overall length: 192.6 in. Overall height: 50.3 in. Overall width: 72.8 in. Front tread: 60 in. Rear tread: 60.9 in. Front headroom: 37 in. Rear headroom: 35.6 in. Front legroom: 43.0 in. Rear legroom: 29.8 in. Front shoulder room: 57.5 in. Rear shoulder room: 56.3 in. Front hip room: 56.3 in. Rear hip room: 42.8 in. Cargo volume: 12.4 cu. ft. (31 cu. ft. with rear seat back down). Standard tires: P235/55R-16 black-letter steel-belted radial.

Z28 Convertible: Wheelbase: 101 in. Overall length: 192.6 in. Overall height: 50.3 in. Overall width: 72.8 in. Front tread: 60 in. Rear tread: 60.9 in. Front headroom: 37 in. Rear headroom: 35.6 in. Front legroom: 43.0 in. Rear legroom: 29.8 in. Front shoulder room: 57.5 in. Rear shoulder room: 56.3 in. Front hip room: 56.3 in. Rear hip room: 42.8 in. Cargo volume: 5.2 cu. ft. Standard tires: P235/55R-16 black-letter steel-belted radial.

TECHNICAL

Base RS Coupe: Transmission: (Standard): Five-speed manual. (Optional) Four-speed overdrive automatic. Steering: re-circulating ball. Front suspension: MacPherson struts with coil springs, lower control arms and stabilizer bar. Rear suspension: rigid axle and torque tube with longitudinal control arms, Panhard rod, coil springs and stabilizer bar, Brakes: front disc, rear drum, four-wheel discs available. Body construction: unibody. Fuel tank capacity: 15.5 gal.

Camaro RS Convertible: Transmission: (Standard): Five-speed manual. (Optional) Four-speed overdrive automatic. Steering: re-circulating ball. Front suspension: MacPherson struts with coil springs, lower control arms and stabilizer bar. Rear suspension: rigid axle and torque tube with longitudinal control arms, Panhard rod, coil springs and stabilizer bar, Brakes: front disc, rear

The Z28 received a new spoiler and rocker panels, new wheels and two new exterior colors for 1991.

Jerry Heasley photo

The muscular new 1991 Z28 replaced the IROC-Z in the Camaro lineup.

Jerry Heasley photo

drum, four-wheel discs available. Body construction: unibody. Fuel tank capacity: 15.5 gal.

Z28 Coupe: Transmission: (Standard): Five-speed manual. (Optional) Four-speed overdrive automatic. (Required option with L98 V-8) Four-speed overdrive automatic. Steering: re-circulating ball. Front suspension: Modified MacPherson strut with coil springs, lower control arms and large-diameter stabilizer bar. Rear suspension: rigid axle and torque arm with longitudinal control arms, Panhard rod, coil springs, large-diameter stabilizer bar and Delco-Bilstein gas-pressure shock absorbers. Brakes: front disc, rear drum, four-wheel discs available. Body construction: unibody. Fuel tank capacity: 15.5 gal.

Z28 Convertible: Transmission: (Standard): Five-speed manual. (Optional) Four-speed overdrive automatic. (Required option with L98 V-8) Four-speed overdrive automatic. Steering: re-circulating ball. Front suspension: Modified MacPherson strut with coil springs, lower control arms and large-diameter stabilizer bar. Rear suspension: rigid axle and torque arm with longitudinal control arms, Panhard rod, coil springs, large-diameter stabilizer bar and Delco-Bilstein gas-pressure shock absorbers. Brakes: front disc, rear drum, four-wheel discs available. Body construction: unibody. Fuel tank capacity: 15.5 gal.

OPTIONS

RS coupe base equipment group included with model (no cost). RS coupe base equipment group with UN6 radio (add $160). RS coupe base equipment group with U1C radio (add $396). RS coupe base equipment group with UL5 radio delete ($165 credit). RS coupe preferred equipment group number 1, including air conditioning, ETR AM/FM stereo (with seek-and-scan, cassette tape, digital clock and extended-range sound system), body side moldings and front and rear color-keyed carpeted floor mats for package price of $1,060 or $236 additional with U1C radio. RS coupe preferred equipment group number 2 includes air conditioning, ETR AM/FM stereo (with seek-and-scan, cassette tape, digital clock and extended-range sound system), body side moldings and front and rear color-keyed carpeted floor mats, power door locks, speed control with resume, power hatch release, cargo area cover and mirror with dual reading lamps for package price of $1,847 or $236 additional with U1C radio. Z28 base equipment group included with model (no cost). Z28 base equipment group with UN6 radio (add $160). Z28 base equipment group with U1C radio (add $396). Z28 base equipment group with UL5 radio delete ($165 credit). Z28 preferred equipment group number 1 includes air conditioning, body side moldings and front and rear color-keyed carpet mats for package price of $900 (with UN6 radio add $160 or with U1C radio add $396). Z28 coupe preferred equipment group number 2, including air conditioning, body side moldings, front and rear color-keyed carpet mats, ETR AM/FM stereo (with seek-and-scan, cassette tape, digital clock and extended-range sound system), power door locks, speed control with resume, power hatch release, cargo area cover, body side moldings and front and rear color-keyed carpeted floor mats for package price of

$1,847 or $236 additional with U1C radio. Z28 coupe preferred equipment group number 3, including air conditioning, ETR AM/FM stereo (with seek-and-scan, cassette tape, digital clock and extended-range sound system), power windows, power driver's seat, power door locks, speed control with resume, power hatch release, dual power sport-type outside rearview mirrors, cargo area cover, body side moldings, front and rear color-keyed carpeted floor mats and mirror with dual reading lamps for package price of $2,228 or $236 additional with U1C radio. RS convertible base equipment group (no cost). RS convertible base equipment group with UN6 radio (add $160). RS convertible base equipment group with U1C radio (add $236). RS convertible base equipment group with UL5 radio delete ($165 credit). RS convertible preferred equipment group number 1, including air conditioning, ETR AM/FM stereo (with seek-and-scan, cassette tape, digital clock and extended-range sound system), body side moldings and front and rear color-keyed carpeted floor mats for package price of $1,060 (or $236 additional with U1C radio). RS convertible preferred equipment group number 2, including air conditioning, ETR AM/FM stereo (with seek-and-scan, cassette tape, digital clock and extended-range sound system), power windows, power door locks, speed control with resume, body side moldings and front and rear color-keyed carpeted floor mats for package price of $1,705 (or $236 additional with U1C radio). Z28 convertible base equipment group (no cost). Z28 convertible base equipment group with UN6 radio (add $160). Z28 convertible base equipment group with UL5 radio delete ($165 credit). Z28 convertible preferred equipment group number 1, including air conditioning, body side moldings and front and rear color-keyed carpet mats for package price of $900 (add $160 for UN6 radio or $236 for U1C radio). Z28 convertible preferred equipment group number 2, including air conditioning, ETR AM/FM stereo (with seek-and-scan, cassette tape, digital clock and extended-range sound system), power windows, power door locks, speed control with resume, body side moldings and front and rear color-keyed carpeted floor mats for package price of $1,705. Z28 convertible preferred equipment group number 3 including air conditioning, ETR AM/FM stereo (with seek-and-scan, cassette tape, digital clock and extended-range sound system), power windows, power driver's seat, power door locks, speed control with resume, dual power sport-type outside rearview mirrors, body side moldings and front and rear color-keyed carpeted floor mats for package price of $2,086 (or $236 additional with U1C radio). C2 cloth bucket seats (no cost). F2 custom cloth bucket seats ($327). F2 custom cloth bucket seats $(327). A2 custom leather bucket seats ($800). Solid color exterior paint (no cost). LHO 3.1-liter MFI V-6 in RS coupe only, as standard equipment (no cost). LB9 5.0-liter TPI V-8 in Z28 coupe and convertible only, as standard equipment (no cost). L03 5.0-liter EFI V-8, standard in RS convertible, optional in RS coupe ($350). B2L 5.7-liter V-8 in Z28 ($300). C60 air conditioning, including increased-capacity cooling system ($805). G92 performance ratio, includes performance exhaust system, without C60 air conditioning ($675). G92 performance ratio, includes performance exhaust system, with C60 air conditioning

($267). VK3 front license plate bracket (no cost). C49 electric rear window defogger ($160). AU3 electric power door lock system ($190). YF5 California emissions requirements, including all testing and certification necessary for registration in California ($100). NA5 standard emissions equipment (no cost). A90 power hatch release ($50). K05 engine block heater ($20). DE1 rear window louvers ($210). DG7 electric twin remote Sport mirrors ($91). Note: All stereo radios include extended-range sound system. UN6 ETR AM/FM stereo with seek-and-scan, cassette tape and digital clock (available in packages only). U1C ETR stereo with seek-and-scan, stereo cassette tape, search-and-repeat and digital clock (available in packages only). UL5 radio delete (available in packages only). CC1 removable glass roof panels including locks ($866). QMT P235/55R16 steel-belted radial-ply black sidewall tires, standard on Z28, on RS ($170 extra). QLC P245/50ZR16 steel-belted radial-ply black sidewall tires ($400). MM5 five-speed manual transmission, standard on Z28 coupe and convertible ($515 credit). MXO automatic overdrive transmission, standard on RS coupe and convertible ($515). N96 16-in. cast-aluminum wheels with locks and P245/50ZR16 steel-belted radial-ply black sidewall tires (no cost).

HISTORICAL FOOTNOTES

Jim C. Perkins was Chevrolet's general manager during 1991. Model-year sales were 51,974 units. Calendar year sales were 54,383 or 1.8 percent of the middle specialty car segment. Model-year production included 92,306 coupes and 8,532 convertibles for a total of 100,838 (excluding 1991 models introduced in the 1990 model year). The Van Nuys, California, plant built all of these cars (and all 50,247 Firebirds). Of the Camaros built, 84.6 percent had automatic transmission, 15.4 percent had a five-speed manual transmission, 52.6 percent had a 5.0-liter TBI V-8, 9.9 percent had a 5.0-liter TPI V-8, 6 percent had a 5.7-liter TPI V-8, 31.5 percent had a 3.1-liter fuel-injected V-6, 100 percent had power steering, 95.1 percent had power front disc brakes, 4.9 percent had power four-wheel disc brakes, 16.2 percent had a limited-slip differential, 100 percent had steel-belted radial tires, 66.3 percent had power door locks, 64.6 percent had power windows, 100 percent had reclining bucket seats, 11.2 percent had a power seats, 100 percent had a driver's side airbag, 100 percent had tilt steering, 100 percent had tinted glass, 96.6 percent had manual air conditioning, 64.6 percent had cruise control, 100 percent had delay windshield wipers, 3.6 percent had an ETR AM/FM radio, 85.8 percent had a ETR stereo cassette player, 0.1 percent had a Bose/JBL sound system, 8.1 percent had a CD player, 0.8 percent had no factory radio, 100 percent had a digital clock, 56.7 percent had an electric rear window defogger, 0.7 percent had a rear window wiper, 72.2 percent had a manual remote-control left-hand outside rearview mirror, 27.8 percent had a power left-hand rearview mirror, 27.8 percent had a power right-hand rearview mirror, 100 percent had aluminum styled wheels and 38.5 percent had T-tops. A total of 53,566 new Camaros were registered in the U.S. during calendar year 1991. That was down from 76,415 in 1990.

Camaro

This Z28 convertible was one of 1,254 produced for 1992.

Twenty-five years after the debut of the Camaro, Chevrolet marked the anniversary with a "Heritage Edition" package. Consisting primarily of bold hood and rear deck lid striping, it was available on RS and Z28 coupes and convertibles.

Engine and transmission options were basically the same as in 1991. Chevrolet built 66,191 Camaro coupes and 3,816 convertibles and as was the case for the past few years, all were made at the Van Nuys, California, factory.

I.D. DATA

Chevrolets again had a 17-symbol vehicle identification number (VIN) on the upper left surface of the instrument panel, visible through the windshield. The first symbol identifies country of origin: 1=USA, 2=Canada. The second symbol identifies the manufacturer: G=General Motors. The third symbol indicates make: 1=Chevrolet, 7=GM of Canada. The fourth and fifth symbols indicated the car line and series: F/P=Camaro Sport Coupe and Camaro convertible. The sixth symbol indicated body type: 2=two-door hatchback style 87, 3=two-door convertible style 67. The seventh symbol indicated the type of restraint system: 1=manual belts, 3=driver airbag and 4=automatic belts. The eighth symbol indicates the engine type: T=RPO LH0 3.1-liter (190-cid) V-6 with Multiport Fuel Injection, E=RPO LO3 5.0-liter (305-cid) V-8 with electronic fuel injection, F=RPO LB9 5.0-liter (305-cid) V-8 with Tuned Port Injection, 8=RPO L98 5.7-liter (350-cid) V-8 with TPI. The ninth symbol is a check digit. The 10th symbol indicates model year: N=1992. The 11th symbol indicates the assembly plant: L=Van Nuys, California.

COLORS

Polo Green II, Purple Haze Metallic, Medium Quasar Blue Metallic, Dark Gray Green Metallic, Black, Bright Red and Arctic White.

CAMARO RS - SERIES F/P - V-6/V-8

All Camaros, even those without the Heritage Edition option, had a special "25th Anniversary" instrument panel badge. Both series featured coupe and convertible models. The base engine for the RS line was the 3.1-liter V-6. Other standard equipment included manual lap/shoulder front safety belts with a visual and audible warning system, manual rear lap belts, an energy-absorbing steering column, an energy-absorbing instrument panel, energy-absorbing front seat tops, laminated safety windshield glass, safety glass side windows, safety glass rear window, safety interlocking door latches, passenger-guard inside door lock handles, inertia locking folding front seat backs, safety armrests, front head restraints, side marker lights and reflectors, parking lamps that illuminated with the headlights, four-way hazard warning flashers, back-up lights, a center high-mounted stop lamp, direction signals with lane-change feature, a windshield defroster, a windshield washer system, multi-speed windshield wipers, an inside rearview mirror with vinyl bonded glass, dual outside rearview mirrors, a dual-chamber brake master cylinder and brake system warning light, a starter safety switch, a dual-action hood latch system, low-glare instrument panel finish, low-glare windshield moldings, low-glare wiper arms and blades, low-glare metallic steering wheel surfaces, illuminated heater and defroster controls, tires with built-in wear indicators, an audible reminder for ignition key removal, a theft-deterrent steering column lock, a visible VIN number, marked body parts, a PASS-Key vehicle anti-theft system (VATS), a 3.1-liter V-6 engine with Multiport Fuel Injection, an AM/FM stereo (with seek-and-scan, a digital clock and an extended-range sound system), basecoat/clearcoat paint, a black windshield molding, black concealed windshield wipers, body tape striping, a carpeted cargo floor, cloth reclining bucket seats, dual color-keyed sport style outside rearview mirrors (left-hand remote and right-hand manual), 15 x 7-in. cast-aluminum wheels, a front air dam, ground-effects type rocker panel moldings, power front disc brakes with audible wear sensors, power rear drum brakes, power steering, a power ventilation system, P215/65R-15 steel-belted radial-ply touring tires, a rear deck lid spoiler, a rear hatch with automatic pull-down, side window defoggers, special instrumentation with a tachometer and a sport suspension.

Model Number	Body/Style Number	Body Type & Seating	Factory Price	Shipping Weight	Production Total
CAMARO RS SPORT COUPE - SERIES F/P - (V-6)					
F/P	87	2d coupe	$12,075	3,103 lbs.	Note 1
CAMARO RS CONVERTIBLE - SERIES F/P-Z08 - (V-6)					
F/P	67	2d convertible	$18,055	3,203 lbs.	Note 2
CAMARO RS SPORT COUPE - SERIES F/P - (V-8)					
F/P	87	2d coupe	$12,444	3,384 lbs.	Note 1
CAMARO RS CONVERTIBLE - SERIES F/P-Z08 - (V-8)					
F/P	67	2d convertible	$18,424	3,484 lbs.	Note 2

Note 1: Model year production of 1992 Camaro RS coupes was 60,994.
Note 2: Model year production of 1992 Camaro RS convertibles was 2,562.

CAMARO Z28 SERIES F/P - V-8

The Z28 coupe and convertible offered Black, Bright Red, Artic White or Purple Haze Metallic exterior colors. The 5.0-liter TPI V-8 was the base engine for both the Z28 coupe and the Z28 convertible. Both body styles could also be ordered with the 5.7-liter TPI V-8. The base transmission was the five-speed manual. A four-speed automatic was standard in coupes with the 5.7-liter V-8 and otherwise optional. Removable T-tops were another popular option. Other standard equipment included manual lap/shoulder front safety belts with visual/audible warning system, manual rear lap belts, an energy-absorbing steering column, an energy-absorbing instrument panel, energy-absorbing front seat tops, laminated safety windshield glass, safety glass side windows, safety glass rear window, safety interlocking door latches, passenger-guard inside door lock handles, inertia locking folding front seat backs, safety armrests, front head restraints, side marker lights and reflectors, parking lamps that illuminated with the headlights, black painted headlight openings, halogen fog lamps, four-way hazard warning flashers, back-up lights, a center high-mounted stop lamp, direction signals with lane-change feature, a windshield defroster, a windshield washer system, multi-speed windshield wipers, an inside rearview mirror with vinyl bonded glass, dual outside rearview mirrors, a dual-chamber brake master cylinder and brake system warning light, a starter safety switch, a dual-action hood latch system, low-glare instrument panel finish, low-glare windshield moldings, low-glare wiper arms and blades, low-glare metallic steering wheel surfaces, illuminated heater and defroster controls, tires with built-in wear indicators, an audible reminder for ignition key removal, a theft-deterrent steering column lock, a visible VIN number, marked body parts, a PASS-Key vehicle anti-theft (VATS) system, a 5.0-liter V-6 engine with electronic fuel injection, an AM/FM stereo (with seek-and-scan, a digital clock and an extended-range sound system), basecoat/clearcoat paint, a black windshield molding, black concealed windshield wipers, body tape striping, a carpeted cargo floor, cloth reclining bucket seats, dual color-keyed sport style outside rearview mirrors (left-hand remote and right-hand manual), 16-in. cast-aluminum wheels, P235/55R-16 black-

The flashy "Heritage Edition" package was available as a convertible or coupe and could be ordered on both the RS and Z28 models.

Sarah Werbelow photo

The 1992 Z28 was offered with two engine choices and could be ordered without the hood and deck lid stripes.

T-tops were a popular option for the 25th Anniversary Camaros.

Sarah Werbelow photo

letter steel-belted radial tires, a five-speed manual transmission, a leather-wrapped gearshift knob, specific body striping, special instrumentation with a tachometer, a front air dam, ground-effects type rocker panel moldings, power front disc brakes with audible wear sensors, power rear drum brakes, power steering, a power ventilation system, a rear deck lid spoiler, a rear hatch with automatic pull-down, side window defoggers, a special performance ride and handling suspension, a visor vanity mirror and specific taillights.

Model Number	Body/Style Number	Body Type & Seating	Factory Price	Shipping Weight	Production Total
CAMARO Z28 - SERIES F/P - (V-8)					
F/P	87/Z28	2d coupe	$16,055	3,319 lbs.	Note 3
CAMARO Z28 CONVERTIBLE - SERIES F/P-ZO8 - (V-8)					
F/P	67/Z28	2d convertible	$21,500	3,400 lbs.	Note 4

Note 3: Model-year production of 1992 Camaro Z28 coupes was 5,197.
Note 4: Model-year production of 1992 Camaro Z28 convertibles was 1,254.
Note 5: During the 1992 model year the optional 1LE competition package was ordered for 705 Camaro Z28s.

CAMARO HERITAGE EDITION - F/P - V-8

The Camaro 25th Anniversary "Heritage Edition" option package was available for all models and body styles. While not truly a separate model, cars with the Heritage Edition package are of particular interest to Camaro collectors. In addition to the standard equipment for each model listed above, the Heritage Edition package added 25th Anniversary emblems, special hood stripes, special rear deck lid stripes, a specific body-color grille, black-finished headlight "pockets" and a body-color treatment on the 16-in. cast-aluminum wheels. The Heritage Edition package was coded as regular production option ZO3 and carried a price of $175.

Model Number	Body/Style Number	Body Type & Seating	Factory Price	Shipping Weight	Production Total
HERITAGE EDITION CAMARO RS SPORT COUPE - SERIES F/P + ZO3 - (V-6)					
F/P	87	2d coupe	$12,250	3,103 lbs.	Note 6
HERITAGE EDITION CAMARO RS CONVERTIBLE - SERIES F/P + ZO3 - (V-6)					

F/P	67	2d convertible	$18,230	3,203 lbs.	Note 6

HERITAGE EDITION CAMARO RS SPORT COUPE - SERIES F/P + ZO3 - (V-8)

F/P	87	2d coupe	$12,619	3,384 lbs.	Note 6

HERITAGE EDITION CAMARO RS CONVERTIBLE - SERIES F/P + ZO3 - (V-8)

F/P	67	2d convertible	$18,599	3,484 lbs.	Note 6

HERITAGE EDITION CAMARO Z28 - SERIES F/P + ZO3 - (V-8)

F/P	87/Z28	2d coupe	$16,230	3,319 lbs.	Note 6

HERITAGE EDITION CAMARO Z28 CONVERTIBLE - SERIES F/P + ZO3 - (V-8)

F/P	67/Z28	2d convertible	$21,675	3,400 lbs.	Note 6

Note 6: The number of coupes and convertibles having the ZO3 Heritage Edition package was not determined at publication date.

ENGINES

LH0 V-6: 60-degree, overhead-valve V-6. Cast-iron block and head. Bore & stroke: 3.50 x 3.31 in. Displacement: 191 cid (3.1 liters). Compression ratio: 8.8:1. Brake horsepower: 140 at 4400 rpm. Torque: 180 lbs.-ft. at 3600 rpm. Induction system: Multiport Fuel Injection. Standard in Camaro RS hatchback coupe. VIN Code T.

LO3 base V-8: 90-degree, overhead-valve V-8. Cast-iron block and head. Bore & stroke: 3.74 x 3.48 in. Displacement: 305 cid (5.0 liters). Compression ratio: 9.3:1. Brake horsepower: 170 at 4000 rpm Torque: 255 lbs.-ft. at 2400 rpm Five main bearings. Hydraulic valve lifters. Induction system: electronic fuel injection. Optional in Camaro RS hatchback coupe, standard in Camaro RS convertible and Z28. VIN Code: E.

LB9 TPI V-8: 90-degree, overhead-valve V-8. Cast-iron block and head. Bore & stroke: 3.74 x 3.48 in. Displacement: 305 cid (5.0 liters). Compression ratio: 9.3:1. Brake horsepower: 230 at 4400 rpm (195 hp with automatic transmission). Torque: 285 lbs.-ft. at 2400 rpm. Five main bearings. Hydraulic valve lifters. Electronic spark control. Induction system: Tuned Port Injection. Optional in Z28. VIN Code: F.

B2L TPI V-8: 90-degree, overhead-valve V-8. Cast-iron block and head. Bore & stroke: 4.00 x 3.48 in. Displacement: 350 cid (5.7 liters). Compression ratio: 9.3:1. Brake horsepower: 245 at 4400 rpm Torque: 345 lbs.-ft. at 3200 rpm. Five main bearings. Hydraulic valve lifters. Electronic spark control. Induction system: Tuned Port Injection. Optional in Z28. VIN Code: 8.

CHASSIS

Base RS Coupe: Wheelbase: 101 in. Overall length: 192.6 in. Overall height: 50.4 in. Overall width: 72.4 in. Front tread: 60 in. Rear tread: 60.9 in. Front headroom: 37 in. Rear headroom: 35.6 in. Front legroom: 43 in. Rear legroom: 29.8 in. Front shoulder room: 57.5 in. Rear shoulder room: 56.3 in. Front hip room: 56.3 in. Rear hip room: 42.8 in. Cargo volume: 12.4 cu. ft. (31 cu. ft. with rear seat back down). Standard tires: P215/65R-15 black sidewall steel-belted radial.

Base RS Convertible: Wheelbase: 101 in. Overall length: 192.6 in. Overall height: 50.4 in. Overall width: 72.4 in. Front tread: 60 in. Rear tread: 60.9 in. Front headroom: 37 in. Rear headroom: 35.6 in. Front legroom: 43 in. Rear legroom: 29.8 in. Front shoulder room: 57.5 in. Rear shoulder room: 56.3 in. Front hip room: 56.3 in. Rear hip room: 42.8 in. Cargo volume: 5.2 cu. ft. Standard tires: P215/65R-15 black sidewall steel-belted radial.

Z28 Coupe: Wheelbase: 101 in. Overall length: 192.6 in. Overall height: 50.4 in. Overall width: 72.4 in. Front tread: 60 in. Rear tread: 60.9 in. Front headroom: 37.0 in. Rear headroom: 35.6 in. Front legroom: 43.0 in. Rear legroom: 29.8 in. Front shoulder room: 57.5 in. Rear shoulder room: 56.3 in. Front hip room: 56.3 in. Rear hip room: 42.8 in. Cargo volume: 12.4 cu. ft. (31 cu. ft. with rear seat back down). Standard tires: P235/55R-16 black-letter steel-belted radial.

Z28 Convertible: Wheelbase: 101 in. Overall length: 192.6 in. Overall height: 50.4 in. Overall width: 72.4 in. Front tread: 60 in. Rear tread: 60.9 in. Front headroom: 37 in. Rear headroom: 35.6 in. Front legroom: 43 in. Rear legroom: 29.8 in. Front shoulder room: 57.5 in. Rear shoulder room: 56.3 in. Front hip room: 56.3 in. Rear hip room: 42.8 in. Cargo volume: 5.2 cu. ft. Standard tires: P235/55R-16 black-letter steel-belted radial.

TECHNICAL

Base RS Coupe: Transmission: (Standard): Five-speed manual. (Optional) Four-speed overdrive automatic. Steering: re-circulating ball. Front suspension: MacPherson struts with coil springs, lower control arms and 30-mm. Solid steel stabilizer bar (34-mm hollow steel with 16-in. tires). Rear suspension: rigid axle and torque tube with longitudinal control arms, Panhard rod, coil springs and 18-mm solid steel stabilizer bar (21-mm solid steel with 16-in. tires). Brakes: front disc, rear drum, four-wheel discs available. Body construction: unibody. Fuel tank capacity: 15.5 gal.

Camaro RS Convertible: Transmission: (Standard): Five-speed manual. (Optional) Four-speed overdrive automatic. Steering: re-circulating ball. Front suspension: MacPherson struts with coil springs, lower control arms and 30-mm. Solid steel stabilizer bar (34-mm hollow steel with 16-in. tires). Rear suspension: rigid axle and torque tube with longitudinal control arms, Panhard rod, coil springs and 18-mm solid steel stabilizer bar (21-mm solid steel with 16-in. tires). Brakes: front disc, rear drum, four-wheel discs available. Body construction: unibody. Fuel tank capacity: 15.5 gal.

Z28 Coupe: Transmission: (Standard): Five-speed manual. (Optional) Four-speed overdrive automatic. (Required option with L98 V-8) Four-speed overdrive automatic. Steering: re-circulating ball. Front suspension: Modified MacPherson strut with coil springs, lower control arms and 34-mm hollow steel stabilizer bar. Rear suspension: rigid axle and torque arm with longitudinal control arms, Panhard rod, coil springs, 21-mm solid steel stabilizer bar and Delco-Bilstein gas-pressure shock absorbers. Brakes: front disc, rear drum, four-wheel discs available. Body construction: unibody. Fuel tank capacity: 15.5 gal.

Z28 Convertible: Transmission: (Standard): Five-speed manual. (Optional) Four-speed overdrive automatic. (Required option with L98 V-8) Four-speed overdrive automatic. Steering: re-circulating ball. Front suspension: Modified MacPherson strut with coil springs, lower control arms and 34-mm hollow steel bar. Rear suspension: rigid axle and torque arm with longitudinal control arms, Panhard rod, coil springs, 21-mm solid steel stabilizer bar and Delco-Bilstein gas-pressure shock absorbers. Brakes: front disc, rear drum, four-wheel discs available. Body construction: unibody. Fuel tank capacity: 15.5 gal.

OPTIONS

RS coupe base equipment group included with model (no cost). RS coupe base equipment group with UN6 radio (add $160). RS coupe base equipment group with U1C radio (add $396). RS coupe base equipment group with UL5 radio delete ($165 credit). RS coupe preferred equipment group number 1, including air conditioning, ETR AM/FM stereo (with seek-and-scan, cassette tape, digital clock and extended-range sound system), body side moldings and front and rear color-keyed carpeted floor mats for package price of $1,085 or $855 additional with UU8 radio or $236 additional with U1C radio. RS coupe preferred equipment group number 2 air conditioning, ETR AM/FM stereo (with seek-and-scan, cassette tape, digital clock and extended-range sound system), body side moldings and front and rear color-keyed carpeted floor mats, power door locks, speed control with resume, power hatch release, cargo area cover and mirror with dual reading lamps for package price of $1,937 or $855 additional with UU8 radio or $236 additional with U1C radio. Z28 base equipment group included with model (no cost). Z28 base equipment group with UN6 radio (add $160). Z28 base equipment group with U1C radio (add $396). Z28 base equipment group with UL5 radio delete ($165 credit). Z28 preferred equipment group number 1 includes air conditioning, body side moldings and front and rear color-keyed carpet mats for package price of $925 (with UN6 radio add $160, with UU8 radio add $1,015 and with U1C radio add $396). Z28 coupe preferred equipment group number 2 includes air conditioning, ETR AM/FM stereo (with seek-and-scan, cassette tape, digital clock and extended-range sound system), body side moldings and front and rear color-keyed carpeted floor mats, power door locks, speed control with resume, power hatch release, cargo area cover and mirror with dual reading lamps for package price of $1,937 or $855 additional with UU8 radio or $236 additional with U1C radio. Z28 coupe preferred equipment group number 3, including air conditioning, ETR AM/FM stereo (with seek-and-scan, cassette tape, digital clock and extended-range sound system), power windows, power driver's seat, power door locks, speed control with resume, power hatch release, dual power sport-type outside rearview mirrors, cargo area cover, body side moldings, front and rear color-keyed carpeted floor mats and mirror with dual reading lamps for package price of $2,332 or $855 additional with UU8 radio or $236 additional with U1C radio. RS convertible base equipment group (no cost). RS convertible base equipment group with UN6 radio (add $160). RS convertible base equipment group with U1C radio (add $236). RS convertible base equipment group with UL5 radio delete ($165 credit). RS convertible preferred equipment group number 1, including air conditioning, ETR AM/FM stereo (with seek-and-scan, cassette tape, search-and-repeat, digital clock and extended-range sound system), body side moldings and front and rear color-keyed carpeted floor mats for package price of $1,085 (or $236 additional with U1C radio). RS convertible preferred equipment group number 2, including air conditioning, ETR AM/FM stereo (with seek-and-scan, cassette tape, digital clock and extended-range sound system), body side moldings and front and rear color-keyed carpeted floor

mats, power door locks, speed control with resume for package price of $1,785 or $236 additional with U1C radio. Z28 convertible base equipment group (no cost). Z28 convertible base equipment group with UN6 radio (add $160). Z28 convertible base equipment group with U1C radio (add $396). Z28 convertible base equipment group with UL5 radio delete ($165 credit). Z28 convertible preferred equipment group number 1, including air conditioning, body side moldings and front and rear color-keyed carpet mats for package price of $925 (add $160 for UN6 radio or $236 for U1C radio). Z28 convertible preferred equipment group number 2, including air conditioning, ETR AM/FM stereo (with seek-and-scan, cassette tape, digital clock and extended-range sound system), body side moldings and front and rear color-keyed carpeted floor mats, power door locks, speed control with resume for package price of $1,785 or $236 additional with U1C radio. Z28 convertible preferred equipment group number 3, including air conditioning, ETR AM/FM stereo (with seek-and-scan, cassette tape, digital clock and extended-range sound system), power windows, power driver's seat, power door locks, speed control with resume, dual power sport-type outside rearview mirrors, body side moldings and front and rear color-keyed carpeted floor mats for package price of $2,181 (or $236 additional with U1C radio. C2 cloth bucket seats (no cost). F2 custom cloth bucket seats ($327). A2 custom leather bucket seats ($850). Solid color exterior paint (no cost). LHO 3.1-liter MFI V-6 in RS coupe only, as standard equipment (no cost). LB9 5.0-liter TPI V-8 in Z28 coupe and convertible only, as standard equipment (no cost). L03 5.0-liter EFI V-8, standard in RS convertible, in RS coupe ($369). B2L 5.7-liter V-8 in Z28 ($300). C60 air conditioning including increased-capacity cooling system ($830). G92 performance ratio, includes performance exhaust system, without C60 air conditioning ($675). G92 performance ratio, includes performance exhaust system, with C60 air conditioning ($466). VK3 front license plate bracket (no cost). D42 rear compartment cover ($69). C49 electric rear window defogger ($170). R9W rear window defogger not desired (no cost). AU3 electric power door lock system ($190). YF5 California emissions requirements, including all testing and certification necessary for registration in California ($100). NA5 standard emissions equipment (no cost). B34 front color-keyed carpeted floor mats ($20). Rear color-keyed carpeted floor mats ($15). A90 power hatch release ($50). K05 engine block heater ($20). ZO3 Heritage Edition appearance package, including striping and exterior badging, body-color grille and black headlamp pockets ($175). DE1 rear window louvers ($210). DC4 mirror with dual reading lamps ($23). DG7 electric twin remote Sport mirrors ($91). B84 body side moldings ($60). (Note: All stereo radios include extended-range sound system.) UN6 ETR AM/FM stereo with seek-and-scan, cassette tape and digital clock (available in packages only). UU8 GM Delco/Bose music system with ETR AM/FM stereo with seek-and-scan, stereo cassette tape with auto reverse and digital clock (available in packages only). U1C ETR stereo with seek-and-scan, stereo cassette tape, search-and-repeat and digital clock (available in packages only). UL5 radio delete (available in packages only). CC1 removable glass

Jerry Heasley photo

Arctic White was one of four exterior colors offered for the 1992 Z28, which also sported telltale striping.

roof panels including locks ($895). AC3 power driver's seat ($305). K34 electric speed control ($225). QPH P215/65R15 steel-belted radial-ply black sidewall tires, standard on RS coupe and convertible (no cost). QMT P235/55R16 steel-belted radial black sidewall tires, standard on Z28 coupe and convertible ($219). QLC P245/50ZR16 steel-belted radial-ply black sidewall tires ($400). MM5 five-speed manual transmission, standard (no cost). MXO automatic overdrive transmission ($530). N96 16-in. cast-aluminum wheels with locks, standard Z28 coupe and convertible (no cost). A31 power windows ($265).

HISTORICAL FOOTNOTES

Chevrolet promoted the 1992 Camaro as "a veteran American muscle car on the street and at the racetrack." This turned out to be a fitting description when a Camaro marked its 50th win in Sports Car Club of America Trans-Am Series racing in May of 1992. That victory gave the Camaro the most first-place finishers for any single model in 26 years of Trans-Am competition. Model-year sales were 64,444 units. Calendar-year sales were 54,383. Model-year production included 66,191 coupes and 3,816 convertibles for a total of 70,007. The Van Nuys, California, plant built all of these cars (and all 27,566 Firebirds). Of the Camaros built, 79.7 percent had automatic transmission, 20.3 percent had a five-speed manual transmission, 34.1 percent had a 3.1-liter fuel-injected V-6, 61.6 percent had a 5.0-liter TBI V-8, 4.3 percent had a 5.7-liter TPI V-8, 100 percent had power steering, 94.8 percent had power front disc brakes, 5.2 percent had power four-wheel disc brakes, 10.2 percent had a limited-slip differential, 100 percent had steel-belted radial tires, 71.8 percent had power door locks, 69 percent had power windows, 100 percent had reclining bucket seats, 7.4 percent had a power

Jerry Heasley photo

The Z28 could be ordered with the optional 5.7-liter TPI V-8.

seats, 100 percent had a driver's side airbag, 95.1 percent had tilt steering, 100 percent had tinted glass, 98.5 percent had manual air conditioning, 70.9 percent had cruise control, 100 percent had delay windshield wipers, 1.5 percent had an ETR AM/FM radio, 84.7 percent had a ETR stereo cassette player, 3.2 percent had a Bose/JBL sound system, 8.9 percent had a CD player, 100 percent had a digital clock, 62.3 percent had an electric rear window defogger, 69.1 percent had a manual remote-control left-hand outside rearview mirror, 30.9 percent had power rearview mirrors, 27.8 percent had a power right-hand rearview mirror, 100 percent had aluminum styled wheels, 100 percent had an electronic vehicle anti-theft system, 100 percent had electronic gauges and 40 percent had T-tops. A total of 58,081 new Camaros were registered in the U.S. during calendar year 1992.

Camaro

The fourth-generation Camaro was resigned for 1993, making it longer and wider than in the past. There were only two offerings – the Sport Coupe (above) and the Z28.

The fourth-generation Camaro was built in a new factory in Ste. Therese, Quebec, Canada, and was a totally new product from nose to tail. It was longer, taller and wider than its third-generation predecessor. Gone were the convertible and RS models, which left the base Sport Coupe and Z28 coupe.

Among the new Camaro's most striking and attractive appearance features were a windshield with a steep 68-degree slope, a low hood line, a smooth roofline and an integral spoiler with a built-in center high-mounted stop lamp. Just forward of the windshield there was a raised cowl panel designed to shield the windshield wipers and reduce turbulence.

Chevrolet made extensive use of dent-resistant, rust-proof body panels in the fourth-generation Camaro. The roof, doors, hatchback panel and rear deck spoiler were made of sheet molded compound (SMC) made of chopped glass in a polyester resin. Reaction injection molded (RIM) panels were used in manufacturing the front fenders and front fascia. The rear fascia was polyurethane reinforced with Wollastokup. Rust-resistant two-side galvanized steel was used for the rear quarter and hood panels. A remote hatch release was optional.

Standard features included dual airbags, ABS, a wraparound instrument panel, a state-of-the-art sound system and GM's PASS-Key II theft-deterrent system. The base engine was a 3.4-liter V-6 mated to a five-speed manual transmission. The Z28 got the 5.7-liter LT1 Corvette V-8 fitted with a Borg-Warner T56 six-speed manual transmission. A four-speed automatic was optional in both cars. The '93 Camaro was the first GM car to feature R-134a air conditioning refrigerant.

Also new was a short-and-long arm front suspension.

The base coupe had front disc/rear drum brakes, but four-wheel discs were standard on the Z28. A 1993 Camaro Z28 paced the Indy 500 and replicas of the pace car were built and sold to the public.

I.D. DATA

Chevrolets again had a 17-symbol vehicle identification number (VIN) on the upper left surface of the instrument panel, visible through the windshield. The first symbol identifies country of origin: 2=Canada. The second symbol identifies the manufacturer: G=General Motors. The third symbol indicates make: 1=Chevrolet, 7=GM of Canada. The fourth and fifth symbols indicated the car line and series: F/P=Camaro Sport Coupe. The sixth symbol indicated body type: 2=two-door coupe style 87. The seventh symbol indicated the type of restraint system: 1=active manual belts, 2=active manual belts with driver and passenger airbags, 3=active manual belts with driver airbag. 4=passive automatic belts and 5=passive automatic belts with driver airbag. The eighth symbol indicates the engine type: S=RPO L32 3.4-liter (207-cid) V-6 with Multiport Fuel Injection, P=RPO LT1 5.7-liter (350-cid) V-8 with SFI. The ninth symbol is a check digit. The 10th symbol indicates model year: P=1993. The 11th symbol indicates the assembly plant: 2=Ste. Therese, Providence of Quebec (Canada).

COLORS

Black, Bright Red, Purple Pearl Metallic, Medium Quasar Blue Metallic (late production), Medium Patriot Blue Metallic, Dark Green-Gray Metallic and Arctic White.

CAMARO — SERIES 1F — V-6

Standard features included a serpentine belt accessory drive system, four-wheel antilock brakes, a brake/transmission interlock feature with automatic transmission, power front disc/rear drum brakes, 5-mph front and rear energy-absorbing bumpers with body-color fascias, side window defoggers, a stainless steel exhaust system, Solar-Ray tinted glass, miniquad halogen headlights, dual black-finished sport outside rearview mirrors (left-hand remote controlled, right-hand manual), a two-component clearcoat paint system, gas-charged monotube shock absorbers, integral front and rear spoilers, front and rear stabilizer bars, power rack-and-pinion steering, a Firm Ride & Handling suspension, a four-wheel coil spring suspension with computer-selected springs, a front short/long arm (SLA) suspension, the PASS-Key II theft deterrent system, a compact high-pressure spare tire, P215/60R16 black sidewall tires, a five-speed manual transmission, 16-in. steel bolt-on wheel covers, intermittent windshield wipers, driver and front passenger airbags, full carpeting in driver compartment and passenger compartment and cargo area, a center console with cupholder and lighted storage compartment, Scotchguarded interior fabric and door panel protection, front carpeted floor mats, a gauge package with tachometer, a low oil level indicator light, a dome light, a day/night inside rearview mirror with dual reading and courtesy lights, an ETR AM/FM stereo radio (with seek-and-scan, digital clock, stereo cassette tape, search-and-repeat and extended-range speakers), a headlamps-on reminder, a driver's four-way seat with manual adjuster, a rear seat with full-folding seat backs, front reclining bucket seats with cloth trim and integral headrests, a tilt steering wheel, door panel storage compartments, dual covered visor-vanity mirrors and a check-gauges warning light. A 3.4-liter SFI V-6 was the only engine available in the base Camaro.

Model Number	Body/Style Number	Body Type & Seating	Factory Price	Shipping Weight	Production Total
F/P	87	2d coupe-4P	$13,339	3,241 lbs.	Note 1

Note 1: Model-year production of 1993 base Camaro coupes was 21,253.

CAMARO Z28 — SERIES 1F — V-8

The Z28 coupe received Corvette's 5.7-liter LT1 V-8 as its only engine. It came fitted with a Borg-Warner T56 six-speed manual transmission. The high-performance engine included platinum-tip spark plugs. Although this engine was basically the same as the Corvette LT1, the Camaro version had some distinctions. It featured two-bolt (instead of four-bolt) main bearing caps. The accessories were mounted on the right, while the Corvette had them on the left. The Camaro version lacked a shield covering the injector nozzles. The exhaust manifolds had rear outlets compared to center outlets on the Corvette version. The Camaro version's exhaust system had a single three-way catalyst, one stainless steel muffler and dual tailpipes. The valve covers were stamped steel rather than composite material. The Camaro's LT1 V-8 did not require synthetic oil like the Corvette type. The location of the A.I.R. pump was on the engine block rather than remote, as in the Corvette. Standard equipment included a serpentine belt accessory drive system, a limited-slip rear axle, four-wheel antilock brakes, a brake/transmission interlock feature with automatic transmission, four-wheel power disc brakes, 5-mph front and rear energy-absorbing bumpers with body-color fascias, side window defoggers, a stainless steel exhaust system, Solar-Ray tinted glass, miniquad halogen headlights, dual black-finished sport outside rearview mirrors (left-hand remote controlled, right-hand manual), a two-component clearcoat paint system, a special black roof treatment, gas-charged mono-tube shock absorbers, integral front and rear spoilers, front and rear stabilizer bars, power rack-and-pinion steering, a Performance Ride & Handling suspension, a four-wheel coil spring suspension with computer-selected springs, a front short/long arm (SLA) suspension, the PASS-Key II theft deterrent system, a compact high-pressure spare tire, P235/55R16 black sidewall tires, 16 x 8-in. aluminum front wheels, 16 x 11-in. aluminum rear wheels, intermittent windshield wipers, driver and front passenger airbags, full carpeting in driver compartment and passenger compartment and cargo area, a center console with cupholder and lighted storage compartment,

The 1993 Z28 coupe came with a base sticker price of about $16,800.

Scotchguard interior fabric and door panel protection, front carpeted floor mats, a gauge package with 115-mph speedometer and tachometer, a low-coolant-level indicator system, a low oil level indicator light, a dome light, a day/night inside rearview mirror with dual reading and courtesy lights, an ETR AM/FM stereo radio (with seek-and-scan, digital clock, stereo cassette tape, search-and-repeat and extended-range speakers), a headlamps-on reminder, a driver's four-way seat with manual adjuster, a rear seat with full-folding seat backs, front reclining bucket seats with cloth trim and integral headrests, a tilt steering wheel, door panel storage compartments, dual covered visor-vanity mirrors and a check-gauges warning light.

Model Number	Body/Style Number	Body Type & Seating	Factory Price	Shipping Weight	Production Total
F/P+Z28	87	2d coupe-4P	$16,799	3,373 lbs.	Note 2

Note 2: Model-year production of 1993 Camaro Z28 coupes was 17,850.
Note 3: The Z28 production total above included 19 cars with the optional 1LE competition package.
Note 4: The Z28 production total above included 633 cars with an optional Indy Pace Car package.

ENGINES

L32 V-6: 60-degree, overhead-valve V-6. Cast-iron block and head. Bore & stroke: 3.62 x 3.31. Displacement: 207 cid (3.4 liters). Compression ratio: 9.0:1. Brake horsepower: 160 at 4600 rpm. Torque: 200 lbs.-ft. at 3600 rpm. Hydraulic valve lifters. Induction system: Sequential fuel injection. Standard in base Camaro. VIN Code S.

LT1 V-8: 90-degree, overhead-valve V-8. Cast-iron block and head. Bore & stroke: 4.00 x 3.48 in. Displacement: 350 cu. in. (5.7 liters). Compression ratio: 10.5:1. Brake horsepower: 275 at 5000 rpm. Torque: 325 lb.-ft. at 2400 rpm. Hydraulic valve lifters. Sequential fuel injection. Standard in Z28. VIN Code P.

CHASSIS

Base Camaro: Wheelbase: 101.1 in. Overall length: 193.2 in. Height: 51.3 in.; Width: 74.1 in. Front headroom: 37.2 in. Rear headroom: 35.3 in. Front legroom: 43 in. Rear legroom: 26.8 in. Front shoulder room: 57.4 in. Rear shoulder room: 55.8 in. Luggage capacity: (rear seat up) 12.9 cu. ft.; (rear seat down) 32.8 cu. ft. Front tread: 60.7 in. Rear tread: 60.6 in. Standard tires: P215/60R16; (Camaro Z28) P235/55R16.

Z28: Wheelbase: 101.1 in. Overall length: 193.2 in. Height: 51.3 in.; Width: 74.1 in. Front headroom: 37.2 in. Rear headroom: 35.3 in. Front legroom: 43 in. Rear legroom: 26.8 in. Front shoulder room: 57.4 in. Rear shoulder room: 55.8 in. Luggage capacity: (rear seat up) 12.9 cu. ft.; (rear seat down) 32.8 cu. ft. Front tread: 60.7 in. Rear tread: 60.6 in. Standard tires: P235/55R16.

The base Camaro engine for 1993 was a 3.4-liter V-6 attached to a five-speed manual transmission.

The Z28 coupe had only one engine option - the 5.7-liter TPI V-8 borrowed from the Corvette.

**Z28 Indy Pace Car replicas were sold to the public.
A total of 633 were built for 1993.**

TECHNICAL

Base Camaro: Transmission: Five-speed manual. Steering: rack and pinion. Front suspension: SLA/Coil over monotube gas shocks, tubular stabilizer bar with links. Rear suspension: Solid axle/torque arm, trailing arm, coil springs, track bar, monotube gas shocks and solid stabilizer bar with links. Brakes: Front disc/rear drum with antilock. Body construction: unibody. Fuel tank: (Camaro) 15.5 gal.

Z28: Transmission: Six-speed manual. Steering: rack and pinion. Front suspension: SLA/Coil over monotube gas shocks, and 30-mm tubular stabilizer bar with links.

The interior of the Z28 was not lacking in style and comfort.

Rear suspension: Solid axle/torque arm, trailing arm, coil springs, track bar, monotube gas shocks and 19-mm solid stabilizer bar with links. Brakes: Four-wheel discs with antilock. Body construction: unibody. Fuel tank: (Camaro) 15.5 gal.

OPTIONS

Preferred equipment group No. 1 included air conditioning, electronic speed control with resume speed feature, fog lamps and remote hatch release (net price $1,240). Preferred equipment group No. 2 included air conditioning, electronic speed control with resume speed feature, fog lamps, remote hatch release, power door lock system, power windows with driver's side "express down" feature, twin remote electric sport mirrors, leather-wrapped steering wheel, leather-wrapped gear shifter handle and leather-wrapped parking brake handle (net price $1,901). B84 body side moldings ($60). CC1 transparent removable roof panels ($895). C60 air conditioning ($895). AU3 power door lock system ($220). AC3 six-way power driver's seat ($270). C49 rear window defogger ($170). UU8 Delco/Bose electronically tuned AM/FM radio with cassette player ($275). U1T Delco/Bose electronically tuned AM/FM radio with compact disc player ($531). KO5 engine block heater ($20). G92 performance axle ratio ($110). MXO four-speed automatic transmission ($595). P245/50ZR16 performance tires ($144). The 1993 base Camaro could be ordered with the 1LE Special Performance Suspension package that included a 32-mm front stabilizer bar, a 21-mm rear stabilizer bar, higher-rate stabilizer bar bushings, higher-rate upper and lower control arm bushings, stiffer front and rear shock absorber valving and increased-capacity cooling system. There was also a special equipment option package SEO B4C for cars used in police work. It included the LT1 engine, a choice of the automatic or six-speed manual transmissions, the performance suspension, 16-in. aluminum wheels, P245/50ZR16 black sidewall tires, four-wheel disc brakes, a limited-slip axle (3.23:1 ratio with automatic transmission and 3.42:1 ratio with manual gearbox), an engine oil cooler, an automatic transmission cooler for cars so-equipped, a 140-amp alternator, air conditioning and a 150-mph speedometer.

HISTORICAL FOOTNOTES

The Ste. Therese factory, which dated to 1965, was completely revamped to build General Motors' fourth-generation Camaros and Firebirds. The workers were formed into teams, with each department functioning independently, but with the overall goal of producing defect-free automobiles. The North American model-year production (U.S. and Canada) of 1993 Camaros was only 40,224 units due to the new model's late introduction in January. Domestic model-year production (U.S. only) was even lower at 39,103 units. A Camaro Z28 driven by Chevrolet General Manager Jim Perkins paced the 1993 Indianapolis 500. During the 1993 Sports Car Club of America Trans-Am racing series competition, versions of the new Z28 were fielded by Jack Baldwin and Scott Sharp. Baldwin had been the series champion in 1992 and Sharp took the title in 1991. Model-year sales were 45,293 units. Calendar-year sales were 68,773. The Ste. Therese plant built all of these cars (and all 15,475 Firebirds). Of the Camaros built, 81 per-cent had automatic transmission, 8.5 percent had a five-speed manual transmission, 10.5 percent had a six-speed manual transmission, 54 percent had a 3.4-liter MFI V-6, 46 percent had a 5.7-liter MFI V-8, 100 percent had power steering, 100 percent had ABS brakes, 10.2 percent had a limited-slip differential, 100 percent had steel-belted radial tires, 84.3 percent had power door locks, 82.9 percent had power windows, 100 percent had reclining bucket seats, 49.5 percent had a power seats, 100 percent had dual front airbags, 100 percent had tilt steering, 100 percent had tinted glass, 99.6 percent had manual air conditioning, 98.4 percent had cruise control, 100 percent had delay windshield wipers, 46.5 percent had a ETR stereo cassette player, 26 percent had a Bose/JBL sound system, 26 percent had a Bose/JBL sound system with CD, 78.4 percent had an electric rear window defogger, 89.5 percent had a manual remote-control left-hand outside rearview mirror, 10.5 percent had power rearview mirrors, 27.8 percent had a power right-hand rearview mirror, 89 percent had aluminum styled wheels, 100 percent had an electronic vehicle anti-theft system, 100 percent had electronic gauges, 50 percent had remote keyless entry and 4.1 percent had T-tops. A total of 61,845 new Camaros were registered in the U.S. during calendar year 1993.

Scott Moyer photo

The Z28 was back as the Indy Pace Car for 1993.

Camaro

Jerry Heasley photo

More than 40,000 new Z28s hit the streets in 1994.

A convertible returned to the Camaro lineup as a mid-season addition in 1994. Base and Z28 ragtops joined the coupes in both series. New standard features included a keyless entry system, "flood light" interior illumination and a compact disc system with new co-axial speakers. Leather seating surfaces in Grahite and Beige became available late in the production.

The Z28's 5.7-liter V-8 received sequential fuel injection for 1994 to provide a smoother idle and lower emissions. The T56 six-speed transmission utilized Computer-Aided Gear Selection to improve fuel economy. Production rose to 119,934 cars this year and included over 7,200 convertibles.

I.D. DATA

Chevrolets again had a 17-symbol vehicle identification number (VIN) on the upper left surface of the instrument panel, visible through the windshield. The first symbol identifies country of origin: 2=Canada. The second symbol identifies the manufacturer: G=General Motors. The third symbol indicates make: 1=Chevrolet, 7=GM of Canada. The fourth and fifth symbols indicated the car line and series: F/P=Camaro Sport Coupe and Convertible. The sixth symbol indicated body type: 2=two-door coupe style 87 and 3=two-door convertible style 67. The seventh symbol indicated the type of restraint system: 1=active manual belts, 2=active manual belts with driver and passenger airbags, 3=active manual belts with driver airbag, 4=passive automatic belts, 5=passive automatic belts with driver airbag and 6=passive automatic belts with driver and passenger airbags. The eighth symbol indicates the engine type: S=RPO L32 3.4-liter (207-cid) V-6 with Multiport Fuel Injection, P=RPO LT1 5.7-liter (350-cid) V-8 with SFI. The ninth

symbol is a check digit. The 10th symbol indicates model year: R=1994. The 11th symbol indicates the assembly plant: 2=Ste. Therese, Providence of Quebec (Canada).

COLORS

Black, Medium Quasar Blue Metallic, Dark Green-Gray Metallic, Polo Green Metallic, Pearl Purple Metallic, Bright Red, Bright Teal Metallic and Artic White.

CAMARO — SERIES 1F — V-6

Coupes utilized the five-speed manual transmission as standard while the convertibles had the 4L60-E electronic four-speed automatic transmission as base offering. Standard features included a serpentine belt accessory drive system, four-wheel antilock brakes, a brake/transmission interlock feature with automatic transmission, power front disc/rear drum brakes, 5-mph front and rear energy-absorbing bumpers with body-color fascias, side window defoggers, a stainless steel exhaust system, Solar-Ray tinted glass, miniquad halogen headlights, dual black-finished sport outside rearview mirrors (left-hand remote controlled, right-hand manual), a two-component clearcoat paint system, gas-charged monotube shock absorbers, integral front and rear spoilers, front and rear stabilizer bars, power rack-and-pinion steering, a Firm Ride & Handling suspension, a four-wheel coil spring suspension with computer-selected springs, a front short/long arm (SLA) suspension, the PASS-Key II theft deterrent system, a compact high-pressure spare tire, P215/60R16 black sidewall tires, a five-speed manual transmission, 16-in. steel bolt-on wheel covers, intermittent windshield wipers, driver and front passenger airbags, full carpeting in driver compartment and passenger compartment and cargo area, a center console with cupholder and lighted storage compartment, Scotchguard interior fabric and door panel protection, front carpeted floor mats, a gauge package with tachometer, a low oil level indicator light, a dome light, a day/night inside rearview mirror with dual reading and courtesy lights, an ETR AM/FM stereo radio (with seek-and-scan, digital clock, stereo cassette tape, search-and-repeat and extended-range speakers), a headlamps-on reminder, a driver's four-way seat with manual adjuster, a rear seat with full-folding seatbacks, front reclining bucket seats with cloth trim and integral headrests, a tilt steering wheel, door panel storage compartments, dual covered visor-vanity mirrors and a check-gauges warning light. The convertible also featured a power-operated top that folded flush with the body, a three-piece hard tonneau cover, a full headliner and a heated glass backlight.

Model Number	Body/Style Number	Body Type & Seating	Factory Price	Shipping Weight	Production Total
F/P	87	2d coupe-4P	$13,339	3,247 lbs.	Note 1
F/P	67	2d convertible-4P	$18,745	3,342 lbs.	Note 2

Note 1: Model-year production of 1994 base Camaro coupes was 76,531.
Note 2: Model-year production of 1994 base Camaro convertibles was 2,328.

CAMARO Z28 — SERIES 1F — V-8

The Z28s again used Corvette's 5.7-liter LT1 V-8 fitted to a Borg-Warner T56 six-speed manual transmission. The four-speed automatic was the optional transmission in Z28s. The Z28's 5.7-liter V-8 received sequential fuel injection for 1994 to provide a smoother idle and lower emissions. The T56 six-speed transmission utilized Computer Aided Gear Selection (CAGS) to improve fuel economy. Standard equipment included a serpentine belt accessory drive system, a limited-slip rear axle, four-wheel antilock brakes, a brake/transmission interlock feature with automatic transmission, four-wheel power disc brakes, 5-mph front and rear energy-absorbing bumpers with body-color fascias, side window defoggers,

a stainless steel exhaust system, Solar-Ray tinted glass, miniquad halogen headlights, dual black-finished sport outside rearview mirrors (left-hand remote controlled, right-hand manual), a two-component clearcoat paint system, a special black roof treatment, gas-charged monotube shock absorbers, integral front and rear spoilers, front and rear stabilizer bars, power rack-and-pinion steering, a Performance Ride & Handling suspension, a four-wheel coil spring suspension with computer-selected springs, a front short/long arm (SLA) suspension, the PASS-Key II theft deterrent system, a compact high-pressure spare tire, P235/55R16 black sidewall tires, 16 x 8-in. aluminum front wheels, 16 x 11-in. aluminum rear wheels, intermittent windshield wipers, driver and front passenger airbags, full carpeting in driver compartment and passenger compartment and cargo area, a center console with cupholder and lighted storage compartment, Scotchguard interior fabric and door panel protection, front carpeted floor mats, a gauge package with 115-mph speedometer and tachometer, a low coolant level indicator system, a low oil level indicator light, a dome light, a day/night inside rearview mirror with dual reading and courtesy lights, an ETR AM/FM stereo radio (with seek-and-scan, digital clock, stereo cassette tape, search-and-repeat and extended-range speakers), a headlamps-on reminder, a driver's four-way seat with manual adjuster, a rear seat with full-folding seatbacks, front reclining bucket seats with cloth trim and integral headrests, a tilt steering wheel, door panel storage compartments, dual covered visor-vanity mirrors and a check-gauges warning light. The convertible also featured a power-operated top that folded flush with the body, a three-piece hard tonneau cover, a full headliner and a heated glass backlight.

Model Number	Body/Style Number	Body Type & Seating	Factory Price	Shipping Weight	Production Total
F/P+Z28	87	2d coupe-4P	$16,799	3,424 lbs.	Note 3
F/P	67	2d convertible-4P	$22,075	3,524 lbs.	Note 4

Note 3: Model-year production of 1994 Camaro Z28 coupes was 36,008.

Jerry Heasley photo

Both the base Camaro (above) and Z28 were available as convertibles for 1994.

The Z28's 5.7-liter V-8 received sequential fuel injection for 1994.

Jerry Heasley photo

Note 4: Model-year production of 1994 Camaro Z28 convertibles was 4,932.
Note 5: The Z28 production total above included 135 cars with the optional 1LE competition package.

ENGINES

L32 V-6: 60-degree, overhead-valve V-6. Cast-iron block and head. Bore & stroke: 3.62 x 3.31. Displacement: 207 cid (3.4 liters). Compression ratio: 9.0:1. Brake horsepower: 160 at 4600 rpm. Torque: 200 lbs.-ft. at 3600 rpm. Hydraulic valve lifters. Induction system: Sequential fuel injection. Standard in base Camaro; not available in Z28. VIN Code S.

LT1 V-8: 90-degree, overhead-valve V-8. Cast-iron block and head. Bore & stroke: 4.00 x 3.48 in. Displacement: 350 cid. (5.7 liters). Compression ratio: 10.5:1. Brake horsepower: 275 at 5000 rpm. Torque: 325 lbs.-ft. at 2400 rpm. Hydraulic valve lifters. Sequential fuel injection. Standard in Z28; not available in base Camaro. VIN Code P.

CHASSIS

Base Camaro: Wheelbase: 101.1 in. Overall length: 193.2 in. Height: 51.3 in.; Width: 74.1 in. Front headroom: 37.2 in. Rear headroom: 35.3 in. Front legroom: 43 in. Rear legroom: 26.8 in. Front shoulder room: 57.4 in. Rear shoulder room: 55.8 in. Luggage capacity: (rear seat up) 12.9 cu. ft.; (rear seat down) 32.8 cu. ft. Front tread: 60.7 in. Rear tread: 60.6 in. Standard tires: P215/60R16.

Z28: Wheelbase: 101.1 in. Overall length: 193.2 in. Height: 51.3 in.; Width: 74.1 in. Front headroom: 37.2 in. Rear headroom: 35.3 in. Front legroom: 43 in. Rear legroom: 26.8 in. Front shoulder room: 57.4 in. Rear shoulder room: 55.8 in. Luggage capacity: (rear seat up) 12.9 cu. ft.; (rear seat down) 32.8 cu. ft. Front tread: 60.7 in. Rear tread: 60.6 in. Standard tires: P235/55R16.

TECHNICAL

Base Camaro: Transmission: Five-speed manual. Steering: rack-and-pinion. Front suspension: SLA/Coil over monotube gas shocks, tubular stabilizer bar with links. Rear suspension: Solid axle/torque arm, trailing arm, coil springs, track bar, monotube gas shocks and solid stabilizer bar with links. Brakes: Front disc/rear drum with antilock. Body construction: unibody. Fuel tank: (Camaro) 15.5 gal.

Z28: Transmission: Six-speed manual. Steering: rack-and-pinion. Front suspension: SLA/Coil over monotube gas shocks, and 30-mm tubular stabilizer bar with links. Rear suspension: Solid axle/torque arm, trailing arm, coil springs, track bar, monotube gas shocks and 19-mm solid stabilizer bar with links. Brakes: Four-wheel discs with antilock. Body construction: unibody. Fuel tank: (Camaro) 15.5 gal.

OPTIONS

Coupe preferred equipment group No. 1 included air conditioning, electronic speed control with resume speed feature, fog lamps and remote hatch release (net price $1,240 with automatic transmission $1,350 with six-speed manual transmission). Coupe preferred equipment group No. 2 included air conditioning, electronic speed control with resume speed feature, fog lamps, remote hatch release, power door lock system, power windows with driver's side "express down" feature, twin remote electric sport mirrors, remote keyless entry, leather-wrapped steering wheel, leather-wrapped gear shifter handle and leather-wrapped parking brake handle (net price $2,036 with automatic transmission $2,146 with six-speed manual transmission). Convertible preferred equipment group No. 1 included air conditioning, electronic speed control with resume speed feature, fog lamps and remote hatch release (net price $1,240 with automatic transmission $1,350 with six-speed manual transmission). Convertible preferred equipment group No. 2 included air conditioning, electronic speed control with resume speed feature, fog lamps, remote hatch release, power door lock system, power windows with driver's side "express down" feature, twin remote electric sport mirrors, remote keyless entry, leather-wrapped steering wheel, leather-wrapped gear shifter handle and leather-wrapped parking brake handle (net price $2,036 with automatic transmission $2,146 with six-speed manual transmission). C2 cloth bucket seats (no cost). A2 leather bucket seats ($499). C60 air conditioning ($895). GU5 performance axle includes engine oil cooler, Z28 only ($65 with 1LE performance package or $175 without 1LE performance package). VK3 front license plate bracket (no cost). C49 rear window defogger ($170). R9W rear window defogger not desired (no cost). AU3 power door lock system ($220). YF5 California emissions ($100). FE9 federal emissions (no cost). NB8 California/New York override (no cost). NC7 federal emissions override (no cost). B35 rear floor covering ($15). B84 body side moldings ($60). 1LE Performance package including engine oil cooler and Special Handling suspension, Z28 coupe only ($310). [Note: All audio options include extended-range sound system UU8 Delco/Bose electronically tuned AM/FM radio with cassette player ($275 extra as part of all PEGs)]. U1T Delco/Bose electronically tuned AM/FM radio with compact disc player ($531 as part of all PEGs). U1C ETR AM/FM stereo with seek-and-scan, digital clock, CD player, extended-range speakers and Delco Loc II, in convertibles only ($226 as part of all convertible PEGs). CC1 transparent removable coupe roof panels with storage provisions ($970). AC3 six-way power driver's seat ($270). DE4 removable coupe roof sunshade panels ($25). QPE P215/60R16 steel-belted radial black sidewall tires on base coupe and convertible (no cost). QMT P235/55R16 steel-belted radial black sidewall tires on Z28 coupe and convertible (no cost). QLC P245/50ZR16 steel-belted radial black sidewall tires and 150-mph speedometer for Z28 coupe ($225). MXO four-speed automatic transmission ($750). MM5 five-speed manual transmission in base Camaro coupe or convertible (no cost) MN6 six-speed manual transmission in Z28 coupe or convertible (no cost). N96 cast-aluminum wheels with locks on Z28 coupe or convertible only ($275). QB3 16-in. cast steel wheels with bolt-on wheel covers for base coupe or convertible (no cost). L32 3.4-liter sequentially fuel-injected V-6 in base coupe or convertible (no cost). LT1 5.7-liter sequentially fuel-injected V-8 in Z28 coupe or convertible (no cost).

HISTORICAL FOOTNOTES

All 1994 Camaro coupes and convertibles were built at the refurbished factory in Ste. Therese, Quebec, Canada. Computer-aided gear selection (or CAGS) was added to the six-speed manual transmission in 1994. It improved fuel economy by directing the driver from first to fourth gear under light acceleration. Rapid acceleration automatically cancelled the 1-to-4 shift. A lamp lit up when the transmission was in "skip shift" mode. The Camaro's model-year sales were 124,121 units. Calendar-year sales were 116,592. The North American model-year production (U.S. and Canada) of 1994 Camaros was 125,244 units. Domestic model-year production (U.S. market only) was 119,799 units and included 112,539 coupes and 7,260 convertibles. The Ste. Therese plant built all of these cars (and all 45,922 Firebirds). Of the Camaros built, 74.9 percent had automatic transmission, 17.8 percent had a five-speed manual transmission, 7.3 percent had a six-speed manual transmission, 65.3 percent had a 3.4-liter SFI V-6, 34.7 percent had a 5.7-liter MFI V-8, 100 percent had power steering, 100 percent had ABS brakes, 34.7 percent had a limited-slip differential, 100 percent had steel-belted radial tires, 100 percent had power door locks, 65.9 percent had power windows, 100 percent had reclining bucket seats, 49.5 percent had a power seats, 100 percent had dual front airbags, 85 percent had tilt steering, 100 percent had tinted glass, 100 percent had manual air conditioning, 69.7 percent had cruise control, 96.5 percent had delay windshield wipers, 45.5 percent had a ETR stereo cassette player, 26.4 percent had a Bose/JBL sound system, 24.1 percent had a Bose/JBL sound system with CD, 69.7 percent had an electric rear window defogger, 3.9 percent had another brand CD, 24.1 percent had a manual remote-control left-hand outside rearview mirror, 75.9 percent had power rearview mirrors, 27.8 percent had a power right-hand rearview mirror, 87.5 percent had aluminum styled wheels, 100 percent had an electronic vehicle anti-theft system, 100 percent had electronic gauges and 35.6 percent had T-tops. A total of 117,503 new Camaros were registered in the U.S. during calendar year 1994.

Inside, the Z28 got a new CD system, in addition to its already lengthy list of amenities.

Jerry Heasley photo

Camaro

In 1995, Z28s again featured the LT1 V-8 attached to a Borg-Warner T56 six-speed manual transmission, with a four-speed automatic transmission optional.

Camaro returned in 1995 with the same model line-up. New features included body-colored outside dual sport mirrors on base models, an optional monochromatic roof treatment on Z28 coupes (and base coupes with T-tops), optional chrome-plated wheel covers and aluminum wheels. A speed-rated performance tires package with a 150-mph speedometer and an optional Acceleration Slip Regulation traction-control system was planned for 1995 Z28s, but didn't actually arrive until 1998.

The base coupe was powered by the 3.4-liter V-6 fitted to a five-speed manual transmission. The convertible used the 5.7-liter LT1 V-8 mated to an electronic four-speed automatic transmission. Z28s again featured the LT1 attached to a Borg-Warner T56 six-speed manual transmission, with a four-speed automatic transmission listed as optional equipment.

I.D. DATA

Chevrolets again had a 17-symbol vehicle identification number (VIN) on the upper left surface of the instrument panel, visible through the windshield. The first symbol identifies country of origin: 2=Canada. The second symbol identifies the manufacturer: G=General Motors. The third symbol indicates make: 1=Chevrolet, 7=GM of Canada. The fourth and fifth symbols indicated the car line and series: F/P=Camaro Sport Coupe and Convertible. The sixth symbol indicated body type: 2=two-door coupe style 87 and 3=two-door convertible style 67. The seventh symbol indicated the type of restraint system: 1=active manual belts, 2=active manual belts with driver and passenger airbags, 3=active manual belts with driver airbag, 4=passive automatic belts, 5=passive automatic belts with driver airbag and 6=passive automatic belts with driver and passenger airbags. The eighth symbol indicates the engine type: S=RPO L32 3.4-liter (207-cid) V-6 with Multiport Fuel

Injection, K=RPO L36 3.8-liter (231-cid) V-6 with SFI, P=RPO LT1 5.7-liter (350-cid) V-8 with SFI. The ninth symbol is a check digit. The 10th symbol indicates model year: S=1995. The 11th symbol indicates the assembly plant: 2=Ste. Therese, Providence of Quebec (Canada).

COLORS

Black, Bright Red, Dark Purple Metallic, Medium Quasar Blue Metallic, Medium Patriot Red Metallic, Sebring Silver Metallic, Artic White, Bright Teal Metallic, Polo Green Metallic and Mystic Teal Metallic. Interiors came in Medium Beige (not with Sebring Silver exterior), Graphite, Medium Gray and Flame Red (with Black, Bright Red, Sebring Silver and Artic White exterior colors only).

CAMARO — SERIES 1F — V-6

"Camaro is the American sports machine for people who love to drive and one turn behind the wheel is guaranteed to transform just about anybody into a Camaro enthusiast," stated the 1995 Camaro sales catalog. Camaro returned in 1995 with the same lineup. A coupe and a convertible were offered in both the base and Z28 series. New features included body-colored outside Sport mirrors on base models. The base coupe was powered by the 3.4-liter V-6 fitted to a five-speed manual transmission. A 3.8-liter V-6 teamed with an electronically controlled four-speed automatic transmission was a new option. Another new-for-1995 option was a monochromatic roof treatment on base coupes with T-tops. Standard equipment included manual lap and shoulder safety belts, driver and front passenger airbags, an energy-absorbing steering column, an energy-absorbing instrument panel, interlocking door latches, inertia-type folding front seat locks, safety armrests, a breakaway inside rearview mirror, security door locks and door retention components, urethane-bonded laminated windshield glass, integral front head restraints, side-door beams, passenger-guard inside door lock handles, front and rear crush zones, side marker lights and reflectors, parking lamps, four-way hazard warning flashers, back-up lights, directional signal control, windshield defrosters, washers and multi-speed wipers, an inside day/night rearview mirror, outside rearview mirrors, a brake system with a dual master cylinder plus brake warning light, a center high-mounted stop lamp, a starter safety switch, a dual-action hood latch, a low-glare finish inside windshield molding, low-glare wiper arms and blades, low-glare metallic steering wheel surfaces, illuminated heater and defroster controls, tires with built-in tread wear indicators, audible disc brake lining-wear indicators, antilock brakes, a brake/transmission shift interlock (with automatic transmission), basecoat/clearcoat paint, dual sport mirrors (left-hand remote controlled), a front air dam, halogen headlights, a rear deck lid spoiler, auxiliary lighting, carpeted front floor mats, a center console with storage compartment and cupholder, a deep-well luggage area, driver and front passenger-side airbags, an intermittent windshield wiper system, the PASS-Key II theft-deterrent system, Scotchguard protector on fabrics and carpets, cloth-trimmed reclining front bucket seats, special instrumentation with a tachometer, side window defoggers, a tilt adjustable steering wheel, an AM/FM stereo with cassette tape player, a 3.4-liter V-6 with sequential-port fuel injection, a five-speed manual transmission, power front disc/rear drum ABS brakes, a Delco Freedom II battery, power rack-and-pinion steering, rear-wheel drive, single serpentine belt engine accessory drive, a stainless steel exhaust system, a Firm Ride & Handling suspension, 16 x 7 1/2-in. wheels with bolt-on wheel covers and P215/60R-16 touring tires. The convertible also had a standard rear window defogger, a fully lined power-operated folding top and a form-fitting three-piece tonneau cover for a sleek top-down appearance.

Model Number	Body/Style Number	Body Type & Seating	Factory Price	Shipping Weight	Production Total
CAMARO - SERIES F/P - (V-6)					
F/P	87	2d coupe-4P	$14,250	3,251 lbs.	Note 1
F/P	67	2d convertible-4P	$19,495	3,342 lbs.	Note 2

Note 1: Total Camaro and Camaro Z28 coupe production was 115,365.
Note 2: Total Camaro and Camaro Z28 convertible production was 7,360.

CAMARO Z28 — SERIES 1F — V-8

Z28s again featured the LT1 5.7-liter V-8 fitted to the Borg-Warner T56 six-speed manual transmission as standard equipment. The four-speed automatic was optional. New-for-1995 options included a monochromatic roof treatment on Z28 coupes, as well as optional chrome-plated wheel covers and aluminum wheels. Also available on the Z28 were speed-rated performance tires (with a 150-mph speedometer) and an optional traction-control system. Standard equipment included manual lap and shoulder safety belts, driver and front passenger airbags, an energy-absorbing steering column, an energy-absorbing instrument panel, interlocking door latches, inertia-type folding front seat locks, safety armrests, a breakaway inside rearview mirror, security door locks and door retention components, urethane-bonded laminated windshield glass, integral front head restraints, side-door beams, passenger-guard inside door lock handles, front and rear crush zones, side marker lights and reflectors, parking lamps, four-way hazard warning flashers, back-up lights, directional signal control, windshield defrosters, washers and multi-speed wipers, an inside day/night rearview mirror, outside rearview mirrors, a brake system with a dual master cylinder plus brake warning light, a center high-mounted stop lamp, a starter safety switch, a dual-action hood latch, a low-glare finish inside windshield molding, low-glare wiper arms and blades, low-glare metallic steering wheel surfaces, illuminated heater and defroster controls, tires with built-in tread wear indicators, audible disc brake lining-wear indicators, antilock brakes, a brake/transmission shift interlock (with automatic transmission), basecoat-

The 1995 Z28s coupe received a new optional monochromatic roof treatment.

Jerry Heasley photo

Daniel B. Lyons photo

The 1995 Z28 convertible had a standard rear window defogger, a fully lined power-operated folding top and a form-fitting three-piece tonneau cover.

/clearcoat paint, dual sport mirrors (left-hand remote controlled), a front air dam, halogen headlights, a rear deck lid spoiler, auxiliary lighting, carpeted front floor mats, a center console with storage compartment and cup holder, a deep-well luggage area, driver and front passenger-side airbags, an intermittent windshield wiper system, the PASS-Key II theft-deterrent system, Scotchguard protector on fabrics and carpets, cloth-trimmed reclining front bucket seats, special instrumentation with a tachometer, side window defoggers, a tilt adjustable steering wheel, an AM/FM stereo with cassette tape player, the 5.7-liter V-8 with tuned-port-injection system, a six-speed manual transmission, power four-wheel disc ABS brakes, a limited-slip rear axle, a Delco Freedom II battery, power rack-and-pinion steering, rear-wheel drive, single serpentine belt engine accessory drive, a stainless steel exhaust system, a Performance Ride & Handling suspension, 16 x 8-in. cast-aluminum wheels and P235/55R-16 touring tires. The convertible also had a standard rear window defogger, a fully lined power-operated folding top and a form-fitting three-piece tonneau cover for a sleek top-down appearance.

Model Number	Body/Style Number	Body Type & Seating	Factory Price	Shipping Weight	Production Total
CAMARO Z28 - SERIES F/P - (V-8)					
F/P+Z28	87	2d coupe-4P	$17,915	3,390 lbs.	Note 3
F/P+Z28	67	2d convertible -4P	$22,075	3,480 lbs.	Note 4

Note 3: Total Camaro and Camaro Z28 coupe production was 115,365.
Note 4: Total Camaro and Camaro Z28 convertible production was 7,360.

ENGINES

L32 V-6: 60-degree, overhead-valve V-6. Cast-iron block and head. Bore & stroke: 3.62 x 3.31. Displacement: 207 cid (3.4 liters). Compression ratio: 9.0:1. Brake horsepower: 160 at 4600 rpm. Torque: 200 lbs.-ft. at 3600 rpm. Hydraulic valve lifters. Induction system: Sequential fuel injection. Standard in base Camaro and used in 66.5 percent of 1995 models. VIN Code S.

L36 V-6: 60-degree, overhead-valve V-6. Cast-iron block and head. Bore & stroke: 3.80 x 3.40. Displacement: 231 cid (3.8 liters). Compression ratio: 9.4:1. Brake horsepower: 200 at 5300 rpm. Hydraulic valve lifters. Induction system: Sequential fuel injection. Avail-able in base Camaro in late-1995 production, used in only .4 percent of 1995 production. VIN Code K.

LT1 V-8: 90-degree, overhead-valve V-8. Cast-iron block and head. Bore & stroke: 4.00 x 3.48 in. Displacement: 350 cid (5.7 liters). Compression ratio: 10.5:1. Brake horsepower: 275 at 5000 rpm. Torque: 325 lbs.-ft. at 2400 rpm. Hydraulic valve lifters. Sequential fuel injection. Standard in Z28. VIN Code P.

CHASSIS

Base Camaro Coupe: Wheelbase: 101.1 in. Overall length: 193.2 in. Height: 51.3 in. Width: 74.1 in. Front headroom: 37.2 in. Rear headroom: 35.3 in. Front legroom: 43 in. Rear legroom: 26.8 in. Front shoulder room: 57.4 in. Rear shoulder room: 55.8 in. Front hiproom: 52.8 in. Rear hiproom: 44.4 in. Luggage capacity: (rear seat up) 12.9 cu. ft.; (rear seat down) 32.8 cu. ft. Front tread: 60.7 in. Rear Tread: 60.6 in. Standard tires: P215/60R16.

Base Camaro Convertible: Wheelbase: 101.1 in. Overall length: 193.2 in. Height: 52 in. Width: 74.1 in. Front headroom: 38 in. Rear headroom: 39 in. Front legroom: 43 in. Rear legroom: 26.8 in. Front shoulder room: 57.4 in. Rear shoulder room: 43.5 in. Front hiproom: 52.8 in. Rear hiproom: 43.7 in. Luggage capacity: (rear seat up) 7.6 cu. ft. Front tread: 60.7 in. Rear tread: 60.6 in. Standard tires: P215/60R16.

Z28 Coupe: Wheelbase: 101.1 in. Overall length: 193.2 in. Height: 51.3 in. Width: 74.1 in. Front headroom: 37.2 in. Rear headroom: 35.3 in. Front legroom: 43 in. Rear legroom: 26.8 in. Front shoulder room: 57.4 in. Rear shoulder room: 55.8 in. Front hiproom: 52.8 in. Rear hiproom: 44.4 in. Luggage capacity: (rear seat up) 12.9 cu. ft.; (rear seat down) 32.8 cu. ft. Front tread: 60.7 in. Rear tread: 60.6 in. Standard tires: P235/55R16.

Z28 Convertible: Wheelbase: 101.1 in. Overall length: 193.2 in. Height: 52 in. Width: 74.1 in. Front headroom: 38.0 in. Rear headroom: 39 in. Front legroom: 43 in. Rear legroom: 26.8 in. Front shoulder room: 57.4 in. Rear shoulder room: 43.5 in. Front hiproom: 52.8 in. Rear hiproom: 43.7 in. Luggage capacity: (rear seat up) 7.6 cu. ft. Front tread: 60.7 in. Rear tread: 60.6 in. Standard tires: P235/55R16.

TECHNICAL

Base Camaro: Transmission: Five-speed manual. Steering: rack and pinion. Front suspension: SLA/Coil over monotube gas shocks, tubular stabilizer bar with links. Rear suspension: Solid axle/torque arm, trailing arm, coil springs, track bar, monotube gas shocks and solid stabilizer bar with links. Brakes: Front disc/rear drum with antilock. Body construction: unibody. Fuel tank: (Camaro) 15.5 gal.

Z28: Transmission: Six-speed manual. Steering: rack and pinion. Front suspension: SLA/Coil over monotube gas shocks, and 30-mm tubular stabilizer bar with links. Rear suspension: Solid axle/torque arm, trailing arm, coil springs, track bar, monotube gas shocks and 19-mm solid stabilizer bar with links. Brakes: Four-wheel discs with antilock. Body construction: unibody. Fuel tank: (Camaro) 15.5 gal.

OPTIONS

1SA Coupe base equipment group (PEG) included with model, no radio upgrade allowed (no cost). Coupe preferred equipment group No. 1 included air conditioning, electronic speed control with resume speed feature, fog lamps and remote hatch release (net price $1,240 with automatic transmission). PEG 1 with UU8 radio upgrade ($350 additional). PEG 1 with U1T radio upgrade ($606 additional). PEG No. 2 included air conditioning, electronic speed control with resume speed feature, fog lamps, remote hatch release, power door lock system, power windows with driver's side "express down" feature, twin remote electric sport mirrors, remote keyless entry, leather-wrapped steering wheel, leather-wrapped gear shifter handle and leather-wrapped parking brake handle (net price $2,036 with automatic transmission $2,146 with six-speed manual transmission). PEG 1 with UU8 radio upgrade ($350 additional). PEG 1 with U1T radio upgrade ($606 additional). Convertible PEG No. 1 included air conditioning, electronic speed control with resume speed feature, fog lamps and remote hatch release (net price $1,240 with automatic transmission $1,350 with six-speed manual transmission). Convertible PEG No. 2 included air conditioning, electronic speed control with resume speed feature, fog

lamps, remote hatch release, power door lock system, power windows with driver's side "express down" feature, twin remote electric sport mirrors, remote keyless entry, leather-wrapped steering wheel, leather-wrapped gear shifter handle and leather-wrapped parking brake handle (net price $2,036 with automatic transmission $2,146 with six-speed manual transmission). C2 cloth bucket seats (no cost). A2 leather bucket seats ($499). C60 air conditioning ($895). GU5 performance axle includes engine oil cooler, Z28 only ($65 with 1LE performance package or $175 without). 1LE performance package. VK3 front license plate bracket (no cost). C49 rear window defogger ($170). R9W rear window defogger not desired (no cost). AU3 power door lock system ($220). YF5 California emissions ($100). FE9 federal emissions (no cost). NB8 California/New York override (no cost). NC7 federal emissions override (no cost). B35 rear floor covering ($15). B84 body side moldings ($60). 1LE Performance package including engine oil cooler and Special Handling suspension, Z28 coupe only ($310). [Note: All audio options include extended-range sound system UU8 Delco/Bose electronically tuned AM/FM radio with cassette player ($275 extra as part of all PEGs).] U1T Delco/Bose electronically tuned AM/FM radio with compact disc player ($531 as part of all PEGs). U1C ETR AM/FM stereo with seek-and-scan, digital clock, CD player, extended-range speakers and Delco Loc II, in convertibles only ($226 as part of all convertible PEGs). CC1 transparent removable coupe roof panels with storage provisions ($970). AC3 six-way power driver's seat ($270). DE4 removable coupe roof sunshade panels ($25). QPE P215/60R16 steel-belted radial black sidewall tires on base coupe and convertible (no cost). QMT P235/55R16 steel-belted radial black sidewall tires on Z28 coupe and convertible (no cost). QLC P245/50ZR16 steel-belted radial black sidewall tires and 150-mph speedometer for Z28 coupe ($225). MXO four-speed automatic transmission ($750). MM5 five-speed manual transmission in base Camaro coupe or convertible (no cost) MN6 six-speed manual transmission in Z28 coupe or convertible (no cost). N96 cast-aluminum wheels with locks on Z28 coupe or convertible only ($275). QB3 16-in. cast steel wheels with bolt-on wheel covers for base coupe or convertible (no cost). L32 3.4-liter sequentially fuel-injected V-6 in base coupe or con-

The base Camaro coupe came with two different V-6 engines in 1995.

vertible (no cost). LT1 5.7-liter sequentially fuel-injected V-8 in Z28 coupe or convertible (no cost). L36 3.8-liter sequentially fuel-injected V-6 in base coupe or convertible

HISTORICAL FOOTNOTES

Jim C. Perkins was the general manager of Chevrolet Motor Division as the 1995 model year began, but he was soon to be followed by John G. Middlebrook, who would hold the title by 1996. The Camaro's model-year sales were 98.806 units. Calendar-year sales were 97,525. Industry trade journals reported model-year production of 115,365 coupes and 7,360 convertibles for a total of 122,725 units. The Ste. Therese, Quebec, plant built all of these cars (and all 50,986 Firebirds). Of the Camaros built, 77.8 percent had automatic transmission, 13.8 percent had a five-speed manual transmission, 8.4 percent had a six-speed manual transmission, 66.5 percent had a 3.4-liter SFI V-6, 0.4 percent had a 3.8-liter SFI V-6, 33.1 percent had a 5.7-liter MFI V-8, 2.5 percent had traction control, 100 percent had power steering, 100 percent had ABS brakes, 34.7 percent had a limited-slip differential, 100 percent had steel-belted radial tires, 77.5 percent had power door locks, 74.5 percent had power windows, 100 percent had reclining bucket seats, 48.1 percent had a power seats, 100 percent had dual front airbags, 100 percent had tilt steering, 100 percent had tinted glass, 98.5 percent had manual air conditioning, 98.2 percent had cruise control, 100 percent had delay windshield wipers, 46.9 percent had a ETR stereo cassette player, 22 percent had a Bose/JBL sound system, 22.6 percent had a Bose/JBL sound system with CD, 8.5 percent had another brand CD, 63.6 percent had an electric rear window defogger, 25.5 percent had a manual remote-control left-hand outside rearview mirror, 74.5 percent had power rearview mirrors, 27.8 percent had a power right-hand rearview mirror, 88.9 percent had aluminum styled wheels, 74.3 percent had remote keyless entry and 38.9 percent had T-tops. A total of 98,938 new Camaros were registered in the U.S. during calendar year 1995.

The base price of the 1995 Z28 convertible was $22,075.

Daniel B. Lyons photo

Camaro

Jerry Heasley photo

The SS returned to the Camaro lineup for the first time in 24 years in 1996. SLP Engineering teamed up with GM to produce 2,410 cars with the SS package, which was optional for the Z28.

In 1996, Camaro buyers had their choice of three Camaro coupes and three convertibles in base, RS or Z28 trim. They shared a new standard 3.8-liter Series II 3800 V-6 with base Camaros. A new V-6 Performance Handling package was offered for these cars and V-6 Camaros with automatic transmission got a new second gear select switch that allowed second gear starting for an improved "launch" on slippery surfaces. The base line featured a five-speed manual transmission as standard equipment. A four-speed automatic transmission was optional. T-tops were again available as optional equipment on coupes and an antitheft system was also available for all Camaro models.

To keep enthusiasts happy, an SS performance package for the Z28 was introduced at midyear. The first Camaro SS in 24 years was actually a team effort by Chevrolet Motor Division and SLP Engineering of Troy, Michigan. "SLP" originally stood for "Street Legal Performance" and this car was marketed through Chevy dealers for those who appreciated muscle cars.

I.D. DATA

Chevrolets again had a 17-symbol vehicle identification number (VIN) on the upper left surface of the instrument panel, visible through the windshield. The first symbol identifies country of origin: 2=Canada. The second symbol identifies the manufacturer: G=General Motors. The third symbol indicates make: 1=Chevrolet, 7=GM of Canada. The fourth and fifth symbols indicated the car line and series: F/P=Camaro Sport Coupe and Convertible. The sixth symbol indicated body type: 2=two-door coupe style 87 and 3=two-door convertible style 67. The seventh symbol indicated the type of restraint system: 1=active manual belts, 2=active manual belts with driver and passenger airbags, 3=active manual belts with driver airbag, 4=passive automatic belts, 5=passive automatic belts with driver airbag, 6=passive automatic belts with driver and passenger airbags and 7=active manual belts with driver and passenger airbags. The eighth symbol indicates the engine type: K=RPO L36 3.8-liter (231-cid) V-6 with Multiport Fuel Injection, P=RPO LT1 5.7-liter (350-cid) V-8 with SFI. The ninth symbol is a check digit. The 10th symbol indicates model year: T=1996. The 11th symbol indicates the assembly plant: 2=Ste. Therese, Providence of Quebec (Canada).

COLORS

Arctic White, Black, Bright Red, Bright Teal Metallic, Cayenne Red Metallic, Dark, Purple Metallic, Medium Quasar Blue Metallic, Mystic Teal Metallic, Polo Green Metallic, Sebring Silver.

CAMARO — SERIES 1F — V-6

Standard equipment included manual lap and shoulder safety belts, driver and front passenger airbags, an energy-absorbing steering column, an energy-absorbing instrument panel, interlocking door latches, inertia-type folding front-seat locks, safety armrests, a breakaway inside rearview mirror, security door locks and door retention components, urethane-bonded laminated windshield glass, integral front head restraints, side-door beams, passenger-guard inside door lock handles, front and rear crush zones, side marker lights and reflectors, parking lamps, four-way hazard warning flashers, back-up lights, directional signal control, windshield defrosters, washers and multi-speed wipers, an inside day/night rearview mirror, outside rearview mirrors, a brake system with a dual master cylinder plus brake warning light, a center high-mounted stop lamp, a starter safety switch, a dual-action hood latch, a low-glare finish inside windshield molding, low-glare wiper arms and blades, low-glare metallic steering wheel surfaces, illuminated heater and defroster controls, tires with built-in tread wear indicators, audible disc brake lining-wear indicators, antilock brakes, a brake/transmission shift interlock (with automatic transmission), basecoat-/clearcoat paint, dual sport mirrors (left-hand remote controlled), a front air dam, halogen headlights, a rear deck lid spoiler, auxiliary lighting, carpeted front floor mats, a center console with storage compartment and cup holder, a deep-well luggage area, driver and front passenger-side airbags, an intermittent windshield wiper system, the PASS-Key II theft-deterrent system, Scotchguard protector on fabrics and carpets, cloth-trimmed reclining front bucket seats, special instrumentation with a tachometer, side window defoggers, a tilt adjustable steering wheel, an AM/FM stereo with cassette tape player, a 3.8-liter V-6 with sequential-port fuel injection, a five-speed manual transmission, power front disc/rear drum ABS brakes, a Delco Freedom II battery, power rack-and-pinion steering, rear-wheel drive, single serpentine belt engine accessory drive, a stainless steel exhaust system, a Firm Ride & Handling suspension, 16 x 7 1/2-in. wheels with bolt-on wheel covers and P215/60R-16 touring tires. The convertible also had a standard rear window defogger, a fully lined power-operated folding top, air conditioning, a full headliner, rear seat and trunk courtesy lamps, a glass rear window and a form-fitting three-piece hard boot with storage bag.

Model Number	Body/Style Number	Body Type & Seating	Factory Price	Shipping Weight	Production Total
F/P	87	2d coupe-4P	$14,990	3,306 lbs.	31,528
F/P	67	2d convertible-4P	$21,270	3,440 lbs.	2,994

CAMARO RS — SERIES 1F — V-6

The Camaro RS, with its "ground effects" lower body panels, was a new model for 1996. The standard power plant for RS models was the 3.8-liter V-6. The new V-6 Performance Handling package was offered for the RS, as was the new second gear select switch for V-6s with automatic transmissions. In addition to or in place of standard equipment on the base Camaro, the RS coupe and convertible featured the ground effects package, air conditioning, P235/55R16 tires and 16-in. aluminum wheels.

Model Number	Body/Style Number	Body Type & Seating	Factory Price	Shipping Weight	Production Total
F/P	87	2d coupe-4P	$17,490	3,306 lbs.	8,091
F/P	67	2d convertible-4P	$22,720	3,440 lbs.	905

CAMARO Z28 — SERIES 1F — V-8

The Z28 again used the 5.7-liter V-8 as its standard engine. It came standard linked to a six-speed manual transmission. The four-speed automatic was optional. In addition to or in place of base Camaro equipment, the Z28 featured air conditioning, a limited-slip rear axle, four-wheel power ABS disc brakes, the 5.7-liter sequen-

tial fuel injected V-8, a low-coolant-level indicator, two way manual seat adjustment, platinum tip spark plugs, a special coupe roof treatment with black mirrors, a 150-mph speedometer. A Performance Ride & Handling suspension, P235/55R16 black sidewall radial tires, a high-pressure compact spare tire, a six-speed manual transmission and 16-in. aluminum wheels.

Model Number	Body/Style Number	Body Type & Seating	Factory Price	Shipping Weight	Production Total
F/P+Z28	87	2d coupe-4P	$19,390	3,466 lbs.	14,906
F/P+Z28	67	2d coupe-4P	$24,490	3,593 lbs.	2,938

CAMARO SS — SERIES 1F — V-8

A Michigan company named SLP Engineering teamed up with General Motors to issue an all-new Camaro SS model in 1996. SLP (which originally stood for Street Legal Performance) was founded by ex-drag racer Ed Hamburger and began specializing in modifying Pontiac Firebirds in the 1970s. SLP worked hand in hand with both Pontiac and Chevrolet to create super-high-performance versions of both F-cars based on new Camaros and Firebirds. The modifications gave the 1996 Camaro SS extra horsepower and gave the car appearance, handling and braking upgrades to go along with the added power. The new Camaro SS was featured in 35 automotive publications during 1996 and appeared on the cover of 17 leading magazines. The base engine was a 305-hp LT1 V-8. An optional performance exhaust system added 5 hp. Other standard Camaro SS coupe content included an underhood forced-air induction system, a restyled rear deck lid spoiler, a restyled suspension on coupe and T-top models, B.F. Goodrich Comp T/A tires (size P275/40ZR17), 17 x 9-in. ZR-1 styled cast-aluminum alloy wheels, Quaker State Synquest synthetic engine oil, exterior SS badges replacing Z28 logos and a Camaro SS interior plaque. Camaro SS convertibles retained the stock Camaro suspension and had 16-in. B.F. Goodrich Comp T/A tires and 16 x 8-in. styled cast-aluminum wheels.

Model Number	Body/Style Number	Body Type & Seating	Factory Price	Shipping Weight	Production Total
F/P+Z28	87	2d coupe-4P	—	—	Note 7
F/P+Z28	67	2d convertible-4P	—	—	Note 7

NOTE 1: Included in the Camaro Z28 production totals given above were 2,410 Camaro Z28s with the SS package

ENGINE

L36 V-6: 60-degree, overhead-valve V-6. Cast-iron block and head. Bore & stroke: 3.80 x 3.40. Displacement: 231 cid (3.8 liters). Compression ratio: 9.4:1. Brake horsepower: 200 at 5300 rpm. Hydraulic valve lifters. Induction system: Sequential fuel injection. Standard in base Camaro and Camaro RS. VIN Code K.

LT1 V-8: 90-degree, overhead-valve V-8. Cast-iron block and head. Bore & stroke: 4.00 x 3.48 in. Displacement: 350 cid (5.7 liters). Compression ratio: 10.5:1. Brake horsepower: 275 at 5000 rpm. Torque: 325 lbs.-ft. at 2400 rpm. Hydraulic valve lifters. Sequential fuel injection. Standard in Z28. VIN Code P.

LT1 V-8: 90-degree, overhead-valve V-8. Cast-iron block and head. Bore & stroke: 4.00 x 3.48 in. Displacement: 350 cu. in. (5.7 liters). Brake horsepower: 305 at 5500 rpm. Torque: 325 lbs.-ft. at 2400 rpm. Hydraulic

The Brickyard 400 got the Z28 as a pace car in 1996.

valve lifters. Sequential fuel injection. Standard in Camaro SS. VIN Code P.

LT1 V-8: 90-degree, overhead-valve V-8. Cast-iron block and head. Bore & stroke: 4.00 x 3.48 in. Displacement: 350 cid (5.7 liters). Brake horsepower: 310 at 5500 rpm. Torque: 325 lbs.-ft. at 2400 rpm. Hydraulic valve lifters. Sequential fuel injection. Performance exhaust system. Optional in Camaro SS. VIN Code P.

CHASSIS

Base Camaro Coupe: Wheelbase: 101.1 in. Overall length: 193.2 in. Height: 51.3 in. Width: 74.1 in. Front headroom: 37.2 in. Rear headroom: 35.3 in. Front legroom: 43 in. Rear legroom: 26.8 in. Front shoulder room: 57.4 in. Rear shoulder room: 55.8 in. Front hip room: 52.8 in. Rear hip room: 44.4 in. Luggage capacity: (rear seat up) 12.9 cu. ft.; (rear seat down) 32.8 cu. ft. Front tread: 60.7 in. Rear tread: 60.6 in. Standard tires: P215/60R16.

Base Camaro Convertible: Wheelbase: 101.1 in. Overall length: 193.2 in. Height: 52 in. Width: 74.1 in. Front headroom: 38 in. Rear headroom: 39 in. Front legroom: 43 in. Rear legroom: 26.8 in. Front shoulder room: 57.4 in. Rear shoulder room: 43.5 in. Front hip room: 52.8 in. Rear hip room: 43.7 in. Luggage capacity: (rear seat up) 7.6 cu. ft. Front tread: 60.7 in. Rear tread: 60.6 in. Standard tires: P215/60R16.

Camaro RS Coupe: Wheelbase: 101.1 in. Overall length: 193.2 in. Height: 51.3 in. Width: 74.1 in. Front headroom: 37.2 in. Rear headroom: 35.3 in. Front legroom: 43 in. Rear legroom: 26.8 in. Front shoulder room: 57.4 in. Rear shoulder room: 55.8 in. Front hip room: 52.8 in. Rear hip room: 44.4 in. Luggage capacity: (rear seat up) 12.9 cu. ft.; (rear seat down) 32.8 cu. ft. Front Tread: 60.7 in. Rear Tread: 60.6 in. Standard Tires: P235/55R16.

Camaro RS Convertible: Wheelbase: 101.1 in. Overall length: 193.2 in. Height: 52 in. Width: 74.1 in. Front headroom: 38 in. Rear headroom: 39 in. Front legroom: 43 in. Rear legroom: 26.8 in. Front shoulder room: 57.4 in. Rear shoulder room: 43.5 in. Front hip room: 52.8 in. Rear hip room: 43.7 in. Luggage capacity: (rear seat up) 7.6 cu. ft. Front tread: 60.7 in. Rear tread: 60.6 in. Standard tires: P235/55R16.

Z28 Coupe: Wheelbase: 101.1 in. Overall length: 193.2 in. Height: 51.3 in. Width: 74.1 in. Front headroom: 37.2 in. Rear headroom: 35.3 in. Front legroom: 43 in. Rear legroom: 26.8 in. Front shoulder room: 57.4 in. Rear shoulder room: 55.8 in. Front hip room: 52.8 in. Rear hip room: 44.4 in. Luggage capacity: (rear seat up) 12.9 cu. ft.; (rear seat down) 32.8 cu. ft. Front tread: 60.7 in. Rear tread: 60.6 in. Standard tires: P235/55R16.

Z28 Convertible: Wheelbase: 101.1 in. Overall length: 193.2 in. Height: 52 in. Width: 74.1 in. Front headroom: 38 in. Rear headroom: 39 in. Front legroom: 43 in. Rear legroom: 26.8 in. Front shoulder room: 57.4 in. Rear shoulder room: 43.5 in. Front hip room: 52.8 in. Rear hip room: 43.7 in. Luggage capacity: (rear seat up) 7.6 cu. ft.

Front tread: 60.7 in. Rear tread: 60.6 in. Standard tires: P235/55R16.

Camaro SS Coupe: Wheelbase: 101.1 in. Overall length: 193.2 in. Height: 52 in. Width: 74.1 in. Front headroom: 38 in. Rear headroom: 39 in. Front legroom: 43 in. Rear legroom: 26.8 in. Front shoulder room: 57.4 in. Rear shoulder room: 43.5 in. Front hip room: 52.8 in. Rear hip room: 43.7 in. Luggage capacity: (rear seat up) 7.6 cu. ft. Front tread: 60.7 in. Rear tread: 60.6 in. Standard tires: B.F. Goodrich Comp T/A P275/40ZR17.

Camaro SS Convertible: Wheelbase: 101.1 in. Overall length: 193.2 in. Height: 52 in. Width: 74.1 in. Front headroom: 38 in. Rear headroom: 39 in. Front legroom: 43 in. Rear legroom: 26.8 in. Front shoulder room: 57.4 in. Rear shoulder room: 43.5 in. Front hip room: 52.8 in. Rear hip room: 43.7 in. Luggage capacity: (rear seat up) 7.6 cu. ft. Front tread: 60.7 in. Rear tread: 60.6 in. Standard tires: 16-in. B.F. Goodrich Comp T/A.

TECHNICAL

Base Camaro: Transmission: Five-speed manual. Steering: rack and pinion. Front suspension: SLA/Coil over monotube gas shocks, tubular stabilizer bar with links. Rear suspension: Solid axle/torque arm, trailing arm, coil springs, track bar, monotube gas shocks and solid stabilizer bar with links. Brakes: Front disc/rear drum with antilock. Body construction: unibody. Fuel tank: (Camaro) 15.5 gal.

RS: Transmission: Five-speed manual. Steering: rack and pinion. Front suspension: SLA/Coil over monotube gas shocks, tubular stabilizer bar with links. Rear suspension: Solid axle/torque arm, trailing arm, coil springs, track bar, monotube gas shocks and solid stabilizer bar with links. Brakes: Front disc/rear drum with antilock. Body construction: unibody. Fuel tank: (Camaro) 15.5 gal.

Z28: Transmission: Six-speed manual. Steering: rack and pinion. Front suspension: SLA/Coil over monotube gas shocks and 30-mm tubular stabilizer bar with links. Rear suspension: Solid axle/torque arm, trailing arm, coil springs, track bar, monotube gas shocks and 19-mm solid stabilizer bar with links. Brakes: Four-wheel discs with antilock. Body construction: unibody. Fuel tank: (Camaro) 15.5 gal.

SS: Transmission: Six-speed manual. Steering: rack and pinion. Front suspension: Modified SLA/Coil over monotube gas shocks and tubular stabilizer bar with links. Rear suspension: Modified solid axle/torque arm, trailing arm, coil springs, track bar, monotube gas shocks and solid stabilizer bar with links. Brakes: Four-wheel discs with anti-lock. Body construction: unibody. Fuel tank: 15.5 gal. (Note: The Camaro SS convertible retained the stock Camaro Z28 suspension).

OPTIONS

1SA Camaro coupe base equipment group, included with model, no radio upgrades allowed (no cost). 1SB Camaro coupe preferred equipment group 1 includes air conditioning, fog lights, remote control hatch release and electric speed control with resume feature ($1,240). 1SB Camaro coupe preferred equipment group 1 includes air conditioning, fog lights, remote control hatch release and electric speed control with resume fea-

ture and UU8 radio upgrade ($1,590). 1SB Camaro coupe preferred equipment group 1 includes air conditioning, fog lights, remote control hatch release and electric speed control with resume feature and U1T radio upgrade ($1,846). 1SC Camaro coupe preferred equipment group 2 includes air conditioning, fog lights, remote control hatch release, electric speed control with resume feature, power lock system, leather-wrapped steering wheel, leather-wrapped brake handle, leather-wrapped shifter, electric sport mirrors, remote keyless entry with illuminated interior feature, theft deterrent alarm system and power windows with driver's side express down ($2,126). 1SC Camaro coupe preferred equipment group 2 includes air conditioning, fog lights, remote control hatch release, electric speed control with resume feature, power lock system, leather-wrapped steering wheel, leather-wrapped brake handle, leather-wrapped shifter, electric sport mirrors, remote keyless entry with illuminated interior feature, theft deterrent alarm system, power windows with driver's side express down and UU8 radio upgrade ($2,476). 1SC Camaro coupe preferred equipment group 2 includes air conditioning, fog lights, remote control hatch release, electric speed control with resume feature, power lock system, leather-wrapped steering wheel, leather-wrapped brake handle, leather-wrapped shifter, electric sport mirrors, remote keyless entry with illuminated interior feature, theft deterrent alarm system, power windows with driver's side express down and U1T radio upgrade ($2,732). 1SD Camaro convertible base equipment group, included with model (no cost). 1SD Camaro convertible base equipment group, included with model and U1C radio upgrade ($226). 1SE Camaro convertible preferred equipment group 1 includes power door lock system, fog lights, remote control trunk release and electric speed control with resume feature ($565). 1SE Camaro convertible preferred equipment group 1 includes power door lock system, fog lights, remote control trunk release, electric speed control with resume feature and U1C radio upgrade ($791). 1SF Camaro convertible preferred equipment group 2 includes power door lock system, fog lights, remote control trunk release, electric speed control with resume feature, leather-wrapped steering wheel, leather-wrapped brake handle, leather-wrapped shifter, electric sport mirrors, remote keyless entry with illuminated interior feature, theft-deterrent alarm system and power windows with driver's side express down ($1,231). 1SF Camaro convertible preferred equipment group 2 includes power door lock system, fog lights, remote control trunk release, electric speed control with resume feature, leather-wrapped steering wheel, leather-wrapped brake handle, leather-wrapped shifter, electric sport mirrors, remote keyless entry with illuminated interior feature, theft deterrent alarm system, power windows with driver's side express down and U1C radio upgrade ($1,457). 1SN Camaro RS coupe base equipment group, included with model, no radio upgrades allowed (no cost). 1SP Camaro RS coupe preferred equipment group 1 includes electric speed control with resume feature, power lock system, remote hatch release and fog lights ($565). 1SP Camaro RS coupe preferred equipment group 1 includes electric speed control with resume feature, power lock system, remote hatch release, fog lights and UU8 radio upgrade ($915). 1SP Camaro RS coupe preferred equipment group 1 includes electric speed control with resume feature, power lock system, remote hatch release, fog lights and U1T radio upgrade ($1,170). 1SQ Camaro RS coupe preferred equipment group 2 includes power door lock system, remote control hatch release, electric speed control with resume feature, fog lights, leather-wrapped steering wheel, leather-wrapped brake handle, leather-wrapped shifter, electric sport mirrors, remote keyless entry with illuminated interior feature, theft deterrent alarm system and power windows with driver's side express down ($1,231). 1SQ Camaro RS coupe preferred equipment group 2 includes power door lock system, remote control hatch release, electric speed control with resume feature, fog lights, leather-wrapped steering wheel, leather-wrapped brake handle, leather-wrapped shifter, electric sport mirrors, remote keyless entry with illuminated interior feature, theft deterrent alarm system, power windows with driver's side express down and UU8 radio upgrade ($1,581). 1SQ Camaro RS coupe preferred equipment group 2 includes power door lock system, remote control hatch release, electric speed control with resume feature, fog lights, leather-wrapped steering wheel, leather-wrapped brake handle, leather-wrapped shifter, electric sport mirrors, remote keyless entry with illuminated interior feature, theft deterrent alarm system, power windows with driver's side express down and U1T radio upgrade ($1,837). 1SR Camaro RS convertible base equipment group, included with model (no cost). 1SR Camaro RS convertible base equipment group, included with model and U1C radio upgrade ($226). 1SS Camaro RS convertible preferred equipment group 1 includes power door lock system, fog lights, remote control trunk release and electric speed control with resume feature ($565). 1SS Camaro RS convertible preferred equipment group 1 includes power door lock system, fog lights, remote control trunk release, electric speed control with resume feature and U1C radio upgrade ($791). 1SF Camaro RS convertible preferred equipment group 2 includes power door lock system, fog lights, remote control trunk release, electric speed control with resume feature, leather-wrapped steering wheel, leather-wrapped brake handle, leather-wrapped shifter, electric Sport mirrors, remote keyless entry with illuminated interior feature, theft-deterrent alarm system and power windows with driver's side express down ($1,231). 1SF Camaro RS convertible preferred equipment group 2 includes power door lock system, fog lights, remote control trunk release, electric speed control with resume feature, leather-wrapped steering wheel, leather-wrapped brake handle, leather-wrapped shifter, electric sport mirrors, remote keyless entry with illuminated interior feature, theft-deterrent alarm system, power windows with driver's side express down and U1C radio upgrade ($1,457). 1SG Camaro Z28 coupe base equipment group, included with model, no radio upgrades allowed (no cost). 1SH Camaro Z28 coupe preferred equipment group 1 includes electric speed control with resume feature, power lock system, remote hatch release, fog lights and four-way manual driver's seat adjustment ($600). 1SH Camaro Z28 coupe preferred equipment group 1 includes electric speed control with

resume feature, power lock system, remote hatch release, fog lights, four-way manual driver's seat adjustment and UU8 radio upgrade ($950). 1SH Camaro Z28 coupe preferred equipment group 1 includes electric speed control with resume feature, power lock system, remote hatch release, fog lights, four-way manual driver's seat adjustment and U1T radio upgrade ($1,206). 1SJ Camaro Z28 coupe preferred equipment group 2 includes power door lock system, remote control hatch release, electric speed control with resume feature, fog lights, leather-wrapped steering wheel, leather-wrapped brake handle, leather-wrapped shifter, electric Sport mirrors, remote keyless entry with illuminated interior feature, theft deterrent alarm system, four-way manual driver's seat adjustment and power windows with driver's side express down ($1,266). 1SJ Camaro Z28 coupe preferred equipment group 2 includes power door lock system, remote control hatch release, electric speed control with resume feature, fog lights, leather-wrapped steering wheel, leather-wrapped brake handle, leather-wrapped shifter, electric Sport mirrors, remote keyless entry with illuminated interior feature, theft deterrent alarm system, power windows with driver's side express down, four-way manual driver's seat adjustment and UU8 radio upgrade ($1,616). 1SJ Camaro Z28 coupe preferred equipment group 2 includes power door lock system, remote control hatch release, electric speed control with resume feature, fog lights, leather-wrapped steering wheel, leather-wrapped brake handle, leather-wrapped shifter, electric sport mirrors, remote keyless entry with illuminated interior feature, theft deterrent alarm system, power windows with driver's side express down, four-way manual driver's seat adjustment and U1T radio upgrade ($1,872). 1SK Camaro Z28 convertible base equipment group, included with model (no cost). 1SK Camaro Z28 convertible base equipment group, included with model and U1C radio upgrade ($226). 1SL Camaro Z28 convertible preferred equipment group 1 includes power door lock system, fog lights, remote control trunk release and electric speed control with resume feature ($565). 1SL Camaro Z28 convertible preferred equipment group 1 includes power door lock system, fog lights, remote control trunk release, electric speed control with resume feature and U1C radio upgrade ($791). 1SM Camaro Z28 convertible preferred equipment group 2 includes power door lock system, fog lights, remote control trunk release, electric speed control with resume feature, leather-wrapped steering wheel, leather-wrapped brake handle, leather-wrapped shifter, electric sport mirrors, remote keyless entry with illuminated interior feature, theft-deterrent alarm system and power windows with driver's side express down ($1,231). 1SM Camaro Z28 convertible preferred equipment group 2 includes power door lock system, fog lights, remote control trunk release, electric speed control with resume feature, leather-wrapped steering wheel, leather-wrapped brake handle, leather-wrapped shifter, electric sport mirrors, remote keyless entry with illuminated interior feature, theft-deterrent alarm system, power windows with driver's side express down and U1C radio upgrade ($1,457). C60 air conditioning ($895). GU5 optional performance axle ($250). VK3 front license plate bracket (no cost). C49 rear window defogger

The Z28 had a standard 5.7-liter V-8 attached to a six-speed manual transmission. It also featured a high-performance suspension, four-wheel ABS, a limited-slip rear end and 150-mph speedometer.

($170). R9W rear window defogger not desired in coupes (no cost). AU3 power door lock system ($220). FE9 federal emissions (no cost). NG1 New York and Massachusetts emissions (no cost). YF5 California emissions (no cost). NB8 California and Massachusetts emissions override (no cost). NC7 federal emissions override (no cost). B35 rear carpeted floor mats ($15). B84 color-keyed body side moldings ($60). 1LE performance package includes Special Handling suspension, larger stabilizer bars, stiffer springs, dual adjustable shocks and bushings, Z28 coupe only ($310). Y87 performance handling package includes limited-slip axle, four-wheel disc brakes, dual outlet exhaust and sport steering ration on base and RS models only ($400). UU8 Delco Bose music system (packages only). U1C ETR AM/FM stereo (with packages only). U1C ETR AM/FM stereo (with packages only). D82 monochromatic roof treatment including body-color roof and mirrors on base or RS coupe, requires CC1 roof panels or on Z28 replaces standard black roof (no cost). CC1 removable roof panels ($970). AGF1 six-way power driver's seat ($270). AR9 leather bucket seat ($499). DE4 sunshades for removable roof panels ($25). QCB P235/55R16 tires ($132). QLC P245/50ZR16 tires ($225). QFZ P245/50ZR16 performance tires for Z28s and convertibles ($225). MXO four-speed automatic transmission with brake/shift interlock ($790). N96 16-in. silver aluminum wheels ($275). N98 16-in. chrome wheels with Z28 ($500).

CAMARO SS OPTIONS

Performance exhaust system. Level II Bilstein Sport suspension.Torsen limited-slip differential includes performance lubricant package. Hurst six-speed short-throw shifter. Engine oil cooler. B.F. Goodrich Comp T/A 17-in. tires, available only as a second set shipped to Chevrolet dealer on 17-in. wheels and recommended for track usage by an experienced driver. Performance lubri-cants package with premium synthetic media engine oil filter, rear axle lube and semi-synthetic power steering fluid.

HISTORICAL FOOTNOTES

The Camaro's model-year sales were 75,336 units. Calendar-year sales were 66,866. Model-year production was 54,525 coupes and 6,837 convertibles for a total of 61,362 units. The Ste. Therese, Quebec, plant built all of these cars (and all 30,937 Firebirds). Of the Camaros built, 71.7 percent had automatic transmission, 16.4 percent had a five-speed manual transmission, 11.1 percent had a six-speed manual transmission, 70.5 percent had a 3.8-liter SFI V-6, 29.5 percent had a 5.7-liter MFI V-8, 11.3 percent had traction control, 100 percent had power steering, 100 percent had ABS brakes, 26 percent had a limited-slip differential, 100 percent had steel-belted radial tires, 76.8 percent had power door locks, 70.9 percent had power windows, 100 percent had reclining bucket seats, 46.4 percent had a power seats, 27.4 percent had leather seats, 100 percent had dual front airbags, 100 percent had tilt steering, 100 percent had tinted glass, 99.2 percent had manual air conditioning, 95.7 percent had cruise control, 100 percent had delay windshield wipers, 42.8 percent had a ETR stereo cassette player, 15.9 percent had a Bose/JBL sound system, 34.1 percent had a Bose/JBL sound system with CD, 7.2 percent had another brand CD, 65.4 percent had an electric rear window defogger, 29.2 percent had a manual remote-control left-hand outside rearview mirror, 70.8 percent had power rearview mirrors, 27.8 percent had a power right-hand rearview mirror, 88.1 percent had aluminum styled wheels, 70.5 percent had remote keyless entry and 43.8 percent had T-tops. A total of 68,106 new Camaros were registered in the U.S. during calendar year 1996.

Camaro

The 1997 RS came with a ground effects package, air conditioning and aluminum wheels.

The Camaro observed its 30th anniversary in 1997 and Chevrolet marked the occasion by offering an orange-striped 30th Anniversary package for Z28s. Standard features on all Camaros now included automatic daytime running lamps, four-wheel ABS disc brakes, dual airbags, an electronically controlled AM/FM stereo with cassette player (and extended range speakers) and a reinforced steel safety cage with steel side-door beams and front and rear crush zones. The standard power plant of the base model was a 200-hp V-6.

The Camaro model lineup was unchanged, but there were numerous technical refinements. A new instrument panel and floor console featured built-in power outlets and cupholders, coupes got a new 200-watt sound system, taillamps were switched to an international tri-color design, new uplevel five-spoke wheels were introduced and automatic transmission became standard equipment in Z28s.

I.D. DATA

Chevrolets again had a 17-symbol vehicle identification number (VIN) on the upper left surface of the instrument panel, visible through the windshield. The first symbol identifies country of origin: 2=Canada. The second symbol identifies the manufacturer: G=General Motors. The third symbol indicates make: 1=Chevrolet, 7=GM of Canada. The fourth and fifth symbols indicated the car line and series: F/P=Camaro Sport Coupe and Convertible. The sixth symbol indicated body type: 2=two-door coupe style 87 and 3=two-door convertible style 67. The seventh symbol indicated the type of restraint system: 2=active manual belts with driver and passenger front airbags, 4=active manual belts with driver and passenger front and side airbags. The eighth symbol indicates the engine type: K=RPO L36 3.8-liter (231-cid) V-6 with MFI, P=RPO LT1 5.7-liter (350-cid) V-8 with SFI. The ninth symbol is a check digit. The 10th

symbol indicates model year: V=1997. The 11th symbol indicates the assembly plant: 2=Ste. Therese, Quebec (Canada).

COLORS

Arctic White, Black, Bright Green Metallic, Bright Purple, Metallic, Bright Red, Sebring Silver Metallic.

CAMARO — SERIES 1F — V-6

The Camaro lineup again was comprised of three coupes and three convertibles offered in base, RS or Z28 trim. Standard equipment included automatic daytime running lamps, manual lap and shoulder safety belts, driver and front passenger airbags, an energy-absorbing steering column, an energy-absorbing instrument panel, interlocking door latches, inertia-type folding front seat locks, safety armrests, a breakaway inside rearview mirror, security door locks and door retention components, urethane-bonded laminated windshield glass, integral front head restraints, side-door beams, passenger-guard inside door lock handles, front and rear crush zones, side marker lights and reflectors, parking lamps, four-way hazard warning flashers, back-up lights, directional signal control, windshield defrosters, washers and multi-speed wipers, an inside day/night rearview mirror, outside rearview mirrors, a brake system with a dual master cylinder plus brake warning light, a center high-mounted stop lamp, a starter safety switch, a dual-action hood latch, a low-glare finish inside windshield molding, low-glare wiper arms and blades, low-glare metallic steering wheel surfaces, illuminated heater and defroster controls, tires with built-in tread wear indicators, audible disc brake lining-wear indicators, four-wheel disc ABS brakes, a brake/transmission shift interlock (with automatic transmission), basecoat/clearcoat paint, dual Sport mirrors (left-hand remote controlled), a front air dam, halogen headlights, a rear deck lid spoiler, auxiliary lighting, carpeted front floor mats, a center console with storage compartment and cupholder, a deep-well luggage area, driver and front passenger side airbags, an intermittent windshield wiper system, the PASS-Key II theft-deterrent system, Scotchguard protector on fabrics and carpets, cloth-trimmed reclining front bucket seats, special instrumentation with a tachometer, side window defoggers, a tilt adjustable steering wheel, an ETR AM/FM stereo with cassette tape player with extended-range speakers, a 3.8-liter V-6 with sequential port fuel injection, a five-speed manual transmission, power front disc/rear drum ABS brakes, a Delco Freedom II battery, power rack-and-pinion steering, rear-wheel drive, single serpentine belt engine accessory drive, a stainless steel exhaust system, a Firm Ride & Handling suspension, 16 x 7 1/2-in. wheels with bolt-on wheel covers, P215/60R-16 touring tires and a reinforced steel safety cage that included steel side-door beams and front and rear crush zones. The convertible also had a standard rear window defogger, a fully lined power-operated folding top, air conditioning, a full headliner, rear seat and trunk courtesy lamps, a glass rear window and a form-fitting three-piece hard boot with storage bag.

Model Number	Body/Style Number	Body Type & Seating	Factory Price	Shipping Weight	Production Total
F/P	87	2d coupe-4P	$16,215	3,294 lbs.	Note 1
F/P	67	2d convertible-4P	$21,770	3,446 lbs.	Note 2

Note 1: Total Camaro, Camaro RS and Camaro Z28 coupe production was 48,292.
Note 2: Total Camaro, Camaro RS and Camaro Z28 convertible production was 6,680.

CAMARO RS — SERIES 1F — V-6

The power plant for Camaro RS models was the 3.8-liter V-6. In addition to or in place of standard equipment on the base Camaro, the RS coupe and convertible featured a ground effects package, air conditioning, P235/55R16 tires and 16-in. aluminum wheels.

Model Number	Body/Style Number	Body Type & Seating	Factory Price	Shipping Weight	Production Total
F/P	87	2d coupe-4P	$17,970	3,307 lbs.	Note 3
F/P	67	2d convertible-4P	$23,170	3,455 lbs.	Note 4

Note 3: Total Camaro, Camaro RS and Camaro Z28 coupe production was 48,292.
Note 4: Total Camaro, Camaro RS and Camaro Z28 convertible production was 6,680.

CAMARO Z28 — SERIES 1F — V-8

The Camaro observed its 30th anniversary in 1997 and Chevrolet marked the occasion by offering a 30th Anniversary Package for the Z28. The package consisted of a paint scheme that used Arctic White with Hugger Orange stripes that was reminiscent of the package on the Camaro that paced the 1969 Indianapolis 500. Also part of the package were door handles finished in white, white five-spoke aluminum wheels and a white front fascia intake. Seats in this anniversary Z28 were also Arctic White with cloth black-and-white houndstooth inserts. In addition, the floor mats and headrests had 30th Anniversary five-color embroidery. The Z28 again used the 5.7-liter V-8 as its standard engine. It came standard linked to a six-speed manual transmission. In addition to, or in place of base Camaro equipment, the Z28 featured air conditioning, a limited-slip rear axle, four-wheel power ABS disc brakes, the 5.7-liter SFI V-8, a low-coolant-level indicator, two-way manual seat adjustment, platinum tip spark plugs, a special coupe

roof treatment with black mirrors, a 150-mph speedometer, a Performance Ride & Handling suspension, P235/55R16 black sidewall radial tires, a high-pressure compact spare tire, a six-speed manual transmission and 16-in. aluminum wheels.

Model Number	Body/Style Number	Body Type & Seating	Factory Price	Shipping Weight	Production Total
F/P+Z28	87	2d coupe-4P	$20,115	3,433 lbs.	Note 5
F/P+Z28	67	2d convertible -4P	$25,520	3,589 lbs.	Note 6

Note 5: Total Camaro, Camaro RS and Camaro Z28 coupe production was 48,292.
Note 6: Total Camaro, Camaro RS and Camaro Z28 convertible production was 6,680.

CAMARO SS — SERIES 1F — V-8

Chevrolet built Camaros and SLP Engineering, of Troy, Michigan, turned new Camaro coupes and convertibles into a Camaro SS. SLP offered a choice of two engines, beginning with a 305-hp version of the LT1 V-8. This could be boosted to 310 hp with the addition of an optional performance exhaust system. Other standard Camaro SS coupe content included an underhood forced-air induction system, a restyled rear deck lid spoiler, a restyled suspension on coupe and T-top models, B.F. Goodrich Comp T/A tires (size P275/40ZR17), 17 x 9-in. ZR-1 styled cast-aluminum alloy wheels, Quaker State Synquest synthetic engine oil, exterior SS badges replacing Z28 logos and a Camaro SS interior plaque. Camaro SS convertibles retained the stock Camaro suspension and had 16-in. B.F. Goodrich Comp T/A tires and 16 x 8-in. styled cast-aluminum wheels. The Camaro SS was offered in standard exterior colors of Artic White, Black, Bright Red and Polo Green. Sebring Silver Metallic finish was optional. All colors were available with Dark Gray or Medium Gray interiors. All but Sebring Silver cars could have a neutral color interior and all but Polo Green cars could have a red interior. Also available was a new special edition, low-volume "30th Anniversary SS" with Artic White finish, bold Hugger Orange dual stripes on the hood, roof, deck lid and rear spoiler, white SS wheels, exterior SS emblems, a commemorative dash plaque, two key fobs and a premium quality car cover with locking cable and tote bag. The 30th Anniversary SS option required Chevrolet options 1SJ, Z4C and AG1 on coupes and 1SM, Z4C and AG1 on convertibles. SLP Engineering projected that it would build a total of 3,000 Camaro Z28s with the SS package (coupes and convertibles combined) in 1997 and that 1,000 of them would receive the "30th Anniversary SS" option, but actual production fell short of these goals.

Model Number	Body/Style Number	Body Type & Seating	Factory Price	Shipping Weight	Production Total
F/P+Z28	87	2d coupe-4P	$24,114	—	Note 7
F/P+Z28	67	2d convertible-4P	$29,513	—	Note 7

Note 7: Included in the production totals given above were 3,035 Camaro Z28s with the SS package.

ENGINE

L36 V-6: 60-degree, overhead-valve V-6. Cast-iron block and head. Bore & stroke: 3.80 x 3.40. Displacement: 231 cid (3.8 liters). Compression ratio: 9.4:1. Brake horsepower: 200 at 5300 rpm. Hydraulic valve lifters. Induction system: Sequential fuel injection. Standard in base Camaro and Camaro RS. VIN Code K.

The base Camaro coupe received a few upgrades, like daytime running lamps and four-wheel ABS, and came standard with a 200-hp V-6.

LT1 V-8: 90-degree, overhead-valve V-8. Cast-iron block and head. Bore & stroke: 4.00 x 3.48 in. Displacement: 350 cid (5.7 liters). Compression ratio: 10.5:1. Brake horsepower: 275 at 5000 rpm. Torque: 325 lbs.-ft. at 2400 rpm. Hydraulic valve lifters. Sequential fuel injection. Standard in Z28. VIN Code P.

LT1 V-8: 90-degree, overhead-valve V-8. Cast-iron block and head. Bore & stroke: 4.00 x 3.48 in. Displacement: 350 cid (5.7 liters). Brake horsepower: 305 at 5500 rpm. Torque: 325 lbs.-ft. at 2400 rpm. Hydraulic valve lifters. Sequential fuel injection. Standard in Camaro SS. VIN Code P.

LT1 V-8: 90-degree, overhead-valve V-8. Cast-iron block and head. Bore & stroke: 4.00 x 3.48 in. Displacement: 350 cid (5.7 liters). Brake horsepower: 310 at 5500 rpm. Torque: 325 lbs.-ft. at 2400 rpm. Hydraulic valve lifters. Sequential fuel injection. Performance exhaust system. Optional in Camaro SS. VIN Code P.

CHASSIS

Base Camaro Coupe: Wheelbase: 101.1 in. Overall length: 193.2 in. Height: 51.3 in. Width: 74.1 in. Front headroom: 37.2 in. Rear headroom: 35.3 in. Front legroom: 43 in. Rear legroom: 26.8 in. Front shoulder room: 57.4 in. Rear shoulder room: 55.8 in. Front hip room: 52.8 in. Rear hip room: 44.4 in. Luggage capacity: (rear seat up) 12.9 cu. ft.; (rear seat down) 32.8 cu. ft. Front tread: 60.7 in. Rear tread: 60.6 in. Standard tires: P215/60R16.

Base Camaro Convertible: Wheelbase: 101.1 in. Overall length: 193.2 in. Height: 52 in. Width: 74.1 in. Front headroom: 38 in. Rear headroom: 39 in. Front legroom: 43 in. Rear legroom: 26.8 in. Front shoulder room: 57.4 in. Rear shoulder room: 43.5 in. Front hip room: 52.8 in. Rear hip room: 43.7 in. Luggage capacity: (rear seat up) 7.6 cu. ft. Front tread: 60.7 in. Rear tread: 60.6 in. Standard tires: P215/60R16.

Camaro RS Coupe: Wheelbase: 101.1 in. Overall length: 193.2 in. Height: 51.3 in; Width: 74.1 in. Front headroom: 37.2 in. Rear headroom: 35.3 in. Front legroom: 43 in. Rear legroom: 26.8 in. Front shoulder room: 57.4 in. Rear shoulder room: 55.8 in. Front hip room: 52.8 in. Rear hip room: 44.4 in. Luggage capacity: (rear seat up) 12.9 cu. ft.; (rear seat down) 32.8 cu. ft. Front tread: 60.7 in. Rear tread: 60.6 in. Standard tires: P235/55R16.

Camaro RS Convertible: Wheelbase: 101.1 in. Overall length: 193.2 in. Height: 52 in. Width: 74.1 in. Front headroom: 38 in. Rear headroom: 39 in. Front legroom: 43 in. Rear legroom: 26.8 in. Front shoulder room: 57.4 in. Rear shoulder room: 43.5 in. Front hip room: 52.8 in. Rear hip room: 43.7 in. Luggage capacity: (rear seat up) 7.6 cu. ft. Front tread: 60.7 in. Rear tread: 60.6 in. Standard Tires: P235/55R16.

Z28 Coupe: Wheelbase: 101.1 in. Overall length: 193.2 in. Height: 51.3 in. Width: 74.1 in. Front headroom: 37.2 in. Rear headroom: 35.3 in. Front legroom: 43 in. Rear legroom: 26.8 in. Front shoulder room: 57.4 in. Rear shoulder room: 55.8 in. Front hip room: 52.8 in. Rear hip room: 44.4 in. Luggage capacity: (rear seat up) 12.9 cu. ft.; (rear seat down) 32.8 cu. ft. Front tread: 60.7 in. Rear tread: 60.6 in. Standard tires: P235/55R16.

Z28 Convertible: Wheelbase: 101.1 in. Overall length: 193.2 in. Height: 52 in. Width: 74.1 in. Front headroom: 38 in. Rear headroom: 39 in. Front legroom: 43 in. Rear legroom: 26.8 in. Front shoulder room: 57.4 in. Rear shoulder room: 43.5 in. Front hip room: 52.8 in. Rear hip room: 43.7 in. Luggage capacity: (rear seat up) 7.6 cu. ft. Front tread: 60.7 in. Rear tread: 60.6 in. Standard tires: P235/55R16.

Camaro SS Coupe: Wheelbase: 101.1 in. Overall length: 193.2 in. Height: 52 in. Width: 74.1 in. Front headroom: 380 in. Rear headroom: 39 in. Front legroom: 43 in. Rear legroom: 26.8 in. Front shoulder room: 57.4 in. Rear shoulder room: 43.5 in. Front hip room: 52.8 in. Rear hip room: 43.7 in. Luggage capacity: (rear seat up) 7.6 cu. ft. Front tread: 60.7 in. Rear tread: 60.6 in. Standard tires: B.F. Goodrich Comp T/A P275/40ZR17.

Camaro SS Convertible: Wheelbase: 101.1 in. Overall length: 193.2 in. Height: 52 in. Width: 74.1 in. Front headroom: 38 in. Rear headroom: 39 in. Front legroom: 43 in. Rear legroom: 26.8 in. Front shoulder room: 57.4 in. Rear shoulder room: 43.5 in. Front hip room: 52.8 in. Rear hip room: 43.7 in. Luggage capacity: (rear seat up) 7.6 cu. ft. Front tread: 60.7 in. Rear tread: 60.6 in. Standard tires: 16-in. B.F. Goodrich Comp T/A.

TECHNICAL

Base Camaro: Transmission: Five-speed manual. Steering: rack and pinion. Front suspension: SLA/Coil over monotube gas shocks, tubular stabilizer bar with links. Rear suspension: Solid axle/torque arm, trailing arm, coil springs, track bar, monotube gas shocks and solid stabilizer bar with links. Brakes: Front disc/rear drum with antilock. Body construction: unibody. Fuel tank: 15.5 gal.

RS: Transmission: Five-speed manual. Steering: rack and pinion. Front suspension: SLA/Coil over monotube gas shocks, tubular stabilizer bar with links. Rear suspension: Solid axle/torque arm, trailing arm, coil springs, track bar, monotube gas shocks and solid stabilizer bar with links. Brakes: Front disc/rear drum with antilock. Body construction: unibody. Fuel tank: 15.5 gal.

Z28: Transmission: Six-speed manual. Steering: rack and pinion. Front suspension: SLA/Coil over monotube gas shocks, and 30-mm tubular stabilizer bar with links. Rear suspension: Solid axle/torque arm, trailing arm, coil springs, track bar, monotube gas shocks and 19-mm solid stabilizer bar with links. Brakes: Four-wheel discs with antilock. Body construction: unibody. Fuel tank: 15.5 gal.

SS: Transmission: Six-speed manual. Steering: rack and pinion. Front suspension: Modified SLA/Coil over monotube gas shocks and tubular stabilizer bar with links. Rear suspension: Modified solid axle/torque arm, trailing arm, coil springs, track bar, monotube gas shocks and solid stabilizer bar with links. Brakes: Four-wheel discs with antilock. Body construction: unibody. Fuel tank: 15.5 gal. (Note: The Camaro SS convertible retained the stock Camaro Z28 suspension).

OPTIONS

1SA Camaro coupe base equipment group, included with model (no cost). 1SA Camaro coupe base equipment group with UL0 radio upgrade ($215). 1SA Camaro coupe base equipment group with UN0 radio upgrade ($315). 1SB Camaro coupe preferred equipment group 1 includes fog lights, remote control hatch release and electric speed control with resume feature ($345). 1SB

Camaro coupe preferred equipment group 1 includes fog lights, remote control hatch release and electric speed control with resume feature and UL0 radio upgrade ($560). 1SB Camaro coupe preferred equipment group 1 includes fog lights, remote control hatch release and electric speed control with resume feature and UN0 radio upgrade ($660). 1SC Camaro coupe preferred equipment group 2 includes fog lights, remote control hatch release, electric speed control with resume feature, power lock system, leather-wrapped steering wheel, leather-wrapped brake handle, leather-wrapped shifter, electric Sport mirrors, remote keyless entry with illuminated interior feature, theft deterrent alarm system and power windows with driver's side express down ($1,231). 1SC Camaro coupe preferred equipment group 2 includes fog lights, remote control hatch release, electric speed control with resume feature, power lock system, leather-wrapped steering wheel, leather-wrapped brake handle, leather-wrapped shifter, electric Sport mirrors, remote keyless entry with illuminated interior feature, theft deterrent alarm system, power windows with driver's side express down and UL0 radio upgrade ($1,446). 1SC Camaro coupe preferred equipment group 2 includes fog lights, remote control hatch release, electric speed control with resume feature, power lock system, leather-wrapped steering wheel, leather-wrapped brake handle, leather-wrapped shifter, electric Sport mirrors, remote keyless entry with illuminated interior feature, theft deterrent alarm system, power windows with driver's side express down and UN0 radio upgrade ($1,546). 1SD Camaro convertible base equipment group, included with model (no cost). 1SD Camaro convertible base equipment group, included with model and UL0 radio upgrade ($215). 1SD Camaro convertible base equipment group, included with model and UN0 radio upgrade ($315). 1SE Camaro convertible preferred equipment group 1 includes power door lock system, fog lights, remote control trunk release and electric speed control with resume feature ($565). 1SE Camaro convertible preferred equipment group 1 includes power door lock system, fog lights, remote control trunk release, electric speed control with resume feature and UL0 radio upgrade ($780). 1SE Camaro convertible preferred equipment group 1 includes power door lock system, fog lights, remote control trunk release, electric speed control with resume feature and UL0 radio upgrade ($1,446). 1SE Camaro convertible preferred equipment group 1 includes power door lock system, fog lights, remote control trunk release, electric speed control with resume feature and UL0 radio upgrade ($1,446). 1SF Camaro convertible preferred equipment group 2 includes power door lock system, fog lights, remote control trunk release, electric speed control with resume feature, leather-wrapped steering wheel, leather-wrapped brake handle, leather-wrapped shifter, electric Sport mirrors, remote keyless entry with illuminated interior feature, theft deterrent alarm system and power windows with driver's side express down ($1,231). 1SF Camaro convertible preferred equipment group 2 includes power door lock system, fog lights, remote control trunk release, electric speed control with resume feature, leather-wrapped steering wheel, leather-wrapped brake handle, leather-wrapped shifter, electric

Sport mirrors, remote keyless entry with illuminated interior feature, theft deterrent alarm system, power windows with driver's side express down and UL0 radio upgrade ($1,456). 1SF Camaro convertible preferred equipment group 2 includes power door lock system, fog lights, remote control trunk release, electric speed control with resume feature, leather-wrapped steering wheel, leather-wrapped brake handle, leather-wrapped shifter, electric Sport mirrors, remote keyless entry with illuminated interior feature, theft deterrent alarm system, power windows with driver's side express down and UL0 radio upgrade ($1,556). 1SN Camaro RS coupe base equipment group, included with model, no radio upgrades allowed (no cost). 1SN Camaro RS coupe base equipment group, included with UL0 radio upgrade ($215). 1SN Camaro RS coupe base equipment group, included with UN0 radio upgrade ($315). 1SP Camaro RS coupe preferred equipment group 1 includes electric speed control with resume feature, power lock system, remote hatch release and fog lights ($565). 1SP Camaro RS coupe preferred equipment group 1 includes electric speed control with resume feature, power lock system, remote hatch release, fog lights and UL0 radio upgrade ($780). 1SP Camaro RS coupe preferred equipment group 1 includes electric speed control with resume feature, power lock system, remote hatch release, fog lights and UN0 radio upgrade ($880). 1SQ Camaro RS coupe preferred equipment group 2 includes power door lock system, remote control hatch release, electric speed control with resume feature, fog lights, leather-wrapped steering wheel, leather-wrapped brake handle, leather-wrapped shifter, electric Sport mirrors, remote keyless entry with illuminated interior feature, theft deterrent alarm system and power windows with driver's side express down ($1,231). 1SQ Camaro RS coupe preferred equipment group 2 includes power door lock system, remote control hatch release, electric speed control with resume feature, fog lights, leather-wrapped steering wheel, leather-wrapped brake handle, leather-wrapped shifter, electric Sport mirrors, remote keyless entry with illuminated interior feature, theft deterrent alarm system, power windows with driver's side express down and UUS radio upgrade ($1,446). 1SQ Camaro RS coupe preferred equipment group 2 includes power door lock system, remote control hatch release, electric speed control with resume feature, fog lights, leather-wrapped steering wheel, leather-wrapped brake handle, leather-wrapped shifter, electric Sport mirrors, remote keyless entry with illuminated interior feature, theft deterrent alarm system, power windows with driver's side express down and U1T radio upgrade ($1,546). 1SR Camaro RS convertible base equipment group, included with model (no cost). 1SR Camaro RS convertible base equipment group, included with model and UL0 radio upgrade ($215). 1SR Camaro RS convertible base equipment group, included with model and UN0 radio upgrade ($315). 1SS Camaro RS convertible preferred equipment group 1 includes power door lock system, fog lights, remote control trunk release and electric speed control with resume feature ($565). 1SS Camaro RS convertible preferred equipment group 1 includes power door lock system, fog lights, remote control trunk release, electric speed control with resume feature and UL0 radio upgrade ($780). 1SS

Camaro RS convertible preferred equipment group 1 includes power door lock system, fog lights, remote control trunk release, electric speed control with resume feature and UN0 radio upgrade ($780). 1ST Camaro RS convertible preferred equipment group 2 includes power door lock system, fog lights, remote control trunk release, electric speed control with resume feature, leather-wrapped steering wheel, leather-wrapped brake handle, leather-wrapped shifter, electric Sport mirrors, remote keyless entry with illuminated interior feature, theft deterrent alarm system and power windows with driver's side express down ($1,231). 1ST Camaro RS convertible preferred equipment group 2 includes power door lock system, fog lights, remote control trunk release, electric speed control with resume feature, leather-wrapped steering wheel, leather-wrapped brake handle, leather-wrapped shifter, electric Sport mirrors, remote keyless entry with illuminated interior feature, theft deterrent alarm system, power windows with driver's side express down and UL0 radio upgrade ($1,446). 1ST Camaro RS convertible preferred equipment group 2 includes power door lock system, fog lights, remote control trunk release, electric speed control with resume feature, leather-wrapped steering wheel, leather-wrapped brake handle, leather-wrapped shifter, electric Sport mirrors, remote keyless entry with illuminated interior feature, theft deterrent alarm system, power windows with driver's side express down and UN0 radio upgrade ($1,446). 1SG Camaro Z28 coupe base equipment group, included with model (no cost). 1SG Camaro Z28 coupe base equipment group, plus UL0 radio upgrade ($215). 1SG Camaro Z28 coupe base equipment group, plus UN0 radio upgrade ($315). 1SH Camaro Z28 coupe preferred equipment group 1 includes electric speed control with resume feature, power lock system, remote hatch release, fog lights and four-way manual driver's seat adjustment ($600). 1SH Camaro Z28 coupe preferred equipment group 1 includes electric speed control with resume feature, power lock system, remote hatch release, fog lights, four-way manual driver's seat adjustment and UL0 radio upgrade ($815). 1SH Camaro Z28 coupe preferred equipment group 1 includes electric speed control with resume feature, power lock system, remote hatch release, fog lights, four-way manual driver's seat adjustment and UN0 radio upgrade ($915). 1SJ Camaro Z28 coupe preferred equipment group 2 includes power door lock system, remote control hatch release, electric speed control with resume feature, fog lights, leather-wrapped steering wheel, leather-wrapped brake handle, leather-wrapped shifter, electric Sport mirrors, remote keyless entry with illuminated interior feature, theft deterrent alarm system, four-way manual driver's seat adjustment and power windows with driver's side express down ($1,266). 1SJ Camaro Z28 coupe preferred equipment group 2 includes power door lock system, remote control hatch release, electric speed control with resume feature, fog lights, leather-wrapped steering wheel, leather-wrapped brake handle, leather-wrapped shifter, electric Sport mirrors, remote keyless entry with illuminated interior feature, theft deterrent alarm system, power windows with driver's side express down, four-way manual driver's seat adjustment and UUS radio upgrade ($1,481). 1SJ Camaro Z28 coupe preferred

The 1997 Z28 coupe was largely unchanged from 1996, but automatic transmission became standard equipment.

equipment group 2 includes power door lock system, remote control hatch release, electric speed control with resume feature, fog lights, leather-wrapped steering wheel, leather-wrapped brake handle, leather-wrapped shifter, electric Sport mirrors, remote keyless entry with illuminated interior feature, theft deterrent alarm system, power windows with driver's side express down, four-way manual driver's seat adjustment and U1T radio upgrade ($1,581). 1SK Camaro Z28 convertible base equipment group, included with model (no cost). 1SK Camaro Z28 convertible base equipment group, included with model and UL0 radio upgrade ($215). 1SK Camaro Z28 convertible base equipment group, included with model and UN0 radio upgrade ($315). 1SL Camaro Z28 convertible preferred equipment group 1 includes power door lock system, fog lights, remote control trunk release and electric speed control with resume feature ($565). 1SL Camaro Z28 convertible preferred equipment group 1 includes power door lock system, fog lights, remote control trunk release, electric speed control with resume feature and UL0 radio upgrade ($780). 1SL Camaro Z28 convertible preferred equipment group 1 includes power door lock system, fog lights, remote control trunk release, electric speed control with resume feature and UL0 radio upgrade ($780). 1SM Camaro Z28 convertible preferred equipment group 2 includes fog lights, leather-wrapped steering wheel, leather-wrapped brake handle, leather-wrapped shifter, electric Sport mirrors, remote keyless entry with illuminated interior feature, theft deterrent alarm system, power windows with driver's side express down and U1C radio upgrade ($1,231). 1SM Camaro Z28 convertible preferred equipment group 2 includes fog lights, leather-wrapped steering wheel, leather-wrapped brake handle, leather-wrapped shifter, electric Sport mirrors, remote keyless entry with illuminated interior feature, theft deterrent alarm system, power windows with driver's side express

down and UL0 radio upgrade ($1,456). 1SM Camaro Z28 convertible preferred equipment group 2 includes fog lights, leather-wrapped steering wheel, leather-wrapped brake handle, leather-wrapped shifter, electric Sport mirrors, remote keyless entry with illuminated interior feature, theft deterrent alarm system, power windows with driver's side express down and UL0 radio upgrade ($1,556). GU5 optional performance axle ($300). VK3 front license plate bracket (no cost). C49 rear window defogger ($170). R9W rear window defogger not desired in coupes (no cost). AU3 power door lock system ($220). FE9 federal emissions (no cost). NG1 New York and Massachusetts emissions (no cost). YF5 California emissions (no cost). NB8 California and Massachusetts emissions override (no cost). NC7 federal emissions override (no cost). LT36 3.8-liter SFI V-6 (no cost in base coupe and RS; not available in Z28). LT1 5.7-liter SFI V-8 (in Z28 no charge). B35 rear carpeted floor mats ($15). K05 engine block heater ($20). AU0 remote keyless entry, as a separate option ($225). B84 color-keyed body side moldings ($60). 1LE performance package includes special handling suspension, Z28 coupe only ($1,175). Y87 performance handling package includes limited-slip axle, four-wheel disc brakes, dual outlet exhaust and sport steering ration on base and RS models only ($400). Ul0 ETR AM/FM stereo ($350). UN0 ETR AM/FM stereo and CG player ($450). U1S 12-disc CD player ($595). D82 monochromatic roof treatment includes body-color roof and mirrors on base or RS coupe requires CC1 roof panels or on Z28 replaces standard black roof (no cost). CC1 removable roof panels ($995). AGF1 six-way power driver's seat ($270). AR9 leather bucket seat ($499). Z4C 30th Anniversary Edition package includes white monochromatic exterior with orange stripes, white five-spoke aluminum wheels, 30th Anniversary embroidered emblems on front floor mats and 30th Anniversary embroidered emblems on headrests ($575). QEA

P215/60R16 black sidewall tires for standard coupe or convertible (no cost). QCB P235/55R16 tires ($132). QLC P245/50ZR16 tires ($225). QFZ P245/50ZR16 performance tires for Z28s and convertibles ($225). MN6 six-speed manual transmission (no cost). MM5 five-speed manual transmission (no cost). MXO four-speed automatic transmission with brake/shift interlock ($790). N96 16-in. silver aluminum wheels ($275). N98 16-in. chrome wheels with Z28 ($500). N98 16-in. chrome wheels with Z28 ($775).

CAMARO SS OPTIONS

Performance exhaust system. Level II Bilstein sport suspension. Torsen limited-slip differential includes performance lubricant package. Hurst six-speed short-throw shifter. Engine oil cooler. B.F. Goodrich Comp T/A 17-in. tires for Camaro SS Coupe, available only as a second set shipped to Chevrolet dealer on 17-in. wheels and recommended for track usage by an experienced driver. Performance lubricants package with premium synthetic media engine oil filter, rear axle lube and semi-synthetic power steering fluid. Fitted car cover with locking cable, tote bag and silk-screened Camaro SS logo on cover and bag (standard with 30th Anniversary package). Premium front floor mats with embroidered Camaro SS logo. Sebring Silver Metallic exterior color.

HISTORICAL FOOTNOTES

The Camaro's model-year sales were 58,152 units. Calendar-year sales were 55,973. According to industry trade journals domestic model-year production was 48,292 coupes and 6,680 convertibles for a total of 54,972 units. The Ste. Therese, Quebec, plant built all of these cars (and all 30,754 Firebirds). Of the Camaros built, 71.5 percent had automatic transmission, 14.9 percent had a five-speed manual transmission, 13.6 percent had a six-speed manual transmission, 66 percent had a 3.8-liter SFI V-6, 34 percent had a 5.7-liter MFI V-8, 13.7 percent had traction control, 100 percent had power steering, 100 percent had ABS brakes, 27.4 percent had a limited-slip differential, 100 percent had steel-belted radial tires, 81.3 percent had power door locks, 78.8 percent had power windows, 100 percent had reclining bucket seats, 47.3 percent had a power seats, 22 percent had leather seats, 100 percent had dual front airbags, 100 percent had tilt steering, 100 percent had tinted glass, 99.2 percent had manual air conditioning, 93.4 percent had cruise control, 100 percent had delay windshield wipers, 30 percent had a ETR stereo cassette player, 15.9 percent had a name brand sound system, 3.8 percent had a name brand sound system with CD, 20.3 percent had another brand CD, 64 percent had an electric rear window defogger, 29.2 percent had a manual remote-control left-hand outside rearview mirror, 70.8 percent had power rearview mirrors, 27.8 percent had a power right-hand rearview mirror, 18 percent had chrome styled wheels, 82 percent had aluminum styled wheels, 76.6 percent had remote keyless entry and 43.3 percent had T-tops. A total of 55,437 new Camaros were registered in the U.S. during calendar year 1997.

The "30th Anniversary" Camaros were white-and-orange SS models that were destined to be collector cars.

Jerry Heasley photo

The 1998 Z28 convertible carried a price tag of $27,975.

The big news for 1998 was a restyled front end for all Camaros and a new Corvette-derived LS1 V-8 engine in SS and Z28 models. Chevy dropped both RS Camaros in 1998 and offered an optional Sport Appearance package instead. It was available for all Camaros except Z28 SS models. A factory-direct SS Performance/Appearance package replaced the previous limited-edition performance car made at SLP Engineering.

Exterior revisions included a redesigned hood, front fenders and front fascia, composite headlamps with reflector optics and optional fog lamps. A new four-wheel disc brake system was standard on all Camaros, as was a one-piece all-welded exhaust system.

The Z28 received a Gen III 5.7-liter 305-hp LS1 "Corvette" aluminum-block V-8. Base Camaros again featured the 3.8-liter V-6 and a five-speed manual transmission. The 4L60-E four-speed automatic was standard in Z28s and optional in base Camaros. Z28s offered an optional six-speed manual transmission.

I.D. DATA

Chevrolets again had a 17-symbol vehicle identification number (VIN) on the upper left surface of the instrument panel, visible through the windshield. The first symbol identifies country of origin: 2=Canada. The second symbol identifies the manufacturer: G=General Motors. The third symbol indicates make: 1=Chevrolet, 7=GM of Canada. The fourth and fifth symbols indicated the car line and series: F/P=Camaro Sport Coupe and Convertible. The sixth symbol indicated body type: 2=two-door coupe style 87 and 3=two-door convertible style 67. The seventh symbol indicated the type of restraint system: 2=active manual belts with driver and passenger front airbags, 4=active manual belts with driver and passenger front and side airbags. The eighth symbol indicates the engine type: K=RPO L36 3.8-liter (231-cid) V-6 with Multiport Fuel Injection, G=RPO LS1 5.7-

liter (350-cid) V-8 with SFI. The ninth symbol is a check digit. The 10th symbol indicates model year: W=1998. The 11th symbol indicates the assembly plant: 2=Ste. Therese, Quebec (Canada).

COLORS

Sport Gold Metallic, Navy Blue Metallic, Black, Bright Green Metallic, Bright Purple Metallic, Bright Red, Cayenne Red Metallic, Sebring Silver Metallic, Mystic Teal Metallic, Arctic White

CAMARO — SERIES 1F — V-6

New features for the first-rung F-car included four-wheel disc brakes, a standard PASS-Key II anti-theft system, the new front end styling, body-color door handles and new colors of Sport Gold and Navy Blue. Standard equipment for the base Camaro coupe included a 3.8-liter V-6, a five-speed overdrive manual gearbox, a battery with run-down protection, rear-wheel drive, a 3.23:1 rear axle ratio, a stainless steel exhaust system, a firm ride suspension, independent front suspension with an anti-roll bar, front coil springs, front shocks, a rear suspension with an anti-roll bar, rear coil springs, rear shocks, power rack-and-pinion steering, four-wheel disc ABS brakes, a 15.5-gal. fuel tank, a rear wing spoiler, body-color front and rear bumpers, and monotone body paint. In addition to or in place of these items, the base convertible featured an electrically operated lined convertible top, automatic halogen sealed beam headlights, daytime running lamps, a center high-mounted stoplight, a manual remote control left-hand outside rearview mirror, 16 x 7.5-in. steel wheels, full wheel covers, P215/60SR16 black sidewall tires, a compact spare tire on a steel spare wheel, air conditioning, an AM/FM stereo (with clock, seek-and-scan, cassette, four speakers and fixed antenna), two power accessory outlets, retained accessory power, analog instrumentation (with a tachometer, oil pressure gauge, water temperature indicator, voltmeter, trip odometer and various warning indicators), dual airbags, an ignition disable feature, tinted windows, variable intermittent windshield wipers, four-passenger seating with front bucket seats, front headrests, a center armrest with storage provision, a four-way-adjustable driver's seat, a fixed folding rear bench seat, cloth seat trim, cloth door trim inserts, a full cloth headliner, full carpeting, carpeted floor mats, interior lights, a tilt-adjustable sport steering wheel, visor-vanity mirrors, a day/night inside rearview mirror, a full floor console, a lighted lockable glove box, a front cupholder, driver and passenger door storage bins, a carpeted cargo area, a plastic trunk lid, a cargo area cover, a cargo area light and black door handles. In addition to or in place of these items the base Camaro convertible featured an electrically operated lined convertible top, a glass rear window, a sound system with four performance speakers, a rear window defroster and a carpeted cargo floor.

Model Number	Body/Style Number	Body Type & Seating	Factory Price	Shipping Weight	Production Total
F/P	87	2d coupe-4P	$17,150	3,294 lbs.	Note 1
F/P	67	2d convertible-4P	$22,650	3,446 lbs.	Note 2

Note 1: Domestic model-year production of Camaro and Camaro Z28 coupes was 43,360.
Note 2: Domestic model-year production of Camaro and Camaro Z28 convertibles was 3,858.

CAMARO Z28 — SERIES 1F — V-8

The Z28 got a slightly de-tuned version of the Corvette LS1 engine for 1998. This V-8 replaced the LT1 used from 1995 through 1997. The Z28 also had the new front-end styling, a black roof treatment and the same two new colors. Standard equipment for the Camaro Z28 coupe included a 5.7-liter V-8, a four-speed electronic overdrive transmission, a battery with run-down protection, rear-wheel drive, a limited-slip differential, a 2.73 rear axle ratio, a stainless steel exhaust system with chrome tips, a Sport ride suspension, independent front suspension with an anti-roll bar, front coil springs, front shocks, a rear suspension with an anti-roll bar, rear coil springs, rear shocks, power rack-and-pinion steering, four-wheel disc ABS brakes, a 15.5-gal. fuel tank, a rear wing spoiler, body-color front and rear bumpers, and monotone body paint. In addition to or in place of these items, the base convertible featured an electrically-operated lined convertible top, automatic halogen sealed beam headlights, daytime running lights, a center high-mounted stoplight, a manual remote control left-hand outside rearview mirror, 16 x 8-in. silver alloy wheels, P235/55TR16 black sidewall tires, a compact spare tire on a steel spare wheel, air conditioning, an AM/FM stereo (with clock, seek-and-scan, cassette, four speakers and fixed antenna), two power accessory outlets, retained accessory power, analog instrumentation (with a tachometer, oil pressure gauge, water temperature indicator, voltmeter, trip odometer and various warning indicators), dual airbags, an ignition disable feature, tinted windows, variable intermittent windshield wipers, four-passenger seating with front bucket seats, front headrests, a center armrest with storage provision, a four-way-adjustable driver's seat, a fixed folding rear bench seat, cloth seat trim, cloth door trim inserts, a full cloth headliner, full carpeting, carpeted floor mats, interior lights, a tilt-adjustable sport steering wheel, visor-vanity mirrors, a day/night inside rearview mirror, a full floor console, a lighted lockable glove box, a front cupholder, driver and passenger door storage bins, a car-

The Z28 featured a version of the Corvette LS1 5.7-liter V-8 for 1998.

peted cargo area, a plastic trunk lid, a cargo area cover, a cargo area light and black door handles. In addition to or in place of these items the Camaro Z28 convertible featured traction control, an electrically operated fully lined convertible top, a glass rear window, a sound system with four performance speakers, a rear window defroster and a carpeted cargo floor.

Model Number	Body/Style Number	Body Type & Seating	Factory Price	Shipping Weight	Production Total
F/P+Z28	87	2d coupe-4P	$20,995	3,433 lbs.	Note 3
F/P+Z28	67	2d convertible -4P	$27,975	3,589 lbs.	Note 4

Note 3: Domestic model-year production of Camaro and Camaro Z28 coupes was 43,360.

Note 4: Domestic model-year production of Camaro and Camaro Z28 convertibles was 3,858.

CAMARO SS — SERIES 1F — V-8

Chevrolet built Camaros and SLP Engineering, of Troy, Michigan, turned new Camaro coupes and convertibles into a Camaro SS with the WU8 "SS Performance & Appearance" option. SLP offered a choice of two engines beginning with a 315-hp version of the LS1 V-8. This could be boosted to 320 hp with the addition of an optional performance exhaust system. Other standard Camaro SS coupe content included an under-hood forced-air induction system, a unique spoiler, a high performance suspension package, P275/40ZR17 Goodyear Eagle F1 tires, 17-in. cast-aluminum alloy wheels, Quaker State Synquest synthetic engine oil, exterior SS badges replacing Z28 logos and a Camaro SS interior plaque.

Model Number	Body/Style Number	Body Type & Seating	Factory Price	Shipping Weight	Production Total
F/P+WU8	87	2d coupe-4P	$24,495	—	Note 5
F/P+WU8	67	2d convertible-4P	$31,475	—	Note 6

Note 5: The production total above included 2,397 Camaro Z28 coupes with the SS option.

Note 6: The production total above included 478 Camaro Z28 convertibles with the SS option.

ENGINE

L36 V-6: 60-degree, overhead-valve. Cast-iron block and head. Bore & stroke: 3.80 x 3.40. Displacement: 231 cid (3.8 liters). Compression ratio: 9.4:1. Brake horsepower: 200 at 5200 rpm. Torque: 225 lbs.-ft. at 4000 rpm. Hydraulic valve lifters. Induction system: Sequential fuel injection. VIN Code K.

LS1 V-8: Overhead valve. Cast-aluminum block and head. Bore & stroke: 3.90 x 3.62 in. Displacement: 346 cid (5.7 liters). Compression ratio: 10.1:1. Brake horsepower: 305 at 5200 rpm. Torque: 335 lb.-ft. at 4000 rpm. Hydraulic valve lifters. Sequential fuel injection. Standard in Z28. VIN Code G.

LS1 V-8: Overhead valve. Cast-aluminum block and head. Bore & stroke: 3.90 x 3.62 in. Displacement: 346 cid (5.7 liters). Brake horsepower: 315. Hydraulic valve lifters. Sequential fuel injection. Standard in SS. VIN Code G.

LS1 V-8: Overhead valve. Cast-aluminum block and head. Bore & stroke: 3.90 x 3.62 in. Displacement: 346 cid (5.7 liters). Brake horsepower: 320. Hydraulic valve lifters. Sequential fuel injection. Performance exhaust system. Optional in SS. VIN Code G.

CHASSIS

Base Camaro Coupe: Wheelbase: 101.1 in. Overall length: 193.5 in. Height: 51.3 in. Width: 74.1 in. Front headroom: 37.2 in. Rear headroom: 35.3 in. Front legroom: 42.9 in. Rear legroom: 26.8 in. Front shoulder room: 57.4 in. Rear shoulder room: 55.8 in. Front hip room: 52.8 in. Rear hip room: 44.4 in. Luggage capacity: (rear seat up) 12.9 cu. ft.; (rear seat down) 32.8 cu. ft. Front tread: 60.7 in. Rear tread: 60.6 in. Standard tires: P215/60SR16.

Base Camaro Convertible: Wheelbase: 101.1 in. Overall length: 193.5 in. Height: 52 in. Width: 74.1 in. Front headroom: 38 in. Rear headroom: 39 in. Front legroom: 43 in. Rear legroom: 26.8 in. Front shoulder room: 57.4 in. Rear shoulder room: 43.5 in. Front hip room: 52.8 in. Rear hip room: 43.7 in. Luggage capacity: (rear seat up) 7.6 cu. ft. Front tread: 60.7 in. Rear tread: 60.6 in. Standard tires: P215/60R16.

Z28 Coupe: Wheelbase: 101.1 in. Overall length: 193.5 in. Height: 51.3 in. Front headroom: 37.2 in. Rear headroom: 35.3 in. Front legroom: 43 in. Rear legroom: 26.8 in. Front shoulder room: 57.4 in. Rear shoulder room: 55.8 in. Front hip room: 52.8 in. Rear hip room: 44.4 in. Luggage capacity: (rear seat up) 12.9 cu. ft.; (rear seat down) 32.8 cu. ft. Front tread: 60.7 in. Rear tread: 60.6 in. Standard tires: P235/55TR16.

Z28 Convertible: Wheelbase: 101.1 in. Overall length: 193.5 in. Height: 52 in. Width: 74.1 in. Front headroom:

The SS Camaro again had several performance and appearance upgrades.

Jerry Heasley photo

38 in. Rear headroom: 39 in. Front legroom: 43 in. Rear legroom: 26.8 in. Front shoulder room: 57.4 in. Rear shoulder room: 43.5 in. Front hip room: 52.8 in. Rear hip room: 43.7 in. Luggage capacity: (rear seat up) 7.6 cu. ft. Front tread: 60.7 in. Rear tread: 60.6 in. Standard tires: P235/55TR16.

Camaro SS Coupe: Wheelbase: 101.1 in. Overall length: 193.5 in. Height: 51.3 in. Width: 74.1 in. Front headroom: 38 in. Rear headroom: 39 in. Front legroom: 43 in. Rear legroom: 26.8 in. Front shoulder room: 57.4 in. Rear shoulder room: 43.5 in. Front hip room: 52.8 in. Rear hip room: 43.7 in. Luggage capacity: (rear seat up) 7.6 cu. ft. Front tread: 60.7 in. Rear tread: 60.6 in. Standard tires: B.F. Goodrich Comp T/A P275/40ZR17.

Camaro SS Convertible: Wheelbase: 101.1 in. Overall length: 193.5 in. Height: 52 in. Width: 74.1 in. Front headroom: 38 in. Rear headroom: 39 in. Front legroom: 43 in. Rear legroom: 26.8 in. Front shoulder room: 57.4 in. Rear shoulder room: 43.5 in. Front hip room: 52.8 in. Rear hip room: 43.7 in. Luggage capacity: (rear seat up) 7.6 cu. ft. Front tread: 60.7 in. Rear tread: 60.6 in. Standard tires: 16-in. B.F. Goodrich Comp T/A.

TECHNICAL

Base Camaro: Transmission: Five-speed manual. Steering: rack and pinion. Front suspension: SLA/Coil over monotube gas shocks, tubular stabilizer bar with links. Rear suspension: Solid axle/torque arm, trailing arm, coil springs, track bar, monotube gas shocks and solid stabilizer bar with links. Brakes: Front disc/rear drum with antilock. Body construction: unibody. Fuel tank: 15.5 gal.

Z28: Transmission: Four-speed electronic overdrive transmission. Steering: rack and pinion. Front suspension: SLA/Coil over monotube gas shocks, and 30-mm tubular stabilizer bar with links. Rear suspension: Solid axle/torque arm, trailing arm, coil springs, track bar, monotube gas shocks and 19-mm solid stabilizer bar with links. Brakes: Four-wheel discs with antilock. Body construction: unibody. Fuel tank: 15.5 gal.

SS: Transmission: Six-speed manual. Steering: rack and pinion. Front suspension: Modified SLA/Coil over monotube gas shocks and tubular stabilizer bar with links. Rear suspension: Modified solid axle/torque arm, trailing arm, coil springs, track bar, monotube gas shocks and solid stabilizer bar with links. Brakes: Four-wheel discs with antilock. Body construction: unibody. Fuel tank: 15.5 gal. (Note: The Camaro SS convertible retained the stock Camaro Z28 suspension).

OPTIONS

U15 12-disc CD changer, requires ULO, not available with UNO ($595). GU5 3.23 performance axle ratio for Z28, requires QFZ or QLC, not available with MN6 ($300). MXO four-speed automatic transmission in base Camaro, includes second-gear start and 3.23 axle, not available with Y87 teamed with MM5 ($815). MN6 six-speed manual transmission in Z28, includes 3.42 axle, not available with GU5 (no cost). AG1 six-way power driver's seat in base Camaro ($270). NW9 acceleration slip regulation in Z28, QFC tires recommended, not available with 1SF ($450). YF5 California emissions ($170). B84 color-keyed body side moldings on base coupe ($60).

C49 electric rear window defogger on coupes, not available with R9W ($170). Leather seating surface, not available with 1SF ($499). New York, Massachusetts, Connecticut emissions ($170). Y87 performance handling package with MM5, includes sport steering ratio, dual outlet exhaust and limited-slip differential, requires QCB and N96 or N98, not available with 1SA or 1SD ($225). 1LE Z28 coupe performance package, includes special handling suspension system, larger stabilizer bars, stiffer springs, dual adjustable shock absorbers and bushings and power steering cooler ($1,175). 1SA base coupe preferred equipment group includes vehicle with standard equipment (no cost). 1SB base coupe preferred equipment package includes electronic speed control, remote hatch release, power door lock system and fog lamps ($565). 1SC base coupe preferred equipment package includes electronic speed control with resume feature, remote hatch lid release, power door lock system, fog lamps, power windows with river's side express down, dual electric remote-control sport mirrors, a leather-wrapped steering wheel, a leather gearshift knob, remote keyless entry, illuminated entry, remote hatch release and theft-deterrent alarm system ($1,231). 1SD base convertible preferred equipment group includes vehicle with standard equipment (no cost). 1SE base convertible preferred equipment group includes power door lock system, electronic speed control with resume, remote hatch release, fog lamps, power windows with driver's side express down, electric dual remote control sport mirrors, leather-wrapped steering wheel, leather gearshift knob, remote keyless entry, illuminated entry, panic alarm, remote hatch release, theft-deterrent alarm system, color-keyed lower body side moldings and rear carpet floor mats ($1,306). 1SF Z28 coupe preferred equipment group, includes vehicle with standard equipment (no cost). 1SG Z28 coupe preferred equipment group includes power door lock system, electronic speed control with resume, remote hatch release, fog lamps, power windows with driver's side express down, electric dual remote control sport mirrors, leather-wrapped steering wheel, leather gearshift knob, remote keyless entry, illuminated entry, panic alarm, remote hatch release, theft-deterrent alarm system, six-way power driver's seat, color-keyed lower body side moldings and rear carpet floor mats ($1,576). 1SH Z28 convertible preferred equipment group includes power door lock system, electronic speed control with resume, remote hatch release, fog lamps, power windows with driver's side express down, electric dual remote control sport mirrors, leather-wrapped steering wheel, leather gearshift knob, remote keyless entry, illuminated entry, panic alarm, remote hatch release, theft-deterrent alarm system, six-way power driver's seat, color-keyed lower body side moldings and rear carpet floor mats (no cost). ULO AM/FM stereo with automatic tone control and cassette in coupes, includes digital clock, theft lock, speed-compensated volume, 200-watt amplifier and eight speakers ($350). ULO AM/FM stereo with automatic tone control and cassette in convertibles, includes digital clock, theft lock, speed-compensated volume, 200-watt amplifier and eight speakers ($215). UNO AM/FM stereo with Automatic Tone Control and CD in convertibles, includes digital clock, theft lock, speed-compensated volume, 200-watt amplifier and eight speakers ($315). UNO AM/FM stereo with Automatic Tone Control and CD in coupes, includes digital clock, theft lock, speed-compensated volume, 200-watt amplifier and eight speakers ($450). B35 rear carpet floor mats in base coupe ($15). R9W rear window defogger not desired in coupes (no cost). AUO remote keyless entry in base coupe, includes illuminated entry, theft-deterrent alarm system, panic alarm and remote hatch release ($225). Y3F Sport Appearance package for base Camaro, includes rocker and rear fascia moldings, 16-in. aluminum wheels and P235/55R15 all-season black sidewall tires ($1,755). Y3F Sport Appearance package for Z28 includes rocker moldings, front fascia moldings, rear fascia moldings, spoiler extension, 16-in. aluminum wheels and P235/55R16 all-season black sidewall tires ($1,348). WU8 SS performance and appearance package for Z28, includes 320-hp engine, forced air induction hood, a unique spoiler, 17-in. aluminum wheels, P275/40ZR17 Goodyear Eagle F1 tires, high performance ride & handling package and SS badging ($3,500). QCB P235/55R16 black sidewall tires on base Camaros ($132). QFZ P245/50ZR16 black sidewall all-season performance tires on Z28s ($225). QLC P245/50ZR16 black sidewall performance tires on Z28s ($225). CC1 transparent removable roof panels, includes locks, lockable stowage and sun shade ($995). N96 16-in. aluminum wheels on base Camaro ($275). N98 16-in chrome aluminum wheels on base Camaros ($775). N98 16-in. chrome aluminum wheels on Camaro Z28s ($500).

HISTORICAL FOOTNOTES

John G. Middlebrook was the general manager of Chevrolet Motor Division in 1998, but Kurt L. Ritter held the new title of general manager of marketing by 1999.

The Camaro's model-year sales were 48,806 units. Calendar-year sales were 47,577. According to industry trade journals domestic model-year production was 45,630 coupes and 3,858 convertibles for a total of 49,218 units. The Ste. Therese, Quebec plant built all of these cars (and all 32,157 Firebirds). Of the Camaros built, 72.9 percent had automatic transmission, 13.8 percent had a five-speed manual transmission, 13.3 percent had a six-speed manual transmission, 63.5 percent had a 3.8-liter SFI V-6, 36.5 percent had a 5.7-liter MFI V-8, 100 percent had power steering, 100 percent had four-wheel disc brakes with ABS, 17.2 percent had traction control, 100 percent had automatic headlamps (DRLs), 28.5 percent had a limited-slip differential, 100 percent had steel-belted radial tires, 89 percent had power door locks, 86.1 percent had power windows, 100 percent had reclining bucket seats, 55.7 percent had a power seats, 21.3 percent had leather seats, 100 percent had dual front airbags, 100 percent had tilt steering, 100 percent had tinted glass, 100 percent had manual air conditioning, 89 percent had cruise control, 100 percent had delay windshield wipers, 46.6 percent had a ETR stereo cassette player, 15 percent had a name brand sound system with CD, 38.4 percent had another brand CD, 78.8 percent had an electric rear window defogger, 25.2 percent had a manual remote-control left-hand outside rearview mirror, 74.8 percent had power rearview mirrors, 27.8 percent had a power right-hand rearview mirror, 29.5 percent had chrome styled wheels, 58 percent had aluminum styled wheels, 78 percent had remote keyless entry, 78 percent had an anti-theft device and 49.2 percent had T-tops. A total of 47,624 new Camaros were registered in the U.S. during calendar year 1998.

All 1998 Camaros, including the Z28, got restyled front ends.

Camaro

A total of 38,800 Camaro coupes were built in 1999, starting at a price of $16,625.

The big change for 1999 Camaros was a Zexel Torsen differential to replace all limited-slip rear axle applications. Traction control was made available with the 3800 V-6 engine and a Monsoon premium sound system was added to the convertible's options list. A new electronic throttle control was featured with V-6 Camaros and a new telltale light that monitored oil life was incorporated into the instrument cluster in all Camaros. Another change was a larger fuel tank so that Camaro lovers could go further on a tank of gas.

"Why settle for just any sports car, when you can get something with attitude?" asked Chevrolet's 1999 Camaro sales catalog. "That's what the Camaro is all about."

I.D. DATA

Chevrolets again had a 17-symbol vehicle identification number (VIN) on the upper left surface of the instrument panel, visible through the windshield. The first symbol identifies country of origin: 2=Canada. The second symbol identifies the manufacturer: G=General Motors. The third symbol indicates make: 1=Chevrolet, 7=GM of Canada. The fourth and fifth symbols indicated the car line and series: F/P=Camaro Sport Coupe and Convertible. The sixth symbol indicated body type: 2=two-door hatchback/liftback style 87 and 3=two-door convertible style 67. The seventh symbol indicated the type of restraint system: 2=active manual belts with driver and passenger front airbags, 4=active manual belts with driver and passenger front and side airbags. The eighth symbol indicates the engine type: K=RPO L36 3.8-liter (231-cid) V-6 with MFI, G=RPO LS1 5.7-liter (350-cid) V-8 with SFI. The ninth symbol is a check digit. The 10th symbol indicates model year: X=1999. The 11th symbol indicates the assembly plant: 2=Ste. Therese, Providence of Quebec (Canada).

COLORS

Black, bright Blue Metallic, Navy Blue Metallic, Sebring Silver Metallic, Hugger Orange, Light Pewter Metallic, Bright Red, Mystic Teal Metallic, Arctic White.

CAMARO — SERIES 1F — V-6

Standard equipment for the base Camaro coupe included the 3.8-liter 200-hp V-6, a five-speed overdrive manual gearbox, dent resistant body panels (doors, roof, hatch lid and front fenders), a left-hand remote control Sport-style outside rearview mirror, a right-hand manual Sport-style rearview mirror, composite headlights with automatic exterior lamp control, CFC-free air conditioning, battery run-down protection, carpeted front floor mats, full instrumentation with a tachometer, next-generation dual airbags, the PASS-Key II theft-deterrent system, retained power accessory, cloth-trimmed reclining front bucket seats with Scotchguard protection, a rear seat with a full folding back and Scotchguard fabric protection, door trim with Scotchguard fabric protection, full carpeting with Scotchguard fabric protection, a tilt wheel steering column, Solar-Ray tinted glass on all windows, an AM/FM stereo with a cassette player, power four-wheel disc brakes with ABS, power rack-and-pinion steering, a Firm Ride & Handling suspension, 16-in. bolt-on wheel covers and P215/60R-16 black sidewall touring tires. The convertible added a fully lined power top (in White, Neutral or Black), a three-piece hard tonneau cover and a glass rear window with an electric defogger. A new option for V-6-powered base Camaros was traction control. Ten exterior colors were available for 1999 Camaros. Cars painted Black, Light Pewter Metallic, Bright Red and Artic White could be had with all four interior colors that were Dark Gray, Neutral, Red Accent and White. The exterior colors Navy Blue Metallic, Bright Green Metallic, Hugger Orange and Mystic Teal Metallic came with all but the Red Accent interior. Bright Blue

Metallic came only with Dark Gray or White interiors and Sebring Silver came with all but Neutral. Mystic Teal Metallic finish was not available with the Sport Appearance package.

Model Number	Body/Style Number	Body Type & Seating	Factory Price	Shipping Weight	Production Total
F/P	87	2d coupe-4P	$16,625	3,306 lbs.	Note 1
F/P	67	2d convertible-4P	$22,125	3,340 lbs.	Note 2

Note 1: Domestic model-year production of Camaro and Camaro Z28 coupes was 38,800.
Note 2: Domestic model-year production of Camaro and Camaro Z28 convertibles was 3,298.

CAMARO Z28 — SERIES 1F — V-8

The Z28 boasted four-wheel disc brakes with ABS, a new heavy-duty Torsen limited-slip differential, a special Sport suspension and the LS-1 V-8 as standard equipment. A four-speed automatic transmission was standard, but a six-speed manual transmission was a no-cost option. Standard equipment also included dent-resistant body panels (doors, roof, hatch lid and front fenders), a left-hand remote control Sport-style outside rearview mirror, a right-hand manual Sport-style rearview mirror, composite headlights with automatic exterior lamp control, CFC-free air conditioning, battery run-down protection, carpeted front floor mats, full instrumentation with a tachometer, next-generation dual airbags, the PASS-Key II theft-deterrent system, retained power accessory, cloth-trimmed reclining front bucket seats with Scotchguard protection, a rear seat with a full folding back and Scotchguard fabric protection, door trim with Scotchguard fabric protection, full carpeting with Scotchguard fabric protection, a tilt wheel steering column, Solar-Ray tinted glass on all windows, an AM/FM stereo with a cassette player, power four-wheel disc brakes with ABS, power rack-and-pinion steering, a Firm Ride & Handling suspension, 16 x 8-in. cast aluminum wheels and P235/55R-16 black sidewall touring tires. The Z28 convertible added a fully lined power top (in white, neutral or black), a three-piece hard tonneau cover and a glass rear window with an electric defogger.

Model Number	Body/Style Number	Body Type & Seating	Factory Price	Shipping Weight	Production Total
F/P+Z28	87	2d coupe-4P	$20,870	3,446 lbs.	Note 3
F/P+Z28	67	2d convertible -4P	$27,850	3,565 lbs.	Note 4

Note 3: Domestic model-year production of Camaro and Camaro Z28 coupes was 38,800.
Note 4: Domestic model-year production of Camaro and Camaro Z28 convertibles was 3,298.

CAMARO SS — SERIES 1F — V-8

Technically, the Camaro SS was a Z28 performance/appearance option sourced from SLP Engineering, of Troy, Michigan. "Think of it as the extreme Z28," said the 1999 Camaro sales brochure. This WU8 "SS Performance & Appearance" option pumped the LS1 V-8 up to 320 hp. Other standard Camaro SS coupe content included a forced air induction system, a special air scoop hood, a new low-restriction exhaust system, a Torsen limited-slip performance axle, an exclusive high-level rear spoiler, a high-performance ride & handling suspension package, speed-rated P275/40ZR17 Goodyear Eagle F1 tires, 17-in. lightweight cast-aluminum alloy wheels, Quaker State Synquest synthetic engine oil, exterior SS badges replacing Z28 logos and a Camaro SS interior plaque. The Camaro SS convertible was based on the Z28 convertible, but shared the 320-hp V-8, 17-in. wheels and functional hood scoop with the SS coupe.

Model Number	Body/Style Number	Body Type & Seating	Factory Price	Shipping Weight	Production Total
F/P+Z28	87	2d coupe-4P	$24,370	3,446 lbs.	Note 5
F/P+Z28	67	2d convertible-4P	$31,350	3,565 lbs.	Note 5

Note 5: The production totals given above included 810 Camaro Z28 coupes with the SS option.
Note 6: The production totals given above included 3,207 Camaro Z28 T-tops with the SS option.
Note 7: The production totals given above included 800 Camaro Z28 convertibles with the SS option.
Note 8: Of the 4,817 cars with the Camaro SS option, 222 were built for the Canadian market.

Leonard Goffe photo

This 1999 Z28 convertible came in Mystique Teal with chrome wheels.

ENGINE

L36 V-6: 60-degree, overhead-valve V-6. Cast-iron block and head. Bore & stroke: 3.80 x 3.40. Displacement: 231 cid (3.8 liters). Compression ratio: 9.4:1. Brake horsepower: 200 at 5200 rpm. Torque: 225 lbs.-ft. at 4000 rpm. Hydraulic valve lifters. Induction system: Sequential fuel injection. VIN Code K. Standard in base Camaro; not available in Z28.

LS1 V-8: Overhead valve. Cast-aluminum block and head. Bore & stroke: 3.90 x 3.62 in. Displacement: 346 cid (5.7 liters). Compression ratio: 10.1:1. Brake horsepower: 305 at 5200 rpm. Torque: 335 lbs.-ft. at 4000 rpm. Hydraulic valve lifters. Sequential fuel injection. Standard in Z28. VIN Code G. Standard in base Z28; not available in base Camaro.

LS1 V-8: Overhead-valve. Cast-aluminum block and head. Bore & stroke: 3.90 x 3.62 in. Displacement: 346 cid (5.7 liters). Brake horsepower: 320. Hydraulic valve lifters. Sequential fuel injection. Performance exhaust system. Optional in SS. VIN Code G.

CHASSIS

Base Camaro Coupe: Wheelbase: 101.1 in. Overall length: 193.2 in. Height: 51.3 in. Width: 74.1 in. Front headroom: 37.2 in. Rear headroom: 35.3 in. Front legroom: 43 in. Rear legroom: 26.8 in. Front shoulder room: 57.4 in. Rear shoulder room: 55.8 in. Front hip room: 52.8 in. Rear hip room: 44.4 in. Luggage capacity: (rear seat up) 12.9 cu. ft.; (rear seat down) 32.8 cu. ft. Front tread: 60.7 in. Rear tread: 60.6 in. Standard tires: P215/60SR16.

Base Camaro Convertible: Wheelbase: 101.1 in. Overall length: 193.2 in. Height: 52 in. Width: 74.1 in. Front headroom: 38 in. Rear headroom: 39 in. Front legroom: 43 in. Rear legroom: 26.8 in. Front shoulder room: 57.4 in. Rear shoulder room: 43.5 in. Front hip room: 52.8 in. Rear hip room: 43.7 in. Luggage capacity: (rear seat up) 7.6 cu. ft. Front tread: 60.7 in. Rear tread: 60.6 in. Standard tires: P215/60R16.

Z28 Coupe: Wheelbase: 101.1 in. Overall length: 193.2 in. Height: 51.3 in. Width: 74.1 in. Front headroom: 37.2 in. Rear headroom: 35.3 in. Front legroom: 43 in. Rear legroom: 26.8 in. Front shoulder room: 57.4 in. Rear shoulder room: 55.8 in. Front hip room: 52.8 in. Rear hip room: 44.4 in. Luggage capacity: (rear seat up) 12.9 cu. ft.; (rear seat down) 32.8 cu. ft. Front tread: 60.7 in. Rear tread: 60.6 in. Standard tires: P235/55R16.

Z28 Convertible: Wheelbase: 101.1 in. Overall length: 193.2 in. Height: 52 in. Width: 74.1 in. Front headroom: 38 in. Rear headroom: 39 in. Front legroom: 43 in. Rear legroom: 26.8 in. Front shoulder room: 57.4 in. Rear shoulder room: 43.5 in. Front hip room: 52.8 in. Rear hip room: 43.7 in. Luggage capacity: (rear seat up) 7.6 cu. ft. Front tread: 60.7 in. Rear tread: 60.6 in. Standard tires: P235/55R16.

Camaro SS Coupe: Wheelbase: 101.1 in. Overall length: 193.2 in. Height: 51.3 in. Width: 74.1 in. Front headroom: 37.2 in. Rear headroom: 35.3 in. Front legroom: 43 in. Rear legroom: 26.8 in. Front shoulder room: 57.4 in. Rear shoulder room: 55.8 in. Front hip

The 1999 Camaro SS convertible was billed as the "extreme Z28."

Kevin Lupo photo

This Z28 coupe featured a new heavy-duty Torsen limited-slip differential, a special Sport suspension and the LS-1 V-8 as standard equipment. It is one of only 778 1999 models that had white interior.

room: 52.8 in. Rear hip room: 44.4 in. Luggage capacity: (rear seat up) 12.9 cu. ft.; (rear seat down) 32.8 cu. ft. Front tread: 60.7 in. Rear tread: 60.6 in. Standard tires: P275/40ZR17 Goodyear Eagle F1 speed-rated on lightweight 17-in. wheels.

Camaro SS Convertible: Wheelbase: 101.1 in. Overall length: 193.2 in. Height: 52 in. Width: 74.1 in. Front headroom: 38 in. Rear headroom: 39 in. Front legroom: 43 in. Rear legroom: 26.8 in. Front shoulder room: 57.4 in. Rear shoulder room: 43.5 in. Front hip room: 52.8 in. Rear hip room: 43.7 in. Luggage capacity: (rear seat up) 7.6 cu. ft. Front tread: 60.7 in. Rear tread: 60.6 in. Standard tires: P275/40ZR17 Goodyear Eagle F1 speed-rated on lightweight 17-in. wheels.

TECHNICAL

Base Camaro: Transmission: Five-speed manual. Steering: rack and pinion. Front suspension: SLA/Coil over monotube gas shocks, tubular stabilizer bar with links. Rear suspension: Solid axle/torque arm, trailing arm, coil springs, track bar, monotube gas shocks and solid stabilizer bar with links. Firm Ride & Handling suspension standard. Brakes: Front disc/rear drum with anti-lock. Body construction: unibody. Fuel tank: 16.8 gal.

Z28: Transmission: Four-speed electronic overdrive transmission. Steering: rack and pinion. Front suspension: SLA/Coil over monotube gas shocks, and 30-mm tubular stabilizer bar with links. Rear suspension: Solid axle/torque arm, trailing arm, coil springs, track bar, monotube gas shocks and 19-mm solid stabilizer bar with links. Performance Ride & Handling suspension standard. Brakes: Four-wheel discs with anti-lock. Body construction: unibody. Fuel tank: 16.8 gal.

SS: Transmission: Six-speed manual. Steering: rack and pinion. Front suspension: Modified SLA/coil over monotube gas shocks and tubular stabilizer bar with links. Rear suspension: Modified solid axle/torque arm, trailing arm, coil springs, track bar, monotube gas shocks and solid stabilizer bar with links. Brakes: Four-wheel discs with anti-lock. Body construction: unibody. Fuel tank: 16.8 gal. (Note: The Camaro SS convertible retained the stock Camaro Z28 suspension).

OPTIONS

U15 12-disc CD changer, requires ULO, not available with UNO ($595). GU5 3.23 performance axle ratio for Z28, requires QFZ or QLC, not available with MN6 ($300). MXO four-speed automatic transmission in base Camaro, includes second-gear start and 3.23 axle, not available with Y87 teamed with MM5 ($815). MN6 six-speed manual transmission in Z28, includes 3.42 axle, not available with GU5 (no cost). AG1 six-way power driver's seat in base Camaro ($270). NW9 acceleration slip regulation in Z28, QFC tires recommended, not available with 1SF ($450). YF5 California emissions ($170). B84 color-keyed body side moldings on base coupe ($60). C49 electric rear window defogger on coupes, not available with R9W ($170). Leather seating surface, not available with 1SF ($499). New York, Massachusetts, Connecticut emissions ($170). Y87 performance handling package with MM5, includes sport steering ratio, dual outlet exhaust and limited-slip differential, requires QCB and N96 or N98, not available with 1SA or 1SD ($225). 1LE Z28 coupe performance package, including special handling suspension system, larger stabilizer bars, stiffer springs, dual adjustable shock absorbers and bushings and power steering cooler ($1,175). 1SA base coupe preferred equipment group includes vehicle with standard equipment (no cost). 1SB base coupe preferred equipment package includes electronic speed control, remote hatch release, power door lock system and fog lamps ($565). 1SC base coupe preferred equipment package includes electronic speed control with resume feature, remote hatch lid release, power door lock system, fog lamps, power windows with river's side express down, dual electric remote-control sport mirrors, a leather-wrapped steering wheel, a leather gearshift knob, remote keyless entry, illuminated entry, remote hatch release and theft-deterrent alarm system ($1,231). 1SD base convertible preferred equipment group includes vehicle with standard equipment (no cost). 1SE base convertible preferred equipment group includes power door lock system, electronic speed control with resume, remote hatch release, fog lamps, power windows with driver's side express down, electric dual remote control sport mirrors, leather-wrapped steering wheel, leather gearshift knob, remote keyless entry, illuminated entry, panic alarm, remote hatch release, theft-deterrent alarm system, color-keyed lower body side moldings and rear carpet floor mats ($1,306). 1SF Z28 coupe preferred equipment group, includes vehicle with standard equipment (no cost). 1SG Z28 coupe preferred equipment group includes power door lock system, electronic speed control with resume, remote hatch release, fog lamps, power windows with driver's side express down, electric dual remote control sport mirrors, leather-wrapped

steering wheel, leather gearshift knob, remote keyless entry, illuminated entry, panic alarm, remote hatch release, theft-deterrent alarm system, six-way power driver's seat, color-keyed lower body side moldings and rear carpet floor mats ($1,576). 1SH Z28 convertible preferred equipment group includes power door lock system, electronic speed control with resume, remote hatch release, fog lamps, power windows with driver's side express down, electric dual remote control sport mirrors, leather-wrapped steering wheel, leather gearshift knob, remote keyless entry, illuminated entry, panic alarm, remote hatch release, theft-deterrent alarm system, six-way power driver's seat, color-keyed lower body side moldings and rear carpet floor mats (no cost). ULO AM/FM stereo with automatic tone control and cassette in coupes, includes digital clock, theft lock, speed-compensated volume, 200-watt amplifier and eight speakers ($350). ULO AM/FM stereo with automatic tone control and cassette in convertibles, includes digital clock, theft lock, speed-compensated volume, 200-watt amplifier and eight speakers ($215). UNO AM/FM stereo with Automatic Tone Control and CD in convertibles, includes digital clock, theft lock, speed-compensated volume, 200-watt amplifier and eight speakers ($315). UNO AM/FM stereo with Automatic Tone Control and CD in coupes, includes digital clock, theft lock, speed-compensated volume, 200-watt amplifier and eight speakers ($450). B35 rear carpet floor mats in base coupe ($15). R9W rear window defogger not desired in coupes (no

The 1999 Camaro coupe came standard with a 3.8-liter 200-hp V-6 and a five-speed overdrive manual gearbox.

cost). AUO remote keyless entry in base coupe, includes illuminated entry, theft-deterrent alarm system, panic alarm and remote hatch release ($225). Y3F Sport Appearance package for base Camaro, includes rocker and rear fascia moldings, 16-in. aluminum wheels and P235/55R15 all-season black sidewall tires ($1,755). Y3F Sport Appearance package for Z28 includes rocker moldings, front fascia moldings, rear fascia moldings, spoiler extension, 16-in. aluminum wheels and P235/55R16 all-season black sidewall tires ($1,348). WU8 SS performance and appearance package for Z28, includes 320-hp engine, forced air induction hood, a unique spoiler, 17-in. aluminum wheels, P275/40ZR17 Goodyear Eagle F1 tires, high-performance ride & handling package and SS badging ($3,500). QCB P235/55R16 black sidewall tires on base Camaros ($132). QFZ P245/50ZR16 black sidewall all-season performance tires on Z28s ($225). QLC P245/50ZR16 black sidewall performance tires on Z28s ($225). CC1 transparent removable roof panels, includes locks, lockable stowage and sunshade ($995). N96 16-in. aluminum wheels on base Camaro ($275). N98 16-in chrome aluminum wheels on base Camaros ($775). N98 16-in. chrome aluminum wheels on Camaro Z28s ($500).

HISTORICAL FOOTNOTES

The Camaro's model-year sales were 41,412 units. Calendar-year sales were 40,7267. According to industry trade journals domestic model-year production was 38,800 coupes and 3,298 convertibles for a total of 42,098 units. The Ste. Therese, Quebec, plant built all of these cars (and all 41,226 Firebirds). Of the Camaros built, 70.8 percent had automatic transmission, 11.8 percent had a five-speed manual transmission, 17.4 percent had a six-speed manual transmission, 58.7 percent had a 3.8-liter SFI V-6, 41.3 percent had a 5.7-liter MFI V-8, 100 percent had power steering, 100 percent had four-wheel disc brakes with ABS, 33.9 percent had traction control, 100 percent had automatic headlamps (DRLs), 12.6 percent had a limited-slip differential, 100 percent had steel-belted radial tires, 83.6 percent had power door locks, 83.6 percent had power windows, 100 percent had reclining bucket seats, 68.1 percent had a power seats, 35.3 percent had leather seats, 100 percent had dual front airbags, 100 percent had tilt steering, 100 percent had tinted glass, 100 percent had manual air conditioning, 90 percent had cruise control, 100 percent had delay windshield wipers, 12.5 percent had a ETR stereo cassette player, 19.2 percent had a name brand sound system with CD, 68.5 percent had another brand CD, 73.9 percent had an electric rear window defogger, 24 percent had a manual remote-control left-hand outside rearview mirror, 76 percent had power rearview mirrors, 27.8 percent had a power right-hand rearview mirror, 29.9 percent had chrome styled wheels, 63.3 percent had aluminum styled wheels, 78 percent had remote keyless entry, 78 percent had an anti-theft device and 56.8 percent had T-tops. A total of 39,384 new Camaros were registered in the U.S. during calendar year 1999.

Black

Bright Blue Metallic

Navy Blue Metallic

Sebring Silver Metallic

Hugger Orange

Light Pewter Metallic

Bright Red

Mystic Teal Metallic

Arctic White

The Camaros were again available in a wide range of colors for 1999.

Camaro

Jerry Heasley photo

New body-color side mirrors were one of the only changes for the 2000 Z28.

The Canadian-built Camaro continued as one of North America's top-selling sports cars in 2000. A new Monterey Maroon Metallic body color was added to the Camaro's palette. The Z28 also got new body-colored outside rearview mirrors on both sides of the car, plus a leather-wrapped steering wheel with "redundant" radio controls inside. Integrated child seat tether anchors were added to all models. The car also had new 16-in. aluminum wheels came standard with painted finish or with optional polished finish.

On the inside, an ebony-colored interior selection replaced dark gray to provide a "true" black interior. A medium gray cloth interior replaced the former Artic White leather option and accent interior cloth replaced red accent. New cloth fabrics were used on the seats and door trim. Also new was a redundant radio control steering wheel. The Monsoon radio with CD player was made to be compatible with the trunk-mounted 12-disc CD changer. Both the V-6 and V-8 engines were revised to meet Low Emission Vehicle regulations in California and states requiring California emissions.

In the spirit of the original 1967-1969 Camaro Z28, Chevrolet Motor Division and Westech Automotive teamed up to build a new "302 Camaro" show car that appeared at the 2000 SEMA show. It featured a high-revving 302-cid LS1-based V-8. SLP Engineering, which teamed with Chevrolet to build the Camaro SS, con-tributed a lightweight flywheel, an aluminum differential cooler and a heavy-duty axle assembly. The 302 also fea-tured a carbon fiber driveshaft and its chassis was stiff-ened with Hotchkiss springs, sway bars, rear control arms, a panhard bar and a strut tower brace.

Koni double adjustable shocks and Baer Racing 14-in. cross-drilled brake rotors and PBR calipers helped the 302 corner at high speeds. The interior was complete with an L.G. Motorsports roll bar, special Recaro seats with five-point safety belts and a Billet Hurst six-speed shifter. The exterior featured an SLP "Bow Tie" grille assembly and special striping and "302" badging. The show car rode on 18-in. American Racing Torq-Thrust II wheels with B.F. Goodrich Z-rated ultra-high perform-ance tires.

I.D. DATA

Chevrolets again had a 17-symbol vehicle identifica-tion number (VIN) on the upper left surface of the instrument panel, visible through the windshield. The first symbol identifies country of origin: 2=Canada. The second symbol identifies the manufacturer: G=General Motors. The third symbol indicates make: 1=Chevrolet, 7=GM of Canada. The fourth and fifth symbols indicated the car line and series: F/P=Camaro Sport Coupe and Convertible. The sixth symbol indicated body type: 2=two-door hatchback/liftback style 87 and 3=two-door convertible style 67. The seventh symbol indicated the type of restraint system: 2=active manual belts with driver and passenger front airbags, 4=active manual belts with driver and passenger front and side airbags, 5=active manual belts with driver and passenger front airbags and driver side airbag, 6=active manual belts with driver and passenger air bags and automatic occupant sensor and 7=active manual belts with driver and front passenger front and side airbags and rear passenger side airbags. The eighth symbol indicates the engine type: K=RPO L36 3.8-liter (231-cid) V-6 with Sequential Fuel Injection, G=RPO LS1 5.7-liter (350-cid) V-8 with SFI. The ninth symbol is a check digit. The 10th symbol indicates model year: Y=2000. The 11th symbol indicates the assembly plant: 2=Ste. Therese, Quebec (Canada).

COLORS

Monterey Maroon Metallic, Onyx Black, Navy Blue Metallic, Artic White, Light Pewter Metallic, Bright Rally Red, Mystic Teal Metallic and Sebring Silver Metallic. Interior color choices were Medium Gray, Ebony or Accent (in cloth door trim and seat inserts only). Optional leather seats were available in Ebony or Neutral.

CAMARO — SERIES 1F — V-6

Standard equipment for the base Camaro coupe included driver and front passenger airbags, CFC-free air conditioning, a center console with cupholders and storage provisions, an engine oil life monitor, cloth-trimmed reclining front bucket seats, a full-folding rear seat, a tilt steering wheel, daytime running lamps (DRLs) with automatic exterior lamp control, a body-color left-hand remote-control outside rearview mirror, a body-color manual right-hand outside rearview mirror, P215/60R-16 touring tires, 16-in. steel bolt-on wheel covers, power four-wheel disc brakes with ABS, a 3800 SFI V-6 engine, power rack-and-pinion steering, a Firm Ride and Handling suspension, the PASS-Key II theft-deterrent system, a five-speed manual transmission, theatre lighting, carpeted front floor mats, a gauge package with a 125-mph speedometer and tachometer and digital odometer, Retained Accessory Power, a closeout panel for the rear cargo area and Solar-Ray tinted glass, extensive anti-corrosion measures (includes the use of composites, two-sided galvanized steel components and electro-deposition primer), sheet-molded compound body parts (for roof, doors, hatch and spoiler), reaction injected molded front fenders and fascia, a stainless steel exhaust system, a clutch/starter safety switch, a brake/transmission shift interlock, a second-gear start feature (except V-6 models with optional traction control), a remote hood release, laser-etched vehicle identification numbering, and an electronically tuned AM/FM stereo with cassette player, seek-and-scan, digital clock and extended-range speakers. In addition to, or in place of, the above equipment, the Camaro convertible also featured power door locks, an electric rear window defogger, a leather-wrapped steering wheel with redundant radio controls, remote keyless entry, a 200-watt Monsoon ETR AM/FM premium sound system (with cassette player, seek-and-scan, digital clock, TheftLock, speed-compensated volume and

Automatic Tone Control), power windows with driver's side "express down," fog lamps, twin power mirrors, carpeted rear floor mats, body-color body side moldings, a remote trunk release, a power convertible top (in Artic White, black or neutral colors), a tonneau cover, a tonneau cover storage bag and cruise control.

Model Number	Body/Style Number	Body Type & Seating	Factory Price	Shipping Weight	Production Total
F/P	87	2d coupe-4P	$16,840	3,306 lbs.	Note 1
F/P	67	2d convertible-4P	$21,140	3,500 lbs.	Note 2

Note 1: Domestic model-year production of Camaro and Camaro Z28 coupes was 41,825.
Note 2: Domestic model-year production of Camaro and Camaro Z28 convertibles was 3,636.

CAMARO Z28 — SERIES 1F — V-8

The 2000 Camaro Z28 was Chevrolet's "modern muscle car." New Z28s got body-color outside rearview mirrors. Standard equipment for the Camaro Z28 Sport Coupe included driver and front passenger airbags, CFC-free air conditioning, a center console with cupholders and storage provisions, an engine oil life monitor, cloth-trimmed reclining front bucket seats, a full-folding rear seat, a tilt steering wheel, a 200-watt Monsoon ETR AM/FM premium sound system (with cassette player, seek-and-scan, digital clock, TheftLock, speed-compensated volume and Automatic Tone Control), daytime running lamps (DRLs) with automatic exterior lamp control, a body-color left-hand remote-control outside rearview mirror, a body-color manual right-hand outside rearview mirror, P235/55R-16 touring tires, 16-in. aluminum wheels, power four-wheel disc brakes with ABS, a 5.7-liter LS1 SFI V-8 engine, a dual-outlet exhaust system, a limited-slip rear axle with Zexel Torsen differential, power rack-and-pinion steering, a Performance Handling suspension package, the PASS-Key II theft-deterrent system, a four-speed electronically controlled automatic transmission (or six-speed manual transmission at no extra cost), theatre lighting, carpeted front floor mats, a gauge package with a 155-mph speedometer and tachometer and digital odometer, Retained Accessory Power, a closeout panel for the rear cargo area and Solar-Ray tinted glass, extensive anti-corrosion measures (includes the use of composites, two-sided galvanized steel components and electro-deposition primer, sheet-molded compound body parts (for roof, doors, hatch and spoiler), a special black roof treatment, reaction injected molded front fenders and fascia, a stainless steel exhaust system, a brake/transmission shift interlock, cruise control, a remote trunk release, remote keyless entry, a second-gear start feature, a remote hood release and laser-etched vehicle identification numbering. In addition to or in place of the above equipment, the Camaro Z28 convertible also featured a six-way power driver's seat, a leather-wrapped gear shifter, a leather-wrapped parking brake release handle, power door locks, an electric rear window defogger, a leather-wrapped steering wheel with redundant radio controls, power windows with driver's side "express down," fog lamps, twin power mirrors, carpeted rear floor mats, body-color body side moldings, a remote trunk release, a power convertible top (in Artic White, black or neutral colors), a tonneau cover, a tonneau cover storage bag and cruise control.

The SS Sport Coupe used a 320-hp version of the LS1 V-8, forced-air induction, and a special fiberglass (SMC) air scoop hood.

Model Number	Body/Style Number	Body Type & Seating	Factory Price	Shipping Weight	Production Total
F/P+Z28	87	2d coupe-4P	$21,265	3,439 lbs.	Note 3
F/P+Z28	67	2d convertible-4P	$28,365	3,574 lbs.	Note 4

Note 3: Domestic model-year production of Camaro and Camaro Z28 coupes was 41,825.
Note 4: Domestic model-year production of Camaro and Camaro Z28 convertibles was 3,636.

CAMARO SS — SERIES 1F — V-8

Technically, the Camaro SS was a Z28 performance/appearance option sourced from SLP Engineering. It had a base price of $3,700, but the actual cost of each car depended upon individual buyer's preferences in equipment and trim. This so-called WU8 "SS Performance & Appearance" option included a 320-hp version of the LS1 V-8, forced-air induction with a special fiberglass (SMC) air scoop hood, a low-restriction exhaust system with dual 2 3/4-in. tailpipes, a Torsen limited-slip performance axle, an exclusive high-level rear spoiler, a high-performance ride & handling suspension package, speed-rated P275/40ZR17 Goodyear Eagle F1 tires, 17-in. lightweight cast-aluminum alloy wheels, a power steering cooler, Quaker State Synquest synthetic engine oil, exterior SS badges replacing Z28 logos and a Camaro SS interior plaque. The Camaro SS convertible was based on the Z28 convertible, but shared the 320-hp V-8, 17-in. wheels and functional hood scoop with the SS coupe.

Model Number	Body/Style Number	Body Type & Seating	Factory Price	Shipping Weight	Production Total
F/P+Z28	87	2d coupe-4P	$24,965	—	Note 5,6,7
F/P+Z28	67	2d convertible-4P	$32,065	—	Note 5,6,7

Note 5: The production totals given above included 1,085 Camaro Z28 coupes with the SS option.
Note 6: The production totals given above included 6,255 Camaro Z28 T-tops with the SS option.
Note 7: The production totals given above included 1,572 Camaro Z28 convertibles with the SS option.
Note 8: Of the 4,817 cars with the Camaro SS option, 224 were build for the Canadian market.

ENGINE

L38 V-6: 60-degree, overhead-valve V-6. Cast-iron block and head. Bore & stroke: 3.80 x 3.40. Displacement: 231 cid (3.8 liters). Compression ratio: 9.4:1. Brake horsepower: 200 at 5200 rpm. Torque: 225 lbs.-ft. at 4000 rpm. Hydraulic valve lifters. Induction system: Sequential fuel injection. VIN Code K.

LS1 V-8: Overhead-valve V-8. Cast-aluminum block and head. Bore & stroke: 3.90 x 3.62 in. Displacement: 346 cid (5.7 liters). Compression ratio: 10.1:1. Brake horsepower: 305 at 5200 rpm. Torque: 335 lbs.-ft. at 4000 rpm. Hydraulic valve lifters. Sequential fuel injection. Standard in Z28. VIN Code G.

LS1 V-8: Overhead-valve V-8. Cast-aluminum block and head. Bore & stroke: 3.90 x 3.62 in. Displacement: 346 cid (5.7 liters). Brake horsepower: 320. Hydraulic valve lifters. Sequential fuel injection. Performance exhaust system. Optional only in SS. VIN Code G.

CHASSIS

Base Camaro Coupe: Wheelbase: 101.1 in. Overall length: 193.5 in. Height: 51.2 in. Width: 74.1 in. Front headroom: 37.2 in. Rear headroom: 35.3 in. Front legroom: 43 in. Rear legroom: 26.8 in. Front shoulder room: 57.4 in. Rear shoulder room: 55.8 in. Front hip room: 52.8 in. Rear hip room: 44.4 in. Luggage capacity: (rear seat up) 12.9 cu. ft.; (rear seat down) 32.8 cu. ft. Front tread: 60.7 in. Rear tread: 60.6 in. Standard tires: P215/60SR16.

Base Camaro Convertible: Wheelbase: 101.1 in. Overall length: 193.5 in. Height: 51.8 in. Width: 74.1 in. Front headroom: 37.2 in. Rear headroom: 39 in. Front legroom: 43 in. Rear legroom: 26.8 in. Front shoulder room: 57.4 in. Rear shoulder room: 43.5 in. Front hip room: 52.8 in. Rear hip room: 43.7 in. Luggage capacity: (rear seat up) 7.6 cu. ft. Front tread: 60.7 in. Rear tread: 60.6 in. Standard tires: P215/60R16.

Z28 Coupe: Wheelbase: 101.1 in. Overall length: 193.5 in. Height: 51.2 in. Width: 74.1 in. Front headroom: 37.2 in. Rear headroom: 35.3 in. Front legroom: 43 in. Rear legroom: 26.8 in. Front shoulder room: 57.4 in. Rear shoulder room: 55.8 in. Front hip room: 52.8 in. Rear hip room: 44.4 in. Luggage capacity: (rear seat up) 12.9 cu. ft.; (rear seat down) 32.8 cu. ft. Front tread: 60.7 in. Rear tread: 60.6 in. Standard tires: P235/55R16.

Z28 Convertible: Wheelbase: 101.1 in. Overall length: 193.5 in. Height: 51.8 in. Width: 74.1 in. Front headroom: 38 in. Rear headroom: 39 in. Front legroom: 43 in. Rear legroom: 26.8 in. Front shoulder room: 57.4 in. Rear shoulder room: 43.5 in. Front hip room: 52.8 in. Rear hip room: 43.7 in. Luggage capacity: (rear seat up) 7.6 cu. ft. Front tread: 60.7 in. Rear tread: 60.6 in. Standard tires: P235/55R16.

Camaro SS Coupe: Wheelbase: 101.1 in. Overall length: 193.2 in. Height: 51.3 in. Width: 74.1 in. Front headroom: 37.2 in. Rear headroom: 35.3 in. Front legroom: 43 in. Rear legroom: 26.8 in. Front shoulder room: 57.4 in. Rear shoulder room: 55.8 in. Front hip room: 52.8 in. Rear hip room: 44.4 in. Luggage capacity: (rear seat up) 12.9 cu. ft.; (rear seat down) 32.8 cu. ft. Front tread: 60.7 in. Rear tread: 60.6 in. Standard tires: P275/40ZR17 Goodyear Eagle F1 speed-rated on light-weight 17-in. wheels.

Camaro SS Convertible: Wheelbase: 101.1 in. Overall length: 193.2 in. Height: 52 in. Width: 74.1 in. Front headroom: 38 in. Rear headroom: 39 in. Front legroom: 43 in. Rear legroom: 26.8 in. Front shoulder room: 57.4 in. Rear shoulder room: 43.5 in. Front hip room: 52.8 in. Rear hip room: 43.7 in. Luggage capacity: (rear seat up) 7.6 cu. ft. Front tread: 60.7 in. Rear tread: 60.6 in. Standard tires: P275/40ZR17 Goodyear Eagle F1 speed-rated on lightweight 17-in. wheels.

TECHNICAL

Base Camaro: Transmission: Five-speed manual. Steering: rack and pinion. Turning diameter (curb-to-curb): 40.8 ft. Turning diameter (wall-to-wall): 42.6 ft. Front suspension: SLA/Coil over monotube gas shocks, tubular stabilizer bar with links. Rear suspension: Solid axle/torque arm, trailing arm, coil springs, track bar, monotube gas shocks and solid stabilizer bar with links. Firm Ride & Handling suspension standard. Brakes: Front disc/rear drum with antilock. Body construction: unibody. Fuel tank: 16.8 gal.

Z28: Transmission: Four-speed electronic overdrive transmission. Steering: rack and pinion. Turning diameter (curb-to-curb): 40.1 ft. Turning diameter (wall-to-wall): 41.1 ft. Front suspension: SLA/Coil over monotube gas shocks, and 30-mm tubular stabilizer bar with links. Rear suspension: Solid axle/torque arm, trailing arm, coil springs, track bar, monotube gas shocks and 19-mm solid stabilizer bar with links. Performance Ride & Handling suspension standard. Brakes: Four-wheel discs with antilock. Body construction: unibody. Fuel tank: 16.8 gal.

SS: Transmission: Six-speed manual. Steering: rack and pinion. Turning diameter (curb-to-curb): 40.1 ft. Turning diameter (wall to wall): 41.1 ft. Front suspension: Modified SLA/Coil over monotube gas shocks and tubular stabilizer bar with links. Rear suspension: Modified solid axle/torque arm, trailing arm, coil springs, track bar, monotube gas shocks and solid stabilizer bar with links. Brakes: Four-wheel discs with antilock. Body construction: unibody. Fuel tank: 16.8 gal. (Note: The Camaro SS convertible retained the stock Camaro Z28 suspension).

OPTIONS

U15 12-disc CD changer, requires ULO, not available with UNO ($595). GU5 3.23 performance axle ratio for Z28, requires QFZ or QLC, not available with MN6 ($300). MXO four-speed automatic transmission in base Camaro, includes second-gear start and 3.23 axle, not available with Y87 teamed with MM5 ($815). MN6 six-speed manual transmission in Z28, includes 3.42 axle, not available with GU5 (no cost). AG1 six-way power driver's seat in base Camaro ($270). NW9 acceleration slip regulation in Z28, QFC tires recommended, not available

with 1SF ($450). YF5 California emissions ($170). B84 color-keyed body side moldings on base coupe ($60). C49 electric rear window defogger on coupes, not available with R9W ($170). Leather seating surface, not available with 1SF ($499). New York, Massachusetts, Connecticut emissions ($170). Y87 performance handling package with MM5, includes sport steering ratio, dual outlet exhaust and limited-slip differential, requires QCB and N96 or N98, not available with 1SA or 1SD ($225). 1LE Z28 coupe performance package, includes special handling suspension system, larger stabilizer bars, stiffer springs, dual adjustable shock absorbers and bushings and power steering cooler ($1,175). 1SA base coupe preferred equipment group includes vehicle with standard equipment (no cost). 1SB base coupe preferred equipment package includes electronic speed control, remote hatch release, power door lock system and fog lamps ($565). 1SC base coupe preferred equipment package includes electronic speed control with resume feature, remote hatch lid release, power door lock system, fog lamps, power windows with river's side express down, dual electric remote-control sport mirrors, a leather-wrapped steering wheel, a leather gearshift knob, remote keyless entry, illuminated entry, remote hatch release and theft-deterrent alarm system ($1,231). 1SD base convertible preferred equipment group includes vehicle with standard equipment (no cost). 1SE base convertible preferred equipment group includes power door lock system, electronic speed control with resume, remote hatch release, fog lamps, power windows with driver's side express down, electric dual remote control sport mirrors, leather-wrapped steering wheel, leather gearshift knob, remote keyless entry, illuminated entry, panic alarm, remote hatch release, theft-deterrent alarm system, color-keyed lower body side moldings and rear carpet floor mats ($1,306). 1SF Z28 coupe preferred equipment group, includes vehicle with standard equipment (no cost). 1SG Z28 coupe preferred equipment group includes power door lock system, electronic speed control with resume, remote hatch release, fog lamps, power windows with driver's side express down, electric dual remote control sport mirrors, leather-wrapped steering wheel, leather gearshift knob, remote keyless entry, illuminated entry, panic alarm, remote hatch release, theft-deterrent alarm system, six-way power driver's seat, color-keyed lower body side moldings and rear carpet floor mats ($1,576). 1SH Z28 convertible preferred equipment group includes power door lock system, electronic speed control with resume, remote hatch release, fog lamps, power windows with driver's side express down, electric dual remote control sport mirrors, leather-wrapped steering wheel, leather gearshift knob, remote keyless entry, illuminated entry, panic alarm, remote hatch release, theft-deterrent alarm system, six-way power driver's seat, color-keyed lower body side moldings and rear carpet floor mats (no cost). ULO AM/FM stereo with Automatic Tone Control and cassette in coupes, includes digital clock, TheftLock, speed-compensated volume, 200-watt amplifier and eight speakers ($350). ULO AM/FM stereo with Automatic Tone Control and cassette in convertibles, includes digital clock, TheftLock, speed-compensated volume, 200-watt amplifier and eight speakers ($215). UNO AM/FM stereo with

Automatic Tone Control and CD in convertibles, includes digital clock, TheftLock, speed-compensated volume, 200-watt amplifier and eight speakers ($315). UNO AM/FM stereo with Automatic Tone Control and CD in coupes, includes digital clock, TheftLock, speed-compensated volume, 200-watt amplifier and eight speakers ($450). B35 rear carpet floor mats in base coupe ($15). R9W rear window defogger not desired in coupes (no cost). AUO remote keyless entry in base coupe, includes illuminated entry, theft-deterrent alarm system, panic alarm and remote hatch release ($225). Y3F Sport Appearance package for base Camaro, includes rocker and rear fascia moldings, 16-in. aluminum wheels and P235/55R15 all-season black sidewall tires ($1,755). Y3F Sport Appearance package for Z28 includes rocker moldings, front fascia moldings, rear fascia moldings, spoiler extension, 16-in. aluminum wheels and P235/55R16 all-season black sidewall tires ($1,348). WU8 SS performance and appearance package for Z28, includes 320-hp engine, forced air induction hood, a unique spoiler, 17-in. aluminum wheels, P275/40ZR17 Goodyear Eagle F1 tires, high performance ride & handling package and SS badging ($3,500). QCB P235/55R16 black sidewall tires on base Camaros ($132). QFZ P245/50ZR16 black sidewall all-season performance tires on Z28s ($225). QLC P245/50ZR16 black sidewall performance tires on Z28s ($225). CC1 transparent removable roof panels, includes locks, lockable stowage and sun shade ($995). N96 16-in. aluminum wheels on base Camaro ($275). N98 16-in chrome aluminum wheels on base Camaros ($775). N98 16-in. chrome aluminum wheels on Camaro Z28s ($500).

HISTORICAL FOOTNOTES

Kurt L. Ritter was the general manager of marketing for Chevrolet Motor Division in 2000. The Camaro's model-year sales were 41,962 units. Calendar-year sales were 42,131. Domestic model-year production was 41,825 coupes and 3,636 convertibles for a total of 45,461 units. The Ste. Therese, Quebec, plant built all of these cars (and all 31,826 Firebirds). Of the Camaros built, 69.3 percent had automatic transmission, 10.9 percent had a five-speed manual transmission, 19.8 percent had a six-speed manual transmission, 55.1 percent had a 3.8-liter SFI V-6, 44.9 percent had a 5.7-liter MFI V-8, 100 percent had power steering, 100 percent had four-wheel disc brakes with ABS, 50 percent had traction control, 100 percent had automatic headlamps (DRLs), 44.9 percent had a limited-slip differential, 100 percent had steel-belted radial tires, 84 percent had power door locks, 84 percent had power windows, 100 percent had reclining bucket seats, 61.1 percent had a power seats, 41 percent had leather seats, 100 percent had dual front airbags, 100 percent had tilt steering, 100 percent had tinted glass, 100 percent had manual air conditioning, 88.1 percent had cruise control, 100 percent had delay windshield wipers, 18.1 percent had a ETR stereo cassette player, 63 percent had a name brand sound system with CD, 68.5 percent had another brand CD, 82.7 percent had an electric rear window defogger, 24 percent had a manual remote-control left-hand outside rearview mirror, 76 percent had power rearview mirrors, 27.8 percent had a power right-hand rearview mirror, 10.8 percent had chrome styled wheels, 79.6 percent had aluminum styled wheels, 78 percent had remote keyless entry, 78 percent had an anti-theft device and 58 percent had T-tops. A total of 42,006 new Camaros were registered in the U.S. during calendar year 2000.

Camaro

Despite rumors that it would be disappearing soon, the 2001 Camaro apeared in the Chevrolet lineup.

By early 2001, rumors that the Camaro was getting near the end of the line were flying and they ultimately proved to be true. Sales of Chevrolet's hot sporty car were on the decline and it seemed that only contracts with Canadian autoworkers at the Camaro assembly plant would keep the car alive through 2002.

With GM planning to discontinue the nameplate after 2002, there was little motivation to make major product changes. A new "de-contented" Z28 package was introduced and a few alterations in color schemes were made. The latter changes included the addition of a new Sunset Orange Metallic exterior color and the discontinuation of Sebring Silver Metallic. A total of 29,009 Camaros were built for worldwide distribution this year. That included 5,328 ragtops and 6,332 Camaro SS models.

On September 26 (the same day the Camaro was introduced in 1967), national newspapers announced that GM would stop making Camaros and Firebirds. "GM loses some old muscle," said the headline in *The Detroit News* that morning.

I.D. DATA

Chevrolets again had a 17-symbol vehicle identification number (VIN) on the upper left surface of the instrument panel, visible through the windshield. The first symbol identifies country of origin: 2=Canada. The second symbol identifies the manufacturer: G=General Motors. The third symbol indicates make: 1=Chevrolet, 7=GM of Canada. The fourth and fifth symbols indicated the car line and series: F/P=Camaro Sport Coupe and Convertible. The sixth symbol indicated body type: 2=two-door coupe style 87 and 3=two-door convertible style 67. The seventh symbol indicated the type of restraint system: 1=active manual belts, 2=active manual belts with driver and passenger front airbags, 3=active manual belts with driver airbag, 4=active manual belts with driver and passenger front and side airbags,

5=active manual belts with driver and passenger front and driver side airbags, 6=active manual belts with driver and passenger airbags and automatic passenger sensor and 7=active manual belts with driver/passenger front airbags and rear passenger side airbags. The eighth symbol indicates the engine type: K=RPO L36 3.8-liter (231-cid) V-6 with Multiport Fuel Injection, G=RPO LS1 5.7-liter (350-cid) V-8 with SFI. The ninth symbol is a check digit. The 10th symbol indicates model year: 1=2001. The 11th symbol indicates the assembly plant: 2=Ste. Therese, Quebec (Canada).

COLORS

11U=Light Pewter Metallic, 41U=Onyx Black, 81U=Bright Rally Red, 10U=Artic White, 28U=Navy Blue Metallic, 44U=Monterey Maroon Metallic, 71U=Sunset Orange Metallic and 79U=Mystic Teal Metallic.

CAMARO — SERIES 1F — V-6

The base model got a new 16-in. chrome wheels option, re-valved shock absorbers and new Sunset Orange Metallic paint choice. Standard equipment for the base Camaro coupe included the 3.8-liter 200-hp V-6, rear-wheel drive, 16-in. steel wheel rims, P215/60R16 tires, a Space-Saver spare tire on a steel spare wheel, full wheel covers, front independent suspension, front and rear stabilizer bars, front disc/rear drum ABS brakes, child seat anchors, an anti-theft system with an engine immobilizer, daytime running lights, intermittent windshield wipers, four-passenger total seating, cloth-trimmed front bucket seats, cloth-trimmed rear bucket-style seats, an AM/FM cassette stereo, tilt-adjustable power steering, remote control exterior mirrors, front and rear cupholders, front door pockets, air conditioning, front reading lights, dual visor-vanity mirrors, front floor mats, a tachometer, a clock and a rear spoiler. In addition to or in place of the standard equipment for the base coupe, the base convertible included front fog lights, a power convertible roof, a glass rear window, a rear window defogger, remote power door locks, one-touch power windows, a Bose premium brand 500-watts stereo system with eight speakers, cruise control, audio and cruise control buttons on the steering wheel, remote control driver and passenger mirrors, a remote trunk release, a leather-wrapped steering wheel, a leather-trimmed gearshift knob, front floor mats and rear floor mats.

Model Number	Body/Style Number	Body Type & Seating	Factory Price	Shipping Weight	Production Total
F/P	87	2d coupe-4P	$17,880	3,306 lbs.	Note 1
F/P	67	2d convertible-4P	$25,175	3,500 lbs.	Note 2

Note 1: Total North American model-year production of Camaro and Camaro Z28 coupes was 23,681.
Note 2: Total North American model-year production of Camaro and Camaro Z28 convertibles was 5,328.

CAMARO Z28 — SERIES 1F — V-8

For 2001 the Z28 had the same changes as the base model (re-valved shocks, Sunset Orange Metallic paint choice and 16-in. chrome wheel option), plus more horsepower to help it compete better with the rival Mustang. Its 5.7-liter LS1 V-8 churned out 310 hp at 5200 rpm, 50 more than the Mustang's 5.0-liter V-8. A four-speed automatic transmission was standard, but a six-speed manual transmission was a no-cost option. Standard equipment for the Camaro Z28 coupe included the LS1 V-8, four-speed automatic transmission, rear-wheel drive, 16-in. alloys, P235/55R16 tires, a Space-Saver spare tire on a steel spare wheel, full wheel covers, front independent suspension, front and rear stabilizer bars, front disc/rear drum ABS brakes, child seat anchors, an anti-theft system, an engine immobilizer, daytime running lights, intermittent windshield wipers, four-passenger total seating, cloth-trimmed front bucket seats, cloth-trimmed rear bucket-style seats, power outside rearview mirrors, a Bose premium brand 500-watts stereo system with eight speakers, tilt-adjustable power steering, remote control exterior mirrors, front and rear cupholders, front door pockets, air conditioning, front reading lights, dual visor-vanity mirrors, front floor mats, a tachometer, a clock and a rear spoiler. In addition to or in place of the standard equipment for the Z28 coupe, the Z28 convertible included front fog lights, a power convertible roof, a glass rear window, a rear window defogger, remote power door locks, 1-touch power windows, cruise control, audio and cruise control buttons on the steering wheel, remote control driver and passenger mirrors, a remote trunk release, a 6-way power driver's seat, a leather-wrapped steering wheel, a leather-trimmed gear shift knob, front floor mats and rear floor mats.

Model Number	Body/Style Number	Body Type & Seating	Factory Price	Shipping Weight	Production Total
F/P+Z28	87	2d coupe-4P	$22,450	3,439 lbs.	Note 3
F/P+Z28	67	2d convertible-4P	$29,555	3,574 lbs.	Note 4

Note 3: Total North American model-year production of Camaro and Camaro Z28 coupes was 23,681.
Note 4: Total North American model-year production of Camaro and Camaro Z28 convertibles was 5,328.
Note 5: Total North American production of Z28s was 6,320 coupes and convertibles.

A clock and a tachometer were among the standard features found inside the 2001 Camaros.

combined.

CAMARO SS — SERIES 1F — V-8

Camaro buyers who checked off the SS performance option got a real muscle car that delivered 325 hp thanks to its functional hood scoop, forced-air induction system and big, fat exhausts. The SS ran from 0 to 60 mph in a tad over 5 seconds and could do the quarter mile in 13.5 seconds. The complete contents of this WU8 SS Performance/Appearance package included the 325-hp engine, the forced-air induction hood, a specific SS spoiler, 17-in. aluminum wheels, P275/40ZR17 Goodyear Eagle F1 tires, a high-performance ride and handling package, a power steering cooler, a low-restriction dual outlet exhaust system and SS badging. The package also included a 3.23:1 ratio rear axle with the MX0 automatic transmission or a 3.42:1 ratio rear axle with the MN6 six-speed manual transmission. It was available for Z28s, but was not available with the Y3F Sport Appearance package.

Model Number	Body/Style Number	Body Type & Seating	Factory Price	Shipping Weight	Production Total
F/P+Z28	87	2d coupe-4P	$26,400	—	5,468
F/P+Z28	67	2d convertible-4P	$33,505	—	864

ENGINE

L36 V-6: 60-degree, overhead-valve V-6. Cast-iron block and head. Bore & stroke: 3.80 x 3.40. Displacement: 231 cid (3.8 liters). Compression ratio: 9.4:1. Brake horsepower: 200 at 5200 rpm. Torque: 225 lbs.-ft. at 4000 rpm. Hydraulic valve lifters. Induction system: Sequential fuel injection. VIN Code K.

LS1 V-8: Overhead valve. Cast-aluminum block and head. Bore & stroke: 3.90 x 3.62 in. Displacement: 346 cid (5.7 liters). Compression ratio: 10.1:1. Brake horsepower: 310 at 5200 rpm. Torque: 340 lbs.-ft. at 4000 rpm. Hydraulic valve lifters. Sequential fuel injection. Standard in Z28. VIN Code G.

LS1 V-8: Overhead valve. Cast-aluminum block and head. Bore & stroke: 3.90 x 3.62 in. Displacement: 346 cid (5.7 liters). Brake horsepower: 325. Torque: 350 lbs.-ft. at 4000 rpm. Hydraulic valve lifters. Sequential fuel injection. Performance exhaust system. Optional in SS. VIN Code G.

CHASSIS

Base Camaro Coupe: Wheelbase: 101.1 in. Overall length: 193.2 in. Height: 51.3 in. Width: 74.1 in. Front headroom: 37.2 in. Rear headroom: 35.3 in. Front legroom: 43 in. Rear legroom: 26.8 in. Front shoulder room: 57.4 in. Rear shoulder room: 55.8 in. Front hip room: 52.8 in. Rear hip room: 44.4 in. Luggage capacity: (rear seat up) 12.9 cu. ft.; (rear seat down) 32.8 cu. ft. Front tread: 60.7 in. Rear tread: 60.6 in. Standard tires: P215/60SR16.

Base Camaro Convertible: Wheelbase: 101.1 in. Overall length: 193.2 in. Height: 52 in. Width: 74.1 in. Front headroom: 38 in. Rear headroom: 39 in. Front legroom: 43 in. Rear legroom: 26.8 in. Front shoulder room: 57.4 in. Rear shoulder room: 43.5 in. Front hip room: 52.8 in. Rear hip room: 43.7 in. Luggage capacity: (rear seat up) 7.6 cu. ft. Front tread: 60.7 in. Rear tread: 60.6 in. Standard tires: P215/60R16.

Z28 Coupe: Wheelbase: 101.1 in. Overall length: 193.2 in. Height: 51.3 in. Width: 74.1 in. Front headroom: 37.2 in. Rear headroom: 35.3 in. Front legroom: 43 in. Rear legroom: 26.8 in. Front shoulder room: 57.4 in. Rear shoulder room: 55.8 in. Front hip room: 52.8 in. Rear hip room: 44.4 in. Luggage capacity: (rear seat up) 12.9 cu. ft.; (rear seat down) 32.8 cu. ft. Front tread: 60.7 in. Rear tread: 60.6 in. Standard tires: P235/55R16.

Z28 Convertible: Wheelbase: 101.1 in. Overall length: 193.2 in. Height: 52 in. Width: 74.1 in. Front headroom: 38 in. Rear headroom: 39 in. Front legroom: 43 in. Rear legroom: 26.8 in. Front shoulder room: 57.4 in. Rear shoulder room: 43.5 in. Front hip room: 52.8 in. Rear hip room: 43.7 in. Luggage capacity: (rear seat up) 7.6 cu. ft. Front tread: 60.7 in. Rear tread: 60.6 in. Standard tires: P235/55R16.

Camaro SS Coupe: Wheelbase: 101.1 in. Overall length: 193.2 in. Height: 51.3 in. Width: 74.1 in. Front headroom: 37.2 in. Rear headroom: 35.3 in. Front legroom: 43 in. Rear legroom: 26.8 in. Front shoulder room: 57.4 in. Rear shoulder room: 55.8 in. Front hip

A rear deck lid spoiler was used to set off the sporty looks of all the 2001 Camaros.

room: 52.8 in. Rear hip room: 44.4 in. Luggage capacity: (rear seat up) 12.9 cu. ft.; (rear seat down) 32.8 cu. ft. Front tread: 60.7 in. Rear tread: 60.6 in. Standard tires: P275/40ZR17 Goodyear Eagle F1 speed-rated on lightweight 17-in. wheels.

Camaro SS Convertible: Wheelbase: 101.1 in. Overall length: 193.2 in. Height: 52 in. Width: 74.1 in. Front headroom: 38 in. Rear headroom: 39 in. Front legroom: 43 in. Rear legroom: 26.8 in. Front shoulder room: 57.4 in. Rear shoulder room: 43.5 in. Front hip room: 52.8 in. Rear hip room: 43.7 in. Luggage capacity: (rear seat up) 7.6 cu. ft. Front tread: 60.7 in. Rear tread: 60.6 in. Standard tires: P275/40ZR17 Goodyear Eagle F1 speed-rated on lightweight 17-in. wheels.

TECHNICAL

Base Camaro: Transmission: Five-speed manual. Steering: rack and pinion. Front suspension: SLA/Coil over monotube gas shocks, tubular stabilizer bar with links. Rear suspension: Solid axle/torque arm, trailing arm, coil springs, track bar, monotube gas shocks and solid stabilizer bar with links. Firm Ride & Handling suspension standard. Brakes: Front disc/rear drum with anti-lock. Body construction: unibody. Fuel tank: 16.8 gal.

Z28: Transmission: Four-speed electronic overdrive transmission. Steering: rack and pinion. Front suspension: SLA/Coil over monotube gas shocks, and 30-mm tubular stabilizer bar with links. Rear suspension: Solid axle/torque arm, trailing arm, coil springs, track bar, monotube gas shocks and 19-mm solid stabilizer bar with links. Performance Ride & Handling suspension standard. Brakes: Four-wheel discs with anti-lock. Body construction: unibody. Fuel tank: 16.8 gal.

SS: Transmission: Six-speed manual. Steering: rack and pinion. Front suspension: Modified SLA/Coil over monotube gas shocks and tubular stabilizer bar with links. Rear suspension: Modified solid axle/torque arm, trailing arm, coil springs, track bar, monotube gas shocks and solid stabilizer bar with links. Brakes: Four-wheel discs with anti-lock. Body construction: unibody. Fuel tank: 16.8 gal. (Note: The Camaro SS convertible retained the stock Camaro Z28 suspension).

OPTIONS

1SA convertible with base equipment group, includes vehicle with standard equipment (no cost). 1SA hatchback base equipment group, includes vehicle with standard equipment; not available with 1SB (no cost). 1SB hatchback preferred equipment group 1 includes remote keyless entry, theft-deterrent alarm system, cruise control, fog lights, twin electric remote-control sport mirrors, power door locks, power windows with driver's side express down feature and remote hatch release; not available with 1SA ($1,170). 1SB convertible preferred equipment group 1, includes vehicle with standard equipment (no cost). 1SC Z28 hatchback preferred equipment group 2, includes vehicle with standard equipment; not available with 1SD (no cost). 1SD Z28 hatchback preferred equipment group 1 includes remote keyless entry, theft-deterrent alarm system, electronic cruise control, twin electric remote-control sport mirrors, power door locks, power windows with driver's side express down feature, remote hatch release; power six-way driver's seat, leather-wrapped steering wheel with redundant radio controls, leather-trimmed gear shift knob, leather-wrapped parking brake handle, rear carpeted floor mats and color-keyed body side moldings; not available with 1SC ($1,715). AG1 six-way power driver's seat ($270). AR9 leather accent bucket seats ($500). B35 rear carpet mats ($35). B84 body-color body side moldings on hatchback ($60). BBS Hurst performance shift linkage for Z28, includes short-throw shift linkage, requires six-speed manual transmission ($325). C49 hatchback rear window defogger ($170). CC1 transparent removable hatch roof panels, includes locks, lockable storage provisions and sunshades ($995). FE9 federal emissions requirements (no cost). GU5 3.23:1 ratio performance rear axle; requires MX0 automatic transmission and QLC or QFZ tires ($300). MN6 six-speed manual transmission in Z28, includes "skip-shift" feature (no cost). MX0 four-speed overdrive automatic transmission ($815). N96 16-in. silver cast-aluminum wheels ($275). NB8 California and Northeast states emissions override, requires FE9 (no cost). NC7 federal emissions override, requires YF5 or NG1 (no cost). NG1 Northeast states emissions override (no cost). NW9 traction control ($250). PW7 16-in. chrome cast-aluminum wheels on base Camaro, requires QCB tires ($975). PW7 16-in. chrome cast-aluminum wheels on Camaro Z28; not available with WU8 Camaro SS package ($725). QCB P235/55R16 black sidewall tires for base Camaro, requires N96 or PW7 wheels ($135). P245/50ZR16 Goodyear Eagle RSA all-season performance tires on Z28, recommended with NW9 traction control; not available with WU8 SS package ($225). P245/50ZR16 Goodyear Eagle GS-C performance tires on Z28; not available with WU8 SS package ($225). New Jersey cost surcharge ($93 to dealer no cost to buyer). U1S trunk-mounted 12-disc CD changer in base convertible and all Z28s, requires UNO ($595). U1S trunk-mounted 12-disc CD changer in base coupe, requires ULO or UNO ($595). UK3 leather-wrapped steering wheel in base coupe, includes leather-wrapped steering wheel rim, redundant radio controls, leather-trimmed gear shift knob and leather-wrapped parking brake handle, requires 1SB and ULO or UNO ($170). UK3 leather-wrapped steering wheel in Z28 coupe, includes leather-wrapped steering wheel rim, redundant radio controls, leather-trimmed gear shift knob and leather-wrapped parking brake handle, requires 1SC and included in 1SD ($170). ULO Monsoon 500-watts sound system in base coupe, includes Monsoon 500-watt sound system, ETR AM/FM stereo radio with seek-and-scan, digital clock, Auto Tone Control, cassette player, TheftLock, speed-compensated volume, eight speakers and auxiliary amplifier ($350). UNO Monsoon 500-watts sound system with CD player in base convertible and all Z28s, includes Monsoon 500-watt sound system, ETR AM/FM stereo radio with seek-and-scan, digital clock, Auto Tone Control, CD player, TheftLock, speed compensated volume, eight speakers and auxiliary amplifier ($100). UNO Monsoon 500-watts sound system with CD player in base coupe, includes Monsoon 500-watt sound system, ETR AM/FM stereo radio with seek-and-scan, digital clock, auto-tone control, CD player, TheftLock, speed-compensated volume, eight speakers and auxiliary amplifier ($450). V12 power steering cooler in Z28 ($100). WU8 SS Performance-/Appearance package for Z28, includes 325-hp engine, forced-air induction hood, a specific SS spoiler, 17-in. aluminum wheels, P275/40ZR17 Goodyear Eagle F1 tires, a high-performance ride and handling package, a power steering cooler, a low-restriction dual outlet exhaust system, SS badging, a 3.23:1 ratio rear axle with the MX0 automatic transmission or a 3.42:1 ratio rear axle with the MN6 six-speed manual transmission; available for Z28s, but was not available with Y3F Sport Appearance package ($3,950). Y38 RS package, for base coupe, includes dual silver or black Heritage stripes on hood, roof and deck lid, RS interior and exterior badging and Z28-type exhaust system with silver painted dual outlets; not available with Y87 or Y3F (no cost). Y3F Sport Appearance package for base Camaros, includes front fascia extension, rocker panel moldings, spoiler extension, rear fascia molding, 16-in. silver cast-aluminum wheels and P235/55R16 black sidewall ties; not available with Y3B ($1,755). Y3F Sport Appearance package for Z28s, includes front fascia extension, rocker panel moldings, spoiler extension and rear fascia molding; not available with WU8 ($1,348). Y87 Performance Handling package for base convertible, includes Zexel Torsen limited-slip differential, dual outlet exhausts and sport steering ratio, requires QCB and N96 ($275). Y87 Performance Handling package for base coupe, includes Zexel Torsen limited-slip differential, dual outlet exhausts and sport steering ratio, requires 1SB, QCB and N96; not available with Y3B ($275). YF5 California emissions requirements (no cost). ($275)

HISTORICAL FOOTNOTES

The 2001 model year saw a total of 29,009 Camaros built for distribution throughout the world. This included 12,652 cars with the LS1 V-8 and 16,357 cars with the 3800 V-6. A total of 1,697 of the V-6 Camaros had the Y87 package. A total of 398 Camaros were ordered with the Y3B SLP Rally Sport package. According to Camaro expert Tony Hossain, there was little interest among collectors and enthusiasts in the RS package, since they were more excited about the SS model with SLP options plus the 35th Anniversary SS option that was due in 2002. On Sept. 26, 2001, General Motors surprised no one by announcing that it would stop making, at least for the time being, the Chevrolet Camaro and Pontiac Firebird. GM also said that it would shut down the Canadian plant where both cars were made and that it would take a $300 million pretax charge to its earnings as a result of the move, reducing earnings by 35 cents a share after taxes in the third quarter. Industry analysts saw the discontinuation of the F-car as necessary and overdue. "It was long in coming," Rod Lache, an analyst at Deutsche Bank, told *The New York Times*. He said demand for Camaros and Firebirds had fallen so much that the plant that produced them, in Ste. Therese, Quebec, was making less than a third of the vehicles it was able to produce. But Camaro enthusiasts saw it as a sad turn of events in Camaro history. GM said that the 1,100 blue-collar workers at the Canadian plant (plus 300 that had already been laid off) would be eligible for early retirement or that they could stay on the payroll and keep their benefits for up to three years. *USA Today* reported that Camaro sales were down 25 percent through August 2001 (and Firebird sales were down 28 percent). Despite a write-in campaign to GM, Camaro owners weren't surprised by the announcement. "Naturally, we are going to miss it," Gene Forguson, president of Classic Camaro of Central Florida, commented in *USA Today*. "I think they could have taken it to greater heights. But there are millions out there to restore." GM said it would offer a 35th Anniversary Edition Camaro and Collector Edition Firebird Trans Am in 2002. In addition, the company made comments that left the door open for the return of a totally revised F-car at a later date.

Camaro

A special 2002 limited edition 35th Anniversary SS was produced to mark the Camaro's farewell year.

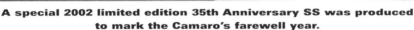

In the fall of 2001, Chevrolet Motor Division announced that production of the Camaro would end after the 2002 model year, although the gate was left open for the development of a new type of Camaro sometime in the future.

Returning this year was Sebring Silver Metallic finish. A new limited-edition Camaro 35th Anniversary package was introduced for cars with the SS package. Its special features included Rally Red paint, unique badging and striping, a unique grille and tail panel appliqué, special 17-in. wheels, embroidery on the front seat headrests and front floor mats and a luxurious Ebony leather interior.

The second-gear start feature was eliminated on Camaro base coupes and convertibles equipped with the V-6 engine and automatic transmission. An eight-speaker Monsoon stereo system became standard and convertibles with a manual trunk got a new entrapment release handle. P245/55R16 tires were made standard on Z28 coupes and convertibles, while both base models got P235/55R16 tires.

I.D. DATA

Chevrolets again had a 17-symbol vehicle identification number (VIN) on the upper left surface of the instrument panel, visible through the windshield. The first symbol identifies country of origin: 2=Canada. The second symbol identifies the manufacturer: G=General Motors. The third symbol indicates make: 1=Chevrolet, 7=GM of Canada. The fourth and fifth symbols indicated the car line and series: F/P=Camaro Sport Coupe and Convertible. The sixth symbol indicated body type: 2=two-door coupe style 87 and 3=two-door convertible style 67. The seventh symbol indicated the type of restraint system: 1=active manual belts, 2=active manu-

al belts with driver and passenger front airbags, 3=active manual belts with driver airbag, 4=active manual belts with driver and passenger front and side airbags, 5=active manual belts with driver and passenger front and driver side airbags, 6=active manual belts with driver and passenger airbags and automatic passenger sensor and 7=active manual belts with driver/passenger front airbags and rear passenger side airbags. The eighth symbol indicates the engine type: K=RPO L36 3.8-liter (231-cid) V-6 with Multiport Fuel Injection, G=RPO LS1 5.7-liter (350-cid) V-8 with SFI. The ninth symbol is a check digit. The 10th symbol indicates model year: 2=2002. The 11th symbol indicates the assembly plant: 2=Ste. Therese, Quebec (Canada).

COLORS

Navy Blue Metallic, Monterey Maroon Metallic (not available on SS), Onyx Black, Light Pewter Metallic, Sunset Orange Metallic, Arctic White, Bright Rally Red, Sebring Metallic.

CAMARO — SERIES 1F — V-6

Standard equipment for the base Camaro coupe included the 3.8-liter 200-hp V-6, a five-speed manual transmission, rear-wheel drive, 16-in. aluminum wheels, P235/55R16 tires, a Space-Saver spare tire on a steel spare wheel, full wheel covers, front independent suspension, front and rear stabilizer bars, ventilated front disc/solid rear disc ABS brakes, child seat anchors, an anti-theft system, an engine immobilizer, intermittent windshield wipers, four-passenger total seating, cloth-trimmed front bucket seats, cloth-trimmed rear bucket-style folding seats, power outside rearview mirrors, an AM/FM CD stereo, tilt-adjustable power steering, front and rear cupholders, front door pockets, a front 12-volt power outlet, a front console with storage, air conditioning, front reading lights, dual visor-vanity mirrors, front and rear floor mats, a tachometer and a clock. In addition to or in place of the standard equipment for the base coupe, the base convertible included a remote anti-theft system, front fog lights, a power convertible roof, a glass rear window, a rear window defogger, remote power door locks, one-touch power windows, Monsoon premium brand 500-watts stereo system with eight speakers, cruise control, audio and cruise control buttons on the steering wheel, a remote trunk release, a leather-wrapped steering wheel and a leather-trimmed gearshift knob.

Model Number	Body/Style Number	Body Type & Seating	Factory Price	Shipping Weight	Production Total
F/P	87	2d coupe-4P	$18,655	3,306 lbs.	Note 1
F/P	67	2d convertible-4P	$26,650	3,500 lbs.	Note 1

Note 1: Production unavailable at publication date.

CAMARO Z28 — SERIES 1F/P — V-8

Standard equipment for the base Camaro coupe included the 5.7-liter 310-hp V-8, a four-speed automatic transmission, rear-wheel drive, 16-in. aluminum wheels, P245/50ZR16 tires, a Space-Saver spare tire on a steel spare wheel, full wheel covers, front independent suspension, front and rear stabilizer bars, ventilated front disc/solid rear disc ABS brakes, child seat anchors, an anti-theft system, an engine immobilizer, intermittent windshield wipers, four-passenger total seating, cloth-trimmed front bucket seats, cloth-trimmed rear bucket-style folding seats, power outside rearview mirrors, a Monsoon premium AM/FM cassette stereo with eight speakers, tilt-adjustable power steering, a leather-wrapped steering wheel, a leather-trimmed gearshift knob, front and rear cupholders, front door pockets, a front 12-volt power outlet, a front console with storage, air conditioning, front reading lights, dual visor-vanity mirrors, front and rear floor mats, a tachometer and a clock. Standard equipment for the base Z28 convertible also included a remote anti-theft system, front fog lights, a power convertible roof, a glass rear window, a rear window defogger, remote power door locks, one-touch power

windows, cruise control, audio and cruise control buttons on the steering wheel, a remote trunk release, P245/50ZR16 tires, a six-way power driver's seat, a height-adjustable driver's seat and a rear spoiler.

Model Number	Body/Style Number	Body Type & Seating	Factory Price	Shipping Weight	Production Total
F/P+Z28	87	2d coupe-4P	$23,070	3,439 lbs.	Note 2
F/P+Z28	67	2d convertible-4P	$30,165	3,574 lbs.	Note 2

Note 2: Production unavailable at publication date.

CAMARO SS — SERIES 1F — V-8

At the 2002 Chicago Auto Show the "final" Camaro SS received heavy promotion. The code WU8 SS Performance and Appearance package was a $3,625 option for the Z28. The contents of this option package included a 5.7-liter 325-hp V-8, a forced-air induction hood, a specific SS spoiler, 17-in. aluminum wheels, P275/40ZR17 Goodyear Eagle F1 tires, a high-performance ride and handling package, a power steering cooler, a low-restriction dual outlet exhaust system and SS badging. The package also included a 3.23:1 ratio rear axle with the MX0 automatic transmission or a 3.42:1 ratio rear axle with the MN6 six-speed manual transmission. It was available for Z28s, but was not available with the Y3F Sport Appearance package. A special limited-edition 35th anniversary model was the big news for Camaro SS fans in 2002. It was actually a $2,500 option for the Camaro Z28 coupe and convertible with the SS package only.

Model Number	Body/Style Number	Body Type & Seating	Factory Price	Shipping Weight	Production Total
F/P+Z28	87	2d coupe-4P	$26,695	—	Note 3
F/P+Z28	67	2d convertible-4P	$33,790	—	Note 3

Note 3: Production unavailable at publication date.

ENGINE

L36 V-6: 60-degree, overhead-valve V-6. Cast-iron block and head. Bore & stroke: 3.80 x 3.40. Displacement: 231 cid (3.8 liters). Compression ratio: 9.4:1. Brake horsepower: 200 at 5200 rpm. Torque: 225 lbs.-ft. at 4000 rpm. Hydraulic valve lifters. Induction system: Sequential fuel injection. VIN Code K.

GM and SLP Engineering again teamed up to build the 2002 Camaro SS. This coupe was loaded with options, produced 325 hp and carried a window price of $35,515.

Erick Lieder photo

The SS option package included a 5.7-liter 325-hp V-8.

LS1 V-8: Overhead valve. Cast-aluminum block and head. Bore & stroke: 3.90 x 3.62 in. Displacement: 346 cid (5.7 liters). Compression ratio: 10.1:1. Brake horsepower: 310 at 5200 rpm. Torque: 340 lbs.-ft. at 4000 rpm. Hydraulic valve lifters. Sequential fuel injection. Standard in Z28. VIN Code G.

LS1 V-8: Overhead valve. Cast-aluminum block and head. Bore & stroke: 3.90 x 3.62 in. Displacement: 346 cid (5.7 liters). Brake horsepower: 325. Torque: 350 lbs.-ft. at 4000 rpm. Hydraulic valve lifters. Sequential fuel injection. Performance exhaust system. Optional in SS. VIN Code G.

CHASSIS

Base Camaro Coupe: Wheelbase: 101.1 in. Overall length: 193.2 in. Height: 51.3 in.; Width: 74.1 in. Front headroom: 37.2 in. Rear headroom: 35.3 in. Front legroom: 43.0 in. Rear legroom: 26.8 in. Front shoulder room: 57.4 in. Rear shoulder room: 55.8 in. Front hip room: 52.8 in. Rear hip room: 44.4 in. Luggage capacity: (rear seat up) 12.9 cu. ft.; (rear seat down) 32.8 cu. ft. Front tread: 60.7 in. Rear tread: 60.6 in. Standard tires: P235/55R16.

Base Camaro Convertible: Wheelbase: 101.1 in. Overall length: 193.2 in. Height: 52 in.; Width: 74.1 in. Front headroom: 38 in. Rear headroom: 39 in. Front legroom: 43 in. Rear legroom: 26.8 in. Front shoulder room: 57.4 in. Rear shoulder room: 43.5 in. Front hip room: 52.8 in. Rear hip room: 43.7 in. Luggage capacity: (rear seat up) 7.6 cu. ft. Front tread: 60.7 in. Rear tread: 60.6 in. Standard tires: P235/55R16.

Z28 Coupe: Wheelbase: 101.1 in. Overall length: 193.2 in. Height: 51.3 in.; Width: 74.1 in. Front headroom: 37.2 in. Rear headroom: 35.3 in. Front legroom: 43 in. Rear legroom: 26.8 in. Front shoulder room: 57.4 in. Rear shoulder room: 55.8 in. Front hip room: 52.8 in. Rear hip room: 44.4 in. Luggage capacity: (rear seat up) 12.9 cu. ft.; (rear seat down) 32.8 cu. ft. Front tread: 60.7 in. Rear tread: 60.6 in. Standard tires: P245/55ZR16.

Z28 Convertible: Wheelbase: 101.1 in. Overall length: 193.2 in. Height: 52 in.; Width: 74.1 in. Front headroom: 38 in. Rear headroom: 39 in. Front legroom: 43 in. Rear legroom: 26.8 in. Front shoulder room: 57.4 in. Rear shoulder room: 43.5 in. Front hip room: 52.8 in. Rear hip room: 43.7 in. Luggage capacity: (rear seat up) 7.6 cu. ft. Front tread: 60.7 in. Rear tread: 60.6 in. Standard tires: P245/50ZR16.

Camaro SS Coupe: Wheelbase: 101.1 in. Overall length: 193.2 in. Height: 51.3 in.; Width: 74.1 in. Front headroom: 37.2 in. Rear headroom: 35.3 in. Front legroom: 43 in. Rear legroom: 26.8 in. Front shoulder room: 57.4 in. Rear shoulder room: 55.8 in. Front hip room: 52.8 in. Rear hip room: 44.4 in. Luggage capacity: (rear seat up) 12.9 cu. ft.; (rear seat down) 32.8 cu. ft. Front tread: 60.7 in. Rear tread: 60.6 in. Standard tires: P275/40ZR17 Goodyear Eagle F1 speed-rated on lightweight 17-in. wheels.

Camaro SS Convertible: Wheelbase: 101.1 in. Overall length: 193.2 in. Height: 52 in.; Width: 74.1 in. Front headroom: 38 in. Rear headroom: 39 in. Front legroom: 43 in. Rear legroom: 26.8 in. Front shoulder room: 57.4 in. Rear shoulder room: 43.5 in. Front hip room: 52.8 in. Rear hip room: 43.7 in. Luggage capacity: (rear seat up) 7.6 cu. ft. Front tread: 60.7 in. Rear tread: 60.6 in. Standard tires: P275/40ZR17 Goodyear Eagle F1 speed-rated on lightweight 17-in. wheels.

TECHNICAL

Base Camaro: Transmission: Five-speed manual. Steering: rack and pinion. Front suspension: SLA/Coil over monotube gas shocks, tubular stabilizer bar with links. Rear suspension: Solid axle/torque arm, trailing arm, coil springs, track bar, monotube gas shocks and solid stabilizer bar with links. Firm Ride & Handling suspension standard. Brakes: Front disc/rear drum with antilock. Body construction: unibody. Fuel tank: 16.8 gal.

Z28: Transmission: Four-speed electronic overdrive transmission. Steering: rack and pinion. Front suspension: SLA/Coil over monotube gas shocks, and 30-mm tubular stabilizer bar with links. Rear suspension: Solid axle/torque arm, trailing arm, coil springs, track bar, monotube gas shocks and 19-mm solid stabilizer bar with links. Performance Ride & Handling suspension standard. Brakes: Four-wheel discs with antilock. Body construction: unibody. Fuel tank: 16.8 gal.

SS: Transmission: Six-speed manual. Steering: rack and pinion. Front suspension: Modified SLA/Coil over monotube gas shocks and tubular stabilizer bar with links. Rear suspension: Modified solid axle/torque arm, trailing arm, coil springs, track bar, monotube gas shocks and solid stabilizer bar with links. Brakes: Four-wheel discs with antilock. Body construction: unibody. Fuel tank: 16.8 gal. (Note: The Camaro SS convertible

This Camaro with the SLP option package was all muscle from any angle.

retained the stock Camaro Z28 suspension).

OPTIONS

1SA convertible with base equipment group, includes vehicle with standard equipment (no cost). 1SA hatchback base equipment group, includes vehicle with standard equipment; not available with 1SB (no cost). 1SB hatchback preferred equipment group 1 including remote keyless entry, theft-deterrent alarm system, cruise control, fog lights, twin electric remote-control sport mirrors, power door locks, power windows with driver's side express down feature and remote hatch release; not available with 1SA ($1,170). 1SB convertible preferred equipment group 1, includes vehicle with standard equipment (no cost). 1SC Z28 hatchback preferred equipment group 2, includes vehicle with standard equipment; not available with 1SD (no cost). 1SD Z28 hatchback preferred equipment group 1 includes remote keyless entry, theft-deterrent alarm system, electronic cruise control, twin electric remote-control sport mirrors, power door locks, power windows with driver's side express down feature, remote hatch release; power sixway driver's seat, leather-wrapped steering wheel with redundant radio controls, leather-trimmed gearshift knob, leather-wrapped parking brake handle, rear carpeted floor mats and color-keyed body side moldings; not available with 1SC ($1,700). AG1 six-way power driver's seat ($270). AR9 leather accent bucket seats ($500). B84 body-color body side moldings on hatchback ($60). BBS Hurst performance shift linkage for Z28, includes short-throw shift linkage, requires six-speed manual transmission ($325). C49 hatchback rear window defogger ($170). CC1 transparent removable hatch roof panels, includes locks, lockable storage provisions and sunshades ($995). GU5 3.23:1 ratio performance rear axle; requires MX0 automatic transmission and QLC or QFZ tires ($300). MN6 six-speed manual transmission in Z28, includes "skip-shift" feature (no cost). MX0 four-speed overdrive automatic transmission ($725). NW9 traction control ($250). PW7 16-in. chrome cast-aluminum wheels on base Camaro ($725). PW7 16-in. chrome cast-aluminum wheels on Camaro Z28; not available with WU8 Camaro SS package ($725). QLC P245/50ZR16 Goodyear Eagle GS-C performance tires on Z28, not available with WU8 SS package ($225). R6M New Jersey cost surcharge ($93 to dealer no cost to buyer). U1S trunk-mounted 12-disc CD changer, requires UNO ($595). UK3 leather-wrapped steering wheel in base coupe, includes leather-wrapped steering wheel rim, redundant radio controls, leather-trimmed gearshift knob and leather-wrapped parking brake handle, requires 1SB and ULO or UNO ($170). UNO Monsoon 500-watts sound system with CD player in base convertible and all Z28s, includes Monsoon 500-watt sound system, ETR AM/FM stereo radio with seek-and-scan, digital clock, Auto Tone Control, CD player, TheftLock, speed compensated volume, eight speakers and auxiliary amplifier ($350). WU8 SS Performance/Appearance package for Z28, includes 325-hp engine, forced-air induction hood, a specific SS spoiler, 17-in. aluminum wheels, P275/40ZR17 Goodyear Eagle F1 tires, a high-performance ride and handling package, a power steering cooler, a low-restriction dual outlet exhaust system,

The SS interior had all the best features GM could offer.

Erick Lieder photo

SS badging, a 3.23:1 ratio rear axle with the MX0 automatic transmission or a 3.42:1 ratio rear axle with the MN6 six-speed manual transmission; available for Z28s, but was not available with Y3F Sport Appearance package ($3,625). Y38 RS package, for base coupe, includes dual silver or black Heritage stripes on hood, roof and deck lid, RS interior and exterior badging and Z28-type exhaust system with silver painted dual outlets; not available with Y87 or Y3F ($1,345). Y87 Performance Handling package for base hatchback, includes Zexel Torsen limited-slip differential, dual outlet exhausts and sport steering ratio, requires QCB and N96 ($275). Z4C 35th Anniversary package for Z28 convertible with the SS package, includes traction control, 12-disc CD changer, 17 x 9-in. custom black machine-faced aluminum wheels, black anodized brake calipers, custom silver embroidery on head restraints, ebony leather seating surfaces with pewter leather inserts and custom trophy floor mats, requires WU8 ($2,500).

HISTORICAL FOOTNOTES

The Camaro entered its final year of availability – at least for now – in the fall of 2001. Generating the most excitement for the 2002 model year were three specialty models created as a joint effort between Chevrolet Motor Division and SLP Engineering. The 2002 Camaro RS package offered by SLP could be added to V-6-powered Camaros for $849. It was available for cars finished in Artic White, Light Pewter Metallic, Silver Metallic, Navy Blue Metallic, Onyx Black, Monterey Maroon Metallic, Sunset Orange Metallic, Mystic Teal Metallic and Bright Rally Red. The RS content included a front grille with the Chevrolet bow-tie logo, an interior plaque with RS badge, three exterior RS badges, a dual-outlet exhaust system with a high-performance muffler (adds 5 hp and a throaty exhaust note) and black or silver striping. The black striping was not available for Oynx Black or Navy Blue cars and the silver striping was not available for Light Pewter or Sunset Orange cars. SLP also offered the SS package (with a new 345-hp option available at extra cost), plus the 35th anniversary package listed with 2002 options. The latter was available only for the Camaro Z28 with the SS package and was on display at the 2002 Chicago Automobile Show in February.

The 1967 Camaro Indy Pace Car (in back), shown here with a 1997 Brickyard 400 Pace Car, was an RS/SS 396 convertible.

35 Special Camaros

1967 Camaro Indianapolis 500 Pace Car

In 1967, Chevrolet got the chance to show off its newest product at the Indy 500, where the all-new Camaro paced the racing cars. The cars supplied were RS/SS-396 convertibles. Chevrolet employee and two-time 500 winner Mauri Rose (1947, 1948) drove the car and A.J. Foyt got to keep a Camaro for winning the event. Instead of offering replicas to dealers, Chevrolet built only 104 of the Camaros and let Indianapolis Motor Speedway VIPs use them during the month of May. Most

of these "Indy Pace Cars" were SS-350s with Powerglide automatic. The 396s used for track purposes had the new Turbo-Hydra-Matic installed. When the race was over, the replicas were sold through local dealers as used cars.

For a comprehensive history of this model refer to *The Official Chevrolet Indy Pace Car Book* by D.M. Crispino and John R. Hooper.

1967 Chevrolet Super Yenko Camaro (SYC)

Don Yenko, of Canonsburg, Pennsylvania, became one of the first Chevrolet factory dealers to turn a Camaro into a hot rod. During the early '60s, Yenko had turned out race-modified Corvettes and Corvairs. Starting in 1967, his Yenko Sportscars dealership started dropping RPO L72 427-cid "rat" motors into Camaros.

After the mechanics at his dealership put together a few cars, Yenko helped to establish a distributorship called Span, Inc., based in Chicago. The original Super Yenko Camaro concept had actually been the brainchild of Dickie Harrell, a drag racer. Harrell had previously worked for another performance-car specialist — Nickey Chevrolet of Chicago. Span was set up in Chicago to market the muscular Camaros nationwide.

Most of the cars were probably modified in Chicago. Yenko added decals, badges and other special features at

his Pennsylvania dealership. To help sell the cars, Yenko sent sales literature out to other performance-minded Chevy dealers like Fred Gibbs.

A Span advertisement from 1967 offered the Super Yenko Camaro/410 with a 427-cid 410-hp engine, hydraulic lfters, a Super GT Hydro (three-speed automatic) transmission, metallic brakes and other performance upgrades for $4,245. It also offered the Super Yenko Camaro/450 with a 427-cid, 450-hp V-8, mechanical lifters, four-speed close-ratio transmission and additional modifications for the same price as the "410" package. In addition, there was a "Stormer" Z/28 competition package for $6,000 and individual special options like an L88 engine, side exhausts and a high-rise intake manifold.

1968 Chevrolet Super Yenko Camaro (SYC)

Jerry Heasley photo

The hot Yenko 427 Camaro was built using the Chevrolet Central Office Production Order System.

The early 427-powered Camaros assembled by Yenko Sportscars and distributed by Span, Inc., led to the first Camaros with factory-installed 427-cid V-8s. Yenko's mechanics could hardly keep up with the early demand for such conversions.

In 1968, Yenko and his father visited Chevrolet to talk about getting cars with factory-installed 427s. It was decided to use the COPO — a.k.a. Central Offiice Production Order — system to create such cars and to provide 100 of them to Yenko Sportscars in 1969.

Until those COPO 9561 Camaros became available, Yenko's mechanics worked on dropping 427-cid V-8s in other special-order cars. In fact, the rarest Yenko Camaro was a 1968 model built under COPO 8008.

1969 Camaro RS/SS-396 Indy Sport Convertible Z11

The 1969 Indy Pace Car, shown here with its 1997 relative, could be had with several engine setups ranging from 325 to 375 hp.

After making a hit at the "Brickyard" in 1967, Chevy was invited to bring the Camaro back for a repeat performance in 1969. This time the company took better advantage of sales promotional opportunities by releasing a pace car replica option package.

The genuine Indianapolis 500 Pace Cars were 375-hp SS-396 convertibles with Hugger Orange racing stripes, rear spoilers and black and orange hound's-tooth upholstery. About 100 copies were built to pace the race and transport dignitaries and members of the press around Indianapolis. Chevrolet then released the Indy Pace Car replica option (RPO Z11) and sold 3,674 replicas to the general public.

The Z11 was actually just a $37 striping package for convertibles only. But other extras, such as the $296 SS option and the special interior were also required. Buyers could order the pace car treatment on either RS/SS-350 or RS/SS-396 ragtops. The 350-cid/300-hp versions are most common. More desirable are pace car replicas with a big-block V-8. They came in four variations: L35 ($63) with 325 hp, the L34 ($184) with 350 hp, the L78 ($316) with 375 hp and the L89 ($711) with aluminum heads and 375 hp. The 375-hp ragtops were good for 7-second 0 to 60-mph acceleration and 15-sec. quarter-mile runs.

For a comprehensive history of this model refer to *The Official Chevrolet Indy Pace Car Book* by D.M. Crispino and John R. Hooper.

1969 Camaro Z10 Hardtop

The Z10 is a rare hardtop version of the 1969 Indy Pace Car that was built for only a couple of weeks. They had white bodies and Hugger Orange pace car stripes. About 200 of these cars were made as a reaction to complaints by some Chevrolet dealers that they could not get enough Z11 Indy Pace Car convertibles.

The Z10 package included RS/SS features, a cowl-induction hood and a V-8 engine (350- or 396-cid). A large percentage of the cars had air conditioning.

For a brief, but detailed history of this model refer to *The Official Chevrolet Indy Pace Car Book* by D.M. Crispino and John R. Hooper.

1969 Chevrolet Super Yenko Camaro 427

The 1969 Super Yenko Camaro 427 was clocked at 114.5 mph in the quarter mile.

Jerry Heasley photo

After making SYC (Super Yenko Camaro) models available to enthusiasts through a small number of selected factory dealers during 1967 and 1968, Don Yenko wanted to expand his operation in 1969. Once again, the basic plan was to base the racecars on 1969 Camaros obtained from Chevrolet via the COPO (Central Office Production Order) arrangement. This type of purchase allowed Yenko to order special equipment, as long as building the car did not upset the normal stream of output at the factory. The original '69 Yenkos were produced under order No. 9561 and were fitted with 427-cid, 425-hp L72 V-8 engines. They also got M21 or M22 four-speed gearboxes (or an M40 Turbo-Hydra-Matic), front disc brakes, a special Zl2 ducted hood, a heavy-duty radiator, a special suspension, a 4.10:1 positraction rear axle and a rear spoiler.

Yenko also ordered a batch of COPO 9737 Camaros, which had 15-in. wheels, Goodyear Wide Tread GT tires, a 140-mph speedometer and a beefy 1-inch front stabilizer bar. Between 100 and 201 Yenko SYC Camaros were made, depending upon which source you refer to.

Yenko's SYC Camaros came only in seven colors: Hugger Orange, LeMans Blue, Fathom Green, Daytona Yellow, Rally Green and Olympic Gold. The cars had a base price of $3,895, including shipping. Available options included front and rear bumper guards ($25), front and rear floor mats ($12), an AM-FM push-button radio ($134), heavy-duty Air Lift shocks ($45), traction bars ($50) and chrome exhaust extensions ($38).

On April 19, 1969 a Yenko Camaro with factory-installed headers and racing slicks, driven by Ed Hedrick, did the quarter mile at a drag strip in York, Pennsylvania, in 11.94 seconds at 114.5 mph.

1969 Chevrolet COPO Camaros

Muscle car fans could get a fast factory Camaro by ordering a 1969 COPO model.

Jerry Heasley photo

Like Don Yenko, Chevrolet dealers Fred Gibb of LeHarpe, Illinois, and Nickey Chevrolet of Chicago specialized in dropping 427-cid "big-block" V-8s into Camaros for drag racing. To help them accomplish this, Chevrolet came up with the idea of letting dealers employ the seldom-used Central Office Production Order system to provide such cars through factory channels. This continued in 1969.

The 1969 COPO cars began life as L78 Camaros with a 396-cid 325-hp engine. They then had about 14 modifications. The COPO cars were made at the Norwood, Ohio, and Van Nuys, California, assembly plants. Prices ranged from about $3,500 at the low end to $4,500, depending on what regular Camaro options were also ordered. It is believed that about 1,015 cars were built in total, 822 with four-speed manual transmissions and 193 with automatics.

Although Yenko inspired the production of COPO units, they were technically available through any Chevrolet dealer. Berger Chevrolet, of Grand Rapids, Michigan, also ordered 40 to 50 COPO Camaros for its high-performance department. Dana Chevrolet, of South Gate, California, was another dealership that handled COPO cars, but less is known about this operation.

Nickey Chevrolet also continued to do many of its own 427 transplants in 1969. They were advertised nationally in *Hot Rod* magazine. Motion Performance, of Baldwin (Long Island) New York was another supplier. In 1969, this company offered the 427-cid 450-hp SS-427 "Baldwin-Motion" Camaro for $3,895 and the 427-cid 500-hp Phase III SS-427 Camaro for $4,999.

1969 Chevrolet Camaro ZL1

Jerry Heasley photo

The 1969 Camaro ZL1 is a rare and classic American muscle car.

During 1968, Chevy performance dealer Fred Gibb talked to the legendary Vince Piggins about constructing the ultimate Camaro muscle car with an all-aluminum 427-cid V-8 for Super Stock drag racing. National Hot Rod Association (NHRA) rules said a minimum of 50 cars had to be built to qualify the ZL1 for competition. Chevrolet general manager Pete Estes told Gibb that Chevrolet would build the first cars before the end of the year, if the dealer would take 50 of them at a proposed price of $4,900.

Gibb accepted and the Central Office Production Order system was utilized to order the cars. The first ZL1s built were a pair of Dusk Blue cars made at the Norwood, Ohio, assembly plant on Dec. 30, 1968. They arrived at the LeHarpe, Illinois, dealership the next day, covered with snow. Unfortunately, the factory invoice price had climbed to $7,269!

All 50 ZL1s were virtually identical, except for color

and transmission. They had the COPO 9560 option with the aluminum 427. An additional 19 Camaro ZL1s were built for other dealers. Equipment on all 69 cars included the Z22 RS option, J50 power brakes, N40 power steering, a V10 tachometer, racing mirrors, dual exhausts with resonators and tailpipe extensions, a special steering wheel, F70-15 black sidewall tires with raised gold letters, special lug nuts and wheel center caps, a special instrument cluster, special identification decals on the hood, grille and rear panel and an extra-wide front valance panel.

According to the February 1969 issue of *Super Stock* magazine, a ZL-1 Camaro in racing trim could cover the quarter mile in 10.41 sec. at 128.10 mph with a stock Holley 850-cfm carburetor. Dickie Harrell raced a ZL1 for Gibb. He took four wins and had a best performance of 10.05 sec. at 139 mph.

1969 Chevrolet Camaro Caribe Concept

The two-seat 1969 Camaro Caribe Concept Car had a pickup-like box instead of a trunk.

This rather unique factory concept vehicle was a heavily modified 1969 Camaro convertible. It had a special roadster-style windshield, a wrapover "roll bar" behind the seats and instead of a trunk, it had a large open bin or tub. Probably the neatest thing about the car was the styled wheels and unique "dotted line" tires it wore.

1978 Chevrolet Camaro Indy 500 Official Car

In 1978, a silver-and-black Corvette was used to pace the Indy 500 race in honor of the Corvette's 25th anniversary (these cars should not be confused with another 1978 model called the Silver Anniversary Edition Corvette). As part of the pace car promotion, Chevrolet also loaned the Indianpolis 500 a number of parade vehicles and support vehicles. They included a fleet of 54 special Camaros and Monte Carlos. The special Camaros had Indianapolis Motor Speedway decals above the rear wheel openings.

1982 Chevrolet Camaro Indy 500 Commemorative Edition

The 1982 Indy 500 Camaro was a tricked-out Z28 with an appealing silver and blue paint job.

There was an all-new Camaro for 1982 and the Z28 version was exciting enough to draw an invitation from the Indianapolis Motor Speedway Corp. to have it pace the Indy 500 that year. Chevrolet cranked out the actual track cars, as well as 6,360 copies that were marketed as Indy 500 Commemorative Editions.

All of the Indy Pace Car replicas sold to the public had Silver and Blue Metallic finish, Indy 500 logos, four-color lower body accents, red-accented silver aluminum wheels and Goodyear Eagle GT white-letter tires. The Indy Pace Car's blue-cloth-and-silver-vinyl interior included a Lear-Siegler Conteur driver's seat, along with special instrumentation, a leather-wrapped steering wheel and an AM/FM radio.

Racecar driver Jim Rathmann piloted the actual Camaro pace car on the day of the race.

1985 Chevrolet Camaro GTZ Concept

The 1985 Camaro GTZ Concept car was wrapped in custom accessories.

The 1985 Camaro GTZ concept vehicles was a customized version of the then-current Z28 model with a competition-car look to it. It featured aero headlamp covers with a "smoked glass" look, a special finned hood with two rows of large air louvers, hood hold-down pins, a special front air dam with air intake slots ahead of the wheels, special rocker panel skirting with air intake slots ahead of the rear wheels, a unique "whale tail" spoiler, a competition-style exposed gas filler cap and special six-spoke billet wheels.

1989 Chevrolet Concept California Camaro IROC

A sneak peak at the fourth-generation Camaros was offered with the 1989 Concept California Camaro.

This smoothly styled Camaro concept car was a design study that aimed at providing the car-buying public with a glimpse of possible future 2+2 sports cars. The car, which grew from a scale model to a full-size running prototype in just six months, was obviously an advance look at the fourth-generation Camaro.

The original scale model of the car came out of the General Motors Advanced Design Concept Center in Newbury Park, California, where John Schinella was director at the time. It had a smooth and rounded shape with a hood that dipped aggressively to a point where it was flanked by high, rounded wheel wells. The angle of the hood continued its swoop up the front of the car, angling the windshield over the engine compartment in a dramatic sweep. Flush-mounted glass and integrated side-view mirrors combined to create sleek body sides that flowed into a "raked" rear end.

The Concept Camaro IROC also had a gull-wing door that pulled up at a 45-degree angle to the front of the car, taking part of the roof with it. This made getting into the red front seats and black rear seats a lot easier than with a conventional door. The car had a 104-in. wheelbase, a 186.4-in. overall length and a double-overhead-cam V-6 engine.

1989 Chevrolet PPG XT-2 Pace Truck

The futuristic XT-2 Pace Truck could cover the quarter mile in 13.1 seconds.

The XT-2 (for "Experimental Truck #2") was essentially an IROC Camaro with a 360-hp V-6 and a pickup truck bed. The unique vehicle could do 0 to 60 mph in 6 seconds and there was a good reason for its performance potential. By the spring of 1989, the XT-2 would be playing "leader of the pack" as one of Chevrolet's co-sponsor PPG's CART (Indy car series) pace vehicles.

The truck featured an aerodynamic windshield that was also its hood (the engine underneath it pivoted upwards, on gas struts, for servicing), a removable pickup bed floor at the rear (to provide drive train access) and a complete array of CART-required features such as a fire extinguishing system, dual batteries and fuel tanks, strobe lights, rollover safety features and racing-type passenger restraints.

The truck had a 117-in. wheelbase and a 204.5-in. overall length with independent front and rear suspensions, a six-speed manual gearbox and different size front and rear tires. It could do 0 to 60 mph in 6 seconds and cover the quarter mile in 13.1 sec. It was finished in a purplish blue PPG color with special graphics accents.

1992 Chevrolet Camaro "Heritage Edition"

The 1992 "Heritage Edition" Camaro was a $175 option available on the RS and Z28 models.

Chevrolet marked the Camaro's 25th birthday with a new ZO3 "Heritage Edition" package. The $175 option package was available for RS and Z28 models. In addition to standard equipment for the Camaro or Camaro RS coupe or convertible, the Heritage Edition content included 25th Anniversary emblems, special hood stripes, special rear deck lid stripes, a specific body-color grille, black-finished headlight "pockets" and 16-in. cast-aluminum wheels with body-color accents. All Camaros — even those that did not have the Heritage Edition option — had a special "25th Anniversary" badge on the instrument panel.

1993 Camaro Indy Pace Car

The 1993 Indy Pace Car was hard to miss with its black-and-white exterior and body accents.

The 1993-1995 Camaro Z28 models are nearly identical. They differ in details such as what type of fuel-injection system they use, transmission, axle ratio, colors of the dashboard numbers, etc. However, if you want one that stands out, get yourself a 1993 Indianapolis 500 pace car replica.

The Camaro paced the Indy 500 for the fourth time that year (the previous years for Camaro pace cars were 1967, 1969 and 1982). Chevrolet provided the Indianapolis Motor Speedway with three "Official Pace Cars" and replicas for track officials. In addition, dealers were supposed to get 500 copies, with another 20 reserved for Canada. The actual total built was 633, which puts the 1993 Camaro Indy pace car in the limited-production class.

The 1993 Indy Pace Car came only as a coupe, with a special black-and-white exterior and multi-colored body accents. Interiors featured the same color combination, with a new 3D knitting process used on the seats and door panels. A gold hood emblem topped it all off. Mechanically, the Camaro Z28's 350-cid 275-hp LT1 Corvette V-8 met Indianapolis Motor Speedway's requirements without modification. "Performance-wise, every 1993 Camaro Z28 is capable of pacing Indy," said Jim Perkins, Chevrolet general manager and driver of the pace car for the 500.

Camaro Indy Pace cars were fitted with automatic transmissions. Chevrolet installed the 4L60 Hydra-Matic with a .70 fourth gear. The rest of the Z28 driveline and underpinnings were just fine for track duty.

1993-1996 Callaway Camaro C8

The Calloway SuperNatural C8 is a really cool adaptation of the fourth-generation F-car. Callaway Cars described it as "the logical and philosophical extension of the Callaway Corvette's heritage applied to GM's 1993-1996 Chevrolet Camaro and Pontiac Firebird." Since the year-to-year changes in the Callaway Camaro C8 were largely a function of customer preference, the four years of production can be lumped together.

Like the famed Callaway Corvette, the C8 represented a carefully conceived concept followed by thorough development by Callaway engineers. One version of the car called the "CamAerobody" was for Camaros only, while other Callaway SuperNatural C8 package contents were equally applicable to both Camaros and Firebirds.

The upgraded LT1 engine — labeled the SuperNatural 383 after getting Callaway modifications — was claimed to provide performance comparable to a Ferrari 355 or a Dodge Viper in a 2+2 coupe. It required just 4.7 seconds to accelerate from 0 to 60 mph and did the quarter mile in 13.1 seconds at 110 mph with factory emissions gear and off-the-shelf Pirelli tires. This outstanding go power was complemented by suspension, brake, wheel ands tire enhancements that made the car "docile enough for your Mom's shopping trips" according to Callaway. The company said that only regular factory maintenance was required and that the C8 was backed by a three-year/36,000-mile warranty.

The Callaway CamAerobody was a distinctive and aerodynamically effective kit of parts that made the Gen IV Camaro look even more aerodynamic. Priced at $4,500, the kit included a complete replacement nose, a replacement rear bumper section, gill panels, new rocker panels and restyled door cladding. Callaway noted, "In keeping with the Callaway 'complete car' concept, the designation 'Callaway C8' applies only to those Camaros equipped with both the SuperNatural 383 engine and the CamAerobody (package)."

The C8 modifications could be installed at Callaway headquarters in Old Lyme, Connecticutt, or at Callaway dealers across the country or at a shop of the customer's chosing.

1993 DRM Camaro

In this "tuner" Camaro's name the initials DRM stood for Doug Rippie Motorsports. This Plymouth, Minnesota, company was owned by Doug Rippie, who was well known for his race driving in the 1989 Corvette Challenge Series and the 1992 World Challenge Championship. Rippie decided to work some magic on the fourth-generation Camaro soon after it arrived on the scene.

Like other modern tuners such as Callaway and SLP, Rippie offered his customers a range of options. Things started off with the DRM/375 Camaro, which carried a 375-hp version of the LT-1 under its hood. The extra power came mainly from breathing and exhaust improvements and included a cold-air-induction box and tubular exhaust manifolds. The DRM/400 was a little more powerful and added a few heavy-duty suspension bits, like Bilstein shocks and Hyperco high-rate springs. At the top of the heap was the get-out-of-my-way DRM/430 option, which was essentially a DRM/400 bored .030 over to 383 cid. The optional power plant also featured a 3.75-in. stroke Callies crankshaft, Oliver 6-in. rods, Ross forged pistons and ported cylinder heads. An aero body kit was optional for all DRM Camaros.

According to *Chevy High Performance* magazine, the DRM/400 with the 383-cid engine option was good for 4.9-second 0-to-60 times and covered the quarter mile in 13.40 seconds at 109.70 mph!

1994 Camaro ZL1

Chevrolet's special vehicles genius, Jon Moss, built the jet-black 1994 Camaro ZL1 concept car on a dare. Several automotive writers who talked to Moss during the debut of the Gen IV Camaro suggested that a big-block Camaro would never be seen again. To prove them wrong, Moss shoe-horned a 572-cid all-aluminum monster mill into the tight-fitting engine bay of a new Camaro.

The tall-deck engine was fitted with a custom-fabricated cross-ram intake manifold that fed a pair of LT1 throttle bodies. This setup was hooked to a five-speed gearbox and Dana 60 rear end. It cranked up 636 hp and 670 lbs.-ft. of torque.

Chassis upgrades on the subtle concept car included polyurethane suspension bushings and racing disc brakes. The suspension mounting points were beefed up and Moss added a Corvette hood scoop, a ground effects package, Goodyear GS-C tires and 17-in. aluminum wheels. Even equipped with a stereo and air conditioning, the ZL1 could do 200 mph.

1996 Camaro SS

The 1996 Camaro SS was clocked at 13.8 seconds in the quarter mile.

Ed Hamburger first got involved in the high-performance field by drag racing Chrysler (Mopar) products in the 1960s. Later, in the 1980s, he created SLP Engineering, of Red Bank, New Jersey, a company that converted Pontiac Firebirds into "street legal performance" machines. His 1992 Firehawk version of the Firebird was a successful venture for SLP and Pontiac dealers who sold the SLP package.

In 1996, Hamburger started working in conjunction with Chevrolet Motor Division to produce a Camaro muscle car that could be sold by Chevrolet dealers as a high-priced, factory-approved option package. The secret behind this 1996 Camaro SS was a special air-induction system combined with an optional low-restriction exhaust system. This setup boosted the horsepower of the 10.4:1 compression 350-cid LT1 V-8 to 305 at 5000 rpm and torque to 325 ft.-lbs. at 2400 rpm. The engine had a cast-iron block and aluminum cylinder heads. It came with a sequential port fuel injection system and was hooked up to a six-speed manual transmission.

Like any *real* muscle car, the 1996 Camaro SS needed an image and a "feel" to suit its higher-than-standard performance capabilities. Therefore, the SS package also included a special composite hood with an "ant eater" air scoop, 17 x 9.0-in. Corvette ZR1-style wheels, BF Goodrich Comp T/A tires and special SS badges. It also featured a Torsen limited-slip differential, Bilstein shock absorbers, progressive-rate springs and performance-altered lower rear control arms.

The Camaro SS was a roughly $28,000 package. It weighed in at 3,565 lbs. and, while that didn't exactly make it a lightweight, it could accelerate from 0 to 60 mph in 5.3 seconds. It handled the quarter mile in 13.8 seconds at 101.4 mph. Speaking of handling, it could brake from 60 mph in 117 feet and registered 0.88 gs in lateral acceleration testing. For model year 1996, a total of 2,410 Camaro Z28s had the SS option package ordered for them.

1997 Camaro Z28 '96 Brickyard 400 Pace Car

The 1997 Brickyard 400 Pace Car (front) and its predecessors (left to right) from 1967, 1969, 1982 and 1993.

If you think the dating on this entry seems confusing, there's an interesting historical highlight involved. On August 3, 1996, the public got an advanced look at the 1997 30th Anniversary Edition Camaro Z28 when one of the earliest examples was used to pace the Brickyard 400 stock car race at Indianapolis Motor Speedway. The special 30th Anniversary Camaro featured lengthwise orange racing stripes and hounds-tooth upholstery like the 1969 Indy 500 Pace car.

This was the fifth time a Chevrolet Camaro had served as the pace car for a race at the famous Brickyard, although the racing cars had been open-wheel types up to this point. Camaros had been used to pace the traditional Indy 500 race in 1967, 1969, 1982 and 1993. The new Brickyard 400 Pace Car was about as exciting as an Indy 500 Pace Car to Camaro lovers. It sported a flip-up light bar, T-tops and a large black light bar underneath the front air dam.

1997 Camaro 30th Anniversary Edition

Chevrolet used the Z28 for its 30th Anniversary Camaro in 1997.

The Camaro observed its 30th anniversary in 1997 and Chevrolet marked the occasion by offering a 30th Anniversary package for the Z28 models. The $575 option consisted of Artic White paint with Hugger Orange stripes, a combination patterned after the collectible 1969 Camaro Indy Pace car. Also included in the package were white door handles, white five-spoke aluminum wheels and a white front fascia air intake. The seats inside the 30th Anniversary Camaro were trimmed in Artic White with black-and-white hounds-tooth cloth inserts. The floor mats and headrests had five-color 30th Anniversary embroidery.

The Z28 came in coupe and convertible models for 1997. The closed car sold for $20,115 and weighed 3,433 lbs. The open car had a base retail price of $25,520 and weighed 3,589 lbs. All Camaros came with daytime running lights, four-wheel ABS disc brakes, dual airbags, an electronically controlled AM/FM stereo with cassette player, steel side-door guard beams and a reinforced steel safety cage. The Z28 included a 5.7-liter sequential fuel injected V-8 and a six-speed manual transmission. The 350-cid V-8 engine developed 285 hp at 5200 rpm and 325 lbs.-ft. of torque at 2400 rpm.

Berger Camaro

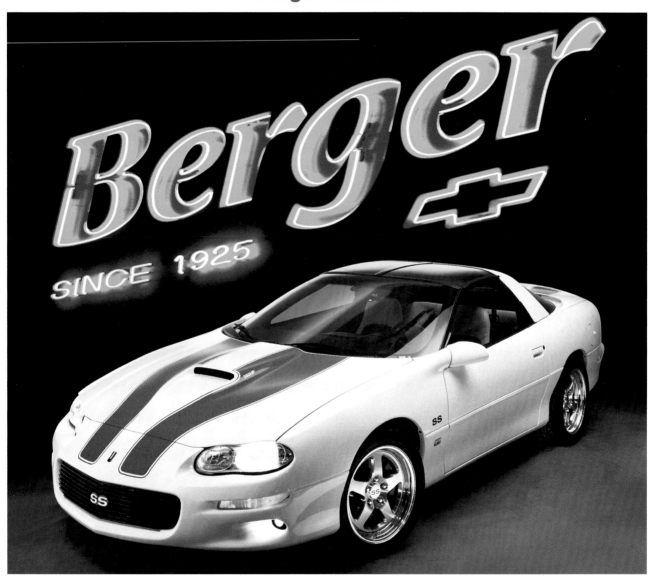

This 1997 Camaro SS was one in a long line of hot Berger Camaros.

Berger Chevrolet of Grand Rapids, Michigan, made a name for itself in the muscle car market back in the 1960s by selling factory supercars. The dealership did some conversions, but gained more of a reputation for setting up racers and performance-car enthusiasts with powerhouse cars straight from the assembly line. The earlierst Berger Camaros are definite collector cars and some of the fastest street machines every produced in Detroit.

The dealership is still catering to the muscle car crowd today with dressed-up SS Camaros that feature 380 hp and figure to be collector cars of the future.

1997 Camaro SS

The 1997 Camaro SS came standard with a 305-hp LT1 V-8.

In 1997, SLP Engineering, of Troy, Michigan, continued to turn new Camaros into hot SS models. They came standard with a 305-hp version of the LT1 V-8. Optional was a 310-hp version featuring a cool performance exhaust system. The Camaro SS included a forced-air induction system, a restyled rear deck lid spoiler, a restyled suspension (on coupe and T-top models), P275/40ZR17 B.F. Goodrich Comp T/A tires, 17 x 9-in. ZR-1 styled cast-aluminum alloy wheels, Quaker State Synquest synthetic engine oil, exterior SS badges and a Camaro SS interior plaque. Camaro SS convertibles retained the stock Camaro suspension and had 16-in. B.F. Goodrich Comp T/A tires and 16 x 8-in. styled cast-aluminum wheels.

The Camaro SS was offered in standard exterior colors of Artic White, Black, Bright Red and Polo Green. Sebring Silver Metallic finish was optional. All colors were available with Dark Gray or Medium Gray interiors. All but Sebring Silver cars could have a neutral color interior and all but Polo Green cars could have a red interior.

Also available on the SS was the 30th Anniversary package. SLP Engineering noted that the 30th Anniversary SS option required Chevrolet options 1SJ, Z4C and AG1 on coupes and 1SM, Z4C and AG1 on convertibles. SLP projected that it would build a total of 3,000 Camaro Z28s with the SS package (coupes and convertibles combined) in 1997 and that 1,000 of them would receive the "30th Anniversary SS" option. Total model-year production wound up at 3,055.

1998 Camaro SS

Jerry Heasley photo

The 1998 Camaro SS featured a factory-installed option package, rather than an aftermarket package.

In 1998, the Camaro SS was changed from a "factory-approved" aftermarket option installed by an outside "partner" company into an extra installed at the Chevrolet factory. SLP Engineering continued to provide the special hardware.

Cataloged as the WU8 SS Performance and Appearance package, the SS option included an upgrade to a 320-hp V-8, a forced-air-induction hood, a rear deck lid spoiler, 17-in. aluminum wheels, a high-performance Ride and Handling package and special SS badging. The option was available only for Z28s. It retailed for $3,500. A six-speed manual gearbox was again used with V-8 engines.

Chevrolet produced 2,397 Camaro SS coupes in 1998 and 1,485 had the six-speed, while 910 had an automatic transmission. This included 248 White cars, 316 Silver cars, 238 Navy Blue cars, 967 Black cars, 29 Gold cars and 598 Red cars. In addition, 478 Camaro SS convertibles were built — including 197 with the six-speed manual gearbox and 281 with the automatic transmission. Of these, 114 were White, 58 were Silver, 45 were Navy Blue, 109 were Black, seven were Gold, one was Teal and 144 were painted Red.

1999 Camaro Z28 SS

The 1999 Z28 SS got high marks for its handling and road manners.

The 1999 Camaro Z28 SS was the top dog in a comparison test that *Car and Driver* magazine conducted in August 1999. The faceoff pitted the convertible version of Chevy's muscular pony car against counterpart ragtops wearing Pontiac Firebird Trans Am and Ford SVT Cobra Mustang badges.

Powering the Camaro SS was a 346-cid, 16-valve Chevrolet LS1 V-8 with an aluminum block and aluminum cylinder heads. It had General Motors' engine-control system with port fuel injection. This system generated 320 hp at 5200 rpm and 335 lbs.-ft. of torque at 4000 rpm. The available factory transmission options included a six-speed manual gearbox or a four-speed automatic.

The $33,955 fully equipped Camaro SS ragtop used in the road test did 0 to 60 mph in just 5.3 seconds, 0 to 100 mph in 12.8 seconds and 0 to 130 mph in 24.6 seconds. The quarter mile took all of 13.9 seconds with a trap speed of 103 mph. The car's top speed was recorded as 160 mph.

The Camaro SS was not the fastest car in the *Car and Driver* test, but it was right up there and it really excelled where it came to driving and handling. The original equipment P275/40ZR-17 Goodyear Eagle F1 GS tires were a big plus and it had a tight suspension, excellent steering and great brakes. The Camaro SS could stop from 70 mph in just 175 feet and turned 0.86 gs on a skidpad. It also turned in the best performance when a professional driver, Paul Gentilozzi, put it through its paces on a road course.

Car and Driver said that the Camaro SS was the best car to drive on an everyday basis and suggested that ABS braking and traction control were important considerations when it came to daily driving in such a machine.

This year the SS option was installed on 2,647 coupes and 365 convertibles with the six-speed manual transmission and on 1,380 coupes and 437 convertibles with automatic transmission. In addition, eight of the SS models had the 1LE competition suspension (seven with the six-speed gearbox and one with automatic transmission).

1999 "SEMA" Camaro ZL1

A special Camaro ZL1 was right at home at the 1999 SEMA (Specialty Equipment Market Association) show in Las Vegas. The 770-hp beast was jam-packed with performance parts and drew attention and lustful stares from the hot rodders and buff-book readers. The SEMA ZL1's modifications included an 8.4-liter aluminum-block pushrod V-8 that produced 770 hp at 6900 rpm and 683 lbs.-ft of torque at 5200 rpm hooked to a five-speed manual transmission and a three-disc hydraulic clutch setup.

The Camaro ZL1 began life in 1993 as a study in power and torque. It originally had a 0-to-60 time of just 2.7 seconds and a 230-mph-plus top speed and ran the quarter mile in 10.410 seconds (137.19 mph). Then it was tweaked and fine-tuned as it evolved into the SEMA show car for 1999. The myriad performance add-ons included everything from a Hamburger Hi-Torque starter and Crower forged steel crankshaft with 4.5-in. stroke, to a Dart intake manifold reworked for fuel injection with a K&N air filter and Exhaust Tech dual 3.5-in. inlet and outlet mufflers. The chassis was reinforced and stiffened to better handle the onslaught of speed and power. The front suspension employed spindles modified for Brembo four-piston caliper stopping power, with Koni shocks and 540 lb.-in. springs. At the rear, the lower control arms were reworked to house 18-in. wheels shod with Goodyear Z-rated performance Eagle F-1 tires. Modified stabilizer bars were used front and rear.

After SEMA 99, the ZL1 made special appearances at various Chevy-sanctioned events around the country.

2000 Chevrolet SLP Camaro RS

SLP's RS package for the 2000 Camaro was merchandised as an $849 Chevrolet dealer option with code Y3B. Ingredients of the SLP package included the Camaro Z28 dual-slot exhaust system and black longitudinal racing stripes, plus "RS" badges on the fenders and dash. A second RS package costing $699 added 8 x 16-in. five-spoke alloy wheels.

The changes brought the price of the Camaro up to about $20,000. They added a little performance, but made the Camaro look really cool. Technically speaking, the 231-cid V-6 from the stock Camaro was tweaked to generate 205 hp at 5200 rpm and 225 lbs.-ft. of torque at 4000 rpm.

Car and Driver (December, 2000) found the RS good enough to produce a 7.5-second 0-to-60 time and a 15.8-second quarter mile at 86 mph. The magazine pointed out that such performance wasn't likely to win any modern-day street races, but outdid the performance of the 350-cid V-8 used in the original "Bandit" Trans Ams that SLP created back in 1987.

2000 Camaro SS

The 2000 Camaro SS came with a 320-hp, 5.7-liter V-8.

Chevrolet's Camaro entered the new millennium continuing to play its traditional role as one of the greatest values among modern muscle cars. The 2000 Camaro was offered in a choice of coupe and convertible body styles with prices ranging from a low of about $17,500 to a high of $35,000. Regardless of where you purchased on the Camaro price spectrum, you wound up with a lot of car for your hard-earned bucks.

For muscle car lovers, the hot ticket was the SS, which came stuffed with a tweaked 5.7-liter motor that cranked up 320 hp and promised 5.2-second 0 to 60-mph times, even with a 3,306-lb. curb weight.

A total of 4,772 Camaro SS coupes with six-speed manual transmission were made. Of these, 1,591 were Black, 892 were Red, 718 were Pewter, 619 were Silver, 573 were Navy Blue, 378 were White and one was Sunset Orange Metallic. A total of 2,569 Camaro SS coupes with automatic transmission were made. Of these, 679 were Black, 498 were Red, 451 were Pewter, 308 were Silver, 306 were Navy Blue and 327 were White. A total of 802 Camaro SS convertibles with six-speed manual transmission were made. Of these, 274 were Black, 144 were Red, 154 were Pewter, 93 were Silver, 88 were Navy Blue, 48 were White and one was Sunset Orange Metallic. A total of 770 Camaro SS convertibles with automatic transmission were made. Of these, 165 were Black, 173 were Red, 154 were Pewter, 101 were Silver, 66 were Navy Blue, 146 were White and one was Sunset Orange Metallic.

2001 Camaro RS

Option No. Y3B identified the Camaro RS Package created by SLP Engineering for the 2001 V-6 Camaro coupe. Standard features of the new RS package included a grille with a Chevrolet bow tie logo, one special interior plaque and three "RS" exterior badges and a dual outlet exhaust system with a high-performance muffler that added 5 hp and a more "throaty" exhaust note.

The RS was available on Arctic White, Light Pewter Metallic, Navy Blue Metallic, Onyx Black, Monterey Maroon Metallic, Sunset Orange Metallic, Mystic Teal Metallic and Bright Rally Red cars. The RS dual stripe package could be ordered in black for cars with exterior colors other than Navy Blue or Black or in silver with body colors other than Light Pewter or Sunset Orange.

You could not team the RS package with the WU8 Camaro SS Package, the Z28 Special Performance package, the Y3F Camaro ground effects package, the Y87 performance enhancement package or the MM5 five-speed manual transmission in California or Florida. Optional equipment for the Camaro RS included 16 x 8-in. SS-style wheels and a suspension package that used standard V-8 front (32mm) and rear (19mm) anti-sway bars.

2001 Camaro SS

The new 2001 Camaro SS reflected a number of subtle updates that distinguished it from previous models. They included a new free-flowing intake manifold and a new higher-lift camshaft. SS buyers still got a real muscle car that delivered 310 hp thanks to its functional hood scoop, forced-air induction system and big, fat exhausts. With the ram-air hood the output jumped to 325 hp.

The complete contents of this WU8 SS Performance/Appearance package also included a specific SS rear deck lid spoiler, 17-in. aluminum wheels, P275/40ZR17 Goodyear Eagle F1 tires, a high-performance ride and handling package, a power steering cooler, a low-restriction dual outlet exhaust system and SS badging. The package also included a 3.23:1 ratio rear axle with the MX0 automatic transmission or a 3.42:1 ratio rear axle with the MN6 six-speed manual transmission. It was available for Z28s, but was not available teamed with the Y3F Sport Appearance package.

The 2001 Camaro SS could move from 0 to 60 mph in a tad over 5 seconds and would do the quarter mile in 13.5 seconds.

2002 Camaro RS

The 2002 Camaro RS package offered by SLP could be added to V-6-powered Camaros for $849. It was available for cars finished in Artic White, Light Pewter Metallic, Silver Metallic, Navy Blue Metallic, Onyx Black, Monterey Maroon Metallic, Sunset Orange Metallic, Mystic Teal Metallic and Bright Rally Red. The RS content included a front grille with the Chevrolet bow-tie logo, an interior plaque with RS badge, three exterior RS badges, a dual outlet exhaust system with a high-performance muffler (adds 5 hp and a throaty exhaust note) and black or silver striping. The black striping was not available for Oynx Black or Navy Blue cars and the silver striping was not available for Light Pewter or Sunset Orange cars.

2002 Camaro SS

At the 2002 Chicago Auto Show the "final" Camaro SS received heavy promotion. The code WU8 SS Performance and Appearance package was a $3,625 option for the Z28. The contents of this option package included a 5.7-liter 325-hp V-8, a forced-air induction hood, a specific SS spoiler, 17-in. aluminum wheels, P275/40ZR17 Goodyear Eagle F1 tires, a high-performance ride and handling package, a power steering cooler, a low-restriction dual outlet exhaust system and SS badging. New this year was a 345-hp engine option. It featured a high-flow induction system and either of two proven optional exhaust systems. The SS package also included a 3.23:1 ratio rear axle with the MX0 automatic transmission or a 3.42:1 ratio rear axle with the MN6 six-speed manual transmission. It was available for Z28s, but was not available with the Y3F Sport Appearance package.

2002 Camaro Z28 SS 35th Anniversary

The 35th Anniversary Z28 SS had the best of everything to celebrate the end of the Camaro.

A limited-availability 35th Anniversary package was offered only on Z28 Sport Coupes and convertibles with the SS option to honor the last season of Camaro production. This car was powered by the 5.7-liter LS1 V-8 that produced 325 hp at 5200 rpm and 350 lbs.-ft. of torque at 4000 rpm. It came standard with a four-speed automatic transmission, but a six-speed manual gearbox was a no-extra-cost option.

Only Bright Rally Red exterior finish was featured and it was set off with a special graphics package, plus a black-accented hood air scoop and a red roof band on coupes. There were fog lamps up front, dual electric sport mirrors on the body sides and special SS wheels with machined edges underneath. A silver-embossed Camaro nameplate decorated the front grille and the rear fascia. Four-wheel disc brakes with ABS were included, along with anodized brake calipers. Topping off the package were 35th Anniversary body badges and a special trophy mat made of heavy vinyl with an embroidered 35th Anniversary logo.

On the inside, the anniversary package included a Monsoon 500-watt peak power premium sound system with a stereo and CD player, power door locks, power windows, a power hatch/trunk release, a six-way power driver's seat, remote keyless entry, electronic cruise control, a leather-wrapped shifter and steering wheel, 35th Anniversary instrument panel badging, a 35th Anniversary emblem embroidered on the headrests, ebony/pewter leather seating surfaces and a special owner's portfolio.

2002 Camaro Z28 Indy 500 Festival Car

Although the 50th Anniversary Corvette was picked to be the Indy 500 Official Pace Car in 2002, a fleet of 55 specially finished 2002 Sebring Silver Camaro Z28 convertibles was provided to Indianapolis Motor Speedway for use in conjunction with the year's Indianapolis 500. The silver cars were destined for use in the Indy 500 Festival Parade and as public relations vehicles for officials from the Speedway, the Indy Racing League (IRL) and City of Indianapolis Officials. Camaro brand manager Scott Settlemire pointed out that the Camaro had been used extensively over the years at Indianapolis and served every year at the Brickyard 400 NASCAR race at Indianapolis Motor Speedway.

2002 Camaro Z28 Florida State Patrol cars

When driving in Florida, keep an eye out for a black Camaro Z28 coming up on your bumper. Two hundred 2002 Camaros capable of hitting 100 mph in 14 seconds were purchased by the Florida Highway Patrol to catch speeders. Each black and cream Camaro cost $23,000, about $2,000 more than a full-size Ford Crown Victoria, the standard cruiser in Florida.

The Camaros used a 5.7-liter engine that churned out 310 hp and could reach nearly 160 mph at top end. They were 10 seconds quicker than Crown Victorias in quarter-mile acceleration tests conducted by the Michigan State Police. The Camaro's "career" with the patrol would be short because 2002 was its last year in production. FHP normally trades a cruiser in after 65,000 to 75,000 miles (keep an eye out for FHP equipment auctions in the next year or so).

Officers say the Camaros' fast looks make them a deterrent to drivers who might have try to outrun a standard cruiser. In Pensacola, Escambia County sheriff's deputies, who have nine Camaros in their traffic division, can vouch for their effectiveness in stopping speeders. "We're on them before they can even think about running," said sheriff's Sgt. Alan Barton. "A lot of times we'll see them just pull right over."

Camaro

1968 SS convertible (left), 1980 Z28 (center), and 1968 RS/SS 396.

Camaro Price Guide

Vehicle Condition Scale

1: Excellent: Restored to current maximum professional standards of quality in every area, or perfect original with components operating and apearing as new. A 95-plus point show car that is not driven.

2: Fine: Well-restored or a combination of superior restoration and excellent original parts. Also, extremely well-maintained original vehicle showing minimal wear.

3. Very Good: Complete operable original or older restoration. Also, a very good amateur restoration, all presentable and serviceable inside and out. Plus, a combination of well-done restoration and good operable components or a partially restored car with all parts necessary to compete and/or valuable NOS parts.

4: Good: A driveable vehicle needing no or only minor work to be functional. Also, a deteriorated restoration or a very poor amateur restoration. All components may need restoration to be "excellent," but the car is mostly useable "as is."

5. Restorable: Needs complete restoration of body, chassis and interior. May or may not be running, but isn't weathered, wrecked or stripped to the point of being useful only for parts.

6. Parts car: May or may not be running, but is weathered, wrecked and/or stripped to the point of being useful primarily for parts.

1967 Camaro, V-8

	6	5	4	3	2	1
2d IPC	1,400	4,200	7,000	14,000	24,500	35,000
2d Cpe	950	2,900	4,800	9,600	16,800	24,000
2d Conv	1,200	3,600	6,000	12,000	21,000	30,000
2d Z28 Cpe	1,750	5,300	8,800	17,600	30,800	44,000
2d Yenko Cpe	3,200	9,600	16,000	32,000	56,000	80,000

NOTE: Deduct 5 percent for six-cylinder, (when available). Add 15 percent for Rally Sport Package, (when available; except incl. w/Indy Pace Car). Add 25 percent for SS-350 (when available; except incl. w/Indy).

1968 Camaro, V-8

	6	5	4	3	2	1
2d Cpe	850	2,500	4,200	8,400	14,700	21,000
2d Conv	1,000	3,000	5,000	10,000	17,500	25,000
2d Z28	1,100	3,350	5,600	11,200	19,600	28,000
2d Yenko Cpe	2,650	7,900	13,200	26,400	46,200	66,000

NOTE: Deduct 5 percent for six-cylinder (when available). Add 10 percent for A/C. Add 15 percent for Rally Sport Package (when available). Add 25 percent for SS package. Add 15 percent for SS-350 (when available).

Eugene Stransky photo

1970 Rally Sport

1969 Camaro, V-8

	6	5	4	3	2	1
2d Spt Cpe	900	2,650	4,400	8,800	15,400	22,000
2d Conv	1,100	3,250	5,400	10,800	18,900	27,000
2d Z28	1,100	3,250	5,400	10,800	18,900	27,000
2d IPC	1,250	3,700	6,200	12,400	21,700	31,000
2d ZL-1	3,100	9,350	15,600	31,200	54,600	78,000
2d Yenko	2,050	6,100	10,200	20,400	35,700	51,000

NOTE: Deduct 5 percent for six-cylinder, (when available). Add 10 percent for A/C. Add 10 percent for Rally Sport (except incl. w/Indy Pace Car). Add 25 percent for SS-
350 (when available, except incl. w/Indy Pace Car).

1970 Camaro, V-8

	6	5	4	3	2	1
2d Cpe	700	2,050	3,400	6,800	11,900	17,000
2d Z28	850	2,500	4,200	8,400	14,700	21,000

NOTE: Deduct 5 percent for six-cylinder, (except Z28). Add 35 percent for the 375-hp 396, (L78 option). Add 35 percent for Rally Sport and/or Super Sport options.

1971 Camaro, V-8

	6	5	4	3	2	1
2d Cpe	700	2,050	3,400	6,800	11,900	17,000
2d Z28	800	2,400	4,000	8,000	14,000	20,000

NOTE: Add 35 percent for Rally Sport and/or Super Sport options.

1972 Camaro, V-8

	6	5	4	3	2	1
2d Cpe	700	2,150	3,600	7,200	12,600	18,000
2d Z28	850	2,500	4,200	8,400	14,700	21,000

NOTE: Add 35 percent for Rally Sport and/or Super Sport options.

1973 Camaro, V-8

	6	5	4	3	2	1
2d Cpe	700	2,150	3,600	7,200	12,600	18,000
2d Z28	800	2,400	4,000	8,000	14,000	20,000

NOTE: Add 35 percent for Rally Sport and/or Super Sport options.

1979 Berlinetta

1982 Indy 500 Pace Car

1974 Camaro, V-8

	6	5	4	3	2	1
2d Cpe	700	2,100	3,500	7,000	12,300	17,500
2d LT Cpe	700	2,150	3,600	7,200	12,600	18,000

NOTE: Add 10 percent for Z28 option.

1975 Camaro, V-8

	6	5	4	3	2	1
Cpe	650	1,900	3,200	6,400	11,200	16,000
Type LT	700	2,050	3,400	6,800	11,900	17,000

NOTE: Add 30 percent for Camaro R/S.

1976 Camaro, V-8

	6	5	4	3	2	1
2d Cpe	600	1,800	3,000	6,000	10,500	15,000
2d Cpe LT	650	1,900	3,200	6,400	11,200	16,000

1977 Camaro, V-8

	6	5	4	3	2	1
2d Spt Cpe	500	1,450	2,400	4,800	8,400	12,000
2d Spt Cpe LT	500	1,500	2,500	5,000	8,750	12,500
2d Spt Cpe Z28	600	1,800	3,000	6,000	10,500	15,000

1978 Camaro, V-8

	6	5	4	3	2	1
2d Cpe	240	720	1,200	2,400	4,200	6,000
2d LT Cpe	260	780	1,300	2,600	4,550	6,500
2d Z28 Cpe	360	1,080	1,800	3,600	6,300	9,000

1979 Camaro, V-8

	6	5	4	3	2	1
2d Spt Cpe	232	696	1,160	2,320	4,060	5,800
2d Rally Cpe	256	768	1,280	2,560	4,480	6,400
2d Berlinetta Cpe	264	792	1,320	2,640	4,620	6,600
2d Z28 Cpe	276	828	1,380	2,760	4,830	6,900

NOTE: Deduct 20 percent for 6-cyl.

1980 Camaro, 6-cyl.

	6	5	4	3	2	1
2d Cpe Spt	244	732	1,220	2,440	4,270	6,100
2d Cpe RS	252	756	1,260	2,520	4,410	6,300
2d Cpe Berlinetta	256	768	1,280	2,560	4,480	6,400

1991 Z28

1993 Z28

1980 Camaro, V-8

	6	5	4	3	2	1
2d Cpe Spt	260	780	1,300	2,600	4,550	6,500
2d Cpe RS	268	804	1,340	2,680	4,690	6,700
2d Cpe Berlinetta	272	816	1,360	2,720	4,760	6,800
2d Cpe Z28	360	1,080	1,800	3,600	6,300	9,000

1981 Camaro, 6-cyl.

	6	5	4	3	2	1
2d Cpe Spt	248	744	1,240	2,480	4,340	6,200
2d Cpe Berlinetta	256	768	1,280	2,560	4,480	6,400

1981 Camaro, V-8

	6	5	4	3	2	1
2d Cpe Spt	264	792	1,320	2,640	4,620	6,600
2d Cpe Berlinetta	272	816	1,360	2,720	4,760	6,800
2d Cpe Z28	368	1,104	1,840	3,680	6,440	9,200

1982 Camaro, 6-cyl.

	6	5	4	3	2	1
2d Cpe Spt	252	756	1,260	2,520	4,410	6,300
2d Cpe Berlinetta	260	780	1,300	2,600	4,550	6,500

1982 Camaro, V-8

	6	5	4	3	2	1
2d Cpe Spt	268	804	1,340	2,680	4,690	6,700
2d Cpe Berlinetta	276	828	1,380	2,760	4,830	6,900
2d Cpe Z28	376	1,128	1,880	3,760	6,580	9,400

NOTE: Add 20 percent for Indy Pace Car.

1983 Camaro, 6-cyl.

	6	5	4	3	2	1
2d Cpe Spt	256	768	1,280	2,560	4,480	6,400
2d Cpe Berlinetta	264	792	1,320	2,640	4,620	6,600

1983 Camaro, V-8

	6	5	4	3	2	1
2d Cpe Spt	272	816	1,360	2,720	4,760	6,800
2d Cpe Berlinetta	360	1,080	1,800	3,600	6,300	9,000
2d Cpe Z28	380	1,140	1,900	3,800	6,650	9,500

1984 Camaro, V-8

	6	5	4	3	2	1
2d Cpe	264	792	1,320	2,640	4,620	6,600
2d Cpe Berlinetta	272	816	1,360	2,720	4,760	6,800
2d Cpe Z28	364	1,092	1,820	3,640	6,370	9,100

NOTE: Deduct 10 percent for six-cylinder.

1985 Camaro, V-8

	6	5	4	3	2	1
2d Cpe Spt	268	804	1,340	2,680	4,690	6,700
2d Cpe Berlinetta	276	828	1,380	2,760	4,830	6,900
2d Cpe Z28	368	1,104	1,840	3,680	6,440	9,200
2d Cpe IROC-Z	384	1,152	1,920	3,840	6,720	9,600

NOTE: Deduct 30 percent for 4-cylinder. Deduct 20 percent for V-6.

1986 Camaro

	6	5	4	3	2	1
2d Cpe	272	816	1,360	2,720	4,760	6,800
2d Cpe Berlinetta	360	1,080	1,800	3,600	6,300	9,000
2d Cpe Z28	380	1,140	1,900	3,800	6,650	9,500
2d Cpe IROC-Z	400	1,200	2,000	4,000	7,000	10,000

1987 Camaro

	6	5	4	3	2	1
2d Cpe V-6	276	828	1,380	2,760	4,830	6,900
2d Cpe LT V-6	360	1,080	1,800	3,600	6,300	9,000
2d Cpe V-8	368	1,104	1,840	3,680	6,440	9,200
2d Cpe LT V-8	372	1,116	1,860	3,720	6,510	9,300
2d Cpe Z28 V-8	388	1,164	1,940	3,880	6,790	9,700
2d Cpe IROC-Z V-8	400	1,200	2,050	4,100	7,150	10,200
2d Conv IROC-Z V-8	800	2,400	4,000	8,000	14,000	20,000

NOTE: Add 20 percent for 350 V-8 where available. Add 10 percent for Anniversary Edition.

1988 Camaro V-6

	6	5	4	3	2	1
2d Cpe	220	660	1,100	2,200	3,850	5,500

1988 Camaro, V-8

	6	5	4	3	2	1
2d Cpe	240	720	1,200	2,400	4,200	6,000
2d Conv	560	1,680	2,800	5,600	9,800	14,000
2d IROC-Z Cpe	420	1,260	2,100	4,200	7,350	10,500
2d IROC-Z Conv	700	2,150	3,600	7,200	12,600	18,000

1989 Camaro V-6

	6	5	4	3	2	1
2d RS Cpe	240	720	1,200	2,400	4,200	6,000

1989 Camaro, V-8

	6	5	4	3	2	1
2d RS Cpe	260	780	1,300	2,600	4,550	6,500
2d RS Conv	640	1,920	3,200	6,400	11,200	16,000
2d IROC-Z Cpe	340	1,020	1,700	3,400	5,950	8,500
2d IROC-Z Conv	720	2,160	3,600	7,200	12,600	18,000

1990 Camaro V-6

	6	5	4	3	2	1
2d RS Cpe	240	720	1,200	2,400	4,200	6,000

1990 Camaro, V-8

	6	5	4	3	2	1
2d RS Cpe	264	792	1,320	2,640	4,620	6,600
2d RS Conv	600	1,800	3,000	6,000	10,500	15,000
2d IROC-Z Cpe	520	1,560	2,600	5,200	9,100	13,000
2d IROC-Z Conv	680	2,040	3,400	6,800	11,900	17,000

1991 Camaro, V-6

	6	5	4	3	2	1
2d Cpe	240	720	1,200	2,400	4,200	6,000
2d Conv	560	1,680	2,800	5,600	9,800	14,000

1991 Camaro, V-8

	6	5	4	3	2	1
2d RS Cpe	260	780	1,300	2,600	4,550	6,500
2d RS Conv	580	1,740	2,900	5,800	10,150	14,500
2d Z28 Cpe	420	1,260	2,100	4,200	7,350	10,500
2d Z28 Conv	660	1,980	3,300	6,600	11,550	16,500

1992 Camaro, V-6

	6	5	4	3	2	1
2d RS Cpe	400	1,200	2,000	4,000	7,000	10,000
2d RS Conv	600	1,800	3,000	6,000	10,500	15,000
2d Z28 Cpe	540	1,620	2,700	5,400	9,450	13,500
2d Z28 Conv	680	2,040	3,400	6,800	11,900	17,000

NOTE: Add 10 percent for V-8 where available.

1993 Camaro

	6	5	4	3	2	1
2d Cpe, V-6	420	1,260	2,100	4,200	7,350	10,500
2d Cpe Z28, V-8	540	1,620	2,700	5,400	9,450	13,500

NOTE: Add 10 percent for Pace Car.

1994 Camaro

	6	5	4	3	2	1
2d Cpe, V-6	340	1,020	1,700	3,400	5,950	8,500
2d Conv, V-6	380	1,140	1,900	3,800	6,650	9,500
2d Z28 Cpe, V-8	420	1,260	2,100	4,200	7,350	10,500
2d Z28 Conv, V-8	500	1,500	2,500	5,000	8,750	12,500

1995 Camaro, V-6 & V-8

	6	5	4	3	2	1
2d Cpe, V-6	350	1,000	1,700	3,400	5,950	8,500
2d Conv, V-6	400	1,150	1,900	3,800	6,650	9,500
2d Z28 Cpe, V-8	400	1,250	2,100	4,200	7,350	10,500
2d Z28 Conv, V-8	500	1,500	2,500	5,000	8,750	12,500

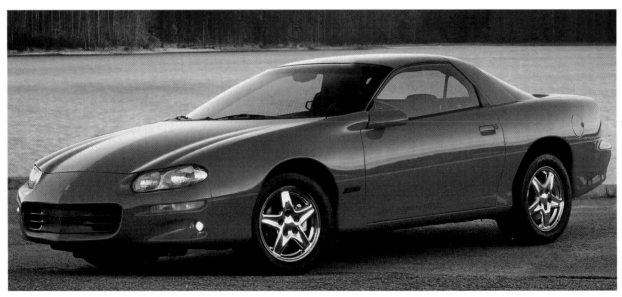

1998 Z28